Best Literature By and About Blacks

Best Literature By and About Blacks

Phillip M. Richards, Ph.D.
Neil Schlager

GALE GROUP

Detroit
San Francisco
London
Boston
Woodbridge, CT

Phillip M. Richards, Ph.D. and Neil Schlager

Gale Group Staff:
Coordinating Editor: Beverly Baer
Contributing Editors: Nancy Franklin, Elizabeth Manar
Managing Editor: Debra M. Kirby

Composition Manager: MaryBeth Trimper
Assistant Production Manager: Eveline Abou-el-Seoud
Manufacturing Manager: Dorothy Maki
Buyer: Stacy L. Melson
Product Design Manager: Cynthia Baldwin
Art Director: Pamela Galbreath

Manager, Data Entry Services: Ronald D. Montgomery
Sr. Data Entry Associate: Beverly Jendrowski
Data Entry Associate: Nancy Sheridan

Manager, Technical Support Services: Theresa Rocklin
Programmer/Analysts: Charles Beaumont, Magdalena Cureton

ISBN 0-7876-0507-7

Printed in the United States of America

10 9 8 7 6 5 4 3 2 1

Table of Contents

Introduction

Best Literature By and About Blacks seeks to provide the reader with a guide to information on significant writers and works in African American literature and history. This book will direct students, teachers, librarians and researchers to fiction, nonfiction, poetry, drama, and literary criticism either written by or about blacks. Writers and their works are arranged first within the major periods of African American historical experience and then within specific genres. To be sure, this book is intended to be of use to readers looking for the works of individual authors such as Toni Morrison or Alexander Crummell. However, it is also the intention of the authors to place the literature in a series of contexts--authors, genres and historical periods. By doing so, this book helps to create a sense of the world in which the works were written as well as a framework for other texts, ideas, and personalities in which the book should be read. The purpose of the book is to prepare the reader for the best use of the text by defining the most plausible and available contexts surrounding it. In that sense, then, this is a book to be consulted not only for a particular author or work, but also a book to be quickly skimmed and browsed for the context it can give for locating other individuals and publications which may be of interest to the user.

Organization of This Book

Books are grouped by historical era and then by genre within the era. The era essays provide a broad overview of the contexts in which African American literature developed during the time frame. The eras used are 1750-1860, 1860-1900, 1900-1940 and 1940-present. Eras are then divided into five genres: fiction, nonfiction, poetry, drama and literary criticism. Each of the 1867 entries include the author's name, title of the work, bibliographic data, subjects covered by the book, and awards won, if any. A brief annotation describes the work, and, if pertinent, its significance to black literature. An index provides access to authors, titles, subjects and keywords.

About the Authors

Phillip M. Richards is an associate professor in the Department of English at Colgate University. He has also taught at the University of North Carolina, Chapel Hill and Boston University. He has been a Fellow at the National Humanities Center and a teaching/research Fulbright Fellow at the Université Omar Bongo in Gabon. Dr. Richards has published a number of articles on African American literature and culture in a variety of academic and literary journals.

Neil Schlager is the founder and president of Schlager Information Group, an editorial services company based in Chicago. He has worked in the reference industry for a decade and is the editor of *When Technology Fails* (Gale Research, 1994) and *The St. James Press Gay and Lesbian Almanac* (St. James Press, 1998). He is currently compiling an encyclopedia about the history of science.

Comments Are Welcome

Best Literature By and About Blacks is intended to serve as a useful reference tool for a wide audience, so your comments about this work are encouraged. Send comments and suggestions to: Editor, *Best Literature By and About Blacks*, Gale Group, Inc., 25700 Drake Rd., Farmington Hills, Michigan 48331-3535. You may also call us toll-free at 1-800-347-GALE or fax to 248-699-8074.

1750-1860

African American literature emerged out of the central concerns of seventeenth century Anglophone writing in the British New World. For the most part, early Americans wrote and published public documents concerned with the building, ordering, and reproduction of a predominantly white Anglo-Saxon society in British North America. The British settlers in the New World expressed their social, political, and economic concerns in religious language. The desire to create a New World of God had brought many of these settlers to North America. In their literature, they conceived of their lives as defined by the covenant language of British Protestantism and the Old Testament patriarchs. Significantly, the New World British defined the place of blacks too. The place of black slaves in the law, in the household, in the congregation, and in government was frequently spelled out in the language and literary texts of English Puritanism.

The fundamental proposition of covenant Protestantism was bound up in the relationship between God and the believer. In return for the believer's faith and moral action, God promised earthly protection and heavenly salvation. Christian families, congregations, towns, colonies, and ultimately the American nation could enter into this relationship with God. A critical aspect of early American society was the cultivation of religious piety and moral action associated with faith, and much early American writing concerned with African Americans dealt with piety and morality as it relates to slaves.

As early as the l630s, the English Puritan theologian Richard Baxter wrote on the education and keeping of black slaves in the household. This tradition was continued in similar New World texts by George Fox, Cotton Mather, and others. Religious diaries and household letters such as those of Samuel Sewall, Cotton Mather, and Ezra Stiles also display Puritan household patriarchs in the midst of the religious care of their slaves.

The covenant privileges of religious settlements and colonies also depended upon the day to day ordering of town and colony life. Slaves were the subjects of American laws forbidding freedom to baptized bondsmen as well as an increasing set of eighteenth century regulations limiting the geographical movements of slaves, their education, miscegenation, and their social status. Not surprisingly, given the New World's wide spaces and relative absence of law enforcement officials, many slaves ran away--as did white apprentices and indentured servants. As newspapers came into being in the American colonies, advertisements for runaway slaves became commonplace.

Slaves figured too in other kinds of New England writing that gradually developed into popular art forms. Englishmen brought with them to North America the practice of public executions accompanied by cautionary and evangelical sermons. The high crime rate among blacks--and the growing fears of black disorder throughout the eighteenth century--made the autobiographies of executed black criminals and cautionary sermons addressed to the black public into popular broadside and pamphlet literature. Similarly, some of the increasingly popular captivity narratives associated with the Indian Wars involved blacks, such as the narrative of Jupiter Hammon.

The Puritan aim of a morally and spiritually pure community led white colonists to question the religious and ethical status of slavery itself. Englishmen such as Ralph Sandiford had condemned slavery on moral grounds. In Puritan New England, a tradition beginning with Samuel Sewall's *The Selling of Joseph* in 1700 and continuing through the anti-slavery writings of Samuel Hopkins would condemn slavery on the same grounds. Other writers, such as Cotton Mather in *Bonifacius,* were equivocal on the morality of slave-holding while vociferous against the continuance of the trade--whose horrors were openly visible in such North American docks as Boston, Newport, and Philadelphia. By the late eighteenth century, many of the New England colonies had banded to end slavery within their boundaries. In 1808, American participation in the slave trade had been forbidden by the federal government.

Published writing by blacks begins in the late eighteenth century as figures such as Phillis Wheatley and Jupiter Hammon establish themselves respectively as a popular poet and preacher. Their work reflects traditions of Puritan piety and political rhetoric. They address not only the conventional New England themes of Protestant social morality and religious observance, but also the Revolutionary-era issues of the founding of the new nation. Significantly, both belonged to households where they were educated and proselytized by wealthy white masters. At about the same time, Lemuel Haynes, a mulatto who was to become a minister and theologian in the early nineteenth century, began to write poems.

An important historical factor in the development of black writing was the institutionalization of black life in the North--from before the Revolution to the coming of the Civil War. The political, social, and economic lives of northern blacks became more complex as an increasing black population moved to cities such as Boston, Worcester, Newport, New York, Albany, Philadelphia, and Baltimore. There they frequently formed Benevolent and School societies to assist in the process of settlement, the dislocation of new migrants, and the education of children in cities where schools were frequently settled. These developments produced increased literacy and social organization among blacks.

Blacks in the cities also formed churches in the midst of the second Great Awakening, which gathered steam in the late eighteenth century and reached full tilt in the opening decades of the nineteenth century. The widespread formation of churches, as well as black entry into expanded white denominations and church associations, had an important effect upon black literature. A number of early black slave narratives such as those by John Jea, George White, and Jarena Lee show the impact of the professional requirements of an expanded Protestant ecclesiastical bureaucracy upon the lives of black intellectuals and spiritualists.

These religious and benevolent societies had a broader political thrust that parallels the emergent nationalist symbolism and ideologies of the new nation. A number of these black religious and benevolent groups, as well as some regional white groups, supported the resettlement of part of western Africa by American ex-slaves. Samuel Hopkins and Ezra Stiles had just before the American Revolution begun a project intended to educate two blacks and to send them as missionaries to Sierra Leone. The Newport Benevolent Society, a black group with whom Hopkins worked, also tried to set up a settlement in Sierra Leone. White and black ministers frequently spoke to black audiences on the subject of the return of black Americans to Africa. Among those black writers and activists who wrote on colonization were Lemuel Haynes and Phillis Wheatley, who corresponded with black missionaries such as Philip Quaque, Prince Saunders, and Absolom Jones.

This trend was transformed in the 1820s when a growing number of African American intellectuals, ministers, and political activists began to support the immediatist anti-slavery movement, which was guided by a white anti-slavery activist named William Lloyd Garrison. Colonizationists had supported a gradual end to slavery and advocated the deportation of freed slaves to Africa. Immediatists called for an immediate end to slavery; stressed that there was no mild slavery; demanded that slaves, however, not resist their masters; and sought to prepare ex-slaves for life in the United States. A number of black political and religious groups quickly became some of Garrison's most critical supporters. Most importantly, the Garrisonian abolitionists began to make use of black ex-slave orators as speakers against slavery. The speeches of such orators such as William Wells Brown, James Pennington, and Frederick Douglass became the basis of the slave narrative--a classic form of autobiography in American and African American letters. The anti-slavery movement also supported in Garrison's paper, *The Liberator*, such early black prose writers as Maria Stewart, and the poets George Moses Horton and Frances E.W. Harper.

The abolitionist period was a particularly important period because it brought a wide variety of black thinkers and writers such as Martin Delany, Alexander Crummell, and William Whipper into contact with each other, with white abolitionists, and with a host of other thinkers and activists. In the 1850s, the Fugitive Slave Act and the Kansas-Nebraska Act caused tensions throughout the abolitionist, temperance, feminist, and Protestant organizations. The fracture of the abolitionist movement was reflected in the increasing tendency of black writers to challenge immediatist abolitionist ideology in their narratives, as did Frederick Douglass in his second autobiography, *My Bondage and My Freedom* and Linda Brent (the pseudonym of Harriet A. Jacobs) in *Incidents in the Life of a Slave Girl*. During this time, intellectuals such as Delany and Crummell experimented with conceptions of a national black convention, black nationalism, and the return to Africa. Delany wrote *Blake*, a novel of slave revolt, while Crummell, who developed an important strand of black nationalist thought, went to Africa.

Fiction

During this period, black and mulatto characters play slender conventional roles in fiction by white writers such as Washington Irving and James Fenimore Cooper. However, the first novels by blacks emerged during the era immediately preceding the Civil War. This was a period of experimentation with the forms of the slave narrative, abolitionist fiction, and the sentimental novel. William Wells Brown's novel, *Clotel; or the President's Daughter: A Narrative of Slave Life in the United States* was published in 1853 in England and is considered the first novel written by an African American. It incorporates elements of the sentimental novel to tell the story of the illegitimate mulatto daughter of Thomas Jefferson and one of his slaves. As with most of the fiction and nonfiction by blacks during this period, this work denounces the institution of slavery by depicting the horrors of the slave market, the conditions of slave life, and the destruction of families and lives. Another early work of fiction, considered the first by an African American woman, was Harriet E. Wilson's *Our Nig; or Sketches From the Life of a Free Black*, which was published in 1859. Unlike Brown's novel, Wilson's does not deal directly with slavery, but with the lives of blacks in the Northern states, who, though they were technically free, were nonetheless enslaved by poverty and prejudice.

1 **William Wells Brown**

Clotel; or, The President's Daughter: A Narrative of Slave Life in the United States

(London, England; Partridge & Oakey, 1853)

Summary: This novel was the first ever penned by an African American. Drawing on Brown's own experiences as a slave and as the son of a white man and a slave woman, the novel offers a panoramic view of slavery in nineteenth-century America. The novel's title character, Clotel, is the light-skinned daughter of a slave woman and Thomas Jefferson, third President of the United States. The novel follows Clotel as she fights slavery, endures other hardships, and suffers disappointments in love. Filled with countless anecdotes from Brown's life as a slave and sometimes overwhelmed by the author's sentimentality and his preoccupation with the cause of abolition, the novel is nonetheless a groundbreaking work of fiction in American literature. The novel's plot featuring Thomas Jefferson would prove prescient more than a century later, when DNA tests in 1998 revealed that Jefferson had indeed fathered children by his slave, Sally Hemings.

Subject(s): Slavery, Abolition, Miscegenation

2   Our Nig
(Pseudonym of Harriet E. Wilson)

Our Nig; or Sketches from the Life of a Free Black
(Boston, MA; G.C. Rand & Avery, 1859)

Summary: This semi-autobiographical novel, originally published in 1859, is now believed to be the first novel written in English by a female African American. The story of Alfrado, the heroine, begins with her abandonment, at age six, by her white mother after the death of her black father. She is left at the house of a white family to become an indentured servant in their New England home, but in actuality is treated as a slave by most of the members of the family. She is beaten and verbally abused until she turns eighteen, at which point she has completed her servitude and leaves the family. She marries a fugitive slave and has a child with him, but he eventually deserts the family, leaving her to fend for herself and her child. Wilson states in the preface that she is writing the novel to support her son, just as Frado works to do the same in the novel. The novel was republished in 1983 with Henry Louis Gates, Jr. as the editor.

Subject(s): Servants, Slavery, Race Relations

3   Frank J. Webb

The Garies and Their Friends
(London, England; G. Routledge & Co., 1857)

Summary: In his only full-length novel and one of the earliest novels written by a black American, Webb used numerous situations and themes--such as middle-class issues, racial pride, mixed marriages, the color line, and passing for white--that became earmarks of later African American novels. *The Garies and Their Friends* is a melodrama covering two generations of three families in Philadelphia. Clarence Garie, a white southern aristocrat with a mulatto wife, heads the title family. Their "friends" are the Ellises, a middle-class black family. "Slippery" George Stevens, the novel's villain, is a greedy white, Mr. Garie's cousin, and head of the third family. A son from

each family mirrors the fathers. The book has an underlying message about the abolition movement and the effects of racial oppression, particularly the destruction of the family by prejudice.

Subject(s): Prejudice, Racial Conflict, Middle Classes

Nonfiction

The earliest prose by African Americans concerned the function of community organizations. The execution narratives dictated by African American convicts before hanging were part of an elaborate ritual designed to warn their fellows from crime. The early sermons of figures such as Jupiter Hammon and Lemuel Haynes were aimed at the evangelization of the population. The letters of Phillis Wheatley often concerned social piety and the organization of missionary efforts. And the papers of the Newport Benevolent Association show the workings of an early African American relief organization.

In the early nineteenth century, this largely organizational prose increased with black involvement in the colonization and later the abolitionist movements. The orations celebrating the abolition of the slave trade in 1808 were a major source of African American prose. In addition, the writing of abolitionists such as David Walker, Henry Highland Garnett, and Martin Delany were an important source of political expression.

Finally, the development of the abolitionist slave narrative marked the high point of African American nonfiction prose during the period. The slave narrative had emerged in the eighteenth century accounts of captivity and adventure. In 1770, James Albert Ukawsaw Gronniosaw dictated the tragic story of his life to a sympathetic Dutch woman. As a teenaged Nigerian prince, Gronniosaw was persuaded by a duplicitous merchant to join him in travel, but instead was forced into American slavery. Religious narratives such as those by John Jea and George White appeared in the early nineteenth century. The slave narrative became a prolific form after the 1830s, when the "immediatist" abolitionists began to use the stories of ex-slaves in order to campaign against slavery. Among the most famous anti-slavery narratives were those of Frederick Douglass, James Pennington, and William Wells Brown. In the case of Douglass and Brown, the composition of a slave narrative marked the beginning of an important literary career.

4   Herbert Aptheker, Editor

A Documentary History of the Negro People of the United States. Volumes 1-3
(New York, NY; Citadel Press, 1969)

Summary: Using original letters, articles, and other documents, Marxist Historian Herbert Aptheker's *Documentary History of the Negro People in the United States* takes readers on a well-researched journey through the saga that parallels the family history of many African Americans. In the first of the work's three volumes, Aptheker outlines the brutal way of life endured by many Africans newly arrived at U.S. farms and plantations, their gradual fight for freedom, emancipation, and their movement to the industrial cities of the North in search of paying jobs and a new life. The volume, which contains a preface by black leader W.E.B. Du Bois, concludes at the time Du Bois founded the National Association for the Advancement of Colored People (NAACP) in 1909. In volume two, Aptheker takes readers through the early years of the twentieth century, as black culture flourished during such cultural movements as the Harlem Renaissance. The depression years through World War II are outlined in volume three.

Subject(s): History, Slavery, African Americans

5   William Wells Brown

The American Fugitive in Europe: Sketches of Places and People Abroad
(Boston, MA; John P. Jewett, 1855)

Summary: Author, orator, and amateur historian William Wells Brown published his *Three Years in Europe; or, Places I Have Seen and People I Have Met* in London in 1852. The book was expanded and revised for a U.S. readership in 1855 as *The American Fugitive in Europe: Sketches of Places and People Abroad*. A popular speaker for the abolitionist cause and well known as the author of a widely read slave narrative, Brown traveled to Europe to attend the Paris Peace Conference of 1849 as a delegate from Boston and to win converts to the abolitionist cause. The letters he sent across the sea to friends, as well as articles on his European excursion that he submitted to pro-abolition newspapers, were collected in 344 pages, most of which were taken up with the contents of twenty-three letters containing vivid descriptions of notable people, events, and places that Brown had encountered during his travels. Concerned over his status as a fugitive slave, Brown remained in Great Britain until he was forty years old, during which time he traveled more than 25,000 miles, addressed more than one thousand public meetings, and lectured at numerous antislavery societies. With the help of friends and through his lectures, publication of newspaper articles, and books such as *The American Fugitive in Europe*, Brown not only paid for the entire trip but sent both of his daughters to school in France and England.

Subject(s): Slavery, Abolition, Travel

6   William Wells Brown

Narrative of William W. Brown, a Fugitive Slave
(Boston, MA; Anti-Slavery Office, 1847)

Summary: A man who became a masterful and tireless orator on behalf of the abolitionist cause, William Wells Brown was born into slavery in 1814. He was hired out to numerous employers before reaching the age of eight, attempted escape several times during his teens, and was convinced by his experiences that the fight to end slavery was his calling. In 1833 he successfully fled North and, after eight days, found shelter with a Quaker named Wells Brown, whose name Brown would

adopt as an expression of gratitude. Written after its author learned to read and became strongly affiliated with the abolitionist cause, Brown's *Narrative of William W. Brown, a Fugitive Slave, Written by Himself* went through four editions and sold over ten thousand copies in the first two years of its publication. Brown's detached point of view serves to focus readers' attention on the horrors of the institution of slavery as a whole rather than on the unfortunate circumstances of the narrator. The split between the narrator's dispassionate voice and his melodramatic topic (somewhat fictionalized for heightened effect) reflects the black authors' typical quandary when writing for a white audience: to gain support for abolitionism, Brown could not afford to alienate his readers through overt sarcasm, bitterness, or rage.

Subject(s): Slavery, Abolition, History

7   William Wells Brown

Three Years in Europe; or, Places I Have Seen and People I Have Met
(London, England; C. Gilpin, 1852)

Summary: A tireless orator on behalf of the abolitionist cause, William Wells Brown was born into slavery in 1814, escaping to freedom in 1833. He published the travelogue *Three Years in Europe; or, Places I Have Seen and People I Have Met* while in London in 1852. Renowned as the author of a popular slave narrative, Brown followed in the footsteps of Frederick Douglass, traveling to Europe to win converts to the abolitionist cause. Letters sent back home to friends and articles on his experiences in Europe were collected in 344 pages as *Three Years in Europe;* the book was expanded and revised for a U.S. readership in 1855 as *The American Fugitive in Europe: Sketches of Places and People Abroad*. Fearing capture under the Fugitive Slave Law passed in 1850, Brown remained in Europe for three years, travelling widely and speaking before many groups.

Subject(s): Slavery, Abolition, History

8   Samuel Eli Cornish

The Colonization Scheme Considered, in Its Rejection by the Colored People...
(Newark, NJ; A. Guest, 1840)

Summary: Presbyterian minister Samuel Eli Cornish (1795-1858) dedicated much of his adult life to the abolitionist cause. As editor of the *Colored American* and other black-run newspapers, he promoted a conservative strategy to eliminate slavery, and this conservatism led to his views being overshadowed by those of younger abolitionists by the mid-1800s. In *The Colonization Scheme Considered, in Its Rejection by the Colored People*, Cornish expressed what he considered to be the problems of the colonization movement promoted by many blacks and whites; he also wrote in opposition to the use of force in preventing the enforcement of the fugitive slave laws enacted in the 1830s.

Subject(s): Abolition, Slavery, Resistance Movements

**9   Alexander Crummell
Wilson Jeremiah Moses,** Editor

Destiny and Race: Selected Writings, 1840-1898
(Amherst, MA; University of Massachusetts Press, 1992)

Summary: Founder of the American Negro Academy, Alexander Crummell (1819-1898) was a key voice in the vociferous nineteenth century debates over the future of black Americans. While his earliest writings focus on the dilemmas faced by southern blacks with regard to education, employment, religion, gender, and battling prejudice, Crummell's later works set forth his vision of a Pan-African culture and discuss his personal spirituality. Highly educated, Crummell was an ordained Episcopalian priest who became pastor of Washington, D.C.'s St. Luke's Church in 1870.

Subject(s): Pan-Africanism, Religion, American South

10   Alexander Crummell

The Man, the Hero, the Christian!: A Eulogy on the Life and Character of Thomas Clarkson: Delivered in the City of New York, December, 1846
(New York, NY; Egbert, Hovey, & King, 1847)

Summary: Thomas Clarkson was a noted abolitionist whose work *Essay on the Slavery and Commerce of the Human Species, Particularly the African* was highly influential in its day. *The Man, the Hero, the Christian! A Eulogy on the Life and Character of Thomas Clarkson* is the transcription of the speech given by fellow abolitionist Alexander Crummell upon Clarkson's death in 1846. Crummell, an Episcopalian priest, was allied to Clarkson in his support of Pan-African ideas.

Subject(s): Abolition, Slavery, Human Rights

**11   Paul Cuffe
Rosalind Cobb Wiggins,** Editor

Captain Paul Cuffe's Logs and Letters, 1808-1817: A Black Quaker's "Voice from within the Veil"
(Washington, DC; Howard University Press, 1996)

Summary: Edited by Rosalind Cobb Wiggins, *Captain Paul Cuffe's Logs and Letters, 1808-1817: A Black Quaker's Voice from within the Veil* is a collection of correspondence and ship's logs written by Cuffe (1759-1817), an African American Quaker. Covering the years between 1808 and 1817, the documents reveal Cuffe's efforts to undercut the slave trade by forming a trading cooperative in Sierra Leone, as well as the many hardships and obstacles Cuffe faced, despite help from an organization of blacks that supported his efforts within the United States.

Subject(s): Slavery, Ships

12   Philip D. Curtin, Editor

Africa Remembered: Narratives by West Africans from the Era of the Slave Trade
(Madison, WI; University of Wisconsin Press, 1967)

Summary: In *Africa Remembered: Narratives by West Africans from the Era of the Slave Trade* Philip D. Curtin collects ten rare, personal narratives that recall the experiences of West African natives who were taken abruptly from their home and families, chained, and shipped to the New World under often horrifying conditions. Candid in their views about the passage as well as their treatment at the hands of slavers, each narrator frames his or her story within a non-Western understanding of the experiences encountered.

Subject(s): Slavery, Africa, American History

13   Martin Delany

The Condition, Elevation, Emigration, and Destiny of the Colored People of the United States
(Philadelphia, PA; Privately published, 1852)

Summary: Frederick Douglass embodies the abolitionist movement of nineteenth century America. Though also working for the cessation of slavery, Martin R. Delany (1812-1885) advocated for a solution that put him in opposition with Douglass. While each man recognized the importance of Africa and in the need for abolition, Delany allied himself with the American Colonization Society in promoting as a solution to the "color problem" the return of freed slaves to Africa. Historians have viewed Delany's work as key in the development of the Pan-African movement advocated by such activists as W.E.B. Du Bois in the next century.

Subject(s): Slavery, Emigration and Immigration, Africa

**14   Frederick Douglass
John W. Blassingame,** Editor

The Frederick Douglass Papers: Speeches, Debates, and Interviews. Volumes 1-5
(New Haven, CT; Yale University Press, 1979)

Summary: Though he was born into slavery, Frederick Douglass rose to become one of the most respected African Americans of the Civil War era. Escaping to freedom by the time he was twenty, Douglass's skills as an orator came to the attention of Boston's Anti-Slavery Society, which featured the former slave at abolitionist rallies it staged around the country. In his many speeches, as well as in a series of debates that are also included in the five-volume work *The Frederick Douglass Papers*, Douglass spoke of the horrors of slavery and chastised the "Christian" churches of the South that would condone such treatment of the black man (and woman) at the hands of a white elite. Notable among the selections are a series of talks he gave while in England in the mid-1840s to avoid capture as a runaway slave, and his July 1848 speech at the Seneca Falls Women's Suffrage meeting organized by Elizabeth Cady Stanton. Douglass's skills as an orator and his sophisticated understanding of political issues--clearly apparent in a reading of his collected speeches--called into question his claimed birth into slavery, prompting him to pen his well-known autobiography, *The Narrative of the Life of Frederick Douglass, an American Slave.*

Subject(s): Abolition, Slavery, Civil War

15 Frederick Douglass

Narrative of the Life of Frederick Douglass, an American Slave
(Boston, MA; Anti-Slavery Office, 1845)

Summary: Born into slavery in approximately 1818, orator and abolitionist leader Frederick Douglass was encouraged to set down his recollections of his life in 1844 by Boston abolitionist William Lloyd Garrison. Escaping from his Baltimore owners and making his way to the northern states in the late 1830s, the well-spoken and charismatic Douglass began what would be a lifelong career as a defender of the equal rights of blacks, as well as of women, in the United States. His autobiography, which went through several editions as Douglass refined it for a changing readership, recounts his early family life, the horrors he endured and witnessed as a slave, and his flight to ultimate freedom via the Underground Railroad. It was published in 1855 as *My Bondage and My Freedom* and then as *Life and Times of Frederick Douglass: The Complete Autobiography*, in 1881. Later editions of the work expand upon his family life, while in all editions the names of those individuals who aided him in his escape are omitted for their protection.

Subject(s): Slavery, Civil War, Autobiography

16 Henry Highland Garnet

An Address to the Slaves of the United States of America
(New York, NY; J.H. Tobitt, 1848)

Summary: *An Address to the Slaves of the United States of America* is one of the most noted speeches of radical abolitionist and activist Henry Highland Garnet (1815-1882). A black Presbyterian minister and later the first black to receive a diplomatic appointment, Garnet and his militant ideology, as promoted in this work, was rejected by Frederick Douglass, although several of Garnet's "radical" views would later be adopted by Garnet's fellow abolitionists. Given in 1843, the "Address to the Slaves of the United States of America" would serve as a touchstone for future generations of black militants.

Subject(s): Slavery, Abolition, Resistance Movements

17 Henry Highland Garnet

The Past and Present Condition, and the Destiny of the Colored Race
(Troy, NY; J.C. Kneeland, 1848)

Summary: Black abolitionist, activist, Presbyterian minister, and educator, Henry Highland Garnet (1815-1882) was one of the most well-known black abolitionists of his day. Although Garnet was frequently in disagreement with his colleague Frederick Douglass, several of Garnet's "radical" views were later adopted by an increasingly militant abolitionist movement. *The Past and Present Condition, and the Destiny of the Colored Race* collects several of the writings that caused Garnet's contemporaries to view him either as a violent revolutionary or, conversely, as a puppet of such racist groups as the American Colonization Society. Garnet would be the first African American to receive a diplomatic appointment.

Subject(s): Slavery, Abolition, Resistance Movements

18 James M. Gregory

Frederick Douglass the Orator
(Springfield, MA; Wiley & Co., 1893)

Summary: Published two years before Douglass's death at the age of 78, *Frederick Douglass the Orator* recall's the former slave's dedication to the cause of abolition through his work speaking on behalf of the Massachusetts Anti-Slavery Society from 1843 to 1847. After the close of the Civil War, Douglass found new channels for his skills as a compelling speaker, serving in a variety of public offices, speaking on behalf of women's suffrage--he was among those who spoke at the first rally for women's suffrage, organized by Elizabeth Cady Stanton at Seneca Falls, New York, in 1848--and as U.S. minister to Haiti beginning in 1889.

Subject(s): Biography, History, Abolition

19 C. Peter Ripley, Editor

The Black Abolitionist Papers: The British Isles, 1830-1865
(Chapel Hill, NC; University of North Carolina Press, 1985)

Summary: *The Black Abolitionist Papers: The British Isles, 1830-1865* is volume one of a five-volume work containing edited and annotated representative documents recounting the ambitious history of a generation of African Americans and their involvement in the international movement to abolish the "peculiar institution" of slavery. Abolitionist activities emanating within England, Ireland, and Scotland and ending with the American Civil War are accounted for in this volume; three volumes focus on black abolitionists in the United States, while abolitionist activities in Canada are covered in the final volume.

Subject(s): Abolition, Journalism, Reference

20 David Walker

Walker's Appeal, in Four Articles: Together with a Preamble, to the Coloured Citizens of the World
(Boston, MA; D. Walker, 1829)

Summary: When it first appeared in Boston in 1829, David Walker's *Walker's Appeal, in Four Articles* sparked a reward for its author's head. Considered the most radical work to be written by a nineteenth century African American, Walker refuted each of the arguments used to sanction slavery and called on black slaves to rise up against their masters. Serving as an inspiration to abolitionists in the North, the document accelerated the conflicts that led to Civil War, refuting the belief of some that blacks played little part in acquiring their own freedom. Walker would be killed less than a year after publishing this work.

Subject(s): Slavery, Resistance Movements, Abolition

21 Irma Watkins-Owens

Blood Relations: Caribbean Immigrants and the Harlem Community, 1900-1930
(Bloomington, IN; Indiana University Press, 1996)

Summary: In *Blood Relations: Caribbean Immigrants and the Harlem Community, 1900-1930* author Irma Watkins-Owens examines the role of immigrants from both the Caribbean and the postwar South in shaping the character of Harlem during the years of its cultural renaissance. Watkins-Owens, a professor at Fordham University, draws on in-depth research into primary sources and oral histories to highlight the role of organized religion and community organizations within the lives of immigrants, and to note their contributions to black New York culture. She also suggests that the voluntary and involuntary segregation of such groups away from the American mainstream contributed to their eventual radicalization.

Subject(s): Harlem Renaissance, Urban Affairs, Emigration and Immigration

22 William M. Wightman, Editor

Life of William Capers, D.D.: One of the Bishops of the Methodist Episcopalian Church, South
(Nashville, TN; Southern Methodist Publishing House, 1858)

Summary: Edited by William D. Wightman, the *Life of William Capers, D.D.* details the life of a southern-born bishop and missionary who, as the owner of slaves, opposed abolition but dedicated much of his career to establishing slave missions. Capers (1790-1855), a preacher for the Methodist Episcopal church beginning in 1808, supported evangelization of slaves as an alternative to emancipation. He became a source of controversy when his slaveholder status made him an inappropriate figurehead of the church as a whole, and in 1845 he assumed leadership of the Methodist Episcopal Church, South.

Subject(s): Religion, Slavery, American South

23 John Woolman

Life and Travels of John Woolman
(Philadelphia, PA; Friends Book Association, 1774)

Summary: In his *Life and Travels of John Woolman* Quaker abolitionist John Woolman (1720-1772) recounts his ministry and his efforts against the exploitation of people of color. Born in New Jersey, Woolman began his traveling ministry in 1743 while working at a series of odd jobs. During a trip through the southern colonies he became convinced of the evils of slaveholding, publishing *Some Considerations on the Keeping of Negroes* and other works encouraging his fellow Quakers to commit to an official abolitionist stance. Woolman's work also extended to defending Native Americans against their exploitation by white traders, and his journal was distributed throughout the United States and England after his death.

Subject(s): Slavery, Abolition, Religion

Poetry

African American poetry emerged in the context of long-standing English traditions in colonial American poetry. The writing of polite personal and private verse was a highly developed tradition in the British world from the time of the sixteenth century. This tradition--which British colonials carried to the New World--furnished an important precedent for African American writing. In both the southern and northeastern British colonies of North America, occasional verse written about current religious, political, personal, or nature related issues quickly established itself as a dominant art form, evident in the poetry of such white poets as Anne Bradstreet, Edward Taylor, and Samuel Sewall.

The religious aspect of this verse was particularly important. The Puritan and evangelical traditions of New World British Protestants encouraged the writing of meditative spiritual poetry, didactic moral verse, elegies, verse prayer, and biblical paraphrases. Popular English religious poets such as Isaac Watts and Richard Blackmore offered important precedents for such verse.

The political, military, and social crises of the New World also provided ample opportunity for writing about blacks by whites and African Americans. The first extant black poem concerns, significantly, an Indian attack in western Massachusetts during the French and Indian War. Along with Jupiter Hammon, Phillis Wheatley continued the tradition of writing poems celebrating important events in the lives of late eighteenth-century white colonists. Much of her didactic verse concerns specifically the problem of preparing the population--particularly the youth--for life in the dawning American Republic.

The traditions of occasional religious, social, and political verse would continue through the late eighteenth and early nineteenth century on the part of white as well as black poets. The occasional poetry of George Moses Horton--much of it written for schoolboys at the University of North Carolina, Chapel Hill--implicitly continued an African American tradition of didactic, personal, and social celebratory verse. This verse was, in many ways, part of a larger American tradition of popular didactic religious verse, a tradition that died by the twentieth century.

The democratization of British poetry in the late eighteenth and early nineteenth centuries--when new groups of people began writing poetry on a vocational basis--left an important mark on African American poetry. The writing of early American black poets shows not only the borrowing of poets taught outside of the traditional educational institutions but also the innovation of the new group of traditional English poets.

African American literature of the early nineteenth century continued many of the same trends of the previous century. The anti-slavery, reform, and evangelical movements of the period provided a political and religious context that made blacks and their plight an inevitable subject for white writers such as William Cullen Bryant and John Greenleaf Whittier. Moreover, writers such as Frances E.W. Harper continued Wheatley and Horton's earlier emphasis on topical religious and political verse. Indeed, her verse shows a sustained interest in political, religious, and social themes during the periods of abolition, the Civil War, and beyond.

24   **Frances E.W. Harper**

"The Drunkard's Child"

Poems on Miscellaneous Subjects
(Boston, MA; J.B. Yerrinton & Son, 1854)

Summary: The child of this poem's title is dying, and his drunken father staggers out of the saloon just in time to see him die. The poem is a didactic, cautionary piece about the evils of alcohol; the bloated, unkempt drunkard is contrasted with his dying but beautiful, golden-haired son. The poem consists of five stanzas of eight lines each.

Subject(s): Alcoholism, Children

25   **Frances E.W. Harper**

"Eliza Harris"

The Liberator
(1853)

Summary: One of Harper's best-known and most-anthologized poems, "Eliza Harris" originally appeared in the famed publication of abolitionist William Lloyd Garrison, *The Liberator*. The poem is based on an incident from Cincinnati, Ohio—and also used by Harriet Beecher Stowe in her novel *Uncle Tom's Cabin*—in which a young slave mother makes a daring escape to freedom with her young son in her arms. The poem, which is told in an aabb rhyme scheme in fourteen quatrains, was later revised by Harper.

Subject(s): Slavery, Abolition

26   **Frances E.W. Harper**

"Eva's Farewell"

Poems on Miscellaneous Subjects
(Boston, MA; J.B. Yerrinton & Son, 1854)

Summary: This simple poem epitomizes Frances E.W. Harper's religious poetry, a sizable segment of her poetic output. In the poem, Eva bids farewell to her father because she is dying; rather than focusing on her death, however, she focuses on the glories she hopes to find in heaven.

Subject(s): Religion, Christianity, Death

27   **George Moses Horton**

"The Creditor to His Proud Debtor"

The Poetical Works of George M. Horton, the Colored Bard of North Carolina
(Hillsborough, NC; Heartt, 1845)

Summary: This poem appeared in Horton's second collection, which was published sixteen years after his first. The poem is told from the vantage point of a man who is owed money by a proud and haughty debtor. The creditor mocks the younger man and his obnoxious ways: "dear boy, you would be trash / If your accounts were paid." The poem is typical of the makeup of Horton's 1845 volume in that it contains virtually no references to his status as a slave. With Horton still legally a slave in a slave-owning state (North Carolina) in which it was a crime for him to write and publish, Horton and his publisher were careful about which poems they allowed into public scrutiny. As critics have pointed out, words such as "freedom," "liberty," and "slavery" do not appear in a single poem in the volume.

Subject(s): Slavery, Poetry, Money

28   **George Moses Horton**

"Division of an Estate"

The Poetical Works of George M. Horton, the Colored Bard of North Carolina
(Hillsborough, NC; Heartt, 1845)

Summary: In this poem from his 1845 collection, Horton describes the aftermath of a slaver-owner's death, when his estate is divided and sold. Horton focuses on the confusion and apprehension of the man's slaves, who have no say in their fate and may be sold to other owners in piecemeal fashion—thus separating them from family and friends. The poem consists of a single stanza with no formal rhyme scheme; included are references to Greek mythology.

Subject(s): Slavery, Family, Death

29   **George Moses Horton**

"Liberty and Slavery"

The Hope of Liberty, Containing a Number of Poetical Pieces
(Raleigh, NC; J. Gales & Son, 1829)

Summary: In bold and forthright terms, Horton in this poem speaks out against his status as a slave and calls for an end to the "foul oppression" of slavery. Though Horton is careful not to address his owner specifically, he does refer to slavery in general as "barbarism" and a "sad disgrace," amazingly strong terms for a poet who was still subject to the whims of his owner. By the time of this volume's appearance, Horton and his supporters had already begun making appeals for his owner to free him, and they hoped that proceeds from *The Hope of Liberty* would make it even easier to secure his freedom. However, Horton's owner refused all such requests. Horton was not freed for another thirty years, when Abraham Lincoln issued the Emancipation Proclamation in 1863.

Subject(s): Slavery

30   George Moses Horton

"On Hearing the Intention of a Gentleman to Purchase the Poet's Freedom"

The Hope of Liberty, Containing a Number of Poetical Pieces (Raleigh, NC; J. Gales & Son, 1829)

Summary: This poem was composed in response to the first serious attempt by Horton's friends to secure his freedom, an 1829 campaign that ended unsuccessfully. The poem is composed of rhymed couplets, which Horton dictated to friend and novelist Caroline Lee Hentz, who in turn produced the written version.

Subject(s): Slavery, Poetry

31   George Moses Horton

"On Summer"

The Hope of Liberty, Containing a Number of Poetical Pieces (Raleigh, NC; J. Gales & Son, 1829)

Summary: This poem is a meditation on the sights and sounds of summer in North Carolina, where Horton was born and lived for most of his life as a slave. Horton mentions the town of Esteville, refers to the zodiac sign of Cancer, and makes observations about insects and animals. Like most of his poetry, "On Summer" contains a formal rhyme scheme. Though the poem is written in twelve quatrains, it must be remembered that at the time of this volume's publication Horton had not yet learned how to write. Thus, he dictated this and other poems in the volume to novelist Caroline Lee Hentz.

Subject(s): Slavery, Summer, Nature

32   George Moses Horton

"Praise of Creation"

The Hope of Liberty, Containing a Number of Poetical Pieces (Raleigh, NC; J. Gales & Son, 1829)

Summary: This poem from Horton's pioneering first collection is a simple and straightforward celebration of God's creation of the universe. Born into slavery, from which he was not freed until the 1863 Emancipation Proclamation—more than 30 years after this volume was published—Horton taught himself to read. Like the other poems in this collection, "Praise of Creation" was dictated by Horton to local North Carolina novelist Caroline Lee Hentz; Horton did not learn to write until 1832.

Subject(s): Slavery, Education, Religion

33   George Moses Horton

"The Slave's Complaint"

The Hope of Liberty, Containing a Number of Poetical Pieces (Raleigh, NC; J. Gales & Son, 1829)

Summary: In this poem from his first collection, Horton offers a heartfelt plea for God to deliver him and all slaves from their bondage. This plea is remarkable given that Horton was still a slave at the time of this volume's appearance; in fact, "The Slave's Complaint" and other similar poems in the collection likely represent the first time a slave had protested his status in published verse. Horton and his admirers hoped that the proceeds from *The Hope of Liberty* would be enough compensation to convince Horton's owner to free him, but that did not happen. Horton continued to compose poetry during another 30 years of slavery, until he was freed with the Emancipation Proclamation in 1863.

Subject(s): Slavery, Religion

34   George Moses Horton

"To Eliza"

The Hope of Liberty, Containing a Number of Poetical Pieces (Raleigh, NC; J. Gales, 1829)

Summary: Bittersweet and tender, "To Eliza" is a poem about a spurned lover. The speaker of the poem laments the deception of his beloved, Eliza, and regrets wooing her while another man has won her heart. In spite of his bitterness, the speaker infuses his poem with tender salutations such as "sweet lass" and "fare thee well!" The poem includes a traditional rhyme scheme (abab).

Subject(s): Love

35   Lucy Terry

"Bar's Flight"

The Norton Anthology of African American Literature (New York, NY; W.W. Norton & Co., 1997)

Summary: First published in Springfield, Massachusetts in 1855, this poem is the earliest known piece of literature by an African American. Though its date of composition is unknown, the poem was maintained orally until its first publication in 1855. The poem, composed in rhymed couplets of iambic tetrameter, describes an ambush of two white families by Native Americans in Deerfield, Massachusetts, on August 25, 1746. Terry herself was born in Africa, then kidnapped, sold into slavery, and brought to America as an infant. She gained her freedom in 1756 upon marriage to a wealthy free black, Obijah Prince. Until her death in 1821, she was known as a prominent orator and defender of the rights of African Americans.

Subject(s): Slavery, Murder, Indians of North America

36 Frances Ellen Watkins

(Also known as Frances E.W. Harper)

"Ethiopia"

Poems on Miscellaneous Subjects. 2nd Edition
(Boston, MA; J.B. Yerrinton, 1854)

Summary: Throughout her life, Frances E. W. Harper crusaded for the abolition of slavery and black civil rights, for women's and children's rights, and on behalf of Christian morality. Several of these themes are evident in "Ethiopia," which in Harper's era was often meant to refer to "black Africa" in general. In the poem, Harper foresees the eventual freedom of Ethiopia and of Africa's enslaved blacks, a freedom that will be achieved through "the mighty hand of God." Harper also sees an end to the practice of slave traders working in Africa: "Nor human tigers hunt for prey / Within her peaceful bowers." The poem, which consists of seven quatrains, contains a formal rhyme scheme and a consistent meter, both of which were typical in Harper's poetry.

Subject(s): Slavery, Africa, Abolition

37 Frances Ellen Watkins

(Also known as Frances E.W. Harper)

"The Slave Mother"

Poems on Miscellaneous Subjects. 2nd Edition
(Boston, MA; J.B. Yerrinton, 1854)

Summary: In this poem from her 1854 collection, Harper presents a strong protest against the common habit of slave owners breaking up slave families by selling the family members to different owners. Harper uses a mythical slave mother and her young son as representative examples of this practice. Harper's slave mother is long suffering ("Saw you the sad, imploring eye? / Its every glance was pain"), while the mother's son is a frightened child who is torn from "her circling arms, / Her last and fond embrace." Like many of Harper's poems, "The Slave Mother" is didactic and sentimental. Nonetheless, it would have achieved a passionate power when read orally, as was Harper's practice throughout her life.

Subject(s): Slavery, Children, Poetry

38 Phillis Wheatley

An Elegiac Poem, on the Death of that Celebrated Divine, and Eminent Servant of Jesus Christ, the Reverend and Learned George Whitefield

(Boston, MA; Ezekiel Russell & John Boyles, 1770)

Summary: Though there is some doubt as to whether this poem is Wheatley's first published piece (as scholars had long thought), there is no doubt that this poem was the work that first brought Wheatley international acclaim as a poet. First published as a pamphlet in New England in 1770 and then published again in London in 1771, the poem is an ode to George Whitefield, who was chaplain to the Countess of Huntingdon, a wealthy abolitionist who assisted Wheatley with her early literary efforts. The poem is written in iambic pentameter and is composed of rhymed couplets.

Subject(s): Abolition, Christianity

39 Phillis Wheatley

"Goliath of Gath"

Poems on Various Subjects, Religious and Moral
(London, England; Archibald Bell, 1773)

Summary: In this poem from her first published collection, Wheatley depicts the Biblical story of David and Goliath, in which the young David slew the evil giant Goliath. The poem is a lengthy ballad composed in rhymed couplets, a poetic form that Wheatley often used.

Subject(s): Biblical Story, Christianity, Religion

40 Phillis Wheatley

"Hymn to the Evening"

Poems on Various Subjects, Religious and Moral
(London, England; Archibald Bell, 1773)

Summary: In this companion piece to "Hymn to the Morning," Wheatley describes the sights and sounds of an evening thunderstorm in spring. The poem ends with a reference to nighttime and the eventual dawning of a new day.

Subject(s): Nature, Spring

41 Phillis Wheatley

"Hymn to the Morning"

Poems on Various Subjects, Religious and Moral
(London, England; Archibald Bell, 1773)

Summary: In this poem from her 1773 collection, Wheatley references the zodiac in a brief ode to morning. After celebrating the rise of the sun—"the illustrious king of day"—Wheatley abruptly cuts short her celebration and the poem: "I feel his fervid beams too strong, / And scarce begun, concludes the abortive song." The poem is a companion piece to "Hymn to the Evening."

Subject(s): Nature

42 Phillis Wheatley

"Niobe in Distress for Her Children Slain by Apollo: From Ovid's Metamorphoses, Book 6th, and from a View of the Painting of Mr. Richard Wilson"

Poems on Various Subjects, Religious and Moral
(London, England; Archibald Bell, 1773)

Summary: In this poem, Wheatley depicts scenes from Greek mythology, in particular Apollo's destruction of the children of Niobe, who then turned into stone while grieving for her dead children. Such classical themes, told in the formal poetic style of the day, represented accepted subjects for Wheatley and other poets of this era.

Subject(s): Poetry, Mythology, Murder

43 **Phillis Wheatley**

"On Being Brought from Africa to America"

Poems on Various Subjects, Religious and Moral
(London, England; Archibald Bell, 1773)

Summary: The subject of this poem is Wheatley's enslavement in West Africa in approximately 1761, at about the age of seven, and her subsequent journey to America. Once in America, the frail girl was bought by John Wheatley of Boston, who taught her to read. Recognizing her literary gifts, John Wheatley allowed Phillis to live a relatively pampered life. In this poem, Phillis Wheatley gives thanks for being rescued from her "pagan land" and introduced to Christianity, but she also admonishes whites to recognize that "Negroes black as Cain / May be refined, and join the angelic train." The poem consists of a single eight-line stanza comprising four rhymed couplets.

Subject(s): Slavery, Christianity, Africa

44 **Phillis Wheatley**

"On Imagination"

Poems on Various Subjects, Religious and Moral
(London, England; Archibald Bell, 1773)

Summary: In this poem from her 1773 collection, Wheatley sings the praises of imagination: "At thy command joy rushes on the heart, / And through the glowing veins the spirits dart." Wheatley makes heavy use of nature imagery in this poem, particularly in a stanza in which she describes imagination's power to drive away winter with the sights, smells, and sounds of springtime.

Subject(s): Nature, Imagination

45 **Phillis Wheatley**

"On Recollection"

Poems on Various Subjects, Religious and Moral
(London, England; Archibald Bell, 1773)

Summary: This poem is a testament to memory, including the anguish it causes as well as the joy it brings. In both the poem's form—rhymed couplets of iambic pentameter—as well as its subject, Wheatley follows the poetic conventions of colonial America. Though modern critics have sometimes dismissed Wheatley's poetry for its lack of comment on slavery and servitude, the protest poetry written by African Americans in the twentieth century could not have been conceived in Wheatley's lifetime.

Subject(s): Slavery, Memory, Colonial America

46 **Phillis Wheatley**

"Thoughts on the Works of Providence"

Poems on Various Subjects, Religious and Moral
(London, England; Archibald Bell, 1773)

Summary: This poem epitomizes the numerous religious poems in Wheatley's pioneering 1773 collection. Composed of ten stanzas of uneven length, the poem's rhymed couplets are written in iambic pentameter. Wheatley was approximately nineteen years of age when this collection appeared and was already a literary celebrity in both America and England.

Subject(s): Christianity, Religion

47 **Phillis Wheatley**

"To a Gentleman, On His Voyage to Great Britain for the Recovery of His Health"

Poems on Various Subjects, Religious and Moral
(London, England; Archibald Bell, 1773)

Summary: As its descriptive title suggests, this poem was written for a sick friend on his way to England. Following the strict poetic conventions of her day, Wheatley uses a formal rhyme scheme (though not rhymed couplets as in most of her other poems) in iambic pentameter. She also makes heavy use of religious imagery in wishing her friend, whom she addresses only as "R___", recovery from his illness.

Subject(s): Illness, Friendship, Religion

48 **Phillis Wheatley**

"To Maecenas"

Poems on Various Subjects, Religious and Moral
(London, England; Archibald Bell, 1773)

Summary: This poem from Wheatley's first published collection (and the first published collection of poetry written by an African American) is a variation of a poem by the Roman lyric poet Horace. In her version, Wheatley converts the original friendship ode into a celebration of Jesus. The poem epitomizes the classical foundation of much of Wheatley's poetry and her fondness for religious themes. It is composed in rhymed couplets, a literary form often used by Wheatley. At the time of this volume's publication, Wheatley—though a slave—was already a literary phenomenon in both America and in England, where this volume was published following a trip by Wheatley in 1771.

Subject(s): Religion, Slavery, Christianity

49 Phillis Wheatley

"To S.M., A Young African Painter: On Seeing His Works"

Poems on Various Subjects, Religious and Moral
(London, England; Archibald Bell, 1773)

Summary: This single-stanza poem is a tribute to an African painter whom Wheatley identifies only as "S.M.," in reality a slave named Scipio Moorhead. In the poem, Wheatley describes the inspiration that arises in her after she views the painter's work. As was standard for her, Wheatley composed this poem in rhymed couplets of iambic pentameter.

Subject(s): Painting

50 Phillis Wheatley

"To the University of Cambridge, in New-England"

Poems on Various Subjects, Religious and Moral
(London, England; Archibald Bell, 1773)

Summary: This poem, heavily religious in its imagery, is addressed to the students of what would become Harvard University in Boston. Wheatley counsels the students to "Improve your privileges while they stay" and warns them, "Let sin, that baneful evil to the soul / By you be shunn'd, nor once remit your guard."

Subject(s): Education, Religion

Drama

During the 1700s, black characters appeared mainly in stereotyped and comic roles in a handful of plays by white authors. Minstrelsy in the early 1800s became a common entertainment, practiced mainly by whites (in blackface make-up) and occasionally blacks as well. But, also during this time, there were some black playwrights who began to write about serious topics dealing with slavery and other black issues and black actors were beginning to appear in more challenging roles. The first black playwright in America was William Henry Brown, who began the African Grove Company in 1821 and in 1823 produced his play, *The Drama of King Shotaway*. Two important actors were associated with the African Grove Company. One, James Hewlet was the principal actor in Brown's play and also performed Shakespearean roles in the United States and abroad. The other, Ira Aldridge earned international recognition for his abilities playing Shakespeare's Othello while touring Europe from the 1820s to the 1860s. Both men were recognized by all audiences for their skill in performing the roles of both black and white characters. Ex-slave and man of letters, William Wells Brown, was the first African American to publish a play in America. *The Escape; or A Leap for Freedom* was published in 1858 and read from the lectern. Reflecting both the slave narrative and abolitionist fiction, its plot includes a slave couple who marry in secret and escape to Canada. New Orleans-born

Victor Sejour was the most productive black playwright during this period. Sejour lived in France and had at least twenty-one plays produced in Paris before his death in 1874.

51 Ira Aldridge, Adapter

The Black Doctor

Black Theater, U.S.A.: Forty-Five Plays by Black Americans, 1847-1974
(New York, NY; Free Press, 1974)

Summary: Ira Aldridge (1807-1867) adapted this play by French author Anicet-Bourgeoise for the English stage in 1846. The story concerns a black doctor, described by Aldridge as a "Mulatto," who falls in love with the daughter of a French aristocrat. When the love affair is discovered, the doctor is imprisoned. He goes insane, but in the play's final act, he saves his lover from a mob by taking a bullet meant for her. Aldridge's achievement in adapting and staging the play is considerable, although he was forced to leave the United States to do so.

Subject(s): Class Conflict, Exile

52 William Wells Brown

The Escape; or, A Leap for Freedom: A Drama in Five Acts

(Boston, MA; R.F. Wallcut, 1858)

Summary: The first published play by an African American, *The Escape; or, A Leap for Freedom* is a tale based on William Wells Brown's own life. A former slave who escaped to the North in 1834, Brown later became a renowned author, orator, and abolitionist. *The Escape* features the story of two slaves, Glen and Melinda, who marry in secret, then escape from their abusive owner to a new life in Canada. The work, with its melodramatic structure and comedic style infused with autobiographical elements, became a popular model for subsequent generations of African American writers.

Subject(s): Slavery

53 Victor Sejour

The Brown Overcoat

Black Theater, U.S.A.: Forty-Five Plays by Black Americans, 1847-1974
(New York, NY; Free Press, 1974)

Summary: This early comedy does not concern itself with race, but it is notable for its author's life and success. Born in New Orleans, Sejour traveled to Paris at the age of seventeen and stayed there the rest of his life. He became a renowned playwright in France, writing light comedies and historical romances that were popular at the time. He became an early example of an African American artist (later examples include James Baldwin, Richard Wright, and Josephine Baker) finding a freedom and success in Paris that would have been impossible in America. Written in 1858 and first produced in Paris a year later, a translated version of *The Brown Overcoat* was finally produced in America in a 1972 off-Broadway production.

Literary Criticism

There is no evidence of formal literary criticism written by blacks in this period. An early sustained criticism of African American literature was made by Thomas Jefferson about the writing of Phillis Wheatley and Ignatius Sancho in *Notes on the State of Virginia*. Jefferson judged the writing of both negatively and implied that their productions indicated a deficiency in black intellect. The writing of Phillis Wheatley, however, was variously noted by both American and European intellectuals, including Benjamin Rush and Francois-Marie Aruoet Voltaire, as a sign of the literary competency of blacks.

1860-1900

The historical experience that produced the black literature of the period between 1860 and 1900 was driven by complex political and social dynamics. Within the already established black northern bourgeoisie of New York, Boston, and Philadelphia, this era saw the further institutionalization of black churches, social clubs, benevolent groups, and religious clubs, many of which had been deeply politicized by the anti-slavery movements and its vicissitudes during the 1850s. During the Civil War, northern black communities contributed troops and important support to the northern forces, and they played an important role in the white- and black-supported Protestant missionary initiatives in the South during the Reconstruction era. Black expatriation from West Africa and Haiti, the Negro Conventions, and rebellion against Garrisonian abolitionism provided the black middle class and intellectuals in particular with important antecedents in black intellectual independence. This experience was deepened by their participation in the growth of black schools such as Fisk, Howard, Wilberforce, and Tuskegee.

The period of Reconstruction in the South from 1863 to 1867 might be seen as a new period of Americanization paralleling that which some northern blacks had experienced during the late eighteenth and early nineteenth centuries. This period saw the importation of northern and Republican control of black and white southern life, through institutions such as the Freedman's Bureau. A number of blacks took up independent farming. Many entered the newly opened sphere of politics through voting, political organization, and finally participation in state and national legislatures. A number of missionary groups from the North helped in the establishment of the predominantly black colleges, and although the results of black reconstruction were mixed, they did--as a number of historians have shown--involve the improvement of public services in education, health, and urban life throughout the South. Black political participation in Reconstruction, newly gained social and economic autonomy, as well as the creation of a middle class black society stimulated the viciously anti-black backlash of Reconstruction. During this period, whites instituted legalized segregation of public facilities, drove blacks out of political office and intimidated them from political organization, and

launched a campaign of terror against the black population in general.

To a large extent, both the northern and southern response to the terror of the post-Reconstruction South was dictated by the absorption of a middle class black culture in both the North and South. This culture had, in antebellum America, been cultivated upon anti-slavery politics, evangelical religions, and broad-based reform movements that splintered into the problematic radicalism of the 1850s. It is therefore no wonder that black American intellectuals and literary figures of this period were influenced so deeply by Harriet Beecher Stowe's *Uncle Tom's Cabin*, which combined all of these elements into a widely selling popular novel. This group of intellectuals could self-consciously take up the morally and spiritually edifying culture that is reflected in much of the black women's fiction of the period. In addition, these intellectuals were deeply influenced by the exotic romance and adventure elements--as well as the lyrical romanticism--of the New England "Fireside" poets such as Henry Wadsworth Longfellow, William Cullen Bryant, and John Greenleaf Whittier. And finally, this was a culture that had been politicized by the anti-slavery movement, the Civil War, and the attempted reconstruction of the South. It had, moreover, a recurring sense of black nationalism that extended from the colonization movement earlier in the century, particularly the radical colonization experiments of the 1850s and the experiences of expatriates such as Martin Delany and Alexander Crummell. Under the influence of literary models such as Whittier and later Joel Chandler Harris, it had increasingly absorbed the culture of the South. Figures such as Frederick Douglass had experimented in free market capitalism. And writers such as William Wells Brown and Frances E.W. Harper had, in various ways and contexts, experimented with literary careers. Most importantly, young black intellectuals such as W.E.B. Du Bois, William Monroe Trotter, and William Ferris had begun to enter major universities such as Harvard and Yale.

To a large extent, the response to the backlash against Reconstruction in the post-1877 South involved the re-creation of a broad-based protest effort that included church organizations, women's organizations, and political societies. These groups directly protested the terrors of lynching, the ferocious dehumanization of blacks in southern culture, and the exclusion of blacks from political participation in the North. Reflections of the movement appeared in literature, evident in the protest anti-racist poetry of Harper and her racial uplift novel, *Iola Leroy*, and the political fiction of Pauline Hopkins, including her novel *Contending Forces*. By the end of the century, this politicization led to a serious division between accomodationists such as Booker T. Washington, who sought to create a place for blacks in the economic rehabilitation of the South while withdrawing from political participation, and the overtly political activism of W.E.B. Du Bois, who led the Niagara Movement to its eventual culmination in the formation of the National Association for the Advancement of Colored People (NAACP).

To be sure, however, Washington and Du Bois shared a common conservative Victorian and Christian black American culture that was able to increasingly access mainstream elite American institutions and that was influenced by cosmopolitan European forces. To a large extent, this must be seen as the common cultural world from which figures such as the poets Albery Whitman, George McClellan, and Frances E.W. Harper worked, as well as the novelist Pauline Hopkins. In addition, highly successful writers such as Paul Laurence Dunbar and Charles W. Chesnutt were important antecedents to the Harlem Renaissance of the 1920s and early 1930s.

Fiction

If there was a single most important fictional source for African American writing in the second half of the nineteenth century, it was Harriet Beecher Stowe's *Uncle Tom's Cabin*. This novel addressed the themes of northern anti-slavery propaganda, domesticity, the Gothic, and antebellum plantation life, all of which would be adopted by black writers of the period. Such novels as Frances E.W. Harper's *Iola Leroy* and Pauline Hopkins's *Contending Forces* made use of light-skinned mulatto heroines and the theme of commitment to the improvement of the race.

A second major influence on the African American novel of the period was the evangelical novel. The growth of black churches and religious societies during the period inevitably led to the development of a novel that centered on the themes of evangelism and conversion. Fiction such as Emma Dunham Kelley's *Megda* and *Four Girls at Cottage City* (written as Emma D. Kelley-Hawkins) exemplified this trend. Much of this fiction depicted black family life during a period when many families had been destroyed both by the aftermath of slavery and by the racist attacks on black men. Finally, these novels preached the possibility of racial progress through the formation of new kinship units that would be at the core of the middle class.

A third variety of novel derived from the traditions of black nationalism that had been established by *David Walker's Appeal* and Martin Delany's pre-Civil War fiction *Blake*. This sentiment was evident in the work of Sutton Griggs, who pub-

lished a series of four black nationalist novels: *Imperium in Imperio, Overshadowed, Unfettered* and *Pointing the Way*.

The greatest advance in fiction was made by Charles W. Chesnutt in two short story collections, *The Conjure Woman* and *The Wife of His Youth*, and three novels, *The Colonel's Dream, The Marrow of Tradition*, and *The House Behind the Cedars*. The novels combined the regionalist accounts of Reconstruction and post-Reconstruction southern culture with a depth of psychological insight that had not appeared previously in African American fiction. This insight was directed toward the inner dynamics of intellectual blacks as they interacted with white superiors and with less-educated blacks.

Also explored in great detail were the inner conflicts of tragic mulattos as well as the precarious balance of interracial peace in the post-Reconstruction South. In many ways, Chesnutt not only looked back to the moral allegories of Nathaniel Hawthorne but also ahead to the psychology of racial identity to be explored in the work of such Harlem Renaissance writers as Langston Hughes, Zora Neale Hurston, and Nella Larsen.

54 Lorenzo Dow Blackson

The Rise and Progress of the Kingdoms of Light & Darkness: Or, The Reign of Kings Alpha and Abadon
(Philadelphia, PA; J. Nicholas, 1867)

Summary: This early novel offers an original take on the battle between Jesus Christ and Satan for control of the Earth. Told in the style of a folk tale, the novel follows King Alpha (Jesus) as he battles King Abadon (Satan) through the centuries before defeating him at the time of the U.S. Civil War of the 1860s. The novel is illustrated.

Subject(s): Folk Tales, Civil War, Christianity

55 M.L. Burgess

Ave Maria
(Boston, MA; Press of the Monthly Review, 1895)

Summary: This short work (only thirty-three pages) features four stories, each of which deals in some way with Catholicism. Burgess was a nurse.

Subject(s): Catholicism, Literature

56 Charles W. Chesnutt

The Conjure Woman
(Boston, MA; Houghton, Mifflin and Company, 1899)

Summary: In the few years prior to 1899, Charles W. Chesnutt began establishing his literary reputation with short stories built around the character of Uncle Julius, a wise former slave. For his first full-length book, Houghton, Mifflin decided to collect several of these tales in addition to commissioning Chesnutt to write a handful of new ones. The format of each story is the same: Uncle Julius relates tales—in the rural southern dialect that was being popularized by such writers as Paul Laurence Dunbar and Joel Chandler Harris—of slavery-era plantation days to a white Ohio man. Though utilizing folk tales and humor, Chesnutt broke new ground with these stories by including realistic depictions of slave life, featuring miserly slave owners seeking profit at the expense of their slaves' dignity and well-being.

Subject(s): American South, Slavery, Folk Tales

57 Charles W. Chesnutt

The House Behind the Cedars

(Boston, MA; Houghton, Mifflin and Company, 1900)

Summary: Originally planned with the title of "Rena Walden," *The House Behind the Cedars* tells the story of a light-skinned black woman (seven-eighths white) who tries to pass for white. Following in the footsteps of her brother, Rena attempts to enter white upper-class society in a town in South Carolina. At first she succeeds, becoming engaged to a white gentleman named George Tryon. However, Rena's ruse is discovered, and she seeks redemption by returning to her African American roots in another locale. Despite her efforts, however, Rena is relentlessly harassed by Tryon and a local schoolteacher, and she eventually dies of exposure while trying to escape to her mother's house. In this and other works, Chesnutt argued passionately that until racism was exonerated, light-skinned blacks had a moral right to pass for white if they so chose.

Subject(s): American South, Race Relations, Miscegenation

58 Charles W. Chesnutt
Sylvia Lyons Render, Editor

The Short Fiction of Charles W. Chesnutt

(Washington, DC; Howard University Press, 1974)

Summary: This volume collects the short stories of Charles W. Chesnutt, whose literary efforts at the turn of the twentieth century revealed him to be an astute observer of racial issues. Included are Chesnutt's early "Uncle Julius" stories, featuring the trickster ex-slave Uncle Julius; his "color line" stories of the turn-of-the-century, in which he examines such controversial issues as miscegenation; and his later stories, in which he continued to explore race relations while crafting stories with more diverse settings and situations. The stories date from 1885 to 1930 and provide an in-depth look at Chesnutt's development as a literary pioneer.

Subject(s): American South, Race Relations, Miscegenation

59 Charles W. Chesnutt

The Wife of His Youth and Other Stories of the Color Line

(Boston, MA; Houghton Mifflin, 1899)

Summary: Chesnutt's second collection of short stories displays the author's continued development as a pioneering

writer of realistic stories about race. Unlike his first collection, *The Conjure Woman*, this collection includes only one story set during slavery. The remainder of the stories are set in the postwar "New South" and focus primarily on the issue of miscegenation—sexual relations between members of different races. Himself a product of a racially mixed union, Chesnutt used these stories to explore not only unions between blacks and whites but also the racial tensions between light-skinned blacks and dark-skinned blacks. Chesnutt did not advocate miscegenation but merely held a mirror up to prejudicial attitudes and their legacy.

Subject(s): American South, Race Relations, Miscegenation

60 Martin Delany

Blake; or, The Huts of America: A Novel

(Boston, MA; Beacon Press, 1970)

Summary: Written in the mid-1800s but not published in complete form until 1970, Martin Delany's only novel revolves around an educated black man from the West Indies who is kidnapped into slavery and brought to the United States. Once there, his Mississippi owner sells his wife to another man, prompting the protagonist to plot revenge through a secret organization. Delany was a pioneering physician and magazine publisher and was the first black high-ranking field officer in the Unites States Army; during the Civil War, he organized two regiments of former slaves to fight on behalf of the union.

Subject(s): Slavery, Civil War

61 Thomas Detter

Nellie Brown, or, The Jealous Wife, with Other Sketches

(San Francisco, CA; Cuddy & Hughes, 1871)

Summary: This 1871 work is notable for its depiction of life in the American West, specifically Nevada and Idaho, a fictional terrain explored by few if any other black writers of the period. Interestingly, the book includes a preface in which Detter apologizes to the reader for his literary shortcomings. He explains these shortcomings due to the lack of educational opportunities for blacks in his native Washington, D.C.

Subject(s): American West, Education

62 Paul Laurence Dunbar

Folks from Dixie

(New York, NY; Dodd, Mead and Company, 1898)

Summary: Written during a two-year period in which Dunbar was living in Washington, D.C., and in which he secretly married writer Alice Ruth Moore, *Folks from Dixie* contains twelve short stories. Half of the stories are set during the slavery era, while the other half are set after Reconstruction. Thematically, the stories range from an indictment of the "Jim Crow" laws that denied civil rights to post-emancipation blacks, to a discussion of the ill effects of northern migration on southern blacks, to an expose of labor union practices in barring blacks from membership. Prior to 1898, Dunbar had become famous for his dialect poems, but he turned to fiction in the hope that it would allow him a larger forum in which to examine the problems faced by African Americans at the time.

Subject(s): Reconstruction, Slavery, Civil Rights

---

63 **Paul Laurence Dunbar**

The Love of Landry

(New York, NY; Dodd, Mead and Company, 1900)

Summary: This novel, Dunbar's second, is a slight western-themed romance set in Colorado, where Dunbar himself had lived during 1899 and 1900 while trying to keep his tuberculosis at bay. The plot concerns the love affair between Mildred Osbourne, who travels west to regain her health, and Landry Thaler, a rugged cowboy who saves Mildred from a cattle stampede. Like Dunbar's novels *The Uncalled* and *The Fanatics,* this work focuses on white rather than black characters, as Dunbar tried in vain to establish himself as a respected novelist with a broad thematic canvas.

Subject(s): Romance, Country Life

---

64 **Paul Laurence Dunbar**
E.W. Kemble, Illustrator

The Strength of Gideon, and Other Stories

(New York, NY; Dodd, Mead & Company, 1900)

Summary: This 1900 collection of short stories is significant among Dunbar's fictional oeuvre for its protest of racial discrimination and its treatment of numerous issues of importance to African Americans at the turn of the twentieth century. Among the collection's twenty stories are pieces that denounce lynching, explore the difficulties of black migration from the South to the North, and expose the hollowness of blacks who forfeit racial justice for social improvement. Though white critics at the time of the collection's publication tended to ignore the stories of social protest in favor of the more humorous, plantation-era pieces, later critics have applauded the breadth of characters and thematic concerns in the collection.

Subject(s): Racism, American South

---

65 **Paul Laurence Dunbar**

The Uncalled: A Novel

(New York, NY; Dodd, Mead and Company, 1898)

Summary: Set in Dexter, Ohio, during the late-1800s and somewhat reminiscent of Nathaniel Hawthorne's classic novel, *The Scarlet Letter,* Dunbar's first novel examines a young minister's fight with an intolerant community. The protagonist, Frederick Bent, returns from seminary to be the pastor of Dexter Baptist Church; he also becomes engaged to the daughter of the church's pastor emeritus. However, he breaks with his fiancee and with the community when they insist that he condemn a woman who has given birth to an illegitimate child.

Though a modest commercial success, the novel was criticized by reviewers who longed for the local color of Dunbar's dialect poetry and who wondered why Dunbar had chosen to write a novel that did not include any black characters.

Subject(s): Religion, Intolerance

---

66 **Victoria Earle**
Mary L. Payne, Illustrator

Aunt Lindy: A Story Founded on Real Life

(New York, NY; Press of J.J. Little & Co., 1893)

Summary: This short story, published in book form, features black characters as part of a tale about a fire and its aftermath in a fictional Georgia town. The story was illustrated by Mary L. Payne.

Subject(s): City and Town Life, Fires

---

67 **Sutton Griggs**

Imperium in Imperio

(Cincinnati, OH; Editor Pub. Co., 1899)

Summary: In his acclaimed first novel, Griggs reimagines the political reality of late-nineteenth-century America. He depicts a United States that contains a separate, black-dominated state known as the "Imperium." In portraying this world, Griggs follows the lives of two central characters: Belton, a poor but indomitable black man who becomes a conservative assimilationist; and Bernard, a wealthy mulatto who becomes a militant black nationalist and who fights to preserve the purity of the black race despite his own racially mixed heritage. Most remarkable about this 1899 novel are the militant calls for a proud, separate black state that foreshadowed the Black Nationalist movement of the 1960s by six decades. However, Griggs also implies in the novel that sympathetic whites are the key to solving racism, an attitude more in keeping with turn-of-the-century society.

Subject(s): Racism, Black Nationalism, Miscegenation

---

68 **Frances E.W. Harper**
(Also known as Frances Ellen Watkins)

Iola Leroy; or, Shadows Uplifted

(Philadelphia, PA; Garrigues Brothers, 1892)

Summary: Set just prior to the start of the American Civil War (1861-1865), Harper's best-known novel is about a fiercely independent woman who strives to improve the lives of fellow African Americans. Iola Leroy is a blond-haired mulatto who is unaware of her true racial identity. When she eventually discovers her identity, she embraces it wholeheartedly. In the novel, Harper also sets up a love triangle between Iola, a white physician, and a black physician whom Iola eventually marries. Sentimental in the style of other post-war fiction, *Iola Leroy* was the first widely distributed American novel by an African American woman.

Subject(s): Civil War, Slavery, Identity

69 Pauline Hopkins
R. Emmett Owen, Illustrator

Contending Forces: A Romance Illustrative of Negro Life North and South
(Boston, MA; Colored Co-operative Publishing Co., 1900)

Summary: Though Hopkins was a published writer in several genres, she is best known for this novel in which she wove racial and social themes into the context of nineteenth century women's romances. The melodramatic story has many sub-plots; its main characters are brother and sister Will and Dora Smith and their two boarders, Sappho Clark and John Langley. Through these characters Hopkins highlights problems, such as lynching, voting rights, and employment, faced by blacks in post-Reconstruction America, and she advocates education and political rights. However, Hopkins's major theme was women's issues, especially the slavery and sexual exploitation of black women (as evinced by the beautiful Sappho's experiences and victimization), and women's need for self-reliance.

Subject(s): Women, Sexism, Social Chronicle

70 James H.W. Howard

Bond and Free: A True Tale of Slave Times
(Harrisburg, PA; E.K. Meyers, 1886)

Summary: Howard's 1886 novel focuses on fugitive slaves and their attempts to gain freedom. The slave-owning Maxwell family is a well-established Virginia clan; among their slaves are Elva, her daughter Purcey, and her sons Henry and Joseph. Purcey eventually marries another slave, William; by the end of the novel, these two have escaped, along with their son, to freedom in the North.

Subject(s): Slavery, Freedom, Family

71 Amelia E. Johnson

The Hazeley Family
(Philadelphia, PA; American Baptist Publication Society, 1894)

Summary: The aim of Johnson in this 1894 novel is to highlight the benefits of Christian living. The story centers on Flora Hazeley, who lives with her two aunts until one of the women dies. Flora then returns home bent on reforming everyone in her immediate family. Didactic and high-minded, the novel's most interesting feature is its lack of racial reference. Nothing in the story identifies the characters or the author as black, while the book's illustrations depict whites.

Subject(s): Race Relations, Christianity

72 J. McHenry Jones

Hearts of Gold: A Novel
(Wheeling, WV; Daily Intelligencer, 1896)

Summary: The backdrop for this 1896 work is the Reconstruction Period of 1865 to 1877, in which freed slaves made some political and social gains but were still often overwhelmed by racist violence and oppression. These injustices are extensively depicted in the novel, which revolves around the issue of miscegenation and the effects it has on the protagonist, Regina.

Subject(s): Reconstruction, Racism, Miscegenation

73 Emma Dunham Kelley
(Also known as Emma D. Kelley-Hawkins)

Megda
(Boston, MA; J.H. Earle, 1891)

Summary: This novel, in which most of the characters appear to be white, centers on Megda, a young agnostic whose friends convert to Christianity. Megda loses Reverend Stanley to the religious Ethel, who dies on the eve of her wedding. Inspired by the dying Ethel, Megda promises to spread a message of religious faith and later marries Stanley herself. When another of Megda's acquaintances from school dies, she and Stanley promise to take in the woman's daughter as their own.

Subject(s): Religion, Christianity, Marriage

74 Emma D. Kelley-Hawkins
(Also known as Emma Dunham Kelley)

Four Girls at Cottage City
(Boston, MA; J.H. Earle, 1898)

Summary: A Christian moral tale centering on white characters, this novel follows four girls, sisters Jessie and Garnet and their friends Allie and Vera, as they go on vacation to the Cape Cod resort of Cottage City. On the way there, they meet two young men: Fred, who is Jessie and Garnet's cousin, and his friend Erford. The girls stay at an elderly couple's cottage, which they remember as being the place where their fictional heroine Megda stayed. They meet a poor widow and her crippled son, Robin. Later, the group pays a Boston physician to operate on Robin. Among the young people, Vera marries Fred and Jessie marries Erford.

Subject(s): Doctors, Sisters, Christianity

75 Alice Ruth Moore
(Also known as Alice Ruth Moore Dunbar Nelson, Alice Dunbar-Nelson)

Violets and Other Tales
(Boston, MA; Monthly Review, 1895)

Summary: Nelson's first published collection contains poems and essays as well as short stories. The title story, which tells of a woman in love who dies of a broken heart, is a mixture of romance and death imagery, both of which Nelson would examine in much of her later work. In addition to the story "Violets," the collection includes a poem of the same title that works as a compressed version of the story. The image of the violet would play a recurring role in Nelson's life and art throughout her career.

Subject(s): Love, Flowers, Death

76 **Alice Ruth Moore Dunbar Nelson**

(Also known as Alice Dunbar-Nelson, Alice Ruth Moore)

The Goodness of St. Rocque, and Other Stories

(New York, NY; Dodd, Mead, 1899)

Summary: Published as a companion piece to *Poems of Cabin and Field* by Paul Laurence Dunbar, to whom Alice Ruth Moore Dunbar Nelson was married at the time, this collection focuses on the black Creole culture of New Orleans, Louisiana. The stories in the collection mix standard English with black rural southern dialect (a dialect perfected by Paul Laurence Dunbar in his works) and feature romantic situations and religious imagery. The title story, for instance, follows an exotic Creole woman as she combines Catholic prayer with voodoo practices to win back her beloved from a rival woman. This collection established Nelson's reputation as a skilled writer of southern regional fiction.

Subject(s): Love, Religion, American South

77 **Sanda**

(Pseudonym of Walter H. Stowers, William H. Anderson)

Appointed: An American Novel

(Detroit, MI; Detroit Law Printing Co., 1894)

Summary: With action ranging from Detroit to the South, this story depicts the friendship between a black and a white man. Their relationship ends in the lynching of the black friend, John Saunders. The novel provides one of the first fictional descriptions of the lynching of a black man.

Subject(s): Racism, American South, Lynching

Nonfiction

To a large extent, the writing of the era between the Civil War and 1900 represented the record of a rising black middle class in both the North and South. The Emancipation Proclamation of 1863 abolished slavery and the Civil Rights Act of 1875 established a semblance of equality, but in 1896 the U.S. Supreme Court decided in *Plessy v. Ferguson* that "separate but equal" facilities did not violate the Constitution. As a result, much of the writing between these years was concerned primarily with the economic, social, political, and cultural conditions of blacks under slavery and afterwards, and it took the form of

journalism, scholarship, politics, and the advocacy of "uplifting" the race.

The growing intellectual world of the A.M.E. church provided an important repository for the literary culture of figures such as Daniel Payne and Frances E.W. Harper. Works included literary criticism, biography, autobiography, theology, church history, and political tracts. These writers reflected Victorian Christian culture and advocated bourgeois stability, literary cultivation, and middle-class aspirations.

Women such as Harriet A. Jacobs, Harriet Tubman, Sojourner Truth and Charlotte Forten Grimke were writing, speaking and politically active during this period. Jacob's wrote her slave narrative *Incidents in the Life of a Slave Girl*, which was published in 1861. It was the first slave narrative by an African American woman, and addressed not only the issues that men's slave narratives addressed, but also frankly discussed the sexual abuse suffered at the hands of white men. Though Tubman and Truth were illiterate, they became prominent figures; Tubman's autobiography was published in 1869 and some of Truth's speeches before and after the Civil War about abolition, religion and women's issues were recorded. Grimke, on the other hand, was well educated and kept a series of diaries that are indicative of what the life of a free woman of color was like during this period.

Frederick Douglass, who had published his slave narrative in 1845, was an extremely influential figure throughout this period. His appeals for the abolition of slavery prior to the Civil War changed to calls for political activism for equality and social reform after the Emancipation Proclamation. As the century came to an end, his biographical memoirs, speeches and essays all served as inspirational literature for the next generation of writers.

Following in Douglass' footsteps, another major figure who began writing during this period was W.E.B. Du Bois. One year after Douglass' death and in the same year as the *Plessy* verdict (1896), Du Bois published *The Suppression of the African Slave Trade to the United States*, the first volume in the Harvard Historical Studies series. This book detailed the overt racism and oppression of blacks which still existed in the South and which Du Bois encountered while a student at Fisk University.

78 **Richard Allen**

The Life, Experience, and Gospel Labors of the Rt. Rev. Richard Allen

(Philadelphia, PA; Lee and Yeocum, 1887)

Summary: This autobiographical work provides insight into the life of Richard Allen. Born a slave, he was the first black to be ordained and licensed to preach in America. The book shows how tensions between black and white members of St. George's Methodist Episcopal Church in Philadelphia led to his establishing the African Methodist Episcopal Church. The volume also includes an argument by Allen against criticism of blacks in nursing services during Philadelphia's yellow fever epidemic as well as an inspirational address to blacks in the United States.

Subject(s): Religion, Slavery, Nursing

79 **William Francis Allen,** Compiler

Slave Songs of the United States
(New York, NY; A. Simpson & Co., 1867)

Summary: Citing the general popularity of slave songs and their subsequent imitations in the early nineteenth century, as well as a renewal of interest in them following an 1861 educational mission to the Port Royal Islands, this book offers a collection of slave songs from around the United States. The book, which was published shortly after the Civil War, organizes the songs by region and provides directions for singing.

Subject(s): Slavery, Music

80 **Ruth Bogin,** Editor
Bert James Loewenberg, Co-editor

Black Women in Nineteenth-Century American Life: Their Words, Their Thoughts, Their Feelings
(University Park, PA; Pennsylvania State University Press, 1976)

Summary: *Black Women in Nineteenth-Century American Life: Their Words, Their Thoughts, Their Feelings* is a collection of primary documents--letters, diaries, and other original writings--that reflects the day-to-day lives, as well as the shifting social and political attitudes, of American women of color throughout the tumultuous 1800s. Co-edited by historian and educator Ruth Bogin, the book attempts to focus, in particular, on those women who, as members of political and social groups existing outside the "elite" white society, would not have been heard without her research. By uncovering and including the writings of these women into the public record, Bogin intends to realign the written history of nineteenth century women and counterbalance the public sentiments and community activities of a minority of outspoken, albeit noteworthy, female figures against the opinions, activities, and beliefs held by many more lower and middle-class women.

Subject(s): Women's Rights, Letters, Family Life

81 **William Wells Brown**

Black Man: His Antecedents, His Genius, and His Achievements
(New York, NY; T. Hamilton, 1863)

Summary: A compelling orator on behalf of the abolitionist cause, former slave and author William Wells Brown published his first major historical work, *The Black Man: His Antecedents, His Genius, and His Achievements*, in 1863. Containing a short memoir by the author, who had published his widely read slave narrative in 1847, *The Black Man* contains two sections: the essay "Antecedents," which pushes for freedom for black slaves by mustering historical comparisons between Anglo-Saxon and African societies; and a collection of over fifty biographical sketches, mostly of noteworthy African Americans and Haitians, that provides the volume's bulk. The popularity of Brown's book, fueled no doubt by his numerous speaking engagements, resulted in two editions and four printings overall, the last in 1865. While historians have faulted the work for its numerous inaccuracies, they also cite Brown for his effort to draw African American contributions to U.S. culture into the light of history.

Subject(s): Slavery, Abolition, American History

82 **William Wells Brown**

My Southern Home; or, The South and Its People
(Boston, MA; A.G. Brown, 1880)

Summary: A masterful and tireless orator on behalf of the abolitionist cause, William Wells Brown was the first African American to publish a novel, play, travel book, full-length military study of Afro-Americans, and study of black sociology. Born into slavery in 1814, Brown's last book, *My Southern Home; or The South and Its People*, is considered by many critics to be the best showcase of his strengths as both a writer and chronicler. The first part of the volume details slave life, reviving the abolitionist materials, historical writings, and realistic and romanticized fictions Brown created earlier in his writing career. The second section of *My Southern Home* recounts the author's trip to the South in the winter of 1879-80. Brown documents with dramatic intensity the growing despair and oppression felt by southern blacks, foreshadowing W.E.B. Du Bois's 1903 work, *The Souls of Black Folk*. He also includes transcriptions of the African American slave and folk songs he heard during his trip, thereby preserving them for future generations.

Subject(s): American History, Social Chronicle, American South

83 **William Wells Brown**

The Negro in the American Rebellion: His Heroism and His Fidelity
(Boston, MA; Lee & Shepard, 1867)

Summary: A former slave-turned-abolitionist, William Wells Brown became well known as a chronicler of African American accomplishments. *The Negro in the American Rebellion: His Heroism and His Fidelity* was the first treatment of the role of African Americans during the Civil War, and it also briefly covered black participation in the two other "American" wars: the Revolutionary War and the War of 1812. Unfortunately, the work sold few copies, and those left unsold and warehoused were destroyed during the great Boston fire of 1872. While large portions of *The Negro in the American Rebellion* are compiled from other sources, some sections clearly come more from Brown's fertile imagination than from the historical record. In one section, Brown describes President Andrew Johnson as: "Intensely in love with himself, egotistical, without dignity, tyrannical, ungrateful, and fond of flattery, Mr. Johnson was entirely unprepared to successfully resist the overtures of the slaveholding aristocracy, by whom he had so long wished to be recognized."

Subject(s): Civil War, American Revolution, History

84 William Wells Brown

The Rising Son; or, The Antecedents and Advancement of the Colored Race
(Boston, MA; A.G. Brown, 1874)

Summary: Born into slavery in 1814, Brown escaped into freedom, learned to read, and dedicated most of his life to abolitionist and, then, temperance work. *The Rising Son; or, The Antecedents and Advancement of the Colored Race* would be Brown's last, longest volume of history. "After availing himself of all the reliable information obtainable, the author is compelled to acknowledge the scantiness of materials for a history of the African race," admits Brown in the preface of his work, and the lack of factual detail would seem to bear him out. While little time was devoted to research, Brown lavished attention on the human aspect of his study, compiling individual histories of over one hundred African Americans whose stories would otherwise have been lost. The book's general organization is based on Brown's 1863 work, *The Black Man,* which critics have noted is clearer and more forceful in its impact.

Subject(s): Biography, African Americans, History

85 Alexander Crummell

Africa and America: Addresses and Discourses
(Springfield, MA; Wiley & Co., 1891)

Summary: A mentor to NAACP-founder W.E.B. Du Bois and an outspoken critic of the assimilationist philosophy of Booker T. Washington, Crummell (1819-1898) was among the most prominent speakers in nineteenth century discussions of "the Negro Problem." Born to free blacks in New York City, he graduated from Oneida Institute in 1837, became an ordained Episcopalian priest in 1840, earned a degree from Cambridge University in 1853, and taught in Liberia in the 1860s. Many of the speeches in *Africa and America* focus on Crummell's Pan-African ideas and his spiritual approach to life.

Subject(s): Pan-Africanism, Spirituality, Africa

86 Alexander Crummell

The Future of Africa: Being Addresses, Sermons, etc., etc., Delivered in the Republic of Liberia
(New York, NY; Scribner, 1862)

Summary: *The Future of Africa: Being Addresses, Sermons, etc., etc., Delivered in the Republic of Liberia* collects the public pronouncements of Episcopalian priest and educator Alexander Crummell, many featuring Crummell's spiritual views and his support of a Pan-African future. Educated in the United States and at Cambridge University, Crummell left England in the 1860s to teach in the fledgling nation of Liberia. Returning to the United States in 1870, he served as pastor of St. Luke's Episcopal Church in Washington, D.C., until his death in 1898. Founder of the American Negro Academy,

Crummell was also a noted voice in discussions of the "Negro Problem" in post-Civil War America.

Subject(s): Pan-Africanism, Spirituality, Christianity

87 Alexander Crummell

The Greatness of Christ and Other Sermons
(New York, NY; Thomas Whittaker, 1882)

Summary: A Pan-Africanist who taught in Liberia for several years, Alexander Crummell (1819-1898) was also an ordained Episcopalian priest. In *The Greatness of Christ and Other Sermons* he collected what he considered his most moving sermons. These sermons espouse his spiritual views regarding African Americans as they attempted to deal with the aftermath of slavery and "the Negro Problem" that resulted in the founding of the African nation of Liberia. In 1870 Crummell returned to Washington, D.C., serving as pastor of that city's St. Luke's Episcopal Church.

Subject(s): Pan-Africanism, Religion, Spirituality

88 Alexander Crummell

The Relations and Duties of Free Colored Men in America to Africa: A Letter to Charles B. Dunbar by the Rev. Alex. Crummell
(Hartford, CT; Press of Case, Lockwood and Company, 1861)

Summary: *The Relations and Duties of Free Colored Men in America to Africa* reflects the pro-Africa beliefs of Alexander Crummell (1819-1898). A prominent voice in both spiritual matters and discussions of the "Negro Problem" following the Civil War, Crummell expounds in this volume upon the responsibility of African Americans not only to pursue education, spirituality, and integrity, but also to forge a renewed relationship to Africa in light of their newfound freedom. Crummell himself actively supported emigrating African Americans. In addition to raising funds for the founding of Liberia while in England, he worked as a missionary in Africa and taught in Liberia before returning to become pastor of an Episcopal parish in the United States, where he served until his death.

Subject(s): Pan-Africanism, Africa, Responsibility

89 W.E.B. Du Bois
Herbert Aptheker, Editor

The Correspondence of W.E.B. Du Bois. Volumes 1-33840
(Amherst, MA; University of Massachussets Press, 1973)

Summary: Twenty years before his death in the early 1960s, noted black scholar and writer W.E.B. Du Bois chose a white man and fellow Marxist, Herbert Aptheker, to edit his correspondence. In 1961 Du Bois gave Aptheker over one hundred thousand letters as well as other personal papers. The daunting task handed to Aptheker resulted in the three-volume *The Cor-*

respondence of W.E.B. Du Bois, which has been praised for providing a balanced portrait of the black leader. Du Bois, a black American of international stature and founder of the National Association for the Advancement of Colored People (NAACP), engaged in voluminous correspondence with other social leaders, and his letters are interesting in that they reflect his belief in the equality of the races and his gradual embrace of Communism, despite its unpopularity during the Cold War era. Aptheker illuminates Du Bois' letters with notes explaining the background of the correspondence and the identities of the individuals mentioned in the letters. The selection process involved research in numerous private and public archives.

Subject(s): Biography, Communism, Civil Rights

90 **W.E.B. Du Bois**

The Suppression of the African Slave-Trade to the United States of America, 1638-1870
(New York, NY; Longmans, Green, and Co., 1896)

Summary: W.E.B. Du Bois was among the most noted civil rights activists of the twentieth century. Raised in Massachusetts, he had little contact with overt racism until he moved south to attend Fisk University. While obtaining his Ph.D. at Harvard, he wrote his doctoral thesis on the slave trade. Published in 1896 as *The Suppression of the African Slave Trade to the United States of America, 1638-1870,* the work reflects its author's reaction to the oppressive treatment of blacks by whites, as well as the anger he felt upon encountering vestiges of the southern slave culture during his tenure at Fisk. Du Bois's lifelong desire to separate himself from the white culture that had enslaved his race would fuel his efforts to establish the National Association for the Advancement of Colored People little over a decade later.

Subject(s): Slavery, History, American South

91 **Fisk University. Social Science Institute**
Clifton H. Johnson, Editor

God Struck Me Dead: Religious Conversion Experiences and Autobiographies of Negro Ex-Slaves
(Nashville, TN; Pilgrim Press, 1945)

Summary: This book is a collection of six brief autobiographies and other narratives of men and women of color who once wore the yoke of slavery. Through their experiences of attaining freedom, their spiritual beliefs, and their views of nineteenth century America, modern readers can gain a deeper understanding of what it truly meant to be slave and to be free. The material for this work was collected during the Fisk Social Science Institute's massive study on race relations during the 1930s.

Subject(s): Spirituality, Slavery, Autobiography

92 **Henry Ossian Flipper**

A Colored Cadet at West Point: Autobiography of Lieut. Henry Ossian Flipper, U.S.A., First Graduate of Color from the U.S. Military Academy
(New York, NY; H. Lee & Co., 1878)

Summary: Henry Ossian Flipper was the first African American to enroll at the prestigious West Point Military Academy. In his *A Colored Cadet at West Point* Flipper recounts his experiences up to and including his graduation from the Academy. One of the more colorful African American figures of the nineteenth century, Flipper remained in service to the U.S. military, and several of his considerable accomplishments are also recounted here. Unfortunately, his career would later have a setback; Flipper was court-martialed and dismissed from military duty in 1882.

Subject(s): Military Life, Racism, Autobiography

93 **Harriet A. Jacobs**
Lydia Maria Child, Editor

Incidents in the Life of a Slave Girl
(Boston, MA; Privately printed, 1861)

Summary: Similar to 1845's *Narrative of the Life of Frederick Douglass,* Harriet Ann Jacobs' *Incidents in the Life of a Slave Girl* details the author's life as a slave, her efforts to resist the advances of her master, and her eventual attainment of freedom for both her children and herself. Unlike slave narratives written by men, Jacobs' autobiography shows her desire for freedom as a result of her treatment as a slave rather than an exposure to "book learning." Characterized by critics as a proto-feminist work due to its candid depiction of sexuality, *Incidents* shows the institution of slavery from a woman's point of view; as Jacobs writes: "Slavery is terrible for men; but it is far more terrible for women." Jacobs' autobiography was reissued by Harvard University Press in 1987.

Subject(s): Slavery, Autobiography, Sexual Abuse

94 **Bert James Loewenberg,** Editor

Black Women in Nineteenth-Century American Life: Their Words, Their Thoughts, Their Feelings
(University Park, PA; Pennsylvania State University Press, 1976)

Summary: This work offers a diversity of life experiences from black American women of the nineteenth century. The book includes their written or recorded observations. Among the more widely known women represented in the book are Sojourner Truth, Harriet Tubman, and Charlotte Forten Grimke. Lesser known individuals reveal their personal insights as well.

Subject(s): Women

95 **Daniel Alexander Payne**

Recollections of Seventy Years
(Nashville, TN; Publishing House of the A.M.E. Sunday School Union, 1888)

Summary: Born to free parents in Charleston, South Carolina, Daniel Alexander Payne opened a school for other free blacks. Following the Nat Turner slave rebellion, Payne went north to study theology. He joined the African Methodist Episcopal Church and was later made a bishop. As the president of Wilburforce University, he became the nation's first black college president. In his 1888 autobiography, Payne discusses these and other events from his life, including his work as an abolitionist.

Subject(s): Religion, Education, Abolition

96 **G.D. Pike**

The Jubilee Singers, and Their Campaign for Twenty Thousand Dollars
(Boston, MA; Lee and Shepard, 1873)

Summary: Written by G.D. Pike, *The Jubilee Singers, and Their Campaign for Twenty Thousand Dollars* documents the first years of the famous Fisk University singing group. Founded in 1871 by music instructor George L. White as a way to raise much needed funds for the university, the Jubilee Singers toured the northern United States, performing black work songs and spirituals before captivated audiences. Sponsored by Brooklyn pastor Henry Ward Beecher, the group raised over $150,000, far exceeding their goal, funding the construction of Jubilee Hall at Fisk, and becoming a permanent part of Fisk campus.

Subject(s): Music, Students, Performing Arts

Poetry

In the period after the Civil War, black poetry began to thrive during an era when the mainstream of American poetry defined itself as the morally edifying literary entertainment of the New England and northern American middle class. In particular, the literary production of African American poetry benefited from the institutionalization of black educational, religious, and cultural institutions such as magazines. Poetry during this time was largely written by members of the black middle class; they created poetry not unlike that produced by the "Fireside" school of poets.

To a large extent, poets like James Madison Bell, Albery Allson Whitman, and George McClellan reflected the romanticism, nationalism, and regionalism of earlier white poets such as William Cullen Bryant, Henry Wadsworth Longfellow, James Russell Lowell, and others. These black poets wrote not only morally edifying romantic poetry but also nature lyrics, narratives that interpreted the country's birth and western movement, tales of black heroes, and strong anti-slavery and

political poems. The poets saw themselves as offspring of the central line of English verse extending from Britain. Moreover, they sought to maintain the energy of lofty literary conventions with the zeal of the New England missionary societies that had founded so many of the black colleges in the South after the Civil War and during the period of Reconstruction.

A third major factor in the development of this poetry was the emergence of literary regionalism and the development of a broader American audience that slowly opened to blacks. Black artists began to explore the possibilities of literary dialect, such as the southern regional experiments of Joel Chandler Harris. However, the major beneficiary of this trend was Paul Laurence Dunbar. Born in Dayton, Ohio, and largely self-educated, Dunbar had a remarkable gift for the production of stylized dialect speech in rhyming verse. In addition, though, he could produce remarkable set pieces and sustained narratives capturing the drama of antebellum southern plantation life. His work appealed to an American public already enthused with the fashion of dialect verse, and he became the first African American poet of major popularity and a significant black cultural hero in late nineteenth and early twentieth century America.

97 **James Madison Bell**

An Anniversary Poem Entitled the Progress of Liberty
(San Francisco, CA; Agnew & Deffebach, 1866)

Summary: Like his earlier poem "The Day and the War," this long poem was written in honor of an anniversary—in this case, the third anniversary—of the Emancipation Proclamation, the January 1863 order by Abraham Lincoln that freed all slaves. Stretching to 850 lines, virtually all in rhyming iambic tetrameter, this poem takes the reader from 1862 through the end of the Civil War and Lincoln's assassination in the spring of 1865.

Subject(s): Civil War, Slavery, Poetry

98 **James Madison Bell**

"Modern Moses, or 'My Policy' Man"
Early Black Poets: Selections with Biographical and Critical Introductions
(Dubuque, IA; W.C. Brown Co., 1969)

Summary: This lengthy satiric poem, written in 1867, takes aim at Andrew Johnson, who succeeded Abraham Lincoln as President of the United States, serving from 1865 to 1869. Bell heaps scorn and ridicule on Johnson for unseemly personal traits such as drinking alcohol and for policy decisions that, among other things, betrayed freed slaves by restoring lands, promised to them, to their former Confederate owners instead. Like most of his best-known poems, "Modern Moses" is told in rhyming lines of iambic tetrameter.

Subject(s): Civil War, Slavery, Poetry

99   James Madison Bell

A Poem Entitled the Day and the War
(San Francisco, CA; Agnew & Deffebach, 1864)

Summary: This lengthy poem of 750 lines was composed for the first anniversary of the Emancipation Proclamation, the order issued by President Abraham Lincoln on January 1, 1863, that freed all slaves. The poem features Bell's trademark use of rhyming lines of iambic tetrameter and takes the reader from slavery's height to the early years of the Civil War and finally to the Emancipation Proclamation. Though somewhat conventional, this and other Bell poems were acclaimed for their inspirational qualities and were especially popular in the dramatic readings Bell did during his reading tours.

Subject(s): Civil War, Slavery, Poetry

100   Joseph Seamon Cotter, Sr.

"Answer to Dunbar's 'After a Visit'"
Links of Friendship
(Louisville, KY; Bradley & Gilbert Company, 1898)

Summary: As the title suggests, this poem is a response to a poem written by African American poet Paul Laurence Dunbar after a visit to Kentucky. In his poem, Dunbar praised the hospitality of the people of Kentucky and expressed his desire to return. Here, Cotter treats Dunbar's work with bemusement and irony, noting that Dunbar likely did not experience all that Kentucky had to offer. Cotter implies that if Dunbar were to return, he might be carried into "the stronghold of despair," a reference to the racist and hostile atmosphere of the American South in the late nineteenth century.

Subject(s): American South, Poetry, Racism

101   Joseph Seamon Cotter, Sr.

"On Hearing James W. Riley Read: From a Kentucky Standpoint"
Links of Friendship
(Louisville, KY; Bradley & Gilbert Company, 1898)

Summary: This poem's title references James W. Riley (1849-1916), a popular late nineteenth century poet who wrote sentimental verse in his native Indiana dialect. In the poem, Cotter expresses his admiration for Riley's poetry in five stanzas that use traditional rhymes and verse structure.

Subject(s): Poetry

102   Paul Laurence Dunbar

"An Ante-Bellum Sermon"
Majors and Minors: Poems
(Toledo, OH; Hadley & Hadley, 1895)

Summary: In this poem, Dunbar depicts a slavery-era black preacher giving a sermon to fellow blacks. The sermon deals with how God helped Moses free the enslaved Israelites, a story told in the Bible's Old Testament. The preacher makes direct comparisons between the Israelites and American slaves and counsels his flock that God will one day set them free as well. Written in rural black dialect, the poem consists of eleven stanzas of eight lines each.

Subject(s): American South, Bible, Slavery

103   Paul Laurence Dunbar

"The Colored Soldiers"
Majors and Minors: Poems
(Toledo, OH; Hadley & Hadley, 1895)

Summary: This poem from Dunbar's 1895 collection is an ode to the bravery of black soldiers who fought during the American Civil War (1861-1865) and who were thus instrumental in abolishing slavery. Written in standard English and consisting of rhyming, evenly measured eight-line stanzas, the poem is written to a white audience: "They were comrades then and brothers, / Are they more or less today?" In the poem, Dunbar references well-known battles in which African Americans played important roles, including battles at Fort Donelson and Fort Henry.

Subject(s): Civil War, Courage, Slavery

104   Paul Laurence Dunbar

"The Corn-Stalk Fiddle"
Majors and Minors: Poems
(Toledo, OH; Hadley & Hadley, 1895)

Summary: In this poem from his acclaimed 1895 collection, Dunbar paints a romantic portrait of life among southern rural blacks. The poem's subjects work hard in the fields during the day and then celebrate in the evening with dancing and music played on corn stalks. Dunbar's idealized southern landscapes, in which the hardships suffered by blacks in the post-Civil War South are never hinted at, earned him significant fame during his lifetime. The poem is written in standard English and consists of seven six-line stanzas that are evenly measured and contain a formal rhyme scheme.

Subject(s): Singing, Dancing, Civil War

105   Paul Laurence Dunbar

"Deacon Jones' Grievance"
Majors and Minors: Poems
(Toledo, OH; Hadley & Hadley, 1895)

Summary: This humorous poem tells the story of a church deacon who is offended by his church's choir ("they'll need some extry trainin' / 'Fore they jine the heavenly choir"). Though he is best known for his poems written in southern rural black dialect, Dunbar also wrote a number of poems—including this one—using white rural vernacular. Here, Dunbar mimics the midwestern dialect made popular by the poet James W. Riley.

Subject(s): American South, Religious Life, Singing

106   **Paul Laurence Dunbar**

"Harriet Beecher Stowe"

Lyrics of the Hearthside
(New York, NY; Dodd, Mead and Company, 1899)

Summary: This poem is an ode to Harriet Beecher Stowe (1811-1896), an American writer whose 1852 antislavery novel, *Uncle Tom's Cabin*, had a significant impact on the movement to abolish slavery. This poem consists of a single stanza of fourteen lines and contains a consistent rhyme scheme.

Subject(s): Slavery, Abolition, Literature

107   **Paul Laurence Dunbar**

"A Negro Love Song"

Majors and Minors: Poems
(Toledo, OH; Hadley & Hadley, 1895)

Summary: The "love song" of this poem is told by a southern black man, who exults in the affections of his girlfriend. Like most of Dunbar's popular dialect poems, "A Negro Love Song" depicts an idealized rural landscape in which slaves labor happily and post-war freedmen have little to trouble them. Dunbar would later be criticized for perpetuating the plantation-era stereotypes made popular by white writers in the late nineteenth century.

Subject(s): Slavery, Love, American South

108   **Paul Laurence Dunbar**

"The Paradox"

Lyrics of the Hearthside
(New York, NY; Dodd, Mead and Company, 1899)

Summary: This poem from Dunbar's 1899 collection is a rumination on paradox, "the mother of sorrows" and "the ender of grief." The year of this collection's publication was filled with personal crises for the author, who suffered a near-fatal bout with pneumonia, which in turn brought on the tuberculosis that would eventually claim his life in 1906 at the age of thirty-three.

Subject(s): Illness

109   **Paul Laurence Dunbar**

"Sympathy"

Oak and Ivory
(Dayton, OH; Press of United Brethren Publishing House, 1893)

Summary: Though chiefly famous for the dialect verse about rural southern blacks that made him the most popular African American poet of his time, Dunbar also wrote many poems in standard English. In this poem from his first collection, Dunbar uses standard English to express his sympathy for the "caged bird," noting that he understands its song of longing and hope. The poem's last line, "I know why the caged bird sings!," was

used a century later as the source for both a poem and a hugely popular autobiography by Maya Angelou.

Subject(s): American South, Poetry

110   **Paul Laurence Dunbar**

"We Wear the Mask"

Majors and Minors: Poems
(Toledo, OH; Hadley & Hadley, 1895)

Summary: This poem's subject is hiding one's pain behind a mask of "grin and lies." Though Dunbar here writes of "tortured souls" and emotional suffering, he does not address racial issues. In fact, Dunbar rarely dealt with socio-political matters such as racism or the hardships suffered by nineteenth-century African Americans.

Subject(s): Racism

111   **Paul Laurence Dunbar**

"When All Is Done"

Lyrics of the Hearthside
(New York, NY; Dodd, Mead and Company, 1899)

Summary: This poem from Dunbar's 1899 collection is a romantic piece that extols the joy of life after death. It consists of four stanzas, each with two rhyming couplets. Though Dunbar's best-known poetry was written in black rural vernacular, he himself preferred his larger body of works in standard English, of which this poem is one.

Subject(s): Death

112   **Paul Laurence Dunbar**

"When de Co'n Pone's Hot"

Majors and Minors: Poems
(Toledo, OH; Hadley & Hadley, 1895)

Summary: This poem from Dunbar's second collection epitomizes the dialect verse and optimistic outlook that made him one of the first important African American writers. An enthusiastic poem extolling the joys of sitting down to a meal, the piece utilizes the stylized rural southern black dialect that Dunbar made famous in his verse. Despite its unconventional language, the poem is nevertheless traditionally structured, with rhyming, consistently metered twelve-line stanzas. Dunbar's idealized portraits of life among southern slaves were extremely popular during his lifetime but have been criticized by subsequent generations of scholars.

Subject(s): American South, Rural Life, Slavery

113   **Paul Laurence Dunbar**

"When Malindy Sings"

Majors and Minors: Poems
(Toledo, OH; Hadley & Hadley, 1895)

Summary: This poem is a celebration by a slave of a fellow slave's beautiful singing voice—and a tribute by Dunbar to his mother. The narrator describes the woman—the Malindy of the poem's title—singing well-known spirituals such as "Swing Low, Sweet Chariot." As in much of his most popular poetry, Dunbar here depicts plantation life as joyous and satisfying, in so doing perpetuating stereotypes held by white writers in the latter half of the nineteenth century.

Subject(s): Slavery, Singing, American South

114 **Frances E.W. Harper**

"Aunt Chloe"

Sketches of Southern Life
(Philadelphia, PA; Merrihew & Son, Printers, 1872)

Summary: Aunt Chloe is one of two major narrators for the poems in Harper's 1872 collection, along with Uncle Jacob. Both are former slaves who speak in wise, sentimental, yet politically astute terms about their lives as slaves. In their political consciousness, they differ from the characters seen in the works of Joel Chandler Harris. The poem "Aunt Chloe" consists of numerous smaller parts that describe, among other incidents, the sale of her children and their separation while still slaves, the beginning of the Civil War, and Abraham Lincoln issuing the Emancipation Proclamation, which freed all slaves.

Subject(s): Slavery, Civil War, Poetry

115 **Frances E.W. Harper**

"The Burial of Sarah"

The Martyr of Alabama and Other Poems
(Philadelphia, PA; George S. Ferguson, 1895)

Summary: This poem tells the Biblical story of Abraham and his search for a place to bury his wife, Sarah. He finally finds a place—the Cave of Machpelah—in what is now Hebron, on Jerusalem's West Bank. The poem is told in one of Harper's favorite constructions, with ten quatrains using an abcb rhyme scheme.

Subject(s): Religion, Biblical Story

116 **Frances E.W. Harper**

(Also known as Frances Ellen Watkins)

"Bury Me in a Free Land"

The Liberator
(January 14, 1864)

Summary: First published in the prominent abolitionist periodical *The Liberator*, "Bury Me in a Free Land" is a passionate plea by an African American to be buried anywhere but "in a land where men are slaves." The poem consists of eight quatrains of rhymed couplets. At the time of the poem's first publication, the Civil War was still raging and many blacks were still enslaved, despite President Abraham Lincoln's Emancipation Proclamation of January 1863.

Subject(s): Slavery, Death, Civil War

117 **Frances E.W. Harper**

"Christ's Entry into Jerusalem"

Poems
(Philadelphia, PA; George S. Ferguson, 1900)

Summary: Another of Harper's religious-themed poems, this piece describes the entry of Jesus into Jerusalem, where he will eventually be betrayed and then crucified. The poem consists of seven quatrains. The rhyme scheme of abcb is seen frequently in Harper's poetry, as it is in much of nineteenth century poetry in general.

Subject(s): Religion, Christianity, Biblical Story

118 **Frances E.W. Harper**

"A Double Standard"

Atlanta Offering, Poems
(Philadelphia, PA; George S. Ferguson, 1895)

Summary: In "A Double Standard," Frances E.W. Harper offers a stinging indictment of nineteenth century society's hypocritical stance that a woman who bore a child out of wedlock would be stripped of her honor while the father would suffer no such criticism. Despite her forthright anger at the convention of the day, Harper ends the poem in a hopeful note, predicting that God will judge men and women equally.

Subject(s): Religion

119 **Frances E.W. Harper**

"The Dying Mother"

Poems
(Philadelphia, PA; Merrihew & Son, 1871)

Summary: Much of Frances E.W. Harper's poetry is written in the sentimental, religious style popular among nineteenth century poets. In this piece, a dying woman counsels her husband to love their children and instruct them in the promise of Christianity. The poem's six quatrains are told in an abcb rhyme scheme.

Subject(s): Religion, Christianity, Death

120 **Frances E.W. Harper**

"The Martyr of Alabama"

The Martyr of Alabama and Other Poems
(Philadelphia, PA; George S. Ferguson, 1895)

Summary: The title poem from Frances E.W. Harper's 1894 collection opens with a newspaper item from December, 1894, which describes how a group of white men beat and shot to death an African American boy named Tim Thompson for refusing to dance for them; the boy had refused to dance on the grounds that it was against his religious beliefs. The poem includes Harper's account of this incident, told in twenty-one quatrains.

Subject(s): Murder, Racism, American South

121   Frances E.W. Harper

Moses: A Story of the Nile

(Philadelphia, PA; Merrihew, 1869)

Summary: Frances E.W. Harper's 1869 work is considered by many modern critics to be her most-accomplished work of poetry. The volume is a blank verse allegory about the life of Old Testament figure Moses. Although Harper makes no overt references to race, she implies that contemporary African Americans need to exhibit the same qualities of self-sacrifice and leadership that characterized Moses's life.

Subject(s): Religion, Biblical Story

122   Frances E.W. Harper

"To Bishop Payne"

The Martyr of Alabama and Other Poems
(Philadelphia, PA; George S. Ferguson, 1895)

Summary: Harper precedes this poem with an explanatory note: "Written for the special celebration of the fortieth anniversary of Daniel A. Payne as bishop of the A.M.E. Church, 1892." Using an abcb rhyme scheme, one of her favorite constructions, Harper offers a loving tribute to Bishop Payne.

Subject(s): Religion

123   George Moses Horton

"George Moses Horton, Myself"

Naked Genius
(Raleigh, NC; Wm. B. Smith & Co., Southern Field and Fireside Book Publishing House, 1865)

Summary: In this sad and revealing poem from his final collection, Horton admits his bitterness about his advancing age and his earlier years as a slave, when his bondage kept him from pursuing his poetry as he would have wished. He compares his poetic skills, his "genius," to a caged bird that longs to "let her songs be loudly heard, / And dart from world to world."

Subject(s): Slavery, Poetry

124   George Moses Horton

"Imploring to Be Resigned at Death"

Naked Genius
(Raleigh, NC; Wm. B. Smith & Co., Southern Field and Fireside Book Publishing House, 1865)

Summary: This poem from Horton's final collection of poetry appeared about a year before he moved from North Carolina north to Philadelphia, where he lived until his death in the early 1880s. Though relieved to finally be a free man following the Emancipation Proclamation of 1863 and the end of the Civil War in 1865, Horton apparently was beset by loneliness in the North. In this poem, Horton expresses his desire to be brave, unafraid, and happy when death comes.

Subject(s): Slavery, Death, Civil War

125   George Moses Horton

"Jefferson in a Tight Place: The Fox Is Caught"

Naked Genius
(Raleigh, NC; W.B. Smith, 1865)

Summary: The subject of this poem is Jefferson Davis, president of the fledgling Confederacy during the American Civil War of 1861 to 1865. In the poem, Horton predicts the eventual downfall of Davis and, by extension, of the Confederacy that fought for the right to retain slavery. The poem has an interesting rhyme scheme (aaabcccb) but falls within Horton's typical reliance on traditional poetic forms.

Subject(s): Slavery, Civil War

126   George Moses Horton

"Slavery"

Naked Genius
(Raleigh, NC; W.B. Smith, 1865)

Summary: "Slavery" is another of Horton's remarkable poems protesting the institution of slavery—remarkable because for all but the final years of his life, Horton himself was a slave. Similar to his other poems about slavery, this piece contains lofty rhetoric and religious imagery but protests slavery only generally; there is no reference to Horton's personal situation. The formal rhyme scheme (abab) and evenly metered quatrains are hallmarks of Horton's poetry.

Subject(s): Slavery

127   George Marion McClellan

"The Feet of Judas"

Poems
(Nashville, TN; A.M.E. Church Sunday School Union, 1895)

Summary: This poem is a rumination on the Biblical story of Jesus washing the feet of his friend Judas, who would later betray him. Consisting of five consistently measured, rhyming quatrains, the poem epitomizes the thematic territory favored by McClellan. He focused his verse on themes of nature, love, and religion, rather than addressing social themes such as race or injustice. While some of McClellan's fiction would reveal his bitter resentment toward racial discrimination, he hid such resentments behind a passive stoicism in his poetry.

Subject(s): Bible, Racism, Literature

128   George Marion McClellan

"A January Dandelion"

Poems
(Nashville, TN; A.M.E. Church Sunday School Union, 1895)

Summary: In this poem from his first collection, McClellan crafts an ode to a pitiable dandelion that rose from the soil and bloomed in January. Misled by a few days of warm weather in Nashville, Tennessee, the dandelion bloomed, only to be doomed by the inevitable return of winter. In McClellan's accomplished hands, the poem becomes a rumination on the dangers that accompany overeager youth.

Subject(s): Childhood, Nature, Winter

129 George Marion McClellan

"Lines to Mount Glen"

Poems
(Nashville, TN; A.M.E. Church Sunday School Union, 1895)

Summary: In this poem from his 1895 collection, McClellan visits a southern mountain on which he played as a boy. The poet contrasts his youthful escapades to the mountain, when he was filled with innocence and dreams, with his disillusioned and besieged adult self. With its references to Greek mythology and its traditional, restrained diction and structure, the poem epitomizes McClellan's interest in creating mainstream verse for a white public that preferred sentimental poetry concerned with romantic subjects such as nature, youth, and beauty. However, despite his success in this venture, McClellan came to feel alienated from that white culture as well as from his native black culture. As he notes in this poem, "A stranger at thy base I lie to-day / To all but thee, save this soft yielding grass."

Subject(s): Friendship, Nature, Childhood

130 George Marion McClellan

"Love Is a Flame"

Poems
(Nashville, TN; A.M.E. Church Sunday School Union, 1895)

Summary: This short poem, which consists of two quatrains with a pair of rhymed couplets in each stanza, focuses on a standard romantic subject—love. McClellan was committed to writing traditional romantic lyric verse devoted to themes such as nature, truth, and beauty, and he followed this commitment while eschewing subjects such as racial injustice.

Subject(s): Beauty, Nature, Love

131 George Marion McClellan

"A September Night"

Poems
(Nashville, TN; A.M.E. Church Sunday School Union, 1895)

Summary: This poem from McClellan's first collection of poetry is a description of an evening in Anguilla, Mississippi, in 1892. Filled with lush images of nature, such as insects and flowers, the poem is a sentimental ode to the author's beloved southern landscape. The piece's carefully measured lines and genteel imagery epitomize McClellan's commitment to crafting traditional, restrained verse that fit within the mainstream literary culture of the period. He did not experiment with the dialect verse popularized by other African American writers of the period (chiefly Paul Laurence Dunbar), nor did he address specifically black themes in his poetry. Later in his career he grew alienated from his native black culture as well as from the white culture at which his poetry was directed.

Subject(s): American South, Nature, Race Relations

132 George Marion McClellan

"The Sun Went Down in Beauty"

Poems
(Nashville, TN; A.M.E. Church Sunday School Union, 1895)

Summary: Written in Tiptonville, Tennessee, overlooking the Mississippi River in August, 1892, this poem is a perfect example of the nostalgic, sentimental verse for which McClellan is known. The poem features McClellan's trademark themes of friendship, nature, and God, as well as his fondness for restrained diction and traditional verse structure. The poem consists of nine stanzas of eight lines each and contains a formal rhyme scheme and consistent meter.

Subject(s): Friendship, Nature, Religion

133 Albery Allson Whitman

Not a Man, and Yet a Man

(Springfield, OH; Republican Printing Co., 1877)

Summary: Considered one of the most important African American poets between Phillis Wheatley and Paul Laurence Dunbar, Whitman is known for his sensuous imagery and traditional verse forms. His 1877 work is chiefly remembered for its lengthy title poem, which stretches for approximately 5,000 lines. This epic poem follows Rodney, a slave who helps rescue a white slave-owner's daughter after she is kidnapped by Native Americans. Despite his bravery, Rodney is sold to a brutal slave-owner in the Deep South. There, Rodney falls in love with a lightskinned Creole slave, Leeona, and the two eventually escape to freedom in Canada. Rodney eventually fights for the Union Army during the Civil War.

Subject(s): Civil War, Slavery, Indians of North America

134 Albery Allson Whitman

The Rape of Florida

(St. Louis, MO; Nixon-Jones Print. Co., 1884)

Summary: This book-length poem, Whitman's second major work after *Not a Man and Yet a Man,* is the story of two Seminole chieftains, the aging Palmecho and the younger Atlassa. Betrayed and hounded by whites, the chieftains and their people are exiled from Florida to Mexico. The poem also features a love story between Atlassa and Ewald, who is Palmecho's daughter.

Subject(s): Indians of North America, Love, Racial Conflict

Drama

During the period from 1860 to 1900, most black performers appeared in conventional roles within white plays celebrating the southern plantation tradition. Also, black entertainers began to participate in minstrel shows in place of white performers using black face paint. By the late 1800s, in a departure from the debasing images that many believed minstrelsy created, musicals were being produced which offered more positive expressions of talent and creativity. Yet relatively few of these musicals were translated from or into serious drama and no important plays were published by or about blacks during this period of time.

Literary Criticism

During the period from 1860 to 1900, there were few authors writing literary criticism about black literature, mainly because the body of literature was so small and, at this point, not considered important by many white critics. Though none of the work done in this field is considered significant now, these years did see the beginning of advances in the criticism of African American authors, particularly by other black writers. Black-edited magazines and newspapers such as the *A.M.E. Church Review* were an important source of commentary about African American literature.

1900-1940

The turn of the century marked a critical transformation in African American literature. *Up from Slavery* by Booker T. Washington, *The Souls of Black Folk* by W.E.B. Du Bois, and *The Autobiography of an Ex-Coloured Man* by James Weldon Johnson were among the finest intellectual fruits of the Victorian Christian culture that had emerged in the post-Reconstruction world. Washington's *Up from Slavery* considered a grand project for the economic integration of the Negro into the world of the industrializing New South. *The Souls of Black Folk* not only explored the psychological question of black identity but promulgated a bold new stance of civil rights activism as a political strategy; and Johnson's *The Autobiography of an Ex-Coloured Man* was a bold psychological novel which assessed the cost of racism upon the inward development of a light-skinned mulatto *petit bourgeois.* All of these works marked the result of an intense black intellectual engagement with not only the idea of but also the reality of an American society. And in doing so, these works helped to propel the movements of protest and artistic renaissance that lay ahead.

One of the responses of the black intelligentsia to the continuation of white lynching and terror in the South was the formation of a protest movement. This protest was a central concern of W.E.B. Du Bois, who was a major leader in the Niagara Movement that resulted finally in the formation of the National Association for the Advancement of Colored People (NAACP). Protest against lynching also became a critical subject in the art of the period. Black activism against southern terror was promoted by the experience of many black military men abroad during World War I, when they experienced the relative racial freedom of a Europe that had never known an era of black slavery such as that in the United States. The era of protest deepened and broadened after the War during the early 1920s.

A second element that played an enormous role in the black intellectual response to the early twentieth century was the Great Migration. The migration of blacks from the South seeking productive, peaceful lives in the North continued throughout the first half of the century until well into the 1960s. This migration resulted in the creation of the urban ghettoes of the North, as the southern newcomers were crowded into segregated housing in northern industrial cities such as New York,

Detroit, and Chicago. The southern migrants created their own institutions and had an enormous impact on the political formation of the black urban communities of the North. In addition, they brought remnants of an already dying southern folk culture with blues, jazz, and other forms of music. Their presence within the world of the urban North was an important impetus to the self-consciousness of northern intellectuals.

One result of this self-consciousness was the creation of a movement to help integrate the black population into American culture through the presentation of brilliant new artists. This movement was brokered by now-established older black intellectuals, such as Du Bois and Johnson, who promoted a new generation of young black poets and writers such as Langston Hughes, Arna Bontemps, Zora Neale Hurston, and Claude McKay. Figures such as Du Bois helped to arrange white patrons for these new authors, promoted literary competitions, and published them in their literary organs. In New York this artistic upsurge corresponded with a new interest in black culture on the part of the literary and cultural worlds at large. Plays about blacks by writers such as Eugene O'Neill appeared on Broadway, while the bars and speakeasies of Harlem became favorite watering holes for artistic and cultural innovators.These developments brought even more attention to the new writers whom Du Bois and others promoted. Langston Hughes was working in a restaurant when he attracted the attention of the distinguished literary editor and writer Carl Van Vechten.

A number of things happened in the new literature of the Harlem Renaissance. First, black writing grew in psychological complexity. Spurred by the work of Du Bois and James Weldon Johnson, writers such as Nella Larsen, Jean Toomer, and McKay began to explore the psychological effects of living in a color-conscious society with great penetration and depth. The theme of the quest for an authentic racial identity assumed enormous importance in the work of all three of these writers and in the work of Langston Hughes and Countee Cullen as well. Secondly, writers drew upon all of the literary resources of folk tradition in order to shape their work. Folk customs, traditions, patterns of life, games, vernacular, and religion all began to play an intensely important role in the shaping of African American literature. The most important figure in this field was Zora Neale Hurston, who wrote some of the most memorable folk stories produced during the Harlem Renaissance. Langston Hughes began to use the black folk music of the blues to establish his poetry towards the end of the period.

The commencement of the Harlem Renaissance's literary scene was signaled by Jean Toomer's *Cane*, which was published in 1923. In a series of vignettes, its many narrators come to reveal themselves as autobiographical personae of the author. The book records the movement of a struggling artist from life in the South--where he observes southern black folk--to the North, and finally back South. The central theme of the work is the artist's failure to embody and express the vitality and cultural strengths that he finds in the South. As a work of the observation of black folk and as an account of the quest for identity, *Cane* builds solidly upon Du Bois's *The Souls of Black Folk*. Following *Cane* in the mid-1920s came a flurry of works, including the poetry of Langston Hughes, Claude McKay, and Countee Cullen. This art also defines the themes of the black man's double consciousness in American society. McKay's poetry drew upon the memories of his black Jamaican past, while Countee Cullen in the long poem "Heritage" dramatized a cultivated black person's futile attempt to establish a link with his African past. Langston Hughes captured some of the same themes in *The Weary Blues*.

The younger black writers may be divided into two groups. First, there is the group including Nella Larsen and Jessie Redmon Fauset that preferred to explore the lives of cultivated middle-class blacks. One such book is Nella Larsen's *Quicksand*, which concerns the inability of the heroine to come to terms with life in the black South, Harlem, or Denmark. At the core of this inability is her failure to grasp her viable sexual and social identity.

A second group of black writers rejected outright Du Bois' notion that black art was a means of promoting black integration within American society. These writers--Zora Neale Hurston, Langston Hughes, Wallace Thurman, and Bruce Nugent (who also wrote as Richard Bruce)--founded an avant garde magazine called *Fire*. In the spirit of this movement, Zora Neale Hurston wrote a set of brilliant stories that sought to recapture the consciousness of rural southern black life. These stories anticipate her landmark novel, *Their Eyes Were Watching God*.

In many ways, the period of the 1930s during the Depression represented the fruition of the artistic movements begun by the Harlem Renaissance. In the late twenties, Langston Hughes had written his autobiographical novel, *Not Without Laughter*, and continued to write poetry. Zora Neale Hurston wrote her major novels, *Jonah's Gourd Vine* and *Their Eyes Were Watching God*. Similarly productive in writing novels during this period were Claude McKay, who wrote *Banana Bottom* and Wallace Thurman whose work was titled *The Blacker the Berry*. At the same time as the culmination of the Harlem Renaissance, a new naturalistic movement in fiction was taking place. It was influenced not only by the growth of the ghetto but by the realistic fiction experiments of writers Sinclair Lewis and Theodore Dreiser among others. This movement produced writers such as Ann Petry and--most notably--the young Richard Wright, who during this period wrote an excellent book of short stories, *Uncle Tom's Children*, and the

novel *Native Son*.. Drawing upon a sociological understanding of the Great Migration and the northern urban ghetto, these works explored the lives of the underclass in the slums with great penetration.

Fiction

The period from 1900 to l940 is one of important transition in African American fiction. The turn of the century brought the creation of important realist works such as Paul Lawrence Dunbar's *The Sport of the Gods*. In l912, James Weldon Johnson, deeply influenced by W.E.B. Du Bois's *The Souls of Black Folk*, published his psychologically probing *The Autobiography of an Ex-Coloured Man*, an account of a sensitive mulatto intellectual. The Harlem Renaissance was heralded by Jean Toomer's experimental collage *Cane*, a work that reflected the main currents of Modernism and Cubism. The Renaissance itself saw the emergence of one major female writer, Nella Larsen, whose *Quicksand* and *Passing* were subtle examples of the psychological novel. Other significant black writers of the period included Claude McKay and Zora Neale Hurston, who continued to publish significant novels or short stories during the thirties. The thirties saw the emergence of a groundbreaking black writer of fiction, Richard Wright, who published his first collection of short stories, *Uncle Tom's Children*, in l938. In 1940, he would go on to publish the important novel *Native Son*.

135 **Clayton Adams**
(Pseudonym of Charles Henry Holmes)

Ethiopia, the Land of Promise: A Book with a Purpose
(New York, NY; Cosmopolitan Press, 1917)

Summary: The "purpose" alluded to in the subtitle of this 1917 novel is highlighting the abuse of blacks by whites in Ethiopia, a country in northeastern Africa. One of the activities the author examines is lynching.

Subject(s): Africa, Lynching, Slavery

136 **Aaron Eugene Aiken**

Exposure of Negro Society and Societies
(New York, NY; J.P. Wharton, 1916)

Summary: Aiken's 1916 work is a collection of twenty short stories. All of the pieces are set in New York City's Harlem neighborhood, which a decade later would be the birthplace of the Harlem Renaissance cultural movement.

Subject(s): Literature

137 Anonymous

Confessions of a Negro Preacher
(Chicago, IL; Canterbury Press, 1928)

Summary: Anonymously penned, this 1928 novel is a story about the virtue of nature. In the novel, a preacher fails both as a minister and later as a writer. He then becomes a farmer, and his re-acquaintance with the land provides him with character and hope.

Subject(s): Literature, Religion, Farm Life

138 John Arthur
(Pseudonym of Arthur Joseph)

Dark Metropolis
(Boston, MA; Meador Publishing Company, 1936)

Summary: This novel looks at life in Harlem. Its characters range from Jerry Ricks, a young black man troubled by racism, to a well-off black doctor named Ferguson and his wife. The story is framed by the experiences of two white men, a banker and a lawyer, as they twice pass through Harlem. Appalled by the poverty of the area when the story opens, the banker and lawyer on a subsequent trip find themselves stranded in Harlem and receive a warm reception at a hotel by Ricks and the Fergusons.

Subject(s): Racism, Poverty, City and Town Life

139 William Mobile Ashby

Redder Blood: A Novel
(New York, NY; Cosmopolitan Press, 1915)

Summary: The issue of mixed-race heritage is at the heart of Ashby's 1915 novel. In the work, liberal white Stanton Birch is happy in marriage until he discovers that his light-skinned wife actually has an African American ancestry. Stunned, he abandons her, but he later resolves his concerns and returns to her.

Subject(s): Literature, Miscegenation, Marriage

140 William Attaway

Let Me Breathe Thunder
(Chatham, NJ; Chatham Bookseller, 1939)

Summary: Attaway's first novel is unusual in that its chief characters are white. However, Attaway's creations are white migrant workers, a poor and despised class of workers who fall outside of the middle-class mainstream and who thus face some of the same hurdles as blacks. As in his second novel, *Blood on the Forge*, Attaway here exposes the class conflict inherent in American economic life.

Subject(s): Class Conflict, Poverty

141 Arna Bontemps

Black Thunder
(New York, NY; Macmillan and Company, 1936)

Summary: In this 1936 novel, Bontemps tells a fictional story based on the 1800 slave revolt known as the "Gabriel Insurrection," which occurred outside of Richmond, Virginia. Following the savage beating of a slave for a minor offense, Gabriel Prosser recruits slaves, free blacks, and even some whites in a rebellion whose aim is to seize Richmond. In the first part of the novel, Bontemps depicts the demise of the rebellion due to a fierce rainstorm and last-minute betrayals, and in the novel's second half, he recounts the capture and punishment of the insurrectionists. Praised for its historical accuracy and for Bontemps's rhythmic prose, *Black Thunder* remains the author's most acclaimed novel.

Subject(s): Slavery, American South, Resistance Movements

142 Arna Bontemps

Drums at Dusk: A Novel
(New York, NY; Macmillan and Company, 1939)

Summary: Like Bontemps's 1935 novel *Black Thunder*, this 1939 work tells the story of a slave revolt. In this case, the setting is 1890s Haiti, when slaves under the leadership of Toussaint L'Ouverture rebelled against the French colonial government. The novel revolves around a sympathetic white man who, with the help of his friend Toussaint, escapes from the angry mobs and flees the country with his girlfriend. Although not as accomplished as *Black Thunder*, *Drums at Dusk* nevertheless displays the author's trademark lush and lyrical prose style.

Subject(s): Slavery, Haitians, Resistance Movements

143 Arna Bontemps

God Sends Sunday
(New York, NY; Harcourt, Brace and Company, 1931)

Summary: Bontemps's first novel is the story of Little Augie, a successful black jockey in St. Louis whose luck during the 1890s runs out and who subsequently becomes a penniless wanderer. Bontemps earned praise for his lyrical prose and realistic depiction of southern blacks. Following the novel's success, Bontemps collaborated with Countee Cullen on a play adaptation of the work titled *St. Louis Woman*, which ran for more than 100 performances on Broadway in 1946.

Subject(s): Gambling, American South

144 Med Bridgeforth

God's Law and Man's
(Privately published, 1927)

Summary: In his 1927 novel, Med Bridgeforth offers a didactic tale about the way in which humans have corrupted God's law for materialistic purposes. The story asks for God to give humankind a second chance, a request implied when the novel was reprinted in 1951 under the title *Another Chance.*

Subject(s): Religion, Literature

145 Charlotte Hawkins Brown

"Mammy," an Appeal to the Heart of the South

(Boston, MA; Pilgrim Press, 1919)

Summary: This 1919 protest novel is set during the Civil War after the Emancipation Proclamation was issued. In the work, former slaves Mammy and Pappy are ordered by the plantation owner to remain and take care of his wife, as he leaves to join the war. They do so willingly, unable to break free of their life-long bondage, and end up destroyed in the process.

Subject(s): Civil War, Slavery

146 Handy Nereus Brown

The Necromancer; or, Voo-Doo Doctor: A Story Based on Facts

(Opelika, AL; H.N. Brown, 1904)

Summary: Told in the manner of a folk tale, Handy Brown's 1904 novel is one of numerous didactic, religious novels by early African American writers. In Brown's version, characters named "Mr. Truth" and "Mr. Lie" vie for power.

Subject(s): Religion, Literature, Folk Tales

147 Olivia Ward Bush

Driftwood

(Cranston, RI; Atlantic Printing Co., 1914)

Summary: Bush's 1914 work contains twenty-four poems and three prose works. The title refers to the plight of African Americans: once rooted firmly as trees, they are now uprooted, cast about, and oppressed by forces beyond their control. The book's three prose compositions focus on elements of African American history.

Subject(s): Racism, History

148 Charles W. Chesnutt

The Colonel's Dream

(New York, NY; Doubleday, Page & Company, 1905)

Summary: Of all of Chesnutt's pioneering novels about racism and race relations in the post-Civil War American South, *The Colonel's Dream* is perhaps his most realistic. Its detailed description of life in small-town North Carolina features a white protagonist, Colonel French, who returns to his native region and begins to overhaul the unjust systems of education and industry. French believes that enlightened race relations, economic cooperation, and white well-meaning can begin to lift the region out of its economic depression and can improve the lives of blacks and whites alike. However, his

dreams are crushed by a corrupt and powerful local politician, and he gives up and returns to the North. Like Chesnutt's previous novels about the South, *The Colonel's Dream* was not a commercial success, and its failure led the author to abandon the thematic terrain of the South for other issues. Today, however, his novels about the South are viewed as astute naturalistic novels that broke new ground in dealing with racial issues.

Subject(s): American South, Race Relations, Racism

149 Charles W. Chesnutt

The Marrow of Tradition

(Boston, MA; Houghton, Mifflin, 1901)

Summary: This sweeping epic, which is Chesnutt's longest and most complex exploration of the racial attitudes underlying southern life, is set in a fictional town in North Carolina. Chesnutt features two opposing families: the racist white Carterets and the progressive, racially mixed Millers. In the novel, Phillip Carteret's reactionary attitudes and attempt to gain political power result in a race riot in which Dr. Adam Miller's son is killed. Later, however, Carteret's own son falls ill, prompting his father to ask Miller for help. Miller eventually puts aside his bitter resentment over the death of his son to help Carteret's child. Alongside this main plot line are dozens of subplots and secondary characters. Chesnutt's achievement in *The Marrow of Tradition* was to expose the falsehood of the progressive "New South," a place in which racial harmony had supposedly dawned. In reality, argued Chesnutt, the brutally racist culture that had built and defended the institution of slavery continued to control the South even at the turn of the twentieth century.

Subject(s): American South, Race Relations, Racism

150 Albert Evander Coleman

The Romantic Adventures of Rosy, the Octoroon, with Some Account of the Persecution of the Southern Negroes during the Reconstruction Period

(Boston, MA; Meador Publishing Company, 1929)

Summary: This work's lengthy title provides an accurate description of the novel's content. An octoroon, as mentioned in the title, is a person whose heritage is one-eighth black. During the Reconstruction Period (1865-1877), which followed the end of the Civil War, freed slaves in the South gained some rights but were vigorously opposed by southern whites, who fought to maintain the privileges they enjoyed during slavery.

Subject(s): Reconstruction, Race Relations, American South

151 James D. Corrothers

The Black Cat Club

(New York, NY; Funk & Wagnalls Co., 1902)

Summary: One of the most celebrated black writers working at the turn of the twentieth century, James D. Corrothers, was best known for his dialect poetry. However, he also produced short fiction, including *The Black Cat Club,* a collection of eight short sketches that had previously been published in the *Chicago Evening Journal.* Featuring the exploits of Sandy Jenkins and eight of his friends and told in black rural dialect, these sketches make use of African American folk tales for their story lines. The overall depiction of Sandy and his sidekicks is a humorous one, as the friends constantly bicker and fight among themselves. In portraying black characters as simple buffoons and utilizing elements of slapstick comedy, Corrothers was adhering to a popular literary style of the era.

Subject(s): Comedy, Rural Life

152 Joseph Seamon Cotter, Sr.

Negro Tales

(New York, NY; Cosmopolitan Press, 1912)

Summary: This collection of short fictional pieces, which comprises Cotter's only fictional output, was one of only four fiction collections by black authors to appear between 1906 and 1922. Of the seventeen pieces in *Negro Tales,* ten deal with black characters and issues and seven do not; of the ten that do, four are told in the black rural southern dialect that was popular among writers of the era. The tales in the collection range widely among styles and genres, from comic stories to fairy tales to naturalistic pieces.

Subject(s): American South, Rural Life

153 Countee Cullen

One Way to Heaven

(New York, NY; Harper & Brothers, 1932)

Summary: This 1932 work, Cullen's only novel, contains two plot lines that are only marginally connected. The chief plot involves the relationship between Mattie Johnson, a serious-minded Harlem woman, and Sam Lucas, a comical character modeled after the "trickster" figure in African American folklore. Sam fakes a religious conversion to get Mattie to marry him, and then afterward he carries on an affair with another woman. Only on his deathbed does Sam perform a selfless act—in this case feigning a second religious conversion to ease Mattie's fears that he will go to hell. The secondary plot involves a Harlem intellectual salon run by a wealthy socialite. Based on Cullen's own experiences as one of the most famous members of the Harlem Renaissance literary movement in the 1920s, this secondary story line pokes fun at the intellectual pretensions of that era. Though Cullen dreamed of becoming a successful novelist, this work's cool critical reception ended that hope.

Subject(s): Harlem Renaissance, Folklore

154 Victor Daly

Not Only War: A Story of Two Great Conflicts

(Boston, MA; Christopher Publishing House, 1932)

Summary: Daly's 1932 novel focuses on the plight of African American soldiers who served during World War I, but it is also a tragic love story. In the novel, a white soldier and a black soldier find themselves in love with the same woman; she is African American and loves the white soldier. At the story's end, the two men fight together in France, and both are killed as the black soldier attempts to save the life of the white soldier.

Subject(s): World War I, Race Relations, Love

155 John T. Dorsey

The Lion of Judah

(Chicago, IL; Fouche Company, 1924)

Summary: Ethiopia, an ancient country in the northeastern part of Africa, has long figured in African American literature as a metaphor for a free, black-dominated state. In John T. Dorsey's 1924 novel, the author depicts an attempt by European imperialists to take control of Ethiopia.

Subject(s): Africa, Independence

156 Henry F. Downing

The American Cavalryman: A Liberian Romance

(New York, NY; Neale Publishing Company, 1917)

Summary: The central issue of Downing's 1917 novel is miscegenation and its effects, a theme that engaged numerous American writers during the later 1800s and early 1900s. The work is set both in the United States and in the west African country of Liberia, a country that was settled mainly by freed slaves during the 1800s.

Subject(s): Africa, Miscegenation, Romance

157 Herman Dreer

The Immediate Jewel of His Soul: A Romance

(St. Louis, MO; St. Louis Argus Publishing Company, 1919)

Summary: In this romantic 1919 work, Herman Dreer tells the story of an African American man trying to make his way in the world. The work reflects some of the issues highlighted by Booker T. Washington, who counseled blacks to pursue success through hard work and education.

Subject(s): Education, Romance

158 W.E.B. Du Bois

Dark Princess: A Romance

(New York, NY; Harcourt, Brace, 1928)

Summary: Though best known for his nonfiction writings, famed twentieth century intellectual and activist W.E.B. Du Bois also wrote fiction throughout his life. Typically, his fictional works explored the themes that animated his political work. *Dark Princess* is no exception. In the work, considered both fantasy and satire, Du Bois depicts the efforts of people of color throughout the world to organize for their advancement. The main characters are an African American man and a Hindu princess.

Subject(s): Racial Conflict, Romance, Politics

159 **W.E.B. Du Bois**
H.S. DeLay, Illustrator

The Quest of the Silver Fleece
(Chicago, IL; McClurg, 1911)

Summary: The "silver fleece" of this novel's title is cotton, which symbolizes generations of poverty, lack of education, and educational deprivation for blacks and poor whites in the South. In the novel, protagonists Zora Cresswell and Bles Alwyn move from individual pursuits to a passionate commitment to uplifting the black race through education and economic opportunity. A central theme in the novel is Du Bois's concept of the "talented tenth"—the most-gifted African Americans, whose leadership and courage would improve the lives of ordinary blacks.

Subject(s): American South, Economics, Farm Life

160 **Paul Laurence Dunbar**
Benjamin Brawley, Editor

The Best Stories of Paul Laurence Dunbar
(New York, NY; Dodd, Mead & Company, 1938)

Summary: The twenty stories in this 1938 work were drawn from the four collections of short stories that were published during Dunbar's lifetime. Thematically, the stories range from the issue of lynching to labor problems to the plight of southern blacks transplanted to the urban, industrial North. The collection includes an introduction by noted author and critic Benjamin Brawley.

Subject(s): Urban Affairs, Lynching, City and Town Life

161 **Paul Laurence Dunbar**

The Fanatics
(New York, NY; Dodd, Mead and Company, 1901)

Summary: Dunbar's third novel, a historical novel set in small-town Ohio during the Civil War, is a study of the sectional strife that characterized America during that period. The plot involves two feuding, prominent white families, one of which supports the Union and the other of which supports the Confederacy. Dunbar weaves in a secondary plot about escaped slaves, clearly showing his sympathy with them. However, he also expresses sympathy with the Confederate supporters, who are brave enough to voice their opinions even while living in a region unsympathetic to their views. The novel received a poor critical and commercial reception, once again frustrating Dunbar's efforts to establish himself as a prominent fiction writer.

Subject(s): Slavery, Civil War

162 **Paul Laurence Dunbar**

The Heart of Happy Hollow
(New York, NY; Dodd, Mead and Company, 1904)

Summary: Dunbar's final short story collection contains sixteen pieces set in Happy Hollow, which in Dunbar's words is a fictional place "wherever Negroes colonise in the cities or villages, North or South." The collection covers many of the topics that Dunbar had examined in previous collections: lynching; the northern migration of southern blacks and the conditions in northern ghettos; and the impact of political corruption on average African Americans. By the time of this volume's appearance, Dunbar was nearing the end of his literary output. He died two years later of tuberculosis.

Subject(s): Lynching, Racism, Politics

163 **Paul Laurence Dunbar**

In Old Plantation Days
(New York, NY; Dodd, Mead and Company, 1903)

Summary: The twenty-five stories in this collection are written in the thematic tradition of Dunbar's popular dialect poetry. Containing scenes about daily life on a slave plantation, the stories consist of romantic depictions of contented slaves and benevolent slave owners. Subsequent generations of African American critics and readers savaged Dunbar's literary reputation because these stories, along with some of his poems, appeared to reinforce white stereotypes about the slavery era. However, numerous scholars since the 1960s have rehabilitated Dunbar's reputation, pointing out the skill with which he drew his plantation portraits and examining his numerous works of social protest, such as the novel *The Sport of the Gods*.

Subject(s): Slavery, Racism, American South

164 **Paul Laurence Dunbar**

The Sport of the Gods
(New York, NY; Dodd, Mead and Company, 1902)

Summary: Considered Dunbar's most important work of fiction, this 1902 novel is an indictment of the forces that oppress African Americans and prevent them from improving their status. The plot involves Berry Hamilton, who for ten years has worked as a butler for a southern white man, Maurice Oakley. When Berry is falsely accused of stealing, he is sentenced to ten years of hard labor in a prison. Devastated, his wife and children migrate to New York City in search of better opportunities. Once there, however, they are devoured by the moral corruption of the city's inhabitants, both black and white. When Berry's innocence is finally established after four years of imprisonment, he ventures to New York, reclaims his family, and returns with them to the South. Dunbar's hatred of cities is clearly evident in his treatment of New York City. More importantly, however, his portrayal of Berry Hamilton—a dignified African American who maintains his integrity and strength even through dehumanizing experiences—signaled the development of a new black male character in American literature. Two decades after this novel's appearance, writers of the Harlem Renaissance would build upon Dunbar's creation by offering similar characters of moral strength and purpose.

Subject(s): Racism, Harlem Renaissance, American South

165 John Stephens Durham

"Diane, Priestess of Haiti"

Lippincott's Monthly Magazine
(April 1902)

Summary: This novella appeared in the April 1902, edition of *Lippincott's Monthly Magazine*. As the title suggests, the work is set in Haiti; the background involves business relations between Germans and Haitians.

Subject(s): Business

166 Jessie Redmon Fauset

The Chinaberry Tree: A Novel of American Life

(New York, NY; Frederick A. Stokes Company, 1931)

Summary: *The Chinaberry Tree* focuses on black middle-class life in a fictional New Jersey town. The work functions as a novel of domestic life and social mores, an unusual point of view for a black novel in the early 1930s. In the novel, Fauset explores themes of social superiority and illegitimacy in telling the stories of beautiful Laurentine, ostracized because of her out-of-wedlock birth, and half-siblings Malory and Melissa, who nearly marry before they discover their true heritage.

Subject(s): Family Life, City and Town Life, Race Relations

167 Jessie Redmon Fauset

Comedy, American Style

(New York, NY; Frederick A. Stokes Company, 1933)

Summary: In her final novel, Fauset examines the destruction caused by a black woman who despises her racial heritage and longs to be white. Olivia Cary drives her son to suicide, secures her daughter in an emotionally empty marriage, and torments her other son and her husband, all because of her color mania. Eventually, her son Christopher finds happiness in the form of Phebe Grant, a blonde-haired, blue-eyed African American who proudly proclaims her black heritage and conducts her life with dignity and strength. Critics view *Comedy, American Style* as less sentimental and more direct than Fauset's other works.

Subject(s): Family Life, Race Relations

168 Jessie Redmon Fauset

Plum Bun: A Novel without a Moral

(New York, NY; Frederick A. Stokes Company, 1929)

Summary: Fauset's second novel follows a beautiful light-skinned mulatto, Angela, as she journeys from denial of her racial heritage to acceptance and happiness. In the novel, Angela moves from Philadelphia to New York City to pursue her painting. Once there, though, she decides to "pass" as a white woman. Later, however, she regrets her decision and decides to reveal her black heritage. While her decision costs her the chance to wed her wealthy white boyfriend, Angela is rewarded with a romance with a light-skinned black man. The novel contains fairy-tale romantic elements but also is a complex portrait of the psychological difficulties that arise out of racial discrimination.

Subject(s): Racism, Art

169 Jessie Redmon Fauset

There Is Confusion

(New York, NY; Boni and Liveright, 1924)

Summary: Prominent as both a writer and editor during the Harlem Renaissance literary movement of the 1920s, Fauset is known for entertaining novels about the black middle class that address racial and gender discrimination and social justice. In *There Is Confusion,* her first novel, Fauset presents the stories of two black families who are united through marriage by their offspring. Among other themes, Fauset explores the vocational limitations placed on women during the 1920s; the legacy of discrimination faced by blacks living in northern cities; and the power of black folklore as a means to personal and social liberation.

Subject(s): Harlem Renaissance, Racism, Women's Rights

170 Rudolph Fisher

"The City of Refuge"

Atlantic Monthly
(February 1925)

Summary: Written while Fisher was in medical school, training for his eventual career as a physician, the short story "City of Refuge" is notable as the work that immediately established Fisher as one of the leading writers of the Harlem Renaissance literary movement. The story revolves around a poor black man from the rural South, King Solomon Gillis, who kills a white man in North Carolina and flees to Harlem hoping to find sanctuary. Once there, the naive Gillis is taken advantage of by a drug peddler named Mouse Uggams. Fisher would further examine the theme of the transplanted southerner in his later tales.

Subject(s): Harlem Renaissance, Murder, Drugs

171 Rudolph Fisher

The Conjure-Man Dies: A Mystery Tale of Dark Harlem

(New York, NY; Covici, Friede, 1932)

Summary: Fisher's groundbreaking second novel is considered the first black detective novel ever written. In the novel, two friends—Jinx and Bubber, both of whom appeared in Fisher's first novel, *The Walls of Jericho*--get involved in the mysterious murder of a "conjure-man" (someone who professes to be able to contact the dead). Jinx is framed for the man's murder, and Bubber uses his fledgling detective skills to clear his friend's name. He is assisted by a local doctor, John Archer, and Archer's assistant, Perry Dart. Critics view the Archer character as autobiographically inspired, as Fisher himself was a physician.

Subject(s): Mystery, Murder

172 Rudolph Fisher

The Walls of Jericho

(New York, NY; A.A. Knopf, 1928)

Summary: Rudolph Fisher's first novel depicts the diverse vibrancy of 1920s New York City, specifically the Harlem neighborhood—home to much of the city's black population. In contrast to other Harlem novels of the era, including Carl Van Vechten's *Nigger Heaven* and Claude McKay's *Home to Harlem*, Fisher chose not to focus on the seamy side of Harlem life such as prostitution and gambling. Instead, he examined the interactions between working-class Harlem blacks, their lower-class counterparts (called "rats"), and the better-educated, middle-class Harlemites known as "dickties." In portraying these distinct economic and cultural communities, Fisher displays his knack for subtle, ironic humor and sophisticated observation.

Subject(s): Class Conflict, Working-Class Life

173 Sarah Lee Brown Fleming

Hope's Highway: A Novel

(New York, NY; Neale Publishing Company, 1918)

Summary: In her 1918 novel, Fleming proposes that African Americans can succeed despite the enormous barriers placed in their way. Protagonist Tom Brinley is convicted of a crime he did not commit, but he later escapes from a prison chain gang. With the help of Grace Ennery, a local white woman who is free of prejudice, he eventually attends Oxford University. At the end of the novel, he returns to his home in the South to work towards dismantling racism while helping to build a black college.

Subject(s): Racism, American South, Crime and Criminals

174 Charles H. Fowler

Historical Romance of the American Negro

(Baltimore, MD; Press of Thomas & Evans, 1902)

Summary: In the preface to his novel, Charles H. Fowler states that his purpose in writing the book is to use the genre of historical romance to tell the story of African Americans from the slavery era through the Civil War and Reconstruction. In the story, his heroine, Beulah Jackson, is representative of all blacks and her story illustrates the panorama of black history during the second half of the nineteenth century. Beulah narrates the story of her life, from her birth in 1855 to the present in 1902.

Subject(s): Slavery, Civil War, Reconstruction

175 Carlyle W. Garner

It Wasn't Fair

(New York, NY; Fortuny's, 1940)

Summary: Carlyle W. Garner's 1940 work features two short stories: "It Wasn't Fair" and "The Contemptuous Town Mouse." Both stories are written for young adults and examine adolescent love.

Subject(s): Love, Adolescence

176 Mercedes Gilbert

Aunt Sarah's Wooden God

(Boston, MA; Christopher Publishing House, 1938)

Summary: A work of social realism about life in the American South during the 1930s, this novel focuses on the family life of Sarah, whose life is complicated by the destructive rivalry between her sons William and Jim. In the work, Gilbert deftly portrays the tensions between life in small-town Byron, Georgia, and the larger city of Macon. The book's foreword was written by noted author Langston Hughes.

Subject(s): Family Problems, American South

177 F. Grant Gilmore

"The Problem": A Military Novel

(Rochester, NY; Press of H. Conolly Co., 1915)

Summary: This novel is set during the Spanish-American War of 1898. In the work, protagonist William Henderson is a heroic black sergeant in the war who woos a light-skinned woman, Freda. Unsure of her racial heritage, Freda hesitates, but she agrees to marry William when she discovers that she does indeed have African American ancestry. The issue of mixed-race relationships was a divisive topic that engaged both white and black writers from the 1800s through the early 1900s.

Subject(s): Spanish-American War, Miscegenation, Marriage

178 John Wesley Grant

Out of the Darkness; or, Diabolism and Destiny

(Nashville, TN; National Baptist Publishing Board, 1909)

Summary: Grant's 1909 work features three main black characters—a doctor, a lawyer, and a minister—all of whom occupy respected positions in their community. The author uses their prominent standings to explore the issues of racism and oppression. For instance, the doctor is lynched after falling in love with one of his white patients.

Subject(s): Community Relations, Racism, Lynching

179 **Sutton Griggs**

Overshadowed: A Novel
(Nashville, TN; Orion Pub. Co., 1901)

Summary: A dark portrait of black life in America at the turn of the twentieth century, *Overshadowed* depicts its black characters as overwhelmed by white racism, social injustice, and economic stagnation. Protagonists Erma and Astral fall in love and move to Richmond, Virginia, where they are preyed upon by villainous whites. The pair eventually marry and have a son, but their happiness is short-lived. Erma's brother, on the run after killing a brutal white boss, dies of exposure, leading to Erma's own death by shock. Astral considers moving to Africa but decides against it, believing that injustice and racism are likely to be found throughout the world. Known for his militant beliefs, Griggs in this novel attacks the accommodationist philosophy of Booker T. Washington in favor of the more strident views of W.E.B. Du Bois.

Subject(s): Racism, Romance, Poverty

180 **Sutton Griggs**

Pointing the Way
(Nashville, TN; Orion Publishing Company, 1908)

Summary: Griggs's 1908 novel is less militant than his earlier efforts, but it nonetheless contains the author's examination of issues such as racism and interracial romance. One of the major characters, Letitia, is a light-skinned black woman who urges her niece to marry another light-skinned black so that the black race can continue to be diluted; in this way, hopes Letitia, the suffering of African Americans will eventually end. Other characters refute this viewpoint, and Letitia's niece marries a dark-skinned man and has a child by him. In this novel, Griggs offers no ultimate opinions on the issue of miscegenation, an issue that engaged many black political and intellectual leaders in the early twentieth century.

Subject(s): Racism, Miscegenation

181 **Sutton Griggs**

Unfettered: A Novel
(Nashville, TN; Orion Publishing Company, 1902)

Summary: Didactic and melodramatic, Griggs's 1902 novel depicts an American South peopled by virtuous blacks and hateful whites. In the novel, a heroic black man, Dorlan Worthell, becomes a leader of a new movement for black civil rights. The novel also includes a love story between Dorlan and Morlene, a beautiful black mulatto, as well as political intrigue. Griggs uses the character of Dorlan to espouse his own political philosophy of securing black civil rights through education, economic advancement through land ownership, and agricultural advances, ideas that were also promulgated by black leader W.E.B. Du Bois.

Subject(s): Racism, American South, Economics

182 **George Wylie Henderson**

Ollie Miss: A Novel
(New York, NY; Frederick A. Stokes Company, 1935)

Summary: Although he produced only a small literary output, George Wylie Henderson is an important African American author whose work falls between the Harlem Renaissance literary movement of the 1920s and the social protest literature inaugurated by Richard Wright in the 1940s. Henderson's first novel, *Ollie Miss,* focuses on an alienated eighteen-year-old girl who ventures to her uncle's farm near a small southern town in order to work and live. She falls in love with a local man, Jule, and eventually becomes pregnant by him. However, Jule abandons Ollie for another woman, a move that prompts Ollie to resolve to live her life independently and to rely on her own strength and dignity. Critics praised Henderson's portrayal of a strong, self-reliant black heroine and his depiction of life in the rural South during the 1930s.

Subject(s): Harlem Renaissance, American South, Rural Life

183 **William S. Henry**

Out of Wedlock
(Boston, MA; R.G. Badger, 1931)

Summary: Mary Tanner, the protagonist of William S. Henry's 1931 novel, is the mother of five children. The father of the children is a white man who refuses to marry Tanner, thus bringing shame on her and on their children. In the novel, Tanner dedicates her life to fighting against out-of-wedlock births.

Subject(s): Children, Marriage, Race Relations

184 **John H. Hill**

Princess Malah
(Washington, DC; Associated Publishers, 1933)

Summary: Set in colonial America, this 1933 work offers a sunny portrait of life in pre-Civil War times for a black-Indian slave. Such positive depictions of slave life were more common before 1900; later writers and thinkers sought to debunk the myth of happy slaves eager to serve their white masters.

Subject(s): Indians of North America, Slavery, Colonial America

185 **Pauline Hopkins**

The Magazine Novels of Pauline Hopkins
(New York, NY; Oxford University Press, 1988)

Summary: This volume contains the three novels by Hopkins that were serialized in the *Colored American* magazine form between 1901 and 1903: *Hagar's Daughter: A Story of Southern Caste Prejudice*; *Winona: A Tale of Negro Life in the South and Southwest*; and *Of One Blood; or, The Hidden Self*. The three works are notable for Hopkins's use of popular fictional formulas and her engagement with racial issues that predominated literature around the turn of the century, including miscegenation and light-skinned blacks who "pass" for white.

Subject(s): Racism, Miscegenation, Race Relations

186 Pauline Hopkins

Of One Blood; or, The Hidden Self

Colored American
(1902-1903)

Summary: Hopkins's publishing career began with the founding of the *Colored American* magazine in May 1900. During its nine year existence it carried several of her short stories (some under the name Sarah Allen) and serialized three of her novels. As with her other novels, "Of One Blood" has a complicated plot. Its story about interracial romance emphasizes the common blood of all races and focuses on mystical and mysterious experiences.

Subject(s): Interracial Marriage

187 Pauline Hopkins

Winona: A Tale of Negro Life in the South and Southwest

Colored American
(1902)

Summary: Much of Hopkins's creative output was published in the *Colored American* magazine, including this complicated serialized work that involves adventure, murder, and romance. The title character is Winona, the mixed-race daughter of a white man, who joined an Indian tribe and became its chief, and his fugitive-slave wife, who died giving birth to her. At the story's close, Winona hopes to escape prejudice by going to England with her British lover.

Subject(s): Interracial Marriage, Prejudice, Murder

188 Eugene Henry Huffman

"Now I Am Civilized"

(Los Angeles, CA; Wetzel Publishing Co., 1930)

Summary: In his 1930 novel, Eugene Henry Huffman tells the satirical story of a black man who has worked as a cook for wealthy whites for years. As a result of this experience, the man can speak English beautifully—completely matching the measured, haughty tones of his employers. However, he does not know how to write because he has not been taught. Huffman thus explores the issue of illiteracy in a tale of class and social mores.

Subject(s): Servants, Writing, Race Relations

189 Langston Hughes

Laughing to Keep from Crying

(New York, NY; Holt, 1952)

Summary: Composed of works written in the mid-1930s and the early 1940s, Hughes's second collection of short stories deals primarily with the black experience. Some stories are about blacks whose behavior is servile to or defiant of the white establishment. "Professor," "Trouble with the Angels," and "Little Old Spy" are about self-serving blacks who betray the aspirations of oppressed people, while "On the Road" has a rebellious protagonist. Other stories have black adolescents confronting the issues of racial, economic, and social inequality as they become aware of their ethnic heritage. In "One Friday Morning" a girl attends an awards ceremony and recites the pledge of allegiance despite learning her scholarship to an art institute is to be withdrawn because of her race.

Subject(s): Short Stories, Race Relations

190 Langston Hughes

Not Without Laughter

(New York, NY; A.A. Knopf, 1930)

Summary: Hughes began writing and revising this novel while a student at Lincoln University in Pennsylvania; it was accepted for publication after his graduation. Loosely patterned after his own youth, it tells the story of a typical black family in Kansas. Sandy lives with his religious, washerwoman grandmother Hagar and his domestic mother Anjee, who anxiously waits for her roaming husband to come home. (Hughes's own grandmother, with whom he lived, was not religious and she did not take in wash, and his mother was a stenographer and newspaperwoman. His father did leave the family in search of work.) Hagar's family also includes older daughter Tempy, who has married a mail clerk and taken on the snobbery of middle-class blacks, and younger daughter Harriet, who quit high school to work, party, and follow her dream of becoming a blues singer. After Hagar dies, it is the unlikely Harriet who carries on the mother's values and encourages Sandy to pursue his education.

Subject(s): Family Life, Middle Classes, Working-Class Life

Award(s): Harmon Gold Medal: Literature, 1930

191 Langston Hughes

The Ways of White Folks

(New York, NY; A.A. Knopf, 1934)

Summary: Although Hughes believed people of all races were basically good and could live together, he also was very cognizant of the reality of interracial relations. The stories in this collection are about white domination and about white people who are unable emotionally, psychologically, or culturally to deal honorably with black people. A white patron in "The Blues I'm Playing" insists his protege reject her cultural heritage; a sailor in the "Red-Headed Baby" flees the Haitian prostitute whose son he apparently fathered; a middle-aged women moves out of her apartment in the "Little Dog" rather than face her attraction to the black janitor; an artist uses her servant as a model in "Slave on the Block," then does not protest when her husband fires him at his mother's insistence; a young black musician is strung up in "Berry" for greeting his mentor, a white music teacher, on the street and being suspected of threatening rape. The collection links the restrained literature of the Harlem Renaissance with that of later writers who criticized discrimination.

Subject(s): Racism, Harlem Renaissance, Miscegenation

192 **Zora Neale Hurston**

Jonah's Gourd Vine

(Philadelphia, PA; J.B. Lippincott Company, 1934)

Summary: Associated with the Harlem Renaissance, Hurston is considered one of the great twentieth century African American authors. Her books, containing black myth and legend, reveal her background as an anthropology scholar and folklore collector. Hurston partially patterned the central character in this, her first novel, after her own father. John Buddy Pearson is a Baptist minister in Florida who succumbs to temptations during the week. He attempts to live this double life in a community steeped in white evangelical tradition that finds such behavior shameful, but Pearson's attitude is that there is no real difference between the worlds of the spirit and the flesh. He is frustrated by the different stances, but never reconciles himself to the community.

Subject(s): Harlem Renaissance, Religious Conflict, Folklore

193 **Zora Neale Hurston**

Seraph on the Suwanee: A Novel

(New York, NY; C. Scribner's Sons, 1948)

Summary: Hurston, a well-regarded author of the Harlem Renaissance, is noted for her use of black folklore in her fiction. However, in this novel she wrote about white people. Believing that people (regardless of color) react to stimuli the same way, she aimed to dispel the myth that black writers could not write effectively about whites. The book features Arvay Henson, a poor, neurotic white woman in Florida. Arvay makes a long journey to overcome her feelings of inferiority and worthlessness and emerge as a positive person.

Subject(s): Harlem Renaissance, Mental Health, Folklore

194 **Zora Neale Hurston**

Their Eyes Were Watching God: A Novel

(Philadelphia, PA; J.B. Lippincott Company, 1937)

Summary: Hurston wrote this novel in less than two months after beginning to do folklore research. She so effectively conveyed emotions in the book that it is said to be her best work and a classic of black literature. Protagonist Janie Crawford dreams of genuine happiness. She marries two men, but they have society's view that the measure of success is possessions and that women are helpless. She survives these marriages by retreating within herself. At the age of forty, Janie meets Vergible "Tea Cake" Woods, a mature man several years her junior. He encourages her to enjoy life with him during their brief mar-

riage before his death. Janie remembers him as a "glance from God."

Subject(s): Marriage, Literature

195 **Dennis I. Imbert**

The Colored Gentleman: A Product of Modern Civilization

(New Orleans, LA; Williams Printing Service, 1931)

Summary: In this brief novel, Dennis I. Imbert insists that African Americans should be respected for their humanity and cultural contributions in the same way that whites are. The 1931 edition, which was published in Imbert's home city of New Orleans, Louisiana, contains a directory supplement of prominent African Americans from the city.

Subject(s): African Americans, Culture, Race Relations

196 **E.A. Johnson**

Light Ahead for the Negro

(New York, NY; Grafton Press, 1904)

Summary: In his preface to this 1904 novel, E.A. Johnson states that his goal in the book is to argue for a solution to "the Negro problem" that involves peace and good will. At the time, southern blacks attempting to improve their lives through education and work were met with hostility and brutality by white-dominated society. The fantasy-laden story involves a white man, Gilbert Twitchell, who leaves to teach at a black school in Ebenezer, Georgia, in 1906. However, the airship on which he travels crashes. When Gilbert awakens, the year is 2006, and he has virtually no memory. The rest of the novel focuses on his romance with Irene and his efforts to understand the race relations of the era.

Subject(s): Education, Race Relations, American South

197 **Fenton Johnson**

Tales of Darkest America

(Chicago, IL; Favorite Magazine, 1920)

Summary: Johnson began his writing career early; he had plays produced and poetry published by the age of twenty. However, despite his founding of several literary magazines, including the *Favorite* magazine, he was an obscure author for the last thirty years of his life. This collection of six short stories is one of Johnson's last books. It is noted for addressing the issue of black urban life, a theme that grew out of the great migration of southern rural blacks to northern industrial cities during the early decades of the twentieth century. One story, "A Woman of Good Cheer," contrasts the uncomplicated life of the rural black and the destructive experience of urban blacks.

Subject(s): Rural Life, City and Town Life

198   James Weldon Johnson

The Autobiography of an Ex-Coloured Man
(Boston, MA; Sherman, French, 1912)

Summary: Johnson, a noted civil rights leader, had many careers and experiences during his lifetime. Those experiences, as well as friendships (including that of a boyhood friend who was able to pass as white as an adult), are the sources for this novel, which he began while a consul in Venezuela and which was first published anonymously. Like Johnson, the unnamed narrator is sheltered from racism early in life, and he later engages in many occupations and travels abroad with a patron. In addition, the light-skinned mulatto narrator is able to cross the color line by passing as white. In Europe the protagonist decides to express his racial identity by writing a great musical about African American culture, but while doing research in rural Georgia, he is so overwhelmed by the lynching of a black man that he resolves to move north and again pass for white. As a white, he becomes a successful businessman and marries a white woman, but he realizes in the end that he has surrendered his heritage.

Subject(s): Lynching, Racism, Identity

199   Joshua Henry Jones, Jr.

By Sanction of Law
(Boston, MA; B.J. Brimmer Company, 1924)

Summary: This novel depicts its protagonist's fight for the right to marry his white fiancee. The story presents miscegenation as an affirmative means toward solving racial problems.

Subject(s): Miscegenation, Racism, Judicial System

200   Nella Larsen

Passing
(New York, NY; A.A. Knopf, 1929)

Summary: Larsen's second novel looks at two women from Chicago, both of whom are light enough in skin color to "pass" as white. Irene lives a comfortable middle class life in Harlem with her husband who, unlike her, is willing to leave the United States in order to seek freedom from its racism. The other woman, Clare, marries a racist white man who believes that she too is white. When Clare begins to renew her ties to the black community, Irene feels that her marriage is threatened. At the story's end, Clare dies in a mysterious fall from an apartment window during a party in Harlem. Although contemporary reviewers were divided in their reception of the novel, it continues to be of interest among modern scholarly critics.

Subject(s): Racism, Race Relations, Women

201   Nella Larsen

Quicksand
(New York, NY; A.A. Knopf, 1928)

Summary: The author's autobiographical first novel tells the story of Helga Crane, the racially mixed daughter of a West Indian man and a Danish woman. Her quest for racial and sexual identity takes her from a small black southern college modeled on the Tuskegee Institute to Chicago, Harlem, and Copenhagen. Unable to find a place for herself in either white or black society, Helga marries a black preacher from rural Alabama. The novel ends with Helga exhausted and pregnant with her fifth child. Contemporary reviewers were generally enthusiastic in their reception of the novel, and modern critics have applauded Larsen for her treatment of racial and feminist concerns. The author's two novels place her among the top writers of the Harlem Renaissance cultural movement of the 1920s.

Subject(s): Racism, Sexuality, Harlem Renaissance

Award(s): Harmon Foundation: Bronze Medal, 1928

202   George W. Lee

River George
(New York, NY; Macaulay Company, 1937)

Summary: The hero of this novel is based on a person called River George who was described by the author in his earlier nonfiction work *Beale Street: Where the Blues Began*. Adding autobiographical elements, Lee created Aaron George as *River George*'s protagonist. Following the death of his father, George must abandon his law studies at Alcorn Agricultural and Mechanical College. In order to support his mother, he takes a job as a sharecropper on Beaver Dam Plantation. Here, he finds out that the woman he loves is involved with the white postmaster. George tries to organize the tenant farmers, which leads to a confrontation in which the postmaster is killed. George seeks refuge on Beale Street in Memphis, then joins the army and heads to France. Returning to America, he works on the Mississippi River. Wanting to be reunited with his mother and the woman he loves, he returns to Beaver Dam, where he is lynched for the death of the postmaster. Although critics were generally not impressed with Lee's writing technique, they praised his portrayal of southern sharecropping.

Subject(s): Racism, Miscegenation, Labor Conditions

203   John M. Lee

Counter-Clockwise
(New York, NY; Wendell Malliet and Co., 1940)

Summary: Like many other fictional works by African Americans prior to 1950, *Counter-Clockwise* treats its mixed-race protagonist as a tragic victim. Liom, a beautiful light-skinned mulatto, rejects her mixed-race parents and chooses to live solely in white society. She falls in love with and becomes pregnant by a white man, Herbert Wilton. When Wilton informs Liom that marriage is out of the question because of her African American heritage, she commits suicide. A secondary character in the novel, also a light-skinned mulatto, similarly commits suicide when her white lover spurns her.

Subject(s): Miscegenation, Suicide, Love

204 Harry F. Liscomb

The Prince of Washington Square: An Up-to-the-Minute Story
(New York, NY; Frederick A. Stokes, 1925)

Summary: This novel centers on a group of predominantly white shoeshine and newspaper boys. The story follows Jack as he achieves fame and fortune. Not all the boys have such a charmed life--among the group is a razor-wielding black character named Rastus.

Subject(s): Poverty, City and Town Life

205 Gilbert Lubin

The Promised Land
(Boston, MA; Christopher Publishing House, 1930)

Summary: The African republic of Liberia was founded by freed American slaves in 1847. This novel depicts the effort to create a "Promised Land" for blacks from the United States in the new nation.

Subject(s): Africa, Slavery

206 George Marion McClellan

Old Greenbottom Inn and Other Stories
(Louisville, KY; Privately published, 1906)

Summary: This work is a collection of short stories, all of which focus on black characters. Reminiscent of Charles W. Chesnutt's *The House Behind the Cedars*, the title story tells of the doomed interracial relationship between a young woman of mixed race and a young white man. Following the murder of the young man by a black man and the murderer's subsequent lynching, a southern inn is lost by its white owners and turned into an industrial school for blacks. McClellan viewed the American black experience as a tragedy in which racism acts as a hostile, if indifferent, force against black aspirations. A writer known for his literary conservatism, McClellan modeled his writing not on black cultural or historical figures but on such authors from the Western tradition as Aeschylus and Shakespeare.

Subject(s): Racism, Miscegenation, Lynching

207 George Marion McClellan

The Path of Dreams
(Louisville, KY; J.P. Morton & Company, Incorporated, 1916)

Summary: McClellan's final book is a collection of poems and short stories, most of which appeared in earlier works by the author. In addition to writings from his *Poems*, McClellan added ten new poems to *The Path of Dreams*. He also added one new story to those taken from *Old Greenbottom Inn and Other Stories*. Demonstrating the author's affinity for looking to Western tradition for his inspiration, McClellan bases one of his most ambitious poetic efforts on Richard Wagner's opera,

Tannhauser. The new story "Gabe Yowl" centers on the character Gabe, framed for the murder of a white man, and uses the framework of a mystery story to examine race relations and justice in the American South.

Subject(s): Mystery, American South, Racism

208 James E. McGirt

The Triumphs of Ephraim
(Philadelphia, PA; McGirt Publishing Co., 1907)

Summary: This collection of short stories marks one of the author's last literary efforts. "At the Mercy of a Slave" tells of a black bondsman's loyalty to the family of slaveholder, who is fighting in the Civil War. The title story involves a black protagonist whose heroism wins him the daughter of the president of a black college. "In Love as in War" shows how a black soldier in the Spanish-American War beats out a New Orleans aristocrat to marry a Filipino princess.

Subject(s): Civil War, American South, Spanish-American War

209 Claude McKay

Banana Bottom
(New York, NY; Harper & Brothers, 1933)

Summary: McKay's final novel revolves around Bita Plant, a black Jamaican who is raped as a child and then adopted by white British missionaries. The missionaries send Bita to school in Britain, but she eventually returns to Jamaica. Later, she clashes with her adoptive parents when they try to control her life, and at the end of the novel she reconciles her native island heritage with her European perspective. As in his previous novels and in much of his poetry, McKay—an outsider who left Jamaica for the United States and later Europe—deals primarily with the themes of alienation and dual, often conflicting, heritages.

Subject(s): Emigration and Immigration, Rape, Adoption

210 Claude McKay

Banjo: A Story without a Plot
(New York, NY; Harper & Brothers, 1929)

Summary: Written during a period in which McKay was living in Europe and North Africa, *Banjo* is set in Marseilles, France. Among a group of black seamen who congregate there is Banjo, a working-class black, and Ray, a would-be writer who is forced to work as a laborer. The character of Ray appears to be the same character that McKay presented in his first novel, *Home to Harlem*. A Haiti-born man who struggles as an outsider in American and European society, Ray is clearly modeled after McKay himself. Toward the end of the story, Ray realizes that his intellect means nothing in the face of white racism and economic oppression and that in reality he shares his fate with black common-man laborers such as Banjo.

Subject(s): Working-Class Life, Literature, Racism

211 **Claude McKay**

Gingertown
(New York, NY; Harper & Brothers, 1932)

Summary: Though written while McKay was living in Paris and in Morocco, the twelve stories in this collection are mostly set in Harlem and Jamaica, where McKay was born and raised. The Harlem stories deal with women's rights, lost love, and racial issues, while the Jamaica stories address sexual repression, bureaucracy, and failed marriage. Two stories in the volume are set in the Mediterranean region (including southern Europe and northern Africa).

Subject(s): Women's Rights, Marriage, Racism

212 **Claude McKay**

Home to Harlem
(New York, NY; Harper & Brothers, 1928)

Summary: One of the first commercially successful novels by a black writer, *Home to Harlem* provides a panoramic view of jazz-age Harlem. The plot revolves around Jake, a soldier who has abandoned the war effort and returned home to Harlem. Once there, he meets a prostitute, Felice, who has a strong effect on him. The remainder of the novel focuses on Jake's search for Felice. A secondary character is Ray, a writer from Haiti who struggles to deal with the oppressive influence of white society. The novel's chief importance lies in its depiction of Harlem during the 1910s and 1920s, from its poolrooms and bars to its working-class docks.

Subject(s): Working-Class Life, Prostitution

213 **Oscar Micheaux**

The Conquest: The Story of a Negro Pioneer
(Lincoln, NE; Woodruff Press, 1913)

Summary: Micheaux's early novels are notable for not confronting topics common to his black literary contemporaries: the rural South, northern ghettos, or the results of slavery. Instead, his novels are either inspirational or cautionary tales for black readers. His literary importance lies in his depiction of black middle class life. *The Conquest* is an autobiographical novel. It tells the story of Oscar Devereaux, who in order to better himself, leaves his home in Metropolis, Illinois, and takes over a homestead in Gregory County, South Dakota. He falls in love with a Scottish girl but decides not to marry her because of the racial barrier. The novel ends with his failure to marry the daughter of a black minister. The work emphasizes that blacks should avoid mixed marriages and leave the cities for more rural settings.

Subject(s): Miscegenation, Farm Life, Middle Classes

214 **Oscar Micheaux**

The Forged Note: A Romance of the Darker Races
(Lincoln, NE; Western Book Supply Company, 1915)

Summary: Micheaux was a promoter of the doctrines of Booker T. Washington, who advocated black concentration on accomplishing practical goals to better themselves. Along this line, the autobiographical *The Forged Note* tells the story of Sidney Wyeth, who, like the author, has written a book about his experiences as a homesteader in South Dakota and has gone south on a bookselling tour. Wyeth meets Mildred, who became the mistress of a white man to protect her father in an embezzling scheme. They marry and head west for a better life. In the novel, Micheaux criticizes the black communities in major southern cities for not doing more to address the problems of urban blacks.

Subject(s): Miscegenation, Urban Affairs

215 **Oscar Micheaux**

The Homesteader
(Sioux City, IA; Western Book Supply Company, 1917)

Summary: This novel is a reworking of the author's first novel, *The Conquest*. In this version of his life as a homesteader, Micheaux places greater emphasis on the romantic story line. The protagonist of *The Homesteader* is Jean Baptiste, who sets up a homestead in South Dakota. He falls in love with Agnes, the daughter of a white farmer, but chooses instead to marry the daughter of a black minister, who opposes the marriage. When his wife kills her father and herself, Jean is accused of the crimes, but Agnes hires a detective, leading to his acquittal. Micheaux argues that blacks should reject interracial marriages; Jean and Agnes marry only when she learns that she has black blood. By producing the movie version of *The Homesteader*, Micheaux would begin his career as the first black filmmaker.

Subject(s): Miscegenation, Farm Life, Film

216 **T.E.D. Nash**

Love and Vengeance; or, Little Viola's Victory: A Story of Love and Romance in the South; also Society and Its Effects
(Portsmouth, VA; T.E.D. Nash, 1903)

Summary: This melodramatic romance is set in Washington, D.C., and features the handsome Bertram Heathcourt and his passion for the beautiful Viola. At the novel's beginning, Bertram is in love with another woman--Mona--but eventually he realizes his greater love for Viola. Mona, distraught at the death of her mother and the loss of Bertram, vows to kill Bertram and Viola. She fails, however, and ends up killing herself. By the novel's close, Bertram and Viola are happily ensconced in their marriage.

Subject(s): Love, Romance

217 John H. Paynter

Fugitives of the Pearl

(Washington, DC; Associated Publishers, 1930)

Summary: This novel is set in the period following the American Revolution. John Brent is the descendent of a Virginia planter and a slave. As a "free dealer," Brent is permitted to work in Washington and is able to purchase his freedom. He then buys the freedom of not only his father but also that of the woman he loves. The new family that forms, however, does not remain unaffected by the institution of slavery. The story culminates in the winning of the freedom of two of Brent's sisters-in-law.

Subject(s): American Revolution, Slavery, Family

218 William Pickens

American Aesop: Negro and Other Humor

(Boston, MA; Jordan & More Press, 1926)

Summary: This collection of over two hundred stories opens with an introduction by the author. In "Humor in Speech," he addresses the benefits of using humor to tell stories and uses Abraham Lincoln and Booker T. Washington as examples of good story tellers. He considers humorous stories to be good vehicles to get across more serious messages. He also defends the use of a specific race or class to tell a story. The stories are organized into four main sections: "Negro Stories," "Jew Stories," "Irish Stories," and "Cosmopolite Stories." When possible, these sections are further broken down into categories such as "Religion" and "War."

Subject(s): Humor

219 William Pickens

The Vengeance of the Gods: And Three Other Stories of Real American Color Line Life

(Philadelphia, PA; A.M.E. Book Concern, 1922)

Summary: This collection of short stories reflects the author's determination to go beyond traditional stereotypes found in publishing and present a true picture of blacks. The title story, "The Vengeance of the Gods," recalls the author's childhood memories involving laborers in Arkansas. "Tit for Tat" is based on an actual account of a black military regiment, which when sent to serve in France during World War I is confronted by the racism of white American soldiers.

Subject(s): World War I, Racism, Labor and Labor Classes

220 George Langhorne Pryor

Neither Bond Nor Free (A Plea)

(New York, NY; J.S. Ogilvie Publishing Company, 1902)

Summary: Set in a southern town following the Civil War, this work depicts the lives of former slaves and their subsequent generation. The novel considers the importance of religion in the lives of southern blacks, their relations with whites (the problem of lynchings is critically examined), and the importance of political participation by blacks. The novel argues for the education and industrial training of blacks as the key to future success.

Subject(s): Slavery, American South, Race Relations

221 J.A. Rogers

From Superman to Man

(Chicago, IL; M.A. Donohue & Co., 1917)

Summary: This novel takes place during a train ride from the East coast to the West. An African American porter, Dixon, engages in a lengthy series of conversations with a racist white senator about the differences between blacks and whites. Although the senator at first is incredulous that Dixon considers blacks to be the equal of whites in every respect, he gradually is persuaded by Dixon's reasoned arguments based on his widespread reading of science, anthropology, politics, and history.

Subject(s): Race Relations, Travel

222 Tom Sanders

Her Golden Hour

(Houston, TX; T. Sanders, 1929)

Summary: This novel is set in Texas and features a love story. Its plot involves the discovery of oil on lands to which black families have a rightful claim and the subsequent dispossession of those lands.

Subject(s): Racism, Oil, Business

223 George Samuel Schuyler

Black No More: Being an Account of the Strange and Wonderful Workings of Science in the Land of the Free, A.D. 1933-1940

(New York, NY; Macaulay Co., 1931)

Summary: Schuyler's first novel is a satire in which blacks are turned into white by the use of a cream. The cream, invented by a black physician named Dr. Crookman, also changes hair and facial features to Caucasian. The plot follows the picaresque adventures of the black Max Disher, who becomes the white Matthew Fisher. He then becomes the right-hand man to the leader of a Ku Klux Klan-like organization called the Knights of Nordica and marries the leader's daughter. When research shows that more than half of the so-called Caucasians in the country actually have some black ancestry, Fisher and his new family flee to Mexico with the Knights' treasury. When it turns out that the Black-No-More whites are even lighter than actual Caucasians, dark skin becomes the fashion. Besides the Ku Klux Klan, the novel satirizes the NAACP, both black and white churches, and such figures as W.E.B. Du Bois.

Subject(s): Racism

---

224 George Samuel Schuyler

Slaves Today: A Story of Liberia
(New York, NY; Brewer, Warren & Putnam, 1931)

Summary: Sponsored by publisher George Palmer Putnam and the *The New York Evening Post*, the author traveled to Liberia in 1931 to investigate the nation's slave trade. He wrote six newspaper articles on what he observed. What he found was that the ruling class, which was founded by freed slaves from America, was exploiting the native Africans. Beginning in World War I, the nation's rulers sold native Liberians to work as forced laborers for the Spanish plantation owners on the island of Fernando Po. In his investigation, Schuyler implicated Christian missionaries. This research was also used as the basis for the novel *Slaves Today*. Satirizing the corrupt Liberian leaders, the novel shows how a young Nigerian is sent to the island after trying to rescue his wife, who has been taken as the concubine of a government official. When he is allowed to return, he finds that she has died from a venereal disease. He assassinates the official and, in turn, is killed by a guard.

Subject(s): Africa, Slavery

---

225 Otis M. Shackelford
William Hamilton, Illustrator

Lillian Simmons; or, The Conflict of Sections
(Kansas City, MO; Burton Publishing Company, 1915)

Summary: In this novel, the author demonstrates his interest in breaking from traditional stereotypes and depicting a true representation of blacks, and his concern for the social and economic status of blacks. While the novel is a love story, it also calls attention to the various forms of segregation, including separate schools and public transportation.

Subject(s): Love, Segregation, Education

---

226 O'Wendell Shaw

Greater Need Below
(Columbus, Ohio; Bi-Monthly Negro Book Club, 1936)

Summary: This novel opens as Ellen Vance, a young black student recently graduated from Northern University, is advised that if she wants to teach she should go to the South. She is hired by the Avon State College for Negroes and travels south. On her way there, she meets her romantic interest, Dewalt Brooks, who is also headed to Avon College to teach. Based on the author's own experiences as a faculty member at a similar school, the novel offers a criticism of the conditions at a southern black college.

Subject(s): American South, Racism, Colleges and Universities

---

227 Mary Etta Spencer

The Resentment
(Philadelphia, PA; A.M.E. Book Concern, 1921)

Summary: Set in Philadelphia, this novel follows young Silas Miller from poverty, working for a white farmer, to wealth as the "Hog King." Important to Silas's success are education and religion. Silas shares his success with fellow blacks, demonstrating the importance of business enterprise in racial advancement.

Subject(s): Poverty, Education, Business Enterprises

---

228 Wallace Thurman

The Blacker the Berry: A Novel of Negro Life
(New York, NY; Macaulay Company, 1929)

Summary: The author's first novel centers on Emma Lou Morgan. Considered unacceptable by whites and lighter-colored blacks, she moves from her hometown of Boise, Idaho, to the University of Southern California, and finally to Harlem. Emma takes on the views of those who have discriminated against her and looks down on working-class blacks with darker skin. She becomes involved with Alva, who, because of his lighter skin, is considered handsome. Emma endures Alva's abusive treatment until she sees him engaged in a homosexual embrace. Only then does she make any real change in her own behavior. Although critical response to the novel was generally not enthusiastic, Thurman was commended for addressing the issue of intraracial prejudice.

Subject(s): Racism, Homosexuality/Lesbianism

---

229 Wallace Thurman

Infants of the Spring
(New York, NY; Macaulay Co., 1932)

Summary: Wallace Thurman, an author who was considered part of the Harlem Renaissance, wrote this farcical novel about the times and the people with which he was involved. The novel revolves around a boarding house, called Niggerati Manor, which is run by the generous Euphoria Blake. The characters who fill the boarding house all represent famous figures of the Harlem Renaissance; Alain Locke, Langston Hughes, Countee Cullen and Zora Neale Hurston all appear in some guise. Thurman himself is played by his character Raymond Taylor, a young writer who believes himself only interested in artistic form and far above concerning himself with racial issues. Though all of the characters are interested in high-minded ideals, occasionally pleasure-seeking and gin-swilling get in the way of their good intentions.

Subject(s): Harlem Renaissance, Artists and Art, Identity

230 Wallace Thurman
Abraham L. Furman, Co-author

The Interne
(New York, NY; Macaulay Company, 1932)

Summary: No longer writing about the experiences of blacks in America, Thurman collaborated on this novel with Abraham L. Furman, a white writer. The story is set in City Hospital on New York City's Welfare Island. Examining the training of doctors, the novel illustrates hospital bureaucracy and the lack of ethics shown by its personnel. The young white protagonist finally chooses to set up a medical practice in the country. Reviewers roundly criticized the novel for its sensationalism.

Subject(s): Medicine, Doctors, Ethics

231 Jean Toomer

Cane
(New York, NY; Boni and Liveright, 1923)

Summary: Toomer's literary reputation is based primarily on this work, which integrates prose poems into the narrative as epigraphs to explore the black experience in white America, including northern urban and southern rural cultures. The book uses the analogy of the hard and grinding work required to extract syrup from cane with the fortitude of people resisting physical and psychological oppression.

Subject(s): American South, City and Town Life, Rural Life

232 R. Archer Tracy

The Sword of Nemesis
(New York, NY; Neale Pub. Co., 1919)

Summary: This romance novel features the love between Mary Highfield, daughter of a wealthy plantation owner, and Carl, a strong and virtuous gentleman. Although their love is strained and their initial engagement is broken off because of a misunderstanding, the two eventually realize their error and make amends, thus securing their inevitable marriage.

Subject(s): Love, Romance

233 Carl Van Vechten

Nigger Heaven
(New York, NY; Knopf, 1926)

Summary: Considered an important work in the Harlem Renaissance cultural movement, this controversial novel by white writer Carl Van Vechten is set in the colorful world of Harlem in the 1920s. In the novel, protagonist Byron Kessen journeys from his rural home to New York City's Harlem neighborhood, where he is seduced and ultimately destroyed by the area's big-city vices. The title comes from a slang expression that referred to the uppermost gallery of a theater, to which blacks were typically confined. While some black observers praised the novel, others (including W.E.B. Du Bois) heaped criticism on the novel. Nevertheless, Van Vechten spent con-

siderable energy throughout his career promoting the work of African American writers and intellectuals.

Subject(s): City and Town Life, Harlem Renaissance

234 Thomas Hamilton Beb Walker

Bebbly; or, The Victorious Preacher
(Gainesville, FL; Pepper Publishing and Printing Co., 1910)

Summary: As its title suggests, Walker's 1910 work tells the story of a black minister. The novel is one of many by African American authors to explore religion.

Subject(s): Religion, Literature

235 Thomas Hamilton Beb Walker

J. Johnson, or "The Unknown Man: n Answer to Mr. Thos. Dixon's "Sins of the Fathers"
(De Land, FL; E.O. Painter Printing Co., 1915)

Summary: Thomas H.B. Walker's 1915 work glorifies its African American protagonists. In so doing, the work offers a repudiation of Thomas Dixon's *Sins of the Fathers*, which presents a much less flattering view of African American life. The better-known Sutton Griggs, who, like Walker, was writing at the turn of the twentieth century, also repudiated Dixon's work in his writings.

Subject(s): African Americans, Literature

236 Eric Walrond

Tropic Death
(New York, NY; Boni & Liveright, 1926)

Summary: Set in the American tropics, this story collection emphasizes the connection between human activity and the surrounding environment. In ten stories, Walrond explores such themes as dissipation, poverty, famine, and racial prejudice. Walrond himself was born and raised in Guyana in the Caribbean; he lived for several years in the United States before making his way to Europe, where he lived for the majority of his life.

Subject(s): Poverty, Prejudice

237 Robert Louis Waring

As We See It
(Washington, DC; C.F. Sudwarth, 1910)

Summary: Waring in his 1910 novel offers an impassioned look at southern racism from the view of educated southern blacks. In the work, Waring uses the epithet "cracker" to describe the white racists who populate the story.

Subject(s): American South, Racism, Literature

238 Charles Elmer Waterman

Carib Queens

(Boston, MA; Chapple Publishing Company, 1932)

Summary: Waterman's 1932 work is set in Haiti during the early 1800s, after the African-born slave population had overthrown the French colonial authorities to take control of the island. The "queens" of the title refer to Defilee and Marie-Louise, the wives of two important Haitians; Jean Jacques Dessalines, who was emperor of Haiti from 1804 until his assassination in 1806; and Henri Christophe, who was the leader of Haiti from 1811 to 1820.

Subject(s): Politics, Women, Independence

239 Walter White

The Fire in the Flint

(New York, NY; A.A. Knopf, 1924)

Summary: White wrote *The Fire in the Flint* in two weeks while in New England, a location far different than the novel's Central City, Georgia. The novel takes place in the years following World War I. Educated in Europe, protagonist Kenneth Harper, a young black doctor, returns to his hometown believing he can improve the lives of both black and white residents. But the social conditions he thought would have changed while he was away have not. Horrifying events, such as the murder of a black man by the sheriff's brother and the gang rape of Harper's sister by white men, still take place and go unpunished. Tensions escalate as Harper tries to effect change, and eventually he is killed by a mob. A very popular work, the novel was translated into five foreign languages, and its plot was considered for a stage play and motion picture.

Subject(s): Racial Conflict

240 Lillian E. Wood

Let My People Go

(Philadelphia, PA; A.M.E. Book Concern Printers, 1922)

Summary: This novel, the only one known to have been written by this author, tells the love story of Bob McComb and Helen Adams. Following their days as students, Bob enters the army and Helen works as a nurse during World War I. The McCombs later move to Chicago, where Bob successfully runs for public office. Concerned with racial violence, Bob introduces an anti-lynching bill, which is passed by his fellow members of Congress.

Subject(s): Lynching, World War I, Politics

241 Richard Wright

Native Son

(New York, NY; Harper & Brothers, 1940)

Summary: This novel stands as Wright's most important work of fiction. At its center is Bigger Thomas, a young, impoverished black man in Chicago who takes a job as the chauffeur to a wealthy white family. When Bigger accidentally kills the family's daughter, he burns the body and concocts a kidnapping scheme with the aid of his girlfriend. When the remains of the body are discovered, Bigger attempts to flee from the authorities, murdering his girlfriend in the process. He is captured by the police, and despite the eloquent defense presented by his Communist lawyer, is convicted and condemned to death. Although Wright has been criticized for his portrayal of Bigger, perhaps most notably in an essay by James Baldwin, he purposely made his protagonist unsympathetic. In so doing, the novel provided arguably the first powerful depiction of the dehumanizing effects of racism on blacks and called attention to the state of race relations in the United States. The critical and popular success of the novel solidified Wright's place among the most influential American writers of the twentieth century.

Subject(s): Racism, Murder, Communism

Award(s): National Association for the Advancement of Colored People: Spingarn Medal, 1940

242 Richard Wright

Uncle Tom's Children: Four Novellas

(New York, NY; Harper & Brothers, 1938)

Summary: Wright's first major published work originated as the winning entry for a *Story* magazine contest involving writers associated with the Federal Writer's Project. *Uncle Tom's Children* initially consisted of four stories inspired by the life of a black Communist Wright had known while living in Chicago. Dealing with racial oppression and violence, the stories declare that the Uncle Tom figure from Harriet Beecher Stowe's novel is dead and that his descendents will not submit to their bondage. Although some critics have considered the stories melodramatic and weakened by a reliance on Communist ideology, Wright's striking portrayal of racism in America placed the author on a par with white literary contemporaries. Wright later added an essay and a fifth story to the collection.

Subject(s): Racism, Communism

Award(s): *Story* Magazine Prize, 1938

243 Zara Wright

Black and White Tangled Threads

(Chicago, IL; Barnard & Miller, 1920)

Summary: Set in the American South around the time of World War I, this novel critiques contemporary attitudes about race. On the eve of her engagement to Lord Blankleigh, an English nobleman, heiress Zoleeta Andrews learns that her mother was a mulatto. Zoleeta's aunt, who wants her own daughter, Catherine, to marry Blankleigh, has Zoleeta kidnapped and held in a tower. Catherine instead marries Guy Randolph, but abandons both him and their daughter when she discovers that he is racially mixed. After Zoleeta is rescued, she marries Blankleigh and moves with him to England. Zoleeta later returns to the South to educate white people on the issue of race.

Subject(s): Miscegenation, Race Relations, American South

244 Zara Wright

Kenneth
(Chicago, IL; Barnard & Miller, 1920)

Summary: This novel is the sequel to *Black and White Tangled Threads* and was published under the same cover. Like its predecessor, *Kenneth* is set in the American South around the time of World War I. Kenneth is the son of Guy Randolph, who lives as a white but uses his legal abilities to help fellow blacks. Kenneth's wife almost loses him to the daughter of Zoleeta, the heroine of the first novel. Most of the story, however, revolves around Phillip Grayson, a black doctor whose life and career are endangered by the attentions of a white patient, Alice Blair. Alice becomes a Red Cross nurse in Europe during the war and reconciles with Grayson when they meet in a hospital.

Subject(s): Miscegenation, World War I, American South

Nonfiction

The years between 1900 and 1940 were a time of serious advances in black writing in *belles lettres*, the humanities, and the social sciences. Booker T. Washington, who founded the Tuskegee Institute in Alabama, was one of the most influential figures of the late nineteenth and early twentieth centuries. In 1901 Washington's *Up from Slavery* was published and the publicity earned him a trip to the White House to visit President Theodore Roosevelt, who continued to consult Washington about race issues afterward. Initially W.E.B. Du Bois agreed with most of Washington's views about the status of blacks, but in 1903 he attacked Washington on several issues in his major work of *belles lettres*, *The Souls of Black Folk*,. The book combined autobiography, meditation, history, and sociology into a consideration of the psychological and social condition of American blacks and also included a stinging critique of Washington in the essay "Of Mr. Booker T. Washington and Others." Du Bois founded the National Association for the Advancement of Colored People (NAACP) in 1909 and published the magazine *The Crisis* from 1910 to 1934. Another prominent figure, Marcus Garvey, the leader of the United Negro Improvement Association (UNIA), published two volumes of his essays and other writings during the years from 1923 to 1925 with the help of his wife.

The beginning of important historical and social scientific commentary by other black writers occurred at this time. Some of Arthur Huff Fauset's biographies of famous black people and Monroe Work's studies of black folk culture were published during this era and continued after 1940. The sociologist Charles S. Johnson published sociological works such as *The Negro in American Civilization* and others during this period, as well as editing *Opportunity* magazine, sponsoring new writers and editing anthologies of work from the magazine. In addition to his poetry, essays, novels and editing, James Weldon Johnson wrote a social history of Harlem entitled *Black Manhattan* in 1930 and his autobiography, *Along this Way* in 1933. In many ways this period marked a prelude to the socio-

logical advances in the 1940s and 1950s as well as the accomplishments of literary figures such as James Baldwin.

245 Sterling A. Brown

Outline for the Study of the Poetry of American Negroes
(New York, NY; Harcourt, Brace and Co., 1931)

Summary: Noted among the writers of the Harlem Renaissance of the early twentieth century for his poetry, Sterling Brown also contributed to the African American historic legacy through his critical works, which include *Outline for the Study of the Poetry of American Negroes*. Written to fill a void in available texts for use in his class in American literature while a professor at Howard University, this volume was pioneering in its focus specifically on "black" poetry as a genre. In addition to being strong influences upon Brown's original poetry, the traditions of African American blues and spirituals create unique conventions within African American poetry, according to Brown. The development of these conventions is illustrated through a well-researched chronology of works that form the basis of Brown's "outline."

Subject(s): Poetry, Culture, Literature

246 Harry T. Burleigh

Negro Spirituals: Arranged for Solo Voice
(New York, NY; G. Ricordi, 1922)

Summary: Composer, singer, and music editor Harry T. Burleigh (1866-1949) dedicated his life to raising the stature of Americans of African descent by properly presenting black men and women's traditional music. One of his most significant works, *Negro Spirituals*, sets the spirituals of southern slaves in musical notation, providing arrangements for piano and voice, to allow them to be played and sung outside their formerly oral tradition.

Subject(s): Music, Slavery, Performing Arts

247 Allison Davis
John Dollard, Co-author

Children of Bondage: The Personality Development of Negro Youth in the Urban South
(Washington, DC; American Council on Education, 1940)

Summary: Psychologist, social anthropologist, and educator Allison Davis, who had a long career at the University of Chicago as professor emeritus prior to his death in 1983, published several works based on his studies of the effects of education and class on black youth. Focusing specifically on segregated Southern society during the 1920s and 1930s, Davis was one of the first to correlate inferior educational opportunities with poverty and a propensity to violent behavior in adulthood. His *Children of Bondage*, co-authored with fellow anthropologist

John Dollard, contained the essential findings that would prompt his further study into areas that included intelligence testing and militancy.

Subject(s): Education, American South, Segregation

---

248   **W.E.B. Du Bois**

An ABC of Color

(Berlin, Germany; Seven Seas Publishers, 1963)

Summary: W.E.B. Du Bois helped to establish the National Association for the Advancement of Colored People (NAACP), serving as that organization's publicity director for many years. As the editor of the NAACP journal *The Crisis,* he became well known for his articles and editorials on issues related to African American equality, including black history, the politics of oppression, and Pan-Africanism, which he promoted later in his life. Harvard educated, Du Bois was a prolific writer. He produced a number of books on the history of Africans and African Americans and on the problems of racial prejudice, including *Color and Democracy: Colonies and Peace,* focusing on imperialism, and *Black Folk: Then and Now,* from 1939. Published in the year of Du Bois's death, *An ABC of Color* collects excerpts from several of these works as a way of memorializing the civil rights leader and his message.

Subject(s): Civil Rights Movement, Pan-Africanism, Sociology

---

249   **W.E.B. Du Bois**

Black Folk, Then and Now: An Essay in the History and Sociology of the Negro Race

(New York, NY; H. Holt and Company, 1939)

Summary: Civil rights leader and NAACP founder W.E.B. Du Bois was trained as a sociologist while a student at Harvard University, where he began his documentation of the oppression of African Americans and their efforts to gain equality in the years since the Civil War. In *Black Folk, Then and Now: An Essay in the History and Sociology of the Negro Race* Du Bois outlines the history of black society. He follows African-based culture from its roots in Africa to its place in the New World, as African slaves attempted to navigate the culture of a foreign land where their stature in society was almost nonexistent. By depicting black Africans in their rightful place within a world history that had previously overlooked them, the Du Bois work was groundbreaking. Critics praised the author for his insight, several going so far as to say that Du Bois had proven the case for equality by producing a work equal to that of any of his white colleagues.

Subject(s): American History, Slavery, Cultural Conflict

---

250   **W.E.B. Du Bois**

Darkwater: Voices from within the Veil

(New York, NY; Harcourt, Brace and Howe, 1920)

Summary: W.E.B. Du Bois stood at the vanguard of the civil rights movement in America. Trained as a sociologist at Harvard University, Du Bois began to document the oppression of black people and their efforts to gain equality in the 1890s. His *Darkwater: Voices from within the Veil* is a semi-autobiographical collection of essays, stories, and parables in which he depicts the majority of mankind as being subjugated by an imperialistic white race. A note of bitterness underlies the autobiographical portions of the work, reflecting its author's anger at the inequities suffered by his race. Among the essays included are "The Hands of Ethiopia," "The Servant in the House," and the passionate "The Damnation of Children."

Subject(s): Racism, Civil Rights Movement, Autobiography

---

251   **W.E.B. Du Bois**

The Gift of Black Folk: The Negroes in the Making of America

(Boston, MA; Stratford Co., 1924)

Summary: Raised in Massachusetts and a student at Harvard University, W.E.B. Du Bois stands as one of the most influential black Americans of the first half of the twentieth century. In *The Gift of Black Folk: The Negroes in the Making of America* the civil rights activist sets forth the contributions of black Americans throughout history, from their participation in the discovery of the New World, to their sacrifices in wartime, their many contributions in the arts and literature, and their gift of the unique "spiritual quality" that threads throughout U.S. culture. According to Du Bois, African Americans have been and continue to be an asset to the nation; the "Black Problem," he argues, stems from whites' failure to recognize this fact.

Subject(s): Artists and Art, History, Race Relations

---

252   **W.E.B. Du Bois**

The Souls of Black Folk: Essays and Sketches

(Chicago, IL; A.C. McClurg, 1903)

Summary: A pioneer in the civil rights movement, W.E.B. Du Bois was considered radical due to his beliefs, which encompassed communism and socialism, and for his aggressive stance in support of equal opportunities for African Americans. Du Bois was raised in Massachusetts, and trained as a sociologist at Harvard University. He began documenting the oppression of blacks and their efforts to attain equality while still a student at Harvard. "The problem of the twentieth century is the problem of the color line," he tersely stated in his 1903 work *The Souls of Black Folk: Essays and Sketches,* which collected Du Bois's impressions of prominent African Americans. Reflecting its author's strong opinions, *The Souls of Black Folk* was not well received by either blacks or whites. White Americans were shocked by the unfavorable, if historically accurate depiction of their brutal treatment of blacks throughout history. Blacks, too, were stunned by Du Bois's pronounced opposition to the appeasement policy of leaders like Booker T. Washington, who believed racial tensions could diminish over time if unskilled blacks became trained in new vocations. In more recent years, however, academics have cited *The Souls of Black Folk* as a major influence on the attitudes of younger generations of civil rights activists, one critic citing the work as Du Bois's "greatest achievement as a writer."

Subject(s): Civil Rights Movement, Biography, Race Relations

253 Alice Dunbar-Nelson

(Also known as Alice Ruth Moore Dunbar Nelson, Alice Ruth Moore)

Gloria T. Hull, Editor

Give Us Each Day: The Diary of Alice Dunbar-Nelson

(New York, NY; W.W. Norton, 1984)

Summary: The wife of writer Paul Lawrence Dunbar, Alice Dunbar-Nelson chronicled her life, from her middle-class roots in New Orleans to her long career as both a writer and educator, in *Give Us Each Day*. Born in 1875, she became active in the "Votes for Women" campaign of the early 1900s and other social reforms of the first half of the twentieth century, while also gaining a measure of renown as a published poet and author of short fiction. She describes her frustration over the limited roles afforded to women and her efforts to preserve the written efforts of other African American women through both her own writing and editing and her journalistic assistance with the publication of several periodicals. Of special interest is Dunbar-Nelson's relationship to the writers of the Harlem Renaissance, which sprang up in the years following her most creative period and on which she had a significant influence.

Subject(s): Autobiography, Harlem Renaissance, Women's Rights

254 Paul K. Edwards

The Southern Urban Negro as a Consumer

(New York, NY; Prentice-Hall, Inc., 1932)

Summary: In *The Southern Urban Negro as a Consumer* Paul K. Edwards undertakes the statistical study and analysis of the economic aspects of African American urban living. Based on data gathered by Fisk University over a three year period in and around Nashville, Tennessee, the volume explores such aspects as the type of merchandise consumed, blacks' response to brand name merchandise, the type of advertising that blacks follow, and a wage and occupation study of buying power. The volume, which concludes with suggestions as to how to reach blacks through advertising, would be revised and updated in 1969 and published by Negro Universities Press.

Subject(s): City and Town Life, Economics, Conduct of Life

255 Arthur Huff Fauset
Mabel Betsy Hill, Illustrator

For Freedom: A Biographical Story of the American Negro

(Philadelphia, PA; Franklin Publishing and Supply Co., 1927)

Summary: In this 1927 study of African American culture and history, Arthur Huff Fauset offers a comprehensive examination of notable black Americans throughout history. He begins with a chapter about "The First Slaves" before moving on to such figures as Crispus Attucks, a black man who was among the group of protesters killed during the Boston Massacre; poet Phillis Wheatley; scientist and inventor Benjamin Banneker; and activist Booker T. Washington. Fauset ends the book with a chapter devoted to the literary and artistic figures of the Harlem Renaissance, which was well underway by the time of the book's publication. Among the people he discusses in this final chapter are Langston Hughes, Countee Cullen, and Claude McKay.

Subject(s): Harlem Renaissance, Slavery, Biography

256 Arthur Huff Fauset

Sojourner Truth: God's Faithful Pilgrim

(Chapel Hill, NC; University of North Carolina Press, 1938)

Summary: *Sojourner Truth: God's Faithful Pilgrim* details the life story of a woman who escaped from slavery and became a prominent figure in the abolition movement prior to the Civil War. Written by Philadelphia public school teacher Arthur Huff Fauset as a way to provide his students with books about prominent African Americans who were neglected by mainstream history texts of the time, the biography recounts Truth's ordeals as a slave, her flight to freedom, the publication of her biography, *The Narrative of Sojourner Truth*,--which her inability to read or write forced her to dictate to a neighbor--and her active support of both women's suffrage and the gospel of Jesus Christ in speaking engagements throughout the United States during the years following the Civil War.

Subject(s): Biography, Slavery, Abolition

257 E. Franklin Frazier

The Negro Family in the United States

(Chicago, IL; University of Chicago Press, 1939)

Summary: E. Franklin Frazier's *The Negro Family in the United States* outlines the history of the African American family unit and predicts areas where problems will arise. Relying on case studies and a wealth of statistics, Frazier shows the changes wrought upon the black family unit as a result of the movement of blacks both northward and westward in the wake of the Civil War.

Subject(s): History, Family Life, Family Problems

258 Marcus Garvey
Amy Jacques Garvey, Editor

The Philosophy and Opinions of Marcus Garvey, or, Africa for the Africans. Volumes 1-2
(New York, NY; Universal Pub. Co., 1923)

Summary: This work, *The Philosophy and Opinions of Marcus Garvey; or, Africa for the Africans*, contains essays the noted black leader contributed to the periodicals *Negro World* and *Black Man*, as well as the Jamaican-born Garvey's speeches and writings for the Universal Negro Improvement Association, the Pan-African organization he founded in 1914. Edited by his daughter, Amy Jacques Garvey, *Philosophy and Opinions* reflects Garvey's promotion of black--specifically African--aesthetic standards, a black deity, and a revisionist perspective that praised the previously ignored accomplishments of blacks throughout history. Garvey also actively championed the creation of a united black nation. While his opposition to the philosophy of the NAACP and his radical pro-black stance caused his popularity among African Americans during the decades prior to his death in 1940, Garvey's legacy of racial pride and Pan-Africanism have been reassessed in more recent years.

Subject(s): Pan-Africanism, Racism, Religion

259 Taylor Gordon
Miguel Covarrubias, Illustrator

Born to Be
(New York, NY; Covici, Friede, 1929)

Summary: The early years of Taylor Gordon, who found fame as a singer of Negro spirituals, are the focus of this memoir. Gordon recounts his childhood in the mining boom town of White Sulphur Springs, Montana. He experienced racial prejudice for the first time when he left for the East. In New York, Gordon forged a significant career during the Harlem Renaissance.

Subject(s): Music, Prejudice, Harlem Renaissance

260 Herbert S. Gorman

The Incredible Marquis, Alexandre Dumas
(New York, NY; Farrar & Rhinehart, 1929)

Summary: A biography of French author Alexandre Dumas *pere*, Herbert S. Gorman's work is based on the black writer's memoirs, which relate his colorful life from birth to just before his death in 1870. A writer of romances and plays, Dumas was a man of the world, a successful black man who flourished due to his bravado, his imagination, and his skill as an author. An enthusiastic, if somewhat one-sided, portrayal of Dumas, Gorman's book was praised for its readability and the author's restraint in attempting to psychoanalyze one of the most interesting writers of the nineteenth century.

Subject(s): Biography, Writing, Literature

261 Paul Green

In Abraham's Bosom
(London, England; Allen & Unwin, 1929)

Summary: *In Abraham's Bosom* tells the life story of Abraham, the illegitmate black son of white landowner Colonel McCranie, who has never publicly admitted to being Abraham's father. A self-educated man, Abraham becomes a teacher, marries, and has a son, at which point the Colonel acknowledges the relationship and gives Abraham the gift of a house and 25 acres of land as a christening present for the baby. Abraham fulfills his dream of opening a school for black children of the county, but the tensions between black and white neighbors and interpersonal difficulties with Abraham himself doom the school. Abraham and his wife become low-paid laborers, and life continues a downward spiral. Ultimately, he must turn to Lonnie, his white half-brother, to keep his family together. Playwright Paul Green's explorationn of racial tensions in the American South during the 1920s was awarded the Pulitzer Prize for Drama in 1927.

Subject(s): Race Relations, Racial Conflict, Family Relations

Award(s): Pulitzer Prize: Drama, 1927

262 Lorenzo Johnston Greene
Carter G. Woodson, Co-author

The Negro Wage Earner
(Washington, DC; Association for the Study of Negro Life and History, Inc., 1930)

Summary: *The Negro Wage Earner* was one of the most notable books written by civil rights leader and historian Lorenzo Greene. Greene's deep social commitment and his experience as a member of three presidential commissions--on housing, youth, and human rights under Presidents Herbert Hoover, Dwight D. Eisenhower, and Lyndon B. Johnson--inform this book, which presents an overview of the changing economic status of African Americans throughout U.S. history. A professor of history at Lincoln University, Greene was considered an authority on black American history.

Subject(s): Slavery, Working-Class Life, Economics

263 William E. Hatcher

John Jasper: The Unmatched Negro Philosopher and Preacher
(New York, NY; F.H. Revell Company, 1908)

Summary: Written as a testament to a friend, William E. Hatcher's *John Jasper: The Unmatched Negro Philosopher and Preacher* describes the life of Baptist preacher and orator John Jasper (1812?-1901), who rose from a childhood in slavery to become one of the most original black preachers of the South. As Hatcher noted of Jasper's sermonizing at the Sixth Mount Zion Baptist Church: "In the circle of Jasper's gifts his imagination was preeminent. It was the mammoth lamp in his tower of being." A cofounder of the Sixth Baptist in 1867, Jasper would preach there until the end of his life, drawing crowds to hear such sensationalist rhetoric as his advancement of a geocentric theory encapsulated in his famous "The Sun Do Move" sermon.

Subject(s): Religion, Biography, Imagination

264   Samuel Jackson Holmes

The Negro's Struggle for Survival: A Study in Human Ecology
(Berkeley, CA; University of California Press, 1937)

Summary: In his *The Negro's Struggle for Survival: A Study in Human Ecology* Samuel Jackson Holmes presents an exhaustive study of the vital statistics of African Americans. Adopting a dispassionate scientific perspective, Holmes observes the race problem as a struggle for survival between two competing species. Concluding that while whites were still "ahead" in terms of survival criteria, blacks were gaining in momentum and would be expected to increase their numbers at a faster rate. Viewed as a useful tool for sociologists and anthropologists, Holmes's work also predicted the white push for birth control that would begin to be heard by mid-century.

Subject(s): Anthropology, Race Relations

265   William Henry Holtzclaw

The Black Man's Burden
(New York, NY; Neale Publishing, 1915)

Summary: Now considered a classic, William Henry Holtzclaw's inspiring autobiography *The Black Man's Burden* reflects the author's belief in the importance of education by describing his own rise from poverty with the help of the industrial high school system organized in the rural South during the last decades of the nineteenth century. Booker T. Washington, who devoted his life to advocating African American education as a way of overcoming racism, called Holtzclaw's work "a very important chapter in the history of Negro education." Holtzclaw published his life story to tell "the story of many others like myself who have struggled to get an education and to be of use in the world, but whose efforts will never be known."

Subject(s): Racism, Autobiography, Education

266   C.L.R. James

The Black Jacobins: Toussaint L'Ouverture and the San Domingo Revolution
(New York, NY; Dial, 1938)

Summary: A vividly written account of the Haitian Revolution,*The Black Jacobins: Toussaint L'Ouverture and the San Domingo Revolution* chronicles events in Haiti from 1794 to 1803. Beginning shortly after the French Revolution threw France into chaos, the colony of San Domingo was incited to rebellion by a semi-literate black slave named Toussaint L'Ouverture. The revolution that followed was a model for

countless other colonies wishing to remove colonial oppressors; L'Ouverture and his followers successfully repelled invasions by French, Spanish, and English forces to form the first independent nation in the Caribbean.

Subject(s): Revolution, Rebellion, Colonialism

267   Eva A. Jessye

My Spirituals
(New York, NY; Robbins-Engel, 1927)

Summary: In *My Spirituals* composer and singer Eva Jessye collected and arranged many of the songs she had used in her work as choral director in Oklahoma schools and at Morgan State College in Baltimore, as well as songs she and her group, the Dixie Jubilee Singers, performed at New York City's Capitol Theatre. A talented composer and singer, Jessye had excelled at her musical studies under several noted music theorists, and she would go on to a successful career as both an internationally acclaimed vocalist with the Dixie Singers--later renamed the Eva Jessye Choir--and as choral director of such notable stage works as *Porgy and Bess* and *Four Saints in Three Acts*.

Subject(s): Music, African Americans, Folklore

268   Charles Spurgeon Johnson

The Negro in American Civilization: A Study of Negro Life and Race Relations in the Light of Social Research
(New York, NY; H. Holt and Company, 1930)

Summary: *The Negro in American Civilization* was the result of a conference held in 1926 that featured sixteen organizations active in working toward African American equality. A sociological study of the condition of black Americans following World War I, the work is divided into two parts, the first a fact-based survey of the employment, family, and community life of blacks, and the second a presentation of papers by various sociologists, scholars, and social workers dealing with specific aspects of the current problem. Among contributors to the volume were W.E.B. Du Bois, Niles Carpenter, and Raymond Pearl. Including a wealth of statistical evidence, the work was nonetheless criticized for its lack of a discussion of either causes or solutions to the current inequitable state of affairs.

Subject(s): Sociology, African Americans

269   Guy B. Johnson

Folk Culture on St. Helena Island, South Carolina
(Chapel Hill, NC; University of North Carolina Press, 1930)

Summary: The sea islands off the coast of South Carolina and Georgia have long been the focus of intense scholarly attention because of their unique African American culture. In this 1930 study, Guy B. Johnson examines the folk culture of one of these islands, St. Helena. In addition to discussing the folk songs and folklore of the island, Johnson offers details of the native black dialect known as gullah.

Subject(s): Folklore, Music, Language

---

270 Jack Johnson

Jack Johnson In the Ring and Out
(Chicago, IL; National Sports Publishing, 1927)

Summary: *Jack Johnson In the Ring and Out* is the autobiography of Jack Johnson, a black boxer raised in Galveston, Texas, who rose to greatness as the nation's first black heavyweight champion. Published in 1927--nine years after he won the historic title from Tommy Burns--Johnson's biography has been hailed as entertaining reading, giving a full sense of the man and his determination.

Subject(s): Autobiography, Boxing

---

271 James Weldon Johnson

Along This Way: The Autobiography of James Weldon Johnson
(New York, NY; Viking Press, 1933)

Summary: In *Along This Way* James Weldon Johnson tells his own story. A civil rights leader and, with W.E.B. Du Bois and others, a co-founder of the National Association for the Advancement of Colored People (NAACP), Johnson helped advance the cause of racial equality and human rights through not only his activism but also in his songs, poems, speeches, and books such as *Black Manhattan*.

Subject(s): Autobiography, Civil Rights Movement, Writing

---

272 James Weldon Johnson

Black Manhattan
(New York, NY; A.A. Knopf, 1930)

Summary: Written by James Weldon Johnson, a civil rights leader and co-founder of the NAACP who blazed a trail for racial equality and human rights through his songs, poems, speeches, and other writings, *Black Manhattan* presents the history of New York blacks from the time Manhattan Island was first settled to the Harlem Renaissance that was then taking place. Showing Harlem as it was during the 1920s, the book depicts a community free from racial strife, displaying a vitality in art, literature, and drama. Johnson also includes biographies of notable artists and playwrights of that era, making *Black Manhattan* a valuable reference for those studying the high points of African American culture.

Subject(s): Harlem Renaissance, City and Town Life, Artists and Art

---

273 Laurence C. Jones

Piney Woods and Its Story
(New York, NY; F.H. Revell Co., 1922)

Summary: In his 1922 memoir, Laurence C. Jones offers the heartwarming story of his odyssey from an educated, well-to-do background to the leadership of a school for blacks in poverty-stricken, rural Mississippi. After becoming the principal of the Piney Woods Country Life School, Laurence led a building campaign in which the school's students actually built their own permanent classroom facility.

Subject(s): Education, Rural Life, School Life

---

274 Louise Venable Kennedy

The Negro Peasant Turns Cityward: Effects of Recent Migrations to Northern Centers
(New York, NY; Columbia University Press, 1930)

Summary: In her study *The Negro Peasant Turns Cityward*, sociologist Louise Venable Kennedy examines the migration of African Americans from the southern states to the industrial North between 1915 and 1930. A population shift that would have pronounced effects on several northern cities, including New York City, Detroit, and Chicago, this move by rural blacks was motivated by economic concerns. Examining both the economic and social aspects of the rising clusters of southern blacks in northern cities, Kennedy analyzes the causes and projected effects of this movement in terms of labor, family ties, education, and other quality of life issues.

Subject(s): Migration, Urban Affairs, Sociology

---

275 Benjamin E. Mays
Joseph William Nicholson, Co-author

The Negro's Church
(New York, NY; Institute of Social and Religious Research, 1933)

Summary: *The Negro's Church*, co-authored by prominent clergyman, educator, and civil rights activist Benjamin E. Mays, reflects Mays' efforts to uncover the areas of concern unique to the African American community. While directing a study of the nation's black churches for the Institute of Social and Religious Research, Mays surveyed more than 600 urban and 180 rural houses of worship, obtaining data on the education and training of ministers, congregations' financial resources, and the types of religious and social programs offered, among other things. A synthesis of that study, *The Negro's Church* increased awareness of the social, economic, and community-based forces that combined to form the modern African American church.

Subject(s): Religion, Civil Rights Movement, Autobiography

276 Robert Russa Moton

Finding a Way Out: An Autobiography
(Garden City, NY; Doubleday, Page and Company, 1920)

Summary: *Finding a Way Out: An Autobiography* recounts the life of Robert Russa Moton, the man who rose from slavery to follow Booker T. Washington as the principal of Tuskeegee University. Born on a plantation in the state of Virginia, Moton achieved freedom and set about a course of education that brought him through college and into a career dedicated to helping African Americans achieve equal economic standing with whites. As Moton noted in the introduction to his book, his purpose in setting forth his life story was "helping [people achieve] a clearer understanding of the hopes and aspirations of my own people and the difficulties which they have overcome of the last fifty years."

Subject(s): Autobiography, Slavery, Education

277 Robert Russa Moton

What the Negro Thinks
(Garden City, NY; Doubleday, Doran and Company, Inc., 1929)

Summary: In *What the Negro Thinks*, Tuskegee Institute principal Robert Russa Moton, approaches the problem of race relations from a black viewpoint allied very much to that of his predecessor, Booker T. Washington. In chapters such as "Knowing the White Man" and "The Negro's Reaction," Moton shows why African Americans are discontented with their status as second-rate citizens and expresses the hope that whites, in accord with Christian ideals and a sense of fairness, will realize the benefit of promoting a more equitable, respectful exchange of ideas between the races. Moton's volume was noted for its dispassionate approach and its lack of animosity in the light of the oppression openly visited upon blacks during the early years of the twentieth century.

Subject(s): Race Relations

278 National Urban League

Negro Membership in American Labor Unions
(New York, NY; Alexander Press, 1930)

Summary: The National Urban League produced this study in 1930, just as the Great Depression was beginning in the United States. The book begins with an examination of "The Industrial Status of the Negro" before discussing black membership in specific national unions, including those in the building trades; metals and machinery; clothing and textiles; food, liquor and tobacco; amusements; and other categories. In addition, the book offers information about the status of black unions organizing in select cities and explores the phenomena of independent black unions.

Subject(s): Labor and Labor Classes, Labor Conditions

279 Howard W. Odum
Guy B. Johnson, Co-author

The Negro and His Songs: A Study of Typical Negro Songs in the South
(Chapel Hill, NC; University of North Carolina Press, 1925)

Summary: Praised for making available to folklorists and other scholars a body of work not previously studied, *The Negro and His Songs* includes improvisations of hundreds of songs, many dating to the early years of U.S. slavery. Including religious songs, social songs, and work songs, the songs or song fragments reflect imagery, graphic description, and dramatic effect within their oral tradition. While receiving some criticism for revising song lyrics to make them more palatable to white sensitivies, the authors also alerted a broad audience to the necessity of documenting such songs before the tradition was lost.

Subject(s): Music, Folklore, Slavery

280 Mary White Ovington

Black and White Sat Down Together: The Reminiscences of an NAACP Founder
(New York, NY; Feminist Press, 1995)

Summary: *Black and White Sat Down Together: The Reminiscences of an NAACP Founder* are the recollections of civil rights activist Mary White Ovington. Originally published in the *Baltimore Afro-American* in 1932-33, Ovington chronicles the events of 1909, when she, W.E.B. Du Bois, and numberous others founded the National Association for the Advancement of Colored People. This memoir details the political climate of her time with regard to blacks and women and the reason she was drawn into social activism.

Subject(s): Autobiography, Civil Rights Movement, Women's Rights

281 Ulrich B. Phillips

Life and Labor in the Old South
(Boston, MA; Little, Brown, and Company, 1929)

Summary: Ulrich B. Phillips is considered the founding father of modern southern history; his pioneering research into politics, slavery, and the plantation system in the early twentieth century was based upon primary source materials that he brought to light and published. His *Life and Labor in the Old South* was planned as the first of three volumes encompassing political policy and sectionalism. Focusing on the plantation system, it was planned to be followed by *The Course of the South to Secession*; however, that work was left incomplete at Phillips's death and published posthumously in 1939. The concluding volume, bringing the history of the South up to the early twentieth century, was never completed.

Subject(s): Slavery, American South, Work

282 Mungo Melanchton Ponton

Life and Times of Henry M. Turner
(Atlanta, GA; A.B. Caldwell Pub. Co., 1917)

Summary: Born into a free black family in 1834, Henry M. Turner was responsible for establishing the African Episcopal Church throughout Georgia, as well as advocating the emigration of African Americans to Africa. In *Life and Times of Henry M. Turner* he recalls his early years working alongside slaves in South Carolina cotton fields, and his religious development, from Baptist to Methodist and ultimately to Episcopalian. Putting his education to good use, Turner served as chaplain to black troops during the Civil War and then returned to the South, where he was active in politics until Supreme Court decisions in the late 1800s showed a lack of willingness to support equal rights for blacks.

Subject(s): Slavery, Emigration and Immigration, Autobiography

283 Edward Byron Reuter

The American Race Problem: A Study of the Negro
(New York, NY; Thomas Y. Crowell, 1927)

Summary: Reissued several times since its original publication in 1927, Edward Byron Reuter's *The American Race Problem* is a sociological study of the problems facing blacks in the United States. Beginning with the history of blacks in America, Reuter presents an analysis of the current situation as well as a critique of the proposed solutions to the "black problem." Chapters include "Racial Differences," "Negro Sex and Family Life," and "Economic Status of the Negro." A wealth of social statistics are included that highlight areas such as health, education, and delinquency as they pertain to the African American population.

Subject(s): Sociology, Family Life, Economics

284 Paul Robeson
Philip Foner, Editor

Paul Robeson Speaks: Writings, Speeches, and Interviews, 1918-1974
(New York, NY; Brunner/Mazel, 1978)

Summary: This collection contains the work of Paul Robeson (1898-1976), a noted actor and vocalist who sacrificed a successful career in the United States to advocate on behalf of people of color around the world. Robeson, a graduate of Columbia Law School, placed himself squarely on the side of those who fought racial discrimination through the speeches and writings, interviews, and newspaper reports included in this volume. The volume includes Robeson's contributions to *Freedom*, a political journal he established in New York City that drew on the talents of many other black writers of the mid-twentieth century.

Subject(s): Freedom of Speech, Journalism, Cold War

285 Wulf Sachs

Black Hamlet: The Mind of an African Negro Revealed by Psychoanalysis
(London, England; G. Bles, 1937)

Summary: Originally published in 1937, Wulf Sachs's *Black Hamlet* is a psychological profile of the relationship between Sachs, a physician, and healer-diviner John Chavafambira. Recalling Sachs's term in South Africa, the book is part memoir and part history. It has been praised for its readability as well as for its ruminations on such issues as apartheid, ethnography, political consciousness, and Jungian psychology. The book was published under the title *Black Anger* in 1947.

Subject(s): Medicine, Apartheid, Spiritualism

286 Sterling Denhard Spero
Abram L. Harris, Co-author

The Black Worker: The Negro and the Labor Movement
(New York, NY; Columbia University Press, 1931)

Summary: In *The Black Worker: The Negro and the Labor Movement*, authors Sterling Spero and Abram Harris examine the history of African American laborers in relation to the development of modern U.S. industry as a whole. Citing case after case, the authors show that racial prejudice has infiltrated not only the demand for labor but also trade union politics and organizational structures. They suggest that separatist policies and programs--promoted by radical blacks but often funded by "philanthropic" northern whites as a covert way of keeping blacks economically inferior—should be disavowed in favor of cooperating with whites only when doing so would promote a common good. Harris argues that blacks should try to organize separately to address blacks' unique issues in the U.S. labor market.

Subject(s): Working-Class Life, Labor and Labor Classes, Work

287 Melvin B. Tolson
Robert M. Farnsworth, Editor

Caviar and Cabbage
(Columbia, MO; University of Missouri Press, 1982)

Summary: This volume is a selection of articles by poet Melvin Tolson, a writer who was affiliated with the Harlem Renaissance in the years following World War I. Featuring a discussion of social issues, Tolson's columns also were noted for their sophisticated style; they ended in 1944 when the writer determined to put renewed effort into his poetry. A professor for many years, Tolson would be named poet laureate of the Republic of Liberia in 1953.

Subject(s): Journalism, Social Conditions

288 **Mark Twain**
(Pseudonym of Samuel Clemens)

King Leopold's Soliloquy: A Defense of His Congo Rule

(Boston, MA; P.R. Warren, 1905)

Summary: In *King Leopold's Soliloquy: A Defense of His Congo Rule*, noted American satirist Mark Twain takes aim at Belgium's King Leopold II, under whose rule the colonization of the Belgian Congo region (now part of Zaire) began when Leopold declared it an independent state—and he its king—in 1885. In his book, Twain comments upon Leopold's mistreatment of the native Africans in his zeal to plunder the region's natural resources; international criticism caused the region to be annexed to Belgium in 1908.

Subject(s): Slavery, Africa, Colonialism

289 **John W. Vandercook**

Black Majesty: The Life of Christophe, King of Haiti

(New York, NY; Harper & Brothers, 1928)

Summary: *Black Majesty* is the romanticized account of the life of Henri Christophe, a Haitian slave who rose to become king. Written to inspire readers with an interest in their own history, John W. Vandercook's work describes Christophe's tutelage under Toussaint L'Overture, his eventual overthrow of French colonialist power, and his brief role as king of Haiti before power corrupted his revolutionary ideals. Poet Countee Cullen wrote of the book that it "should serve as a social and moral stimulus to 12 million people who can well-afford the incitement of such short-lived brilliance as is herein inscribed."

Subject(s): Slavery, Colonialism, Resistance Movements

290 **Booker T. Washington**

Up from Slavery

(Garden City, NY; Doubleday, Page & Co., 1901)

Summary: *Up from Slavery* is the autobiography of Booker T. Washington, a mulatto who was born into slavery in Virginia in 1856. Freed with his parents after the Civil War, Washington was educated at Hampton Institute and dedicated his life to educating other blacks. Washington lectured around the nation as a way of motivating blacks to train themselves in skills that would allow the newly freed slaves to support their families. In 1881 Washington founded Alabama's Tuskegee Institute as a means of providing former slaves with the means to gain an economic footing on par with whites. Washington died in 1915.

Subject(s): Autobiography, Slavery, Education

291 **Charles H. Wesley**

Negro Labor in the United States, 1850-1925: A Study in American Economic History

(New York, NY; Vanguard Press, 1927)

Summary: *Negro Labor in the United States, 1850-1925* presents a profile of African American labor from the days of slavery to the massive emigration from southern agricultural areas to the industrialized North that occurred at the beginning of the twentieth century. A work of economic as well as social history, Wesley's book marshals a vast array of statistical and other evidence to show the myriad effects of the black movement from the skilled agricultural labor pool of the south to the unskilled industrial labor pool of the North. Wesley concludes by suggesting that through this relocation blacks will overcome their economic obstacles to full freedom and independence.

Subject(s): Economics, Labor and Labor Classes, Emigration and Immigration

292 **Charles H. Wesley**

Richard Allen, Apostle of Freedom

(Washington, DC; Associated Publishers, 1935)

Summary: In his biography *Richard Allen, Apostle of Freedom* historian Charles H. Wesley profiles the life of Allen (1760-1831), who is credited as the founder of the first black-controlled Christian denomination. Born into slavery in Philadelphia, Allen moved to Delaware, where he was converted to Methodism as a teenager. Founder of the African Methodist Episcopal Church, he parlayed his role as bishop into one as a successful businessman and influential black leader able to address topics of concern to blacks that created a dialogue across denominational lines.

Subject(s): Religion, Biography, Slavery

293 **Sol White**
Jerry Malloy, Compiler

Sol White's History of Colored Base Ball, With Other Documents on the Early Black Game 1886-1936

(Lincoln, NE; University of Nebraska Press, 1995)

Summary: First published in 1907 by the then-legendary player Sol White, *Sol White's History of Colored Base Ball* is a vivid record, copiously illustrated, of the Negro League, a talented group of African American men whose talents were ignored by the Major Leagues only because of the color of their skin. The edition also includes an essay by baseball historian Jerry Malloy describing White's efforts to bolster the success of the Negro League, and it contains several other documents reflecting the color politics of the sports world during the late nineteenth century.

Subject(s): Baseball, African Americans

294 Walter White

Rope & Faggot: A Biography of Judge Lynch

(New York, NY; A.A. Knopf, 1929)

Summary: *Rope & Faggot: A Biography of Judge Lynch* by civil rights activist Walter White was a result of the NAACP co-founder's decade-long investigation of mob violence in the American South. The evidence White uncovered while posing as a local reporter suggested, as he notes in this book, that racially motivated violence had become "an almost integral part of our national folkways." Lynching had its source in southerners' attempts to put unruly blacks in their place after industrialization began to make slavery unnecessary, contends White.

Subject(s): Violence, American South, Lynching

295 Carter G. Woodson

The Mis-Education of the Negro

(Washington, DC; Associated Publishers, 1933)

Summary: Written by Carter G. Woodson, a historian, educator, and founder of the Association for the Study of Negro Life and History, *The Mis-Education of the Negro* profiles the educational system endured by African American children in segregated America. Reprinted almost sixty years after its original publication, the book includes Woodson's observations of social and educational conditions, highlighting the underpinnings of much of the modern bureaucracy controlling U.S. public education today.

Subject(s): Education, Segregation, History

296 Carter G. Woodson, Editor

Negro Orators and Their Orations

(Washington, DC; Associated Publishers, Inc., 1925)

Summary: A collection of noteworthy speeches presented by black Americans throughout the nation's history, *Negro Orators and Their Orations* demonstrates, through its organization and the commentary provided by its editor, historian and educator Carter G. Woodson, the growing sophistication of African Americans within the U.S. public forum. Among the speeches contained are abolitionist addresses, sermons, and other public pronouncements in support of black interests. Woodson collected these works as a way of inspiring future generations of black Americans.

Subject(s): Biography, Education

297 T.J. Woofter, Jr.

Black Yeomanry: Life on St. Helena Island

(New York, NY; H. Holt and Company, 1930)

Summary: In *Black Yeomanry* sociologist T.J. Woofter presents the history of the black settlement on St. Helena Island in South Carolina, where the finest grade of cotton was once grown on lands divided among a group of middle-class landowners. Together with a group of specialists, Woofter lived on the island for nine months, during which time he assembled a vast amount of data on health, education, play, religion, family life, and other aspects of this unique community. The volume includes tables of statistical data collected during this study.

Subject(s): Sociology, Economics, History

298 T.J. Woofter, Jr.

Negro Problems in Cities

(Garden City, NY; Doubleday, Doran & Company, Inc., 1928)

Summary: *Negro Problems in Cities* is a textbook by sociologist T.J. Woofter that is geared toward an academic readership. Focusing on urban communities most affected by the growth and redistribution of the black population following the Civil War years, Woofter cites blacks and whites' mutual interest in working together toward the betterment of all. After contrasting styles of civic leadership, local organizations, and religious and educational opportunities, the volume presents solutions to the race-based problems confronting city-dwelling blacks as well as whites in the 1920s. Woofter expressed particular concern over black education in southern cities, where efforts at conciliation between the races had advanced to a far lesser degree than in northern communities by the date of the book's publication.

Subject(s): Race Relations, Urban Affairs, Sociology

299 Monroe Nathan Work, Compiler

Bibliography of the Negro in Africa and America

(New York, NY; H.W. Wilson, 1928)

Summary: Sold on a service basis, Monroe Nathan Work's *Bibliography of the Negro in Africa and America* encompasses over 17,000 entries listing books, pamphlets, public documents, periodicals, and other written source material referencing African Americans in both the United States and Africa. Including both English and foreign-language publications, the bibliography is divided into 74 sections and includes an author index and a logical arrangement, making it accessible to the general reader. Work was Director of Records at Booker T. Washington's Tuskegee Institute.

Subject(s): Education, Books and Reading

Poetry

Poetry in the period from 1900 to 1940 continued the genteel tradition of the previous century, yet also saw new breakthroughs in style and content. In the years of the Harlem Renaissance and following World War II, there was a time of great productivity by the black elite. In the early years of the 1900s, George McClellan was writing poetry that emulated

Western ideals of gentility, sentimentalism, and the conservative values he held as a minister. Also in the beginning of the century, Paul Laurence Dunbar had become one of the most famous African American poets, though his career was cut short with his early death in 1906. Dunbar had written poetry in standard verse, but also began using black dialect in his poetry. Though this was criticized by some, Dunbar's fame was attributed to the use of this verse and other black poets began experimenting with the form. During the teens, Joseph Seamon Cotter, Sr. wrote modernist folk dialect poetry, a precursor to the verse of the Harlem Renaissance; his son Joseph Seamon Cotter, Jr. also published verse during this time.

Figures such as William Braithwaite perpetuated the genteel tradition during the Harlem Renaissance. Braithwaite's own poetry reflected English romantic tradition, was formally composed, and addressed universal themes of beauty and art. He supported both new black and white writers by sponsoring and editing anthologies of combined works. Countee Cullen also became a major figure during this period. He won the support of black and white critics with his use of traditional forms, but Cullen's poetry addressed more racial and religious issues than Braithwaite's. Another significant poet who addressed racial concerns was Claude McKay. McKay wrote poems in sonnet verse that usually dealt with protest and exile.

But not all of the poetry of the period conformed to traditional verse standards; a vital new folk poetry emerged in the verse of Langston Hughes. James Weldon Johnson's *Book of American Negro Poetry*, published in 1922, was an important anthology that set the work of contemporary poets against the backdrop of early African American traditions in verse and Johnson also published several collections of his own work during this period. In his 1926 work *The Weary Blues*, Hughes uses blues and jazz forms in his verse to give realistic portrayals of Harlem nightlife.

The thirties saw the continual literary production of Hughes, who established himself as a major poet. The literary output of McKay and Cullen also continued, while the groundbreaking folk poetry of Sterling A. Brown was published in *Southern Road* in 1936. Brown had studied ballads, blues and spirituals while he was in the South and used the folklore and language of southern blacks to write his poetry. Though Brown had trouble publishing his second book of poetry soon afterwards, he was later recognized as a skilled and innovative poet.

300 William Stanley Braithwaite

"April"

Lyrics of Life and Love
(Boston, MA; H.B. Turner & Co., 1904)

Summary: This poem is a classic romantic "nature" poem by Braithwaite. In its four stanzas of exact imagery and traditional rhyme schemes, the poet celebrates the dawning of spring. The influence of the English Romantic poets on Braithwaite is clearly visible in this poem.

Subject(s): Nature, Poetry

301 William Stanley Braithwaite

"April's Dream"

Lyrics of Life and Love
(Boston, MA; H.B. Turner & Co., 1904)

Summary: This poem is a brief ode to nature and to spring. As critics have pointed out, this is one of two poems in Braithwaite's 1904 collection with "April" in the title, and one of several poems in which the word "dream" plays a prominent role.

Subject(s): Nature, Dreams and Nightmares

302 William Stanley Braithwaite

"The Departure of Pierrott"

Lyrics of Life and Love
(Boston, MA; H.B. Turner and Company, 1904)

Summary: This poem is a love poem, written to the speaker's beloved and using nature as its source—both standard elements in Braithwaite's poetry. In the poem, the speaker discusses how the lovers passed the long winter by entertaining themselves with poetry from "Tennyson, Shelley, Keats, and Emerson" and how April's arrival signals the end of such entertainment.

Subject(s): Poetry, Love, Nature

303 William Stanley Braithwaite

"Evening"

Lyrics of Life and Love
(Boston, MA; H.B. Turner & Company, 1904)

Summary: This poem from Braithwaite's first collection of poetry exhibits the qualities on which his literary reputation is based: traditional verse (in this case, rhymed couplets) and themes in the tradition of romantic poets such as John Keats (here an ode to the closing of a day). An emphasis on beauty and on universal subjects such as nature, time, and love are the hallmarks of Braithwaite's poetry. The poet felt strongly that poetry should be written for its own sake and thus should be free from social and political issues of the day, including racial issues. Because of this approach, Braithwaite was heavily criticized by black activists and others who were more concerned with social change than with artistic ideals such as beauty and truth.

Subject(s): Poetry, Civil Rights, Nature

304 William Stanley Braithwaite

"The House of Falling Leaves"

The House of Falling Leaves, with Other Poems
(Boston, MA; J.W. Luce and Company, 1908)

Summary: The title poem of Braithwaite's second poetry collection illustrates the poet's guiding philosophy. Heavily influenced by Romantic poets such as John Keats, Braithwaite felt strongly that poetry as an art form should not address social or political issues such as race but should be written merely for its own sake. Accordingly, this collection focuses on nature and love. The title poem, like many others in this collection, is a sonnet sequence (a series of sonnets, which are fourteen-line poems) in four parts.

Subject(s): Love, Nature

---

305 William Stanley Braithwaite

"Keats Was an Unbeliever"

Lyrics of Life and Love
(Boston, MA; H.B. Turner & Company, 1904)

Summary: An homage to Braithwaite's artistic hero, the English Romantic poet John Keats (1795-1821), this poem highlights the aesthetic principles that animated Braithwaite: a pursuit of "Beauty" and a focus on "Nature and Life." The poem's title is from a sketch critical of Keats, which Braithwaite denounces in the poem.

Subject(s): Poetry, Artists and Art

---

306 William Stanley Braithwaite

"Off the New England Coast"

The House of Falling Leaves, with Other Poems
(Boston, MA; J.W. Luce and Company, 1908)

Summary: Dedicated "To John Daniel," this poem consists of four sections. The four have distinct meters and rhyming schemes, but—as with virtually all of Braithwaite's poems—the works are traditional verse compositions. The poem ranges from an ode to a friend, to ruminations on universal themes such as God, life, and time.

Subject(s): Poetry, Friendship

---

307 William Stanley Braithwaite

"She Sleeps Beneath the Winter Snow"

Lyrics of Life and Love
(Boston, MA; H.B. Turner & Co., 1904)

Summary: In this poem, Braithwaite reflects on the death of a loved one, "Ciceline." The poem consists of two stanzas of eight lines each and reflects the poet's fondness for traditional verse and formal rhyming.

Subject(s): Nature, Death

---

308 William Stanley Braithwaite

"Song of a Syrian Lace Seller"

The House of Falling Leaves, with Other Poems
(Boston, MA; J.W. Luce and Company, 1908)

Summary: This traditional verse poem consists of four stanzas, each with three rhymed couplets. As its title suggests, the poem is an ode to a Syrian woman selling lace; her chosen storefront is a sidewalk near St. Paul's Cathedral in London, England. The poem epitomizes the influence of the English Romantic poets on Braithwaite.

Subject(s): Poetry

---

309 William Stanley Braithwaite

"Thanksgiving"

Lyrics of Life and Love
(Boston, MA; H.B. Turner & Co., 1904)

Summary: As its title suggests, this poem is a recitation of the things for which the poet is thankful. In one case, Braithwaite expresses thanks that his mind is free "from creed and doctrine's thrall," an interesting line that reveals his devotion to aesthetic principles rather than to social or political causes—including race.

Subject(s): Poetry

---

310 William Stanley Braithwaite

"To Arthur Upson"

The House of Falling Leaves, with Other Poems
(Boston, MA; J.W. Luce and Company, 1908)

Summary: This sonnet, told using traditional rhyme, is an ode to a friend and a testament to Braithwaite's beloved New England landscape. The poem explores the topic of manhood while using the Charles River as a backdrop. As in all of his poetry, Braithwaite focuses here on craft and aesthetics and pointedly ignores the wider social and political milieu.

Subject(s): Poetry, Friendship, Nature

---

311 William Stanley Braithwaite

"To Dante Gabriel Rossetti"

The House of Falling Leaves, with Other Poems
(Boston, MA; J.W. Luce and Company, 1908)

Summary: This poem is an ode to Dante Gabriel Rossetti (1828-1882), the English poet and painter who founded the Pre-Raphaelite artistic movement and whose mystic poetry had a large influence on Braithwaite. Also mentioned in the poem is another poet whose work influenced Braithwaite: John Keats. The poem's subject matter, devoid of any mention of the socio-political milieu in which Braithwaite lived, is typical of his poetry.

Subject(s): Artists and Art

---

312 William Stanley Braithwaite

"White Magic: An Ode"

The House of Falling Leaves, with Other Poems
(Boston, MA; J.W. Luce and Company, 1908)

Summary: Introduced with the notation "Read at the Centenary Celebration of the Birth of John Greenleaf Whittier at Faneuil Hall, Dec. 17, 1907," this poem is an ode to Whittier (1807-1892), an American poet and abolitionist. Though deeply committed to the fight against slavery, Whittier kept his abolitionist prose writings separate from his poetry—a philosophy that Braithwaite admired. During his life, Braithwaite came under criticism by activists who were unaware of the aesthetic reasons for Braithwaite's reason for creating poetry that did not address the socio-political issues of his day.

Subject(s): Slavery, Abolition

313 Sterling A. Brown

"Children of the Mississippi"
Southern Road
(New York, NY; Harcourt, Brace and Company, 1932)

Summary: Another hardship poem told in the style of a blues song, "Children of the Mississippi" continues the theme of the second section of Brown's 1932 collection. In the poem, Brown depicts the destructive power of the Mississippi River and its fearful hold over the people who live near it. The poem is told in dialect, with main stanzas narrated by an observer offset by brief refrains told in the voices of the people who live by the river.

Subject(s): American South, Rural Life

314 Sterling A. Brown

"Children's Children"
Southern Road
(New York, NY; Harcourt, Brace and Company, 1932)

Summary: In a collection that extols the solace and power of blues music, "Children's Children" is interesting for the ironic light it casts on such music. In the poem, the narrator laments how the children of his generation, who have never known the intense suffering and hardship of previous African American generations, reject the depressing and melodramatic lyrics of blues songs. The poem thus examines not only the long-suffering heritage of African Americans but also the inevitable clash between the old and the young.

Subject(s): American South, Rural Life, Music

315 Sterling A. Brown

"Frankie and Johnny"
Southern Road
(New York, NY; Harcourt, Brace and Company, 1932)

Summary: Unlike many of the poems in Brown's 1932 collection, "Frankie and Johnny" contains political observations that reflect the difficulty of life for African Americans in the rural South in the early decades of the twentieth century. In southern dialect, the poem tells of the love affair between a white woman, Frankie, and a black man, Johnny. Frankie, presented as a willful and malicious gadabout, seduces the hardworking Johnny. At the end of the poem, Frankie's father learns of the affair, and Johnny is lynched.

Subject(s): Lynching, American South, Rural Life

316 Sterling A. Brown

"Long Gone"
Southern Road
(New York, NY; Harcourt, Brace and Company, 1932)

Summary: In this poem, Brown presents a man explaining to his lover why he must leave her side and resume his rail travels. The man acknowledges that he does not know why he travels or where he is going, but notes that his wanderlust is too powerful for him to stay in one place for very long. Using the rural dialect common among African Americans in the South, as Brown does throughout this collection, he dignifies the realities of his protagonist's life without delving into political commentary.

Subject(s): Railroads, American South, Rural Life

317 Sterling A. Brown

"Ma Rainey"
Southern Road
(New York, NY; Harcourt, Brace and Company, 1932)

Summary: This poem is an ode to Ma Rainey, perhaps the first great blues singer, who became popular during the 1920s and 1930s. In the poem, Brown describes rural blacks traveling from all over the South to hear Ma Rainey perform. The blues, a musical form pioneered by blacks that typically explores the hardships of life, emerged out of the South during the early part of the twentieth century and eventually became widely beloved and influential throughout the United States among both blacks and whites.

Subject(s): Music, American South, Rural Life

318 Sterling A. Brown

"Memphis Blues"
Southern Road
(New York, NY; Harcourt, Brace and Company, 1932)

Summary: This poem opens the second section of Brown's 1932 collection, titled "On Restless River." Divided into three stanzas and displaying Brown's trademark use of southern dialect, the poem explores the potential destruction of Memphis, Tennessee—the birthplace of the blues—through flood, fire, tornado, or hurricane. However, the poem suggests, blacks will survive the destruction of Memphis and will endure to rebuild it, if necessary. Among the folk figures Brown utilizes in this poem are the preacher, the musician, the lover, and the gambler.

Subject(s): Music, American South

319 Sterling A. Brown

"Nous n'irons plus au bois"
Southern Road
(New York, NY; Harcourt, Brace and Company, 1932)

Summary: This poem, whose French title translates roughly as "We Will No Longer Go to the Woods," presents a man accusing his lover of throwing away their love—developed in romantic meetings in a forest hut—for a sterile life amid "juvenile" friends and meaningless luxury. As in the other poems in the collection's final section, Brown here uses formal rhymes and eschews themes of race.

Subject(s): Love, Romance

320 Sterling A. Brown

"Odyssey of Big Boy"
Southern Road
(New York, NY; Harcourt, Brace and Company, 1932)

Summary: This poem, which opens Brown's acclaimed 1932 collection *Southern Road*, sets the stage for the collection and for Brown's subsequent literary reputation with its use of southern rural dialect and its elevation of an ordinary African American from the agrarian South into a black "everyman." In the poem, Big Boy lists his life's endeavors: driving steel in Kentucky, mining coal in West Virginia, shucking corn in Maryland, and working on the railroad in Baltimore, among other jobs. He also describes numerous girlfriends. Brown essentially creates a mythic black folk hero in Big Boy, and his technique of relating the realities of southern life without any accompanying commentary is seen in most of his other work. The poem opens the first section of the four-part *Southern Road*. This section, titled "Road So Rocky," is introduced with lines from an old African American spiritual song—a musical form whose themes inform many of the poems in the section. Although often referred to as a poet of the Harlem Renaissance, Brown did most of his best work in the later 1930s, after that literary movement had already run its course.

Subject(s): Harlem Renaissance, American South, Rural Life

321 Sterling A. Brown

"Old King Cotton"
Southern Road
(New York, NY; Harcourt, Brace and Company, 1932)

Summary: This despairing poem about the hardships of picking cotton is representative of Brown's depiction of rural southern blacks in *Southern Road*. Told from the point of view of a cotton picker in heavy southern dialect, the poem chronicles the fickle nature of cotton and the myriad disasters that await cotton growers and pickers, from bad weather to bugs. In keeping with the theme of the volume's second section, "Old King Cotton" is constructed like a blues song.

Subject(s): Farm Life, American South, Rural Life

322 Sterling A. Brown

"Sister Lou"
Southern Road
(New York, NY; Harcourt, Brace and Company, 1932)

Summary: This poem reflects the importance of religious belief among African Americans following centuries of enslavement and discrimination. The poem's protagonist counsels the reader to face death bravely and with relief, since it

finally offers the chance to gain in heaven everything that had been denied here on Earth: a chance to rest, a comfortable bed and a room of one's own, and the right to walk through the front door—in this case the "pearly gates." As elsewhere in this collection, Brown here uses folk stereotypes—the black female servant who cooks and sews and tells stories—to evoke rural southern life.

Subject(s): American South, Rural Life, Religion

323 Sterling A. Brown

"Slim in Hell"
Southern Road
(New York, NY; Harcourt, Brace and Company, 1932)

Summary: The protagonist of "Slim in Hell," Slim Greer, is a character who reappears in several poems in the "On Restless River" section of Brown's 1932 collection. A simple African American man from the South, Slim ventures to Heaven, where St. Peter orders him to travel to Hell and report back on the activities he finds there. Slim finds Hell to be suspiciously similar to the racist South on Earth, with "white devils" continuously attacking blacks. In addition to its portrayal of simple rural African American characters and violent southern whites, the poem pokes fun at Slim for his naivete in assuming that Hell would be any different than the South.

Subject(s): American South, Rural Life, Racism

324 Sterling A. Brown

"Southern Road"
Southern Road
(New York, NY; Harcourt, Brace and Company, 1932)

Summary: The title poem to Brown's 1932 collection contains all of the elements that make the collection notable: use of rural African American dialect, a reliance on folk themes, and a sympathetic portrait of life in the rural South in the early decades of the twentieth century. The narrator of the poem is a member of a prison chain gang, and in singsong dialect that evokes African American spirituals, he describes his hard-luck life.

Subject(s): Music, American South, Rural Life

325 Sterling A. Brown

"Sporting Beasley"
Southern Road
(New York, NY; Harcourt, Brace and Company, 1932)

Summary: The title character of this poem is a prototypical dandy who revels in his flashy clothing and endures the teasing of those around him. He is also a sympathetic character; though he is prideful of his style, it is depicted as a rare joy among life's hardships. The poem utilizes dialect and is structured like a song.

Subject(s): American South, Music, Clothes

326 Sterling A. Brown

"Strong Men"

Southern Road
(New York, NY; Harcourt, Brace and Company, 1932)

Summary: The closing poem of the first section of *Southern Road*, this poem is introduced with two lines from a poem by Carl Sandburg: "The young men keep coming on / The strong men keep coming on." More overtly political than many of the poems in the collection, "Strong Men" describes the violence and outrage of slavery, the later humiliations of economic discrimination, and the political and social conditions that have made life so difficult for generations of African Americans. But it also strikes a hopeful note with its refrain, based on Sandburg's lines, which promises that blacks keep getting stronger and that one day that strength will overwhelm the discrimination that has so long plagued the community.

Subject(s): Racism, Slavery

327 Sterling A. Brown

"Tin Roof Blues"

Southern Road
(New York, NY; Harcourt, Brace and Company, 1932)

Summary: This poem opens the brief third section of *Southern Road*, a section also titled "Tin Roof Blues." The poem's narrator dreams of getting away from his "dirty city" and back home where the people are "mo' lak friends." In its use of southern African American dialect, themes of misfortune and depression, and consistently repeating refrains, "Tin Roof Blues" clearly reflects Brown's interest in blues music.

Subject(s): American South, Rural Life

328 Sterling A. Brown

"To a Certain Lady, in Her Garden"

Southern Road
(New York, NY; Harcourt, Brace and Company, 1932)

Summary: This poem appears early in the fourth and final section of *Southern Road*, titled "Vestiges," and is representative of the dramatic departure of this section from the three that precede it. In the first three sections, Brown uses dialect exclusively and focuses on rural African American characters and folk themes from southern life. In "Vestiges," by contrast, Brown offers a far more formal poetry told in standard English and exploring universal themes such as love and death. "To a Certain Lady, in Her Garden" is an ode to the narrator's lover, and its nine rhyming quatrains do not mention race—a feature found throughout the collection's final section.

Subject(s): Gardens and Gardening, Love

329 Joseph Seamon Cotter, Sr.

"Algernon Charles Swinburne"

A White Song and a Black One
(Louisville, KY; Bradley & Gilbert Co., 1909)

Summary: This poem is an ode to English romantic poet Algernon Charles Swinburne (1837-1909), whose repetitive language and sensual imagery Cotter mimics in the piece. The poem consists of four identically structured stanzas.

Subject(s): Poetry

330 Joseph Seamon Cotter, Sr.

"The Book's Creed"

A White Song and a Black One
(Louisville, KY; Bradley & Gilbert Co., 1909)

Summary: In this poem from his 1909 collection, Cotter outlines a "simple creed" for prospering. He cautions not to give too much weight to one's ancestors but rather to engage the modern world in thought and learning, an approach to black advancement advocated by other African American leaders in the early 1900s, including Booker T. Washington.

Subject(s): Education, Success

331 Joseph Seamon Cotter, Sr.

"The Don't Care Negro"

A White Song and a Black One
(Louisville, KY; Bradley & Gilbert Co., 1909)

Summary: This humorous poem makes use of black folk myths and deals with diverse subjects from political innocence to fun seeking to devil-may-care fatalism. The poem consists of seven four-line stanzas that contain a formal rhyme scheme. Though his poems were often constructed with standard English, "The Don't-Care Negro" is composed of rural southern black dialect, later used to greater effect by writers such as Langston Hughes.

Subject(s): American South, Poetry, Folk Tales

332 Joseph Seamon Cotter, Sr.

"Ned's Psalm of Life for the Negro"

A White Song and a Black One
(Louisville, KY; Bradley & Gilbert Co., 1909)

Summary: This poem, told in dialect, reveals Cotter's lifelong interest in advancing the cause of African American civil rights. In keeping with many black leaders at the beginning of the twentieth century, including Booker T. Washington, Cotter felt that black advancement could best be achieved through hard work and education. In this poem, Cotter also expresses optimism that such efforts would eventually lead to racial harmony between blacks and whites.

Subject(s): Race Relations, Education, Success

333 Joseph Seamon Cotter, Sr.

"William Lloyd Garrison"

A White Song and a Black One
(Louisville, KY; Bradley & Gilbert Co., 1909)

Summary: This poem is an ode to William Lloyd Garrison (1805-1879), the noted abolitionist who founded the influential periodical *The Liberator* as well as the American Antislavery Society. Like most of Cotter's early poetry, this piece is traditionally structured, consisting of seven four-lined stanzas and a formal rhyme scheme.

Subject(s): Slavery, Abolition

334 Countee Cullen

"Brown Boy to Brown Girl: Remembrance on a Hill. For Yolande"
Color
(New York, NY; Harper & Brothers, 1925)

Summary: As implied in its subtitle, this poem is dedicated to a woman Cullen knew—in this case the daughter of his first wife and W.E.B. Du Bois. The poem is in the form of a sonnet, a traditional English poetic form consisting of fourteen lines. Cullen, one of the leading voices of the Harlem Renaissance, typically used traditional English ballads in his poetry.

Subject(s): Harlem Renaissance, Poetry

335 Countee Cullen

"A Brown Girl Dead"
Color
(New York, NY; Harper & Brothers, 1925)

Summary: This brief ode to a dead girl consists of two stanzas of four lines each. As was typical of this first collection (and much of his later poetry as well), Cullen used a traditional rhyme scheme in this poem.

Subject(s): Death, Poetry

336 Countee Cullen

"From the Dark Tower: To Charles S. Johnson"
Copper Sun
(New York, NY; Harper & Brothers, 1927)

Summary: This poem from Cullen's second published collection is dedicated to Charles S. Johnson, a sociologist, founder of the influential magazine *Opportunity,* and a champion of the Harlem Renaissance. "From the Dark Tower" is an angry warning that African Americans will not continue to suffer while others prosper and, like most of Cullen's poetry, it is formally structured.

Subject(s): Racism, Harlem Renaissance

337 Countee Cullen

"Heritage: For Harold Jackman"
Color
(New York, NY; Harper & Brothers, 1925)

Summary: This lengthy poem reflects the concept of "Negritude," an aesthetic philosophy popular among Harlem Renais-sance writers in which the African roots of black culture were affirmed and celebrated. Cullen himself advocated a conservative version of the concept, arguing that black poets should follow Negritude within traditional English verse. In the poem, Cullen reveals a passion and longing for Africa that remain unfulfilled, since he is centuries removed from the continent and now thoroughly American. The poem is dedicated to Harold Jackman, Cullen's best friend and a fringe figure of the Harlem Renaissance.

Subject(s): Harlem Renaissance, Africa

338 Countee Cullen

"Incident: For Eric Walrond"
Color
(New York, NY; Harper & Brothers, 1925)

Summary: This poem describes an incident from Cullen's childhood, when, while living in Baltimore, another child called him "nigger." While Cullen was critical of artists whose preoccupation with social justice overrode their work, he occasionally addressed social matters such as racism in his own work. The poem is dedicated to Eric Walrond, a West Indian writer who, like Cullen, was associated with the Harlem Renaissance of the 1920s.

Subject(s): Harlem Renaissance, Racism

339 Countee Cullen

"The Litany of the Dark People"
Copper Sun
(New York, NY; Harper & Brothers, 1927)

Summary: In this poem from his second collection, told in the form of a prayer, Cullen asks for the salvation of African Americans from the "agony" and "hunger" that they have so long known. The poem, while making references to "the ancient deities" of Africa's past, clearly espouses Christianity as the key to deliverance. For Cullen, an embrace of the cultural traditions of Africa—seen in the philosophy of "Negritude" advocated by many Harlem Renaissance figures—had to be moderated by an acceptance of western values.

Subject(s): Africa, Religion, Christianity

340 Countee Cullen

"The Shroud of Color: For Llewellyn Ransom"
Color
(New York, NY; Harper & Brothers, 1925)

Summary: A long, religious-themed poem, "The Shroud of Color" describes a depressed poet who is weary of living in a racist society and who longs to die. It then follows him as God shows him a glimpse of Heaven and Hell and persuades him that there is reason to live. The turning point of the poet's metaphorical journey is the realization of the countless people who have struggled and died before him. Critics are uncertain of the identity of Llewellyn Ransom, to whom the poem is dedicated.

Subject(s): Racism, Religion

341 Countee Cullen

"Threnody for a Brown Girl"
Copper Sun
(New York, NY; Harper & Brothers, 1927)

Summary: One of Cullen's most-celebrated poems, "Threnody for a Brown Girl" is an elegy for a dead girl (a "threnody" is a lamentation). In ten stanzas of eight lines each, using a traditional rhyme scheme, Cullen mourns the girl's death. By the end of the poem, Cullen presents death as a relief from the brutality and suffering of life.

Subject(s): Death, Poetry

Award(s): *Poetry* magazine: John Reed Memorial Prize, 1925

342 Countee Cullen

"To a Brown Girl: For Roberta"
Color
(New York, NY; Harper & Brothers, 1925)

Summary: Dedicated to Roberta Bosley, a friend of the poet's and a bridesmaid at his first wedding, this poem urges the young woman to cast aside caution and pursue love with vigor. The poem consists of three stanzas of four lines each and contains a formal rhyme scheme. As was often the case in his poetry, Cullen here focused on a universal theme—love—without addressing the larger social and cultural milieu in which he lived.

Subject(s): Love, Poetry

343 Countee Cullen

"Yet Do I Marvel"
Color
(New York, NY; Harper & Brothers, 1925)

Summary: In the opening poem to his first collection of poetry, Cullen displays his erudition—the formally structured poem includes references to Greek mythology—as well as a willingness to address racial matters. Here, Cullen marvels at the mysterious ways of God, who can enforce terrible punishments on His creations but who can also "make a poet black, and bid him sing!" Although he often argued against art that was too preoccupied with socio-political issues, Cullen addressed race and injustice in numerous works.

Subject(s): Mythology

344 Paul Laurence Dunbar

"Douglass"
Lyrics of Love and Laughter
(New York, NY; Dodd, Mead and Company, 1903)

Summary: This poem is an ode to Frederick Douglass (1817-1895), who escaped from slavery and eventually became a prominent journalist and abolitionist. In the poem, Dunbar laments that "we have fall'n on evil days" and longs for Douglass's strong voice to lead society "through the lonely dark." The poem is written in standard English and contains two stanzas of uneven length.

Subject(s): Abolition, Slavery

345 Paul Laurence Dunbar

"The Haunted Oak"
Lyrics of Love and Laughter
(New York, NY; Dodd, Mead and Company, 1903)

Summary: "The Haunted Oak" is a ballad about a lynching, told in sixteen rhyming quatrains. The poem is mostly told from the point of view of the mythical tree, which laments the murder of an innocent black man by a white mob filled with judges, doctors, and ministers. Lyrical and tragic, this poem is one of the few in which Dunbar directly protests racial injustice.

Subject(s): Lynching, Murder, Racism

346 Paul Laurence Dunbar

"The Poet"
Lyrics of Love and Laughter
(New York, NY; Dodd, Mead and Company, 1903)

Summary: In this autobiographical poem, Dunbar regrets his unfulfilled promise as a poet. Always plagued by self-doubt, Dunbar in particular bemoaned the fact that his poems in dialect received far more attention and praise from the public than did his poems in standard English. As he writes in "The Poet," the world ignored his deeper ruminations on love and instead "turned to praise / A jingle in a broken tongue."

Subject(s): Poetry

347 Langston Hughes

"Afro-American Fragment"
The Crisis magazine
(July 1930)

Summary: "Afro-American Fragment" is an homage to Africa and to the inspiration it provides to African Americans. The poem epitomizes the concept of Negritude, popular among figures of the Harlem Renaissance, in which African Americans celebrate the validity of African culture. When the poem appeared in 1959 in his *Selected Poems*, Hughes combined several pairs of lines that stood alone in the poem's earliest version.

Subject(s): Harlem Renaissance, Africa

348 Langston Hughes

"Aunt Sue's Stories"
The Crisis magazine
(July 1921)

Summary: In this early poem, written in the 1920s, Hughes displays the musical rhythms and rich imagery that mark his best poetry. In the piece, Hughes describes a child listening to the stories of "Aunt Sue," from her life as a slave to her experiences on the Mississippi River. The poem, like many of Hughes's early pieces, was published in *The Crisis* magazine, the official publication of the National Association for the Advancement of Colored People (NAACP) that was founded in 1910 by W.E.B. Du Bois.

Subject(s): Rivers, Slavery

349 Langston Hughes

"Bound No'th Blues"

Opportunity magazine
(October 1926)

Summary: This poem is told in the literary blues style for which Hughes is famous. It describes an African American man heading north on foot, leaving Mississippi behind. Using southern rural dialect in the poem's earliest published versions, Hughes later moderated some of the spelling when the poem was published in his 1959 *Selected Poems*.

Subject(s): Music, Poetry, American South

350 Langston Hughes

"Christ in Alabama"

Contempo magazine
(December 1931)

Summary: This provocative poem, which begins with the lines "Christ is a nigger, / beaten and black," was written in response to the infamous "Scottsboro case" that began in 1931. The case involved the arrest of nine African American youths for the rapes of two white women on a train near Painted Rock, Alabama. Upon their imprisonment in nearby Scottsboro, eight of the youths were sentenced to death and the ninth to life in prison. After almost twenty years of appeals and trials, the nine men were released. Hughes visited the youths in prison in 1931, was involved in the fundraising for their defense, and wrote several poems about their case, which coincided with his movement to the political left during the 1930s.

Subject(s): American South, Judicial System, Racial Conflict

351 Langston Hughes

"Dream Variation"

The Crisis magazine
(July 1924)

Summary: First published in *The Crisis* magazine and later included in his 1926 collection, *The Weary Blues,* this poem extols dancing, music, and rest. The brief poem (it contains seventeen lines divided into two stanzas) includes imagery that highlights Hughes's racial pride.

Subject(s): Music, Dancing

352 Langston Hughes

"Good Morning Revolution"

New Masses magazine
(September 1932)

Summary: Langston Hughes moved leftward politically during the 1930s, and this poem epitomizes that change. The poem is a socialist's call to arms, and in it Hughes castigates those with economic power while expressing sympathy for workers and those who are "hungry, cold, oppressed." Some critics feel that the poem is a parody of "Good Morning America" by Carl Sandburg, who ironically was one of Hughes's earliest literary influences.

Subject(s): Politics

353 Langston Hughes

"Negro"

The Crisis magazine
(January 1922)

Summary: Infused with racial pride, "Negro" describes the endurance of blacks throughout history. The poem's imagery ranges from ancient Egypt to the Roman Empire to American slavery. In recounting the journey of blacks through time, Hughes references historical characters including Julius Caesar and George Washington, notes the development of African American musical forms such as ragtime, and mentions contemporary lynchings in Mississippi.

Subject(s): Lynching, Slavery, Africa

354 Langston Hughes

"The Negro Speaks of Rivers"

The Crisis magazine
(June 1921)

Summary: One of Langston Hughes's best-known poems, his first published following high school, "The Negro Speaks of Rivers" is a rumination on the endurance of the human spirit. Via the metaphor of the river, Hughes addresses the strength of humanity from ancient Egypt through the nineteenth century—noting Abraham Lincoln's Mississippi River trip to New Orleans—and to the present. Hughes wrote the poem while passing over the Mississippi on a train bound for Mexico in 1920. He was eighteen years old at the time and at the beginning of a literary career in which he would eventually establish himself as one of the twentieth century's greatest writers.

Subject(s): Rivers

355 Langston Hughes

"Ruby Brown"

The Crisis magazine
(August 1926)

Summary: In this poem, Hughes tells the story of an African American woman who becomes a prostitute for lack of better jobs and "joy." Irony infuses the poem; Hughes describes how

Ruby's white clients pay her far more money for her sexual services than they did "when she worked in their kitchens." Nonetheless, Ruby is shunned by the town's more pious residents.

Subject(s): Prostitution, Employment

356 Langston Hughes

"The Weary Blues"

The Weary Blues
(New York, NY; A.A. Knopf, 1926)

Summary: The title poem in Hughes's 1926 collection is important for many reasons. Its description of a piano player's blues song epitomizes the literary blues style for which Hughes is renowned. In addition, by juxtaposing the black man's emphasis on the "ivory" piano keys, Hughes addresses racial issues with understatement and irony. Finally, the poet's reference to Lenox Avenue in New York City's Harlem highlights the geographical nexus of the burgeoning Harlem Renaissance cultural movement, of which Hughes was at the forefront.

Subject(s): Music, Harlem Renaissance

Award(s): *Opportunity* magazine: First Prize, 1925

357 Langston Hughes

"When Sue Wears Red"

The Weary Blues
(New York, NY; A.A. Knopf, 1926)

Summary: Though a draft of this poem was published in *The Crisis* magazine in 1923, the final version was included in Hughes's first collection of poetry, published in 1926. The poem is an ode to "Susanna Jones," a ravishing figure based on a girl whom Hughes met in high school. The key image in the poem is "Susannah Jones in red," whom Hughes compares to an ancient Egyptian queen.

Subject(s): Love

358 Langston Hughes

"Wide River"

Measure magazine
(June 1926)

Summary: Another example of Hughes's literary blues style—a blues song told in verse—"Wide River" uses humor to tell its story of hardship, in this case a man separated from his beloved by a river. The poem is marked by Hughes's expert use of southern rural dialect and his utilization of the metaphor of the river, a recurring metaphor in black literature.

Subject(s): Music, Rivers, American South

359 Langston Hughes

"Young Gal's Blues"

Four Negro Poets
(New York, NY; Simon and Schuster, 1927)

Summary: In the southern rural dialect at which he was so adept, Hughes describes a young girl who ruminates on death and old age while taking solace in love. This literary blues poem was published in the 1927 anthology compiled by noted editor Alain Locke.

Subject(s): Love, Death, Old Age

360 George Marion McClellan

"Daybreak"

The Path of Dreams
(Louisville, KY; J.P. Morton & Company, 1916)

Summary: This poem is an optimistic call to all African Americans to be prepared for the freedom that is about to arrive. In the poem, McClellan counsels fellow blacks to remain pious, ignore hatred and injustice, and avoid sin, "For they who fight with God must win / On Every battle ground." Consisting of twelve rhyming quatrains, "Daybreak" is a rare poem in which McClellan directly addresses racial matters.

Subject(s): Race Relations

361 George Marion McClellan

"Hydromel and Rue"

The Path of Dreams
(Louisville, KY; J.P. Morton & Company, 1916)

Summary: The title references in this poem from McClellan's 1916 collection are to a honey-water mixture that can be brewed to a potent liquor called hydromel and to the medicinal plant, rue. In the poem, McClellan offers spiritual thanks that he has been fortunate enough, metaphorically, to taste the sweet hydromel by knowing love and fatherhood, even though he has also had the misfortune to taste rue—in other words, been beset by "sorrow, grief, and pain." The poem's dominant Christian imagery is typical of McClellan, who maintained a stoic idealism throughout his poetry.

Subject(s): Christianity, Nature, Poetry

362 George Marion McClellan

"To Theodore"

The Path of Dreams
(Louisville, KY; J.P. Morton & Company, 1916)

Summary: This poem, written in February, 1916, is an anguished piece dedicated to McClellan's son, Theodore, who suffered and eventually died from tuberculosis. At the time of the poem's composition, father and son were living in Colorado in hopes that the mountain air would cure the son's illness; they would later venture to Los Angeles for treatment, only to see Theodore denied admission to a sanitarium because of his race. The younger McClellan died in Los Angeles in January, 1917, less than a year after this poem was written.

Subject(s): Death, Illness, Racism

363 Claude McKay

"Africa"
Harlem Shadows: The Poems of Claude McKay
(New York, NY; Harcourt, Brace and Company, 1922)

Summary: This poem from McKay's 1922 collection reflects the philosophy of Negritude, popular among writers of the Harlem Renaissance movement, in which black Americans celebrated and affirmed the cultural validity of their African heritage. Composed in McKay's favored sonnet form—a fourteen line lyric poem made popular by English poets—"Africa" works as a companion poem to "America," which appears in the same collection.

Subject(s): Harlem Renaissance, Africa

364 Claude McKay

"America"
Harlem Shadows: The Poems of Claude McKay
(New York, NY; Harcourt, Brace and Company, 1922)

Summary: One of McKay's most-anthologized poems, "America," depicts the poet's love-hate relationship with his adopted homeland (he was born and raised in Jamaica). In the sonnet, he castigates America's habit of preying on its black citizens but confesses his love for the country's "cultured hell." At the poem's close, McKay warns of the eventual collapse of America due to its racist ways.

Subject(s): Racism

365 Claude McKay

"Harlem Shadows"
Harlem Shadows: The Poems of Claude McKay
(New York, NY; Harcourt, Brace and Company, 1922)

Summary: One theme seen frequently in McKay's work is the theme of Harlem—a seedy, poverty-stricken, yet culturally vibrant neighborhood in New York City. In this poem about Harlem, McKay depicts the nighttime wanderings of local prostitutes while decrying the "harsh world" that has forced such women into prostitution. Through poems such as "Harlem Shadows," McKay became one of the leading poets of the Harlem Renaissance cultural movement of the 1920s.

Subject(s): Prostitution, Harlem Renaissance, Poverty

366 Claude McKay

"If We Must Die"
The Liberator
(July 1919)

Summary: One of the most influential poems ever produced by a black writer, "If We Must Die" is a stirring appeal to die with dignity in the face of oppression. McKay wrote the poem in response to the racial violence he witnessed during the summer of 1919, but he couched his sentiments in language that did not necessarily have a racial connotation. Appearing as it did in the aftermath of World War I, the poem would later

be viewed in the context of war by readers unaware of its origin. Nonetheless, the poem contains many trademark McKay elements, including the use of the sonnet form, which he learned during his youth in British-dominated Jamaica, and an angry and defiant tone. McKay became one of the leading poets of the Harlem Renaissance cultural movement of the 1920s, and this poem was adopted by some members of that group as an unofficial anthem for the movement.

Subject(s): Violence, Harlem Renaissance, Death

367 Claude McKay

"The Lynching"
Harlem Shadows: The Poems of Claude McKay
(New York, NY; Harcourt, Brace and Company, 1922)

Summary: This poem about the lynching of a black man and the burning of his body displays McKay's unflinching anger at the racial violence of America. Though born and raised in Jamaica, McKay became a passionate critic of his adopted country's flaws. At the end of "The Lynching," McKay remarks on the initiation of young white children—"lynchers that were to be"—into America's racist ways.

Subject(s): Racism, Lynching, Anger

368 Claude McKay

"Spring in New Hampshire"
Spring in New Hampshire and Other Poems
(London, England; Grant Richards, 1920)

Summary: McKay is best known for his protest poetry, and while this poem is not of that category, it contains elements of his trademark defiance. Consisting of two stanzas of six lines each, the poem describes the sights and smells of spring in New England. However, each stanza closes with an angry and despairing sentiment: the poet is missing spring because of overwork and fatigue. Both stanzas have a similar rhyme scheme (ababcc).

Subject(s): Spring, Work

369 Claude McKay

"The Tropics in New York"
Harlem Shadows: The Poems of Claude McKay
(New York, NY; Harcourt, Brace and Company, 1922)

Summary: Upon coming across a fruit stand in New York City, McKay relates his nostalgia for his Jamaican homeland. The poet was born and lived in Jamaica until the age of twenty-three, at which point he came to live in the United States. During the 1920s, he became one of the leading lights of the Harlem Renaissance cultural movement, but much of his work includes the theme of an alien black man longing for his island home.

Subject(s): Harlem Renaissance

370 Claude McKay

"The White House"

Harlem Shadows: The Poems of Claude McKay
(New York, NY; Harcourt, Brace and Company, 1922)

Summary: "The White House" epitomizes the anger and pride that characterize McKay's best protest poetry. Using the White House as a metaphor for America, McKay expresses his rage toward his adopted country's racist spirit and yet declares his intention to maintain his humanity in the face of "the potent poison of your hate." With strong, straightforward, sentiments such as these, McKay distinguished himself from other black writers of the 1920s, including his fellow Harlem Renaissance colleagues.

Subject(s): Racism, Harlem Renaissance

371 Albery Allson Whitman

An Idyl of the South

(New York, NY; Metaphysical Publishing Company, 1901)

Summary: The two parts of this book-length epic poem are "The Southland's Charms and Freedom's Magnitude" and "The Octoroon." The poem is told entirely in ottava rima, a verse form consisting of eight-line stanzas, with each line written in iambic pentameter and following a strict rhyme scheme. In the poem's first section, Whitman offers wide-ranging impressions and opinions of the American South. In the poem's second section, "The Octoroon," Whitman relates the doomed love affair between a handsome white man and a beautiful octoroon slave (an "octoroon" is a person whose ancestry is one-eighth black) owned by his father. Many critics consider "The Octoroon" to be Whitman's finest work of poetry.

Subject(s): American South, Love, Slavery

Drama

The period between 1900 and 1940 saw the flourishing of black drama. Early in the century, plays began to be produced by such minor literary figures as Joseph S. Cotter, Sr., who, in 1901, published *Caleb, the Degenerate*, one of the first dramas published by an African American. Angelina Weld Grimke also began writing drama focused on black main characters; her 1916 play *Rachel* deals with what racist society does to black children. Alice Dunbar-Nelson (also known as Alice Ruth Moore and Alice Moore Dunbar Nelson), and Garland Anderson were also writing plays in the early years of the 20th century. After these playwrights had broken ground, the Harlem Renaissance of the 1920s and early 1930s encouraged the production of plays by dramatists now considered influential. Dramas were written by major figures such as Langston Hughes and Zora Neale Hurston. Other playwrights of the period included Marita Bonner, Georgia Douglas Johnson, John Matheus, and Willis Richardson. Rose McClendon acted in and also directed and promoted African American theatre;

in 1935 she acted in the first African American dramatic play produced on Broadway, Langston Hughes' *Mulatto*. Some other popular actors at this time were Paul Robeson and Charles Gilpin, who acted in both black and white productions. In the aftermath of the Harlem Renaissance, the Works Progress Administration (WPA) created by President Franklin D. Roosevelt began the Federal Writers and Federal Theater Projects. During the years 1935 to 1939, these projects sponsored African American writers and actors in order to generate black productions. Following the discontinuation of these projects, the American Negro Theater was begun in 1940 to encourage portrayals of black life in productions by black playwrights. In the years following the Harlem Renaissance and during the Depression, figures such as Owen Dodson and Randolph Edmonds--who began the first speech and drama department at a black university in 1935 at Dillard University--also began writing for the theatre.

372 Garland Anderson

Appearances

Black Theater, U.S.A.: Forty-Five Plays by Black Americans, 1847-1974
(New York, NY; Free Press, 1974)

Summary: The first full-length play by a black playwright to be produced on Broadway, *Appearances* was written by Garland Anderson in three weeks, between his shifts working as a hotel switchboard operator. The play tells the story of Carl, falsely accused of rape by a white woman. In addition to the somewhat daring subject matter, the play's initial production was notable for using black actors in black roles—something that had not previously been done on Broadway (prior black roles had been played by white actors in "blackface" makeup). At first lauded by white critics but later castigated as amateurish by the same critics, the play was not embraced by black critics, who scorned Anderson for public statements that seemed to support the idea of white racial superiority. Nonetheless, the 1925 play was a modest success on Broadway, toured the United States, and even traveled to London.

Subject(s): Rape, Racism

373 Marita Bonner

The Pot-Maker: A Play To Be Read

Opportunity magazine
(February 1927)

Summary: *The Pot-Maker* is a one-act play featuring the strained relationship between a husband and wife, Elias and Lucinda. Elias has recently become a preacher, and early in the play preaches to Lucinda to give up an affair she has been having with another man and ask God for forgiveness. He cites the parable of the pot-maker, which says that a sinful person— like a pot with a crack in it—can become whole with repentance and redemption. Later in the play, though, Lucinda's lover falls in a well and drowns while coming to meet Lucinda; when Elias refuses to help, Lucinda throws herself in the well too. Elias attempts to save her, but he fails, and both husband and wife also die in the well. The play works as a morality tale about a woman trapped in a loveless marriage and the arrogance of her husband, who does not realize that his own heart is flawed.

Subject(s): Marriage

Marita Bonner

The Purple Flower

The Crisis magazine
(January 1928)

Summary: This allegorical play features as its central motif a giant purple flower. The flower represents happiness and fulfillment, not merely on a personal level but on a societal level as well. On stage, the flower appears at the top of a hill. On the sides of the hill live the "White Devils," who do everything possible to prevent the "Us's"—the play's protagonists, described as being white, brown, or black—from reaching the flower. In a bold repudiation of African American leaders such as Booker T. Washington, Bonner argues that the only way for the "Us's" to reach the purple flower is through violence, an open call for revolution that would not be advocated by other artists and intellectuals until the 1960s.

Subject(s): Violence

Award(s): *Crisis* Contest Award, 1927

Richard Bruce

(Pseudonym of Richard Bruce Nugent)

Sadhji: An African Ballet

Plays of Negro Life: A Source-Book of Native American Drama
(New York, NY; Harper & Brothers, 1927)

Summary: This play, a morality tale that grew out of a short story by Nugent (under the name Richard Bruce), reflects the eccentric author's interest in homosexuality. The drama is set in an African monarchy and revolves around Mrabo's eagerness to see his father, the chieftain, die so that he can marry his beautiful stepmother—the "Sadhji" of the play's title. Unbeknownst to Mrabo, his ardent suitor Numbo resolves to kill the chieftain so that Mrabo can gain happiness. However, after her husband's death, Sadhji's grief is so great that she throws herself on her husband's funeral pyre and commits suicide, thus leaving Mrabo unfulfilled. Known as one of the most bohemian and avant-garde members of the 1920s Harlem Renaissance, Nugent wrote several short stories in addition to working as a visual artist. This play was produced in 1932 at the Eastman School of Music in Rochester, New York.

Subject(s): Harlem Renaissance, Homosexuality/Lesbianism

Mary Burrill

They That Sit in Darkness

Birth Control Review
(September 1919)

Summary: This short play by Burrill was published in the *Birth Control Review* in a special issue devoted to "The Negro's Need for Birth Control as Seen by Themselves." In the play, Burrill advocates for birth control and education for women as a way to escape poverty. The main character, Malinda Jasper, is a frail woman of thirty-eight with six children. Weakened by the ordeal of having and caring for six children, Jasper is in poor health. Despite the efforts of a visiting nurse, Jasper dies, leaving her oldest daughter, seventeen-year-old Lindy, to inherit the task of caring for the remaining children. At the time of the play's publication, the movement to provide women with birth control information was in its earliest stages.

Subject(s): Birth Control, Education, Poverty

Joseph Seamon Cotter, Sr.

Caleb, the Degenerate; A Play in Four Acts: A Study of the Types, Customs, and Needs of the American Negro

(Louisville, KY; Bradley & Gilbert Company, 1903)

Summary: This blank verse drama was the second play to be published by a black American. In it, Cotter supports a view of black advancement similar to that of Booker T. Washington, who argued that blacks would be better served by education and hard work in industry than by political activism that challenged the white establishment. The play tells the story of Caleb, an impressionable young man, and Raheb, a corrupting minister-politician who influences Caleb in several negative ways; Caleb eventually murders his own father. Contrasted against the morally suspect Caleb and Raheb are the Bishop and his daughter, Olivia, who run an industrial school for blacks. It is not known if the play was produced during Cotter's lifetime.

Subject(s): Education

Alice Dunbar-Nelson

(Also known as Alice Ruth Moore Dunbar Nelson, Alice Ruth Moore)

Mine Eyes Have Seen

The Crisis magazine
(1918)

Summary: Published during the final months of World War I, this defiant play challenges the notion that blacks should owe loyalty to a country that shows them no loyalty in return. While denouncing the Germans for their wartime atrocities, Dunbar Nelson presents a complicated story in which she also attacks America's longtime oppression of blacks. The play revolves around a young black man's decision of whether or not to honor his draft notice. The play's end is deliberately ambiguous; Dunbar Nelson leaves it to the reader or theater-goer to determine whether the young man has decided to defy his draft order or to honor the order and fight for his country against the Germans.

Subject(s): World War I, Loyalty, Race Relations

379 Thelma Myrtle Duncan

Black Magic

The Yearbook of Short Plays
(New York, NY; Row, Peterson & Company, 1931)

Summary: Written in black rural dialect, this comedic play focuses on a strained marriage. Convinced that his wife is being unfaithful, a man resorts to voodoo in order to regain the wife's affection. However, he eventually discovers that she has not been having an affair but rather has been searching for a job.

Subject(s): Marriage, Comedy, Magic

380 Thelma Myrtle Duncan

The Death Dance

Negro History in Thirteen Plays
(Washington, DC; Associated Publishers, 1935)

Summary: Duncan's first dramatic work is a one-act musical set in an African village. In the work, a conniving medicine man drugs an accused thief in order to win the heart of a local girl. The plot fails, however, and the accused man is proven innocent. The work, produced in 1923, contains tribal dances in its attempt to authenticate its African setting.

Subject(s): Crime and Criminals, Africa, Dancing

381 Randolph Edmonds

Bad Man

Six Plays for a Negro Theatre
(Boston, MA; Walter H. Baker Company, 1934)

Summary: This melodramatic one-act play, published in Edmonds's groundbreaking collection of six folk plays, explores the brutality of white supremacy and the challenge of surviving its effects. Set in a lumber camp, the play features three men, among them Thea Dugger, the "Bad Man" of the play's title. Afraid of nothing, Thea has killed several men in his lifetime. However, Thea sacrifices himself when a white mob approaches the camp seeking to avenge the murder of a white man. Despite his innocence, Thea gives himself up to the mob and is lynched, thereby saving his companions, at least for the time being. First produced in New York City on NBC radio, 1932.

Subject(s): Lynching, Working-Class Life, Race Relations

382 Randolph Edmonds

Nat Turner

Six Plays for a Negro Theatre
(Boston, MA; Walter H. Baker Company, 1934)

Summary: Published in Edmonds's noted collection of six folk plays, *Nat Turner* examines the life of the man who led an armed revolt of slaves on a Virginia plantation in 1831. Edmonds depicts Turner as a religious leader whose actions grew out of genuine feeling for his fellow slaves. After the defeat of his revolt, Turner questions whether his plan to seek freedom through violence was a wise one.

Subject(s): Slavery, Rebellion, Violence

383 Ruth Gaines-Shelton

The Church Fight

The Crisis magazine
(1926)

Summary: This pioneering drama was one of the first plays by an African American to use comedy and satire. In this case, the target was the church—more specifically, church politics. The use of satire to poke fun at religion was later adopted by such writers as James Baldwin (*Amen Corner*) and Andrew Burris (*You Must Be Bo'n Again*). *The Church Fight*, like many of Gaines-Shelton's other plays, was written for the playwright's own church and club groups.

Subject(s): Comedy, Religious Life

384 Shirley Graham

(Also known as Shirley Graham Du Bois)

It's Morning

Wines in the Wilderness: Plays by African American Women from the Harlem Renaissance to the Present
(New York, NY; Greenwood Press, 1990)

Summary: This emotionally charged one-act play, reminiscent of Greek tragedies, tells the story of a slave woman, Cissie, who plots to kill her teenage daughter rather than let her be sold to a new white owner who obviously intends to sexually assault the girl. On the morning that her daughter is to be sent away, which happens to be January 1, 1863, Cissie hears a horse and rider approaching. Assuming it is her daughter's new owner, Cissie kills her daughter. However, she emerges moments later only to be told that the rider was not the new owner but rather a messenger stating that Abraham Lincoln has issued the Emancipation Proclamation, freeing all slaves. In its sophisticated structure and groundbreaking use of music, dialogue, dancing, and chanting, this play represented a breakthrough in African American drama. Its subject matter prefigures Toni Morrison's acclaimed novel *Beloved,* in which an escaped slave woman kills her baby daughter rather than allow her to be sent back to the plantation. Yale University was the site of the 1940 production.

Subject(s): Slavery, Murder, Freedom

385 Shirley Graham

(Also known as Shirley Graham Du Bois)

Track Thirteen

Yale Radio Plays: The Listener's Theatre
(Boston, MA; Expression Co., 1940)

Summary: This play aired on radio in New Haven, Connecticut, in 1940, when Graham was at work on a Ph.D. at Yale University. A comic one-act drama, the play is set aboard a train leaving Chicago that happens to leave on Track 13. A superstitious black porter becomes terrified that the train will meet disaster, but he turns out to be mistaken: not only is disaster averted, but the porter assists in catching a disguised bank robber who is on the train, thereby earning himself a five-thousand-dollar reward. Graham, who was the first African American composer to have an opera (*Tom-Tom*) professionally produced in the United States, left Yale in 1940. She later married famous educator and activist W.E.B. Du Bois.

Subject(s): Crime and Criminals, Superstition, Trains

386 **Angelina Weld Grimke**

Rachel

Black Theater, U.S.A.: Forty-Five Plays by Black Americans, 1847-1974
(New York, NY; Free Press, 1974)

Summary: Set in New York City, this three-act 1916 drama revolves around Rachel, a woman who struggles continually with how best to proceed in the face of entrenched racism and hostility toward African Americans. During the play, Rachel has to deal with news of her father's lynching, her brother's rage and unhappiness, and her care of a neighborhood orphan. Faced with the prospect of never-ending cruelty for any children she might have, Rachel spurns a marriage proposal. Active during the Harlem Renaissance of the 1920s, Grimke was also an accomplished poet.

Subject(s): Racism, Lynching, Working-Class Life

387 **Abram Hill**

On Strivers Row

Black Theatre USA: Plays by African Americans; The Recent Period, 1935-Today
(New York, NY; Free Press, 1996)

Summary: In this 1939 play, Abram Hill satirizes the social ambitions of the upwardly mobile black middle class that emerged in the 1920s and 1930s. Set in a posh neighborhood in New York's Harlem neighborhood (on a street that became known as "Strivers Row"), the play focuses on the absurd, elitist Van Striven family. They consider themselves superior to all of their neighbors, but underneath their arrogant demeanor are serious problems. This play was a hit when it ran in 1939 and later when it was revived for the American Negro Theater, which Hill co-founded.

Subject(s): Class Conflict, Middle Classes

388 **Langston Hughes**

Emperor of Haiti

Black Drama in America: An Anthology
(Greenwich, CT; Fawcett, 1971)

Summary: This full-length play is set in Haiti during the nineteenth century rebellion against Napoleon's forces and features black soldier Jean Jacques Dessalines, who rose to power after the rebellion. Hughes examines Dessalines's accumulation of power and his eventual corruption by it. In addition, the playwright explores issues of racism—both white against black and black against mulatto; the latter racial conflict led in part to Dessalines's downfall. Produced in 1936, Hughes later adapted this play into an opera, *Troubled Island* (1949) and was still revising the drama as late as 1963.

Subject(s): Race Relations, Rebellion, War

389 **Langston Hughes**

Limitations of Life

Black Theater U.S.A.: Forty-Five Plays by Black Americans, 1847-1974
(New York, NY; Free Press, 1974)

Summary: This brief, one-act 1938 play is a satirical take on a popular 1934 movie titled *Imitation of Life* (the film was remade in 1959). The film traded on stereotypical images of blacks, including the "Mammy" female figure and the tragic mulatto. In his play, Hughes subverts those stereotypes by making the "Mammy" a well-to-do, opera-going black woman and the tragic mulatto a blondhaired, blue-eyed white girl who desperately wants to be black.

Subject(s): Race Relations, Film, Family Life

390 **Langston Hughes**

Little Ham

Black Theater, U.S.A.: Forty-Five Plays by Black Americans, 1847-1974
(New York, NY; Free Press, 1974)

Summary: The title character of this melodramatic 1935 play, set in New York City's poverty-ridden Harlem during the 1920s, is a small, colorful man who shines shoes in addition to gambling on the side. His dual professions—one legal and the other illegal—are shared by other characters in the drama, which works as an exploration of the effects of poverty and corruption on a community. Among Hughes's most important depictions is that of the white police, who make the corruption in Harlem possible by allowing it as long as the operators follow the police's "rules." The play is typical of numerous Hughes works that drew criticism from members of the black community for portraying seamy sides of black life.

Subject(s): Urban Affairs, Gambling, Poverty

391 **Langston Hughes**

Mulatto

Black Drama: An Anthology
(Columbus, OH; Merrill, 1970)

Summary: This tragedy, first produced in an adapted version in 1935 but produced using Hughes's original text in 1939, explores themes of miscegenation and father-son conflict. In the play, a father's rejection of his mulatto son—an event infused with autobiographical elements—leads eventually to the murder of the father by the son, and then to the son's suicide. Hughes draws parallels between the rejection of son by father and the rejection of blacks by whites.

Subject(s): Miscegenation, Family Problems, Fathers and Sons

392 Zora Neale Hurston

The First One

Ebony and Topaz: A Collectanea
(New York, NY; Opportunity Press, 1927)

Summary: Hurston, one of the central figures in the Harlem Renaissance that began in the 1920s, wrote this play not long after arriving in New York City. The play is a retelling of the biblical story of Noah and his son Ham, who was made black after Noah cursed him during a night of celebration; Ham was disparaged because the only gifts he brought to the celebration were his music and joy. The drama reflects Hurston's interest in history and folklore, and she went on to become a renowned folklorist in addition to a celebrated writer.

Subject(s): Religion, Harlem Renaissance, Folklore

393 Georgia Douglas Johnson

Blue Blood

Fifty More Contemporary One-Act Plays
(New York, NY; D. Appleton and Company, 1928)

Summary: This one-act play tackles several serious subjects, among them miscegenation, lynching, and the conflict between light-skinned and dark-skinned African Americans. The play depicts the impending marriage between two light-skinned blacks, whose mothers suddenly realize before the wedding that their betrothed children share the same father, a wealthy white man who impregnated one woman and raped and impregnated the other. The wedding is called off, and the young woman marries another local black man. This play was produced in 1927 by the Krigwa Players in New York City.

Subject(s): Lynching, Race Relations, Miscegenation

394 Georgia Douglas Johnson

Blue-Eyed Black Boy

Wines in the Wilderness: Plays by African American Women from the Harlem Renaissance to the Present
(New York, NY; Greenwood Press, 1990)

Summary: A one-act play attacking the practice of lynching, this work was one of several submitted by Johnson in the 1930s to the Federal Theatre Project of the Works Project Administration. In the play, a young black man is arrested and jailed for innocently brushing up against a white woman. When it becomes clear that a mob of local white people intends to lynch the jailed man, his mother sends an urgent message to the state's governor to save her son; as she makes clear, her son is also the governor's son—the result of a liaison between the woman and the governor twenty-one years prior. The governor receives the message and acts to save his son. The play was not accepted for production by the FTP, whose readers disagreed with Johnson's assertion that black people were subject to lynching for no apparent reason.

Subject(s): Lynching, Race Relations

395 Georgia Douglas Johnson

Frederick Douglass

(Washington, DC; Associated Publishers, 1935)

Summary: One of several plays submitted by Johnson to the Federal Theatre Project of the Works Project Administration in the 1930s, *Frederick Douglass* tells the story of Douglass's escape to freedom. In the play, Douglass is working to buy his way to freedom in the North, where he intends to travel along with his free girlfriend, Ann. However, when he discovers that his old master is searching for him in hopes of sending him back to his old plantation—where he would not be able to buy his freedom—he realizes that he has to escape immediately. *Frederick Douglass* is one of two anti-slavery pieces that Johnson submitted to the FTP; the other was *William and Ellen Craft*.

Subject(s): Slavery, Underground Railroad

396 Georgia Douglas Johnson

Plumes

Anthology of American Negro Literature
(New York, NY; Modern Library, 1944)

Summary: This drama features a popular Harlem Renaissance theme: superstition. In the work, a woman must decide whether to allow a doctor to operate on her gravely ill daughter. Arguing against the operation is the woman's friend, who "foresees" the daughter's death regardless of any operation. Worried that the operation would consume the funds necessary for a decent burial, the woman decides against the operation; her daughter dies. Johnson, who offers an interesting angle on poverty in this play, leaves it to the reader to decide whether the mother was justified in her decision.

Subject(s): Harlem Renaissance, Illness, Poverty

Award(s): *Opportunity* Magazine: First Prize, 1927

397 Georgia Douglas Johnson

Safe

Wines in the Wilderness: Plays by African American Women from the Harlem Renaissance to the Present
(New York, NY; Greenwood Press, 1990)

Summary: This play was written in the mid-1930s and was one of several submitted by Johnson to the Federal Theatre Project of the U.S. government's Works Project Administration. *Safe* is set in 1893 in a small southern town. Written as an anti-lynching exhortation, the play depicts a young mother giving birth in a small cottage. As she nears the final stages of labor, she hears a mob outside dragging a young black boy away to lynch him. Anguished by the boy's cries for help to his mother, the pregnant woman gives birth to her own son. Upon learning of her child's gender, the mother chokes her newborn baby to death, declaring "Now he's safe—safe from the lynchers!" The play was rejected for production by the FTP's readers, some of whom chastised Johnson for implying that lynchings happen for no apparent reason; these readers subscribed to the myth that lynchings resulted only from rapes of white women by black men. *Safe* was lost from public view until 1974, when it was placed in George Mason University's archives.

Subject(s): Lynching, Race Relations, Murder

398 Georgia Douglas Johnson

A Sunday Morning in the South

Black Theater, U.S.A.: Forty-Five Plays by Black Americans, 1847-1974
(New York, NY; Free Press, 1974)

Summary: One of three anti-lynching plays submitted by Johnson to the Federal Theatre Project of the Works Project Administration during the 1930s, *A Sunday Morning in the South* is set in a southern town in 1924. The play opens with Sue Jones receiving word from a neighbor that a local white woman had reported being raped by a black man. Soon after, police arrive, and Sue's grandson Tom is charged with the rape following a vague identification by the white woman. Tom is arrested and taken away, and before Sue has a chance to save him, he is lynched. This work is perhaps Johnson's best known play and is representative of her passionate stand against the practice of lynching.

Subject(s): Lynching, Race Relations

399 Georgia Douglas Johnson

William and Ellen Craft

(Washington, DC; Associated Publishers, 1935)

Summary: One of two plays about slavery submitted by Johnson to the Federal Theatre Project of the Works Project Administration in the 1930s, *William and Ellen Craft* features the story of a beautiful, light-skinned slave who attempts to escape from slavery via the Underground Railroad, along with her fiance. However, when she hears that the Underground Railroad has become dangerous, she agrees to cut her hair and impersonate her white master and father, "Marse Charles." With her fiance now playing the part of her slave, she escapes via train to Philadelphia in the North. Though Johnson was better known as a poet, her plays of the 1930s stand as influential, passionate examples of social protest drama.

Subject(s): Slavery, Underground Railroad

400 Myrtle Smith Livingston

For Unborn Children

Black Theater, U.S.A.: Forty-Five Plays by Black Americans, 1847-1974
(New York, NY; Free Press, 1974)

Summary: This play, the only drama that Livingston ever wrote, is an attack on miscegenation, or mixed-race procreation. Written in 1926, the play features a romance between a black man and a white woman, and in common with other stage plays of the era—by both black and white playwrights—the black man is lynched at the end. However, in this case, the playwright is not at all sympathetic toward the black man. Instead, she voices her opinion through the character of the man's sister,

who feels betrayed by black men seeking romance with white women. At the play's end, the male character accepts his mistake and willingly goes out to face the lynching mob, declaring that his death is "a sacrifice for UNBORN CHILDREN!"

Subject(s): Miscegenation, Lynching, Race Relations

401 John F. Matheus

'Cruiter

Plays of Negro Life: A Source-Book of Native American Drama
(New York, NY; Harper & Brothers, 1927)

Summary: Set in pre-World War I Georgia, this play revolves around the breakup of a poor black family when younger members of the clan decide they must go north to seek better job opportunities. The family's beloved grandmother cannot bring herself to leave the South and thus stays behind. Typical of Matheus's dramas, *'Cruiter* features idealized characters struggling through the harsh living conditions caused by racial discrimination and poverty. Matheus preferred to write drama but was better known for his short stories.

Subject(s): Poverty, Family Relations, Racism

402 May Miller

The Bog Guide

Wines in the Wilderness: Plays by African American Women from the Harlem Renaissance to the Present
(New York, NY; Greenwood Press, 1990)

Summary: This one-act play, written in 1925, reflects an anti-colonialist sentiment, sometimes tinged with racial anger, that is seen in several of the dramas that Miller wrote during the 1920s. In the play, an exiled black woman exacts vengeance on her white English cousin for his part in destroying her father. The play's recognition by *Opportunity* magazine helped fuel Miller's entry into the artistic avant-garde that was flowering in the 1920s in New York City and Washington, D.C.

Subject(s): Race Relations, Colonialism

403 May Miller

Christophe's Daughters

Negro History in Thirteen Plays
(Washington, DC; Associated Publishers, 1935)

Summary: This play is typical of the dramas that Miller wrote in the 1930s because it deals with a well-known black figure from history. In a series of plays, Miller either castigated or monumentalized the well-known figures she featured in her work during this period. In the case of *Christophe's Daughters*, Miller examines the life of Henri Christophe, a former slave and revolutionary who helped liberate Haiti, then served as northern Haiti's tyrant king from 1806 until his suicide in 1820.

Subject(s): Slavery, Haitians, Revolution

404 **May Miller**

Graven Images

Black Theater, U.S.A.: Forty-Five Plays by Black Americans, 1847-1974
(New York, NY; Free Press, 1974)

Summary: Written around 1929, this play represents one of Miller's first efforts to recapture black heroes and heroines from history. Intended for eighth graders, the play tells the story of Zipporah, the Ethiopian wife of Moses as described in the Old Testament, and of the discrimination aimed at their son, Eliezer. Eliezer eventually triumphs over the hostility by using his intelligence.

Subject(s): Interracial Marriage, Racism

405 **May Miller**

Harriet Tubman

Negro History in Thirteen Plays
(Washington, DC; Associated Publishers, 1935)

Summary: This play explores the life of Harriet Tubman, who founded the Underground Railroad as an escape route for slaves. In a manner typical of other historical dramas that Miller wrote in the 1930s, the playwright immortalizes Tubman in this work. Miller was attempting to infuse a sense of historical pride into the African American theater of the time.

Subject(s): Slavery, Underground Railroad

406 **May Miller**

Riding the Goat

Wines in the Wilderness: Plays by African American Women from the Harlem Renaissance to the Present
(New York, NY; Greenwood Press, 1990)

Summary: Written in 1929, this comedic one-act play is unusual in its examination of the black middle class. It features Ant Hetty's attempt to convince a local doctor of the need to remain connected to the less-well-educated black community. The principal event in the play is the parade of a local fraternal lodge, for which men dress up in outlandish garb and ride a goat through the streets. The doctor ridicules this event and refuses to participate, even though the admiring townsmen have elected him Grand Master of the lodge. Eventually, however, Ant Hetty—along with the help of her granddaughter—persuades the doctor of the event's importance in uniting the local community.

Subject(s): Middle Classes, Comedy

407 **May Miller**

Scratches

Carolina Magazine
(April 1929)

Summary: This one-act play examines issues of class difference and racial stereotyping. Set in a pool hall, it features the interaction between poor but honest Dan and dishonest Jeff, who are playing a game of pool. Also featured is the dynamic between two women: Abbie, a mulatto who is much sought-after, and dark-skinned Meldora, who is not. The play was published in a special issue of *Carolina Magazine* devoted to African American folk plays.

Subject(s): Race Relations, Social Classes

408 **May Miller**

Sojourner Truth

Negro History in Thirteen Plays
(Washington, DC; Associated Publishers, 1935)

Summary: This play explores a central incident in the life of Sojourner Truth, the renowned abolitionist, when she used her preaching abilities to lessen hostility. The short drama was one of several historical works that Miller created in an attempt to reclaim African American history and infuse future generations with both knowledge of and pride in their forebears.

Subject(s): Slavery, Abolition, History

409 **Doris D. Price**

The Bright Medallion

University of Michigan Plays
(Ann Arbor, MI; University of Michigan Press, 1932)

Summary: In this tragi-comic play, set in a black ghetto in Texas in 1919, protagonist Samuel Hunt is haunted by a reputation for cowardice. In an attempt to improve his reputation among the local townsfolk, he claims a lost World War I medal as his own. Later, though, he performs a genuine act of bravery, rescuing a child from a burning house, only to die of his own wounds. Price pokes fun at religion in the book with the character of the local illiterate preacher, who amuses his parishioners by pretending to read during his sermons.

Subject(s): Religion, World War I, Hero

410 **Doris D. Price**

The Eyes of the Old

University of Michigan Plays
(Ann Arbor, MI; University of Michigan Press, 1932)

Summary: Set in an unstated year in the American South, this play focuses on the issues of teen pregnancy and poverty. In the play, a young woman has secret plans to drop out of high school and elope with a local man, much as her own mother did. The young woman's grandmother foresees the elopement but refuses to stop it, although she believes the woman will end up as an impoverished single mother.

Subject(s): Poverty, American South, Teen Parents

411 Willis Richardson

The Broken Banjo

Black Writers of America: A Comprehensive Anthology
(New York, NY; Macmillan, 1972)

Summary: This one-act drama focuses on Matt Turner, who is obsessed with playing his banjo, a habit that affords him what little satisfaction he has in a dreary life. When his despised brother-in-law Sam accidentally breaks the banjo, Matt begins to assault him, only to have Sam make a startling announcement: he had seen Matt kill an elderly man in a dispute over the banjo. Matt, who did not realize that his previous assault had killed the old man, then gives himself up to police. The play was awarded first prize in *Crisis* magazine's literary competition in 1925 and was praised by Eugene O'Neill, who was one of the award's judges.

Subject(s): Family Relations, Murder, Music

Award(s): *Crisis* Contest Award, 1925

412 Willis Richardson

The Chip Woman's Fortune

Anthology of the American Negro in the Theatre: A Critical Approach
(New York, NY; Publishers Co., 1967)

Summary: One of the first "serious" plays by an African American to be produced on Broadway, *The Chip Woman's Fortune* played there after opening in Chicago in 1923. The drama concerns a woman, Aunt Nancy, who has lived for years with Silas, nursing his invalid wife in addition to collecting wood for fuel. A dispute arises over Aunt Nancy's small stash of money, however, when Silas faces the prospect of losing his job. He wants it so that he can keep his beloved Victrola, while Nancy wants to keep the money for her son Jim, who will soon be released from prison. The matter is resolved peacefully when Jim returns from prison, learns of the dispute, and brokers a compromise by giving half the money to Silas in thanks for taking care of his mother. Though he never had another play produced on Broadway, Richardson became a prolific and well-regarded playwright.

Subject(s): Family Relations, Money

413 Willis Richardson

The Flight of the Natives

Black Theater, U.S.A.: Forty-Five Plays by Black Americans, 1847-1974
(New York, NY; Free Press, 1974)

Summary: This one-act 1927 drama depicts the brave escape of six slaves from a South Carolina plantation in 1860. Rather than focusing on a central character, Richardson presents the play as a true ensemble piece, with each character contributing to the success of the escape through his own particular strengths. This play was an early example of a literary work by an African American rejecting the myth of slaves as contented simpletons. Richardson depicts the brutality suffered by the slaves and makes clear their desperation to escape from their predicament.

Subject(s): Slavery, Freedom

414 Willis Richardson

The Idle Head

Carolina Magazine
(April 1929)

Summary: Set in the 1920s, this play centers around George Broadus, a man of independent spirit who struggles because he refuses to be subservient to whites. In an attempt to help his mother, George pawns a pin that a white woman forgot to remove from a garment sent to be laundered. When his infraction is discovered, George is carried off to prison with no regard for the circumstances of the crime. As Richardson makes clear, there is little difference between George's treatment for a minor infraction in the 1920s and a slave's treatment for a minor infraction sixty years earlier; both are treated harshly and unfairly.

Subject(s): Slavery, Racism, Criminal Justice

415 Eulalie Spence

Hot Stuff

Wines in the Wilderness: Plays by African American Women from the Harlem Renaissance to the Present
(New York, NY; Greenwood Press, 1990)

Summary: This one-act play, written in 1927, is representative of Spence's works in that it deals with everyday life in Harlem and refuses to idealize its black characters. The protagonist of the play is Fanny King, a decadent woman who gambles, steals, and engages in prostitution (even though she is married) to get what she wants. She is typical of the 1920s Harlem milieu that Spence depicts, which is filled with desperately poor people doing whatever they can to make their lives better. In addition to writing, Spence was actively involved in directing and producing plays—both her own works as well as works by other playwrights.

Subject(s): Poverty, Gambling, Working-Class Life

416 Eulalie Spence

Undertow

Black Theater, U.S.A.: Forty-Five Plays by Black Americans, 1847-1974
(New York, NY; Free Press, 1974)

Summary: Considered perhaps the best craftsman among the playwrights of the Harlem Renaissance, Eulalie Spence chose not to use her plays simply to discuss racial issues. Rather, Spence used race to advance plots, a decision that sometimes generated criticism of her work by leaders such as W.E.B. Du Bois, who felt that the arts should be directly concerned with racial issues. *Undertow*,, written in 1929, is typical of Spence's treatment of race in her work. The play concerns a troubled marriage, in which Hattie is jealous of her husband's old girlfriend. At the heart of Hattie's jealousy is her fear that the other woman is more beautiful than Hattie because her skin color is lighter. Unable to deal with her insecurity, Hattie destroys the lives of her husband and the other woman and is killed by her husband.

Subject(s): Race Relations, Harlem Renaissance, Marriage

417   Jean Toomer

Balo: A Sketch of Negro Life

Black Theater, U.S.A.: Forty-Five Plays by Black Americans, 1847-1974
(New York, NY; Free Press, 1974)

Summary: Best known for his novel *Cane*, which established him as one of the leading lights of the Harlem Renaissance, Toomer wrote only a few plays. *Balo*, first produced around 1924, is representative of all of Toomer's works in its depiction of African American folk life and in its focus on mystical themes. Set in Georgia in 1924, the play concerns a young man's search for God. The man (the "Balo" of the play's title) eventually sees God—in the figure of Jesus—and is transformed.

Subject(s): Harlem Renaissance, Spiritualism, Religion

418   Theodore Ward

Big White Fog: A Negro Tragedy

Black Theater, U.S.A.: Forty-Five Plays by Black Americans, 1847-1974
(New York, NY; Free Press, 1974)

Summary: This drama was the first major work by Ward, who, with his presentation of realistic characters and serious themes, is widely considered one of the pioneers of black theater in the United States. *Big White Fog* was first staged in Chicago in 1938 as part of the Federal Theatre Project of the Works Project Administration. The play is a polemical examination of various political philosophies, among them capitalism and socialism-communism, and the hope that each offers to African Americans. The play concludes that socialism-communism offers black Americans their best hope for advancement, a view that caused significant controversy when the play was first produced. Most of Ward's major theatrical works were written in the next decade, but his influence on black theater was felt into the 1960s and 1970s.

Subject(s): Communism, Social Classes, Capitalism

Literary Criticism

Major African American literary critics begin to appear in the first half of the twentieth century. Their presence was impelled by an increasingly democratized literary culture and the appearance of African American academics in small Southern black colleges. One critic who emerged at this time was Benjamin Brawley, an academic critic who taught first at Shaw University and later at Howard. Another was William Stanley Braithwaite who, in addition to writing his own poetry, began a series of annual anthologies that showcased new African American talent with white writers. The Harlem Renaissance of the twenties was, as one might expect, an important period for African American critics. These included Alain Locke, who played a major role in bringing the Renaissance writers to the notice of the American public. Locke edited the first significant examination of African American literature, *The New Negro: An Interpretation*, which included the poems, short stories, and essays of the significant figures of the Renaissance and helped prove that African Americans were capable of literary genius. During the thirties, the brilliant Howard University critic and poet Sterling A. Brown emerged. His essays in *The Crisis* and *Opportunity* as well as his books on black characterization in American fiction, poetry, and drama established him as a major intellectual presence in African American letters. He was accompanied by the young Saunders Redding, whose *To Make a Poet Black* helped to establish the notion of an African American literary canon. The thirties were an important preparation for the explosion in African American critical writing that would eventually take place in the fifties, sixties, and seventies.

419   Frederick W. Bond

The Negro and the Drama: The Direct and Indirect Contribution Which the American Negro Has Made to Drama and the Legitimate Stage, with the Underlying Conditions Responsible

(Washington, DC; Associated Publishers, 1940)

Summary: One of the first surveys of blacks in the theater, Bond's 1940 work begins with a discussion of the "Backgrounds of Negro Drama," including treatment of such authors as Phillis Wheatley, Jupiter Hammon, and George Horton. He then examines mimicry and the minstrel tradition, including black actors who were active before the twentieth century. Later chapters explore twentieth century actors and playwrights; blacks in operatic music; dance and jazz; movies and radio; and the Federal Theatre Project, inaugurated by Franklin Roosevelt's administration during the Great Depression of the 1930s.

Subject(s): Drama, Music, Dancing

420   Benjamin Brawley

The Negro in Literature and Art in the United States

(New York, NY; Duffield & Company, 1930)

Summary: This 1930 work was one of the first critical works about black literature. In the book, Brawley covers such writers as Phillis Wheatley, Paul Laurence Dunbar, W.E.B. Du Bois, and James Weldon Johnson. He also discusses the fields of drama, painting, sculpture, and music.

Subject(s): Literature, Painting, Music

421 Sterling A. Brown

The Negro in American Fiction
(Washington, DC; Associates in Negro Folk Education, 1937)

Summary: Educator, folklorist, and consummate story-teller Sterling Brown gained renown as both a poet of the Harlem Renaissance and one of the most influential African American literary scholars of the early twentieth century. Contributing to his influence as a critic was *The Negro in American Fiction*, which tracks the appearance of African Americans in U.S. fiction from their earliest appearances in the late eighteenth century through the slave narratives that were published by white abolitionists prior to the Civil War, through the 1930s. Brown's critical insights into the works of such writers as William Hill Brown and William Faulkner are, according to several critics, of great significance. As one of the few black literary critics of his day, Brown was able to view the portrayal of blacks through a black perspective rather than through a white stereotype, however benign that stereotype might be. *The Negro in American Fiction* was published under the subsidy of the Federal Writers' Project, for which Brown served in a key capacity from 1936-39.

Subject(s): Literature, Writing, African Americans

422 Sterling A. Brown

Negro Poetry and Drama
(Washington, DC; Associates in Negro Folk Education, 1937)

Summary: A respected member of the group of writers and artists that comprised the flowering of African American high culture known as the Harlem Renaissance, early twentieth century poet Sterling Brown also contributed to the African American legacy by collecting literature that contained significant depictions of black characters. One of a pair of works completed under the auspices of the Federal Writers' Project of the W.P.A.--the other was *The Negro in American Fiction--Negro Poetry and Drama* critiques works by both black and white authors. Beginning with eighteenth-century writers Jupiter Hammon and Phillis Wheatley and moving on to more recent authors such as Vachel Lindsay and Richard Wright, the volume was pioneering in its scope, and continues to serve as a useful resource, particularly to those studying the role of African Americans in nineteenth- and early twentieth-century literature.

Subject(s): Literature, Culture, African Americans

423 Countee Cullen, Editor

Caroling Dusk: An Anthology of Verse by Negro Poets
(New York, NY; Harper & Brothers, 1927)

Summary: This selection of poems by thirty-eight African American poets includes verse by Paul Laurence Dunbar, W.E.B. Du Bois, Jessie Redmon Fauset, and Sterling A. Brown, among others. The poems are accompanied by biographical notes penned by the poets themselves or by their close family members. Appearing in 1927, this anthology fea-tures numerous writers who were key figures in the Harlem Renaissance cultural movement during the 1920s.

Subject(s): Harlem Renaissance, Poetry

424 Nick Aaron Ford

The Contemporary Negro Novel: A Study in Race Relations
(Boston, MA, United States; Meador Publishing Company, 1936)

Summary: In this 1936 work Ford focuses on novels written by African Americans between 1914 and the mid-1930s, a period which includes the flowering of the Harlem Renaissance cultural movement. In presenting eighteen novels written by eleven authors, Ford focuses on four key areas: common attitudes toward blacks that are condemned by the writers in question; common attitudes toward blacks of which the writers approve; aspects of African American culture that emphasize the differences between racial groups; and the treatment of white characters. Among the writers discussed by Ford are Jessie Redmon Fauset, Langston Hughes, Claude McKay, and Zora Neale Hurston.

Subject(s): Literature, Harlem Renaissance

425 Elizabeth Lay Green

The Negro in Contemporary American Literature: An Outline for Individual and Group Study
(Chapel Hill, NC; University of North Carolina Press, 1928)

Summary: Green divides this early study guide into sections about poetry, drama, fiction, and criticism. She discusses African American authors such as Paul Laurence Dunbar, James Weldon Johnson, Claude McKay, and Countee Cullen, as well as figures such as Booker T. Washington and W. E. B. Du Bois. In the drama section, Green examines the early plays of Eugene O'Neill, which feature black characters. Green closes the book with an examination of the "New Negro Literature" of the Harlem Renaissance, which was at its height when this book was published in 1928.

Subject(s): Literature, Drama, Harlem Renaissance

426 James Weldon Johnson, Editor

The Book of American Negro Poetry
(New York, NY; Harcourt, Brace and Company, 1922)

Summary: This classic anthology, edited by James Weldon Johnson, was one of the first books to highlight the poetic achievements of authors such as Paul Laurence Dunbar, Langston Hughes, Georgia Douglas Johnson, Arna Bontemps, and many others. In his preface to the anthology, Johnson made the bold statement that poetry written in black rural dialect—popularized especially by Dunbar—was severely limited as a poetic form and that it would soon be abandoned by most black writers.

Subject(s): Poetry, Rural Life

427   **Vernon Loggins**

The Negro Author: His Development in America
(New York, NY; Columbia University Press, 1931)

Summary: This 1931 work offers a general survey of writings by African Americans prior to the twentieth century. Loggins examines the "Beginnings of Negro Authorship, 1760-1790", then follows black nonfiction, fiction, and poetry through the Civil War era, and also covers the period from 1865 to 1900.

Subject(s): Poetry, Literature, Biography

428   **J. Saunders Redding**

To Make a Poet Black
(Chapel Hill, NC; University of North Carolina Press, 1939)

Summary: In this influential critical study from 1939, Saunders Redding offers a panoramic overview of black literature, from its eighteenth century origins to its early twentieth century development. Redding argues that African American literature by 1939 could not yet fully be considered an "art," because through its early history it had to be concerned primarily with social issues such as racism rather than aesthetic ones. Another problem faced by black writers according to Redding was the need to consider both a black and a white audience when constructing a work of literature. Redding closes the work with an examination of the writers of the Harlem Renaissance, from Claude McKay to Langston Hughes to Jessie Redmon Fauset.

Subject(s): Literature, Racism, Harlem Renaissance

1940 to Present

The period from 1940 to the present has been the most active and productive period in African American literature. The fruition of the Harlem Renaissance in the 1930s may be said to have led to other periods of extraordinary productivity during World War II and also during the post-war economic miracle in American life. This period saw the consolidation of the presence of black southern migrants in the urban North, first in the urban ghetto and increasingly throughout modern urban America in both the North and the South. This movement of blacks--hitherto a limited oppressed racial caste--into all social, economic, and professional levels of American life was made possible by a number of factors. First, World War II, because of the shortages of labor, accelerated the hiring and education of blacks in numerous fields. Second, a civil rights movement emerged that resulted in the end of legalized segregation through a number of court cases and the legislation of a large body of non-discrimination law. Third, particularly in the late fifties, sixties, and seventies, there was a broad-based democratization of American institutions of education, finance, and production. A better-educated middle class, protected by legislation, fueled an enormous economic expansion and established itself as a remarkable presence in American life. This presence was symbolized by the accession of blacks to the Supreme Court and their entry into national, state, and local politics in every region of the country.

At the center of this transformation was a civil rights movement that had a dynamic of its own. This movement not only brought together a broad assortment of black civil rights groups but also white religious organizations and civic associations, and it led both to school desegregation and to the passage of the Civil Rights Act of 1964. The movement was by no means homogenous, and in the early 1960s a radical separatist black power wing developed, led by figures such as H. Rap Brown and Stokely Carmichael. The appearance of this black power wing corresponded with revolts in the festering urban ghettos that had been created at the beginning third of the century by the segregation of southern rural migrants in the North. As a result of these revolts, a host of American educational institutions opened their doors to blacks. At the same time, white resentment over many of these concessions--and the

implementation of affirmative action programs--would appear in the 1970s, 1980s, and 1990s.

Black writing may be said to have come to one of its highest peaks in this period of extraordinary black progress. An example may be taken from the career of Ralph Ellison, who arrived in New York in the late 1930s and soon thereafter met both Langston Hughes and Richard Wright. Writing in the magazine *New Masses,* Ellison began to establish a literary reputation in the 1940s, and in 1952 he published *Invisible Man*--which today stands as one of the supreme achievements in twentieth century American letters. During the period after the publication of the novel, he was hailed as a major American writer by a white literary establishment that for the first time recognized the universal excellence of a novel written by a black American. In the 1950s and 1960s, Ellison's name was routinely mentioned with that of acclaimed white American authors such as Thomas Pynchon, John Updike, and Saul Bellow. He held a number of distinguished academic posts at major American universities, including the University of Chicago and New York University. His literary eminence might be said to predate that which Toni Morrison enjoys today.

A number of blacks developed similar careers--though not as spectacularly distinguished as Ellison's--during this period. The fifties, sixties, and seventies saw the development of two highly distinguished and nationally recognized poets, Gwendolyn Brooks and Robert Hayden, in addition to the emergence of several eminent playwrights whose pieces appeared on Broadway. This latter group included Lorraine Hansberry, August Wilson, and Adrienne Kennedy. Finally, a set of distinguished literary critics including Ellison and Larry Neal also came to the attention of the American public.

Fiction

African American fiction has grown with the main currents of American literature from the 1940s onward. The major black writer of the 1940s was Richard Wright, who, like his contemporaries William Attaway and Ann Petry, was deeply influenced by realism and naturalism. The late forties and fifties saw the emergence of two important younger writers, Ralph Ellison and James Baldwin. Ellison's book *Invisible Man* won the National Book Award in 1953 and is now widely considered a canonical text of twentieth century literature. Baldwin's early novels made a deep impression in American as well as African American literary life. The careers of writers such as William Gardner Smith, John Williams, and John Killens also began at this time.

The early seventies were distinctive for the emergence of strong writers such as Ernest J. Gaines, John Edgar Wideman and James Alan McPherson, as well as for the satiric fiction of Ishmael Reed. In his most famous work, *The Autobiography of Miss Jane Pittman*, and in his other novels, Gaines uses first person narration and black speaking patterns to realistically portray the lives of African Americans. Wideman began writing novels after he finished his degree as a Rhodes Scholar at Oxford University and was awarded the PEN/Faulkner Award twice for his fiction. In the field of short fiction, McPherson's skills were recognized in 1978 with a Pulitzer Prize. In contrast to the more serious and realistic styles of these authors, Reed's fiction is known for its experimental style and for parodying both black and white culture and establishments, including academia and literary politics. Reed is opposed to the Eurocentric view of history and literature and posits a multicultural tradition that he calls Neo-Hoodooism. All of these authors continue to write fiction.

A number of widely read woman novelists, including Toni Morrison, Alice Walker, Gloria Naylor, and Toni Cade Bambara also emerged during the seventies. Morrison became, in 1993, the first African American writer to win literature's most prestigious award, the Nobel Prize. Her novels include 1987's *Beloved,* which won a Pulitzer Prize for fiction. A Pulitzer also went to Walker for her novel *The Color Purple,* which was adapted and made into a popular movie. All of these women, although influenced by modernism, the writers of the "Black Arts" movement, and contemporary literature, often brought a pronounced feminist perspective to their writing. Other than Bambara, who died in 1995, they are still producing fiction.

429 Lloyd Alexander
Trina Schart Hyman, Illustrator

The Fortune-Tellers
(New York, NY; Dutton Children's Books, 1992)

Summary: Set in West Africa, this children's book tells the story of a young carpenter who goes to a fortune-teller to learn about his future. He receives a prediction that he will become rich. When the fortune-teller mysteriously disappears, the carpenter takes his place and becomes successful and happy giving out similar predictions. The book's bright illustrations contribute to the story's narrative through their depiction of traditional culture.

Subject(s): Children, Africa

430 Alston Anderson

All God's Children: A Novel
(Indianapolis, IN; Bobbs-Merrill Co., 1965)

Summary: The first person narrator of Anderson's 1965 novel, October Pruitt, begins his story by recounting his childhood on the Virginia plantation where he lives as a slave. As a child, October enjoys a relatively good life, as he is allowed to play with his white relatives (October is the grandson of a white slaveowner). After the death of the current owner, however, the estate falls into the hands of the cruel overseer, and October decides to escape to the North. He relates his adventures, from his escape along the Underground Railroad to his experience as a soldier during the Civil War.

Subject(s): Underground Railroad, Slavery, Civil War

431 Alston Anderson

Lover Man
(Garden City, NY; Doubleday, 1959)

Summary: Alston Anderson's 1959 collection of short stories reflects the author's ability in crafting believable, first person narratives using an informal, colloquial prose style. Although most of the stories are set in the Carolinas, some are set in New York City's Harlem neighborhood or in Germany during World War II. Reviewers of the collection praised Anderson's witty prose and his use of regional dialect.

Subject(s): American South, World War II

432 Mignon Holland Anderson

Mostly Womenfolk and a Man or Two: A Collection
(Chicago, IL; Third World Press, 1976)

Summary: The short fictional pieces in Mignon Holland Anderson's 1976 collection are set primarily on the Eastern Shore, a region of Maryland and Virginia on the eastern end of Chesapeake Bay. In the collection, two long sections—one titled "Born" and another titled "And to Die"—are sandwiched around shorter sections titled "A Child" and "To Struggle."

Subject(s): Literature

433 Tina McElroy Ansa

Baby of the Family
(San Diego, CA; Harcourt Brace Jovanovich, 1989)

Summary: Set in the fictional southern town of Mulberry, Ansa's first novel tells the coming-of-age story of Lena McPherson. Lena is born with a caul over her face, which signifies someone who is endowed with extraordinary abilities. As she grows up, surrounded by her nurturing mother, Nellie, and her prosperous father, Jonah, she encounters numerous struggles and challenges. She overcomes these obstacles after a visit by an ancient slave apparition, Rachel.

Subject(s): Supernatural, Coming-of-Age, American South

434 Ethel Nishua Arnold

She Knew No Evil
(New York, NY; Vantage Press, 1952)

Summary: A tale about the conflict between townspeople and an outsider, this 1952 novel is set in a small town. The story follows a well-liked local doctor who decides to marry a beautiful woman from a big city. Unfortunately, the woman turns out to be heartless and unloving, both to her husband and to her children. When it is revealed that the woman was actually a numbers runner in the city, her husband evicts her from their home; she meets her end when her car crashes into a tree and she is killed. The doctor then brings peace to the town by deciding to marry a virtuous local woman.

Subject(s): City and Town Life, Marriage, Community Relations

435 Russell Atkins

Maleficium
(Cleveland, OH; Free Lance Press, 1971)

Summary: The characters in Atkins's 1971 collection of short stories take an ironic delight in the misery that they both experience and cause. In one story, a serial killer muses about trying new forms of murder in a letter to his mother. In another piece, a husband and wife bicker over the lack of generosity of a neighbor who gives the appearance of being a true friend. The dying character of another story in the collection hopes for war to break out upon her death--for London and America to be destroyed. Throughout the pieces, Atkins offers morbid humor and provocative plots.

Subject(s): Death, Murder, Friendship

436 William Attaway

Blood on the Forge: A Novel
(Garden City, NY; Doubleday, Doran & Co., 1941)

Summary: Attaway's second and best-known novel explores the great migration of African Americans from the rural South to the urbanized North during the early 1900s. Like other writers of proletarian novels—works that focused on economic issues such as class conflict—Attaway addresses the powerlessness of black workers in the industrial North. However, he also shows with great skill the alienation and confusion experienced by African Americans who had migrated to the North and who found themselves working in ugly, dehumanizing factories rather than the verdant agricultural landscape of the South.

Subject(s): Class Conflict, American South, Factories

437 Edmund O. Austin

The Black Challenge
(New York, NY; Vantage Press, 1958)

Summary: The protagonist of Edmund O. Austin's 1958 novel, Jeremiah King, is a thirty-six-year-old West Indian man who ventures to Harlem in the late 1920s to start a new life following the dissolution of his marriage. Curious and not very serious, Jeremiah discovers Harlem teeming with life and culture in the midst of an artistic "renaissance" that would make many of its writers and intellectuals famous. Once in Harlem, he befriends Marcus Cox, one of the founders of the Universal Negro Movement of the United States and the World. Though poorly educated, Cox taps into a genuine impulse among blacks of all economic and social classes to better their lives. At the novel's end, Cox has been forced to flee America, but his intention to fight for social justice remains intact--and has even begun to affect Jeremiah. The novel begins with a poem by Austin titled "Ode to the N.A.A.C.P. and Its Freedom Fighters."

Subject(s): Social Classes, Harlem Renaissance

438 James Baldwin

Another Country
(New York, NY; Dial Press, 1962)

Summary: This novel continues the themes of Baldwin's previous fictional effort, *Giovanni's Room*. However, in its examination of the nature of racial and sexual identity and role of pain and suffering in life, *Another Country* is more complex and ambitious in scope than its predecessor. Baldwin weaves together several story lines and characters, including a black jazz drummer, a white homosexual, and an Italian American writer. Throughout the novel, Baldwin incorporates elements from the blues tradition, an important part of African American culture.

Subject(s): Racism, Sexuality, Abuse

439 James Baldwin

Giovanni's Room: A Novel
(New York, NY; Dial Press, 1956)

Summary: In his second novel, James Baldwin offers one of the first serious examinations of homosexuality and sexual identity. The protagonist, David, repeatedly is unable to come to terms with his own homosexual impulses. Fleeing these impulses, David eventually lands in Paris, where in an attempt at social respectability he proposes marriage to a woman, Hella. While awaiting her decision, David has a torrid love affair with Giovanni. Still unable to deal with his feelings, David rejects Giovanni, whose life then takes a tragic turn as he kills his homosexual boss and is sentenced to death. At the novel's end, Hella rejects David's proposal, and David is left alone in Paris. Baldwin's despairing attitude toward homosexuality is an accurate reflection of the attitude of Western society in the mid-1950s, when homosexuality was still considered a disease and gays and lesbians were shunned.

Subject(s): Homosexuality/Lesbianism, Sexuality

440 **James Baldwin**

Go Tell It on the Mountain
(New York, NY; Knopf, 1953)

Summary: James Baldwin's first novel is tinged with autobiographical elements from his own childhood, particularly his tempestuous relationship with his abusive step father and his complex feelings about the fundamentalist religion that pervaded his household. The novel follows protagonist John Grimes from adolescence to maturity, as he deals with his abusive father (a preacher), grapples with his view of Christianity, and struggles with his feelings about his own sexuality. Set in Harlem, where Baldwin himself grew up, the novel was completed four years after Baldwin moved from the United States to Paris, a move that was crucial in his artistic development. The themes in this novel would reappear again and again in Baldwin's writing.

Subject(s): Exile, Religion, Sexuality

441 **James Baldwin**

Going to Meet the Man
(New York, NY; Dial Press, 1965)

Summary: This collection of short stories is chiefly notable for its inclusion of "Sonny's Blues," Baldwin's most acclaimed short story and one of his most important works of fiction. The story includes trademark Baldwin themes such as the question of racial identity and the importance of music—specifically jazz and blues—in African American culture. The story revolves around the strained relationship between the comfortably middle-class narrator and his brother, Sonny, a jazz musician who struggles with drug abuse. At the story's end, the narrator overcomes his distrust of his brother and invites Sonny to come to live with him. In turn, Sonny invites his brother to hear him play in concert. During this experience, the narrator finally realizes that music can help Sonny work through and release his pain and suffering.

Subject(s): Music, Family Relations

442 **James Baldwin**

If Beale Street Could Talk
(New York, NY; Dial Press, 1974)

Summary: This novel features a nineteen-year-old protagonist, Tish, who is unmarried and pregnant. The baby's father, Fonny, is in jail on false rape charges. In many respects, the novel is an attack on the injustice inherent in the American judicial system. The police, prosecutors, and judges are all viewed as accomplices in maintaining a system that ignores the innocence of many of its victims. Another target of Baldwin's criticism is a familiar one from many of his other writings: religion. In this work, Fonny's mother and aunt disown him so that they can maintain their stellar social reputations in church. As in his other novels and essays, Baldwin portrays religion as ineffectual and unconcerned with matters of social justice.

Subject(s): Religion, Judicial System

443 **James Baldwin**

Just Above My Head
(New York, NY; Dial Press, 1979)

Summary: In his final novel, Baldwin continues his exploration of sexual identity and the nature of suffering, both themes that he examined in virtually all of his earlier novels. The work revolves around the sibling relationship between Hall Montana—the narrator—and his older brother, Arthur. In a series of flashbacks, Hall recalls Arthur's life, his struggle to come to terms with his homosexuality, and his ability to work through his pain by using his music. The novel ends on a fairly positive note, suggesting that Baldwin had himself made peace with the themes that had engaged him for nearly twenty-five years. Interestingly, Baldwin also portrays religion in a less antagonistic and hostile manner than he had in earlier works.

Subject(s): Religion, Homosexuality/Lesbianism, Family Relations

444 **James Baldwin**

Tell Me How Long the Train's Been Gone: A Novel
(New York, NY; Dial Press, 1968)

Summary: Generally considered one of Baldwin's weaker novels, this work is nevertheless important for its reflection of Baldwin's own struggle with his role during the black civil rights movement of the 1960s. The novel's protagonist, Leo Proudhammer, is a bisexual black actor who finds himself recovering from a heart attack. In a series of flashbacks, Leo examines his success as an actor and wrestles with the decision about how committed he should be to the civil rights movement. On the one hand, he realizes that he can use his acting success to maintain a comfortable life. On the other, he feels drawn toward a more active role as a spokesman for the movement. At the novel's end, Leo apparently decides that he must play a larger role in the movement, regardless of how that decision impacts his professional life.

Subject(s): Civil Rights Movement, Acting

445 **Toni Cade Bambara**

Gorilla, My Love
(New York, NY; Random House, 1972)

Summary: This collection of short stories, considered by many critics to be Bambara's most important work of fiction, contains fifteen stories. The protagonists of the stories are typically women or girls who use their wit, intelligence, and common sense to succeed despite trying circumstances. In the title story, for instance, the young narrator laments her poor treatment by the adults in her life and the broken promises they continually deliver. However, the girl overcomes her frustrations and turns her attention to the future, resolved to meet whatever challenges she will face.

Subject(s): Childhood

446 Nathan Barrett

Bars of Adamant: A Tropical Novel

(New York, NY; Fleet Pub. Corp., 1966)

Summary: Set in a small Jamaican village, Nathan Barrett's 1966 novel revolves around the arrival of an old man, Benjamin Clark, who declares that he is going home to Morgantown to die amidst his friends and family. Traveling by foot, Clark finds a place to sleep in an inn owned by Martha. Clark, however, dies during his first night in the village, and his death sets in motion a series of changes among the local townspeople. At the end of the novel, Martha too has died. The novel is set during the Christmas season.

Subject(s): Death, Travel, City and Town Life

447 Arthenia J. Bates

Seeds Beneath the Snow

(New York, NY; Greenwich Book Publishers, 1969)

Summary: Set among rural blacks in South Carolina, this collection of twelve short stories focuses on characters who struggle to overcome pain and hardship in their lives. In "Runetta," a young girl dies of pneumonia unnecessarily, while in "Silas," a teenager grows up quickly when his ignorance leads to tragedy. Little known before this collection was published, Bates since 1969 has garnered increasing renown for her fiction, earning comparisons to such writers as Paul Laurence Dunbar and Zora Neale Hurston.

Subject(s): American South, Rural Life

448 Mattie Beason

West to the Ohio River

(Los Angeles, CA; Crescent, 1976)

Summary: A former social worker, Mattie Beason in her 1976 novel examines issues such as teen angst, betrayal, and the devastating consequences of keeping secrets from loved ones. The novel is told through a series of letters between Martha Sullivan and her friend Carol Hudson. Although Carol's life seems serene and charmed, she is stunned when her beloved husband deserts her for a white woman with whom he once had a child. In trying to reach Carol, Martha and her husband swim the Ohio River, after which Martha experiences her own revelation.

Subject(s): Friendship, Marriage, Letters

449 Barry Beckham

My Main Mother

(New York, NY; Walker, 1969)

Summary: Beckham's acclaimed first novel focuses on Mitchell Mibbs, an angry and confused young man who is driven to murder his mother, who had abandoned him in search of a singing career. In addition to depicting the anxieties that beset Mitchell, Beckham also explores the effects of white racism on African Americans in an understated but effective manner. Beckham's literary reputation rests chiefly on this work and his second novel, *Runner Mack.*

Subject(s): Racism, Family Problems, Murder

450 Barry Beckham

Runner Mack

(New York, NY; Morrow, 1972)

Summary: The protagonist of Beckham's second novel is Henry Adams, a naive young man who ventures from his home in the American South to play professional baseball. In a series of picaresque episodes, Henry is cheated of his chance to play baseball, ends up in a bad job, is drafted for a war on Alaska, and finally joins a black revolutionary in a plan to blow up the White House. Despite comic overtones, the underlying despair and chaos of Henry's life amount to an indictment of life in racist and white-dominated America.

Subject(s): Racism, American South, Baseball

451 Claudia Bellinger

Wolf Kitty

(New York, NY; Vantage Press, 1958)

Summary: Bellinger's 1958 novel extols the virtues of Christian living and avoidance of gambling. In the novel, a childless couple takes in a series of orphans and shows them how to live by proper Christian principles. A secondary plot involves Ella Blackman, a severe woman who works very hard but has little love and affection left over to give to her grandchildren.

Subject(s): Childhood, Christianity, Gambling

452 Hal Bennett

The Black Wine

(Garden City, NY; Doubleday, 1968)

Summary: The protagonists of Bennett's second novel, Norman Eisenberg and Viola Anderson, are typical of Bennett's characters in their deluded assumption of spiritual authority and their inevitable struggles as a result of their flawed perspectives. Eisenberg preaches nobility through purpose, but at the end of the novel he alters his perceptions when he is nearly killed by a mob of rioters; he is saved by his mistress. Anderson, for her part, gains a large following through her espousal of murder and her call for self-forgiveness, but her own naivete and her contempt for her followers lead her to disillusionment. Like many other Bennett characters, Eisenberg and Anderson seek an illusory safety in religion from the violence and dehumanization of white racist America.

Subject(s): Religion, Racism

453 Hal Bennett

Lord of Dark Places

(New York, NY; Norton, 1970)

Summary: Bennett's 1970 novel is experimental and technically daring, fulfilling the promise of earlier works such as *A Wilderness of Vines* and *The Black Wine*. The novel features Joe Market, a prophet and visionary who is also a murderer and prostitute, as he journeys from naivete to self-sacrifice. The novel ends with his execution in an electric chair in 1968. The novel contains a dizzying mix of thematic concerns, from religion and sexuality to race relations.

Subject(s): Religion, Race Relations, Sexuality

454 Hal Bennett

Seventh Heaven

(Garden City, NY; Doubleday, 1976)

Summary: The title of Bennett's 1976 novel, another in a string of flamboyant and daring works, refers to a public housing project in Cousinsville, New Jersey. The novel's protagonist, Bill Kelsey, struggles to find a sense of freedom and safety in a world that denies those things to blacks. In the end, he finds a measure of solace in sexual servitude. *Seventh Heaven* typifies the unique quality of Bennett's novels, which hold a distinct status in the pantheon of black literature of the 1960s and 1970s.

Subject(s): Sexuality, Racism, Poverty

455 Hal Bennett

Wait Until the Evening

(Garden City, NY; Doubleday, 1974)

Summary: Kevin Brittain, the protagonist of Bennett's 1974 novel, is a directionless youth until he discovers a compelling reason to live: murder those who anger and irritate him, thereby developing self-esteem in a society that otherwise denies it to blacks. Kevin is inspired by his grandmother, a lonely woman who operates under the same philosophy of redemption-through-murder. Kevin is foiled by his father, a policeman who arrests his son for murders actually committed by Kevin's grandmother. The novel contains the hallmarks of Bennett's fiction: an unusual, controversial storyline and colorful prose.

Subject(s): Family Problems, Race Relations, Murder

456 Hal Bennett

A Wilderness of Vines

(Garden City, NY; Doubleday, 1966)

Summary: Hal Bennett's first novel, like much of his subsequent fiction, is set in Burnside, Virginia, a fictional town in which the racism and violence of American life appear in absurd and tragic fashion. Beginning in 1920 and ending at the start of World War II some twenty years later, *A Wilderness of Vines* exposes the hypocrisy of racism—both by whites against blacks but also by light-skinned blacks against darker-skinned blacks—and the often corrupt confluence of religion and sex.

Subject(s): Racism, American South, Religion

457 Ruth Thompson Bernard

What's Wrong with the Lottery?

(Boston, MA; Meador Publishing Company, 1943)

Summary: As it's title suggests, this 1943 novel by Ruth Thompson Bernard deals with gambling. In the work, Bernard attacks gambling—specifically the "numbers" game, which is featured in numerous works by African Americans of the first half of the twentieth century—as immoral, based on a religious viewpoint.

Subject(s): Literature, Gambling, Religion

458 Eugene H. Berwanger

The Frontier against Slavery: Western Anti-Negro Prejudice and the Slavery Extension Controversy

(Urbana, IL; University of Illinois Press, 1967)

Summary: This work examines the role that prejudice against blacks played in the development of antislavery sentiments in the antebellum United States. The author explores the slavery expansion phase of the antislavery movement, concentrating on those frontier regions that became free states or territories by 1860 but that at some point were faced with the legalization of slavery.

Subject(s): Racism, Slavery, Abolition

459 John Paul Blair

Democracy Reborn

(New York, NY; F. Hubner & Co., 1946)

Summary: Blair's 1946 novel tells the history of slavery in America, from its beginnings in the seventeenth century to its end with the Civil War of 1861 to 1865. The central character in the novel is Uncle Skint.

Subject(s): Slavery, Civil War

460 Alden Bland

Behold a Cry

(New York, NY; C. Scribner's Sons, 1947)

Summary: The great migration of rural southern blacks to northern industrial cities forms the backdrop to this 1947 novel. The protagonist, Ed Tyler, seeks to elude military service in World War I by moving from Georgia to Chicago and starting a new life. Although he begins a relationship with a girlfriend, Mamie, Ed quickly decides to bring his wife and two sons from Georgia to live with him in Chicago. Later, however, Ed again deserts his family by leaving with another woman. Race riots and union activities figure heavily in the novel's plot, but Bland does not focus on friction between blacks and whites. Rather, he offers a naturalistic drama in which his characters deal with common issues such as truth, loyalty, and family.

Subject(s): Race Relations, Family Problems

461 Robert Boles

Curling: A Novel

(Boston, MA; Houghton Mifflin, 1968)

Summary: Boles's 1968 novel is set on Cape Cod, Massachusetts, and the action occurs over a single weekend. In the book, protagonist Chelsea Meredith Burlingame is an engineer in his late twenties. He is struggling with his racial heritage as a black man raised by wealthy white parents. During a weekend on Cape Cod with his white friend Roger and Roger's girlfriend, Burlingame learns new information about his mysterious family past; by the end of the weekend, one of the three characters is dead.

Subject(s): Literature, Identity, Race Relations

462 Robert Boles

The People One Knows: A Novel

(Boston, MA; Houghton Mifflin, 1964)

Summary: In his first novel, Robert Boles presents two days in the life of Saul Beckworth, a lonely soldier who has just survived a suicide attempt. On the first day, Beckworth undergoes observation by psychiatrists at an Army hospital in France. On the second day, he spends time with a longtime white friend and the friend's girlfriend. During the two days, Beckworth makes crucial discoveries about his racial identity.

Subject(s): Suicide, Identity, Race Relations

463 Marita Bonner

Frye Street & Environs: The Collected Works of Marita Bonner

(Boston, MA; Beacon Press, 1987)

Summary: In addition to plays such as *The Pot-Maker,* this collection includes several short stories written by Bonner in the 1930s and 1940s. In "One True Love," a young black woman rejects a marriage proposal to go to law school, only to have her dreams crushed when she fails to pass her entrance exams and then is diagnosed with a terminal disease. Another story, "On the Altar," focuses on the theme of intraracial prejudice, as a grandmother conspires to drive a wedge between her light-skinned granddaughter and her granddaughter's dark-skinned husband. Overall, the collection showcases Bonner's interest in education, prejudice, and self-determination for women.

Subject(s): Education, Prejudice, Women's Rights

464 Arna Bontemps

The Old South: "A Summer Tragedy" and Other Stories of the Thirties

(New York, NY; Dodd, Mead, 1973)

Summary: This collection of fourteen stories is set in the rural South of the Depression-era 1930s, a particularly difficult time and place for African Americans. Recalling his own boyhood in the South, Bontemps in these stories depicts the qualities and concerns of people struggling to improve their lives under difficult circumstances.

Subject(s): Depression (Economic), American South, Rural Life

465 William Bosworth

The Long Search: A Novel

(Great Barrington, MA; Advance Pub. Co., 1957)

Summary: Bosworth's 1957 novel tells the saga of George Murdock, who suffers a stormy childhood living with hostile relatives in the Florida Everglades. As he grows up, George continues to experience loss, frustration, and hostility at every turn, and he eventually becomes a fugitive from justice. By the end of the novel, however, he has resolved his personal crises and gained a measure of self-esteem and inner strength. In the novel, Bosworth parallels George's travails with a series of hurricanes that buffet the Everglades.

Subject(s): Coming-of-Age, Hurricanes

466 David Bradley

The Chaneysville Incident: A Novel

(New York, NY; Harper & Row, 1981)

Summary: Set in rural western Pennsylvania in a town that once served as a stop on the Underground Railroad, this celebrated novel blends fact and fiction while exploring the long-lasting effects of slavery. In the novel, a young history professor explores the mysterious elements of his family's past, eventually discovering a tale of thirteen escaped slaves who chose death over a return to slavery. Critics praised the work for its complex structure and lyrical prose, and the novel won several awards.

Subject(s): Underground Railroad, Slavery, Racism

Award(s): PEN/Faulkner Award: Fiction, 1982; American Academy and Institute of Arts and Letters Award: Literature, 1982

467 David Bradley

South Street

(New York, NY; Grossman Publishers, 1975)

Summary: Bradley's first novel is set in Philadelphia and focuses on life in a ghetto. The novel's protagonist, Adlai Stevenson Brown, is a young poet who begins frequenting a bar in a local neighborhood. The people that he encounters there, and their tales of heartache and courage in the daily struggle of life in the ghetto, form the basis of the book. The novel was inspired by Bradley's own experiences while in college in Philadelphia.

Subject(s): Working-Class Life, Urban Affairs, Poverty

468 | Gwendolyn Brooks

Maud Martha: A Novel

(New York, NY; Harper, 1953)

Summary: Though she is famous for her poetry, Brooks produced this work——her only novel—in 1953 in the early stages of her literary career. The novel features a poor woman, Maud, as she struggles for dignity and self-esteem in a hostile world. Hounded by the worry that she is ugly, Maud eventually overcomes her own doubts and the racism of a white store clerk and gains the dignity she has been seeking. In its inner-city ghetto setting, *Maud Martha* is similar to Brooks's best-known works of poetry, including *A Street in Bronzeville.*

Subject(s): Racism, Women's Rights, Urban Affairs

469 | Cecil M. Brown

The Life and Loves of Mr. Jiveass Nigger: A Novel

(New York, NY; Farrar, Straus & Giroux, 1969)

Summary: Brown's first novel features protagonist George Washington, a young black man disillusioned with the corruption of the society in which he lives. Determined to find out if the rest of the world is as morally bankrupt as America, Washington leaves the United States and travels in Europe, eventually landing in Copenhagen, Denmark. There, he realizes his own foolishness and has his worst fears about humanity confirmed. At the end of the novel, he decides to return to America and become a writer.

Subject(s): Travel, Literature, Racism

470 | Frank London Brown

The Myth Maker: A Novel

(Chicago, IL; Path Press, 1969)

Summary: Published seven years after his death, Brown's second novel was his master's thesis at the University of Chicago in 1960. In the novel, protagonist Ernest Day is a bookish drug addict. One day, for reasons unclear to him, he murders an elderly man who smiles at him underneath an elevated train track in Chicago. During the remainder of the novel, Ernest struggles to come to grips with his crime and with the meaning of life. At the story's end, the police finally come for Ernest while he is making love to his girlfriend, Freda.

Subject(s): Murder, Drug Abuse, Crime and Criminals

471 | Frank London Brown

Trumbull Park: A Novel

(Chicago, IL; Regnery, 1959)

Summary: Brown's first novel is an autobiographical account of his family's move from inner city Chicago to a predominantly white development in the 1950s. In the novel, the black families that move to Trumbull Park are besieged by hostile whites and ignored by an indifferent police force. Facing bomb-ings, mobs, and anonymous violence, some black residents succumb to the intense pressure while others hold firm in their determination to live where they choose. Among those in Brown's fictional milieu who emerge as leaders are women.

Subject(s): Race Relations, Violence, Urban Affairs

472 | Josephine Stephens Brown

The Way of the Shadows: A Novel

(New York, NY; Exposition Press, 1973)

Summary: At the beginning of this novel, the protagonist, George, is a boy of fourteen. He lives with his grandparents in a small town in North Carolina, having been abandoned by his parents. As he grows, he gets a job and eventually attends a technical school. Later, he fights in the Vietnam War before finally returning to his hometown at the end of the novel, at which point he finds his real father.

Subject(s): Vietnam War, Education, Fathers and Sons

473 | Lloyd Louis Brown

Iron City: A Novel

(New York, NY; Masses & Mainstream, 1951)

Summary: Lloyd Louis Brown's first novel is set in the world of mid-twentieth century labor unions, when Communism was seen as a humane alternative to greedy capitalism. In the novel, a Communist labor organizer finds himself under arrest for a murder he did not commit.

Subject(s): Communism, Labor Movement

474 | Mattye Jeanette Brown

The Reign of Terror

(New York, NY; Vantage Press, 1962)

Summary: Set in a fictional southern town not long after the Civil War (1861-1865), Brown's 1962 novel is a tale of racial violence and uncommon courage. In the novel, Knick Jones acquires land in the town of Wickerville and makes plans to send his two daughters to college—actions that raise the ire of local whites. When a violent group of white men arrive in the middle of the night to "question" Knick, his wife fends off the men with a shotgun. In so doing, she saves herself and her children and gives Knick a chance to escape.

Subject(s): American South, Racism, Violence

475 | Ed Bullins

The Hungered One: Early Writings

(New York, NY; Morrow, 1971)

Summary: Though best known for his plays, Bullins has also written works of narrative fiction. This 1971 work collects several of the author's short stories. Like much of his work, these stories are autobiographical in nature and serve to illuminate Bullins's early years in inner-city Philadelphia and his later experiences after moving to Los Angeles. A leader of the "Black Arts" movement that emerged in the late 1960s and early 1970s, Bullins in both his fiction and his drama focuses on life among inner-city blacks, eschewing ineffectual political rhetoric in favor of direct action.

Subject(s): Urban Affairs

476 **Ed Bullins**

The Reluctant Rapist

(New York, NY; Harper & Row, 1973)

Summary: Bullins's first novel features the character of Steve Benson, whose life mirrors the author's in many respects and who appears in several of the author's plays. In the novel, Benson describes his life on the streets of inner-city Philadelphia and his move to Los Angeles, where he finds fulfillment among a group of black intellectuals who are both artistically active and politically engaged. A central event in the novel is based on a real-life event in which Bullins was stabbed in the heart during a fight and briefly stopped breathing. After recovering from the wound, Bullins was determined to follow his literary dreams, and he went on to become one of the most influential dramatists in American theater during the 1960s and 1970s.

Subject(s): Urban Affairs, Literature

477 **Clifton Bullock**

Baby Chocolate and Other Short Stories: Aspects of the Black Experience: An Original Collection

(New York, NY; William-Frederick Press, 1975)

Summary: Written while the author was in prison, the stories in this collection reflect Clifton Bullock's experiences as a black man in a racist, white-dominated society. Some of the pieces are set in the prison world that Bullock himself inhabited, while others focus more generally on themes of love, hate, trust, and religion.

Subject(s): Prisoners and Prisons, Racism

478 **Octavia E. Butler**

"Bloodchild"

Bloodchild and Other Stories
(New York, NY; Four Walls Eight Windows, 1995)

Summary: Written in the 1980s and published in Butler's 1995 collection, this acclaimed novella captured three major science fiction prizes: the Hugo, Nebula, and Locus awards. The story features a race of males on another planet whose childbearing responsibilities define their societal value. Drawing parallels between this race of males and women on Earth, Butler offers a fascinating story of equality and power.

Subject(s): Women's Rights, Science Fiction, Childbirth

Award(s): Hugo Award, 1985; Science Fiction Writers of America: Nebula Award, 1985; Locus Award, 1985

479 **Octavia E. Butler**

Dawn: Xenogenesis

(New York, NY; Warner Books, 1987)

Summary: The opening installment in Butler's "Xenogenesis" trilogy introduces readers to a clash of cultures that takes place on post-nuclear-holocaust Earth in the distant future. *Dawn* features the arrival of nomadic aliens called the Oankali, whose ability to breed with different species provides the remaining humans with a chance to repopulate Earth with a new species containing the best elements of humans and Oankali. The job of manipulating genes to create the new species falls to a third sex called the Ooloi. Butler uses this complex plot line to explore the meaning of hierarchy in a communal setting and the danger hierarchy poses to humanity.

Subject(s): Science Fiction, Genetic Engineering

480 **Octavia E. Butler**

Kindred

(Garden City, NY; Doubleday, 1979)

Summary: Though most of Butler's novels have been part of her "Patternist" and "Xenogenesis" series, *Kindred* is a stand-alone novel that became one of the author's best-known works. In the novel, Dana, a modern-day African American, is carried back in time by her great-great-grandfather, who turns out to have been a white slave owner. Dana is forced to save her ancestor's life in the midst of several threats, because only by keeping him alive can she ensure her own eventual birth. Butler's creative treatment of race and slavery in this novel drew her rave reviews from critics and significant popular approval as well.

Subject(s): Science Fiction, Race Relations, Slavery

481 **Octavia E. Butler**

Patternmaster

(Garden City, NY; Doubleday, 1976)

Summary: One of only a handful of African American writers who work in the field of science fiction, Octavia E. Butler has written several installments in her "Patternist" series. The series is set in a world dominated by specially bred, telepathic beings who survive by killing and assuming the bodies of younger humans. Seeking to establish a race of superhumans, these telepaths are opposed by other immortals who seek a world not built on murder and domination. Though some of the series' novels are set in the late twentieth century, *Patternmaster* is set in an agrarian society in the distant future. In it, communities of peaceful telepaths are at risk from mutated humans who carry a horrible genetic disease. When a Patternist ruler is wounded, his two sons vie for leadership of the telepaths. As is typical in Butler's novels, one son triumphs by learning that compassion and communal responsibility can lead to harmony. Though many of the characters in the "Patternist" books are black females, Butler chooses not to favor such characters but rather to suggest that racial and gender stereotypes thwart human progress.

Subject(s): Science Fiction, Race Relations

482 George Cain

Blueschild Baby

(New York, NY; McGraw-Hill, 1970)

Summary: This heavily autobiographical novel appears to follow Cain's own life and even uses his name for its protagonist. In the novel, the protagonist describes his childhood in Harlem and his secondary school experience as a token black in a snobbish and racist private school. Gifted both intellectually and athletically, the narrator soon makes his way to college. However, despite his potential, he is unable to cope with the stresses of a white-dominated society. He becomes a drug addict and is sent to prison. Following his release, he returns to poverty-stricken Harlem, where he continues to battle drug addiction while also trying to make a new life for himself. He eventually realizes that he has been his own worst oppressor and that only he can free himself. Although *Blueschild Baby* was well received by critics, Cain chose not to continue writing following its publication. It remains his only published work.

Subject(s): Poverty, Drug Abuse, Racism

483 Johnnie Mae Cain

White Bastards

(New York, NY; Vantage Press, 1973)

Summary: Teddy, the protagonist of Johnnie Mae Cain's 1973 novel, is a psychologically disturbed woman of mixed-race origin. A truck driver, she arrives in a small town in Arizona and proceeds to wreak havoc on the town's inhabitants. She first terrorizes the people in a cafe, and later she kills two people at the local hospital. All the while, she rages at the "white bastards" she sees.

Subject(s): Mental Illness, Race Relations, Murder

484 Lewis A.H. Caldwell

The Policy King

(Chicago, IL; New Vistas Publishing House, 1945)

Summary: Caldwell in his 1945 novel presents a study of justice and family loyalty. Set in Chicago, the novel features a clash between siblings. Seventeen-year-old Joe, after clashing with his highly moral father (a preacher), leaves home to join the racketeering machine set up by a South Side kingpin. Joe become successful in the business, but later his sister Helen begins a crusade to outlaw the "policy" racket. Eventually, Joe is killed in gang warfare, but his younger brother Jerry decides to follow in his footsteps. Outraged, Helen works steadily and eventually succeeds in getting Jerry sent to prison. Caldwell casts doubt on the whether Helen's crusade against members of her own family is justified.

Subject(s): Crime and Criminals, Family Problems

485 Steve Cannon

Groove, Bang and Jive Around

(New York, NY; Ophelia Press, 1969)

Summary: Set in New Orleans, Steve Cannon's 1969 novel is filled with illicit sex, profanity, and drug use. In the novel, fourteen-year-old Annette inhabits a nightmarish ghetto world in which frequent, casual sex and drug addiction are the norms. The action is centered in a bar called the "Gumbo House."

Subject(s): Drug Abuse, Sexuality, Poverty

486 Mentis Carrere

Man in the Cane

(New York, NY; Vantage Press, 1956)

Summary: Set in Louisiana during the early part of the twentieth century, this novel focuses on Jimmy and his girlfriend, Antonia. Jimmy, a college-educated farmer, attempts to earn an extra one hundred dollars so that he can refurnish his home for Antonia. However, he is opposed by racist whites at every turn. Eventually, however, Jimmy gets his money, weds Antonia, and is hired as a teacher at a new school for blacks.

Subject(s): Love, Education, Racism

487 Xam Cartier

Muse-Echo Blues

(New York, NY; Harmony Books, 1991)

Summary: In her 1991 novel, Xam Cartier follows the experiences of two similar women living in two different periods. Kat, a musician-composer, lives in present-day San Francisco, while Kitty is a musician in jazz-age Kansas City during the 1930s and 1940s. In telling her story, Cartier features several real-life jazz figures, including Sarah Vaughan and Count Basie.

Subject(s): Jazz, Women, Musicians

488 Alice Childress

Like One of the Family: Conversations from a Domestic's Life

(Brooklyn, NY; Independence Publishers, 1956)

Summary: This 1956 work by Childress contains sketches from the life of Mildred, a black woman who works as a maid for white employers. Defiant, witty, and loving, Mildred upbraids and opposes her employers when she feels it is necessary, including telling them how to raise their children and refusing to do certain tasks that her employers ask her to do. She also, however, occupies a cherished role as someone who is essentially a member of the family. Often serialized in periodicals directed at black audiences, these brief (500 to 700 words) sketches epitomized a gradual shift in attitude among African Americans in literature—a shift away from the powerless victims portrayed earlier in the century toward the much bolder and more confrontational characters that would appear in the 1960s with the advent of the "Black Arts" movement.

Subject(s): Servants, Race Relations

489   Al C. Clark

(Also known as Donald Goines)

Crime Partners

(Los Angeles, CA; Holloway House, 1974)

Summary: *Crime Partners* is the first in a four-book series in which Clark tells a dark saga of ghetto militancy and social justice. In the series' first installment, readers are introduced to Kenyatta, a small-time Detroit revolutionary who has big plans for his militant organization. Kenyatta dreams of eliminating drugs and prostitution from inner-city black ghettos and killing all white policeman. The book illustrates Clark's skill in evoking the racist, violent, spirit-crushing nature of life in black ghettos of the 1970s.

Subject(s): Urban Affairs, Criminal Justice, Black Nationalism

490   Al C. Clark

(Also known as Donald Goines)

Death List

(Los Angeles, CA; Holloway House, 1974)

Summary: In the second installment of his four-book series about a militant black revolutionary with big dreams, Clark shows Kenyatta building his fledgling organization and preparing to move from small-time Detroit to the larger realm of Los Angeles, California. Clark shows Kenyatta using criminal means to move closer to his goal of ridding black ghettos of drugs and prostitution.

Subject(s): Urban Affairs, Criminal Justice, Black Nationalism

491   Al C. Clark

(Also known as Donald Goines)

Kenyatta's Escape

(Los Angeles, CA; Holloway House, 1974)

Summary: *Kenyatta's Escape* is the third of Clark's four-book series about a rising criminal with revolutionary dreams. In this installment, Kenyatta has successfully moved his militant organization to Los Angeles from Detroit, and he finds his organization swelling in members and money. Kenyatta's goals remain the elimination of drugs, prostitution, and white policemen from black urban ghettos. Clark sets up an interesting dynamic, as his central character uses criminal means to rid cities of scourges that the established criminal justice system cannot handle.

Subject(s): Urban Affairs, Criminal Justice, Black Nationalism

492   Al C. Clark

(Also known as Donald Goines)

Kenyatta's Last Hit

(Los Angeles, CA; Holloway House, 1975)

Summary: The final installment in Clark's four-book series about a militant black revolutionary finds Kenyatta closer to realizing his dreams of ridding black ghettos of prostitution, drugs, and white policemen. His organization has swelled from a mere 50 members—during its fledgling days in Detroit—to 2,000 members in the larger realm of Los Angeles. However, Kenyatta meets a violent death just prior to his attempt to assassinate a businessman who is the main drug supplier for Los Angeles. Clark, who has set up an interesting dynamic wherein a black man uses violent means to rid his cities of social ills, seems to say that in the end such revolutionary tactics are doomed to fail. Clark's writing reflects a cynical attitude about the social justice movement of the 1960s and 1970s, when numerous black writers and leaders sought to alleviate the nightmarish conditions of poor, inner-city black ghettos.

Subject(s): Urban Affairs, Criminal Justice, Black Nationalism

493   Austin C. Clarke

The Bigger Light

(Boston, MA; Little, Brown, 1975)

Summary: Born and raised in Barbados but later a resident of Canada, Austin C. Clarke is perhaps best known for his "Toronto" trilogy of novels, which deal directly with the alienation experienced by black West Indian immigrants to Canada. In the trilogy's first two installments, *The Meeting Point* and *Storm of Fortune,* Clarke follows a group of West Indian women who venture to Canada to work as domestic servants for whites. In *The Bigger Light,* which ends the trilogy, Clarke shifts his focus to the husband of one of these women, Boysie Cumberbatch. Boysie is a successful businessman who has achieved the dream of many West Indian immigrants: he owns his own company and his own house. However, Boysie's assimilation into white Canadian culture has come at a price, as he finds himself increasingly estranged from his wife, from his black friends, and from himself. Clarke's depiction of the personal and communal cost of assimilation of West Indian blacks into a white-dominated society brought him widespread recognition from the literary establishment.

Subject(s): Emigration and Immigration, Servants

494   Austin C. Clarke

When He Was Free and Young and He Used to Wear Silks

(Toronto, Canada; Anansi, 1971)

Summary: The stories in Clarke's 1971 collection explore the worlds of Clarke's own life: the Barbados of his youth and the Canada of his adulthood, where he emigrated from his homeland. The stories set in Barbados focus on the divide between rich and poor, white and black in the West Indian country, while the stories set in Canada examine the difficulty faced by black immigrants trying to assimilate into a white-dominated society. Many of these themes are more fully developed in Clarke's acclaimed "Toronto" trilogy of novels, which appeared in the years surrounding the publication of *When He Was Free*. Clarke substantially revised this story collection for an American edition published under the same title in 1973.

Subject(s): Emigration and Immigration

495 Dorothy Randle Clinton

The Maddening Scar: A Mystery Novel

(Boston, MA; Christopher Pub. House, 1962)

Summary: This 1962 murder mystery features white main characters. Vivian Dale, the protagonist, is an aspiring classical music singer whose teacher embarrasses him by calling attention to his speech impediment. When the teacher is found dead, Vivian is the main suspect. However, the real killer is eventually found, and Vivian is given a chance at professional stardom by a concert promoter.

Subject(s): Mystery, Singing, Murder

496 James Nelson Coleman

Seeker from the Stars

(New York, NY; Berkley Publishing Corp., 1967)

Summary: Coleman's 1967 science fiction novel focuses on an inter-planetary chase from Earth to Mars to Venus. Chris Everman, the book's protagonist, is assigned to Earth as part of a peace keeping force. However, he soon discovers that aliens intend to take over the galaxy. When he is captured by those aliens, Chris must find a way to escape so that he can save Earth from the aliens' evil designs. Coleman has been one of the few black writers to work in the genre of science fiction.

Subject(s): Science Fiction, Aliens

497 Wanda Coleman

African Sleeping Sickness: Stories & Poems

(Santa Rosa, CA; Black Sparrow Press, 1990)

Summary: Known for her chronicles of poor African Americans confronting racism and classism in contemporary Los Angeles, Coleman in *African Sleeping Sickness* mixes autobiographical poems with short stories in exploring her trademark urban literary terrain. One story in the collection depicts the protagonist confronting daily, minor incidents of racism (a store clerk examines money to make sure it's not counterfeit; a policeman stops her car for no reason other than race) that become an overwhelming psychological burden; another examines the friendship between an older woman trapped in a poverty-stricken ghetto and a younger woman who has escaped from it. All of the pieces showcase Coleman's use of polemic, anger, and wit to portray the realities of life for African Americans in present-day Los Angeles.

Subject(s): Poverty, Racism, Urban Affairs

498 Cyrus Colter

The Beach Umbrella

(Iowa City, IA; University of Iowa Press, 1970)

Summary: Cyrus Colter's first book, published when he was sixty years old, is a collection of short stories that examine the lives of contemporary African Americans struggling against difficulties ranging from alienation to loneliness to self-delusion. Written in the deterministic style made famous by Russian writers such as Anton Chekhov and Leo Tolstoy, the fourteen stories in this collection all feature African Americans living in Chicago. In the title story, a man borrows money from his teenaged son so that he can buy a beach umbrella. His hope is that the umbrella will allow him to make new friends on a local lakefront beach, but at the end of the day—despite brief interactions that give him hope of transcending his loneliness—he finds that he remains utterly alone and alienated. Rather than focusing on racism as a barrier to happiness, Colter portrays characters facing universal human dilemmas.

Subject(s): Racism, Loneliness

Award(s): University of Iowa School of Letters: Fiction Prize, 1971; Chicago Friends of Literature: Robert F. Ferguson Memorial Award, 1971

499 Cyrus Colter

The Hippodrome

(Chicago, IL; Swallow Press, 1973)

Summary: Controversial and provocative, Colter's second novel opens with a confused man, Yaeger, carrying his wife's head in a bag. Desperate to avoid detection, Yaeger meets a woman named Bea who offers him solace in her home. Once there, however, Yaeger discovers that Bea's true intention is to force him to perform in a hippodrome in her house, in which white customers pay to watch black men and women perform sexual acts with one another. Disgusted by the activity but unable to force himself to leave, Yaeger is finally ejected from the house by Bea. As in his other works, Colter here portrays a character buffeted by forces that he can neither explain nor control.

Subject(s): Murder, Sexual Behavior

500 Cyrus Colter

The Rivers of Eros

(Chicago, IL; Swallow Press, 1972)

Summary: After writing his first work of fiction—the short story collection *The Beach Umbrella*—at the age of sixty, Colter followed with his first novel two years later in 1972. *The Rivers of Eros*, based on the literary style of Greek tragedy, features African American characters buffeted by the past and challenged by universal human struggles that transcend race. The novel's protagonist is Clotilda, who is raising her grandchildren while running a boarding house. Worried that her past mistakes will inevitably doom her and her grandchildren, Clotilda isolates herself—an act that leads to her destruction. Meanwhile, Clotilda's boarders display a range of attitudes about the place of African Americans in contemporary society. While other black writers in the early 1970s were producing works that focused exclusively on African American issues, Colter in his early works explored black issues within the context of a larger human pageant.

Subject(s): Family Problems, African Americans, Boarding Houses

501 Clarence L. Cooper, Jr.

The Dark Messenger

(Evanston, IL; Regency Books, 1962)

Summary: The title of this work refers to a fictional black-owned and -operated newspaper that uses tabloid tactics to cover the news. Under the direction of a greedy management, the *Dark Messenger* capitalizes on the misfortune of those it covers. Cooper uses reporter Lee Merriweather, a conscientious young black man just out of college, to illustrate the parasitic ways of the newspaper.

Subject(s): Newspapers, Urban Affairs

502 Clarence L. Cooper, Jr.

The Farm: A Novel

(New York, NY; Crown Publishers, 1967)

Summary: The "farm" of Cooper's 1967 novel is a federal prison, where the protagonist--serving five years for drug trafficking--is transferred as the story begins. At the farm, the protagonist has an affair with a woman named Sonja. By the story's end, the man finds himself in jail in New York City. The novel is filled with adult language, sexual acts, and violence, all told in the author's trademark prose, in which words are often combined or invented.

Subject(s): Prisoners and Prisons, Sexuality, Violence

503 Clarence L. Cooper, Jr.

The Scene

(New York, NY; Crown Publishers, 1960)

Summary: Clarence Cooper's first novel, *The Scene,* established his reputation for creating searing literature about the urban dispossessed: drug users, prostitutes, and thieves. Set in a nameless urban ghetto, the novel features descriptions of "The Panic," a period in which there are no drugs to be found, and "The Man," a drug kingpin. Cooper wrote the novel while in prison for drug-related offenses.

Subject(s): Crime and Criminals, Drugs, Urban Affairs

504 Clarence L. Cooper, Jr.

Weed

(Evanston, IL; Regency Books, 1961)

Summary: Set amid the poverty-stricken, crime-ridden streets of an urban black ghetto, Clarence Cooper's 1961 novel fea-

tures Ned Land as its protagonist. Like the author himself, who was addicted to drugs and incarcerated for criminal offenses in the 1950s, Ned struggles against drug addiction and the temptations and dangers of the ghetto. Cooper's novels of the late 1950s and 1960s reveal how inner-city African Americans saw their communities ravaged by drugs and crime during this period.

Subject(s): Drug Abuse, Crime and Criminals, Urban Affairs

505 J. California Cooper

Family: A Novel

(New York, NY; Doubleday, 1991)

Summary: In *Family* J. California Cooper, best known for her collections of short stories and her plays, offers a novel that explores the world of slavery. The novel's narrator, Clora, describes her life experiences, as she and her family are ravaged by the white "Masters of the Land" but nevertheless survive with their strength and hope intact.

Subject(s): Slavery, Family, Racism

506 Donald J. Cotton

Sore Foots

(Washington, DC; Libratterian Books, 1972)

Summary: Edward Rois, nicknamed "sore foots" because of a deformity that causes him to limp slightly, is a teenager when this novel opens. The son of a prostitute who abandoned him when he was born, Edward has been raised by his Aunt Martha. Even though Edward gets a college scholarship to fictional Oliver University, Martha berates him for leaving her to attend college. At the end of the novel, Edward returns home.

Subject(s): Education, Family Relations

507 George Peter Crump, Sr.

From Bondage They Came

(New York, NY; Vantage Press, 1954)

Summary: This novel begins with a slave auction in the settlement of Jamestown, Virginia. As the story advances toward the future, the daughter of a slave owner, in order to fulfill her father's wishes, gives each of his freed slaves a tract of land from the Dauson plantation. She dies, however, without a written will to be found, leaving the ex-slaves with the prospect of losing their land to the state. James Dauson, a black alcoholic lawyer, realizes that he can make up for his past failures and win back the woman he loves if he can win this case for the plaintiffs.

Subject(s): Slavery, American South, Law

508 Paul Crump

Burn, Killer, Burn!

(Chicago, IL; Johnson Pub. Co., 1962)

Summary: This 1962 novel about the perils of criminal life is notable chiefly because of its author's lengthy imprisonment. Convicted of murder and sentenced to death in 1953, Crump stayed alive through legal and popular appeals for the next decade. His sentence was commuted in 1962—the same year this novel was published—and he was finally released from prison in 1993. During his early years in prison, Crump became interested in writing as a means to deter other men from committing crimes. His protagonist, Guy Morgan, Jr., is an impulsive, explosive character who is quick to take offense and who acts to protect his manhood from all threats.

Subject(s): Prisoners and Prisons, Crime and Criminals

509 Charles Davis

Two Weeks To Find a Killer
(New York, NY; Carlton Press, 1966)

Summary: This novel centers on Steve Brannon, a crime reporter for the *San Francisco Chronicle*, who enjoys drinking bourbon and attending matinees. When, while at a party, a friend asks him about an elderly woman who died during a mugging, he does not seem to be much affected. Brannon, however, comes to find himself immersed in a search for a serial killer who is targeting the city's women.

Subject(s): Murder, Serial Killer, Newspapers

510 Charles W. Davis

The Nut and Bolt
(New York, NY; Vantage Press, 1972)

Summary: At the beginning of Davis's 1972 novel, the eleven-year-old narrator, his sister, and their father move to Moline, Illinois, to begin a new life. George grows up and eventually fights in World War II. After returning from the war, George struggles with the lack of economic opportunity afforded to blacks at the time. At the end of the novel, he searches for and finds Carol, a white woman with whom he had previously had a son. The two realize that they still love each other, and they marry.

Subject(s): City and Town Life, Race Relations, Love

511 George Davis

Coming Home
(New York, NY; Random House, 1971)

Summary: Davis's 1971 novel is one of the few works by an African American author to focus on the Vietnam War of the 1960s and 1970s. *Coming Home* is a story of dehumanization, racism, brutality, and the horrors of war. The novel focuses on three characters: Ben, a Harvard-educated black man who fights in Vietnam; Childress, a black Air Force pilot; and Stacy, a white man whose racist and sexist attitudes lead to his death. Davis's bleak vision echoes those who saw America's involvement in Vietnam as a doomed action by a racist society bent on domination.

Subject(s): Vietnam War, Racism, Violence

512 Joseph A. Davis

Black Bondage: A Novel of a Doomed Negro in Today's South
(New York, NY; Exposition Press, 1959)

Summary: Set in Richmond, Virginia, this 1959 novel examines a racist, white-dominated political machine and its efforts to crush the spirits of the local African American population. The machine is led by James Crow, a United States senator from Virginia. After a riot in Richmond, Crow manages to persuade local law enforcement and judicial officials to arrest, convict, and sentence seven black men to death for their role in the riot. Despite the innocence of the men, Crow succeeds, and the men are executed. Davis focuses his story on one of the seven men, Wesley Ravenell.

Subject(s): City and Town Life, Judicial System, Racism

513 Corinne Dean

Cocoanut Suite: Stories of the West Indies
(Boston, MA; Meador Pub. Co., 1944)

Summary: This brief collection of short stories contains fourteen pieces. Each deals in some way with the cultural, political, and social life of early twentieth century Puerto Rico.

Subject(s): Politics, Culture

514 Samuel R. Delany

Babel-17
(New York, NY; Ace Books, 1966)

Summary: A groundbreaking science fiction writer in the 1960s and one of a few African American writers working in the genre, Samuel R. Delany in *Babel-17* explores the relationship between language and humanity. The novel features a war between two human civilizations, the intergalactic society known as the Alliance and another civilization called the Invaders. The protagonist, Rydra Wong, is a famous poet who is called upon by her Alliance colleagues to break a secret Invaders code termed Babel-17. In deciphering the code, which is actually a computer program, Rydra comes face to face with a bevy of dangerous contradictions and nearly becomes overwhelmed by them. In the end, however, she is able to view Babel-17 in all of its complexity, and in so doing she helps the Alliance win the war. Among other concepts, Delany uses this novel's plot to critique the way in which language can be used to strip blacks of their identities. Delany's pioneering work in science fiction during the 1960s occurred while other African American writers were forging the "Black Arts" movement, which focused on black themes and issues as a way of revolutionizing white-dominated society.

Subject(s): Science Fiction, Language

Award(s): Science Fiction Writers of America: Nebula Award for Best Novel, 1966

Samuel R. Delany

The Battle of Beta-2
(New York, NY; Ace Books, 1965)

Summary: In this 1965 work, Delany utilizes elements from two main thematic sources: the Christian mythology of the nativity and renunciation, and a 1940s magazine story by famed science fiction practitioner Robert Heinlein about a civil war on a passenger ship. In the novel, a fleet of colonizing ships travels through space; one of the ships, designated Beta-2, is the conduit through which the humans receive communication from an intergalactic god. Delany's habit of referencing well-known myths as well as other literary pieces is seen in much of his other work.

Subject(s): Science Fiction, Christianity, Civil War

516 **Samuel R. Delany**

Dhalgren
(New York, NY; Bantam Books, 1975)

Summary: Experimental and challenging but a huge popular success nonetheless, *Dhalgren* is the story of a young man in search of his identity. Apparently suffering from amnesia, the protagonist enters the chaotic city of Bellona, where he has numerous adventures. He becomes an acclaimed poet and later the leader of a gang of teenagers known as the Scorpions. At the novel's end, he is ejected from the city by a mysterious natural disaster, and his observations upon leaving the city cast doubt on the reality of the city. In addition to subverting typical fictional structural elements such as a linear narrative, Delany relies heavily on symbol and myth and uses unusual linguistic patterns to tell his story. The novel was greeted with wildly divergent critical responses, but its commercial success was instrumental in cementing Delany's stature as one of the most influential science fiction writers of his day.

Subject(s): Science Fiction, Language, Identity

517 **Samuel R. Delany**

Driftglass: Ten Tales of Speculative Fiction
(Garden City, NY; Doubleday, 1971)

Summary: This collection of short stories contains numerous award-winning pieces, including "Aye and Gomorrah...," "We, In Some Strange Power's Employ, Move on a Rigorous Line," and "Time Considered as a Helix of Semi-Precious Stones," which all won Nebula awards. Each of the stories in the collection had been previously published in an anthology or magazine, and each was written while Delany was at work on a longer project—typically a novel.

Subject(s): Science Fiction

518 **Samuel R. Delany**

The Einstein Intersection
(New York, NY; Ace Books, 1967)

Summary: Set on Earth thirty thousand years in the future, this novel is a meditation on the nature of myth and its meaning to society. The novel's basic plot line involves Lo Lobey, one of a new race of beings who are constantly mutating while trying to become more human, who sets out to kill the destructive character of Kid Death and find his beloved, Friza. Unsure of how to proceed in a world defined by irrationality, Lo eventually accepts the realities of his world and chooses a course of action. At the end of the novel, he has killed Kid Death and won and lost Friza. The novel is based on the Incompleteness Theorem (1931) of Austrian-American logician Kurt Godel, which states that some elements of mathematics cannot be proven by using mathematics. Unlike the writers of the "Black Arts" movement in the 1960s, who focused exclusively on black themes and issues, Delany in this and other works treats race as only one part of the larger human question of identity and "difference."

Subject(s): Science Fiction, Mythology, Identity

Award(s): Science Fiction Writers of America: Nebula Award for Best Novel, 1967

519 **Samuel R. Delany**

Empire Star
(New York, NY; Ace Books, 1966)

Summary: *Empire Star* is interesting for its unusual structure, which is modeled after a cycloid—the curve that a point on the circumference of a rolling circle creates as the circle moves on a straight line. Described at the beginning of the novel, the cycloid pattern of the novel actually functions as a spiral, so that the events in the novel do not merely repeat themselves (as in a circular novel) but are moved forward. The basic plot involves the history of a galactic civilization and the freeing of an enslaved race of artisans. In keeping with the novel's structure, there are but a handful of characters, and these characters reappear throughout the novel at different ages; sometimes, a character will even interact with older or younger versions of himself. Another notable feature of the book is that Delany refers to it in his previous published novel, 1966's *Babel-17*. Delany uses this self-referential technique throughout his work to further emphasize the structural element of his fiction.

Subject(s): Science Fiction, Slavery

520 **Samuel R. Delany**

The Fall of the Towers
(New York, NY; Ace Books, 1970)

Summary: This 1970 work comprises a trilogy that includes *Captives of the Flame* (1963), *The Towers of Toron* (1964), and *City of a Thousand Suns* (1965). Written when Delany was in his early twenties, the trilogy is set on a post-apocalyptic Earth island in the distant future. On this island, known as Toromon, the residents are besieged by an out-of-control computer that creates a psychic war existing only in the residents' minds. As in virtually all of his early novels, Delany uses mythological elements to add power and depth to the story lines.

Subject(s): Science Fiction, Mythology, War

521 Samuel R. Delany

The Jewels of Aptor
(New York, NY; Ace Books, 1962)

Summary: Delany's first published novel, written when he was only nineteen years old, reveals the elements that would make him one of the leading science fiction writers of the 1960s and 1970s. Set on Earth in the distant future, the novel follows the basic format of the Greek myth of Jason and the Argonauts. The protagonist, Geo, is part of a crew of sailors that sails to a mysterious island in search of an important jewel. The story culminates in the theft of this jewel from a huge idol. Among the elements that would be seen in Delany's later works are the quest story, the young artist/criminal as protagonist, and the reliance and focus on mythology as a controlling narrative element.

Subject(s): Science Fiction, Mythology, Stealing

522 Samuel R. Delany

Nova
(Garden City, NY; Doubleday, 1968)

Summary: A self-referential novel about the creation of novels and of life itself, *Nova* features standard Delany elements: a battle between civilizations, a quest as a central narrative catalyst, and a use of mythological concepts and ideas. The central character is Lorq Von Ray, who attempts to gain control of civilization and vanquish his enemies by capturing the basic power source in his universe. A long list of secondary characters—including a pair of twins, one of whom is black and the other white—complement the protagonist and provide a forum for additional mythic elements in the story.

Subject(s): Science Fiction, Mythology, Creation

523 Samuel R. Delany

The Tides of Lust
(New York, NY; Lancer Books, 1973)

Summary: Though widely known for his science fiction in the 1960s and 1970s by the early 1970s, Delany was also beginning to move beyond the boundaries of the genre. Comics and adult fantasy would later follow, but in this 1973 work Delany used pornography to explore a new realm of speculative fiction. The novel, intricately structured in the manner of all Delany works, features hetero- and homosexual sex, sadomasochism, mixed-race sex, rape, incest, and orgies. The characters chiefly function as symbolic archetypes, and Delany uses them to explore themes of knowledge, creativity, and chaos. A central motif is modeled on the Faust legend, in which a man sells his soul to the devil in exchange for power and knowledge.

Subject(s): Pornography, Sexuality, Science Fiction

524 Samuel R. Delany

Triton
(New York, NY; Bantam Books, 1976)

Summary: In this 1976 work, Delany presents a psychological utopia in which all forms of social interaction are possible. Although the future world in which *Triton* is set contains many of the chaotic elements seen in his landmark novel *Dhalgren*, here the plot is more stable and accessible to readers. The novel contains two appendices that serve as explanations for the web of semiological thought that is the foundation for the plot.

Subject(s): Science Fiction, Sociology

525 William Demby

Beetlecreek: A Novel
(New York, NY; Rinehart, 1950)

Summary: Based on a short story he wrote for a writing class taught by Robert E. Hayden at Fisk University, William Demby's acclaimed first novel is set in the small-town West Virginia of his own childhood. In the novel, protagonist Johnny Johnson is sent to live with his uncle and aunt in the town of Beetlecreek. Once there, the teenaged Johnny joins a gang of other teenaged boys, a decision that has tragic consequences. When a white man from the area moves beyond what are perceived as "normal" social boundaries, Johnny sees a chance to enforce discipline on the town and secure his status in the gang. Other characters in the novel lead similarly unhappy lives, a situation suggested by the novel's title: "Beetlecreek" refers both to the town and to the brackish creek running through the town in which debris is trapped and stays. In the same way, people are trapped and crushed in Beetlecreek. In his work, Demby—who spent several decades as an expatriate writer living in Italy—treats race as merely one aspect among many that drive humanity.

Subject(s): Gangs, Murder, Teen Relationships

526 William Demby

The Catacombs
(New York, NY; Pantheon Books, 1965)

Summary: Set in Rome, Italy, during the early 1960s—where Demby himself lived at the time—Demby's second novel explores the themes of death, renewal, and self-awareness. The novel features a narrator named Bill Demby, and its chief plot line involves the relationship between a fictional Count and his beloved, Doris. There is significant Christian imagery in the novel; the main characters approach death and are reborn. As in Demby's other works, here he treats race within the context of universal human qualities.

Subject(s): Love, Christianity

527 William Demby

Love Story Black

(New York, NY; Reed, Cannon & Johnson Co., 1978)

Summary: A mixture of fantasy, satire, and realism mark Demby's third novel, which is set in New York City during the late 1960s. The life of the narrator, Edwards, resembles Demby's own life as a former expatriate who has returned to New York and now is a university professor. His life takes a turn when he is hired by a trendy black periodical to profile an aging entertainer, Mona Pariss, with whom he becomes obsessed. Secondary plot lines involve his lover, Hortense Schiller, and the pseudo-revolutionary students who challenge him in class. Unlike his previous novels, in *Love Story Black*, Demby deals directly with issues of race—although he does so with his own unique artistic vision.

Subject(s): Love, Race Relations

528 Henry Denker

Payment in Full

(New York, NY; W. Morrow, 1991)

Summary: The family at the center of Henry Denker's 1991 novel is a nontraditional one. Rebecca and David Rosen are a young immigrant couple in New York City who learn that they will not be able to have children of their own. They decide to adopt an eight-year-old orphaned black girl, Elvira Hitchens. The novel follows this new family from its Depression-era beginnings in the 1930s through the Civil Rights movement of the 1950s and 1960s and in to the 1980s, as the three defy bigotry and narrow-mindedness from every side. In the end, the novel works as a plea for tolerance and understanding.

Subject(s): Family Saga, Adoption, Racism

529 Dorothy Lee Dickens

Black on the Rainbow

(New York, NY; Pageant Press, 1952)

Summary: The protagonist of Dickens's 1952 novel is a conflicted young woman who dreams of stardom in the New York theater world. Light-skinned and ambitious, Hilda Parker decides to "pass" for white once she gets to New York. However, once Hilda's true racial identity is revealed, her managers ruin any chance she has for work. Hilda later joins a dance troupe in Europe but meets misfortune when her boyfriend slashes her face with a knife. Back home in Columbus, Georgia, Hilda finally finds community support, and she meets and marries a conservative local minister.

Subject(s): Race Relations, Identity, Theater

530 Melvin Dixon

Vanishing Rooms

(New York, NY; Dutton, 1991)

Summary: In his fiction, Melvin Dixon explores the nature of identity from his perspective as a gay African American. Nowhere are the two strains of his focus more apparent than in this 1991 novel, which features three alternating narrators: Jesse, a gay black dancer whose white lover, Metro, is brutally gangraped and murdered; Ruella, a fellow dancer and friend of Jesse's; and Lonny, a white teenager who is confused about his sexuality and who contributes to Metro's murder. Jesse eventually begins to see connections between Metro's murder and the racially motivated hatred that is part of the novel's urban landscape.

Subject(s): Race Relations, Homosexuality/Lesbianism, Violence

531 Owen Dodson

Boy at the Window: A Novel

(New York, NY; Farrar, Straus & Giroux, 1951)

Summary: Though perhaps best known as a dramatist, Owen Dodson was also an accomplished poet and novelist. *Boy at the Window,* which is perhaps his most acclaimed work of fiction, is a semi-autobiographical, coming-of-age novel featuring a sensitive boy named Coin Foreman. Growing up in the multicultural landscape of 1920s Brooklyn, New York, Coin is devastated by the death of his mother. He is angered and confused by the fact that his religious conversion was not enough to save his mother's life. Not surprisingly, Dodson used his gifts as a poet to craft prose that is rich in imagery and metaphor.

Subject(s): Childhood, Death, Religion

532 Owen Dodson

Come Home Early, Child

(New York, NY; Popular Library, 1977)

Summary: Written by drama instructor and professor Owen Dodson, the novel *Come Home Early, Child* is a sequel to Dodson's first novel, 1951's *Boy at the Window.* The semiautobiographical work finds protagonist Coin Foreman now grown into manhood and preparing to leave his multi-ethnic working-class Brooklyn neighborhood to join the navy. Coin has a love affair in Italy, then returns to his Brooklyn home to come to terms with a past that includes the loss of his mother and a religious conversion. The novel, which Dodson wrote while on a Guggenheim fellowship in Italy, is richly poetic, its second section bordering on the surrealistic.

Subject(s): Coming-of-Age, Travel, Working-Class Life

533 Mary Drummond

Come Go with Me: High Rock and Spring Bank

(Philadelphia, PA; Dorrance, 1973)

Summary: In her 1973 novel, Mary Drummond pays homage to the beauty of Virginia and to the virtues of strong family ties. The protagonist of the novel, Maggie, remembers her bucolic childhood on a farm in Virginia, where her strong, principled father forged a happy life for his family.

Subject(s): Farm Life, Family Relations, Childhood

---

534 **David Graham Du Bois**

...And Bid Him Sing: A Novel
(Palo Alto, CA; Ramparts Press, 1975)

Summary: David Graham Du Bois, the son of author Shirley Graham Du Bois and the stepson of W.E.B. Du Bois, set this novel in Cairo, Egypt, where he himself lived during the 1960s and early 1970s. The novel follows a group of black American expatriates who move to Africa in search of identity and an escape from racism. These exiles include Suliman, a rebel poet, and Bob Jones, a journalist who also narrates the story. In addition to focusing on the Americans' relationship with their homeland, the novel also explores Egyptian politics, including a growing mistrust of all Americans and the buildup to the 1967 war with Israel.

Subject(s): Africa, Racism

---

535 **Shirley Graham Du Bois**
(Also known as Shirley Graham)

Zulu Heart: A Novel
(New York, NY; Third Press, 1974)

Summary: In her only novel, Shirley Graham Du Bois explores the political and cultural landscape of apartheid-era South Africa. The novel's protagonist, Kirk Vermeer, is a wealthy white Afrikaaner whose promising medical career is suddenly derailed when he suffers a massive heart attack. In order to live, Kirk undergoes a heart transplant in which he receives the heart of a black miner. Afterward, he begins to experience strange dreams and compulsions, and he eventually realizes that his heart belonged to the son of a Zulu chief. Compelled by a destiny that he cannot fight, Kirk casts away his previous life and becomes a leader of the black resistance movement. He is eventually killed in a raid on a notorious prison, but his spirit lives on in the son he has fathered with a black South African woman. The author's achievement in depicting the violent landscape of 1970s South Africa is considerable.

Subject(s): Medicine, Rebellion

---

536 **W.E.B. Du Bois**

Mansart Builds a School
(New York, NY; Mainstream Publishers, 1959)

Summary: In the second installment in his "Black Flame" trilogy, Du Bois covers African American history from 1912, just prior to World War I, to 1932, when Franklin Roosevelt became President of the United States at the beginning of the Great Depression. Focusing the action in Atlanta, Georgia, Du Bois follows Manuel Mansart as he develops and guides the Georgia Colored State College. Numerous historical figures move through the novel, including Booker T. Washington,

entertainer and activist Paul Robeson, and Du Bois's own wife, author Shirley Graham Du Bois.

Subject(s): Racial Conflict, World War I, Education

---

537 **W.E.B. Du Bois**

The Ordeal of Mansart
(New York, NY; Mainstream Publishers, 1957)

Summary: *The Ordeal of Mansart* is the first installment in Du Bois's "Black Flame" trilogy, which depicts African American history from Reconstruction to the beginning of the Civil Rights movement in the 1950s. In this first volume, Du Bois focuses on the period from the Reconstruction era of the 1870s to 1916. The chief protagonist is Manuel Mansart, the son of a former slave who attends college in Atlanta and witnesses key events there, including the race riots of September 1906. At the end of the novel, Manuel rejects an offer to be the head of a school in Indiana so that he can remain in Atlanta and be the "black flame" for social justice.

Subject(s): Race Relations, Reconstruction, Politics

---

538 **W.E.B. Du Bois**

Worlds of Color
(New York, NY; Mainstream Publishers, 1961)

Summary: This novel is the final volume in Du Bois's fictional trilogy known as "The Black Flame." The action begins in the early 1930s, when the United States was mired in the Great Depression and many intellectuals and activists had begun to advocate Communism—which they believed would bring equality and social justice. Although the trilogy's first two installments had been set chiefly in Atlanta, Georgia, *Worlds of Color* ranges widely from Africa to the West Indies to the United States. Du Bois comments on the dying nature of colonial rule and the rise of black freedom around the world. The novel ends in the 1950s with Manuel Mansart's death at the age of seventy-eight.

Subject(s): Race Relations, Africa, Colonialism

---

539 **Henry Dumas**

Ark of Bone, and Other Stories
(Carbondale, IL; Southern Illinois University Press, 1970)

Summary: The oppression and danger experienced by southern blacks during the civil rights movement are key themes of Henry Dumas's first collection of short stories. In "The Crossing," for instance, a group of black children on their way home from Sunday school tease each other mercilessly, only subconsciously aware of the threats to their safety in a racist, violent landscape. That awareness comes to the surface when one of the boys relates the real-life story of Emmett Till, a black teenager from the North who was lynched in 1953 for saying hello to a white girl in a small-town southern store. Another story, "A Boll of Roses," juxtaposes the arrival of civil rights workers from the North—Dumas himself was one—with the cultural and class conflicts that occurred when those workers interacted with poor southern African Americans. Dumas was keenly interested and involved in the civil rights struggles during the 1960s, and his fiction displays his sense of the history of racism, oppression, and poverty that created the need for social change.

Subject(s): Civil Rights Movement, Racism, American South

---

540 **Henry Dumas**

Jonoah and the Green Stone

(Harlem, NY; Random House, 1976)

Summary: The title character of Dumas's unfinished novel is based on the biblical stories of Noah—builder of the Ark and survivor of a great flood—and Jonah, a prophet who became trapped in the belly of a whale. As the novel opens, six-year-old Jonoah struggles to stay alive during terrible flooding in his native Mississippi. His family dies, but he finds a surrogate family after the flood. After he grows up, he leaves his adopted family for the jungle of Harlem in New York City. There, he finds himself stuck inside a metaphorical beast of a depraved environment. He regains his sense of purpose when he returns to his family in the South, determined to assist the civil rights movement of the 1960s. It is not clear how Dumas intended to end the story; similarly, the "Green Stone" of the title remains unexplained in the author's unfinished manuscript. Dumas himself died at the age of thirty-four during the height of the civil rights movement, killed by a policeman on a train platform under mysterious circumstances.

Subject(s): Civil Rights Movement, Biblical Story, American South

---

541 **Larry Duplechan**

Blackbird

(New York, NY; St. Martin's Press, 1986)

Summary: With his second novel, the author revisits his protagonist Johnnie Ray Rousseau, who appeared in his debut novel, *Eight Days a Week*. This time, the story describes Johnnie Ray's "coming out" at the age of seventeen. The book has been acknowledged as the first black, gay coming-out novel.

Subject(s): Homosexuality/Lesbianism, Coming-of-Age

---

542 **Larry Duplechan**

Captain Swing: A Love Story

(Boston, MA; Alyson Publications, 1993)

Summary: The author's fourth novel again features his character Johnnie Ray Rousseau as the story's protagonist. Johnnie Ray is now in his mid-thirties and has lost the man he loved and several friends to AIDS. The story shows how he copes with the death of his estranged father and how he learns to love again.

Subject(s): Homosexuality/Lesbianism, AIDS (Disease), Fathers and Sons

---

543 **Larry Duplechan**

Eight Days a Week: A Novel

(Boston, MA; Alyson Publications, 1985)

Summary: The author's first novel introduces his literary alter ego, Johnnie Ray Rousseau, who is young, black, gay, middle class, and college educated. The partially autobiographical story shows its protagonist involved in an interracial gay relationship and follows his attempt at a singing career. The novel was ignored by the mainstream press but well received by the gay press in general. The author, however, was criticized by some African American gay critics for his portrayal of the main character.

Subject(s): Musicians, Homosexuality/Lesbianism, Miscegenation

---

544 **Larry Duplechan**

Tangled Up in Blue

(New York, NY; St. Martin's Press, 1989)

Summary: In this novel, the author's third, a love triangle serves as the vehicle for an exploration of the threat of AIDS. The story revolves around a young woman, her secretly bisexual husband, and their gay friend. The narrative is told from each individuals point of view and represents the author's concern with creating believable white characters. Having lost several friends to AIDS himself, the author was interested in writing a comic novel about the disease.

Subject(s): Homosexuality/Lesbianism, AIDS (Disease), Marriage

---

545 **Nivi-kofi A. Easley**

The Militants

(New York, NY; Carlton Press, 1974)

Summary: This novel focuses on Nick, a young black man who lives in a slum in New York and has just been promoted to working in his company's all-white office. Nick's anger at society's racism takes the form of militant operations involving train bombings and the killing of a police officer. Nick becomes involved with Gina, one of the white women in his office. When he tells her that he also loves Jackie, a black militant, Gina accepts the situation with little difficulty and the three move in together.

Subject(s): Racism, Miscegenation, Poverty

---

546 **Narena Easterling**

Gifts from God: Two Stories

(New York, NY; Pageant Press, 1953)

Summary: "Gifts from Le Bon Dieu," the first story in this 1953 collection, is set amid the Louisiana Cajun community on Bayou Noir. Jacqueline Latrelle looks forward to seeing her son, who has just become a doctor, as he returns home for Christmas. However, he is not able to make it. Despite her disappointment, Jacqueline directs her positive attitude toward the four young children of a local prostitute who is dying. The collection's second story, "The Gift Supreme," likewise features Louisiana Cajuns. The main character is Chet Ford, who has returned to New Orleans after several years earning his fame as a radio and print journalist abroad.

Subject(s): Love

547 Narena Easterling

A Strange Way Home
(New York, NY; Pageant Press, 1952)

Summary: Angus McBride has come to Beaux Arbres Plantation in Louisiana to investigate the murder of its owner, Colonel Leplan. There, he is quickly confronted with the South's particular form of racism and meets a teenaged girl named Letitia, who, he is shocked to find out, is not white. This girl with the strangely calm demeanor turns out to be the Colonel's illegitimate daughter, and once the crime is solved, she inherits his estate.

Subject(s): American South, Miscegenation, Racism

548 Junius Edwards

If We Must Die
(New York, NY; Urbanite Publishing Company, 1961)

Summary: The title of Edwards's sole novel is taken from a line in a poem by African American writer Claude McKay: "If we must die, let it not be like hogs." The poem was written in the context of World War I, while Edwards's novel is set following the Korean War in the 1950s. The protagonist, Will Harris, is a Korean War veteran who decides to register to vote in his small southern town. He is denied an application, however, and then fired from his job. Later, a group of whites attacks him in a forest, beating him severely and leaving him tied to a tree. While Will is able to free himself and seek help, his survival is doubtful as the novel ends. The novel received lukewarm critical response, with some critics characterizing the novel as an anachronistic throwback to the black novels of the 1920s and 1930s, when African American characters were besieged by forces beyond their control.

Subject(s): Racism, Violence, American South

549 S.W. Edwards

Go Now in Darkness
(Chicago, IL; Baker Press, 1964)

Summary: At the center of this novel is James Hardmore, or Jake, a racially mixed young man. Raised in Chicago, Jake attended a conservative midwestern college where he experienced prejudice before moving back to his hometown. Having once studied music, he now studies English and writes poetry. Jake is hospitalized but he secures his release, an action that only serves to perpetuate his sense of isolation.

Subject(s): Prejudice, Depression, Poetry

550 Teresa Ellis

No Way Back: A Novella
(New York, NY; Exposition Press, 1973)

Summary: The narrator of Ellis's novella recalls her childhood on the outskirts of New Orleans, where she and her siblings reveled in the lush, tropical beauty of Louisiana. The daughter of a white man and a black Creole woman, the narrator begins to experience the effects of racism as she grows older. She eventually marries, but the death of her beloved husband sends her on an emotional and physical journey from which she never recovers.

Subject(s): Marriage, Family Relations, Childhood

551 Trey Ellis

Platitudes
(New York, NY; Vintage Books, 1988)

Summary: Ellis's first novel is a comic tale about sexual politics. The chief characters are novelist Dewayne Wellington and feminist intellectual Isshee Ayam, who agree to collaborate on a novel about two teenagers living in New York City. Infused with song lyrics, restaurant menus, and even photographs purporting to show places mentioned in the novel, *Platitudes* offers an original perspective on relationships and art.

Subject(s): City Life, Sexuality, Comedy

552 Ralph Ellison
John F. Callahan, Editor

Flying Home and Other Stories
(New York, NY; Random House, 1996)

Summary: The thirteen stories in Ralph Ellison's posthumously published collection were written between 1937 and 1954, when Ellison was fairly young and when he was still developing the craft that would lead to the monumental novel *Invisible Man*. In the title story, a young black pilot crashes his plane during a training flight. When an old man and his son arrive at the scene, the pilot realizes that he is separated from the pair by a wide gulf of experience, economic class, and education. Later, however, the old man's experience and quick-thinking save the pilot from difficult circumstances. Other stories examine the practice of lynching and chronicle the exploits of two young friends. Six of the stories were unpublished during Ellison's lifetime.

Subject(s): Lynching, Class Conflict

553 Ralph Ellison

Invisible Man
(New York, NY; Random House, 1952)

Summary: Considered one of the supreme achievements in American literature, Ralph Ellison's *Invisible Man* chronicles the journey from naivete to maturity of an African American man. In telling the story of his protagonist's odyssey, Ellison draws numerous parallels between the main character and African Americans in general, so that the character's journey mirrors the experiences of blacks in America. From the opening scene in which black youths are blindfolded and cast into a violent "Battle Royal," through his move from the South to the urban North, the narrator is continually deceived and injured by those around him. Using a complex variety of images, metaphors, and symbols, Ellison depicts the protagonist's eventual realization that only he can create a meaningful existence for himself in a hostile world. In addition to the book's wide-ranging imagery, Ellison draws upon numerous literary and intellectual sources, from Booker T. Washington and Marcus Garvey to authors such as T.S. Eliot and Walt Whitman, in crafting his story. In the process he stakes his claim to the cultural traditions of both white and black America. The novel was awarded the National Book Award for fiction in 1953.

Subject(s): Coming-of-Age, Racism, Literature

Award(s): National Book Award: Fiction, 1953; National Newspaper Publishers: Russwurm Award, 1953

554   Ralph Ellison
John F. Callahan, Editor

Juneteenth
(New York, NY; Random House, 1999)

Summary: Although Ralph Ellison worked on this novel for nearly forty years, it remained unfinished at the time of his death in 1994. Ellison's literary executor, John F. Callahan, pieced together portions of the unfinished manuscript and published it as *Juneteenth* in 1999. The published story centers on a white politician, Bliss, and the black preacher who raised him. Hickman, the preacher, had hoped that Bliss would grow up to be a champion of racial tolerance; he instead becomes a calculating, racist senator. As he did in his masterpiece, *Invisible Man,* Ellison here examines identity and racism in a wholly American idiom that contains dazzling linguistic passages. The novel's title refers to the celebration of June 19, 1865, the day on which Union soldiers landed in Galveston, Texas, and informed the slaves there that they were free—eighteen months after Abraham Lincoln issued the Emancipation Proclamation.

Subject(s): Slavery, Racism, Politics

555   Rubynn M. English, Sr.

Citizen, U.S.A.
(New York, NY; Pageant Press, 1957)

Summary: The protagonist of English's 1957 novel, Steve Shaw, struggles to overcome generations of Southern racism and oppression and gain a healthier sense of identity. Raised in the South, Steve finds a surprising acceptance from white Europeans during his tour of duty in World War I. Later, after returning to America, he moves to Detroit and finds a job in a manufacturing plant. The novel concludes with a chapter that addresses the state of civil rights for African Americans in the mid-1950s, which is now remembered as the beginning of the Civil Rights movement that would profoundly alter the legal and social landscape in America during the 1960s.

Subject(s): Civil Rights Movement, Racism, American South

556   Ronald L. Fair

Hog Butcher
(New York, NY; Harcourt, Brace & World, 1966)

Summary: A sprawling work about truth, poverty, and corruption, Fair's second novel hinges on the mistaken murder of a promising black athlete and an attempted police cover-up. The young protagonist, Wilford Robinson, witnesses the shooting of the athlete by policeman who mistake him for a criminal. Later, Wilford finds himself besieged on all sides by adults who have something to gain by obscuring the truth. With the support of his mother, a poverty-stricken woman who relies on welfare, Wilford is able to uphold his integrity and tell the truth. For the novel's courtroom scenes, Fair drew upon his own experience working as a court reporter for twelve years.

Subject(s): Murder, Poverty, Law Enforcement

557   Ronald L. Fair

Many Thousand Gone: An American Fable
(New York, NY; Harcourt, Brace & World, 1965)

Summary: Ronald Fair's first novel is a fable set in a fictional town in Mississippi, where a malicious white slave-owning family has managed to defy the Civil War and keep numerous blacks as slaves well into the twentieth century. White rape of young black girls and lynching of black males is commonplace in the town, as the slave owners use force to crush the spirit of their black slaves. The book's hero, Little Jesse, is a rebellious young slave who manages to escape to Chicago to live with his father, who himself earlier escaped from the plantation. Little Jesse grows up to write a book about his town, prompting federal officials to investigate. In the novel's climax, though, it is the enslaved local blacks who save themselves, by revolting and incinerating the town.

Subject(s): American South, Slavery, Civil War

558   Ronald L. Fair

We Can't Breathe
(New York, NY; Harper & Row, 1972)

Summary: Set in Chicago during the 1930s, Fair's autobiographical 1972 novel explores the great migration of southern blacks to northern cities during the early twentieth century. The novel features the story of five boys who encounter poverty, racism, violence, and drugs in the urban ghetto of Chicago. In the end, only the narrator, Ernie, manages to overcome these threats and survive into manhood.

Subject(s): Racism, Violence, Coming-of-Age

Award(s): American Library Association: Best Book Award, 1972

559 Ronald L. Fair

World of Nothing: Two Novellas

(New York, NY; Harper & Row, 1970)

Summary: The two novellas in this award-winning collection are experimental pieces that explore the nature of religious hypocrisy. In "Jerome," an unusual child—the illegitimate offspring of a troubled woman and an unscrupulous preacher—precipitates his own death. Although Jerome is viewed by the townspeople as angelic, his mother perceives him as the devil's child. She eventually stabs him to death, but Fair makes it clear that Jerome was indeed not a devil but a black Christ. The title novella, "World of Nothing," is a fantastical tale set in Chicago that depicts the false promise of religious and political solutions as a means to overcome racism and oppression.

Subject(s): Racism, Religion, Murder

Award(s): National Institute of Arts and Letters: Arts and Letters Award, 1970

560 Ruth A. Fairley

Rocks and Roses

(New York, NY; Vantage Press, 1970)

Summary: Beth Holter has not spent much time in the town of Barton Woods, but in her short term as teacher she has won over both students and citizens alike. Trouble, however, arises when the conniving Eve Waters sees Beth as a threat to her ambition to become principal. Complicating matters still more is the richest man in town, Alf Allen, who, since the deaths of his wife and son in childbirth, has used his influence over the school board to the detriment of the school. Although Allen finally redeems himself before the school board, his action is too late to keep Beth, who by this time has begun to experience success as an artist in New York.

Subject(s): Education, Schools, City and Town Life

561 Clarence Farmer

Soul on Fire

(New York, NY; Belmont Books, 1969)

Summary: This autobiographical novel is narrated by a black writer who hates white America for having always treated him as an animal. He is a drug dealer living in Harlem who does not take drugs himself. For the power that he wields, he is grudgingly treated with respect by the corrupt police. A self-confessed rapist, he has murdered numerous whites, comparing the feeling he gets from murder to sexual excitement. He says that he is not afraid to die but prefers to live for his hate.

Subject(s): Racism, Murder, Drugs

562 Blanche Faulkner

The Lively House

(Los Angeles, CA; Crescent Publications, 1975)

Summary: When Jennifer and Stephanie return from their trip sooner than expected, their mothers realize something dreadful has happened. Jennifer's mother wonders what could have made her once "lively" daughter so silent. Yielding to her mother's insistence, Jennifer agrees to see the family physician. Once at the doctor's office, Jennifer and her fiance, Terrence, decide to unburden themselves. What they reveal is a ghost story in which Jennifer and Stephanie find themselves trapped in a house full of spirits until Terrence ensures the worldly safety of the daughters of two of the ghosts.

Subject(s): Ghosts

563 Ira Lunan Ferguson

The Biography of G. Wash Carter, White: Life Story of a Mississippi Peckerwood, Whose Short Circuit Logic Kept Him Fantastically Embroiled

(San Francisco, CA; Lunan Ferguson Library, 1969)

Summary: Introduced by the author as "a 'laughogenic' satirical novel," this work is based on actual events that Ferguson gleaned from newspaper clippings while living in the South during the 1950s. The protagonist, G. Wash Carter, is a "peckerwood"--local parlance for a poor southern white—and the novel follows his numerous comedic and tragic adventures.

Subject(s): American South, Comedy, Race Relations

564 Ira Lunan Ferguson

Ocee McRae, Texas: A Novel of Passion, Petroleum and Politics in the Pecos River Valley

(New York, NY; Exposition Press, 1962)

Summary: Ocee McRae is the protagonist of this popular romance novel set in the Texas oil industry. At the beginning of the novel, Ocee--initially named Mike Gulbranson--returns from World War II to find that his wife has married another man. Ocee then makes his way to Texas and begins working for an oil company. Strong, kind, and true, he eventually becomes wealthy and popular enough to run for Governor of Texas, a seat he wins on the day that he is assassinated.

Subject(s): Politics, Romance, Oil

565 Ira Lunan Ferguson

Which One of You Is Interracial?: A Novelette and Other Stories

(San Francisco, CA; Lunan Ferguson Library, 1969)

Summary: On the title page of this 1969 work, Ferguson describes the short tales in the book as "3 Enchanting Bedtime Stories for Adults." In addition to the title novella, the work contains "Husband Wanted: Must Be Single!" and "Red's Secretary versus the Lady Admiral." The collection's happy, humorous, apolitical nature places it in stark contrast to the better known works by African Americans of the late 1960s, when the politically engaged, social justice-themed "Black Arts" movement was in place.

Subject(s): Comedy

`566` Amanda Finch

Back Trail: A Novella of Love in the South
(New York, NY; Williams-Frederick Press, 1951)

Summary: This brief tale opens in 1900 with the courtship of Sarah by George. Unbeknownst to Sarah, however, George is only interested in her so that he can get closer to Sarah's younger, prettier sister, Baby. On George and Sarah's wedding day, George and Baby elope. Baby dies a year later, however, leaving George to raise their child on his own; Sarah, for her part, is overwhelmed by bitterness and self-pity. The tale then resumes in 1949, with a renewed meeting and romance between George and Sarah. This time, George goes through with the wedding.

Subject(s): Marriage, Love

`567` John T. Flemister

Furlough from Hell: A Fantasy
(New York, NY; Exposition Press, 1963)

Summary: In this "fantasy," Flemister tells the story of Zeno, who shocks his friends by returning to their lives several years after has died and been buried. Zeno explains that he is on a "furlough from Hell," in which he has been instructed by the Devil to lead several hundred new mortals to Hell. Flemister uses Zeno's story to argue for the civilizing effects of Christianity and its potential as a tool for social justice for African Americans.

Subject(s): Religion, Christianity

`568` Leon Forrest

There Is a Tree More Ancient than Eden
(New York, NY; Random House, 1973)

Summary: Leon Forrest's 1973 novel combines myth, folklore, and psychology to tell the story of a twelve-year-old boy who struggles to come to terms with his mother's recent death. In prose that combines street slang with Biblical references, the novel offers a searing depiction of family violence and pain.

Subject(s): Family Relations, Coming-of-Age, Death

`569` Christine Forte

A View from the Hill
(New York, NY; Vantage Press, 1964)

Summary: Josie Hamilton, the protagonist of Forte's 1964 novel, endures numerous troubles during her life. Her parents die when Josie is young, and later her husband is killed during World War II. When her daughter shamefully bears a child out of wedlock and then abandons her, Josie is forced to raise the child. Through love and guidance, Josie raises the child to be a caring and resourceful woman.

Subject(s): Childhood, Family Problems

`570` Edwina Gaines

Your People Are My People
(London, England; Great Western Pub. Co., 1962)

Summary: This novel opens with a Bible class in which one participant wants to know why blacks are in the worst position of any race. The story then moves to the Jones home, where the father, Newton, lies dying. Two daughters, Bianica and Gaynell, are at odds with other. Gaynell feels that her sister has betrayed her by acknowledging their father's impending death. At Newton's funeral, a white man speaks, saying that the recently deceased Jones was the one who convinced him to love blacks. Gaynell begins to accept her father's death and dreams of his entrance into heaven.

Subject(s): Family, Fathers and Daughters, Sisters

`571` Ernest J. Gaines

The Autobiography of Miss Jane Pittman
(New York, NY; Dial Press, 1971)

Summary: Widely considered Gaines's greatest fictional creation, this 1971 novel features an old woman, Miss Jane Pittman, who lives in a rural Louisiana hamlet. In the novel, Pittman narrates her century-long personal history, describing her own life and the lives of the people she meets and lives among. In telling the story of her own life, however, Pittman also narrates the history of African Americans from the Civil War of the 1860s through the Civil Rights movement of the 1960s.

Subject(s): Rural Life, Civil Rights Movement, Civil War

`572` Ernest J. Gaines

Bloodline
(New York, NY; Dial Press, 1968)

Summary: Each of the short stories in Gaines's 1968 collection is set in Bayonne, Louisiana, the fictional location that serves as the setting for most of the author's works. Thematically, many of the stories involve the relations between older and younger generations, particularly father-son relationships. In exploring these themes, Gaines displays his mastery of rural southern speech patterns, a mastery that would be used to its fullest effect in his 1971 novel, *The Autobiography of Miss Jane Pittman.*

Subject(s): Rural Life, Family Relations, Short Stories

573 Ernest J. Gaines

Catherine Carmier

(New York, NY; Atheneum, 1964)

Summary: Ernest J. Gaines's first novel introduces readers to the Louisiana plantation of Bayonne, a fictional creation that mirrors the rural plantation where Gaines himself was born and raised and which the author uses in many of his later works. In the novel, protagonist Jackson Bradley returns to Bayonne after attending college in California. Once home, Jackson falls in love with Catherine, the daughter of a Creole sharecropper. Catherine's father tries to separate Jackson and Catherine, believing that Jackson's darker skin makes Jackson beneath his daughter both socially and genetically. Another story line involves a clash of cultures that arises out of Jackson's schooling in California, which has given him a wider perspective on the world than can be found in Bayonne. In setting his novel during the Civil Rights movement of the 1960s, but making that movement of secondary concern in the novel, Gaines sets himself apart from other black writers of the 1960s who made political and social justice their primary artistic concern.

Subject(s): Civil Rights Movement, Love, Racial Conflict

574 Ernest J. Gaines

A Lesson before Dying

(New York, NY; A.A. Knopf, 1993)

Summary: Set in 1948 in the fictional Louisiana plantation region of Bayonne, Gaines's 1993 novel tells the story of Jefferson, an innocent and naive twenty-year-old black man who works on a local plantation. Jefferson's life takes a tragic turn when he befriends two white criminals who rob a liquor store, kill the owner, and are themselves killed—leaving Jefferson as the only living accomplice. Jefferson is convicted of murder and sentenced to die by an all-white jury, despite his lawyer's defense argument that Jefferson is merely a dumb animal that acted on command. Enraged by the lawyer's argument, Jefferson's godmother determines that Jefferson will die as a man and not an animal. She enlists the help of a local white teacher, who eventually helps Jefferson grow into his manhood before his execution. In so doing, though, the teacher learns valuable life lessons of his own. The novel was catapulted to the bestseller lists after talk-show host Oprah Winfrey chose it for her televised book club.

Subject(s): Rural Life, Judicial System, Education

575 Ernest J. Gaines

Of Love and Dust

(New York, NY; Dial Press, 1967)

Summary: A story about the challenges posed to the stratified social order of the rural South, Gaines's second novel revolves around a rebellious young black man named Marcus Payne. Marcus is bonded out of prison by a white landowner and put under the supervision of the landowner's brutal Cajun overseer, Sidney Bonbon. After Marcus falls in love with Sidney's wife, the two men eventually clash in a violent confrontation that

leaves Marcus dead. Gaines presents a decaying social and economic system in rural Louisiana in which his characters struggle—ultimately unsuccessfully—to break free.

Subject(s): Rural Life, American South, Racial Conflict

576 Edward Gholson

From Jerusalem to Jericho

(Boston, MA; Chapman & Grimes, 1943)

Summary: Edward Gholson offers a retelling of the Biblical tale of the Good Samaritan in his 1943 work. The story comes from the New Testament story of Luke and depicts a good-hearted traveler who assists a man who has been beaten and robbed.

Subject(s): Biblical Story

577 Donald Goines

(Also known as Al C. Clark)

Black Gangster

(Los Angeles, CA; Holloway House, 1972)

Summary: A complex and cynical depiction of the social justice movement of the early 1970s, *Black Gangster* epitomizes Goines's perspective of life in an urban black ghetto. In the novel, protagonist Prince Walker is released from jail but quickly returns to his criminal ways—dealing drugs, stealing, and extorting. In order to provide cover and fuel for his gang, The Rulers, Prince sets up a bogus social-justice organization called "Freedom Now Liberation Movement" (FNLM). Prince exploits the well-meaning members of FNLM to strengthen his gang. As in his other novels of ghetto realism, Goines paints a grim portrait of life in violent, poverty-stricken inner cities.

Subject(s): Urban Affairs, Drug Abuse, Crime and Criminals

578 Donald Goines

(Also known as Al C. Clark)

Black Girl Lost

(Los Angeles, CA; Holloway House, 1973)

Summary: Perhaps inspired by the 1972 birth of his daughter, Goines in *Black Girl Lost* offers a touching and sympathetic portrait of a young girl trying to make her way through the minefields of an inner-city urban ghetto. The protagonist grows up virtually alone from the age of eight, and Goines depicts her valiant struggle to maintain her dignity and humanity in the face of overwhelming obstacles.

Subject(s): Urban Affairs, Violence, Coming-of-Age

579 Donald Goines

(Also known as Al C. Clark)

Daddy Cool

(Los Angeles, CA; Holloway House, 1974)

Summary: Like virtually all of Goines's novels, *Daddy Cool* is set amid the urban wasteland of an inner-city black ghetto. In the novel, the title character is a successful hit man—a murderer for hire. The protagonist is moved by the love he feels for his daughter, but ultimately that love destroys him. Tellingly, almost all of Goines's protagonists die violent deaths; Goines himself was murdered under suspicious circumstances along with his wife in 1974.

Subject(s): Urban Affairs, Murder, Children

580 **Donald Goines**

(Also known as Al C. Clark)

Dopefiend: The Story of a Black Junkie

(Los Angeles, CA; Holloway House, 1971)

Summary: In his second novel (but first to be published), Goines offers a scathing indictment of heroin addiction—a condition that dominated Goines's own life for most of his adult years. The novel's protagonists are two young black lovers, Teddy and Terry, whose middle-class comfort is gradually replaced by the nightmare of heroin addiction in Detroit's urban ghetto. The third central character is Porky, the sadistic drug kingpin who supplies the heroin and who calls the shots from his hellish dope house. Goines wrote the novel while in prison for larceny; when he was released, he tried to stay drug-free but eventually returned to his heroin-addicted lifestyle.

Subject(s): Urban Affairs, Drug Abuse, Crime and Criminals

581 **Donald Goines**

(Also known as Al C. Clark)

Inner City Hoodlum

(Los Angeles, CA; Holloway House, 1975)

Summary: After Donald Goines was murdered along with his wife in his Detroit home in 1974, friends found a completed manuscript on a shelf by Goines's desk. That manuscript was published as *Inner City Hoodlum* in 1975. Set in the Watts ghetto of south central Los Angeles (where Goines lived for several years), the novel tells the story of a pair of teenaged criminals who exact vengeance on a neighborhood hustler. In the four years prior to his death, the prolific Goines wrote more than fifteen novels and established the genre of ghetto realism, fueled by his own lifetime of criminal experiences in the inner-city ghettos of Detroit and Los Angeles.

Subject(s): Urban Affairs, Murder

582 **Donald Goines**

(Also known as Al C. Clark)

Street Players

(Los Angeles, CA; Holloway House, 1973)

Summary: In *Street Players,* Goines offers another harrowing depiction of life amid the drug dealers, prostitutes, and pimps of an inner-city black ghetto. The novel's protagonist, Earl the Black Pearl, is a successful drug dealer and pimp. However, as often happens in the dog-eat-dog milieu of Goines's fiction, his world falls apart when his girlfriend and best friend are murdered and he loses his wealth. Eventually, Earl too is murdered, in keeping with the author's vision of the ghetto as a place from which no one escapes with his life or soul intact.

Subject(s): Urban Affairs, Drug Abuse, Prostitution

583 **Donald Goines**

(Also known as Al C. Clark)

Swamp Man

(Los Angeles, CA; Holloway House, 1974)

Summary: This 1974 novel is the only Goines effort that is not set in an inner-city black ghetto (usually Goines's birthplace of Detroit or his later hometown of Los Angeles). The novel is set in the swamps of an unnamed southern state. Although the setting is different, the novel's action is consistent with the author's other novels of ghetto realism. The plot features copious sadistic violence and sex. While Goines was never lauded for his prose style or for the complexity of his plot development, many critics consider *Swamp Man* to be his least-accomplished novel.

Subject(s): Urban Affairs, Violence, American South

584 **Donald Goines**

(Also known as Al C. Clark)

White Man's Justice, Black Man's Grief

(Los Angeles, CA; Holloway House, 1973)

Summary: Goines's fourth major novel, a scathing portrait of the racist nature of America's criminal justice system, was published after he moved from Detroit to the Watts ghetto of south central Los Angeles. The novel's protagonist, Chester Hines, finds himself sentenced to four years in prison for carrying a concealed weapon. Once there, he befriends a fellow inmate, Willie Brown, and plans a robbery with Willie once the two are released from prison. Willie, however, is released first and commits the crime on his own. In carrying out the crime, Willie kills a guard. Willie is caught and charged with the crime, at which point he names Chester as his accomplice in the crime. Despite having been in prison hundreds of miles away at the time of the crime, Chester is sentenced to life in prison. Throughout the novel, Goines includes anecdotes about how blacks are treated more harshly than whites in the criminal justice system, and the book contains an "Angry Preface" in which the author argues his case explicitly.

Subject(s): Urban Affairs, Criminal Justice, Crime and Criminals

585 **Donald Goines**

(Also known as Al C. Clark)

Whoreson: The Story of a Ghetto Pimp

(Los Angeles, CA; Holloway House, 1972)

Summary: Considered the inventor of the fictional genre of ghetto realism, Goines wrote his first novel (but second to be published) while in prison for larceny. The novel revolves around Whoreson, a fourteen-year-old black youth who finds himself alone in inner-city Detroit following the death of his prostitute mother. Whoreson becomes a successful pimp who thrives because he understands the brutal reality of life in the ghetto: kill or be killed. The novel sets the tone for Goines's entire oeuvre, which paints a grim portrait of ghetto life in which the options for the poor blacks who live there are to either accept a miserable fate as a victim or join the aggressors who prey on those victims. Goines's protagonists usually choose the latter route, only to discover that being a predator has its spiritual cost and usually leads to a violent death.

Subject(s): Urban Affairs, Murder, Crime and Criminals

586 Marita Golden

Long Distance Life
(New York, NY; Doubleday, 1989)

Summary: Marita Golden's 1989 novel is an intergenerational family saga set in Washington, D.C. In the novel, young Naomi leaves her rural southern home in the 1920s for a better life in Washington. She marries a prosperous man and has children but loses part of herself in the process. Subsequently, her children and grandchildren become involved in the civil rights struggles of the 1960s.

Subject(s): Civil Rights Movement, Children, City and Town Life

587 Jewelle Gomez

The Gilda Stories: A Novel
(Ithaca, NY; Firebrand Books, 1991)

Summary: Gomez's first novel contains elements of numerous literary genres, from science fiction to mystery to lesbian romance. The title character, Gilda, is a runaway slave in the 1850s who becomes an immortal vampire. From 1890s New York to 1950s Massachusetts and into New Hampshire in the twenty-first century, Gilda pursues love while also battling for social justice. Gomez's own dual African American and Native American heritage is reflected in the novel's multicultural cast of vampires.

Subject(s): Slavery, Homosexuality/Lesbianism, Science Fiction

Award(s): Lambda Literary Award: Fiction, 1991; Lambda Literary Award: Science Fiction, 1991

588 Katheryn Campbell Graham

Under the Cottonwood: A Saga of Negro Life in Which the History, Traditions and Folklore of the Negro of the Last Century Are Vividly Portrayed
(New York, NY; W. Malliet and Company, 1941)

Summary: This novel is a family saga set in a small town in Texas and spans the period from the 1860s to the 1930s. Auto-biographically inspired, the story centers on a young girl whose adolescence is shaped by listening to the tales of ex-slaves under a cottonwood tree in town. The girl, Mamie, eventually grows up and attends college before marrying and returning to live in her hometown.

Subject(s): Slavery, Marriage, Rural Life

589 Lorenz Graham

Return to South Town
(New York, NY; Crowell, 1976)

Summary: The concluding segment in a four-volume series of novels for young adults, Lorenz Graham's *Return to South Town* finds protagonist David Williams successfully graduated from medical school and returning to his home town to practice his skills. Beginning with *South Town* in 1958, Graham's series reflects the successes of the civil rights movement, as David and his family find that their efforts to lead a normal life in a southern community grow easier with the passage of time. Graham wrote this and other books for young people to address what he saw as a need for books about black people "he most often saw": neither heroic activists nor the poor and downtrodden, but average men and women attempting to attain the American Dream.

Subject(s): Civil Rights Movement, Education, Small Town Life

590 Wade S. Gray

Her Last Performance
(Omaha, NE; Rapid Printing & Publishing Co., 1944)

Summary: The protagonist of Wade S. Gray's 1944 novel is a pianist. In the work, Gray explores the issues of love and marriage against the backdrop of the music world.

Subject(s): Love, Marriage, Music

591 Sam Greenlee

Baghdad Blues
(New York, NY; Bantam Books, 1976)

Summary: This 1976 novel by Greenlee grew out of his experiences as a foreign service officer in Iran during the 1950s, where he witnessed a revolution in 1958. In the novel, protagonist Dave Burrell finds himself torn between his loyalty to the American government--for whom he works as a service officer--and his sympathy with the local Arabs who are mobilizing to overthrow the American-backed regime. Burrell feels that the Arabs accept his blackness far more than do white Americans. Eventually, he turns down a request by the CIA to spy on his Arab friends, and he resigns from his job in order to study the revolution and possibly carry his knowledge back home to black Americans.

Subject(s): Violence, Rebellion, Racism

592 Sam Greenlee

The Spook Who Sat by the Door: A Novel

(New York, NY; Bantam Books, 1970)

Summary: *The Spook Who Sat by the Door* is a militant protest novel in the tradition of other such works that grew out of the "Black Arts" movement of the late 1960s, when many black artists and intellectuals began advocating violence as a method to end racism and achieve social justice. In the novel, former social worker Dan Freeman is hired by the Central Intelligence Agency (CIA) as a token black. From this position, Freeman uses his intelligence and anger to foment an organized revolution in the United States. Though he is eventually betrayed and killed, Freeman is successful in forcing the white military-industrial complex to reexamine its racism and its economic oppression of blacks.

Subject(s): Violence, Rebellion, Racism

593 John Wesley Groves, IV

Pyrrhic Victory: A Collection of Short Stories

(Philadelphia, PA; United Pub., 1953)

Summary: This collection consists of four short stories. "Stop Thief" concerns a boy who, confronted with poverty and prejudice, opts for of life of crime. The other stories in the volume deal with characters in different environments faced with similar problems. The stories can be traced to the author's interest in sociology and the psychology of the underprivileged black American.

Subject(s): Poverty, Crime and Criminals, Prejudice

594 Rosa Guy

Bird at My Window

(Philadelphia, PA; Lippincott, 1966)

Summary: Rosa Guy's first novel focuses on a family beset by dysfunction and by the corrosive forces of racism and poverty in 1960s Harlem. The central character, Wade, is a middle-aged man whose life has been marked by lost opportunities and violent episodes. Bedeviled and betrayed by his mother and older brother, Wade determines to kill them but instead accidentally kills his beloved sister, Faith. The Trinidad, West Indies-born Guy is best known for her young adult novels.

Subject(s): Racism, Violence, Family Problems

595 Rosa Guy

Ruby: A Novel

(New York, NY; Viking Press, 1976)

Summary: *Ruby* is the second installment in Rosa Guy's acclaimed young adult trilogy about two families living in Harlem. Specifically, the trilogy grew out of Guy's own experience as an African West Indian immigrant to New York City. In this novel, the title character is a lonely and alienated teenager. Although Ruby is ignored by her widowed father and bookish sister, her life improves when she develops a romance with a female friend. When the romance ends abruptly, Ruby tries to commit suicide but is stopped by her father. At the novel's end, he determines to reconnect with his two teenaged daughters. *Ruby* was acclaimed but stirred controversy with its lesbian romance.

Subject(s): Homosexuality/Lesbianism, Family Problems

596 Willie Hagan

The Black Tarnished Image

(New York, NY; Vantage Press, 1974)

Summary: This novel centers on Joe Wright, a black man who passes for white. When he decides to set up a legal consultant's office in a black neighborhood to benefit its residents, he befriends a jobless alcoholic named Al Bennett. While Al turns himself around and eventually is nominated for mayor, Joe murders the man who married his lover, Matherine, and raised his son, Leonard. Hoping to make amends with his son, Joe donates his money to an all-black hospital with fundraising overseen by the philanthropic (and white) Hoffman sisters. Leonard accepts the position of hospital administrator, and when his father dies, he takes to heart what his uncle Al had told him about the healing of wounds.

Subject(s): Murder, Fathers and Sons, Race Relations

597 Frances E.W. Harper
Frances Smith Foster, Editor

A Brighter Coming Day: A Frances Ellen Watkins Harper Reader

(New York, NY; Feminist Press at the City University of New York, 1990)

Summary: Considered perhaps the most important black feminist abolitionist of the nineteenth century, writer and activist Frances E.W. Harper (1825-1911) wrote groundbreaking poetry, short stories, and a landmark novel, *Iola Leroy*. This reader includes a comprehensive collection of her poetry and fiction as well as speeches and letters. In addition, Foster provides an introductory biographical essay as well as critical notes about Harper's writings.

Subject(s): Abolition, Slavery, Women

598 Charlie Avery Harris

Whore-Daughter

(Los Angeles, CA; Holloway House, 1976)

Summary: The title character of Harris's 1976 novel is a third-generation prostitute and the epitome of a femme fatale: she seduces and charms men before crushing them with her cruelty and hatred. Although beautiful and desired, Whore-Daughter resists the attempts of various men to "rescue" her from her life on the streets; one such man is a wealthy white doctor who actually adopts Whore-Daughter. She meets her match, however, in the powerful street gangster Junius. Like his friend and mentor, Donald Goines, Harris made his mark writing about the harsh world of black urban ghettos.

Subject(s): Prostitution, Urban Affairs

599 E. Lynn Harris

Invisible Life

(Atlanta, GA; Consortium Press, 1991)

Summary: The author's first novel is partly autobiographical in nature. The story focuses on Raymond Tyler, a black man who during high school and college is involved in a relationship with a young woman named Nicole. When Raymond finds himself attracted to a man during his senior year, he continues to date women, hiding from them his homosexual experiences. The novel explores the impact of AIDS on his life as well as his interest in having a family.

Subject(s): Homosexuality/Lesbianism, AIDS (Disease), College Life

600 E. Lynn Harris

Just as I Am: A Novel

(New York, NY; Doubleday, 1994)

Summary: The sequel to the novel *Invisible Life*, *Just as I Am* once again illustrates Harris's tremendous commercial appeal. Continuing the story of protagonist Raymond Tyler, and narrated by his former girlfriend, Nicole, the novel was not a favorite among critics but was notable for its treatment of gay life.

Subject(s): Homosexuality/Lesbianism, AIDS (Disease)

Award(s): Blackboard African-American Bestsellers, Inc.: Novel of the Year, 1996

601 James L. Harris

Endurance

(New York, NY; Vantage Press, 1972)

Summary: This novel, set in Harlem, opens on a Sunday. George Wilson attends church with his sister, Gloria, and his religious mother and grandmother. His mother, the head of the household, hosts a dinner that day for Reverend Shields. When Reverend Shields is about to leave, George is crushed by the reverend's embrace and notices the older man's sexual excitement, leaving George wondering if he had liked it, too. The narrative jumps ahead to find George studying law in the city of New York and not limiting himself to relationships with either men or women. George eventually becomes involved with a young woman, Janice, who dies from an illegal abortion after becoming pregnant by another man. The story culminates with George's graduation from law school, at which time he receives the gift of a new home from his lover, Baron.

Subject(s): Mothers and Sons, Homosexuality/Lesbianism, Religion

602 Marcus A. Hart

The Lover with a Killer's Instinct: A Novel

(New York, NY; Exposition Press, 1975)

Summary: The protagonist of Hart's 1975 novel, Rick Lane, is known for his adventures with women as well as his temper. He becomes attracted to a somewhat older woman named Irene, yet despite his interest in her he continues to have affairs with other women. He eventually joins the Air Force, which he believes will help keep him out of trouble. While on leave from basic training, he returns home to see Irene. Again he cheats on her, but manages to convince her to let him speak with her father about how much he has changed.

Subject(s): Military Life, Sexuality

603 Le Roi Rossetti Haskins

The Weak Arm of Justice

(New York, NY; Vantage Press, 1971)

Summary: According to the author in an introduction to the book, this work is a fictional version of true events. In the book, protagonists LeJohn Hyber and his wife Rebecca rent their downstairs flat to a promiscuous woman named Gertie. As the novel progresses, Gertie draws the Hybers deeper into her troubled life, eventually ensnaring LeJohn in a legal fight over financial matters. Although LeJohn is innocent, he is unable to convince the court of the true state of affairs.

Subject(s): Crime and Criminals, Judicial System

604 Christine Hathorn

The Undoing of Miss Abigail Wrigley: A Country Mystery

(New York, NY; Vantage Press, 1973)

Summary: This novel centers on Abbie, a spinster who lives with her cat. The novel's mystery opens when she receives a visit from Miss Samantha. When the two discuss a young man's death, Miss Samantha begins to make a connection between him and a woman who was accused of murdering her adulterous husband and who, following her acquittal, took custody of the mistress's child. At this point, Abbie kills Miss Samantha with a poisoned cup of tea. Miss Samantha is actually Abbie's third victim by this time, but when she attempts to create a fourth, she meets her "undoing."

Subject(s): Mystery, Murder

605 Nathan C. Heard

A Cold Fire Burning

(New York, NY; Simon and Schuster, 1974)

Summary: An interracial romance forms the heart of Heard's third novel. In the book, protagonist Shadow, a poor black man, struggles with his feelings toward Terri, a white social worker. The two are divided by race and class. Ultimately, Heard uses this interracial romance to explore the nature of the racial conflict in America.

Subject(s): Urban Affairs, Racial Conflict, Romance

606 **Nathan C. Heard**

Howard Street: A Novel
(New York, NY; Dial Press, 1968)

Summary: Heard's first novel, written while he was incarcerated in a New Jersey state prison, is set in the 1960s amid the brutal ghetto world of inner-city Newark, New Jersey—where Heard grew up. The novel focuses on two brothers, one of whom is a common criminal and the other of whom tries to live a "straight" life free of crime. It includes a wide assortment of supporting characters drawn from Newark street life: cops, prostitutes, pimps, and drug dealers. Heard was one of several African American writers who began working in the "urban realism" genre during the 1960s and 1970s, a genre that focused on the dehumanizing nature of life in poverty-ridden inner-city ghettos.

Subject(s): Urban Affairs, Crime and Criminals, Poverty

607 **Nathan C. Heard**

To Reach a Dream
(New York, NY; Dial Press, 1972)

Summary: In his second novel, Heard once again returns to the black ghetto world of inner city Newark, New Jersey. The novel's protagonist, Bart, tries to re-establish his worth in the ghetto after being released from prison. Dreaming of becoming a big-time hustler with money, women, and cars to spare, Bart has visions of being the "kept" man of a wealthy black woman for whom he is working. However, conflicts arise when Bart meets and falls in love with the woman's daughter. Eventually, Bart convinces the daughter that they must murder her mother to have any chance at happiness, a decision that leads to Bart's destruction and to the daughter's insanity. The world that Heard depicts in the novel is one in which poverty and despair result in diminished opportunities and crushed humanity.

Subject(s): Urban Affairs, Crime and Criminals, Murder

608 **Marcy Moran Heidish**

A Woman Called Moses: A Novel Based on the Life of Harriet Tubman
(Boston, MA; Houghton Mifflin, 1976)

Summary: In Marcy Heidish's *A Woman Called Moses: A Novel Based on the Life of Harriet Tubman*, the life of one of the most notable conductors on the Underground Railroad is brought to life for younger readers. Tubman escaped from slavery but returned to the South nineteen times, leading over 300 blacks to freedom in the North. Given the name "Moses" due to her selfless efforts to lead her people to freedom, Tubman also served as a spy, nurse, and scout for the Union Army during the Civil War.

Subject(s): Slavery, American South, Civil War

609 **George Wylie Henderson**

Jule
(New York, NY; Creative Age Press, 1946)

Summary: Henderson's second novel is a sequel to his only other novel, 1935's *Ollie Miss*. In this subsequent effort, Henderson focuses on Jule, the illegitimate son of the self-reliant Ollie of the first novel and her boyfriend, Jule the elder. As a young man growing up in rural Alabama, Jule falls in love with a local black girl, but a conflict with a brutally racist white man forces Jule to leave his home for New York City, an event that mirrors the large migration of African Americans from the rural South to the urban North during the 1930s and 1940s. Once in New York City, Jule finds that the cultured North is as racist as the old South; he also is initiated into big-city vices such as liquor and gambling. Despite obstacles, however, Jule calls on the same self-reliance that characterized his mother, eventually finding a measure of safety and job security in New York.

Subject(s): City and Town Life, American South, Rural Life

610 **Frank Hercules**

I Want a Black Doll
(New York, NY; Simon and Schuster, 1967)

Summary: In his second novel, Hercules explores the issue of interracial marriage. His protagonist, Dr. John Lincoln, is a mixed-race African American from the North who is unaware that his father was a white man. He courts and marries a wealthy white woman from the South, Barbara Wakely, but eventually the marriage collapses under the strain of the pair's own prejudices and the pressure of a racist society. Both John and Barbara meet tragic ends: Barbara dies during an abortion, while John is murdered by Barbara's old boyfriend, a racist white man who is in fact John's half-brother.

Subject(s): Murder, Racial Conflict, Marriage

611 **Frank Hercules**

Where the Hummingbird Flies
(New York, NY; Harcourt, Brace, 1961)

Summary: Frank Hercules became a U.S. citizen as an adult, although his early years in the 1920s and 1930s were spent in Trinidad, West Indies, which at that time was a British colony. It is this era that Hercules evokes in his first novel, *Where the Hummingbird Flies*. In the novel, Hercules depicts colonial-era Trinidad as a fading, class- and race-conscious society. Through the character of Dulcina, a laundress, Hercules offers a folk heroine whose strength, pride, and determination point the way toward political self-expression and nationalism for West Indian blacks. Hercules himself was forcibly exiled from Trinidad as an adult for advocating an end to British colonial rule.

Subject(s): Colonialism, Racism, Class Conflict

Award(s): Bread Loaf Writers' Conference, Middlebury College: Fletcher Pratt Memorial Fellowship in Prose, 1961

612 Calvin C. Hernton

Scarecrow

(Garden City, NY; Doubleday, 1974)

Summary: Hernton's provocative 1974 novel takes place on a ship bound for London from New York. All of the ship's passengers, both black and white, struggle with serious psychological problems—a circumstance that reflects the author's viewpoint that unseen social, economic, sexual, and moral evils prevent humanity from achieving any kind of psychological well being. The book's title character, for instance, kills and dismembers his white wife on the voyage in the hopes of starting a new life with Maria, a black woman on the ship. However, Scarecrow and Maria's neuroses make a new life impossible, and by the end of the novel the pair destroy each other in an orgy of violence.

Subject(s): Violence, Sexuality, Psychology

613 Chester Himes

Black on Black: Baby Sister and Selected Writings

(Garden City, NY; Doubleday, 1973)

Summary: This short-story collection contains several short pieces from the first twenty-five years of Chester Himes's career. The featured selection is "Baby Sister," a screenplay treatment set in a squalid black ghetto. In the story, the teen-aged Baby Sister--pregnant by her boyfriend--is sexually assaulted by her brother. Her older sister attempts to rescue her by getting her a job in the theater, while Baby Sister's boyfriend is forced to kill the violent brother as well as a local pimp who lusts for the girl. The screenplay was never filmed.

Subject(s): Urban Affairs, Sexual Assault, Violence

614 Chester Himes

Blind Man with a Pistol

(New York, NY; Morrow, 1969)

Summary: In this final installment of his groundbreaking crime series featuring detectives Grave Digger Jones and Coffin Ed Johnson, Himes offers a bleak depiction of a society in total breakdown at all levels. Violence has overwhelmed this society to such a degree that Jones and Johnson can do little to restore "order" or "peace" to Harlem's innocent citizens. Interestingly, Himes satirizes three main thrusts of the black civil rights movement of the 1960s: the nonviolent effort led by Martin Luther King, Jr.; the Black Power movement led by Malcolm X; and an effort based on Christian theology. In one scene, these three groups converge in a protest march that descends into a riot, with the marchers drunk on alcohol, drugs, and sex. Himes ended his crime series on a bitter and pessimistic note.

Subject(s): Violence, Civil Rights Movement, Drugs

615 Chester Himes

Cast the First Stone: A Novel

(New York, NY; Coward-McCann, 1952)

Summary: This heavily autobiographical novel features a white protagonist, Jim Moore, who is sentenced to prison for committing armed robbery--just as Himes himself was imprisoned for several years during the 1930s for the same offense. In the novel, Jim finds salvation and self-awareness via his intellectual growth and via his relationship with another man, Duke Dido. By the end of the novel, Jim has gained a new understanding of the unfair social conditions that haunt America and has resolved to become a writer. Although Himes was forced by his publisher to tone down the details surrounding the relationship between Jim and Duke, his decision to cast their homosexual relationship as a central part of the novel was remarkable for a fictional work in the 1950s.

Subject(s): Homosexuality/Lesbianism, Crime and Criminals

616 Chester Himes

The Crazy Kill

(New York, NY; Avon, 1959)

Summary: The third novel in Himes's crime series revolves around the attempts of Grave Digger Jones and Coffin Ed Johnson to bring to justice a black mobster who operates in Harlem. In this story, Himes focuses especially on the two detectives' ability to solve the case because they understand their fellow African Americans in Harlem; the white detectives, in contrast, see all blacks as "other" and thus fail to appreciate the cultural forces that operate in black Harlem.

Subject(s): Race Relations, Crime and Criminals

617 Chester Himes

For Love of Imabelle

(Greenwich, CT; Fawcett, 1957)

Summary: After spending the first decade of his career writing bleak protest novels, Chester Himes in 1957 changed direction, publishing the first of numerous crime novels. The change in direction allowed Himes a new and useful venue in which he could explore the plight of African Americans in a violent and racist society. *For Love of Imabelle* follows the conventions of previous American crime novels by such writers as Raymond Chandler. Two black detectives--Grave Digger Jones and Coffin Ed Johnson--seek to find the murderer of an infamous Harlem fraud nicknamed "The Blow." The story revolves around a desperate man's attempts to gain enough money to marry his girlfriend, Imabelle. As in the crime novels that he wrote after this one, Himes depicts a Harlem landscape in which cynical detectives try to solve a crime and impose some order on an otherwise violent and chaotic world.

Subject(s): Crime and Criminals, Criminal Justice

Award(s): Grand Prix de Litterature Policiere, 1958

618   Chester Himes

The Heat's On

(New York, NY; Putnam, 1966)

Summary: In this installment of his crime series featuring Harlem detectives Grave Digger Jones and Coffin Ed Johnson, Himes offers an almost surreal vision of a nightmarish Harlem, beset by drug dealers and horrific violence. In the novel, Grave Digger and Coffin Ed attempt to bring to justice a drug syndicate operating in Harlem. When Grave Digger is wounded in a shootout with members of the syndicate, Coffin Ed goes on a mission to bring the syndicate leaders to justice on his own. In order to survive, he has to descend to the level of the criminals themselves--behaving violently and brutally. In the end, Coffin Ed kills several of the syndicate's members, but the peace he imposes on Harlem is fragile and temporary, as the leaders of the syndicate remain at large and in business. In this novel, Himes began to embellish and transform the standard American crime novel to fit his own distinctive vision.

Subject(s): Crime and Criminals, Criminal Justice, Drugs

619   Chester Himes

If He Hollers Let Him Go

(Garden City, NY; Doubleday, Doran, 1945)

Summary: Set in Los Angeles during World War II, Chester Himes's first novel is a complex, provocative depiction of class and racial issues in the 1940s. The novel's autobiographically inspired protagonist, Bob Jones, ventures to Los Angeles to look for work. Once there, his desire to move up the social ladder of the black middle class is thwarted by his rage at the racism that severely limits his professional and personal options. He veers between threatening violence to racist white men and shouting insults at an ignorant, low-class, racist white woman named Madge, while in the meantime courting the respectable daughter of a wealthy black businessman. Jones is eventually caught in a trap by Madge, who falsely accuses him of rape. He is then spared prison by a judge who instead sentences him to join the U.S. Army, which contains a hierarchical racist system that is little better than prison.

Subject(s): Racism, Class Conflict

620   Chester Himes

Lonely Crusade

(New York, NY; A.A. Knopf, 1947)

Summary: In his second novel, Himes offers a dark view of a racist American society, of capitalism, and of Communist-dominated unions. In the novel, protagonist Lee Gordon finds a new lease on life by marrying Ruth and by becoming a union leader at Comstock Aircraft Organization. However, Lee's feelings of inadequacy eventually lead him to batter his wife and to have an affair with another woman, actions that effectively end his marriage. In addition, his faith in the union is shattered when he sees its leaders completely corrupted by power and vanity. At the end of the novel, Lee decides to take his place in the union leadership and fight for valid workers'

issues, but he does so with no illusions about his potential success; in addition, readers know that Lee will be destroyed, because a white policeman prepares to shoot and kill Lee as he leads a union protest.

Subject(s): Racism, Class Conflict, Communism

621   Chester Himes

Pinktoes

(Paris, France; Olympia Press, 1961)

Summary: Written during the period in which Himes was focusing most of his attention on his crime series, this novel is an unusual piece in Himes's canon. Set in Harlem, the novel offers a humorous and gentle take on the civil rights struggle of the early 1960s as well as the theme of interracial love. Protagonists Joe and Mamie Mason are a politically connected Harlem couple who host gatherings at their apartment to discuss such issues as politics, education, and civil rights. Invariably, these gatherings become sexually themed affairs in which the couple and their guests act out a variety of sexual fantasies. Unlike his earlier novels, in which interracial romance leads to violence and disaster, here Himes treats it as a healthy and harmless pastime.

Subject(s): Sexual Behavior, Civil Rights Movement, Miscegenation

622   Chester Himes

Plan B

(Paris, France; Lieu Commun, 1983)

Summary: This novel, Himes's last fictional effort, was published in incomplete form a year before the author's death. Written in the 1970s, the novel reveals Himes at his most bitter and pessimistic. Although his famed black detective characters Coffin Ed Johnson and Grave Digger Jones appear briefly in the novel, most of the story revolves around an unnamed black revolutionary who murders hundreds of white policemen as they march in a parade in a major American city.

Subject(s): Racial Conflict, Law Enforcement, Murder

623   Chester Himes

The Primitive

(Cleveland, OH; New American Library, 1955)

Summary: As he does in much of his fiction, Himes in this work examines the difficulties of interracial love in America. In the novel, Jesse Robinson is a struggling black writer living in Harlem who is forced to work as a porter to support himself. His life takes a turn when he meets and begins an affair with a wealthy white woman, Kriss Cummings. She agrees to support him only if he will fulfill her fantasy of the stereotypical black male superlover; angered by her views of him and unable to resolve her racial attitudes or his own biases, Jesse eventually kills Kriss in a drunken rage. Himes here offers a portrait of two characters who are unable to view clearly the reality of life in a racist society.

Subject(s): Miscegenation, Racial Conflict

624 **Chester Himes**

The Real Cool Killers
(New York, NY; Avon, 1959)

Summary: Chester Himes's crime series featuring Harlem detectives Grave Digger Jones and Coffin Ed Johnson is often called the first black detective fictional effort. In this installment, Himes's vision of the Harlem world of Jones and Johnson grows noticeably darker and more violent; this trend would continue in later novels in the series. Here, the action opens with a white man being attacked by a black man in a Harlem bar; the white man is then shot and killed by a group of men who appear to be white Muslims but who in fact are black youths. Grave Digger and Coffin Ed expose the masquerade, but they are only able to bring the youths to justice through violent means. In later novels in the series, the two detectives increasingly have to rely on such violence to bring about justice.

Subject(s): Murder, Racial Conflict, Violence

625 **Chester Himes**

Run Man, Run
(New York, NY; Putnam, 1966)

Summary: This novel is the only one of Himes's crime novels that does not feature detectives Grave Digger Jones and Coffin Ed Johnson. Instead, the novel focuses on a brutal white police detective, Matt Walker, and his homicidal pursuit of an innocent black law-school student, Jimmy Johnson. While working as a porter, Jimmy witnesses a drunken Walker senselessly murdering two other porters whom he thinks have stolen his car. Jimmy escapes alive and tells his story to Walker's superiors in the police department, but they do not believe him. After this, Walker continues to stalk Jimmy in order to kill him, and Jimmy eventually realizes that he has to arm himself if he wants to live. In this novel, Himes offers a vision of New York City in which brutal white cops prey on defenseless blacks.

Subject(s): Crime and Criminals, Law Enforcement, Racial Conflict

626 **Chester Himes**

The Third Generation
(Cleveland, OH; World Pub. Co., 1954)

Summary: This novel is Chester Himes's attempt to come to terms with his own family and his traumatic childhood. In the novel, young protagonist Charles Taylor--who is only three generations removed from slavery--sees his family's fortunes decline following the breakup of his parents' marriage. His parents' difficulties are racially tinged, stemming from a clash between his dark-skinned father and his light-skinned, aristocratic mother, who wants to deny the family's black heritage. The family eventually experiences abject poverty in the urban slums of St. Louis and Cleveland, and while Charles resolves

to divorce himself from his family and seek his own promised land elsewhere, no such land ever appears. The novel was completed and published after Himes had left the United States for Europe, where he would live for remaining three decades of his life.

Subject(s): Family Life, Racial Conflict

627 **Chester Himes**

Une Affaire de Viol
(Paris, France; Editions Les Yeux Ouverts, 1963)

Summary: First published in French translation while the author was living in Europe, this novel is about four expatriate black men who are falsely accused of raping and murdering a white woman. (The French title translates as "A Case of Rape.") The prejudice that the men encounter in Paris, France, is similar to that in the United States, allowing Himes to reveal how racism haunts blacks no matter where they live. While Himes lived in Europe for the last thirty years of his life, he never felt at home there and spoke often of the persistent prejudice he felt as a black man living in white European society. The original English edition of this novel was finally published in the United States by Howard University Press in 1984.

Subject(s): Murder, Sexual Assault, Racism

628 **George W. Hodges**

Swamp Angel
(New York, NY; New Voices Pub. Co., 1958)

Summary: This novel is set in the settlement of Freedmen's Hill, located near the town of Green Castle, which, before the Civil War, held slaves. The story looks at the lifelong friendship that grows between two men. King's Highway, whose real name is Floyd Hopkins, received his nickname from an incident at church involving the biblical passage about the highway in the wilderness. He is a trusted farm leader. When a widower named Moses Meade arrives in the area, he is welcomed by Highway and proves himself adept at all sorts of work. He receives the nickname Swamp Angel for his tendency to sing while clearing out swamp land. Religion plays a primary role in both men's lives. Both men are so respected in the community that when they die in their old age, first Angel and then Highway, even the area's white leaders join in the services.

Subject(s): Religion, American South, Friendship

629 **Nathaniel Hooks**

Town on Trial: A Novel of Racial Violence in a Southern Town
(New York, NY; Exposition Press, 1959)

Summary: The setting of this novel is a small southeastern town. When an abusive father finds out that his teenaged daughter has been having sex, he thinks of a young black truck driver whom he saw earlier that day. When he asks if the driver was the man involved, his daughter lies and says yes. The turmoil that follows the father's search for the young man culminates in a trial. The defendant is found innocent of the charges of kidnapping and rape when the daughter finally admits that she was involved with her own brother-in-law.

Subject(s): Racism, American South, Rape

630 Florenz H. Hough

Black Paradise: A Novel
(Philadelphia, PA; Dorrance, 1953)

Summary: This novel focuses on a young black man, Raymond Dupree, who, at the novel's opening, has just graduated from Columbia University. He is in love with a beautiful young woman named Clomaine and plans to continue his education. He goes on to help the United States government design the atomic bomb, for which he is recognized by his fellow scientists. Unable to find happiness with Clomaine, he marries her close friend, Arline.

Subject(s): Education, Science

631 Langston Hughes
Bernhard Nast, Illustrator

The Best of Simple
(New York, NY; Hill & Wang, 1961)

Summary: This work is a collection of short stories based on Hughes's most popular fictional character, Jesse B. Semple of Harlem, whom Hughes first introduced in 1943 in a column he wrote for the *Chicago Defender*. Semple, who came to be called "Simple," tells comical but astute tales symbolic of black life to his bar friend Boyd. Stories in this collection include "There Ought to be a Law," in which Simple makes an appeal for a game preserve for Negroes, and "They Come and They Go," about Simple's eighteen-year-old second cousin and his troubles with his stepfather and mother.

Subject(s): Short Stories, Humor

632 Langston Hughes

Simple Speaks His Mind
(New York, NY; Simon & Schuster, 1950)

Summary: Hughes created the fictional character of Harlem resident Jesse B. Semple, known as Simple, for a column he wrote for the *Chicago Defender* beginning in 1942. Simple's humorous musings cover true-life situations and contemporary themes. In this collection of sketches, Simple ponders such diverse topics as "colored people" being in the image of God; oppression, discrimination, and suppression; relationships with women; interracial relationships; anatomy; fair employment; and voting rights. As Simple sums up in one sketch, white people are "the cause of a lot of inconveniences in my life."

Subject(s): Racism, Race Relations, Interpersonal Relations

633 Langston Hughes

Simple Stakes a Claim
(New York, NY; Rinehart, 1957)

Summary: In Hughes's third collection of columns he wrote for the *Chicago Defender*, his fictional character, Harlem resident Jesse B. Semple, also known as Simple, provides more humorous insights into true-life situations. The central theme of the volume is discrimination. It begins with Simple wondering why there are no female pallbearers at funerals, and he also wonders throughout about the appearance of folks in heaven. In several sketches Simple talks about race relations by expressing his desire for more than a yellow and white egg, which becomes black and white when burned; by lamenting Jim Crow laws; and by speculating how prejudice would by eliminated if people grew from old to young.

Subject(s): Racism, Race Relations

634 Langston Hughes

Simple Takes a Wife
(New York, NY; Simon & Schuster, 1953)

Summary: This volume is the second collection of sketches Hughes wrote for his *Chicago Defender* column. They feature humorous and pointed observations made by the fictional character of Harlem resident Jesse B. Semple, also known as Simple. Simple's musings cover interracial relationships, including hostility by black women toward the white wife of a black man; fear of whites, as told about a mixed-race child afraid to be born in the South; how one drop of blood makes a man black; relationships with women; negative implications of the word *black*; and what changes would make America great for blacks.

Subject(s): Racism, Race Relations, Interpersonal Relations

635 Langston Hughes

Something in Common and Other Stories
(New York, NY; Hill & Wang, 1963)

Summary: In this, his third collection of short fiction, Hughes writes about the black experience as well as about situations with which everyone has "something in common." "Gumption" describes a black family's fight against racial discrimination by the Works Progress Administration, while "Fine Accommodations" reveals a black educator's arrogance toward his own race. Another piece has a father agonizing over his son's apparent homosexuality.

Subject(s): Racism, Homosexuality/Lesbianism

636 Langston Hughes

Tambourines to Glory: A Novel
(New York, NY; J. Day Co., 1958)

Summary: Hughes's 1958 novel is a satiric comment on the rise of unorthodox churches in Harlem in the 1950s, many of which had less-than-noble intentions. In the novel, two out-of-work Harlem women, Laura and Essie, decide to start their own church as a way to make money. Their church is an enormous success, but they eventually meet danger in the form of Big-Eyed Buddy, a handsome con man who has his own ideas for the church. At the story's end, after Laura and Essie jettison Buddy, they decide to use the church for the good of their Harlem neighborhood.

Subject(s): Religion, Comedy

637 Lillie Muse Humphrey

Aggie
(New York, NY; Vantage Press, 1955)

Summary: Set in rural Florida, this 1955 novel tells the story of Aggie, a young schoolteacher. Aggie begins teaching at a small-town school, only to encounter great resistance to her efforts by parents and by other, older teachers, who view Aggie as a threat to their power. Despite these obstacles, Aggie perseveres and eventually helps change the attitude of a community that is hostile to education and to teachers. The novel is based on Humphrey's own experiences as a small-town teacher.

Subject(s): Education, Rural Life

638 Helen Hunter

Magnificent White Men
(New York, NY; Vantage Press, 1964)

Summary: This novel considers two white brothers, Norman Clyde, a patent attorney, and Henry, a nuclear scientist. When Henry announces that he's ready to create babies through an asexual, atomic means, Norman, who has day-dreamed about turning blacks white through a chemical process, introduces Penelope O'Glory, a young black woman, as the woman needed to give birth to the babies. Penelope dies from her experience, which results in the birth of four golden babies endowed with extraordinary powers, proving themselves able to fly and journey to the stars.

Subject(s): Racism, Babies, Mothers

639 Kristin Hunter

God Bless the Child
(New York, NY; Scribner, 1964)

Summary: In her first novel, Hunter shows her talent for realistically depicting black ghetto life and covers her major theme of suffering and deprivation as well as class division based on skin color. Rosalie Fleming is a dark-skinned young girl in Harlem being raised by her promiscuous mulatto mother and uncaring octoroon grandmother. Determined to break away from her slum existence, she works hard at several jobs--some illegal--and even buys a house, but is unable to gain the economic advantages needed to make a true break. The struggle eventually leads to her mental and physical breakdown, and she dies after having an abortion.

Subject(s): Poverty

640 Kristin Hunter

The Landlord
(New York, NY; Scribner, 1966)

Summary: Unlike the main characters in most of her books, Hunter's protagonist in *The Landlord* is a white character. However, typical Hunter elements, including the setting of the black ghetto and the optimistic tone, are again present. In the book, Elgar Enders is a wealthy white man who buys an apartment building to prove himself to his father. He plans to exact a profit, but, as he gets to know his tenants, he undergoes a personal transformation that he channels into both building and community improvements. His good deeds are offset by his affair with a married tenant, whose husband he replaces. The comic style Hunter used in this book led to her being asked to write juvenile novels.

Subject(s): Poverty, Race Relations

641 Kristin Hunter

The Survivors
(New York, NY; Scribner, 1975)

Summary: In this novel Hunter explores what it takes to survive in the ghetto as well as in various types of relationships, including those that cut across class and age barriers. Middle-aged Miss Lena is a successful businesswoman in an inner-city neighborhood being repopulated by whites. She is befriended by B.J., a thirteen-year-old street hustler. He advises her about street life, such as which taxis to take, and she becomes his surrogate mother. Their relationship enables them to survive as their traditional community erodes from drugs and crime.

Subject(s): Interpersonal Relationships, Drugs, Urban Affairs

642 Blyden Jackson

Operation Burning Candle: A Novel
(New York, NY; Third Press, 1973)

Summary: This militant tale is set in Harlem during the late 1960s and early 1970s. In the novel, protagonist Aaron Rogers conceives, plans, and executes a series of terrorist actions in order to bring social justice to African Americans. Rogers gathers fellow former military veterans into a passionate group that eventually robs banks, paralyzes the city with false fire alarms and other acts of civil disobedience, and carries out a plan to murder twelve racist U.S. senators during a Democratic National Convention in New York City. The novel reflects the belief held by many black intellectuals during the period that violence was the only effective means by which to achieve social justice and equality in a racist, white-dominated society.

Subject(s): Violence, Rebellion, Racism

643 Blyden Jackson

Totem: A Novel
(New York, NY; Third Press, 1975)

Summary: The "totem" of this novel's title refers to a long-lost African figurine, the Kabilaote, which is reputed by legend to hold the spirit of all African people. In the novel, two opposing groups attempt to locate the totem. One group, which consists of Africans and African Americans, wants the totem found and returned for the good of all Africans, believing that with the totem modern-day Africa could regain its independence and power. Another group, consisting of CIA operatives, white South African police, and officials in European-controlled African republics, prefers that the totem remain lost. Both groups trace the totem to South Carolina, where it was brought hundreds of years ago by an enslaved African girl, and eventually to New York City's Harlem neighborhood.

Subject(s): Africa, Slavery, Legends

644 W. Warner Jackson

The Birth of the Martyr's Ghost
(New York, NY; Comet Press Books, 1957)

Summary: A religious story about redemption, this novel is narrated by Tou'saint Chaney, a light-skinned mulatto. Raised first by his black mother, Chaney then goes to live with his white father. However, at seventeen, Chaney runs away to California, where he makes a fortune gambling on horses. Later, he is stranded on a desert island for several years when his plane is shot down during World War II. At the end of the novel, he returns to civilization and to his life of wealth and leisure, but he renounces his sinful ways; nonetheless, he is murdered by a vengeful foe at the story's close.

Subject(s): Religion, Gambling, Murder

645 A.Q. Jarrette

Beneath the Sky: A Novel of Love and Murder among the Poor Whites and Negroes of the Deep South
(New York, NY; Weinberg Book Supply Co., 1949)

Summary: A novel about passion, infidelity, and murder, *Beneath the Sky* is set on plantation in South Carolina. Most of the main characters are white. Jim Robinson, who owns the plantation, falls in love with the daughter of his white overseer, Jake Logan. When Jim asks his wife for a divorce so that he can marry the daughter, the wife refuses; Jim then kills her by poisoning her. Jake, meanwhile instigates the lynching of a young black man who works on the plantation. Later, when Jake's daughter tries to marry Jim's son, Jake intervenes to stop it; incensed, his wife kills him so that the young lovers can marry.

Subject(s): Family Problems, Lynching, Love

646 Hawke Jarry

Black Schoolmaster: A Novel
(New York, NY; Exposition Press, 1970)

Summary: Melvin Banks is the title character of this novel about education in the nation's poverty-stricken inner cities. Upon his graduation from college, Banks begins teaching at a high school on Chicago's near west side. His initial excitement and hope are gradually crushed, as he realizes that the school's leadership--and indeed the city's entire public school system--cares little about educating the poor blacks and other minorities who make up the city's school population. By the novel's end, he has become involved in massive, nonviolent demonstrations by blacks about the city's educational system, and he finds himself dismissed from his position. Nonetheless, he resolves to keep working to improve education for poor blacks.

Subject(s): Education, Racism, Urban Affairs

647 Roland S. Jefferson

The School on 103rd Street
(New York, NY; Vantage Press, 1976)

Summary: Jefferson, a psychiatrist, combines various aspects of his observations to create characters and situations. In this novel, two boys disclose details of a friend's murder to Dr. Elwin Carter. Carter's investigation leads him beyond the usual drug and gang motivated violence behind many of the murders in the Watts district and into something much more frightening. Jefferson's novel explores the fear by black America in the 1970s that the government would attempt to incarcerate the entire population.

Subject(s): Government, Fear

648 Deaderick Franklin Jenkins

It Was Not My World: A Story in Black and White That's Different
(Los Angeles, CA; Privately published, 1942)

Summary: Set in Mississippi during the 1930s, this novel presents a one-dimensional portrait of a southern landscape in which all blacks remain semi-enslaved and all whites use brutality to maintain the status quo. Stock characters populate the novel, along with a college-educated author who is modeled after the author. Didactic and heavy-handed, the novel was self published after the author failed to find a commercial publisher willing to release the book.

Subject(s): Racism

649 Deaderick Franklin Jenkins

Letters to My Son
(Los Angeles, CA; Jenkins, 1947)

Summary: Jenkins's 1947 novel is an epistolary work—a novel told entirely in the form of letters. In the book, Jenkins examines numerous contemporary issues and events.

Subject(s): Letters

650 Charles Richard Johnson

Faith and the Good Thing

(New York, NY; Viking Press, 1974)

Summary: Johnson was a twenty-six-year-old doctoral student in philosophy when this novel, reflecting his interest in phenomenology, was accepted for publication. He had previously written six others while working as a cartoonist and journalist, but none had been published. *Faith and the Good Thing* is a folktale about Faith Cross, who sets out from Georgia to find a better life in Chicago. Her experiences take her innocence away and prevent her from finding the "good thing," yet she moves freely in the physical and metaphysical worlds. At her death, her soul returns to the site of her physical and spiritual birth.

Subject(s): Philosophy

651 Charles Richard Johnson

Middle Passage

(New York, NY; Atheneum, 1990)

Summary: Johnson's interest in combining fantasy and black American experiences is reflected in his works, including this novel, which won the prestigious National Book Award for fiction. The book's protagonist is freed slave Rutherford Calhoun. Running away from debts, crimes, and women, Calhoun stows away on a slave ship, where he eventually encounters slaves who are members of a tribe of wizards. The "middle passage" of the book's title refers to the route that slave ships traveled between Africa and the West Indies.

Subject(s): Slavery, Wizards

Award(s): National Book Award: Fiction, 1990

652 William M. Johnson

The House on Corbett Street: A Novel of Negro Stirrings amid Discontent

(New York, NY; William-Frederick Press, 1967)

Summary: The main characters of Johnson's 1967 novel struggle against racism and lack of economic opportunity. Set in the fictional Sprawlingtown, Indiana, the novel revolves around Rebecca, her daughter Moella, and Moella's hard-luck husband, Horace. Rebecca constantly berates Moella and Horace for not being able to support their two young children without her help. Horace eventually does find a factory job, but his inability to provide for Moella leads her to abandon him. At the novel's end, Horace has gone insane and has been committed to a mental hospital, while Rebecca continues to care for her two grandchildren.

Subject(s): Poverty, Family Problems, Mental Illness

653 Gayl Jones

Corregidora

(New York, NY; Random House, 1975)

Summary: Jones, who grew up in segregated Lexington, Kentucky, uses the speech and oral tradition she heard in her community as a child to narrate gothic stories dealing with madness, sexuality, and violence. In Jones' first novel, Ursa Corregidora is a blues singer from Kentucky who is the third-generation progeny of incest by a Portuguese slaveholder in Brazil. Ursa handles the psychic pain caused by the sexual and physical brutality in her background by becoming involved in abusive relationships with men. She eventually comes to reconcile her heritage with her present life.

Subject(s): Miscegenation, Sexual Abuse, Gothic Novels

654 Gayl Jones

Eva's Man

(New York, NY; Random House, 1976)

Summary: Jones uses the same street speech she heard growing up in segregated Lexington, Kentucky, to give voice to the deranged narrator of this novel. In her disjointed, unremorseful narration, Eva Medina Canada relates her personal history, which includes witnessing sexual perversions and being exploited. The sexually aggressive and hostile society in which she lives exacts a psychological toll on her until she breaks, and she is institutionalized for poisoning and sexually mutilating a male acquaintance.

Subject(s): Sexual Abuse, Murder, Racism

655 LeRoi Jones

(Also known as Amiri Baraka)

Tales

(New York, NY; Grove Press, 1967)

Summary: This book features a varied collection of short stories. "The Alternative" offers a look into evening activities in a black male college dormitory. "Answers in Progress" is about spacemen looking for recordings of jazz. "Going Down Slow" depicts the violent reaction of an adulterous husband when he finds out that his wife is also having an affair. In "New Sense," a black man acquires new values. "Uncle Tom's Cabin: Alternate Ending" revolves around a teacher asking a question about a black child. "Words" describes the return of a "prodigal son" to Harlem.

Subject(s): College Life, Jazz, Marriage

656 Elsie Jordan

Strange Sinner

(New York, NY; Pageant Press, 1954)

Summary: This novel follows two black families as they move from the American South to the North at the turn of the century. Joan Brooks marries Larry Blake and later tries to kill him in order continue her affair with his brother. When her husband is scheduled to go to trial for murder after accidentally killing another of her lovers, Joan leaves him. The depiction of Joan's character explores the idea of the evil mulatto.

Subject(s): American South, Marriage, Murder

657 June Jordan

His Own Where

(New York, NY; Crowell, 1971)

Summary: This novel centers on young Buddy, who while spending an evening with his girlfriend, Angela, is confronted by the claustrophobia of Brooklyn. Determined to make a difference in the urban environment, Buddy first remodels his family's house with his father's help. Later, he and Angela make a new home for themselves in an abandoned building in a secluded urban area. The novel demonstrates the author's interest in urban planning.

Subject(s): City and Town Life, Urban Affairs, Architecture

658 Philip B. Kaye

(Pseudonym of Alger Leroy Adams)

Taffy: A Novel

(New York, NY; Crown Publishers, 1950)

Summary: This 1950 novel, written by Alger Leroy Adams under the pseudonym Philip B. Kaye, is set in the colorful world of twentieth century Harlem. In the novel, the protagonist is unable to be at peace with the world around him.

Subject(s): Literature

659 William Melvin Kelley

Dancers on the Shore

(Garden City, NY; Doubleday, 1964)

Summary: Kelley's second major published work is a collection of short stories. The stories in general explore personal and class issues, not racial ones. One of the stories, "Cry for Me," centers on an individual who participates in the fictional exodus from a southern town described in the author's first novel, *A Different Drummer*. Critical reception to the collection was mixed. While reviewers found fault with Kelley's refusal to address the issue of race directly, most critics tended to agree that Kelley had produced a well-written collection of stories.

Subject(s): Individuality

Award(s): *Transatlantic Review* Award, 1964

660 William Melvin Kelley

dem

(Garden City, NY; Doubleday, 1967)

Summary: A satirical novel, *dem* tells the story of Mitchell and Tam Pierce, an upper-middle-class white couple. After participating in a rare fertilization process, Tam gives birth to twins, one white and one black. Mitchell's search for the father of the black child takes him to New York City's Harlem, where he meets the father, Calvin Coolidge Johnson. Cooley's denial of the child's paternity reverses what happened when slave owners would force their male slaves to accept paternity for the masters' illegitimate children. In his depiction of the Pierces, Kelley argues that white America is sterile and cruel. In the opening vignette of the novel, Kelley addresses his concern regarding the Vietnam War; here, a Korean War veteran kills his family and then mows the lawn. Although criticizing the superficiality of the writing, most reviewers gave the novel a positive reception for the questions it raised.

Subject(s): Racism, Slavery, Vietnam War

661 William Melvin Kelley

A Different Drummer

(Garden City, NY; Doubleday, 1962)

Summary: Kelley's first novel takes its name from a famous line by Henry David Thoreau. The story centers on Tucker Caliban, a sharecropper in the southern town of Willson City. Tucker buys the land that he farms and then destroys its farming capabilities by salting it. His personal act of resistance against his near-slave existence sets off a mass exodus of blacks from Willson City. The white community attributes Tucker's actions to his African heritage, which includes a hero who led many slave revolts. The novel was a critical success; reviewers pointed to the author's narrative style as well as his ability to depict realistic people instead of racial abstractions.

Subject(s): Slavery, Racism, Individuality

Award(s): John Hay Whitney Foundation Award, 1963; Rosenthal Foundation Award, 1963

662 William Melvin Kelley

Dunfords Travels Everywheres

(Garden City, NY; Doubleday, 1970)

Summary: This novel has two heroes, Chig Dunford and Carlyle Bedlow. While the first of the two black men is Harvard-educated, the other is from New York City's Harlem. Together, the characters form aspects of what is actually the same personality. Both men are searching for who they are and what their relation to each other might be. The clues presented to them, however, come in a strange dream language. This language was inspired by James Joyce's novel *Finnegans Wake* and Joyce's exploration of being an Irish writer composing in an English context. The language presented to Chig and Carlyle in their dreams is derived from several forms of black speech. Although critics tended to find Kelley's creation of an experimental language lacking, he was nevertheless commended for the artistic undertaking.

Subject(s): Language, Racism, Dreams and Nightmares

Award(s): Black Academy of Arts and Letters: Fiction Award, 1970

663 Arnold Kemp

Eat of Me, I Am the Savior
(New York, NY; William Morrow, 1972)

Summary: The author's first novel was begun while he was in prison and finished at Harvard. It opens with the assassination of Nicholas Said, a Malcolm X-like figure. When Yaquii Laster, a young revolutionary, is released from prison, he goes to Harlem in search of the murderer of his spiritual leader, Said. Through Yaquii's experiences, the novel links a Christ fixation on the part of the black community to a messianic complex shown by its aspiring leaders.

Subject(s): Racism, Religion

664 Randall Kenan

Let the Dead Bury Their Dead and Other Stories
(New York, NY; Harcourt, 1992)

Summary: Kenan's second published work of fiction is a collection of short stories. The title novella revisits the town of Tims Creek, which was seen in the author's earlier novel, *A Visitation of Spirits*. Horace Cross's surname is found to be that of the plantation owner whose escaped slaves founded the town. The history of the town is recorded by Reverend Green from a variety of sources, including oral history, diaries, and letters. Green's unfinished work is used in an academic treatise by the narrator "RK" in the 1990s. Another story depicts an encounter between Booker T. Washington and two former schoolmates in 1909. The collection features conjuring and sensuality, including homoeroticism. The author has received praise for creating complex characters out of racial and sexual types.

Subject(s): Slavery, Homosexuality/Lesbianism, Magic

665 Randall Kenan

A Visitation of Spirits: A Novel
(New York, NY; Grove Press, 1989)

Summary: The author's first novel is set in Tims Creek, a small African American community in North Carolina. The novel uses narrative and chronological leaps to tell its story. In 1984, Horace Thomas Cross, who is at odds with his own homosexuality, relives his and his family's past when he is visited by demons, which may be real or figurative. In 1985, Cross's cousin, the Reverend James Malachai Green, takes his aunt and uncle to visit a dying relative. In the process, the trio provides more perspective on Cross and the history of the town. Critics praised Kenan for his combination of magical and realistic imagery as well as his depiction of complex characters.

Subject(s): American South, Homosexuality/Lesbianism

666 Mark Kennedy

The Pecking Order
(New York, NY; Appleton-Century-Crofts, 1953)

Summary: The author's first novel is set in Chicago and centers on Bruce Freeman, the eleven-year-old son of a middle-class black family. The story takes place during a single day and follows Bruce and his friends: B.J., who has had his share of reform school; the overweight Snag, Bruce's best friend; Henry, who has been left twisted by his southern background; and Johnny, who is only eight. B.J. takes the group through the city, where they meet his prostitute sister and explore a condemned tenement building. This series of adventures, however, culminates in tragedy.

Subject(s): Childhood, Middle Classes, Poverty

667 John Oliver Killens

And Then We Heard the Thunder
(New York, NY; Knopf, 1963)

Summary: The author's second novel is based on his own experience with racism and segregation in the military during World War II. At the center of the story is Solly Saunders, a black law student, who after dropping out of law school and enlisting in the army, is placed in a segregated amphibious military unit. Believing at first that the war is simply one of democracy against fascism, he eventually changes his original assertion that the war is not a racial conflict. Killens illustrates the theme of manhood when Solly defends himself in the face of racism by forfeiting his chance at Officer's Candidate School. At the end of the novel, Solly affirms his African American heritage. While reviewers criticized the novel's style, they warmly praised its characters and message.

Subject(s): World War II, Racism, Military Life

668 John Oliver Killens

The Cotillion; or, One Good Bull Is Half the Herd
(New York, NY; Trident Press, 1971)

Summary: This novel focuses on the Cotillion ball thrown by the Femmes Fatales, an exclusive black women's club in Brooklyn, New York and is written in the tradition of the African American verbal contest. Most of the story's main characters belong to the Lovejoy family. Mrs. Lovejoy, like her fellow women's club members, has no interest in her African American heritage. By the end of the novel, the women of the club are reduced to a confused group of foolish black women exposed for their shallow middle-class values. Killens illustrates the theme of class division by comparing the culturally sterile community of Crowning Heights with the community of Harlem, which is shown as having retained its African American culture. Although some reviewers were critical, the novel received much enthusiastic praise for its satire of black and white society.

Subject(s): Community Relations, Middle Classes, Class Conflict

669 **John Oliver Killens**

'Sippi

(New York, NY; Trident Press, 1967)

Summary: The author's third novel reflects his interest in black militancy and depicts the struggle of black college students working for voting rights in the 1960s. Many of the characters come from two Mississippi families, one black and one white. Malcolm X, Stokely Carmichael and Martin Luther King, Jr., are among the historical figures woven into the novel. Reviewers were divided in their assessments of the work, and the author himself considered it inferior to his previous two novels.

Subject(s): Racism, Civil Rights Movement

670 **John Oliver Killens**

Youngblood

(New York, NY; Dial Press, 1954)

Summary: In his first novel, the author shows what life was like for blacks living in the American South during the first third of the twentieth century. At the center of the story are the Youngbloods, a black family struggling against racism in the town of Crossroads, Georgia. Reflecting the author's faith in the importance of racial brotherhood, one of the town's white men agrees to serve as a donor for Joe Youngblood's blood transfusion at a white hospital. Killens emphasizes the importance of uniting whites and blacks in organized labor movements, as seen in Joe's attempt to start a hotel workers' union. Joe eventually dies as a civil rights martyr. Although Killens's technique was faulted by reviewers, critics praised the novel for its interesting characters and passionate social protest.

Subject(s): Racism, Labor Movement, Civil Rights

671 **Jess Kimbrough**

Defender of the Angels: A Black Policeman in Old Los Angeles

(New York, NY; Macmillan, 1969)

Summary: Set in the early decades of the twentieth century, this novel is a fictionalized account of the author's years working for the Los Angeles police force. When the story's protagonist, Strite Hinton, makes the police force, his assignment is to patrol the black and Mexican ghettos of Los Angeles. Successful at his work, he is promoted to Detective Sergeant. The novel considers the inequities of a racist society as shown through Hinton's experiences as a police officer.

Subject(s): Racism, Crime and Criminals

672 **Jamaica Kincaid**

Annie John

(New York, NY; Farrar, Straus, Giroux, 1985)

Summary: The author's first novel is a coming-of-age story. Set in Antigua, the novel follows Annie John as she enters puberty, experiences the death of a friend, establishes independence from her mother, and goes through a serious illness. At the end of the story, Annie decides to leave Antigua for England. Through its description of Annie's education the novel explores the issue of colonialism. The novel received critical praise for its depiction of Annie's maturation, and Kincaid has been acclaimed for her poetic writing style.

Subject(s): Coming-of-Age, Mothers and Daughters, Colonialism

673 **Richard B. Koiner**

Jack Be Quick

(New York, NY; L. Stuart, 1966)

Summary: The author's first novel is set during America's Great Depression. The story follows its jobless protagonist, Jack Poole, as he escapes shantytown life. Jack's experiences are depicted as he journeys, pursued by hunger, across the continent.

Subject(s): Depression (Economic), Poverty

674 **Florence Ladd**

Sarah's Psalm

(New York, NY; 1996)

Summary: Taking place during the civil rights movement, Florence Ladd's *Sarah's Psalm* tells the story of Harvard doctoral student Sarah Stewart as she finds herself one of the "Negro firsts": a graduate of an exclusive New England women's college, a student at Harvard, and married to Lincoln, another "first" from a well-to-do African American family. Her life and career seem on track until Lincoln becomes caught up in the politics of the civil rights movement and Sarah senses their relationship fragmenting. A trip to Senegal to meet the subject of her doctoral thesis--handsome, married, and wealthy writer Abrahim Mangane--ultimately derails her fast-track life. She divorces her husband and becomes Mangane's lover, and then his wife. In her new role as wife and mother in a traditional African society, she finds she must put her own aspirations aside.

Subject(s): Women's Rights, Africa, Civil Rights Movement

675 **William Lawson**

Zeppelin Coming Down

(Berkeley, CA; Yardbird Wing Editions, 1976)

Summary: This novel centers on Robert Codac, a Pomo Indian sculptor who, fleeing his increasing success, has retreated to his reservation home. With his success seemingly associated with disaster, Codac is disturbed by images of a doomed zeppelin airship. He is linked to others facing their own troubles: Beauty Million, an atheist evangelist preacher with a large television and radio business; Paula Grant, Beauty's daughter and Codac's mistress; and Levi Brown, a black "social technician" who risks the lives of Codac and Paula to investigate the killing of a black man by a white police officer. This novel takes the survival of the nation as its subject, offering a view of America as the Hindenburg.

Subject(s): Sculptors, Religion

676 Audrey Lee

The Clarion People

(New York, NY; McGraw-Hill, 1968)

Summary: The author's first novel focuses on Lillian Peoples, who leaves her rural home to live in the city. The story depicts her experiences in environments including the ghetto and prison. A religious woman, she encounters many spiritually lost people in the ghetto. She herself is saved by a man's faith and love and finally finds peace in a rest home.

Subject(s): City and Town Life, Religion

677 Audrey Lee

The Workers

(New York, NY; McGraw-Hill, 1969)

Summary: In her second novel, Lee tells the story of Harvie Guthrie. Harvie is an expert adding machine operator who is frustrated at working in a mechanized and computerized society. While his girlfriend Nellie sees his salvation in love, Harvie sees it in manual labor. In order to assert his identity, he confesses to a murder he did not commit. The novel ends with his defense attorney using a sculpture called "The Workers" that was made by Harvie as the centerpiece to his closing arguments.

Subject(s): Work, Machines, Identity

678 George W. Lee

Beale Street Sundown

(New York, NY; House of Field, 1942)

Summary: For this collection of short stories, Lee returns to the Beale Street neighborhood of Memphis, Tennessee. The stories vary widely in scope. One story tells how a group of friends tries to prevent the street's name from being changed to Beale Avenue. Another story involves a singer who yearns to be a blues stylist. The figure River George, a character based on a real person, who was seen in Lee's nonfiction *Beale Street: Where the Blues Began* and who was also the basis of Lee's novel *River George*, is also featured in a story. Among the other stories is the tale of a black prostitute who passes for white in a brothel; she faces ostracism, however, when she marries a black man. Less concerned with writing to inspire black Americans as he was in his previous works, Lee was able to write more freely and artistically with this collection.

Subject(s): Racism, Music, Prostitution

679 Mack Leonard

Cover My Rear

(New York, NY; Vantage Press, 1974)

Summary: Set during World War II, this novel follows an army company composed of black soldiers and white officers. Among the officers is Lieutenant Marsh. Leading the troops is Sergeant Farny, whose primary interest is keeping as many of his men alive as possible. The resulting story is based on the author's own experience fighting with the U.S. Army in Europe during the war.

Subject(s): Armed Forces, World War II, Race Relations

680 Julius Lester

Two Love Stories

(New York, NY; Dial Press, 1972)

Summary: *Two Love Stories* consists of two novellas. The first, "Basketball Game," tells the story of how a relationship between a black boy and a white girl in a southern city is destroyed by racial forces. The second, "Catskill Morning," is a tale of sexual awakening involving a young dancer and a counselor at a summer camp. The two stories are united by a theme of unfulfilled love.

Subject(s): Racism, Dancing, Love

681 C. Eric Lincoln

The Avenue, Clayton City

(New York, NY; Morrow, 1988)

Summary: This novel is set in the fictional southern town of Clayton City. Downtown is the starting point for a street that on the white side of town is paved and clean. On the side of town where blacks live, the street has another name, the Avenue, and is unpaved and lined with trash-filled ditches. Nevertheless, the Avenue is the primary residential street for the black community. The story looks at how the life of Walter Tait, a black doctor, is affected by the town's racist status quo.

Subject(s): Racism, Medicine, City and Town Life

682 Ken Lipscomb

Duke Casanova: A Novel

(New York, NY; Exposition Press, 1958)

Summary: The "Casanova" of this novel, Duke Butler, narrates this story about his pursuit of women. He describes his marriage to the pretty, intelligent Barbara, and his subsequent adventures pursuing other women during their marriage. At the end of this comic novel, Duke has sworn to avoid other women and devote himself fully to Barbara.

Subject(s): Love, Marriage

683 Curtis Lucas

Flour Is Dusty

(New York, NY; Dorrance & Company, 1943)

Summary: The hero of *Flour Is Dusty*, Jim Farrell, narrates the story of this novel through flashbacks to his days in Atlantic City, New Jersey. Prior to living there, Jim grew up on his family's farm in Georgia; a fight with his father about Jim's desire to gain an education leads Jim to move to North Carolina to attend school. After graduating, he ventures to Atlantic City. From this point, the plot moves quickly, as Jim develops a romantic attachment. When the girl's mother is murdered, Jim at first is the prime suspect, but he soon is able to point police to the real killer. At the novel's end, Jim and his lover pledge their love for one another. Though somewhat sensational and didactic, the novel includes a measure of political protest at the exclusionary, racist methods used by hotels and restaurants in Atlantic City.

Subject(s): Murder, Racism, Love

684 Curtis Lucas

Lila

(New York, NY; Lion Books, 1955)

Summary: Lucas's 1955 pulp novel features Johnny Martin, who has used every device available to claw his way out of the poverty of his East Harlem youth. Now, having gained the trappings of a luxurious life--a new car, expensive clothes, showy parties, and women--he finds himself nearly destroyed by a woman named Lila. Much of the book is set in Detroit, which in the 1950s was home to a burgeoning population of African Americans of all economic levels.

Subject(s): Middle Classes, Poverty, Success

685 Curtis Lucas

Third Ward, Newark

(New York, NY; Ziff-Davis Publishing Company, 1946)

Summary: Set against the backdrop of a poverty-stricken African American community in Newark, New Jersey, Lucas's second novel is a story of revenge. The book's protagonist, Wonnie, somehow survives a brutal rape and attempted murder by a white man, Earl, though Wonnie's friend does not survive. Several years later, healed physically but determined to exact revenge, Wonnie returns to Newark from college and charges Ernie with rape and murder. The police dismiss her charge. Later, Wonnie provokes a fight with Ernie in his bar, and he murders her. Although Wonnie's husband arrives too late to save her, his presence leads Ernie to commit suicide.

Subject(s): Murder, Racism, Rape

686 Will Anthony Madden

Five More: Short Stories

(New York, NY; Exposition Press, 1963)

Summary: The five short stories in Madden's 1963 collection examine love, betrayal, and murder. In "Phantom Lovers," a man and woman carry on an affair over the telephone and via letters but have trouble cementing their relationship in person. "Thou Shalt Not Kill," meanwhile, features a meek woman who murders her husband and his mistress. Although religious, she feels that she is justified in breaking one of the Ten Commandments. Clarke Branyon, the central character in "A Midnight Supper," is handsome, wealthy, and accomplished, but he is also haunted by depression. After a failed attempt at suicide, he succeeds in killing himself.

Subject(s): Marriage, Suicide, Love

687 William Mahoney

Black Jacob: A Novel

(New York, NY; Macmillan, 1969)

Summary: This novel tells the story of Jacob Blue, a black physician in Mississippi. When his candidacy for a seat in Congress challenges the status quo, he outrages fellow middle-class blacks as well as white racists. Endeavoring to win his constituency, Jacob goes to Tent City, an encampment of blacks who have been driven off their land by the sheriff. Here Jacob meets Jesse, a militant black rebel who travels from one troubled area to another. Jacob is finally killed by a sniper's bullet.

Subject(s): Racism, Politics, Middle Classes

688 Clarence Major

All-Night Visitors

(New York, NY; Olympia Press, 1969)

Summary: Struggling to come to grips with his identity, Eli Bolton is an orphan, a college dropout and a Vietnam War veteran. The novel follows Eli's efforts to understand himself and his world, in the process depicting his sexual relationships with both black and white women. Although much of the material from the original manuscript was cut, the novel still manages to introduce the themes common to the author's fiction, including the difficulty of establishing self-identity in a bigoted world.

Subject(s): Racism, Vietnam War, Sexuality

689 Clarence Major

Reflex and Bone Structure

(New York, NY; Fiction Collective, 1975)

Summary: This work takes the detective novel as its point of departure. The mystery to be solved is the death of the lovers Cora and Dale. The narrator finally reveals that he made them step into a house, which he then made explode; he explains that the action was merely a literary device. By writing a novel in which the story's construction in certain ways has more significance than the story's plot, Major creates a metafictional work in which he encourages the reader to explore the nature of fictive discourse. This novel is among the works that have secured Major's reputation as an acclaimed experimental writer.

Roosevelt Mallory

Subject(s): Mystery, Literature

690 **Roosevelt Mallory**

Radcliff: Double Trouble

(Los Angeles, CA; Holloway House, 1974)

Summary: In this novel, the members of the Organization attempt to rid themselves of Radcliff. They hire a double to impersonate the hitman, and the double begins to murder police officers and federal agents. When Radcliff returns to Los Angeles, he finds himself the object of an intensive manhunt. He discovers that the only one who can clear him is his double, who himself is the object of an Organization contract.

Subject(s): Crime and Criminals, Murder

691 **Roosevelt Mallory**

Radcliff: Harlem Hit

(Los Angeles, CA; Holloway House, 1973)

Summary: Radcliff is the code name for a professional hitman whose real name is unknown to anyone. Having become experienced in killing in Vietnam, Radcliff now murders underworld figures for other underworld criminals. A loner, Radcliff uses his high fees to finance a luxurious lifestyle.

Subject(s): Murder, Crime and Criminals, Vietnam War

692 **Paule Marshall**

Brown Girl, Brownstones

(New York, NY; Random House, 1959)

Summary: Paule Marshall's first novel is an autobiographical work. This coming-of-age story centers on Selina, whose immigrant family lives in the Barbadian American community of Brooklyn, New York. She witnesses the conflict between her mother, who wants to save enough money to buy the brownstone that they rent, and her father, who wants to return to Barbados and live on the land that he has inherited. Selina leaves to attend college and later returns to her family's brownstone. At the novel's end, she decides to travel to the Caribbean. In doing so, she rejects American materialistic values in favor of a desire for black community. Marshall's debut as a writer was widely praised by reviewers but did not find a large reading audience at the time because of its frank portrayal of a young black woman's development. The novel is regarded as a classic female coming-of-age story.

Subject(s): Coming-of-Age, Family Relations

693 **Paule Marshall**

The Chosen Place, the Timeless People

(New York, NY; Harcourt, Brace & World, 1969)

Summary: Marshall, considered a major black female voice of the last half of the twentieth century, set her third novel in the Caribbean island community of Bournehills. A group of American anthropologists working on a development project arrives on the island to help the people but finds that half-measures cannot solve problems rooted in slavery and colonialism. Central to the novel's idea of change is the character Merle Kimbona. Merle returns to the island after having studied in London and given up a child. Confronting her own difficult past, Merle comes to realize that she must act to effect a change in her present life, just as she sees that the island must undergo a similar process. Creating a complex black female character in Merle, Marshall employs her to argue that personal and social change are linked.

Subject(s): Colonialism, Slavery, West Indies

694 **Paule Marshall**

Daughters

(New York, NY; Atheneum, 1991)

Summary: Set in both New Jersey and the fictitious Caribbean island of Triunion, this story follows Estelle, an African American woman who confronted racism in the United States and has married into wealthy Caribbean society, and Ursa, a young urban woman whose mother is American and whose father is West Indian. Estelle and Ursa come to see the racism and imperialism that U.S. projects in the Caribbean involve. In the U.S., Mae Ryland forms a parallel to Estelle and Ursa. Unwilling to support New Jersey's corrupt black politician, Mae chooses instead to focus on her own community. Mae's connection to the politician is reflected in the relationship that Estelle has with her husband and Ursa has with her father. The novel explores the effects of American capitalism on international black communities and examines relations between the sexes within the context of Caribbean identity.

Subject(s): Politics, Racism, West Indies

695 **Paule Marshall**

Soul Clap Hands and Sing

(New York, NY; Atheneum, 1961)

Summary: This collection of four novellas takes its name from a line in William Butler Yeats's poem, "Sailing to Byzantium." The title shows that the stories are united by an emphasis on the importance of spiritual values. The stories are entitled "Barbados," "Brooklyn," "British Guiana," and "Brazil." Each of these works features a particular cultural and historical context. At the center of each novella is an elderly man who has sacrificed certain social values to achieve material success and is left with the alienation of his old age. Each of these men discovers his loss through his relationship with a woman. In this collection, the author expands her setting from the United States to that of the New World, but uses political themes central to most of her other work.

Subject(s): Spiritualism, Politics, Aging

Award(s): National Institute of Arts and Letters: Rosenthal Award, 1962

696   Julian Mayfield

The Grand Parade

(New York, NY; Vanguard Press, 1961)

Summary: The author's third novel was influenced by his changing political views. The story is set in Gainesboro, a fictional city located between the North and the South. Its cast of characters includes a white politician who is murdered by a white supremacist when he tries to integrate a public school, an unethical black politician whose brother is a member of the Communist party, and a black female gang leader. More ambitious in scope than Mayfield's previous novels, *The Grand Parade* explores the interaction of blacks and whites in American politics.

Subject(s): Politics, Racism, Segregation

697   Julian Mayfield

The Hit: A Novel

(New York, NY; Vanguard Press, 1957)

Summary: Based on his one-act play, *417*, the author's first novel focuses on the impoverished Cooley family in 1950s Harlem. The father Hubert takes money from the household budget and bets it on the number 417 in a numbers game. He wins, but when the numbers man fails to pay him, Hubert is left broken. His wife Gertrude is portrayed as the stabilizing influence in the family. Their son James Lee hesitates to marry out of fear of repeating his parents' failure. Reviewers were generally positive in their reception of the novel.

Subject(s): Poverty, Gambling, Family Problems

698   Julian Mayfield

The Long Night

(New York, NY; Vanguard Press, 1958)

Summary: In his second novel, the author returns to both Harlem and the numbers racket. Ten-year-old Steely Brown's father has abandoned the family. Sent by his mother to pick up her winnings from a numbers game, Steely is robbed by members of his own gang. While attempting to raise the money any way he can, Steely encounters a bum who turns out to be his father. The ending suggests that the family will be reunited. As did Mayfield's earlier novel, *The Hit*, *The Long Night* illustrates the oppressive effect that the socioeconomic environment of America can have on the black family.

Subject(s): Poverty, Gambling, Family

699   John McCluskey, Jr.

Look What They Done to My Song: A Novel

(New York, NY; Random House, 1974)

Summary: This novel, considered the author's major work, tells the story of Mack, a young black musician in search of a place where he can play his music. Beginning in Santa Fe, New Mexico, Mack travels the country seeking to spread a message of love. He believes in Malcolm X's teaching about the need for people to know and comprehend each other. During his travels, Mack meets several different characters, learning something from each of them. A couple from Alabama living in Cape Cod and the Reverend Fuller of Boston teach him about the black southern experience. Mack finds that church is the best forum for his music's message. McCluskey has been lauded for his emphasis on history and black culture.

Subject(s): Music, Religion, Racism

700   William P. McKenzie

The Solemn Hour

(New York, NY; Carlton Press, 1972)

Summary: Mckenzie's 1972 novel is a fantasy novel set in the fictional African kingdom of Arcadia. The Emperor, Sar Irafat, and the Empress, Wizero Nemam, preside over a bountiful kingdom until the Empress suffers a heart attack during a New Year's Eve celebration. The action is narrated by an American who visits the kingdom.

Subject(s): Africa, Royalty

701   Reginald McKnight

Moustapha's Eclipse

(Pittsburgh, PA; University of Pittsburgh Press, 1988)

Summary: *Moustapha's Eclipse* is a collection of ten short stories. Some of the stories involve African myths and are told by Idi, a Senegalese English translator, to his friend, a visiting black American anthropologist. The title story involves a peanut farmer who would risk losing his eyesight to witness an eclipse. Along with the tales of West Africa are others belonging to black America. The stories look at adolescence, racism, and beliefs.

Subject(s): Racism, Africa, Mythology

Award(s): Drue Heinz Literature Prize, 1988

702   James Alan McPherson

Hue and Cry: Short Stories

(New York, NY; Little, Brown, 1969)

Summary: *Hue and Cry* is the author's first collection of short stories. The stories portray characters with lives so hopeless that they can only cry out ineffectually against their situations. The story "Gold Coast" centers on the relationship between Robert, a young black man who works as a janitor and wants to be a writer, and an elderly white alcoholic who has worked as a garbage collector for thirty years. The stories depict discrimination based on race, class, sex and age, as well as confronting issues such as homosexuality and the justice system. McPherson has been praised for creating believable characters in sympathetic situations.

Subject(s): Racism, Homosexuality/Lesbianism, Aging

703 Louise Meriwether

Daddy Was a Number Runner

(Englewood Cliffs, NJ; Prentice-Hall, 1970)

Summary: This novel depicts the economic collapse of a black family living in Harlem during the Depression as told through the observations of twelve-year-old Francie Coffin, whose surname represents her family's demise. When Francie's father runs off with another woman, her mother must beg for extra money from a welfare worker, her older brother becomes a pimp, and her younger brother abandons school for a menial job. In the process, she sees the negative perception of blacks held by whites. At the story's end, Francie is pessimistic about her future, in contrast to her literary counterpart, Francie Nolan, the white protagonist of Betty Smith's *A Tree Grows in Brooklyn*. Critics received the novel favorably, praising its portrayal of a black child living without hope.

Subject(s): Depression (Economic), Racism, Poverty

704 Oscar Micheaux

The Case of Mrs. Wingate

(New York, NY; Book Supply Company, 1945)

Summary: This novel is one of several books written by Micheaux after he became a filmmaker. The filmmaker-author borrowed from the ideas of successful movies. The novel is set during World War II and features Nazi spies and a black detective. As were the other books written by Micheaux in his second phase as a novelist, this book was not a notable success.

Subject(s): Film, World War II

705 Oscar Micheaux

The Masquerade: An Historical Novel

(New York, NY; Book Supply Company, 1947)

Summary: The author's last novel is a reworking of Charles W. Chesnutt's *The House behind the Cedars*. Micheaux adds historical background to the story of a young black woman who attempts to pass as white. While Chesnutt's protagonist dies, Micheaux's marries and escapes to the Midwest. After his return to writing books, Micheaux was not able to achieve the success he had found writing novels before his career as a filmmaker.

Subject(s): Racism, Identity

706 Oscar Micheaux

The Story of Dorothy Stanfield: Based on a Great Insurance Swindle, and a Woman!

(New York, NY; Book Supply Company, 1946)

Summary: This novel is one of the works written by the author after he became a filmmaker. Influenced by the author's involvement in movies, the story centers on a female protagonist involved in an insurance scheme, as the book's subtitle explains. The novel, like others written by the author after he began making movies, was not a significant success.

Subject(s): Crime and Criminals

707 Oscar Micheaux

The Wind from Nowhere

(New York, NY; New York Book Supply, 1941)

Summary: Having abandoned the writing of novels for almost thirty years to produce films, Micheaux returned to fiction with *The Wind from Nowhere*. As was his previous book, *The Homesteader*, this novel is a reworking of the story from his first novel, *The Conquest*. This version's protagonist is farmer Martin Eden, who with his racially mixed wife goes east to bring back black families to the prairie and give them a chance for a new life as fellow farmers. The author's return to writing novels, however, was not marked by great success. Micheaux would later adapt this novel into the film *The Betrayal*.

Subject(s): Farm Life, Film

708 Alison Mills

Francisco

(Berkeley, CA; Reed, Cannon & Johnson Communications Co., 1974)

Summary: The narrator of Mills's 1974 novel tells of her doomed love affair with Francisco. The action is set in the early 1970s and ranges from New York to California; the main characters are creative, hard-living people who struggle with the demands and challenges of love and sexuality. Mills uses a prose style devoid of capital letters.

Subject(s): Love, Sexuality

709 Loften Mitchell

The Stubborn Old Lady Who Resisted Change

(New York, NY; Emerson Hall, 1973)

Summary: The narrator of this novel is a New York City social worker who works tirelessly against a society that cares nothing about its elderly, poor, and minority populations. The "stubborn old lady" of the title, Miss Briggs, is a poor elderly white woman who lives in a dilapidated apartment building in Harlem. The narrator works hard to get the building condemned and to get Miss Briggs into a cleaner and safer environment. Along the way, he forms a friendship with the woman. While he succeeds in getting her moved out of the building, he loses his faith in America, which he feels is devouring its weakest citizens.

Subject(s): Old Age, Urban Affairs

710 Marie Eslanda Moore

Little White Shoes

(Hicksville, NY; Exposition Press, 1975)

Summary: Bette, the narrator of Moore's 1975 novel, begins by describing her late-arriving puberty. In the remainder of the novel, she tells of her love for Ward. She details his unhappy marriage to a woman who is having an affair with another man and talks about her son, Ward Alexander.

Subject(s): Childhood, Love

711 Julian Moreau

The Black Commandos: A Novel

(Atlanta, GA; Cultural Institute Press, 1967)

Summary: This novel opens in Oakdale, a rural town near Lake Charles, Louisiana. The religion of the town's whites, the narrator points out, is racism. Segregation of the town's schools prevents the legitimate son of a white man from meeting his illegitimate half-brother, who was born following the rape of his young black mother. The white man's wife is complicit in the town's racist organization. Blacks work in a sawmill or on poorly run farms, and live in a shantytown. Coming from this background, Denis Jackson leads a group called the Black Commandos, who overthrow the governments of the southern states and finally that of the United States.

Subject(s): Racism, Government, American South

712 Earl J. Morris

The Cop: A Novel

(New York, NY; Exposition Press, 1951)

Summary: This book, written by the first black state trooper in Michigan, was the first novel to depict the life of a black police officer. The novel follows the path of its protagonist, Ben Bowie, who serves as a policeman and later dies in World War I.

Subject(s): World War I, Law Enforcement

713 C.T. Morrison

The Flame in the Icebox: An Episode of the Vietnam War

(New York, NY; Exposition Press, 1968)

Summary: As its subtitle expresses, Morrison's 1968 novel is set during the Vietnam War. In the story, a group of American soldiers in Vietnam get captured and become prisoners of war. Eventually, PFCs Hemphauser and Worth find themselves on the verge of freedom, only to have that opportunity destroyed by their own comrades. The novel's conclusion stresses the absurdity and destructiveness of war--regardless of the ideology of the participants.

Subject(s): Vietnam War

714 Toni Morrison

Beloved

(New York, NY; Knopf, 1987)

Summary: Set twelve years after the end of the Civil War, Morrison's most celebrated novel centers on Sethe, an ex-slave who in 1855 escaped with her children from a Kentucky plantation known as Sweet Home. The novel uses flashbacks to narrate the traumatic events of her past, which include her murder of her eldest daughter to save the child from slavery. The story opens with Sethe and her youngest daughter Denver living in an isolated farmhouse near Cincinnati, Ohio. At their home arrives Paul D., a former slave from the Sweet Home plantation, and later the mysterious Beloved, believed by Sethe and Denver to be the incarnation of Sethe's dead child. Although Sethe at first exults in Beloved's presence, Beloved eventually comes to dominate her mother's life. The story concludes with Beloved's departure and Sethe and Denver's reintegration into the local black community. The novel uses the supernatural as a means to examine the crushing legacy of slavery and the bonds of mother-daughter love. The novel received the Pulitzer Prize for fiction.

Subject(s): Slavery, Family, Supernatural

Award(s): Pulitzer Prize: Fiction, 1988; Robert F. Kennedy Award, 1988

715 Toni Morrison

The Bluest Eye

(New York, NY; Holt, Rinehart & Winston, 1970)

Summary: Toni Morrison, who would later win the Nobel Prize for literature, immediately distinguished herself with her provocative first novel. The story centers on Pecola Breedlove, who at eleven-years-old considers herself ugly. Influenced by images from white culture, she longs for blue eyes, believing that they will make her attractive. Pecola is raped by her father and gives birth to a child that dies. She finally sinks into insanity, believing that she has the bluest eyes of anyone. The destructive family life of the ironically named Breedloves is contrasted by the emotionally rich life of the MacTeer family, whose daughters Frieda and Claudia befriend Pecola. Pecola's story is told principally from Claudia's point of view. The novel depicts the destructive effects that white cultural values can have on black identity.

Subject(s): Racism, Family, Rape

716 Toni Morrison

Jazz

(New York, NY; Knopf, 1992)

Summary: The author's sixth novel tells the story of Joe, a middle-aged salesman, his childless wife Violet, and his teenage mistress Dorcas, whom he fatally shoots when he is jilted for a younger lover. This narrative is paralleled by the story of their predecessors. Both tales take place during important periods in African American history, the Jazz Age of the early 1900s and the Reconstruction period of the 1870s. The impact of racism on black Americans is shown in the almost complete absence of the black family in the novel. Instead, black family life is replaced by the attractions of city life. The novel features an unreliable narrator who is surprised when Joe reconciles with Violet. The narrator, having expected another act of violence, admits not being able to present the truth.

Subject(s): Family, City and Town Life, Reconstruction

---

717 Toni Morrison

Paradise
(New York, NY; A.A. Knopf, 1998)

Summary: Intricate and demanding, Morrison's 1998 novel is set in Ruby, Oklahoma, which was founded by the descendants of black freedmen who had left the Reconstruction-era South and headed west. These freedmen settled a town called Haven; when its farmlands turned to dust, their descendants went further west and established Ruby in 1948. After its founding, the town is autonomous and prosperous for more than twenty years. Miles from the town, a convent school that had been closed becomes a refuge for women from all over the nation. As the town begins to change along with the outside world, the male leaders of the town blame the women living at the convent for the town's growing problems. In an attempt at control, they storm the convent and shoot the women. Against a national backdrop of civil rights activism during the 1960s, the town's men destroy what their forefathers had attempted to achieve. The novel pursues themes from previous Morrison novels, such as community, family, and the supernatural.

Subject(s): Family, Civil Rights Movement, City and Town Life

---

718 Toni Morrison

Song of Solomon
(New York, NY; Knopf, 1977)

Summary: Considered one of Morrison's most important works of fiction, this novel centers on Milkman Dead and his quest for identity. Starting from his Michigan home, Milkman journeys southward in a manner that parallels his travels through the generations of his family. In Danville, Pennsylvania, he uncovers the history of his grandfather and in Shalimar, Virginia, that of his great-grandfather. In discovering his bond with his ancestors, Milkman finds himself. The novel differs from Morrison's earlier novels not only in featuring a male protagonist but in providing a broader perspective on black American life. Even though Milkman's fate is left open, the novel shows a more hopeful tone than its predecessors. In this novel, the desire for assimilation into white culture takes the form of land ownership; those who seek to possess the land do so at the expense of community. The author uses myth, folklore, and the supernatural to create transcendent characters who can fly or talk to ghosts. The critical and popular success of the novel established Morrison as one of America's leading writers.

Subject(s): Folklore, Myth, Supernatural

Award(s): National Book Critics Circle: Fiction Award, 1977; American Academy and Institute of Arts and Letters Award, 1977

---

719 Toni Morrison

Sula
(New York, NY; Knopf, 1973)

Summary: Morrison's second novel depicts the friendship of two black women, Nel and Sula. They live in a black hilltop town that is ironically called Bottom. While impoverished, Bottom's communal life is contrasted to the white valley town of Medallion, whose main interest is business. Nel takes on the traditional matriarchal role of wife and mother while Sula leaves town to seek a life separate from family and community. The residents of Bottom label Sula as evil, referring to the supernatural in an effort to explain a woman who does not conform to traditional gender roles. Even after Sula returns to town and has an affair with Nel's husband, Nel does not come to comprehend her friend until after Sula dies. The novel shows the negative impact of white values on the black community when Bottom, reaching for economic benefits, is destroyed by a tunnel project. The novel brought the author both praise and criticism for her writing technique and presentation of black life, and further established Morrison as an important writer.

Subject(s): Poverty, Family, Women

Award(s): Ohioana Book Award, 1975

---

720 Walter Mosley

Devil in a Blue Dress
(New York, NY; Norton, 1990)

Summary: *Devil in a Blue Dress* is the first in a series of mystery novels centering on detective Ezekiel "Easy" Rawlins. The novel is set in 1948 Los Angeles. Easy loses his aircraft industry job and is concerned about money until he is introduced to a wealthy white man who is willing to help him make some quick cash. Easy's job is to find a beautiful blonde who frequents jazz clubs. He takes the assignment, but it turns out to be more dangerous than he realized. Easy's investigation allows Mosley to illustrate the realities of black neighborhoods in postwar Los Angeles, exploring issues of race and class. The novel met with both popular and critical success. Reviewers praised Mosley's creation of a complex and sympathetic protagonist in Easy as well as his use of imagery, dialogue, and humor.

Subject(s): Mystery, World War II, Racism

Award(s): Private Eye Writers of America: Shamus Award, 1990

---

721 Willard Motley

Knock on Any Door
(New York, NY; D. Appleton-Century Company, 1947)

Summary: Motley's first novel centers on Nick Romano, the son of an Italian immigrant. When Nick's father loses his business during the Depression, the family moves to a poor area of Denver, Colorado, where Nick begins to associate with a group of youths who introduce him to petty crime. When he is placed in reform school, Nick is brutalized by both guards and his fellow inmates. Once he is released, his crimes escalate until he is found guilty of murder and executed at the age of twenty-one. The novel argues that poverty is the source of crime and criticizes the penal system for dehumanizing young criminals. Reviewers were generous in their praise of the novel, which was not only a critical success but a popular one as well. The work is considered one of the last great naturalistic American novels.

Subject(s): Prisoners and Prisons, Poverty, Crime and Criminals

722 Willard Motley

Let No Man Write My Epitaph

(New York, NY; Random House, 1958)

Summary: For his third novel, Motley returns to the family of the protagonist from his first novel, *Knock on Any Door*, in which Nick Romano is executed for murder. *Let No Man Write My Epitaph* follows the lives of Nick's son and nephew, both of whom are tested by the problems of urban Chicago, including drugs and crime. In this novel, the author looks at racism by depicting the nephew's interracial relationship with a black woman. Although citing some strengths in the novel, reviews were for the most part not favorable.

Subject(s): Racism, Crime and Criminals, Drugs

723 Willard Motley

Let Noon Be Fair: A Novel

(New York, NY; Putnam, 1966)

Summary: In his final novel, Motley attempted to depict the exploitation of Mexico by the United States. He illustrates the decline of Las Casas, a coastal town based on Puerto Vallarta, from its origins as a fishing village to its development as a resort for the wealthy. At the urging of his publisher, Motley emphasized the sexual exploitation of the Mexican people in order to make the work more commercial. Having died soon after completing the novel's draft manuscript, the author did not participate in its final editing. Reviews of the novel were uniformly negative, pointing to the novel's sensationalism.

Subject(s): Wealth, Poverty

724 Willard Motley

We Fished All Night

(New York, NY; Appleton-Century-Crofts, 1951)

Summary: The author's second novel follows the stories of three white World War II soldiers after they return home from the war. One was an actor before the war. When he returns to Chicago, he becomes involved in politics only to find himself being used by a political boss. Having suffered a nervous breakdown during the war, another character is unable to real-

ize his pre-war dream of becoming a poet. The third protagonist was a popular labor organizer before the war, but he too returns home scarred from his experiences. A conscientious objector during World War II, Motley attempts to illustrate the negative consequences of the war.

Subject(s): World War II, Poetry

725 Horace Mungin

How Many Niggers Make Half a Dozen: Short Stories

(New York, NY; Promoter's Enterprise, 1971)

Summary: The six brief stories in this collection deal with the devastating consequences of drug addiction. In "This Last Conversation," a junkie returns to his apartment with heroin for himself and his girlfriend. However, she overdoses, leading him to leap out the window to his death. Other stories in the collection, including "Ralph" and "The "Rewards of Allah," feature characters trying to fight their way out of drug addiction. One avenue of hope that the author features is religious adherence to the tenets of Islam, a faith that many African Americans adopted during the late 1960s and early 1970s.

Subject(s): Drug Abuse, Islam, Religion

726 Albert L. Murray

Train Whistle Guitar

(New York, NY; McGraw-Hill, 1974)

Summary: This autobiographical novel is a coming-of-age story focusing on Scooter, a black boy who lives in Gasoline Point, Alabama, in the 1920s. Scooter's story differs from most African American coming-of-age stories in that Scooter does not directly encounter white racism. Instead, he learns about it by listening to older members of the community who tell him stories about flights from slavery or conflict with the white sheriff. Having also learned about sex and death, Scooter leaves the town and becomes a storyteller himself; he then returns to receive the town's praise. The novel is notable for its incorporation of the rhythms and idioms of African American music and speech as well as its emphasis on the importance of a communal oral tradition.

Subject(s): Racism, Music, Coming-of-Age

Award(s): Lillian Smith Award: Southern Fiction, 1974

727 Walter Dean Myers

Fast Sam, Cool Clyde, and Stuff

(New York, NY; Viking Press, 1975)

Summary: This highly acclaimed work was the author's first novel for young adults. Set in New York City, the story follows a group of preteen youths making the most of living in the ghetto. As the tale progresses, the children are repeatedly mistakenly arrested, one of their fathers dies, another deserts his family, and an acquaintance involved in drugs is fatally shot.

Through their bonding, the members increase their ability to survive.

Subject(s): Children, Poverty, Urban Affairs

---

728 Walter Dean Myers

It Ain't All for Nothin'

(New York, NY; Viking Press, 1978)

Summary: This young reader's novel focuses on Tippy, a boy who must choose between a life of petty crime with his father or a life that upholds the values instilled in him by his grandmother. Tippy eventually rejects his father's life when he turns his father into the police and decides to live with Mr. Roland, a member of the supportive ghetto community.

Subject(s): Poverty, Fathers and Sons, Crime and Criminals

---

729 Walter Dean Myers
Leo Carty, Illustrator

Where Does the Day Go?

(New York, NY; Parents' Magazine Press, 1969)

Summary: In this picture book for children, the author's first published work, a group of ethnically diverse children takes a long walk. Led by a sensitive black father, the children discuss the ideas they have about day and night. The book was published under his given name Walter M. Myers.

Subject(s): Children, Fathers

Award(s): Council on Interracial Books for Children Award (for the manuscript), 1968

---

730 Walter Dean Myers

The Young Landlords

(New York, NY; Viking Press, 1979)

Summary: In this novel for younger readers, a group of youths living in the ghetto decide to form the Action Group, whose goal is to improve the community. When the Action Group members choose to clean up a rundown apartment building, the building's owner, Mr. Harley, transfers ownership of the building to the group. Confronted with the difficulties of managing a ghetto apartment building, the group learns about responsibility.

Subject(s): Children, Urban Affairs, Poverty

Award(s): Coretta Scott King Award, 1980

---

731 Gloria Naylor

Bailey's Cafe

(New York, NY; Harcourt Brace Jovanovich, 1992)

Summary: This novel was inspired by Edith Wharton's *The House of Mirth* and focuses on how women are defined by society's perceptions of female sexuality. Most of the customers at the magical Bailey's Cafe are residents of the boarding house next door, which is owned by Eve, who heals women who have been exploited for their sexuality. These characters' names and stories show parallels to the lives of Biblical women. Another character is a transvestite who is confronted with racism while searching for a job. Some reviewers found that the novel lacked the unifying structure of Naylor's first novel, *The Women of Brewster Place*, but critics also praised it for its vivid examination of the lives of African American women.

Subject(s): Women, Racism, Magic

---

732 Gloria Naylor

Linden Hills

(New York, NY; Ticknor & Fields, 1985)

Summary: Referred to in the author's first novel, Linden Hills is an exclusive black suburb near the fictional Brewster Place. This novel focuses on the residents of Linden Hills and exposes the moral decay that results when they abandon their past in pursuit of material success. The story shows how two young men, Willie and Lester, learn of the community's hypocrisy and bigotry when they perform jobs for the residents during the Christmas holidays. Critics praised Naylor for her experiment in modeling the suburb of Linden Hills after the nine circles of hell in Dante's *Inferno* to present a social commentary.

Subject(s): Wealth, Social Classes

---

733 Gloria Naylor

Mama Day

(New York, NY; Ticknor & Fields, 1988)

Summary: Naylor's third novel draws on William Shakespeare's play *The Tempest* to combine elements from Shakespeare with black folklore. Having made an appearance in the author's previous novel, *Linden Hills*, the main character of *Mama Day* is Miranda Day, or "Mama." A ninety-year-old woman with magical powers, Mama lives on an island called Willow Springs that her family has owned since it was founded by a slave before the Civil War. Her relative, Cocoa, brings her new husband, George, to the island. When Cocoa falls ill, though, George must believe in Mama's powers to save his wife. A notable theme in the novel is that of the importance of African American identity as seen in the communal life of the island.

Subject(s): Magic, Family, Slavery

---

734 Gloria Naylor

The Women of Brewster Place

(New York, NY; Viking Press, 1982)

Summary: Naylor's first and most celebrated novel looks at the lives of seven women who live in a housing project in an unidentified northern city and their relationships with one another. They face abuse by their lovers, husbands, and even their children, and must deal with living in a racist and sexist society. The protagonists vary in age and background as well as sexual orientation. They are finally united, however, by a common bond of pain and suffering and begin to heal as a community. A popular as well as critical success, the work has been praised for its portrayal of the lives of black women in America.

Subject(s): Women, Homosexuality/Lesbianism, Racism

Award(s): National Book Award: Best First Novel, 1983

---

735 Joseph Nazel

The Black Exorcist

(Los Angeles, CA; Holloway House, 1974)

Summary: In this novel, the members of a church congregation are transformed into murderers. Barbados Sam, leader of the Cult of the Damned, uses voodoo to turn the church members into hit men for the Syndicate. Reverend Moses Johnson dies during the conflict and is replaced by the young Reverend Roger Lee, who, while questioning his own faith, is now confronted by this evil phenomenon.

Subject(s): Religion, Occult, Murder

---

736 Joseph Nazel

Black Fury

(Los Angeles, CA; Holloway House, 1976)

Summary: This novel focuses on "Heavy," an educated factory worker. The monotonous work of the factory has left him frustrated. When Heavy is pushed too far by a white foreman, he lashes out. The violence spreads throughout the town, pitting blacks and whites against each other. Heavy is finally faced with the decision to give himself up or continue to fight.

Subject(s): Factories, Race Relations, Violence

---

737 Joseph Nazel

The Black Gestapo

(Los Angeles, CA; Holloway House, 1975)

Summary: The protagonist of Nazel's 1975 novel, General Ahmed, is a Vietnam veteran who assembles a force of non-militant blacks to help those victimized by the ghetto's ruling crime syndicate. Colonel Kojah, his second in command, believes this fight against the drug suppliers to be futile. He assembles his own militant force and takes over the People's Army. To fund his efforts, Kojah takes over the drug, numbers, and prostitution rackets, and his group becomes even more of a threat to the ghetto than the white syndicate had been. Ahmed, deciding that this situation must end, enters into a new conflict with Kojah.

Subject(s): Crime and Criminals, Drugs, Gambling

---

738 Joseph Nazel

Death for Hire

(Los Angeles, CA; Holloway House, 1975)

Summary: Like most of Nazel's novels, *Death for Hire* is set in an urban ghetto. It centers on an underworld drug king, Sugar

Man, and an assistant district attorney determined to make a conviction. When Tracy and Turtle, two juvenile offenders, decide to murder the prosecutor, Tracy crashes the vehicle into a police car. The novel considers whether juveniles should be treated as adults by the justice system.

Subject(s): Drugs, Crime and Criminals, Judicial System

---

739 Annie Greene Nelson

After the Storm

(Columbia, SC; Hampton Publishing Company, 1942)

Summary: This novel focuses on Nanette, who is forced to leave her home when her mother discovers that she is pregnant out of wedlock. She is befriended by Maw Jennie, a stranger who sees Nanette's strong Christian faith. Later, her baby arrives stillborn. Nanette's doctor falls in love with her and proposes marriage. Now the wife of a doctor, Nanette chooses to serve the community.

Subject(s): Doctors, Christian Life, Pregnancy

---

740 Annie Greene Nelson

The Dawn Appears: A Novel

(Columbia, SC; Hampton Publishing Company, 1944)

Summary: Set around Pee Dee, South Carolina, at the time of World War II, Nelson's 1944 novel has two distinct story lines. The first part of the story considers the situation of an unwed mother. The second features a married couple, Jack and Rachel. Jack is initially skeptical about the participation of blacks in the war but chooses to fight. He decides to preach a message of brotherhood as a minister when the war ends. The novel is religious in tone and considers such issues as democracy and race relations.

Subject(s): Race Relations, Pregnancy, Religion

---

741 Carl Ruthven Offord

The Naked Fear

(New York, NY; Ace Books, 1954)

Summary: This novel tells the story of a white couple, George and Amy Sutton. George steals a baby and brings it home. When, coincidentally, the district attorney's baby is also reported missing, Amy tries to benefit from the situation. When the couple moves to a black tenement house to escape attention, George gains new knowledge about African Americans. He finally takes the child and leaves his wife, who has tried to kill the baby. Considered inferior to Offord's previous novel, *The White Face*, *The Naked Fear* was published originally only in paperback and did not receive attention by reviewers at the time.

Subject(s): Racism, Kidnapping, Race Relations

742 Carl Ruthven Offord

The White Face

(New York, NY; McBride, 1943)

Summary: This novel centers on Chris and Nella Woods, a black couple from Georgia who move to New York after Chris beats his cruel white employer. Living in Harlem, Nella takes a job with a Jewish family while Chris becomes involved with a black fascist. Adopting the fascists' hatred of the Jews, Chris beats the son of Nella's employers, and even attempts to kill Nella, at which point he is fatally shot by the police. The novel shows how racism can destroy relationships. Since it dealt with the topic of subversion during World War II, the novel was widely reviewed. Although noting stereotypes, critics praised the work's examination of racial psychology and its insight into Harlem politics.

Subject(s): Racism, World War II, Politics

743 Ben Okri

The Famished Road

(London, England; J. Cape, 1991)

Summary: In his acclaimed 1991 novel, Nigerian-born author Ben Okri explores modern Nigeria's economic and political problems. The novel tells the story of Azaro, who is an *abiku*, a child involved in an endless cycle of birth and death. His father's involvement in politics to fight on behalf of the poor parallels Azaro's own effort to break free from the spirit world. At the story's affirmative ending, Azaro comes to see the similarities between the *abiku* and his nation, both of whom must make sacrifices to attain a new state of being. Critics have compared Okri's work to the writer Gabriel Garcia Marquez and the school of writing known as magical realism, which combines supernatural and realistic elements. The novel, however, can also be seen as an example of African animistic thought, in which spirits freely take on animal traits. The novel won the prestigious Booker Prize in Great Britain.

Subject(s): Africa, Spiritualism, Politics

Award(s): Booker Prize: Fiction, 1991

744 Cleo Overstreet

The Boar Hog Woman

(Garden City, NY; Doubleday, 1972)

Summary: This novel opens in 1936 as a black man takes an experimental job raising hogs in the Sand Pack Desert. He is disappointed when his giant sow gives birth to only a sexually ambiguous runt. The runt eventually comes to be loved by its owner but disappears in 1943. In 1959, a woman running a barber shop in the black community of Berkeley, California looks like a boar hog and is pregnant. Presented as contemporary myth, the story shows how the Boar Hog Woman wreaks havoc on the lives of those around her.

Subject(s): Mythology

745 Jon Palmer

House Full of Brothers

(Los Angeles, CA; Holloway House, 1973)

Summary: In his first novel, Palmer tells the story of Steven Walls, who moves to Los Angeles from Omaha. Steven obtains what he believes is necessary for success: an education, a prestigious job, and a girlfriend who is white. Steven's plans go awry when he is arrested for a bank robbery and a murder that he did not commit. The novel explores black fraternities as well as the influence of a predominantly white society on middle-class blacks.

Subject(s): Middle Classes, Crime and Criminals, Race Relations

746 Gordon Parks

The Learning Tree

(New York, NY; Harper & Row, 1963)

Summary: Harking back to the author's own childhood, this novel tells the story of Newt Winger, the youngest son of a black family living in a small Kansas town in the 1920s. Newt experiences losing his virginity during a tornado, the death of his mother, and being sent away from his immediate family to live with an aunt in the north. Parks's portrayal of the family is notable because they are respected within their community despite their poverty. Parks later produced and directed the film version of the story in addition to writing the musical score, a first for a black filmmaker.

Subject(s): Poverty, Film, Family

747 Clarence R. Parrish

Images of Democracy (I Can't Go Home)

(New York, NY; Carlton Press, 1967)

Summary: This novel centers on a young black man, Jeff Ransom, who, years before the novel opens, fled Mississippi when he was accused of raping a white girl whom he actually saved from drowning. Jeff is now a successful attorney in New York with his own family. Jeff is drawn to return home when he is asked to defend a racially mixed woman who has been accused of murdering her white lover, the son of the town's sheriff. The town is portrayed as segregated and under the influence of the Ku Klux Klan.

Subject(s): American South, Racism, Miscegenation

748 Charles Perry

Portrait of a Young Man Drowning

(New York, NY; Simon and Schuster, 1962)

Summary: The principal characters in this novel belong to an Irish-American family. Harry lives in a Brooklyn slum with his mother and father. When his father abandons the family, Harry quits school and begins to work for the criminals who control his community. Influenced by his mother's possessiveness, Harry becomes increasingly dangerous, leading to his personal destruction.

Subject(s): Family, Crime and Criminals

---

749 **Richard Perry**

Changes
(Indianapolis, IN; Bobbs-Merrill, 1974)

Summary: Bill Taylor, the protagonist of Perry's 1974 novel, is a black associate professor. Besides facing problems at school and with his wife, Bill is questioning his middle-class values, which he senses have isolated him from his black identity. He meets a character named Bukay, who claims to be an occult scientist and to have invented the white race. Bukay tells Bill that he has a plan to turn everyone in the world black and wants Bill to join him.

Subject(s): Occult, Middle Classes, Race Relations

---

750 **Ann Petry**

Country Place
(Boston, MA; Houghton Mifflin, 1947)

Summary: For her second novel, Petry changed the setting of her story from that of Harlem to the town of Lennox, Connecticut. Her second novel also differs from her first, *The Street*, in that the main characters are white. At the center of the story is Johnnie Roane, who upon returning home from World War II learns that his wife is having an affair. While Johnnie is able to leave the town and pursue a new life as an artist in New York, the other major characters remain spiritually dead or actually die as the story ends. Critics were mainly positive in their reception of *Country Place*, and the novel's reputation has increased with time.

Subject(s): World War II, Marriage

---

751 **Ann Petry**

Miss Muriel and Other Stories
(Boston, MA; Houghton Mifflin, 1971)

Summary: This book collects some of the author's shorter works of fiction. The title story, "Miss Muriel," is told from the perspective of a young girl who watches as two men from different ethnic backgrounds court the affections of her aunt. "The New Mirror" is an autobiographical story that depicts the life of a black family in an all-white town. Both stories confront racial concerns. "The Witness" is written in the tradition of earlier New England writers Nathaniel Hawthorne and Herman Melville and centers on a teacher who discovers the evil within the human heart.

Subject(s): Race Relations

---

752 **Ann Petry**

The Narrows
(Boston, MA; Houghton Mifflin, 1953)

Summary: In her third novel, Petry returns to writing about a small community in Connecticut. The story centers on Link Williams, a young black man, who, although he has graduated from Dartmouth, returns to town and takes a job as a bartender. He falls in love with the daughter of a wealthy white family only to discover that she is married. Link is finally murdered by the heiress's husband and the family matriarch. Once again Petry received favorable reviews for her work, obtaining praise for her characterization and attention to the issue of racism.

Subject(s): Racism, Murder, Social Classes

---

753 **Ann Petry**

The Street
(Boston, MA; Houghton Mifflin, 1946)

Summary: Petry's first novel focuses on Lutie Johnson. After an unhappy experience working for a wealthy white family in Connecticut and learning of her husband's relationship with another woman, Lutie leaves her home in Long Island and attempts to start a new life for herself and her son in Harlem. Unable to secure an honest job and with her son having been introduced to a life of crime, Lutie leaves her son to a probable future of reform school and takes a train heading toward Chicago. Reviewers praised the work, noting its perception and realism. This novel was the first written by a black female author to deal with the problems confronted by disadvantaged black women in the modern city.

Subject(s): Racism, Women, Poverty

---

754 **Robert Deane Pharr**

The Book of Numbers
(Garden City, NY; Doubleday, 1969)

Summary: Pharr was inspired by Sinclair Lewis's *Babbitt* to present a realistic presentation of black American life. *The Book of Numbers* centers on protagonist David Greene, who runs a numbers game in the black ward of a small southern city. In the story of Greene's rise and fall, the reader is introduced to a wide cross-section of black life in 1930s America. The numbers in the novel do not simply refer to gambling but also serve as a metaphor, as the book's Biblical title suggests. The numbers are related to destiny; the novel indicates that destiny for black Americans is determined by white racism. Pharr addresses the question of how blacks can succeed economically when they are confronted by racism. The novel was not only a critical success but a popular one as well.

Subject(s): Racism, Gambling

---

755 Robert Deane Pharr

Giveadamn Brown

(Garden City, NY; Doubleday, 1978)

Summary: This novel follows Lawrence "Giveadamn" Brown, a young black man who moves from Florida to Harlem. When he arrives in the city, his relationship to crime boss Harry Brown is revealed. After the elder Brown is hospitalized because of an accident, Giveadamn attempts to save Harry's criminal empire from his enemies. While the novel was criticized for having a contrived plot, it was also praised for his portrayal of life in Harlem.

Subject(s): Crime and Criminals, Identity

756 Robert Deane Pharr

The Soul Murder Case

(New York, NY; Avon, 1975)

Summary: Pharr's third novel centers on Bobby Dee, a singer turned literary agent. His life lacks meaning, and Bobby must outgrow fear and confront reality. The novel includes Pharr's most explicit depiction of sexuality, including interracial relations, and confronts drug addiction. Published only in paperback, the novel was neither a critical nor a commercial success.

Subject(s): Sexuality, Miscegenation, Drug Abuse

757 Robert Deane Pharr

S.R.O.

(Garden City, NY; Doubleday, 1971)

Summary: The most autobiographical of Pharr's novels, *S.R.O.* centers on Sid Bailey, a college-educated, middle-aged black waiter with an alcohol problem who moves into a single-room-occupancy hotel in Harlem. Here he meets a wide range of characters, including drug addicts and dealers, prostitutes, and an interracial lesbian couple. Given strength by his writing and his relationship with an ex-drug addict, Sid is able to escape from the hopeless life of the hotel. Although offering some praise, reviewers in general did not find this novel to be a worthy follow-up to Pharr's first, *The Book of Numbers*, and it was not a popular success.

Subject(s): Alcoholism, Writing

758 Caryl Phillips

Higher Ground: A Novel in Three Parts

(New York, NY; Viking, 1989)

Summary: *Higher Ground* explores the lingering effects of slavery by connecting the past with the present. The first part, "Heartland," tells the story of an anonymous African captured by European slave traders in the eighteenth century and put to work enslaving fellow Africans. When he finally rebels, he is sent on a slave ship to the Americas. The next part, "The Cargo Rap," focuses on a young black American prisoner named Rudolph Leroy Williams, who writes highly politicized letters about racism in America to his family. By the story's end, Rudi appears to have been defeated by the prison system. The final part, "Higher Ground," is about a Holocaust survivor named Irina who leaves Poland for England. Confronted with anti-immigrant hostility from the British, Irina attempts to establish a relationship with a West Indian immigrant. By referring to his work as "a novel in three parts," Phillips encourages the reader to form thematic connections among the book's stories.

Subject(s): Slavery, Racism

759 Jane Phillips

Mojo Hand

(New York, NY; Trident Press, 1966)

Summary: This novel concerns a young woman, Eunice, who travels in search of a guitarist named Blacksnake Brown. The novel depicts their troubled relationship and concludes with Blacksnake dead at the hands of another woman. Eunice, pregnant with his child, takes shelter at his mother's home.

Subject(s): Music, Interpersonal Relationships, Murder

760 Mike Phillips

Blood Rights

(New York, NY; St. Martin's Press, 1989)

Summary: The author's first crime novel is set in London and centers on a black journalist named Sam Dean. Between assignments and short on money, Dean is made an offer by an old college friend, now a member of Parliament. The man wants Dean to find his missing daughter, who was last seen with a young black man. Among Dean's findings are two corpses in the daughter's flat as well as secrets from the father's past. The novel explores the influence of family and examines the black subculture of London.

Subject(s): Politics, Race Relations, Family

761 Carlene Hatcher Polite

The Flagellants

(New York, NY; Ferrar, Straus & Giroux, 1967)

Summary: The experimental writer's first novel centers on a young black couple, Ideal and Jimson, who fall in love after meeting in New York's Greenwich Village. Their attempt to build a life together is defeated by their inability to transcend the limited roles given to black women and men in a racist society. Full of lyrical prose, the novel consists of stream-of-consciousness passages in which Ideal and Jimson communicate their innermost thoughts. Polite was hailed by critics for her innovative writing as well as for the strength with which she reexamined black male and female roles.

Subject(s): Racism, Sex Roles

762 Carlene Hatcher Polite

Sister X and the Victims of Foul Play
...
(New York, NY; Farrar, Straus, Giroux, 1975)

Summary: The life and death of Sister X Arista Prolo, a black exotic dancer who performed in Paris in the style of Josephine Baker, is told through the conversation of her costume designer, Abyssinia, and her lover, Willis B. Black. Polite uses extended monologues to develop this story even more than in her first novel, *The Flagellants*. The music of the blues is scattered among the pieces of the characters' conservation, which on Abyssinia's part is often grounded in black folklore. Through the pair's dialogue, Sister X's death is shown to be the result of a racist society that kills the aspirations of blacks.

Subject(s): Racism, Dancing, Music

763 Freeman Pollard

Seeds of Turmoil: A Novel of American PW's Brainwashed in Korea
(New York, NY; Exposition Press, 1959)

Summary: When John Hilton, a young black man from Alabama, arrives for duty at a Marine Corps base, he meets Kenneth Tyson, a surprisingly friendly white soldier from Atlanta. The two form a strong friendship. When John is killed in Korea, Kenneth experiences a severe depression. During Kenneth's psychotherapeutic treatment, his doctor reveals that his condition involves an acute schizophrenia which has resulted from being raised in an environment that was at once extremely religious and strongly racist.

Subject(s): Friendship, Racism, Religion

764 Adam Clayton Powell, Sr.

Picketing Hell: A Fictitious Narrative
(New York, NY; Wendell Malliet, 1942)

Summary: This 1942 novel honors the enormous influence of religion in the African American community while at the same time satirizing some of the church's features. The novel's protagonist, Tom Tern, rises from a morally deficient background to become a highly respected and influential minister in Massachusetts. For the most part, this novel does not address issues such as racial conflict or social justice.

Subject(s): Christianity, Religion

765 G. Henderson Puckett

One More Tomorrow
(New York, NY; Vantage Press, 1959)

Summary: Set during the Civil War, this romance novel takes place mainly in the states of Massachusetts and South Carolina. When the story's hero, John, is abducted, he is forced into slavery for a year. With the help of sympathetic whites, John makes his escape. He fights with a black volunteer regiment for the North and is involved in a series of battles.

Subject(s): Civil War, Abolition, Slavery

766 Leroy L. Ramsey

The Trial and the Fire
(New York, NY; Exposition Press, 1967)

Summary: This novel looks at how a small southern town is affected by approaching integration. When a racist white resident lashes out, he murders a young white woman who has associated with black civil-rights workers. Later, he burns down the school and restaurant in the part of town occupied by its black residents. The destruction, however, only contributes to the impending integration of the town.

Subject(s): American South, Racism, Segregation

767 E. Michael Rasmussen

The First Night
(New York, NY; W. Malliet, 1947)

Summary: Set in the Virgin Islands in the late 1930s, during the time when the United States acquired the territory from Denmark, *The First Night* is a story about miscegenation and nationalism. The plot includes a Russian, Dmitri, who sleeps with every island woman who is about to get married, thus fathering many mixed-race children. The novel's protagonist, Lorenson, is an archaeologist who finds love while visiting the territory. Though somewhat stilted in its study of race relations, the novel offers a pleasing romantic tale set in a tropical landscape.

Subject(s): Miscegenation, Romance, Race Relations

768 James-Howard Readus

The Big Hit
(Los Angeles, CA; Holloway House Pub. Co., 1975)

Summary: This novel's story begins when a powerful businessman's son is killed by a stray bullet from the Syndicate, a Los Angeles crime organization. When J.J. is enlisted by the victim's father to take on the Syndicate, the Syndicate is impressed with J.J. and makes him the local godfather. After J.J.'s girlfriend is murdered, he becomes involved in a battle with another godfather.

Subject(s): Crime and Criminals, Murder

769 James-Howard Readus

The Death Merchants
(Los Angeles, CA; Holloway House, 1974)

Summary: This novel centers on Maxwell Noland, who was trained by the army to be a killer. Deciding that he does not want to kill anymore, Noland begins selling drugs. The Syndicate offers him a great deal of money to work for them, but to prove himself he must return to killing. The enjoyment he discovers in murder leads to his own alienation from himself.

Subject(s): Drugs, Crime and Criminals, Murder

---

770   **Saunders Redding**

Stranger and Alone

(New York, NY; Harcourt, Brace, 1950)

Summary: This novel centers on a racially mixed young man, Shelton Howden, the son of a white father and a black mother. Attending both white and black colleges, Shelton remains a loner. When he enters Arcadia College, he meets the school's president, Wimbush, an older version of himself. Under the negative influence of Wimbush and his daughter, Shelton marries for convenience and eventually betrays his black friends to the white politicians of his southern town. Controversial at the time of its publication, the novel was generally well received by critics.

Subject(s): Racism, American South

---

771   **Ishmael Reed**

Flight to Canada

(New York, NY; Random House, 1976)

Summary: This novel is a satire set during the Civil War. It centers on Raven Quickskill, a slave who escapes from Virginia to Canada and returns as a free man to help liberate more slaves. Quickskill writes a poem called "Flight to Canada," which serves as an aesthetic escape from his previous identity as a slave. The novel uses anachronistic elements, such as the television and telephone used by the Virginia slave owner. Robert E. Lee and Abraham Lincoln are among the historic figures who make appearances in the novel. By not focusing on the black aesthetic concept Neo-HooDoo that he presented in his previous three novels, the author is able to concentrate on satirizing the slave narrative, particularly Harriet Beecher Stowe's *Uncle Tom's Cabin*.

Subject(s): Slavery, Civil War

---

772   **Ishmael Reed**

The Free-Lance Pallbearers

(Garden City, NY; Doubleday, 1967)

Summary: Reed's first novel is a satire of the confessional style that has characterized much black American fiction since the slave narratives of the eighteenth century. The story's protagonist, Bukka Doopeyduk, lives in Harry Sam, a white-ruled society headed by a Lyndon B. Johnson-like dictator. The novel depicts Bukka's search for identity and his attempt at social assimilation. At the story's end, he achieves self-awareness but is finally crucified. Reed creates parallels between Bukka and literary figures such as the protagonist in Ralph Ellison's *Invisible Man* and parodies the narrative styles of Zora Neale Hurston's *Their Eyes Were Watching God* and Ellison's novel. In so doing, he signaled his intention to create literature that

moved beyond the social and political confines of previous black fiction.

Subject(s): Racism, Identity

---

773   **Ishmael Reed**

The Last Days of Louisiana Red

(New York, NY; Random House, 1974)

Summary: In his fourth novel, Reed pursues his interest in Neo-HooDoo, the black aesthetic concept presented in his previous two novels. This novel is set in 1970s Berkeley, California, and features voodoo detective Papa LaBas, first seen in *Mumbo Jumbo*. In *The Last Days of Louisiana Red*, Papa LaBas investigates the murder of a business owner, whose Solid Gumbo Works uses spells and charms to fight the effects of Louisiana Red, a hot sauce that Reed uses to depict the division of black people against each other. The novel satirizes the black revolutionary organizations of the era. While some critics have been troubled by the story's representation of women, the novel advanced Reed's reputation as a writer committed to extending the boundaries of African American literature.

Subject(s): Racism, Literature

---

774   **Ishmael Reed**

Mumbo Jumbo

(Garden City, NY; Doubleday, 1972)

Summary: In his third novel, Reed continues to explore his black aesthetic concept, Neo-HooDoo. *Mumbo Jumbo*, which takes its title from the Western designation for black religious rituals as well as black languages, is a parody of the mystery genre and is set during the Harlem Renaissance of the 1920s. It centers on voodoo detective Papa LaBas and follows the spread of Jes Grew, a dance that prevents those who participate in it from functioning in American society. Jes Grew takes its name from Harriet Beecher Stowe's *Uncle Tom's Cabin*, in which Topsy "jes' grew" without antecedents. Reed uses Jes Grew to represent the instinctive impulse of black culture and its opponent Atonism to symbolize the repressive rationalism of the Judeo-Christian tradition. Although lacking much of the humor seen in the author's first two novels, *Mumbo Jumbo* was praised by critics for its use of satire and mythmaking.

Subject(s): Religion, Mythology, Dancing

---

775   **Ishmael Reed**

Yellow Back Radio Broke-Down

(Garden City, NY; Doubleday, 1969)

Summary: Reed's second novel marks the introduction of the author's concept of an alternative black aesthetic, which he terms Neo-HooDoo. Focusing on ancient rites such as magic and voodoo, Neo-HooDoo, Reed asserts, will help rid African Americans and Third World peoples of Judeo-Christian conditioning and aid in restoring their liberty and spiritual sense. The novel is a spoof of western pulp fiction. Set in the Old West town of Yellow Back Radio, the story pits the Loop Garoo Kid, an intuitive Neo-HooDoo cowboy, against Drag Gibson, the town's rational dictator, who shows similarities to former U.S. President Lyndon B. Johnson. At the story's end, Loop Garoo drives off not only Drag Gibson from the town but the Pope as well. Mixing the conventions of the western novel with black jive, Reed models his story on the conflict between Black Osiris and Set, two gods from Egyptian mythology.

Subject(s): Mythology, Westerns, Catholicism

776 **Thomas E. Roach**

Samson

(Boston, MA; Meador Pub Co., 1952)

Summary: The protagonist of this novel is Samson Shylock. The hero introduces a secret weapon that brings an end to war and serves as the catalyst for the creation of an international police force.

Subject(s): War, Weapons

777 **Sadie L. Roberson**

Killer of the Dream: Short Stories

(New York, NY; Carlton Press, 1963)

Summary: This book includes three short stories and an epilogue. The collection opens with "The Color," in which a drifter who overcomes his alcoholism and finds a job is forced back to a life on the road following a racial incident. The next story, "The Creed," features a Jewish brother and sister who find compensation in materialism for their rejection by society. "The Nationality" focuses on a world famous singer who believes that World War II has ruined her career. The epilogue seeks to resolve the issues raised in the preceding stories. The protagonists learn from the Statue of Liberty that the killers of the dream of freedom are prejudice and hatred and that they must enter the world and fight for freedom.

Subject(s): Prejudice, Jews, Music

778 **Arthur Robinson**

Hang That Nigger

(New York, NY; Vantage Press, 1975)

Summary: With a plot as provocative as its title, this novel centers on Art Simmons, a young black man raised and educated in the South. When he moves to a large city in the North, he finds his life less limited. He marries, earns a good income, and becomes involved in politics, yet he misses the South. When he returns there, he attempts to combine the best of his northern and southern lifestyles. Simmons, however, encounters opposition and is charged with the rape of a white woman.

Subject(s): American South, Racism, Politics

779 **J. Terry Robinson**

The Double Circle People

(New York, NY; Suzanna, 1970)

Summary: This novel looks at a group of prostitutes in New York. Among them is Lorraine Evans, who is invited by a fellow prostitute to attend a high-society party as an escort to a handsome man named Clay Dodson. Lorri is attracted to Clay and they are eventually married. Her dreams of happiness, however, are ended when Clay attempts to stop a gun-wielding murderer.

Subject(s): Prostitution, Murder

780 **Rose Robinson**

Eagle in the Air: A Novel

(New York, NY; Crown Publishers, 1969)

Summary: This novel focuses on Jeannie, an impoverished black girl. When she is expelled from college for participating in a sit-in, she first goes to her older boyfriend. When she decides to leave this temperamental boyfriend and discovers that her family cannot help her, she hitchhikes to the West Coast to start a new life. Her experiences on the road, including nearly being raped and her rescue by two white men, help Jeannie to learn not only about herself but also about her relations with whites.

Subject(s): Race Relations, Colleges and Universities, Poverty

781 **Bryant Rollins**

Danger Song

(Garden City, NY; Doubleday, 1967)

Summary: This novel centers on a youth living in the black ghetto of Boston. When he attempts to reach beyond his own environment, he finds himself in touch with the white community. This world seems safer than the danger-filled streets of his ghetto, but he is confronted by a new threat. In the process, he makes a discovery about his own identity.

Subject(s): Racism, City and Town Life, Identity

782 **Sadie Mae Rosebrough**

Wasted Travail

(New York, NY; Vantage Press, 1951)

Summary: The young protagonist of Rosebrough's 1951 work lives on a farm in the American South. She lacks the attention of her mother, who is left exhausted by work. The young woman takes a job driving a bus and later works in a munitions plant. She marries and attends college. Failing to see the injustice in American racial affairs, she feels ashamed of a group of marchers who are protesting the shooting death of a young man caught stealing a car. Narrated in the first person, the novel depicts its protagonist as resolving her emotional conflicts through self-denial.

Subject(s): Racism, American South, Poverty

783 Fran Ross

Oreo
(New York, NY; Greyfalcon House, 1974)

Summary: Christine, called Oreo, is the daughter of a black mother and a Jewish father. In the novel, Oreo experiences picaresque adventures after she sets out to discover the secret of her birth. While the story takes on characteristics of the legend of Theseus, Oreo is presented as a contemporary heroine.

Subject(s): Picaresque Adventure, Jews, Mythology

784 Christopher Rudolph

The Boy Who Cursed God
(New York, NY; Carlton Press, 1975)

Summary: This story begins during the 1940s in Baltimore, where a young black woman is having difficulties with her little boy, whose problematic behavior ranges from stealing to swearing. The mother decides to move to Cheraw, South Carolina, where she has family. For a while, her son's behavior improves but then worsens again. The boy eventually receives advice from his great-grandmother that enables him to control his destructive behavior.

Subject(s): Mothers and Sons, Family, Childhood

785 Saggittarus
(Pseudonym of Carl L. Shears)

Before the Setting Sun: The Age before Hambone
(Washington, DC; Nuclassics and Science Pub. Co., 1974)

Summary: Writing under the pseudonym Saggitarus, Carl L. Shears in this novel offers a tale about African Americans taking over the political system of a disintegrating America. Hambone, referred to in the novel's subtitle, is an idealistic eighteen-year-old as the novel opens. By the novel's end, Hambone has risen to the head of the country's armed forces, at which point he stages a *coup d'etat* and becomes America's first black dictator.

Subject(s): Government, Rebellion

786 Saggittarus
(Pseudonym of Carl L. Shears)

The Count-Down to Black Genocide
(Washington, DC; Nuclassics and Science Pub. Co., 1973)

Summary: This provocative novel describes a plot by the white-dominated United States government to eliminate all blacks from the country. First, however, the government cedes a portion of northern Florida to a group of blacks so that they can set up their own nation called "Afro-America." Only 100,000 blacks are allowed in from a population of 30 million. Afro-America's president, General El, accurately predicts the genocide of those blacks who didn't make it into Afro-America.

Subject(s): Government, Genocide

787 Saggittarus
(Pseudonym of Carl L. Shears)

Niggers and Po' White Trash
(Washington, DC; Nuclassics and Science Pub. Co., 1971)

Summary: The five stories in this collection reflect the darkly comic, pessimistic attitude of Carl L. Shears. In "When You Git to Know the Boys," a poorly educated white man, Wilbur, loses his job. On his first day of being unemployed, he converses with two similarly unemployed African American men. But rather than admitting his lost job, Wilbur pretends that he is rich and spends his family's last dollars paying the two men to mow his grass. In "If There Is a Knock," a law is passed authorizing the authorities to incarcerate all illiterate adults and put their children in child-care institutions. If the adults don't learn to read properly during their incarceration, they are to be sterilized and sent away for good.

Subject(s): Government, Race Relations

788 Anne Scott

Case 999, A Christmas Story
(Boston, MA; Meador Pub. Co., 1953)

Summary: Published in book form, this short story centers on a black grandmother referred to as Granny. Her son's and daughter-in-law's deaths can both be traced back to a riot, which Granny refers to as her "trouble." She struggles to care for her grandson, Sammie, who is involved with a gang. They live without working utilities in the cellar of a tenement house. The Reverend Jones, Doctor Ross, and Miss Rose, a social worker, all attempt to help the pair. Although they are unaware of what awaits them, Granny faces being put in an infirmary and Sammie in a foster home. Relying on coal oil lamps for their heat, Granny and Sammie die from asphyxiation on Christmas Eve.

Subject(s): Race Relations, Poverty, Grandparents

789 Gil Scott-Heron

The Nigger Factory: A Novel
(New York, NY; Dial Press, 1972)

Summary: Set at the all-black Sutton University in Virginia, this novel's central characters are a moderate student leader and the school's conservative president. When they are confronted by an ultimatum issued by militant students calling for sweeping changes at the university, a violent conflict develops.

Subject(s): Colleges and Universities, Race Relations, American South

790 Gil Scott-Heron

The Vulture
(New York, NY; World Pub. Co., 1970)

Summary: Scott-Heron's first novel begins and ends with a view of the lifeless body of John Lee lying on the sidewalk of a New York City street. The story of Lee's murder and the life he led as a junkie and drug pusher is told through the perspective of four other young men who knew him. In telling Lee's tale, the novel offers an illustration of the city's street life as well as its drug trafficking scene.

Subject(s): Drugs, Crime and Criminals

791 Robert Martin Screen

We Can't Run Away from Here: A Novel
(New York, NY; Vantage Press, 1958)

Summary: This novel recounts what happens when three southern black students, John, Emmett, and Edward, attempt to attend a school for whites. Pursued, they take shelter in John's aunt's house but are trapped there by members of the Ku Klux Klan. Over the course of one night, the story explores the hopes that the youths' once held and their current fears as they are killed one after another and the house is engulfed in flames.

Subject(s): American South, Racism, Murder

792 Frank Shackleford

Old Rocking Chair
(New York, NY; Vantage Press, 1975)

Summary: The "old rocking chair" of this novel's title belongs to Mrs. Bandi, an elderly, devoutly Christian woman who is constantly at odds with her neighbors. Among those neighbors are Bessie and her friend Susie, women for whom alcohol and sex are the chief aims in life. In addition to describing the party life that Bessie and her friends lead, the author focuses on Bessie's teenage son Timothy, who revels in New York City's gay subculture.

Subject(s): Homosexuality/Lesbianism, Neighbors and Neighborhoods, City and Town Life

793 Letty M. Shaw

Angel Mink: A Novel
(New York, NY; Comet Press Books, 1957)

Summary: Set in a slum called Sen District, this novel centers on a young girl named Angel Mink, who is mistreated by an aunt, Dollar, whom she believes is her mother. When Angel's father dies, Dollar steals the insurance money and attempts to force Angel into becoming a prostitute. Dollar has her niece thrown into a juvenile detention center when Angel tries to run away. After her aunt and grandmother try to defraud her again, the court puts her in a caring foster home. The novel does not consider the race of its characters.

Subject(s): Family Problems, Poverty, Foster Homes

794 Ann Allen Shockley

Loving Her
(Indianapolis, IN; Bobbs-Merrill, 1974)

Summary: In her pioneering first novel, Shockley tells the story of Renay, a black singer with a child and ex-husband. Renay falls in love with a white female writer. The story shows how Renay develops an awareness of her homosexuality and how she deals with her relationships with her lover, daughter, and former husband. The first novel by a black woman writer to focus on love involving an interracial lesbian couple, the book examines the issue of abusive heterosexual relationships and explores societal attitudes toward interracial as well as lesbian relationships.

Subject(s): Homosexuality/Lesbianism, Racism

795 Minnie T. Shores

Americans in America
(Boston, MA; Christopher Pub. House, 1966)

Summary: Minnie T. Shores in this 1966 work offers a hopeful story about race relations. The novel opens with Larry, a prejudice-free white boy from Tennessee, being run over by a bicycle driven by a young black student, Ralph. Larry eventually grows up to become a man committed to ending racial injustice. Meanwhile, Ralph becomes a prize-winning debater at high school and then in college.

Subject(s): Race Relations, American South

796 Minnie T. Shores

Publicans and Sinners
(New York, NY; Comet Press Books, 1960)

Summary: This melodramatic novel is set in a Missouri city. Centering on a heroine with an impulsive personality, the story features a group of young adults who face difficulties resulting from war and racial discrimination.

Subject(s): War, Racism

797 Herbert A. Simmons

Corner Boy: A Novel
(Boston, MA; Houghton Mifflin, 1957)

Summary: In both of his first two novels, Simmons recreates the life of black urban St. Louis in the 1940s and 1950s. *Corner Boy*, Simmons's debut novel, follows the story of Jake Adams, who pushes drugs for a white underworld boss. When Jake becomes romantically involved with a student named Armenta, his boss agrees to allow him to go to college as long as he continues to sell drugs. When Armenta's father sends her out of state, Jake drops out of college. While going for a ride in his new car with Georgia, the daughter of a white family, the car is involved in an accident and Georgia is killed. The local prosecutor, intent on destroying the crime boss's drug ring, tries to have Jake convicted not only for selling drugs but also for the rape of a white woman. Jake is sent to jail but vows a return to city life. The author's depiction of the destructive effects of economic and racial forces finds some relief in his presentation of black music, particularly jazz.

Subject(s): Racism, Drugs, Jazz

798 Herbert A. Simmons

Man Walking on Eggshells

(Boston, MA; Houghton Mifflin, 1962)

Summary: In his second novel, the author revisits the black urban setting of St. Louis. In this story, however, Simmons emphasizes the positive effect that family support can have on a young person over the pull of the streets. At the center of this coming-of-age story is Raymond Douglas, who is lured away from gang life by the influence of his relatives. His grandfather and uncle teach him the joys of music. His grandmother, in turn, provides him with a sense of family tradition. Raymond goes on to college and then joins a group of radical 1960s musicians before deciding to perform independently. Simmons portrays the artist's music as coming not only from his personal experience but from the collective urban one as well.

Subject(s): Music, Family, Coming-of-Age

799 Theodosia B. Skinner

Dilemma of a College Girl

(Philadelphia, PA; Dorrance, 1972)

Summary: In her 1972 novella, Theodosia B. Skinner tells the story of a troubled romance between Edwina, a talented young college student, and George, a former Army soldier. Through a complex series of circumstances, George confesses that he is the father of two young twins. Edwina despairs that George can never provide her with the love she seeks because his first priority is to his children. However, George convinces her otherwise, and at the end of the story the two plan to get married.

Subject(s): Romance, Parenthood

800 Theodosia B. Skinner

Ice Cream from Heaven

(New York, NY; Vantage, 1962)

Summary: The protagonist of Skinner's 1962 novel is Rebecca Ann, who at the age of seven moves to the North to live with her aunt's family when her mother dies. She marvels at the differences she encounters, including the white students she sees. She refers to snow as ice cream from heaven. Despite the difficulties she goes through when her aunt's family experiences hard times, Rebecca remains grateful for having been able to leave the South. Later, she and her fiancee travel south to bring her grandmother to live with them back in the North.

Subject(s): American South, Family

801 Irene Smalls-Hector
Michael Hays, Illustrator

Jonathan and His Mommy

(Boston, MA; Little, Brown, 1992)

Summary: This children's book follows a five-year-old African American child and his mother as they go for their daily walk through the city. Their walk is highlighted by the imaginative steps that they take, including zigzag, bunny, and slow-motion steps. Illustrated with contemporary images, the book provides a depiction of urban life as well as the love between mother and son.

Subject(s): Children, City and Town Life, Mothers and Sons

802 Daniel Smith

A Walk in the City

(New York, NY; World Pub. Co., 1971)

Summary: Set in a poverty-stricken inner city, the author's first novel centers on Garner Hawkins, who is eight-years-old when the story begins. One of his older brothers, Luther, is tough and street smart but eventually dies at the hands of police. After having dropped out of school himself, the story's conclusion finds an older Garner leaving the city for prep school and a chance at a better life. The novel examines police racism, and Garner comes to realize that an education is the key to overcoming white prejudice.

Subject(s): Poverty, Racism, Education

803 Vern E. Smith

The Jones Men

(Chicago, IL; Regnery, 1974)

Summary: This novel tells the story of twenty-six-year-old Lennie Jack, a Vietnam War veteran who works as a middle-level dealer in heroin, or "jones," as both the drug and the craving it produces are called in the drug subculture. Lennie Jack organizes the hijacking of a large shipment of heroin bound for the drug factory of a powerful wholesaler. Launching a challenge to the drug wholesaler, he tries unsuccessfully to keep ahead of both hired killers and narcotics officers.

Subject(s): Drugs, Crime and Criminals

804 William Gardner Smith

Last of the Conquerors

(New York, NY; Farrar, Straus, 1948)

Summary: Smith's first novel was inspired by his travels in Europe. The work looks at relations between black and white American soldiers in occupied Germany following World War II. The story's protagonist is Hayes Dawkins, who, along with other black soldiers, finds greater acceptance among the Germans than he had in America. When the troops receive a new commander, a prejudiced southern officer, the army unit becomes a microcosm of racist American life. Finally,

Dawkins, in order to avoid court-martial proceedings, leaves behind his German girlfriend and returns to the United States. The author's fiction is linked to the tradition of black social protest novels of the 1940s and 1950s.

Subject(s): Racism, Miscegenation, World War II

805 William Gardner Smith

South Street

(New York, NY; Farrar, Straus and Young, 1954)

Summary: Considered one of the first black militant protest novels, Smith's 1954 novel follows the three Bowers brothers in South Philadelphia. Claude marries a white woman, and tired of the struggle for civil rights, moves to Canada to escape American racism. Michael rejects his brother's interracial marriage and forms a militant group called the Action Society. When the youngest brother, Philip, is killed by a white youth who was beaten in one of Michael's unorganized attacks, Claude decides to leave his wife and provide needed leadership in the Action Society. This book differs from Smith's earlier works, in which the protagonists are powerless to overcome oppression; here, Claude returns to an active role in fighting white racism.

Subject(s): Racism, Miscegenation, Civil Rights

806 William Gardner Smith

The Stone Face: A Novel

(New York, NY; Farrar, Straus, 1963)

Summary: Smith's final novel centers on Simeon Brown, who has been left blind in one eye from a beating by whites. Moving to Paris to escape American racism, he meets other expatriates, from Africa as well as America. He becomes involved with Maria, a Polish woman who is fleeing the horror of the concentration camps. Finding out about the Algerian War, Simeon comes to view the treatment of the Algerians by the French as parallel to the oppression of blacks by whites in America. Influenced by events surrounding the integration of schools in Little Rock, Arkansas, Simeon realizes that he must return to the United States.

Subject(s): Racism, Jewish Holocaust, Segregation

807 Charles A. Smythwick, Jr.

False Measure: A Satirical Novel of the Lives and Objectives of Upper Middle-Class Negroes

(New York, NY; William-Frederick Press, 1954)

Summary: As its subtitle suggests, this novel takes a satirical look at the lives of upper middle-class blacks. Its setting varies from the apartment houses on the edge of Harlem to the expensive summer homes of Martha's Vineyard. The story looks at a group of African Americans who are not as interested in joining the white world as they are in differentiating themselves from lower-income blacks. The novel explores how the mem-

bers of this group have sacrificed their heritage to live in a social setting whose basis is financial.

Subject(s): Middle Classes, Wealth

808 John Stewart

Curving Road: Stories

(Urbana, IL; University of Illinois Press, 1975)

Summary: This book offers a diverse collection of short stories. "Bloodstones" features a woman who is unfaithful while her lover is in prison. In "Early Morning," a man removes the bodies of people who have hanged themselves in Jaipaul. "Julia" follows a young black woman as she attends a freedom rally where the other audience members are white and the singers are black, while "Letter to a Would-be Prostitute" is a brother's response to a sister who is considering prostituting herself. "That Old Madness--1974" depicts the violent intentions of a frustrated black male bank teller.

Subject(s): Racism, Prostitution, Banking

809 John Stewart

Last Cool Days

(London, England; Deutsch, 1971)

Summary: Set on the island nation of Trinidad and Tobago, this novel opens with Marcus Shepard, a black man, being sentenced to a life of hard labor for the death of Anthony Carrington, the son of a wealthy white family. When Marcus is sent to prison, the narrative looks back on his relationship with Anthony as well as with Hille, a white woman, who, following the miscarriage of a child fathered by Marcus, turns him in to the authorities.

Subject(s): Murder, Wealth, Prisoners and Prisons

810 Chuck Stone

King Strut

(Indianapolis, IN; Bobbs-Merrill, 1970)

Summary: Stone's 1970 novel centers on Hiram Elliott Quinault, Jr., a black member of Congress from Chicago. He serves as chair for the Armed Services Committee. When a group of black nationalists declare their independence from the United States and form an independent state, called Blackland, within Mississippi, they ask Quinault to become their president. He accepts their invitation. When Quinault is assassinated, the Blacklanders attack the House of Representatives and kill a dozen members of Congress. The novel ends with the prospect of continuing conflict.

Subject(s): Race Relations, Politics, Black Nationalism

811 Jenny Stow

The House That Jack Built

(New York, NY; Dial Books for Young Readers, 1992)

Summary: This children's book takes the familiar nursery rhyme and places it in a Caribbean setting. The author's own illustrations provide a brightly colored look at island life. The book's images add to the poem's narrative by showing Jack's new wife waving goodbye to him as he leaves for his work as a laborer and presenting the couple surrounded by their animals at sunset.

Subject(s): Islands, Children

812   Charles L. Tarter

Family of Destiny

(New York, NY; Pageant Press, 1954)

Summary: At the beginning of the twentieth century, Laura Jenkins, who carries a lot of pride in her surname, meets Jason Jenkins at a South Carolina post office. She considers the incident to be an act of fate and decides to marry him. Laura rebels against the idea of raising a family in their state, so the Jenkinses move to Baltimore, which is as far as their money will carry them. Laura gives birth to four children, whose development is influenced by her deep religious feeling and her ambitious goals for them.

Subject(s): Family, Mothers, Religion

813   Will Thomas

God Is for White Folks

(New York, NY; Creative Age Press, 1947)

Summary: This novel centers on Beau Beauchamp, who is racially mixed. Influenced by a racist aunt, his white father rejects Beau. He is later betrayed by a darker-skinned black to a lynch mob. Beau manages to escape and returns to become head of his home. The novel was later published with some minor changes under the title *Love Knows No Barriers*.

Subject(s): Racism, Lynching, Miscegenation

814   Carolyn Tillman

Life on Wheels

(Los Angeles, CA; Crescent Publications, 1975)

Summary: Cathy Simmons is a young woman confined to a wheelchair because of polio. When a handsome man named Paul Williams comes to visit her at her parents' house, she begins to fall in love with him. Paul initiates a sexual relationship with Cathy, but when she is rejected by him, she finds it difficult to get on with her life.

Subject(s): Diseases, Relationships

815   Allen Pelzer Turner

Oaks of Eden: A Novel

(New York, NY; Exposition Press, 1951)

Summary: In his 1951 novel, Allen Pelzer Turner offers a story set in a small American town. The work's main themes deal with the gossip and infighting that mark small-town life and the relations between parents and their children.

Subject(s): City and Town Life, Family Relations, A Novel

816   Peter Turner

Black Heat

(New York, NY; Belmont Books, 1970)

Summary: This novel looks at the author's self-named protagonist, Peter Turner, a young black man. After returning from Vietnam, Peter runs into Al Park, a white man who had treated him well in high school, and Al's girlfriend, Victoria Rushton. When Al offers Peter work writing for the *Alternative* paper and Vicky shows a sexual interest in him, he becomes strongly involved in the East Village scene in New York City.

Subject(s): Vietnam War, Newspapers, Miscegenation

817   Mae Caesar Turnor

Uncle Ezra Holds Prayer Meetings in the White House

(New York, NY; Exposition Press, 1970)

Summary: This novel is centered on a people's March on Washington. Leading the march is Uncle Ezra Joshua Jones, who embodies the spirit of Martin Luther King, Jr. A kidnapping occurs during the event, but Uncle Ezra's calming presence prevails at a prayer meeting held once the marchers reach the capital. The novel calls for justice and understanding between the races.

Subject(s): Civil Rights Movement, Race Relations, Religion

818   Waters Edward Turpin

O Canaan!: A Novel

(New York, NY; Doubleday, Doran & Company, Inc., 1939)

Summary: Turpin's second novel continues the saga of the Prince family, recounting the trials and triumphs of both that family and the Benson family in Chicago, which in the early twentieth century was perceived by African Americans as the biblical promised land of Canaan. The prosperity experienced by blacks who built on the city's south side, the devastation brought by the Great Depression, and the determination of characters such as Joe Benson to recover from the ensuing state of disadvantage are all chronicled by Turpin.

Subject(s): Depression (Economic), Family Saga

819   Waters Edward Turpin

The Rootless

(New York, NY; Vantage Press, 1957)

Summary: The third, and last, installment of a five-book saga Turpin planned to write about a black family from the time of the American Revolution to the 1930s, *The Rootless* is set prior to the first two, *These Low Grounds* and *O Canaan!*. It traces the Prince family ba to the birth of a man on a slave ship and follows his determination to earn his freedom. It also traces the gradual deterioration of three generations of slave owners.

Subject(s): American South, Slavery, Family Saga

820 **Waters Edward Turpin**

These Low Grounds

(New York, NY; Harper & Brothers, 1937)

Summary: Set primarily in eastern Maryland, this novel details four generations of the Prince family, beginning with Martha, whom the Civil War freed from slavery. Martha's descendants rise in social status with every generation, making transitions from bondage to domestic service, farming, and teaching. The novel is the first of three novels completed in what was planned as a five-part saga.

Subject(s): Civil War, Social Chronicle, Family Saga

821 **Bert Underwood**

A Branch of Velvet

(New York, NY; Vantage Press, 1973)

Summary: This novel focuses on the Parker family. Descended from the son of a plantation owner and slave, members of the family display the same physical features as whites. Caleb Parker, recently married, decides to leave his relatively well-off home and seek a new life. He and his wife move to Detroit, where Caleb is disturbed by the North's particular brand of racism. Caleb carries a strong sense of family and religion with him up to his death.

Subject(s): Family, Racism, Religion

822 **Henry Van Dyke**

Blood of Strawberries

(New York, NY; Farrar, Straus and Giroux, 1969)

Summary: Van Dyke's second novel continues where his first novel, *Ladies of the Rachmaninoff Eyes,* ended. In this sequel, Oliver narrates the events from a surprising summer in which he explores his friendship with two elderly intellectuals, Max and Orson. Oliver struggles with his identity as a black man, but ultimately Max, Orson, and Oliver's white girlfriend Desdemona help him come to grips with that identity. The novel is set in New York City.

Subject(s): Identity, Race Relations, Friendship

823 **Henry Van Dyke**

Dead Piano

(New York, NY; Farrar, Straus & Giroux, 1971)

Summary: The protagonists of Van Dyke's third novel, Finley and Olga Blake, are an upper-middle-class black couple who enjoy their suburban lifestyle. Their comfortable existence is shattered, however, when a group of militant blacks targets them for betraying their racial heritage. The novel takes place during a single night, when the militants take the Blakes hostage in their own home. The piano of the novel's title symbolizes the shallow facade of success that the Blakes have wrapped themselves in.

Subject(s): Middle Classes, Race Relations, Rebellion

824 **Melvin Van Peebles**

A Bear for the FBI

(New York, NY; Trident Press, 1968)

Summary: This novel focuses on a black youth named Edward. Having lived on the south side of Chicago and moved to the suburbs as a child, Edward eventually graduates from college. The novel explores his sexual development, his relationships with his parents, and the racism that he encounters.

Subject(s): Coming-of-Age, Racism, Education

825 **Melvin Van Peebles**

The True American: A Folk Fable

(Garden City, NY; Doubleday, 1976)

Summary: When black prisoner George Abraham Carver is accidentally killed, he goes to Hell. There he discovers that blacks fare well because the preferential treatment that they receive causes more grief for the whites who make up the majority of the residents of the nether regions. He also meets Dave Stock, a fur-trapping scout who was scalped by Native Americans one-hundred years earlier. Together, they are sent back to earth to experience the Depression, World War II, and the early 1960s. The novel takes a satirical look at American precepts, politics, and racial attitudes.

Subject(s): Racism, Depression (Economic), World War II

826 **Estella V. Vaught**

Vengeance Is Mine

(New York, NY; Comet Press Books, 1959)

Summary: The hardships of this novel's protagonist, Cleo, begin when she is born with six fingers on each hand. As a young girl, she watches with frustration as her father is discriminated against by a local banker and her beloved mother dies. Cleo grows up to be a bitter and vengeful woman who schemes and plots to get her way and to hurt others. Finally, however, Cleo casts off her bitterness and prejudices on her deathbed.

Subject(s): Childhood, Family Life

827 **Berta Verne**

Elastic Fingers

(New York, NY; Vantage Press, 1969)

Summary: This story centers on Mary, who as a young woman was jilted. Subsequently, she managed to avoid a romantic relationship for twenty years by devoting herself to writing music and lecturing. One day she meets a music copyist named Paul and contemplates a possible relationship with him. Their love, however, proves doomed when, after experiencing difficulties with their relationship, Mary takes a trip to Paris, and Paul, oblivious to her whereabouts, commits suicide.

Subject(s): Relationships, Music, Suicide

828 Alice Walker

The Color Purple: A Novel
(New York, NY; Harcourt Brace Jovanovich, 1982)

Summary: Set in the rural South during the early decades of the twentieth century, this epistolary novel--a novel told in the form of letters--tells the triumphant story of an oppressed woman. Impregnated by her father but forced to give up her children, Celie is later brutalized by her husband and is separated from her beloved sister, Nettie. Celie perseveres, however, and eventually gains a measure of self-esteem, in addition to taking control over her destiny. Although she was criticized by some for her negative portrayals of black men, Walker earned tremendous critical praise and commercial success with this novel.

Subject(s): Relationships, Family Saga, American South

Award(s): Pulitzer Prize: Fiction, 1983; American Book Award: Fiction, 1983

829 Alice Walker

"Everyday Use"
In Love & Trouble: Stories of Black Women
(New York, NY; Harcourt Brace Jovanovich, 1973)

Summary: This story from Alice Walker's first collection of short stories is one of her most-celebrated pieces of short fiction and probably her most anthologized. The story follows a young woman, Dee Johnson, who has worked hard to escape racism and poverty but who in the process has separated herself from her true racial heritage—this despite having adopted an Africanized name in keeping with a fad of the times. In the story, Dee returns to her rural home and attempts to commandeer a set of old quilts meant for her sister. The story is narrated by Dee's mother, whose inner peace and calm acceptance of her life's nature is contrasted with her daughter's shallow mindset and her restlessness.

Subject(s): Rural Life, Family Problems

830 Alice Walker

In Love & Trouble: Stories of Black Women
(New York, NY; Harcourt Brace Jovanovich, 1973)

Summary: The stories in this book are about troubled women, who have been dehumanized by oppression and racial and sexual abuse. Their psychological states in turmoil, they resort, despite their victimization, to violence against themselves or others or emotional sacrifice in the hopes of achieving self-determination.

Subject(s): Racism, Violence, Sexual Abuse

Award(s): American Academy and Institute of Arts and Letters Award, 1974

831 Alice Walker

Meridian
(New York, NY; Harcourt Brace Jovanovich, 1976)

Summary: Elegiac in tone and poetic in style, Walker's second novel explores the civil rights movement and its effects on personal transformation. The narrative interweaves memories with the present as the central characters, Meridian Hill and Truman Held, undergo self-examination. They meet when Truman, a civil rights worker, visits Meridian's southern community and she joins the movement. She later identifies with the historical conditions of black women and abandons the movement to become an ascetic, living and working among poor, southern blacks. Her spirituality, however, isolates her. Truman's visits to Meridian are a search for meaning in his own life.

Subject(s): Civil Rights Movement, Relationships, Spiritualism

832 Alice Walker

The Third Life of Grange Copeland
(New York, NY; Harcourt, Brace, Jovanovich, 1970)

Summary: Walker's first novel follows the forty-year history (1920-60) of three generations of Copelands: Grange Copeland and his wife Margaret; his son Brownfield and Brownfield's wife Mem; and Grange's granddaughter Ruth. Subjugated sharecroppers Grange and Brownfield cruelly enact their despair and alienation on their families; Margaret commits suicide after Grange leaves her and Brownfield brutally murders Mem. But a transformed Grange redeems himself in his "third life" when he returns from the North and becomes Ruth's guardian, nurturing her to survive on her own and protecting her, to the point of killing Brownfield and sacrificing himself. With his dying, he leaves Ruth capable of being independent and making choices her female ancestors could.

Subject(s): Family Relations, Survival

833 Alice Walker

You Can't Keep a Good Woman Down
(New York, NY; Harcourt Brace Jovanovich, 1981)

Summary: The central characters in Alice Walker's second collection of short stories are strong women who battle for their beliefs against a backdrop that includes issues such as rape, pornography, abortion, and racism. The stories "Porn" and "Coming Apart: By Way of Introduction to Lorde, Teish and Gardner," for instance, both deal with the way in which pornography threatens relations between black men and women. Other stories confront the dilemma of black artists who lack useful role models and the difficulty of fusing art and life.

Subject(s): Women, Pornography, Abortion

834 **Margaret Walker**

Jubilee

(Boston, MA; Houghton Mifflin, 1966)

Summary: Walker's only novel, *Jubilee*, depicts the slavery and Reconstruction eras through the life story of Vyry, a story pervaded by racism and white brutality. The daughter of a plantation master, Vyry is a house servant brutalized by her father's wife and given to his legitimate daughter. Despite being victimized she is loyal, maternal, nurturing, and averse to violence. She exemplifies the strong African American woman whose spirituality and humanity allow her to survive without bitterness. After the Civil War, Vyry's abilities as a midwife and healer gain her family acceptance by a white community in Alabama and protection against terrorism.

Subject(s): Racism, Slavery, Reconstruction

835 **Elizabeth West Wallace**

Scandal at Daybreak

(New York, NY; Pageant Press, 1954)

Summary: Class conflict, specifically middle-class black snobbery, is the central theme of this 1954 novel set in New Orleans by Elizabeth West Wallace. In the novel, protagonist Helene is able to move with her children from their slum neighborhood, West Bottoms, to a middle-class neighborhood called Quality Hill. Once there, however, Helene encounters financial difficulty, and she is able to survive only by accepting financial help from wealthy black men in the neighborhood in exchange for sex and companionship. A scandal eventually erupts, however, threatening Helene's hard-fought economic status, before a successful lawyer falls in love with Helene and asks her to marry him.

Subject(s): Class Conflict, Love

836 **Thelma Wamble**

All in the Family

(New York, NY; New Voices Pub. Co., 1953)

Summary: Set during the Great Depression, this novel centers on the Westbrooks, a conservative white family. The son, Mark, is a physician with homosexual tendencies. The family acquires more liberal views under Mark's influence as they come to accept Shelby, a "pseudohermaphrodite," as well as his friend, a black law student.

Subject(s): Homosexuality/Lesbianism, Racism, Depression (Economic)

837 **Thomas P. Ward**

The Clutches of Circumstances

(New York, NY; Pageant Press, 1954)

Summary: This novel follows Samuel Lomax from his high school graduation in the South during 1916, through the 1920s, 1930s, and 1940s. Although faced with a terrible stammer since childhood, Samuel overcomes his speech defect to become the valedictorian of his high school graduating class. Later, however, he meets and marries a deranged woman who tries to kill him. Only after re-dedicating himself to his religious beliefs does Samuel extract himself from the marriage and move on with his life.

Subject(s): American South, Religion, Marriage

838 **Doris V. Washington**

Yulan: A Novel

(New York, NY; Carlton Press, 1964)

Summary: The title of Washington's 1964 novel refers to a fictional country in West Africa that is the site of political infighting and betrayal. In the novel, the country is preparing for democratic elections, but the current dictatorial president thwarts the elections by having young radicals killed. The action is witnessed by an embassy secretary modeled after Washington herself, who spent time working for the U.S. State Department in Africa. Washington implies that while many African countries have no racial conflict as does the United States, they are nevertheless troubled by political and class conflict.

Subject(s): Africa, Class Conflict, Politics

839 **Lydia Watson**

(Pseudonym of E.H. White)

Our Homeward Way: A Novel of Race Relations in Modern Life

(New York, NY; Exposition Press, 1959)

Summary: In her 1959 novel, Lydia Watson tells the story of Ruth Haskell, a white, college-age woman who befriends a black man. Other characters include Ruth's husband, Roy, a reporter; his sister Ethel; and Ruth's parents. Written just as the civil rights movement was becoming a national phenomenon, the novel deals with the issues of discrimination, social justice, and love.

Subject(s): Civil Rights Movement, Love, Race Relations

840 **Charles Lewis Webb**

Sasebo Diary

(New York, NY; Vantage Press, 1964)

Summary: Webb's 1964 novel is one of the few works by an African American set during the Korean War of 1950-1953. The narrator of the novel, Carlos V. Conrad, is a World War II veteran who is called back to active duty to serve in Korea. During his stint in the war, he grows stronger both emotionally and physically, even though he doubts whether his presence makes any difference to the war effort.

Subject(s): Korean War

841 Bill Webster

One by One

(Garden City, NY; Doubleday, 1972)

Summary: Written in the early 1970s, when many black leaders and intellectuals advocated militant means to achieve social justice and an end to racism, this novel centers on a murder trial. Ben Waddell is an African American prosecutor who must pursue a trial featuring Vernon Peel, a militant black man who is charged with the murder of three policemen. In the course of the trial, Waddell examines his own past, from his youth in the racist Deep South to his experiences during the Korean War. Although the case against Peel seems strong, Waddell finds himself troubled by a racist, white-dominated society in which African Americans who attempt to break free from oppression are targeted and destroyed.

Subject(s): Crime and Criminals, Racism, Judicial System

842 Dorothy West

The Living Is Easy

(Boston, MA; Houghton Mifflin Co., 1948)

Summary: The protagonist in this novel about false values is Cleo Judson, a woman with a neurotic need to be the one most loved by her mother. She tries to overcome her mother's supposed rejection by doing risky things to gain attention and control and by being malicious. After she marries an older man for his money, she convinces her three sisters to move in with her, thereby destroying their respective marriages. Yet despite her skewed values, she is somewhat vulnerable, as seen when her husband's banana business goes bankrupt, her sisters accept menial jobs, and her husband leaves to find other income.

Subject(s): Greed, Family Relations

843 John B. West

Never Kill a Cop

(New York, NY; New American Library, 1961)

Summary: Rocky Steele, the tough detective at the center of John B. West's series of crime novels, returns from a trip through Africa to find his New York City world in danger. Steele comes under suspicion of murdering a drug kingpin, his mistress, and a policeman. While attempting to clear his name, Steele must also find the real murderer before the killer targets him.

Subject(s): Mystery and Detective Stories, Murder, Drugs

844 John B. West

A Taste for Blood

(New York, NY; New American Library, 1960)

Summary: John B. West is known for his series of mystery novels featuring detective Rocky Steele. In this installment in the series, Steele gets entangled with the beautiful mistress of a powerful politician while attempting to break a drug ring.

Along the way, Steele becomes a murder suspect—and also the target of the real murderer's wrath.

Subject(s): Mystery and Detective Stories, Murder, Drugs

845 Thomas J. White

To Hell and Back at 16

(New York, NY; Carlton Press, 1970)

Summary: Sam, the protagonist of White's 1970 novel, experiences the enormity of white southern racism at the beginning of the novel. Coming home from hunting doves near his rural Texas home in 1948, Sam is viciously assaulted by a group of white policemen who think that Sam has whistled at a white woman. Despite his innocence, Sam is beaten and arrested. As the novel progresses, he fights back, determined to maintain his freedom and unwilling to acquiesce to the brutal whites who want him dead. At the end of the novel, Sam dies in a shootout with police who have come to arrest him for the beating of a white man—whom Sam assaulted for stealing his wallet.

Subject(s): Racism, Law, American South

846 Jim E. Whitney

Wayward O'er Tuner Sheffard

(New York, NY; Carlton Press, 1968)

Summary: This novel features several years in the life of Tuner Sheffard. At the age of fifteen, Tuner leaves his farm in the upper Plains and ventures to Cincinnati, where he works at a jar factory. Eventually making a success of himself, he makes his way back to his family's farm. At the novel's end, Tuner has married, had a child, and is pursuing his education. The novel is a straightforward coming-of-age saga in which racial issues have little or no importance.

Subject(s): Coming-of-Age, Farm Life, Success

847 John Edgar Wideman

A Glance Away

(New York, NY; Harcourt, Brace & World, 1967)

Summary: Wideman's first novel traces a day in the life of Eddie Lawson. Ironically, Eddie is released from a drug rehabilitation program on Easter—a day symbolic of hope—back into a hopeless environment. His hostile mother is dying, his sister is resigned to caring for their mother, his girlfriend is angry about an affair he had with a white woman, and his best friend is an addict. Yet in the end, the sexual partner of Eddie's friend, a white English professor, gives him hope for self-renewal.

Subject(s): Rehabilitation, Drugs

848 John Edgar Wideman

Hurry Home

(New York, NY; Harcourt, Brace & World, 1970)

Summary: In Wideman's second novel, it is often unclear what is real or imagined by protagonist Cecil Otis Braithewaite. Isolated from the black community for unknown reasons, Cecil walks out on his girlfriend on the day he is finally to receive his law degree. His travels eventually take him to Europe, where he ends up with a wealthy white man who treats him as a surrogate son. After breaking away from the man and traveling more, he finally returns home to his girlfriend.

Subject(s): Self-Perception, Travel

849 John Edgar Wideman

The Lynchers

(New York, NY; Harcourt Brace Jovanovich, 1973)

Summary: Wideman's focus expands to the self-destructive nature of the black community in his third novel, *The Lynchers*. The plot involves a group of black men in Philadelphia with a scheme to rouse African Americans against racism and the victimization of blacks. Their plan involves killing a black prostitute then publicly lynching a white policeman (a representative of white society) for the crime. However, without a clear-cut objective for the action and personal motivations driving most of the conspirators, the plan is doomed.

Subject(s): Lynching, Racism, Racial Conflict

850 John Edgar Wideman

Sent for You Yesterday

(New York, NY; Avon Books, 1983)

Summary: In a novel called lyrical by critics, Wideman sympathetically revisits the urban ghetto of Homewood in the third part of a trilogy that also includes *Damballah* and *Hiding Place*. In this final volume, Wideman continues the saga of the community of Homewood, focusing on the descendants of Sybela Owens. In telling his story, Wideman relies heavily on musical expression as a literary device.

Subject(s): Community Relations, Urban Affairs, Music

Award(s): PEN/Faulkner Award: Fiction, 1984

851 Chancellor Williams

Have You Been to the River?

(New York, NY; Exposition Press, 1952)

Summary: Williams based *Have You Been to the River?* on his doctoral dissertation concerning the black storefront church movement that began in the United States in the 1920s. In the novel, Professor Tom Moore tells the story of church founder and leader Charles Amos David and his power over his followers. This power is especially felt by Liza Jackson, whose devotion to David's teachings causes her to destroy her family.

Subject(s): Religious Life, Family Problems

852 Chancellor Williams

The Raven

(Philadelphia, PA; Dorrance, 1943)

Summary: Williams wrote this historical novel, a chronicle of the life of American writer Edgar Allan Poe, during World War II. The story begins in Richmond, Virginia, where Poe is a foster son in a wealthy family, and ends in Baltimore, Maryland, just prior to his mysterious death. The title of the novel is taken from one of Poe's best-known poems.

Subject(s): Literature, Writers

853 Dennis A. Williams
Spero Pines, Co-author

Them That's Not

(New York, NY; Emerson Hall, 1973)

Summary: This novel considers the tension surrounding an integrated high school as seen through the eyes of a student named Nate. When a group of white students hurl racist names, as well as bottles, at a group of black students after school, a riot threatens to break out. The school's mainly white staff, and particularly its principal, find themselves ill-equipped to deal with the situation.

Subject(s): Racism, Schools, Students

854 Edward G. Williams

Not Like Niggers

(New York, NY; St. Martin's Press, 1969)

Summary: Set in the 1930s, this novel centers on a black family, the Petersons, as seen through the eyes of Brad, the family's youngest child. His mother is determined that he and his siblings will grow up "not like niggers." When his parents' strained marriage ends with his father's abandonment of the family, Brad's older brother quits school to help support the household. Despite this setback, his mother continues to urge her children to work hard and receive an education.

Subject(s): Family, Marriage, Education

855 Jerome Aredell Williams

The Tin Box: A Story of Texas Cattle and Oil

(New York, NY; Vantage Press, 1958)

Summary: Set in West Texas, this novel follows the fight over a giant cattle ranch. June Meredith faces the loss of the family ranch when her parents die in an auto accident. Robert Chandler, owner of a real estate and development company, wants to foreclose on the Meredith property so that he can profit from its oil-producing potential. Chandler, however, is undone when he is linked to the Merediths' deaths, while June becomes the successful head of the property's oil operations.

Subject(s): Ranch Life, Oil, Business

856 John A. Williams

The Angry Ones

(New York, NY; Ace Books, 1960)

Summary: In his first published novel, Williams introduces many of the themes of his later works, including black-Jewish relationships, sexual tension, and racism. Set in New York City in the 1950s, the work features Stephen Hill, a young man trying to make a new start following an attempted suicide in Los Angeles. After much searching, he lands a job at a vanity publisher, where he is exploited by the homosexual editor. His friendships with a white couple whose marriage is failing and his affair with a Jewish woman underscore the uncertainty of his life. However, circumstances improve for him in the end when he takes a new job and returns to his childhood sweetheart.

Subject(s): Interpersonal Relations, Racism

857 John A. Williams

Captain Blackman: A Novel

(Garden City, NY; Doubleday, 1972)

Summary: In this 1972 novel, Williams covers U.S. black military history from the Revolutionary War through Vietnam, including racist policies and atrocities. Historic episodes are recounted in the hallucinations career soldier Abraham Blackman has after being struck by a sniper's bullet in Vietnam. The hallucinations flow from the course he has been teaching members of his company. When he regains consciousness, he reviews his own experiences during his military career dating from World War II. In an interesting plot twist, militant African Americans gain control of the country at the end of the novel by seizing the nuclear defense system.

Subject(s): Military Life, War, History

858 John A. Williams

!Click Song

(Boston, MA; Houghton Mifflin, 1982)

Summary: As does *The Man Who Cried I Am*, this novel features the careers of two novelists. Paul Cummings and Cato Caldwell Douglass are long-term friends, having met while in school after World War II. Cummings enjoys wealth and success after he makes his Jewishness known; however, the quality of his writing declines, as does his private life, and he eventually commits suicide. Unlike Cummings, Douglass's writing and private life improve as he acknowledges his blackness, though he does not achieve recognition because of racism in the publishing industry.

Subject(s): Racism, Death, Religion

Award(s): Before Columbus Foundation: American Book Award, 1983

859 John A. Williams

The Junior Bachelor Society

(Garden City, NY; Doubleday, 1976)

Summary: By and large the members of the Junior Bachelor Society returning to Central City, Georgia (first described in *Sissie*) for a reunion are successful middle-class blacks. Moon, a Los Angeles pimp and cop killer, is not. When Swoop, a corrupt police officer who has always been excluded from the JBS, hears that Moon is coming to the reunion, he plans to arrest him, thereby boosting his career and also embarrassing the group. But as the Bachelors rally for Moon, Moon murders Swoop.

Subject(s): Friendship, Murder

860 John A. Williams

The Man Who Cried I Am: A Novel

(Boston, MA; Little, Brown, 1967)

Summary: Williams achieved national and international recognition with this provocative novel about racism. African American journalist and novelist Max Reddick is dying of colon cancer in 1963 when his mentor, Harry Ames, is murdered after he discovers a plot to prevent unification of black Africa. Max then uncovers a genocidal scheme in the United States. After revealing the scheme to Malcolm X-like Minister Q, they both are captured and executed. The novel reflects the influence on Williams of the Black Nationalist movement that arose during the 1960s.

Subject(s): Racism, Black Nationalism, Africa

861 John A. Williams

Mothersill and the Foxes

(Garden City, NY; Doubleday, 1975)

Summary: Perhaps because he had only a part-time father as a child, Odell Mothersill is on a quest as an adult for a stable life. He seeks career fulfillment in social services, administration, and education positions in such far-flung places as Africa and the Caribbean. But it is his sexual encounters, comic to bizarre, that are most elemental to his quest. He eventually finds what he wants with a wife and family.

Subject(s): Sexual Behavior, Africa, Identity

862 John A. Williams

Night Song

(New York, NY; Farrar, Straus and Cudahy, 1961)

Summary: Williams's second novel interweaves the lives of David Hillary, a white failed English professor, Richie Stokes (also known as Eagle), a legendary jazz musician, and Keel Robinson, Eagle's self-appointed protector. Hillary and Eagle connect up on New York City's skid row, and with Robinson's aid, they help each other overcome bouts with substance abuse. Though accepted by the world of black jazz musicians, Hillary resumes his teaching post. In his hometown, Hillary then betrays Eagle, a move that leads to Eagle's death.

Subject(s): Jazz, Alcoholism, Drug Abuse

---

863 **John A. Williams**

Sissie

(New York, NY; Farrar, Straus and Cudahy, 1963)

Summary: Williams devotes a section each to the memories of the three protagonists in his third novel. The title character is dying and wants her children to acknowledge that she did her best raising them while trying to survive in a racist America. Sissie's daughter Iris, a foreign jazz entertainer, whose quest for wealth and fame has left her alone, refuses to forgive her mother her lack of love. Though Sissie's son Ralph seems to accept the past, he doubts his present theatrical success and good marriage because of it.

Subject(s): Racism, Family Relations, Success

---

864 **John A. Williams**

Sons of Darkness, Sons of Light: A Novel of Some Probability

(Boston, MA; Little, Brown, 1969)

Summary: In this novel, Williams explores the use of militancy to advance a cause. An executive of the Institute for Racial Justice, Eugene Browning, decides to hire a professional killer to avenge the death of a black boy by a police officer. He hopes the action will stem racial oppression. Instead, an innocent man, Morris Green, takes credit for the officer's murder, setting off similar murders across the nation and retaliation by police. In a twist, the actual assassin, an Israeli and former terrorist, then makes another hit and implicates Green for it. The book ends with radicals plotting to blow up bridges and members of Congress being blackmailed.

Subject(s): Racial Conflict, Terrorism

---

865 **Rita Williams-Garcia**

Blue Tights

(New York City, NY; Lodestar Books, 1988)

Summary: In this coming-of-age novel, Rita Williams-Garcia tells the story of teenager Joyce Collins. Joyce loves to dance, but her school instructor thinks her body shape is wrong for ballet and keeps her out of the program. Joyce's disappointment and harsh home life cause her to make poor choices before she finds self-worth.

Subject(s): Adolescence, Self-Perception

---

866 **Carl T.D. Wilson**

The Half Caste

(Ilfracombe, England; A.H. Stockwell, 1964)

Summary: This novel is set in the London slum area of Paddington. The story centers on a young widow named Ann Coleman. Surrounded by criminals, drug addicts, and prostitutes, Ann struggles to improve the lives of herself and her daughter, Susan.

Subject(s): Poverty, Widows, Mothers and Daughters

---

867 **Bily Wms-Forde**

Requiem for a Black American Capitalist

(New York, NY; Troisieme Canadian, 1975)

Summary: Donald, the protagonist of this novel, is a middle-aged chauffeur for a black businessman whose wealth is fleeting. Constantly battling his feelings of rage against those who consider him inferior--no matter whether they are white or black. At the story's close, the businessman has been murdered.

Subject(s): Business, Racism

---

868 **Philip Wooby**

Nude to the Meaning of Tomorrow: A Novel of a Lonely Search

(New York, NY; Exposition Press, 1959)

Summary: This novel opens with a young man, Paul Garrity, sitting on a train and being tormented by "black voices" in his head. He has just been forced out of the Order of Brothers Evangelists after having been observed in an indiscretion with a fellow brother-in-Christ. Paul becomes involved in a sexual relationship with a young woman named Lydia while his new boss, Judith, falls in love with him. Confronted by his mother's strong Catholic faith, Paul decides that he will make up his own mind about his future.

Subject(s): Religion, Catholicism, Homosexuality/Lesbianism

---

869 **Odella Phelps Wood**

High Ground: A Novel

(New York, NY; Exposition Press, 1945)

Summary: Jim Clayton, a World War I veteran, is the central character of Wood's 1945 work. When younger men are questioning the nation's claim to their loyalty during World War II, he reaffirms his decision to serve his country. Jim, however, is not untouched by racial injustice. He and his wife Marthana are left deeper in debt following a year's work growing tobacco while their landlord yields a profit. They decide to leave the South and find success through hard work.

Subject(s): Racism, Farm Life, World War II

870 Charles Stevenson Wright

Absolutely Nothing to Get Alarmed About

(New York, NY; Farrar, Straus and Giroux, 1973)

Summary: Wright originally wanted this work to be called "Black Studies: A Journal." Based on nonfiction pieces that he first wrote for the *Village Voice*, this journal-novel blends personal essay with fiction to tell the story of Wright's life as a heavy-drinking dishwasher and porter in the Bowery and Lower East Side sections of New York. Already socially and economically isolated by his work, the assassinations and political failures of the 1960s, and the racism prevalent in America, Wright becomes disillusioned and pessimistic.

Subject(s): Racism, Politics

871 Charles Stevenson Wright

The Messenger

(New York, NY; Farrar, Straus, 1963)

Summary: Wright's novel blurs the line between autobiography and fiction. It tells the story of Charles Stevenson, who has left his native Missouri and now works for a messenger service in Manhattan. While at his job, Charles makes contact with the wealthy and powerful of New York, yet comes to realize that he has little hope of advancing past his own position. His mixed racial background also contributes to his isolation, making him an outcast from black as well as white society. Well-received by readers and critics alike, this novel illustrates the alienation produced in an individual by America's economic and racial forces.

Subject(s): Racism

872 Charles Stevenson Wright

The Wig: A Mirror Image

(New York, NY; Farrar, Straus and Giroux, 1966)

Summary: Having received mixed reviews at its publication, Wright's second novel has since only grown in reputation. It uses hyperbole and fantasy to tell the story of Lester Jefferson, a young man from Harlem who tries to straighten his hair, hoping that his "wig" will help him in his search for success. Success, however, eludes him, and he takes a job in which he crawls around Manhattan in a chicken suit to advertise a restaurant. Now generally considered Wright's most important work, *The Wig* argues that the price of success in America for the black male is one of emasculation and loss of identity.

Subject(s): Racism

873 Richard Wright

Eight Men

(Cleveland, OH; World Pub. Co., 1961)

Summary: *Eight Men* is a significant collection of short stories, including two radio scripts and an autobiographical sketch, published after Wright's death. The stories show great variety and are representative of different periods in the author's career. Considered the most important work in the collection, "The Man Who Lived Underground" centers on Fred Daniels, a black man who has been wrongly accused of murder. To escape from the police, Daniels takes refuge in a sewer. He comes to see the sewer as representative of the human heart. This story has been compared to Dostoyevski's *Notes From the Underground* and appeared in part in 1944, one year before Ralph Ellison began writing *Invisible Man*, whose protagonist also begins to live underground when confronted with a racist society.

Subject(s): Racism, Radio, Murder

874 Richard Wright

The Long Dream: A Novel

(Garden City, NY; Doubleday, 1958)

Summary: Showing similarities to Wright's autobiographical *Black Boy*, *The Long Dream* marks the author's fictional return to racial issues in America. The novel focuses on Fishbelly Tucker, called Fish, and his awakening to the racial injustices in Clintonville, Mississippi and, on a larger scale, in America. Even though he sees that his father's collaboration with the town's immoral white power structure leads to the father's murder, Fish follows his father's path, only to be imprisoned on false charges of raping a white woman. After his release from jail, Fish flies to Paris to begin a new life. As in the previous novels that the author wrote while living in Paris, this one received mainly a negative response from critics, who faulted his style and argued that Wright had been away too long to write accurately about the black American experience.

Subject(s): American South, Racism, Rape

875 Richard Wright

The Outsider

(New York, NY; Harper, 1953)

Summary: One of the first American novels to explore the philosophy of existentialism, *The Outsider* grew out of Wright's friendship with French intellectuals such as Jean-Paul Sartre and Simone de Beauvoir. The story focuses on a black protagonist, but one who is not concerned primarily with racial issues. Given the opportunity to abandon his identity following a train accident, Cross Damon joins the Communist Party in New York out of a fascination with what he perceives as the group's existential views. Confronted with the Party's violation of individual rights, however, he murders two Communists as well as a Fascist. The novel finally rejects existentialism as a sufficient means to cope with modern problems. The novel was generally not well received by American critics, who pointed to a melodramatic plot and a poor integration of philosophy and story. European critics, however, praised the work even more highly than they had Albert Camus's *The Stranger*.

Subject(s): Philosophy, Communism, Murder

876 Richard Wright

Savage Holiday
(New York, NY; Avon Publications, 1954)

Summary: In this novel, Wright adds Freudian psychoanalysis to his continued interest in existentialism. In the story, all of the major characters are white and racial issues are not a main concern. The novel's protagonist is Erskine Fowler, a retired insurance executive in New York, who has repressed his incestuous desires for his mother. Fowler also feels guilty about his role in the accidental death of a boy, a guilt that leads him to propose marriage to the boy's mother, Mrs. Blake, who begins to serve as a substitute for Fowler's mother. Unable to repress his incestuous feelings any longer, Fowler stabs Mrs. Blake to death. Published only as a paperback edition at the time, the novel was not reviewed by the American press. Modern critics tend to consider *Savage Holiday* the least successful of Wright's novels, citing a failure to integrate Freudian theory unobtrusively into an arguably weak plot.

Subject(s): Psychology, Murder

877 Sarah E. Wright

This Child's Gonna Live
(New York, NY; Delacorte Press, 1969)

Summary: Wright's first novel is a prose poem set in the Depression-era town of Tangierneck, a poor oystering and farming community. It uses flashbacks and stream of consciousness to deepen its portrait of Mariah, the main character, and her fight to improve the lives of her children. Struggling against her husband, poverty, and the religious community, Mariah also battles for her own self worth. The novel examines relationships in the town's black community within the context of Western Christianity. Critics enthusiastically received *This Child's Gonna Live*, praising it for its universality as well as the author's use of language.

Subject(s): Depression (Economic), Religion, Family

Award(s): *Baltimore Sun*: Readability Award, 1969

878 James Wylie

The Lost Rebellion: A Novel
(New York, NY; Trident Press, 1971)

Summary: Reflecting the turbulent late 1960s and early 1970s, Wylie's novel tells the story of Miles King. Having once made his living as a pimp and a hustler, he leaves prison with a new philosophy and religion. Dreaming of uniting black people all over the world, he founds the New Brotherhood of Islam. He becomes a leader to thousands and earns international recognition but is murdered while speaking at a crowded meeting hall. King's saga recalls the real-life experiences of Black Nationalist leader Malcolm X.

Subject(s): Racism, Religion, Islam

879 Frank G. Yerby

Benton's Row
(New York, NY; Dial Press, 1954)

Summary: Following the economic successes of his earlier novels, Yerby continued to use the plot devices that had made them so popular. This novel begins with the arrival of Tom Benton in antebellum Louisiana and follows the history of his family into the early part of the next century. *Benton's Row* is among several of the author's novels set in the Old South that would lead to his association with a romanticized version of that era.

Subject(s): American South, Family Saga

880 Frank G. Yerby

Bride of Liberty
(Garden City, NY; Doubleday, 1954)

Summary: Although many of his historical novels focus on the Old South, Yerby also entertained readers with stories set in other periods, in this case the American Revolution. Utilizing plot formulas similar to those found in the author's southern romances, this novel centers on Polly Knowles, a young colonial woman in love with an officer in General Washington's army.

Subject(s): American Revolution, Romance

881 Frank G. Yerby

Captain Rebel
(New York, NY; Dial Press, 1956)

Summary: One among many white protagonists in Yerby's popular historical novels, Tyler Meredith is the rebel captain of the novel's title. During his adventures as a blockade runner for the Confederacy during the Civil War, Meredith becomes involved with a beautiful woman of mixed racial background. While the author's novels of the 1950s and 1960s have for the most part been dismissed by critics, they do often reflect racial concerns.

Subject(s): Civil War, Race Relations

882 Frank G. Yerby

The Dahomean: An Historical Novel
(New York, NY; Dial Press, 1971)

Summary: Having claimed indifference to racial issues for many years, Yerby confronted the matter directly with this novel. *The Dahomean* tells the story of Nyasanu, an African chief's son who is sold into American slavery by jealous relatives. Benefiting from the author's careful historical research, Yerby's depiction of a complex tribal culture dispels American myths about African life. Many reviewers consider this novel to be Yerby's best work.

Subject(s): Slavery, Africa

883   Frank G. Yerby

The Devil's Laughter
(New York, NY; Dial Press, 1953)

Summary: Set during the French Revolution, this novel tells the story of Jean Paul Marin. The son of a wealthy merchant family, Marin becomes involved with the leading figures of the revolution. *The Devil's Laughter* demonstrates Yerby's ability to write a popular novel using carefully researched historical material.

Subject(s): French Revolution

884   Frank G. Yerby

Fairoaks: A Novel
(New York, NY; Dial Press, 1957)

Summary: This novel is one in a long line of Yerby romances set in the Old South. At the center of the story is the aristocratic Guy Falks, owner of a plantation. In *Fairoaks* Yerby would continue to use the plot devices that made his earlier novels popular with many readers, particularly the element of a strong-willed white protagonist.

Subject(s): American South, Romance

885   Frank G. Yerby

Floodtide
(New York, NY; Dial Press, 1950)

Summary: This story is one of Yerby's many historical novels popular with contemporary readers. As with several of his other works, *Floodtide* is set in the Old South. It tells the story of Natchez, Mississippi, architect Ross Pary, and the women in his life. The author's formulaic plotting and romanticized representation of the period would continue to entertain Yerby's readers and frustrate his critics.

Subject(s): American South

886   Frank G. Yerby

The Foxes of Harrow
(New York, NY; Dial Press, 1946)

Summary: Yerby started his career writing critically praised short stories about the plight of contemporary black Americans. But after the rejection by publishers of his first attempt at a novel, he decided to write a popular work of fiction. *The Foxes of Harrow* was the result. A historical novel set in the Old South, it tells the story of Stephen Fox and his rise from poverty to wealth in antebellum New Orleans. Disparaged by critics, the novel was a huge success with the public. Yerby would go on to write several more historical novels with white protagonists, becoming one of the most popular writers of his time.

Subject(s): American South, Poverty, Wealth

887   Frank G. Yerby

The Garfield Honor
(New York, NY; Dial Press, 1961)

Summary: In this novel Yerby continues to follow his popular formula of presenting an adventurous white protagonist in an exciting historical setting. Taking place mainly in post-Civil War Texas, *The Garfield Honor* centers on Roak Garfield and his progression from a penniless war veteran to a position of wealth and social position.

Subject(s): Civil War, American South, Wealth

888   Frank G. Yerby

Gillian
(New York, NY; Dial Press, 1960)

Summary: Returning once again to the South, Yerby sets this historical novel during the Industrial Revolution. The story centers on Gillian MacAllister, the beautiful heiress to an Alabama fortune, and her desire to ruin the lives of those around her. *Gillian* is one of a few of the author's novels to feature a white female as its protagonist.

Subject(s): American South, Industrial Revolution, Wealth

889   Frank G. Yerby

The Girl from Storyville: A Victorian Novel
(New York, NY; Dial Press, 1972)

Summary: One of Yerby's few novels to focus on a white female protagonist, *The Girl from Storyville* is set in turn-of-the-century New Orleans. Having been abandoned by her mother, Fanny Turner eventually succumbs to working in the redlight district of Storyville at her own mother's brothel. At the novel's end, Fanny must attempt to free herself from a life of prostitution.

Subject(s): American South, Prostitution

890   Frank G. Yerby

Goat Song: A Novel of Ancient Greece
(New York, NY; Dial Press, 1967)

Summary: One of Yerby's several historical novels, *Goat Song* takes place in ancient Greece during the Peloponnesian War. The novel tells the story of Ariston, a Spartan youth taken as a slave to Athens, where he becomes one of the city's most powerful men. By using the same plot formulas he had used in his novels of the Old South and changing the locale to foreign lands, Yerby continued to entertain his many readers.

Subject(s): Ancient Greece, War, Slavery

891 **Frank G. Yerby**

The Golden Hawk

(New York, NY; Dial Press, 1948)

Summary: Having focused on southern romances for his first two novels, with *The Golden Hawk* Yerby decided to write a picaresque adventure set in the West Indies of the seventeenth century. Although the story takes place in lands other than the Old South, this novel depends on the same popular formulas that Yerby used for its predecessors, beginning with a larger-than-life white protagonist. The story's hero is Kit Gerado, master of a pirate ship, who seeks revenge on the Spaniard who killed his mother.

Subject(s): Adventure and Adventurers, Pirates

892 **Frank G. Yerby**

Jarrett's Jade: A Novel

(New York, NY; Dial Press, 1959)

Summary: With this novel, Yerby returns to a favorite plot device, that of an Anglo-Saxon hero seeking success in the Old South. Arriving in Savannah, Georgia, in 1736, the Scot James Jarrett is determined to build a New World dynasty. Until Yerby wrote his 1969 novel *Speak Now*, the only sexual attraction depicted by the author between whites and blacks was between white males and black females; and and in this novel, Jarrett becomes involved with a woman bought at a slave auction.

Subject(s): American South, Race Relations, Slavery

893 **Frank G. Yerby**

Judas, My Brother: The Story of the Thirteenth Disciple

(New York, NY; Dial Press, 1968)

Summary: The wealthy Nathan bar Yehudah and the impoverished Yeshu'a meet as youths in Galilee. Eventually, Yeshu'a becomes the leader of a fanatical religious sect and Nathan his protector, the "thirteenth disciple" of the novel's title. In many of his earlier novels, Yerby had been criticized for depicting a romanticized version of the Old South. This novel, in contrast, represents the author's attempt to present a demythologized version of the origin of Christianity.

Subject(s): Christianity, Judaism

894 **Frank G. Yerby**

The Old Gods Laugh: A Modern Romance

(New York, NY; Dial Press, 1964)

Summary: With this novel, Yerby changes his usual approach of locating his story in the past. Set in the contemporary Caribbean nation of Costa Verde, *The Old Gods Laugh* depicts how American foreign correspondent Peter Reynolds becomes involved in the country's revolution. By placing his story in the fictitious Costa Verde, Yerby allows the novel's location to act as a substitute for similar Latin American nations suffering from civil war.

Subject(s): Islands, Revolution

895 **Frank G. Yerby**

Pride's Castle

(New York, NY; Dial Press, 1949)

Summary: Set in late-nineteenth century New York, *Pride's Castle* tells the story of Pride Dawson, who heads east to New York to make his fortune. Quickly becoming one of the nation's richest and most powerful men, Pride's life is complicated—as are the lives of the author's other male protagonists—by his relationships with the women in his life.

Subject(s): Romance, Wealth, Success

896 **Frank G. Yerby**

A Rose for Ana Maria: A Novel

(New York, NY; Dial Press, 1976)

Summary: This novel is based on observations made by the author during more than twenty years of residence in Spain while the nation was under Francisco Franco's dictatorship. The story centers on Diego, a young revolutionary who has murdered the Spanish Consul in France, and his relationship with Ana Maria, the rebellious daughter of an aristocratic family. Diego and Ana Maria are assigned the assassination of another high-ranking Spanish official in exchange for help in returning to Spain.

Subject(s): Murder, Love, Revolution

897 **Frank G. Yerby**

The Saracen Blade: A Novel

(New York, NY; Dial Press, 1952)

Summary: An adventure set during the thirteenth century Crusades, *The Saracen Blade* is the seventh of Yerby's immensely popular novels. It tells the story of Pietro di Donati, the son of a blacksmith, and his connection to Frederick the Second of the Holy Roman Empire. By adding other historical contexts and exotic locations to the plot formulas he had begun using in his novels of the Old South, Yerby continued to engross the reading public with this and later works.

Subject(s): Middle Ages

898 **Frank G. Yerby**

The Serpent and the Staff

(New York, NY; Dial Press, 1958)

Summary: As are many of Yerby's other novels, *The Serpent and the Staff* is set in the Old South. The story centers on Duncan Childers and his climb from poverty to success in turn-of-the-century New Orleans. It is one of the author's many novels to focus on a white male protagonist and his romantic involvements.

Subject(s): American South, Romance, Wealth

899 Frank G. Yerby

Speak Now: A Modern Novel
(New York, NY; Dial Press, 1969)

Summary: This work contrasts markedly with Yerby's earlier historical novels. *Speak Now* is one of the author's few novels to address the problem of racism overtly and his first to depict a sexual relationship between a black male and a white female. The story's protagonist is Harry Forbes, a black jazz musician living in contemporary Paris who through his music finds self-expression. Harry's point of view is a complex one. He hates white American society for what it has done to his people, yet he feels shame at the victimization of black Americans. Though ambivalent, this novel is Yerby's most extensive consideration of American racial issues.

Subject(s): Racism, Jazz, Miscegenation

900 Frank G. Yerby

Tobias and the Angel
(New York, NY; Dial Press, 1975)

Summary: A departure from the author's historical fiction, this novel focuses on Tobias Tobit, who goes south to marry one of his identical twin cousins. On the way, Tobias is involved in a series of sexual misadventures initiated by his guardian angel, Angie. Upon arriving at his destination, Tobias becomes involved with his cousins' murderous and incestuous family.

Subject(s): Murder, Angels, Sexual Behavior

901 Frank G. Yerby

The Treasure of Pleasant Valley
(New York, NY; Dial Press, 1955)

Summary: This novel focuses on Bruce Harkness, the son of a Carolina planter, who at hearing that the woman he loves has married another man, leaves to make his fortune in California. Once there, Bruce falls in love with the beautiful, yet married, Juana and becomes involved with the lawless world surrounding the Gold Rush.

Subject(s): Gold Rush--California, Romance

902 Frank G. Yerby

The Vixens: A Novel
(New York, NY; Dial Press, 1947)

Summary: For his second published novel, Yerby utilized research material that he had not incorporated into his first, *The Foxes of Harrow*. Another southern romance, *The Vixens* centers on Laird Fournois, who is hated by his fellow southerners

for his affiliation with the Yankees during Reconstruction. Here, the author continues to use the plot formulas that had made his first novel so popular with the public: a dominant male protagonist, one or more sexually defined heroines, and a strong conflict.

Subject(s): American South, Reconstruction

903 Frank G. Yerby

The Voyage Unplanned
(New York, NY; Dial Press, 1974)

Summary: Yerby's twenty-fifth novel begins in France during World War II. Here, French-American John Farrow joins the resistance movement and falls in love with fellow resistance fighter Simone, who is captured by the Nazis. Two decades later, his search for Simone takes Farrow back to France, then conflict-ridden Israel, and finally to Spain, where the author himself spent the latter part of his life.

Subject(s): Resistance Movements, World War II

904 Frank G. Yerby

A Woman Called Fancy
(New York, NY; Dial Press, 1951)

Summary: To escape a forced marriage, Fancy Williamson flees her home in the Carolina Hills. Arriving in post-Civil War Augusta, Georgia, she meets Courtland Brantley, son of a once powerful family. When her marriage into Courtland's family proves to be an unhappy one, Fancy refuses to surrender to the despair common to the Brantley women.

Subject(s): Civil War

905 Al Young

Seduction by Light
(New York, NY; Delta Fiction, 1988)

Summary: Returning to the novel form after an eight-year absence, Young tells the story of middle-aged Mamie Franklin, once an actress, now a maid in Los Angeles. In his writing, the author has demonstated an interest in music and black vernacular English. Critics praised Young's work, *Seduction by Light*, for its incorporation of the rhythms of jazz into the black dialect speech of the characters.

Subject(s): Music, Jazz, Language

906 Al Young

Sitting Pretty: A Novel
(New York, NY; Holt, Rinehart and Winston, 1976)

Summary: This novel tells the story of Sidney J. Prettymon, nicknamed Sitting Pretty or just Sit. Having left his family and a good job twenty years earlier, Sit is now a middle-aged janitor working in Palo Alto, California. Sit finds a chance to add focus to his life when he begins to make a series of television commercials for a radio station that he regularly calls. In *Sitting Pretty*, Young pursues his interest in language by taking a character who might otherwise have appeared simple and using dialect to create a complex personality.

Subject(s): Language, Radio, Television

907 Al Young

Snakes: A Novel
(New York, NY; Holt, Rinehart and Winston, 1970)

Summary: Young's first novel tells the story of MC, a young black musician. The success of a record single called "Snakes" allows him to leave behind his native Detroit ghetto and pursue a career as a jazz musician in New York. In his portrayal of MC, Young is just as interested in the protagonist's youth as he is in his race. As the author's later works would continue to do, *Snakes* celebrates black language as well as black music. Not fitting in with the typical 1960s presentation of black ghetto art, the novel shows the importance of transcending stereotypes.

Subject(s): Jazz, Music, Language

908 Al Young

Who Is Angelina?: A Novel
(New York, NY; Holt, Rinehart and Winston, 1975)

Summary: Young's second novel focuses on twenty-six-year-old Angelina Green's personal quest to answer the question posed by the story's title. Her journey begins in Berkeley, California, where she is found suicidal after breaking up with her boyfriend. Traveling to Mexico, she becomes romantically involved with a mysterious stranger named Watusi. Suddenly called to Detroit because of her father's illness, Angelina reacquaints herself with him. After her father helps her come to terms with her life, she returns to California. Considered a sensitive depiction of a young woman seeking self-definition, the novel explores Young's fascination with mystical experiences as well as his continuing interest in African American vernacular issues.

Subject(s): Language, Religion, Family

Nonfiction

The period between 1940 and the present saw the emergence of many important writers in the social sciences, history, and *belles lettres*, and an explosion in the study of blacks in these fields. E. Franklin Frazier, Charles P. Johnson, Allison Davis, and St. Clair Drake were among the young sociologists who began to write in the 1940s. The fifties and sixties saw the continuation of this tradition in the writing of figures such as Kenneth Clark. The eighties and nineties have seen the emergence of a host of major figures in the social sciences, including William J. Wilson and Cornel West.

Also during this period, the field of history by and about blacks has also been particularly rich. In the forties, eminent historians such as John Hope Franklin and Benjamin Quarles began their careers. The seventies and eighties saw the writing of figures such as John Blassingame and Wilson Moses, who continues to write.

Autobiography continued to be an important chronicle of eminent black figures' lives and important events. Richard Wright published his autobiography *Black Boy: A Record of Childhood and Youth* in 1945. In 1958, Paul Robeson published *Here I Stand*, which detailed his life as an actor and political activist. In more recent years, Henry Louis Gates, Jr. released his autobiography, *Colored People* in 1994.

Finally, the essay has become an important form. Major essayists in the recent past have included James Baldwin, Ralph Ellison, Stanley Crouch, and Henry Louis Gates, Jr. Baldwin began publishing essays in 1945 and became a powerful source of commentary on race relations in his three major works of nonfiction *Notes of a Native Son*, *Nobody Knows My Name*, and *The Fire Next Time*. Though Ellison's most recognized work was his novel *Invisible Man*, his book of essays, speeches and other writing, *Shadow and Act* was well-received. In addition to his work in literary criticism and other fields, Henry Louis Gates, Jr. has published important essays in his collection *Loose Canons: Notes on the Culture Wars*.

909 Mathew Ahmann, Editor

Race: Challenge to Religion: Original Essays and "An Appeal to the Conscience"
(Chicago, IL; H. Regnery Co., 1963)

Summary: This volume consists of a collection of essays based on papers delivered at the National Conference on Religion and Race, which was held in Chicago in 1963, one hundred years after the delivery of Abraham Lincoln's Emancipation Proclamation. Attending the conference were representatives from the Jewish, Catholic, and Protestant faiths. The essays in this book are based on the participants' belief that racial discrimination and prejudice are immoral and threaten both church and state.

Subject(s): Racism, Religion, Government

910 Greg Alan-Williams

A Gathering of Heroes: Reflections on Rage and Responsibility: A Memoir of the Los Angeles Riots
(Chicago, IL; Academy Chicago Publishers, 1994)

Summary: *A Gathering of Heroes: Reflections on Rage and Responsibility* was authored by actor and former Marine Greg Alan Williams, a star of the television series *Baywatch*. Detailing his personal memories of the riots that broke out in Los Angeles in April of 1992, Williams reflects on mob violence, individual responsibility, and the consequences of stereotyping. He also recounts his experiences entering the fray to rescue a Japanese man who had been downed in the fighting.

Subject(s): Autobiography, Violence, Intolerance

911 **Amy Alexander,** Editor

The Farrakhan Factor: African American Writers on Leadership, Nationhood, and Minister Louis Farrakhan

(New York, NY; Grove Press, 1998)

Summary: In *The Farrakhan Factor: African American Writers on Leadership, Nationhood, and Minister Louis Farrakhan*, noted journalist and editor Amy Alexander brings together leading black writers and intellectuals to discuss the cultural impact of Louis Farrakhan, minister to the Nation of Islam and one of the most controversial figures of twentieth century America. With an introduction and interview by noted scholar Henry Louis Gates, Jr., the volume includes essays by Michael Eric Dyson, Louis Pitts, Jr., Stanley Crouch, Irene Monroe, Gwendolyn Brooks, and Derrick Bell that focus on issues such as the misogynism and anti-Semitism distilled from Farrakhan's message, and the way it has affected black society. Rather than an endorsement or condemnation of Farrakhan and his principles, Alexander's book responds to the desperation with which many African Americans view their situations and the consequent appeal of black leaders such as Farrakhan when few other solutions are offered. Alexander's purpose in editing the collection is to assist blacks in "rebuilding [their] definition of leadership... [and] establish[ing] a model that is born independently of white Americans' views."

Subject(s): Racism, Civil Rights Movement, Anti-Semitism

912 **Muhammad Ali**

The Greatest: My Own Story

(New York, NY; Random House, 1975)

Summary: With a title reflecting the bravado of its subject, *The Greatest: My Own Story* is the autobiography of three-time world heavyweight boxing champion Muhammad Ali. Ali found fame after winning the light-heavyweight gold medal at the 1960 Olympic Games. Moving quickly to the professional arena, he defeated Sonny Liston to become the heavyweight champion of the world in 1964. His notoriety over refusing the draft, his win over George Foreman that caused him to regain his boxing title in 1974, and the religious conversion that prompted him to change his name are all included in this volume, published five years before Ali's retirement from the sport in 1980. Many commentators cite Ali as the greatest boxer of the twentieth century.

Subject(s): Autobiography, Boxing, Muslims

913 **Gordon Allport**

The Nature of Prejudice

(Cambridge, MA; Addison-Wesley Pub. Co., 1954)

Summary: In his *The Nature of Prejudice* Gordon Allport reflects upon the purpose of prejudice within the human emo-

tional and social makeup and discusses methods by which such instinctual prejudicial reactions are translated into discriminatory behavior. By illuminating the thought processes of bigoted individuals and those who discriminate on the basis of ill-conceived prejudices, Allport aids readers in learning techniques to defuse and deflect racial and ethnic antagonisms. The book, which was studied by civil rights leaders Martin Luther King, Jr., and Malcolm X, was released in a special updated edition in 1988.

Subject(s): Prejudice, Psychology, Racial Conflict

914 **Alan A. Altshuler**

Community Control: The Black Demand for Participation in Large American Cities

(New York, NY; Pegasus, 1970)

Summary: The first volume in the series *Decentralization and the Urban Crisis*, this book analyzes the controversy over community control of public services in the urban ghettoes of the United States. The author reviews the arguments for and against community control and examines the history of the community control movement. In addition to looking at the opposition to community control, Altshuler considers how community control might be implemented. The author concludes with his own evaluation of community control's costs and benefits.

Subject(s): Poverty, Urban Affairs

915 **Alan B. Anderson**
George W. Pickering, Co-author

Confronting the Color Line: The Broken Promise of the Civil Rights Movement in Chicago

(Athens, GA; University of Georgia Press, 1986)

Summary: Theologian and university ethics professor Alan B. Anderson's *Confronting the Color Line: The Broken Promise of the Civil Rights Movement in Chicago* is based on his experiences growing up in the days of the racist Jim Crow laws, working as a Methodist minister in one of Chicago's ethnic neighborhoods, and participating as an activist in the civil rights movement. In 1962 Anderson joined seventy other clergymen for a rally in Albany, Georgia; arrested at the demonstration, he met Dr. Martin Luther King, Jr., when the late civil rights leader visited Anderson in jail. Containing a history of the Coordinating Council of Community Organizations, *Confronting the Color Line* includes a description of King's unsuccessful civil rights campaign in Chicago in 1966, puts King's activism within the context of the history of racism in the United States, proposes ways to move beyond the barriers raised by the movement, and abolish racism where it continues to exist in urban ethnic neighborhoods.

Subject(s): Racism, Civil Rights Movement

916 Elijah Anderson

Streetwise: Race, Class, and Change in an Urban Community
(Chicago, IL; University of Chicago Press, 1990)

Summary: In *Streetwise: Race, Class, and Change in an Urban Community,* Philadelphia native Elijah Anderson contrasts two neighborhoods in his hometown: the upper middle-class suburb where he lived as a young professor, and the impoverished, lower-class ghetto a few blocks away. Studying the ghetto's social and cultural systems, Anderson also interviewed many of its residents, most of whom are African-Americans. His book reveals the poorer community--rife with gang violence, rampant drug abuse, and an attitude of despair from those who believe there is no hope of escape--in marked contrast to the placid, upwardly mobile, and racially integrated suburb. He contends that a lack of jobs contributed to the gradual decay of a once working-class neighborhood into a lawless world run by drug runners and pimps, and cites the erosion of traditional family values as a main factors in the neighborhood's decline. The blame for the current situation, Anderson maintains, is an economic system that rewards more elite communities with enhanced social and cultural services at the expense of expendable lower-class neighborhoods.

Subject(s): Racism, Poverty, Urban Affairs

917 Jervis Anderson

A. Philip Randolph: A Biographical Portrait
(New York, NY; Harcourt Brace Jovanovich, 1973)

Summary: Journalist Jervis Anderson's *A. Philip Randolph: A Biographical Portrait* examines the life of the African American labor leader who founded the Brotherhood of Sleeping Car Porters, a union of railroad employees that Randolph also headed for several years. Anderson, a Jamaican-born staff writer for the *New Yorker* magazine beginning in 1968, recounts Randolph's rise from poverty to a position of leadership during the civil rights era, and details the labor leader's own career as well as his vision of a large-scale civil rights march on Washington, D.C. that became a reality in 1963. Anderson emphasizes the personal integrity that Randolph embodied, a quality that contributed greatly to the confidence he was able to inspire among the working men he unionized.

Subject(s): Biography, Civil Rights Movement, Labor Movement

Award(s): Sidney Hillman Foundation Award, 1973

918 Jervis Anderson

This Was Harlem: A Cultural Portrait, 1900-1950
(New York, NY; Farrar Straus Giroux, 1982)

Summary: In *This Was Harlem: A Cultural Portrait, 1900-1950,* Jamaican-born journalist Jervis Anderson draws readers into the Harlem of an earlier age, a New York community that he describes as "crowded with energy, crowded with talent, crowded with style." Black music had become all the rage by the early years of the twentieth century, and well-heeled whites converged in droves upon Harlem nightspots like the famous Cotton Club. By the 1920s, the mood in Harlem was one ripe with optimism, as blacks saw in their talents and unique culture a way to bridge the gap between black and white, rich and poor. Literary efforts by black writers exploring their roots, such as Langston Hughes, Zora Neal Hurston, and others, sparked the literary movement known as the Harlem Renaissance, one of many aspects of black culture to flourish prior to the onset of the Great Depression.

Subject(s): Urban Affairs, Harlem Renaissance, Depression (Economic)

919 Maya Angelou

Gather Together in My Name
(New York, NY; Random House, 1974)

Summary: The second volume of poet Maya Angelou's autobiography, *Gather Together in My Name* continues her life story. Still a teen, Angelou is also a mother trying to cope with all the responsibilities of work when she meets a man with whom she falls deeply in love. Pitfalls await, however, as the young man proves less than honorable, her baby is kidnapped, and Angelou makes the decision to work as a prostitute to earn money for her lover. As Angelou copes with each successive setback, she retains her dignity, her pride, and her resolve to make something of her life, both for herself and her child.

Subject(s): Autobiography, Childbirth, Unmarried Mothers

920 Maya Angelou

I Know Why the Caged Bird Sings
(New York, NY; Random House, 1970)

Summary: *I Know Why the Caged Bird Sings* is first volume of the poet and playwright Maya Angelou's autobiography. Recounting her early childhood in Arkansas with her grandmother and her experiences of physical and emotional abuse, prejudice, and poverty, the book reflects its author's strong character and resolve to transcend her beginnings. Also, the book illuminates Angelou's use of voice within her writing as a means of connecting with her audience, whether in the form of a play, or in the poetry she would begin to publish in 1970. Ending as Angelou travels to California and becomes pregnant while yet unmarried, *I Know Why the Caged Bird Sings* was followed by *Gather Together in My Name*—the second of five volumes of autobiographical musings—in 1974.

Subject(s): Autobiography, Abuse, Poverty

921 Kwame Anthony Appiah

In My Father's House: Africa in the Philosophy of Culture
(New York, NY; Oxford University Press, 1992)

Summary: Harvard professor Kwame Anthony Appiah draws on memories of his childhood exposure to both Africa and Europe in the book *In My Father's House: Africa in the Philosophy of Culture*. A philosopher, the London-born Appiah uses his own mixed heritage--his father was born in the African city of Kumasi, now part of the Republic of Ghana, and his mother hailed from the western part of England--to interpret the many influences that have coalesced into a unique black culture. His work is deeply influenced by his background in Western philosophy, by his cultural sophistication, and, particularly, by his academic background in black culture and history.

Subject(s): Africa, Europe, Philosophy

922 Bettina Aptheker

Woman's Legacy: Essays on Race, Sex, and Class in American History

(Amherst, MA; University of Massachusetts Press, 1982)

Summary: This work collects essays by the author on the history of African American women written from a Marxist and feminist perspective. She examines the oppression of blacks within the nation's capitalist economy and suggests that the black woman's experience illustrates the connection between class exploitation and sexual oppression. In addition, she proposes an interdependent relationship between black liberation and woman's emancipation. Autobiographical sketches introduce the essays, which cover topics such as black women's contributions to the anti-slavery, suffrage, and anti-lynching movements. The author also considers black women entering the legal and medical professions before the twentieth century, the oppression of black women as domestic servants, and the 1965 Daniel P. "Moynihan Report on the Negro Family in America."

Subject(s): History, Women's Rights, Labor and Labor Classes

923 Herbert Aptheker

American Negro Slave Revolts

(New York, NY; Columbia University Press, 1943)

Summary: Marxist historian Herbert Aptheker has been credited with helping to raise and establish vital questions in Afro-American history and thought. Aptheker's interest in slavery began while he was a student at Columbia University, when he questioned the presentation of the institution of slavery in textbooks penned by elite white European-Americans. Correcting the misperceptions sparked a lifetime interest that resulted in many works, including *American Negro Slave Revolts*. A well-researched presentation of the many instances of rebellion by Africans forced to work the plantations of the South in the years leading up to the Civil War and of those brave individuals who led such rebellions, the book was updated in 1969.

Subject(s): Slavery, Civil War, American South

924 Herbert Aptheker

Anti-Racism in U.S. History: The First Two Hundred Years

(New York, NY; Greenwood Press, 1992)

Summary: In *Anti-Racism in U.S. History,* historian Herbert Aptheker focuses on the period from 1600 through 1860 in his study of anti-racism in the United States. He challenges the accepted position that racism was universally accepted by whites until the outbreak of the Civil War, and cites factual evidence showing a pervasive "anti-racism" philosophy existed in colonial culture and was the predominant viewpoint among most Americans up to the Civil War.

Subject(s): Racism, American Colonies, History

925 Molefi Kete Asante

The Afrocentric Idea

(Philadelphia, PA; Temple University Press, 1987)

Summary: In proposing his theory of "Afrocentricity," the author argues for an understanding of the black American experience as an extension of African history and culture. In advancing his theory, which is philosophical, social, and cultural in its reach, Asante provides a critique of the traditional Eurocentric academic discourse and offers a discourse instead based on a more distinctively African experience.

Subject(s): Africa, History, Philosophy

926 Molefi Kete Asante, Editor

Contemporary Black Thought: Alternative Analyses in Social and Behavioral Science

(Beverly Hills, CA; Sage Publications, 1980)

Summary: Seeing a need in the behavioral and social sciences for an approach more appropriate to Africans and those of African descent, the editors and authors of this volume present alternatives to the Eurocentric view of society. The various contributors explore issues of communication, psychology, rhetoric, economics, technology, religion, and crime. Other writers examine such topics as black American nationalism, interpretations of slavery, history, desegregation, and education.

Subject(s): Economics, History, Education

927 Robert G. Athearn

In Search of Canaan: Black Migration to Kansas, 1879-80

(Lawrence, KS; Regents Press of Kansas, 1978)

Summary: This book tells the story, beginning soon after the end of Reconstruction, of the "Exoduster" movement, the migration of blacks from the South to Kansas and other midwestern and western states. The work considers how the Republican party hoped to win votes as well as reduce the

South's representation in Congress by encouraging the movement. It also demonstrates how blacks were misled by false promises as they sought to escape the new discriminatory laws of the South.

Subject(s): Reconstruction, Frontier and Pioneer Life, American South

928 **William Attaway**

Calypso Song Book
(New York, NY; McGraw-Hill, 1957)

Summary: After working as a fiction writer for several years, black writer William Attaway turned his attention to music. The author of several songs performed by singer Harry Belafonte, Attaway also edited and contributed to *Calypso Song Book,* which he published in 1957. A collection of songs in the musical style that Belafonte made popular during the 1950s after his first big hit, "Jamaica Farewell," *Calypso Song Book* provides the words, music, and chords to a wide variety of songs in the laid-back, call-and-answer style characteristic of the Calypso beat and such songs as "Day-O". The book is geared toward a youthful audience.

Subject(s): Music, Popular Culture

929 **William Attaway**
Carolyn Cather, Illustrator

I Hear America Singing
(New York, NY; Lion Press, 1967)

Summary: African American novelist, playwright, and songwriter William Attaway ended a long but unsuccessful career as a novelist and turned his attention to his first love: music. His *I Hear America Singing,* published in 1967, is the story of the changing face of popular music in the United States. Geared toward a young audience, *I Hear America Singing* covers such musical movements as jazz, the music of the swing bands that held sway during the war years, the country and western music of performers such as Hank Williams, the folk music revival that dominated the 1950s and 1960s, and the development of rock and roll up to 1967, the date of the book's publication.

Subject(s): Popular Culture, Jazz, History

930 **Rob Backus**

Fire Music: A Political History of Jazz
(Chicago, IL; Vanguard Books, 1976)

Summary: This work considers the development of jazz as a reflection of the shaping of black Americans. Tracing the rhythms of jazz back to slavery, the volume follows jazz's history from the antebellum era through the Civil War, Reconstruction, the Depression, World War II, and later. The volume also considers the development of the blues in addition to examining the influence of record companies and the difficulties of musicians. Also explored are the politics of the black musicians' movement of the 1960s and early 1970s.

Subject(s): Jazz, Slavery, Reconstruction

931 **David N. Baker,** Editor
Lida M. Belt, Co-editor
Herman C. Hudson, Co-editor

The Black Composer Speaks
(Metuchen, NJ; Scarecrow Press, 1978)

Summary: Noticing how black composers have been disregarded and ignored in musical society and how their treatment has been misleading regarding the development of musical culture, the editors of this book chose to interview fifteen contemporary black composers. These composers, including Thomas Jefferson Anderson, Herbie Hancock, George Russell, and Olly Wilson, discuss their personal backgrounds, philosophies, motivations, attitudes, and styles. The volume also includes a listing of each composer's work.

Subject(s): Music, Musicians

932 **Josephine Baker**
Jo Bouillon, Co-author

Josephine
(New York, NY; Harper & Row, 1977)

Summary: In *Josephine* readers are introduced to world-renowned entertainer Josephine Baker. Born in 1906, Baker rose above the poverty of her childhood to reach success as a star on Broadway. During World War II, she lived in Paris and worked as a spy for the French Resistance; throughout her life she would work to further the cause of racial equality. Baker's autobiography was praised for reflecting its subject's wit and intelligence. It also contains interviews with friends and colleagues as well as photographs. Baker died in 1975.

Subject(s): Autobiography, Performing Arts, World War II

933 **James Baldwin**

Black Anti-Semitism and Jewish Racism
(New York, NY; R.W. Baron, 1969)

Summary: This volume looks at the problematic relationship between blacks and Jews in America. Including an introduction by Nat Hentoff, the book consists of a series of essays by James Baldwin and other writers, both black and Jewish. The book considers Jewish integration in contrast to black separatism. In turn, the work looks at the relationship of Jews to black self-determination.

Subject(s): Racism, Anti-Semitism

934 **James Baldwin**

The Devil Finds Work: An Essay
(New York, NY; Dial Press, 1976)

Summary: In this work, Baldwin looks at issues of race in American films. The author analyzes such films as *Guess Who's Coming to Dinner*, *In the Heat of the Night*, *Lawrence of Arabia*, and *The Exorcist*, and considers such actors as Sidney Poitier, Joan Crawford, and Bette Davis. Using his own experiences at the movies, including those of his childhood, Baldwin provides insight into what black audiences have perceived in movies produced by whites.

Subject(s): Film, Racism

935 James Baldwin
Nikki Giovanni, Co-author

A Dialogue

(Philadelphia, PA; Lippincott, 1973)

Summary: This book is based on a conversation between James Baldwin and the poet Nikki Giovanni that was taped for the television program "Soul!" in 1971. Representing two different generations, Baldwin and Giovanni discuss issues facing both black and white Americans as well as the changing roles of men and women in contemporary society, paying particular attention to the relationship between the black man and the black woman. The original edition also includes a preface by Ida Lewis and an afterward by Orde Coombs.

Subject(s): Interpersonal Relationships, Racism, Sex Roles

936 James Baldwin

The Fire Next Time

(New York, NY; Dial Press, 1963)

Summary: Published in 1963, respected novelist and playwright James Baldwin's *The Fire Next Time* acquaints readers of all races with the personal beliefs and experiences of a unique African American male and conveys its author's strong sense of urgency regarding the state of racial affairs in the United States during the mid-twentieth century. One of the first commentators to openly recognize the rising negative sentiment bubbling to the surface within the nation's African American community, Baldwin strove, through his work, to accurately depict the reality of blacks during the civil rights era. Among the essays contained in this volume are "Letter from a Region of My Mind" and "My Dungeon Shook: Letter to My Nephew on the One Hundredth Anniversary of the Emancipation Proclamation." Both introspective and analytical, these essays attempt to bring to light such issues as self-identity, assimilation, and cultural reality. Taken as a whole, *The Fire Next Time* served as both an impassioned plea for reconciliation between the races and mandatory reading for black Americans attempting to seek their role within a growing black consciousness. *The Fire Next Time* sold more than a million copies; however, as racial tensions continued to increase throughout the 1960s, its author departed from its conciliatory position, growing increasingly disillusioned and cynical about the future of race relations.

Subject(s): Racism, Cultural Conflict, Civil Rights Movement

Award(s): National Association of Independent Schools: Book Award, 1964

937 James Baldwin

No Name in the Street

(New York, NY; Dial Press, 1972)

Summary: Noted fiction writer and essayist James Baldwin emerged in the 1960s as one of black America's most articulate spokespersons. Growing increasingly disillusioned with the lack of compassion shown by white America toward the now-articulated dilemmas facing blacks, Baldwin reached his most militant point in the early 1970s with the publication of *No Name in the Street*. Based on Baldwin's own observations and experiences, the essays in *No Name* transcend the increasingly angry accusations lobbed by each race toward the other and uncover essential differences in attitudes concerning self-determination, personal pride, and the ability to transcend a life of poverty. After the book's 1972 publication Baldwin was widely criticized for abandoning his efforts at persuasion and conciliation and was accused by several (white) critics of adopting a racist stance.

Subject(s): Racism, Identity, Violence

938 James Baldwin

Nobody Knows My Name: More Notes of a Native Son

(New York, NY; Dial Press, 1961)

Summary: In *Nobody Knows My Name*, James Baldwin's sequel to his 1955 essay collection *Notes of a Native Son*, the noted black novelist continues to share with readers his concerns over the growing discontent felt among African Americans after the concerns they voiced during the civil rights movement fell upon sometimes deaf ears. Revealing himself to be a writer with a strong analytical bent, Baldwin probes beneath the surface contentions between the races to examine such issues as self-determination, identity, and the shape of the African American reality as contrasted with the reality of white America. Baldwin's essays grow in scope: he reflects on the life of an artist and the personal experiences that drew him to political activism and literary and social criticism, then expands his view to include a criticism of the complacency among white Americans in the face of racial strife. Like its predecessor, *Nobody Knows My Name* was widely praised for its optimistic and conciliatory take on race relations in the United States and abroad. The book, which sold more than a million copies, was also cited by critics for its prediction of the outbreak of violence as a desperate response by blacks to ongoing white oppression.

Subject(s): Racism, Violence, Identity

Award(s): National Conference of Christians and Jews: Brotherhood Award, 1962

939 James Baldwin

Notes of a Native Son

(Boston, MA; Beacon Press, 1955)

Summary: Considered one of the most articulate spokespersons for the condition of African Americans in the mid-twentieth century, novelist and playwright James Baldwin added a career as a writer of nonfiction to his diverse talents with the publication of *Notes of a Native Son*. Published in 1955, the book recalls Baldwin's childhood and his treatment at the hands of his stepfather, as well as his developing social consciousness. The novelist and playwright would describe his stepfather--a disillusioned Southern preacher whose approval Baldwin was never able to win--as the only man he ever hated; the title story in *Notes* vividly describes his stepfather's death and funeral. The novelist's ambivalent relationship with the elder Baldwin informs some of Baldwin's best mature writings; the character Gabriel Grimes in Baldwin's 1956 novel *Go Tell It on the Mountain* would be modeled on his stepfather. *Notes of a Native Son* brought Baldwin increased acclaim as an articulate critic of bigotry and social inequality.

Subject(s): American South, Fathers and Sons, Self-Acceptance

940 James Baldwin

One Day, When I Was Lost: A Scenario Based on "The Autobiography of Malcolm X"

(London, England; M. Joseph, 1972)

Summary: Written by prominent African American novelist and essayist James Baldwin, *One Day When I Was Lost* is a screenplay adaptation of novelist Alex Haley's *Autobiography of Malcolm X*. Published in book form but not produced because Baldwin refused to compromise with Columbia Pictures on his perceptions of Malcolm X's life, the work details the life of the Nebraska-born black nationalist leader who gained prominence in the 1950s after he joined the Black Muslims and began promoting the group's nationalist cause. Malcolm X recanted his formerly violent position after a trip to Mecca in the early 1960s; founding the Organization of AfroAmerican Unity in 1964 in an effort to join together the divergent interests of Islam, socialism, and other black factions, the black leader alienated his former Black Muslim associates and was assassinated in 1965 during a solidarity rally in Harlem.

Subject(s): Racism, Violence, Civil Rights Movement

941 James Baldwin
Margaret Mead, Co-author

A Rap on Race

(Philadelphia, PA; Lippincott, 1971)

Summary: *A Rap on Race* is the result of a meeting between prominent anthropologist Margaret Mead and James Baldwin, one of the most noted African American authors of the twentieth century. The two met in 1970, and the volume is a synthesis of their seven-and-a-half hour conversation about race and society. Mead discusses racism within a worldwide context developed over years of studying numerous cultures, while Baldwin contrasts his experiences of racism within the United States. Sometimes emotional, sometimes confrontational, the book is an important document of the civil rights era.

Subject(s): Racism, Anthropology, Social Sciences

942 Lewis V. Baldwin

"Invisible" Strands in African Methodism: A History of the African Union Methodist Protestant and Union American Methodist Episcopal Churches, 1805-1980

(Metuchen, NJ; Scarecrow Press, 1983)

Summary: Written in 1980 as Baldwin's doctoral dissertation at Northwestern University as a response to a perceived gap in the knowledge of African American religious history, this book tells the story of the African Union Methodist Protestant and Union American Methodist Episcopal churches. The work examines the origins of the A.U.M.P. and U.A.M.E. churches within the context of Episcopal Methodism in the United States. The book also explores how these churches have addressed economic, moral, and political problems that have been faced by blacks since coming to America.

Subject(s): Religion, Christian Life

943 Allen B. Ballard

One More Day's Journey: The Story of a Family and a People

(New York, NY; McGraw-Hill, 1984)

Summary: This work looks at how freedmen and their descendants from the South contributed to the shaping of the history of the North. The book shows how, at the time of World War I, blacks fleeing poverty and oppression in the South arrived in Philadelphia and encountered a black community composed of individuals who had been free since the American Revolution. Focusing on his own family, the author follows the migration starting from Greenwood, South Carolina, and demonstrates how the old and new black citizens of Philadelphia created a common culture. The book recounts the development of Philadelphia's black community up to the present time.

Subject(s): American South, Slavery

944 Edward C. Banfield

The Unheavenly City: The Nature and Future of Our Urban Crisis

(Boston, MA; Little, Brown, 1970)

Summary: Challenging the accepted belief that urban America has lost its battle against crime, racism, poverty, and despair, Harvard University professor Edward C. Banfield contends in *The Unheavenly City* that living conditions within major U.S. cities by 1970 had actually improved in quality. The frustration of city dwellers, Banfield argues, is that they harbor unreasonably inflated expectations with which existing social infrastructures are unable to keep pace. Summarizing public policy on both state and federal fronts, Banfield examines the Nixon administration's efforts to deal with the problems plaguing U.S. cities, and he states his central premise: that such problems stem from class rather than race. The work would be revised in 1990 as *Unheavenly City Revisited*.

Subject(s): Urban Affairs, City and Town Life, Poverty

945 Amiri Baraka

(Also known as LeRoi Jones)

The Autobiography of LeRoi Jones

(New York, NY; Freundlich Books, 1984)

Summary: Written in a style its author calls "word jazz," *The Autobiography of LeRoi Jones* tells the story of the writer and political activist who changed his name to Amiri Baraka in the 1960s. Born in 1934, Jones was drawn to the Beat movement in the 1950s, but by the 1960s the "Black Arts" movement had him in its sway. Moving to Harlem, Jones/Baraka adopted the African Islamic faith while continuing to write poems, plays, novels, and other works. Turning from the Black Nationalism ideology in the 1970s, Baraka became a devout Marxist, through which position he has continued to work for the social and political betterment of African Americans.

Subject(s): Autobiography, Islam, Black Nationalism

946 Amiri Baraka

(Also known as LeRoi Jones)

Black Music

(New York, NY; W. Morrow, 1967)

Summary: *Black Music*, a collection of jazz writings by Amiri Baraka (previously known as LeRoi Jones), covers the period 1959 to 1967. In addition to profiles of artists such as Sonny Rollins, Wayne Shorter, Cecil Taylor, and Thelonious Monk, Jones includes the essay "Jazz and the White Critic," which condemns white music critics who judge jazz music using European, rather than African American, criteria. While frequently voicing his anger at white "high" culture, Jones remains a compelling writer.

Subject(s): Music, Racism, Cultural Conflict

947 Floyd B. Barbour, Editor

The Black Power Revolt: A Collection of Essays

(Boston, MA; P. Sargent, 1968)

Summary: The editor of this book defines Black Power as the attempt by black Americans to define and liberate themselves. This volume collects the literature of black American protest writers from the days of slavery to the present period. Essays in the collection include a letter on liberty written by Benjamin Banneker to Thomas Jefferson, an excerpt from *Turner's Confessions* by Nat Turner, as well as writings by Frederick Douglass, W.E.B. Du Bois, Marcus Garvey, Stokely Carmichael, LeRoi Jones, and Malcolm X.

Subject(s): Slavery, Racism, Freedom

948 Floyd B. Barbour, Editor

The Black Seventies

(Boston, MA; P. Sargent, 1970)

Summary: This book is a collection of essays on black thought, moving from the present to the future. The volume begins with a work entitled "Black Declaration of Independence," based on the original American document and made relevant to black Americans. The essays that follow consider issues of black consciousness, nationalism, education, religion, art, and white liberals.

Subject(s): Black Nationalism, Religion, Education

949 Lucius Jefferson Barker
Jessie J. McCorry, Jr., Co-author

Black Americans and the Political System

(Cambridge, MA; Winthrop Publishers, 1976)

Summary: Published in its fourth edition in 1998 as *African Americans and the American Political System*, *Black Americans and the Political System* presents an analysis of how well African Americans fare within the current political, social, and economic system in the United States. Providing a systematic theoretical framework for measuring the well-being of black communities today, in relation to other periods of U.S. history, co-authors Lucius Barker and Jesse J. McCorry, Jr. examine the role of race, class, gender, economics, and the changing nature of African American participation in the political process.

Subject(s): Politics, City and Town Life, African Americans

950 Ben E. Barnes

The River Flows Backward

(Port Washington, NY; Ashley Books, 1975)

Summary: This 1975 memoir by Barnes recounts his colorful life. From his father, the strong and proud Big Syl, Barnes learned valuable lessons about balancing love and compassion with the outrage felt by a black man in a racist, white-dominated society. In recounting his adult years, Barnes catalogues his shifting roles as preacher, teacher, observer, and fighter. Written with Kathlyn Gay, the memoir is in the first person and makes heavy use of street slang.

Subject(s): Autobiography, Family, Racism

951 Daisy Bates

The Long Shadow of Little Rock: A Memoir

(New York, NY; David McKay Co., 1962)

Summary: This work illustrates the role the author played in the events surrounding the racial integration of Central High School in Little Rock, Arkansas, during the 1957-58 school year. Beginning with the murder of her mother at the hands of three white men, the memoir shows the author's fight for civil rights for African Americans. It includes her work as a partner with her husband in the newspaper *The Arkansas State Press* as well as her position as a local leader of the National Association for the Advancement of Colored People, and the events at Little Rock.

Subject(s): Education, Civil Rights Movement, Segregation

952   Allen Overton Battle

Status Personality in a Negro Holiness Sect

(Washington, DC; Catholic University of America Press, 1961)

Summary: This work, an abstract of Battle's thesis at Catholic University of America, studies the correlation between status and personality within a particular group. Specifically, the author considers whether the behavior expected of and carried out by members of a religious sect is correlated with their personality structures. The group studied is the Holiness Church, which was founded in 1908. The Holiness Church emphasizes a belief in possession by the Holy Ghost, which is manifested in the ability to speak in tongues, prophesy, and cure diseases. Members of this sect come from the lower socio-economic stratum of the black population.

Subject(s): Religion, Poverty

953   Derrick Albert Bell, Jr., Editor
Robert Haws, Co-editor

The Age of Segregation: Race Relations in the South, 1890-1945

(Jackson, MS; University Press of Mississippi, 1978)

Summary: This collection of essays addresses the system of segregation that was institutionalized by southern states in the 1890s. The essays in this volume examine the racial imperative in American law, racial discrimination, the impact of segregation on southern whites and politics, the responses of blacks to segregation, and segregation's economic consequences.

Subject(s): Segregation, Law, American South

954   Derrick Albert Bell, Jr.

And We Are Not Saved: The Elusive Quest for Racial Justice

(New York, NY; Basic Books, 1987)

Summary: Authored by law professor and activist Derrick Bell, *And We Are Not Saved: The Elusive Quest for Racial Justice* is a collection of essays that present the hardships faced by African Americans due to the racism that exists in the United States. Bell confronts the proposed "solutions" to racism and both questions and challenges readers' assumptions. The first in a series, *And We Are Not Saved* was followed by *Faces at the Bottom of the Well*.

Subject(s): Racism, History, Judicial System

955   Derrick Albert Bell, Jr.

Gospel Choirs: Psalms of Survival for an Alien Land Called Home

(New York, NY; Basic Books, 1996)

Summary: One of several collections of essays by law professor Derrick Bell, *Gospel Choirs: Psalms of Survival for an Alien Land Called Home* focuses on racism. Through the voice of a fictional 1960s civil rights attorney, as well as his own thoughts, Bell ponders issues such as business practices, the consequences of a renewed political conservatism, sexism, whites' apprehensions about blacks, and the need for African Americans to unite.

Subject(s): Music, Racism, Essays

956   Lerone Bennett, Jr.

What Manner of Man: A Biography of Martin Luther King Jr.

(Chicago, IL; Johnson Pub. Co., 1964)

Summary: Lerone Bennett Jr., executive editor of *Ebony* magazine, has combined his love of American history with his ability to research and report his findings objectively. Considered a pioneer in the field of nineteenth- and twentieth-century black history, Bennett completed his *What Manner of Man* in 1964, four years before the book's subject, civil rights leader Dr. Martin Luther King Jr., was assassinated. The first edition of Bennett's biography details Dr. King's rise from his position as the minister of one of the first black congregations formed in Montgomery, Alabama, in the mid-1950s to his founding of the Southern Christian Leadership Conference in 1957; later editions describe Dr. King's final activities, including his 1963 march on Washington D.C. and his stirring oration recommending nonviolence in advancing the cause of men and women of color. A member of the board of trustees of the Martin Luther King Memorial Center, Bennett imbues his biography of the slain civil rights leader with a sense of respect at King's bravery and dedication to the cause of black Americans.

Subject(s): Civil Rights Movement, Violence, Biography

957   Ira Berlin, Editor
Marc Fayreau, Co-editor
Steven F. Miller, Co-editor

Remembering Slavery: African Americans Talk about Their Personal Experiences of Slavery and Freedom

(New York, NY; New Press, 1998)

Summary: *Remembering Slavery: African Americans Talk about Their Personal Experiences of Slavery and Freedom* includes transcripts of interviews conducted by the Works Progress Administration (WPA) in the 1930s. Traveling the South, writers asked blacks with first-hand knowledge of slavery to recount their experiences. Memories of carrying water to field hands, of precious time with family, of masters who were sometimes harsh, sometimes kindly, and of the day-to-day experiences of living as property to be bought, sold, loaned out, or hunted down, these narratives are a poignant glimpse at an institution that for many years was cursorily described in history texts.

Subject(s): Slavery, Family Life, Autobiography

958 Ira Berlin, Editor
Ronald Hoffman, Co-editor

Slavery and Freedom in the Age of the American Revolution
(Charlottesville, VA; University Press of Virginia, 1983)

Summary: Co-edited by historians Ira Berlin and Ronald Hoffman, *Slavery and Freedom in the Age of the American Revolution* is a collection of essays that demonstrates the importance of the American Revolution in developing the two basic types of African American communities existing in North America during the eighteenth century: those proscribed by the institution of slavery and defined by the plantation holders or other individuals controlling the land on which these communities were established; and those established by free black men and women through commonalities of religion, culture, or some other reason. The essays document many different types of black communities in existence during the years surrounding the Revolutionary War, most of which attained a political and social character independent of their members' African, Creole, or other mixed-race ancestries.

Subject(s): American History, Slavery, Revolutionary War

959 Paul Berman, Editor

Blacks and Jews: Alliances and Arguments
(New York, NY; Delacorte Press, 1994)

Summary: In *Blacks and Jews: Alliances and Arguments*, editor Paul Berman presents a collection of essays reflecting the complex and often volatile relationship between American Jews and African Americans. Featuring essays written from 1960 to the present and authored by writers that include James Baldwin, Cynthia Ozick, Norman Podhoretz, Henry Louis Gates, Jr., Cornell West, bell hooks, Shelby Steele, and others, Berman attempts to present a balanced overview of this long-standing social issue. Divided into four sections, the book presents literary views, political analysis, a discussion of incidents of black-Jewish conflict, and a prediction of the future of the relationship between the two American cultures.

Subject(s): Racism, Cultural Conflict, Jews

960 Faith Berry

Langston Hughes: Before and Beyond Harlem
(Westport, CT; L. Hill, 1983)

Summary: The founder of the Langston Hughes Society, historian and journalist Faith Berry, has authored several works

profiling the life and work of African American poet. In addition to a screenplay and radio broadcast, Berry published *Langston Hughes: Before and Beyond Harlem,* which was the first Hughes biography to include previously unpublished information--the fruit of ten years' worth of research and interviews on Berry's part. The work, which several critics have hailed as a pioneering work of scholarship on the life of a man sometimes called the "poet laureate" of black America, focuses on such personal characteristics as Hughes' humanitarianism, his determination in the face of innumerable odds, as well as his body of work which transcends both race and nationality. Hughes, who died in 1967, was one of the major figures of the literary movement known as the Harlem Renaissance of the early twentieth century.

Subject(s): Biography, Poetry, Harlem Renaissance

961 Jagdish N. Bhagwati, Editor

Economics and World Order from the 1970's to the 1990's
(New York, NY; Macmillan, 1972)

Summary: This book was the first to emerge from the World Law Fund's World Order Models Project, which is concerned with the formulation of governmental policies around the world. This volume begins with an introduction by the editor. Subsequent sections consider underdeveloped nations, socialist economies, and international institutions. The final portion of the book looks at the Third World, with sections devoted to the economies of Latin America, Africa, and Asia.

Subject(s): Economics, International Relations, Africa

962 Darrel E. Bigham

We Ask Only a Fair Trial: A History of the Black Community of Evansville, Indiana
(Bloomington, IN; Indiana University Press, 1987)

Summary: Noting a lack of studies on urban black communities in smaller American cities, as well as literature on blacks in Indiana, the author chose to write a history of Evansville's black community. The book looks at black Evansville from the founding of the city in 1812 to the end of World War II. Bigham examines the city's economy and shows how the area was influenced by its ties to the South. The work also explores how the characteristics of Evansville contributed to the racism experienced by its black citizens.

Subject(s): American South, Racism, City and Town Life

963 Andrew Billingsley

Black Families in White America
(Englewood Cliffs, NJ; Prentice-Hall, 1968)

Summary: In *Black Families in White America* sociologist Andrew Billingsley outlines the history of the black family, beginning with its roots in Africa, its transplantation to the New

World, and its changes through the Civil War and Reconstruction, and into the volatile years of the Civil Rights Movement. While working mothers and elderly grandparents head many families in the black community and others suffer the ill effects of unemployment, increasing violence, and other urban ills, Billingsley argues that the African American family unit is intact and strong. Although blacks share many major cultural influences with whites, they also are influenced by a wide range of subtle influences, a result of the diversity of African ancestry and blacks' roots in the Caribbean and other locations, each with a unique cultural heritage.

Subject(s): Family Life, City and Town Life, Racism

964   Andrew Billingsley

Climbing Jacob's Ladder: The Enduring Legacy of African-American Families
(New York, NY; Simon & Schuster, 1992)

Summary: With a foundation in the author's 1968 work *Black Families in White America*, Andrew Billingsley's *Climbing Jacob's Ladder: The Enduring Legacy of African-American Families* follows the history of the African American family from its roots in Africa, through slavery and Reconstruction, to the late twentieth century. Despite such common influences as technological advances, wars, improved education, and a better standard of living, Billingsley argues that black families, which he views across five social classes, should not be viewed as "dysfunctional" simply because they do not function in accord with white "norms"; their cultural influences, ranging from Africa to the Caribbean, are far more diverse. In addition, trends like single-parent households, which were once condemned and prevalent mainly in the black community, have begun to be felt across the races due to a shift in society as a whole rather than because of the dysfunction of one particular segment.

Subject(s): Family Life, City and Town Life, Racism

965   Janet Mancini Billson

Pathways to Manhood: Young Black Males Struggle for Identity
(New Brunswick, NJ; Transaction Publishers, 1996)

Summary: As is made clear by its subtitle, *Pathways to Manhood: Young Black Males Struggle for Identity* focuses on the ways in which young African American males endeavor to achieve a sense of autonomy and self-worth in U.S. society. Authored by sociologist Janet Mancini Billson, the book focuses on the experience of teens confronted by a world that offers little in the way of economic opportunity or security and, instead, imposes upon them an model for success comprised of a tough attitude, ritualistic behavior, and emotional detachment and a lack of intellectual or artistic aptitude or emotional maturity. The work is an outgrowth of Billson's 1992 volume, a collaborative effort titled *Cool Pose: Dilemmas of Black Manhood in America* that presents the argument that young black mens' adoption of an attitude of detached "coolness" serves to mask

the anger and distrust such teens feel toward the affluent white society from which they are excluded.

Subject(s): Coming-of-Age, Urban Affairs, Adolescence

966   R.J.M. Blackett

Beating Against the Barriers: Biographical Essays in Nineteenth-Century Afro-American History
(Baton Rouge, LA; Louisiana State University Press, 1986)

Summary: Citing a need to explore the lives of lesser-known African American figures, the author presents portraits of several black abolitionists: James W.C. Pennington, William and Ellen Craft, Robert Campbell, John Sella Martin, and William Howard Day. Blackett considers how these individuals responded as the slavery of the antebellum period was supplanted by legal forms of racial discrimination following Reconstruction. Using W.E.B. Du Bois as a model, the author examines the dilemma that these figures faced as black Americans. Showing how one of these individuals chose to move to Africa, the book demonstrates the personal cost paid by those who decided to remain in the United States and work to benefit their race.

Subject(s): Racism, Slavery, Abolition

967   James E. Blackwell, Editor

Black Sociologists: Historical and Contemporary Perspectives
(Chicago, IL; University of Chicago Press, 1974)

Summary: This work is one volume in the Heritage of Sociology series and was created in response to a perceived need to recognize the past accomplishments of black sociologists in the study of race relations. The volume's opening chapters focus on the founding figures among black sociologists W.E.B. Du Bois, Charles S. Johnson, and E. Franklin Frazier. The book also examines the work of black sociologists within a segregated society, with Fisk University given as a specific example. The section on contemporary research looks at black female sociologists. Theoretical issues are considered along with the institutional adaptations made by black sociologists.

Subject(s): Race Relations, Sociology, Colleges and Universities

968   Alice C. Blair

No-Nonsense Principal: The Elementary School Principal's Handbook
(Chicago, IL; Urban Research Institute, 1982)

Summary: This book considers the problems of the elementary school principal and offers a "no-nonsense" approach to solving them. Emphasizing that the principal's primary responsibility must be the children, the author asserts that the principal has to be assertive and a strong disciplinarian. According to Blair, the principal must be able to determine the school's objectives and how to reach them, and the principal must introduce innovations to the school.

Subject(s): Education, Children, Schools

969 John W. Blassingame, Editor

Antislavery Newspapers and Periodicals. Volumes 1-5
(Boston, MA; G.K. Hall, 1980)

Summary: This five-volume collection, published from 1980-1984, provides indexes to several major antislavery publications during the middle 1800s--the period of greatest abolitionist sentiment in the United States. Among the newspapers and periodicals indexed in this work are William Lloyd Garrison's influential newspaper *The Liberator* plus other periodicals including the *Emancipator, Advocate of Freedom,* and the *Observer.* The fourth and fifth volumes in the work were coedited by Jessica M. Dunn.

Subject(s): Slavery, Periodicals, Abolition

970 John W. Blassingame

Black New Orleans, 1860-1880
(Chicago, IL; University of Chicago Press, 1973)

Summary: This work considers the state of black life in New Orleans during the Reconstruction period. Beginning with institutionalized slavery and the participation of blacks in the Civil War, the author shows how the skills developed by blacks during the antebellum period enabled them to compete against whites in the economic realm. The book examines how proscriptions against blacks limited the scale of their business enterprises. Blassingame explores changes in the black family as well as education and segregation within the city.

Subject(s): City and Town Life, Racism, Segregation

971 John W. Blassingame

The Slave Community: Plantation Life in the Antebellum South
(New York, NY; Oxford University Press, 1972)

Summary: Observing that historians had concentrated on plantation owners when studying southern slavery, the author saw a need to focus on slave life. This work relies heavily upon personal records, especially autobiographies, left by slaves. Accounts written by travelers to southern plantations supplement the views presented by slaves and planters. Among the topics included in the book are the Africanization of the South, slave culture and family, plantation institutional roles, and slave personality types.

Subject(s): Slavery, American South, Family

972 Bob Blauner, Editor

Black Lives, White Lives: Three Decades of Race Relations in America
(Berkeley, CA; University of California Press, 1989)

Summary: This book consists of a series of interviews with twenty-eight individuals, sixteen black and twelve white, over a span of approximately twenty years. Each person was interviewed in 1968, then in a period from 1978-79, and finally in 1986. Those questioned were asked about their own lives, their political beliefs and racial attitudes, and the social changes they had witnessed. Given the timing of the first interviews, the assassination of Martin Luther King, Jr. became a primary source for questions. Issues surrounding the civil rights movement included integration, black power, nationalism, and nonviolence. Blacks were asked about the effect of racism on their lives and also about black culture. Whites were asked about racism as well, including the importance of "whiteness" to their personal identity. All together, the interviews provide an opportunity to observe changes in the nation's racial landscape that took place over three decades.

Subject(s): Racism, Civil Rights Movement, Segregation

973 Rhoda Lois Blumberg

Civil Rights: The 1960s Freedom Struggle
(Boston, MA; Twayne Publishers, 1984)

Summary: This book considers the struggle for freedom by blacks in the mid-twentieth century. The work follows the civil rights movement, beginning with the bus boycott by the black citizens of Montgomery, Alabama. It continues through the ascension of Martin Luther King, Jr. as a leader of national prominence, and ends with his assassination and the election of Richard Nixon. Blumberg examines the fight for desegregation and voting rights and traces how activists moved from a philosophy of nonviolence to one of black power and self-defense. The author also looks at the civil rights movement in regard to the escalating war in Vietnam, as well as how frustration with powerlessness and poverty in the ghetto resulted in urban rebellions.

Subject(s): Civil Rights Movement, Poverty, Segregation

974 John B. Boles

Black Southerners, 1619-1869
(Lexington, KY; University Press of Kentucky, 1983)

Summary: One volume in the series "New Perspectives on the South," this book presents an account of slavery in the southern United States from its African background to Reconstruction. The author demonstrates how the institution of slavery changed over time, from its background in the seventeenth and eighteenth centuries to its height in the period from 1820 to 1860. Boles looks at the diversity of the antebellum black experience, including not just agricultural but urban and industrial slavery as well. The work depicts the development of the free black population following the Civil War and shows how slavery evolved into sharecropping.

Subject(s): Slavery, American South, Reconstruction

975 **Aubrey W. Bonnett,** Editor
G. Llewellyn Watson, Co-editor

Emerging Perspectives on the Black Diaspora

(Lanham, MD; University Press of America, 1989)

Summary: In *Emerging Perspectives on the Black Diaspora* editors Bonnett and Watson assemble a number of thought-provoking essays on the growth and social significance of black communities and cultures throughout the New World, including those in Canada, the United States, and Panama. Following the philosophy of black nationalist Marcus Garvey, the editors push for both understanding and social change, as many such communities are threatened by economic disadvantage and a repressive ruling class.

Subject(s): Diaspora, Cultural Conflict, American History

976 **Arna Bontemps,** Editor

The Harlem Renaissance Remembered: Essays

(New York, NY; Dodd, Mead, 1972)

Summary: The essay collection *The Harlem Renaissance Remembered* is edited by poet and literary critic Arna Bontemps, himself a significant figure in the literary movement that flowered in New York City during the early years of the 1900s. Framing the collection of essays describing the flowering of black culture within his own memories of such figures as poet Langston Hughes, Countee Cullen, Zora Neal Hurston, and others, Bontemps's belief in the importance of black heritage and his humanistic concerns inform the anthology. He focuses on the contributions made by Claude McKay, Jean Toomer, Hughes, and Cullen, among others. Publishing his own poetry between 1924 and 1931, editor Bontemps maintains that the creative energy of the Harlem Renaissance was sparked by poetry and then found its way into other art forms, such as novels, paintings, sculpture, dance, and drama.

Subject(s): Harlem Renaissance, Literature, Culture

977 **Arna Bontemps**
Jack Conroy, Co-author

They Seek a City

(Garden City, NY; Doubleday, Doran and Company, Inc., 1945)

Summary: Co-authored by novelist and journalist Jack Conroy and Arna Bontemps, *They Seek a City* examines the movement of African American families from their initial homes in and around Southern plantations to the factories of the Northern states and the rich farmlands of the American Midwest. Discussions focus on the growth of black populations in such cities as New York and Chicago, and the effects the move to a faster-paced, industrial lifestyle had on Southern black families and their traditional culture in the period between the Civil War and World War II.

Subject(s): Reconstruction, Working-Class Life, Family Life

978 **B.A. Botkin,** Editor

Lay My Burden Down: A Folk History of Slavery

(Chicago, IL; University of Chicago Press, 1945)

Summary: Folklorist B.A. Botkin compiled *Lay My Burden Down: A Folk History of Slavery* in 1945. During the Depression years of the 1930s, as many men and women born under slavery and freed by the Emancipation Proclamation were nearing the end of their lives, U.S. President Franklin D. Roosevelt's New Deal Federal Writing Project sent men and women to interview close to 300 such African Americans about their recollections of life under slavery and the changes wrought by freedom.

Subject(s): Slavery, American South, Freedom

979 **Bernard R. Boxill**

Blacks and Social Justice

(Totowa, NJ; Rowman & Allanheld, 1984)

Summary: Starting with Ronald Reagan's administration, the recent trend in American government has been to reverse color-conscious policies. The author aims to rebut this trend, and in so doing, considers the work of Karl Marx and economist Thomas Sowell; he also examines school segregation as well as preferential treatment in education and jobs. Boxill explores black self-segregation, citing figures such as Frederick Douglass, W.E.B. Du Bois, William Monroe Trotter, and Booker T. Washington. In addition, the author calls upon the ideas of Martin Luther King, Jr. to discuss the issue of civil disobedience.

Subject(s): Government, Civil Rights, Education

980 **Taylor Branch**

Parting the Waters: America in the King Years, 1954-63

(New York, NY; Simon and Schuster, 1988)

Summary: The culmination of six years of research, including interviewing, pouring through newspaper files, and listening to FBI tapes, *Parting the Waters: America in the King Years, 1954-1963* profiles the United States during the civil rights era. As the volume's subtitle makes clear, author Taylor Branch positions the late Dr. Martin Luther King, Jr., as the book's focal point, using the civil rights leader's participation in protests and his relationships with other men and women--supporters, colleagues, and opponents in the battle for social change--to investigate the movement's many facets. Beginning with King's appointment as pastor at Montgomery, Alabama's first all-black church, Branch recounts the events leading to the assassination of U.S. President John F. Kennedy in 1963. Among the speeches transcribed and discussed in the book is King's "I have a dream" speech, as well as the early talk--given while leading blacks in a protest of the segregation of Montgomery's buses--that is generally seen as marking the transition between King, the man of the cloth, and King, the civil rights leader. Exploring conflicts existing within the African American community during the 1950s and 1960s, Branch highlights the contributions made by a younger generation of blacks who showed King that true power belongs to those people committed enough to nonviolent protest that they would risk physical injury or jail in defense of their cause. Notable in *Parting the Waters* is its author's stress on the black church and King's own deep religious conviction.

Subject(s): Racism, Biography, Civil Rights Movement

Award(s): Christopher Award, 1988; Pulitzer Prize: History, 1988; National Book Critics Circle Award: Nonfiction, 1989

981   **Russell C. Brignano**

Black Americans in Autobiography: An Annotated Bibliography of Autobiographies and Autobiographical Books Written since the Civil War
(Durham, NC; Duke University Press, 1974)

Summary: Brignano's 1974 work is a comprehensive listing of autobiographical works written by African Americans after the Civil War of the 1860s. In addition to annotating the listings with short descriptions of the works in question, Brignano includes several indexes to help researchers, including indexes of organizations, educational institutions, and occupations.

Subject(s): Autobiography, Civil War

982   **Francis L. Broderick,** Editor
August Meier, Co-editor

Negro Protest Thought in the Twentieth Century
(Indianapolis, IN; Bobbs-Merrill, 1965)

Summary: Revised and expanded in the early 1970s as *Black Protest Thought in the Twentieth Century*, Francis L. Broderick's *Negro Protest Thought in the Twentieth Century* contains excerpts from speeches, editorials, and other public protestations made by outspoken and sometimes militant blacks during the civil rights era. Coverage ranges from a debate on the "separate but equal" doctrine adopted by Southern states in mid-century to the visions of a nation indivisible by race that echo in the speeches of Dr. Martin Luther King, Jr. *Negro Protest Thought*, a rich source of primary material for the study of the history of the U.S. equal rights movement, was edited by educator and attorney Broderick with assistance from other scholars in the field of African American history.

Subject(s): Resistance Movements, Civil Rights Movement, Racial Conflict

983   **Howard Brotz**

The Black Jews of Harlem: Negro Nationalism and the Dilemmas of Negro Leadership
(New York, NY; Free Press of Glencoe, 1964)

Summary: This work considers the history and situation of black Jews in the United States. In addition to demonstrating how blacks came to join the Jewish faith, the book surveys Christianity and explores the relationship between blacks and other Jews. In looking at the search for a black community, Brotz examines figures such as Booker T. Washington and Marcus Garvey as well as the significance of American Communism and black Muslims. Finally, the author investigates black nationalism as a solution to the "Negro Problem."

Subject(s): Religion, Black Nationalism, Jews

984   **Howard Brotz,** Editor

Negro Social and Political Thought, 1850-1920: Representative Texts
(New York, NY; Basic Books, 1966)

Summary: In his anthology titled *Negro Social and Political Thought, 1850-1920*, editor Howard Brotz has collected writings by Booker T. Washington, W.E.B. Du Bois, and Marcus Garvey, among others. Within the essays, collected with the purpose of providing a reader for students of black history, topics range from retraining former slaves for employment in the industrial northern states; proposed plans for blacks to emigrate to Africa; the social rifts between the races that developed following the Civil War; and the quest to redefine the role of blacks within U.S. society. The volume was later reissued as *African American Social and Political Thought, 1850-1920*.

Subject(s): Resistance Movements, Politics, History

985   **Dickson D. Bruce, Jr.**

Archibald Grimke: Portrait of a Black Independent
(Baton Rouge, LA; Louisiana State University Press, 1993)

Summary: This biography of Grimke follows him from his childhood in slavery through his post-emancipation years at Harvard Law School and to his later work as an activist and intellectual. The nephew of noted abolitionists Angelina and Sarah Grimke, Archibald Grimke wrote biographies of Charles Sumner and William Lloyd Garrison; served as ambassador to the Dominican Republic from 1894 to 1898; and helped found the National Association for the Advancement of Colored People (NAACP).

Subject(s): Biography, Slavery

986 **Ralph J. Bunche**
Charles P. Henry, Editor

Ralph J. Bunche: Selected Speeches and Writings
(Ann Arbor, MI; University of Michigan Press, 1995)

Summary: *Selected Speeches and Writings* compiles the oratory and writing of Nobel Prize-winning diplomat and racial pioneer Ralph Bunche. Raised with few advantages as the grandson of a slave, Bunche earned a Ph.D. at Harvard and served in the O.S.S. and U.S. State Department, where he facilitated the founding of the United Nations and the drafting of its charter. His negotiation of the end of the Arab-Israeli conflict in 1949 won him the Nobel Peace Prize in 1950. A respected figure outside his own country, Bunche supported the civil rights movement that would allow successful people of color the same regard within the United States.

Subject(s): Racism, Peace, Civil Rights Movement

987 **Mary Cable**

Black Odyssey: The Case of the Slave Ship Amistad
(New York, NY; Viking Press, 1971)

Summary: Mary Cable's *Black Odyssey: The Case of the Slave Ship Amistad* recounts the chain of events that occurred beginning in August 1839, when an unidentified ship was spotted off the coast of New England. The fate of the 30 Africans aboard would involve a quiet Connecticut community, the courts, and ultimately a former president of the United States (John Quincy Adams) in Cable's well-researched account.

Subject(s): Slavery, Judicial System, Refugees

988 **Cab Calloway**
Bryant Rollins, Co-author

Of Minnie the Moocher & Me
(New York, NY; Crowell, 1976)

Summary: *Of Minnie the Moocher and Me* details the life of jazz singer, orchestra leader, and actor Cab Calloway. Famous for the "scat"-style singing he claimed to have "invented" in 1933 when he forgot the lyrics of a song he was performing and began to improvise, Calloway's memoir recounts his early years performing on vaudeville stages before forming his own orchestra, which featured such jazz nobility as Dizzy Gillespie during its history. Other exploits recounted by the jazz giant include acting stints in a 1953 stage revival of Gershwin's *Porgy and Bess* and motion pictures *St. Louis Blues* and *Stormy Weather*.

Subject(s): Autobiography, Music, Popular Culture

989 **Horace Campbell**

Rasta and Resistance: From Marcus Garvey to Walter Rodney
(Trenton, NJ; Africa World Press, 1987)

Summary: In *Rasta and Resistance: From Marcus Garvey to Walter Rodney*, Horace Campbell, an activist and professor of political science at the University of Dar-es-Salaam in Tanzania, East Africa, examines the Rastafarian movement, from its roots in Jamaica to its later incarnations in the United States and Africa. The book discusses the slave trade, particularly in Brazil, the Haitian Revolution led by Toussaint L'Ouverture, the development of ska and reggae music, and blacks' struggles in Great Britain. Arguing against its classification as a cult, Campbell maintains that Rasta reflects an oppressed people's attempt at resistance and a search for a better life. This was one of the first books to seriously examine Rasta as a political movement.

Subject(s): Resistance Movements, Oppression, Cults

990 **Dominic J. Capeci, Jr.**

Race Relations in Wartime Detroit: The Sojourner Truth Housing Controversy of 1942
(Philadelphia, PA; Temple University Press, 1984)

Summary: This work describes the struggle between black and white World War II government production workers over a group of housing project units called the Sojourner Truth Homes. The book traces Detroit's racial history, particularly the prewar years, as well as the conflict itself, which ended with the occupancy of the project by black defense workers. Overshadowed by the race riot of 1943, this incident is presented by the author as representative of the state of ethnic and racial relations during the time.

Subject(s): Race Relations, Racism, Housing

991 **Stokely Carmichael**
Charles V. Hamilton, Co-author

Black Power: The Politics of Liberation in America
(New York, NY; Random House, 1967)

Summary: Civil rights leader Stokely Carmichael's *Black Power: The Politics of Liberation in America* investigates the meaning of the term "Black Power," which Carmichael, a former Black Panther, is credited with coining. Carmichael, a radical and advocate of a black voice united in its rejection of the need for African Americans to assimilate into an inherently racist white culture, called upon "black people in this country to unite, to recognize their heritage, to build a sense of community...to define their own goals, to lead their own organizations and to support those organizations." The book was viewed by many as a call to revolution; in its preface Carmichael and co-author Hamilton state: "This book presents a political framework and ideology which represents the last reasonable opportunity for this society to work out its racial problems short of prolonged destructive guerilla warfare."

Subject(s): Civil Rights Movement, Pan-Africanism, Resistance Movements

992 **Stokely Carmichael**

Stokely Speaks: Black Power Back to Pan-Africanism
(New York, NY; Random House, 1971)

Summary: *Stokely Speaks: Black Power Back to Pan-Africanism* is a collection of speeches and essays by civil rights leader and former Black Panther, Stokely Carmichael. Radical in his beliefs and outspoken in his support of an African American society united and independent of white America, Carmichael was a brilliant speaker who actively supported the cause of blacks around the world. His speeches and writings stand as a reflection of the attitude of many radical blacks during the civil rights movement. Carmichael would later moderate his radical stance and disavow the Panthers, rejecting the political position many held responsible for instigating much of the racial violence of the era.

Subject(s): Civil Rights Movement, Pan-Africanism, Resistance Movements

993 **Lorene Cary**

Black Ice
(New York, NY; Knopf, 1991)

Summary: *Black Ice* recounts the two years Lorene Cary spent as one of the first African American students to study at St. Paul's, an exclusive New England boarding school. During her two years at St. Paul's, Cary looks back on her shame at her humble Philadelphia roots, and her attempts to fit in to an upper-class, traditional, white world in which she had little experience. Cary tells her story with suprising clarity, revealing the process by which the immature teen, who enrolled at the prestigious boarding school in an attempt to recreate herself, grew into an insightful young woman with a strong appreciation of her African American roots.

Subject(s): Autobiography, Class Conflict, Outcasts

994 **Central State University**

Index to Periodical Articles by and about Blacks
(Boston, MA; G.K. Hall, 1981)

Summary: An ambitious undertaking by Central State University, *Index to Periodical Articles by and about Blacks* lists articles from both major newspapers and magazines as well as from scholarly journals and black publications like *Black Scholar, Freedomways,* and others that focus on topics relevant to African American interests and concerns. Providing the information necessary to allow researchers easy access to periodicals, the *Index* has been updated on a regular basis since its

first publication in 1981, and entries date back to the early part of the twentieth century.

Subject(s): Journalism, Research

995 **Ocania Chalk**

Black College Sport
(New York, NY; Dodd, Mead, 1976)

Summary: This work considers the topic of black male athletes in college sports. The book examines athletes in sports such as baseball, basketball, football, and track and field. It looks at players at both white colleges and black colleges. In the book's final section, Chalk focuses attention on black Olympians.

Subject(s): Olympic Games, Colleges and Universities, Sports

996 **Wilt Chamberlain**
David Shaw, Co-author

Wilt: Just like Any Other Seven-Foot Black Millionaire Who Lives Next Door
(New York, NY; Macmillan, 1973)

Summary: *Wilt: Just like Any Other Seven-Foot Black Millionaire Who Lives Next Door* is former Los Angeles Lakers basketball phenomenon Wilt Chamberlain's account of his rise to greatness in the sports world. Heralded by many as one of the greatest offensive players in the history of basketball, Chamberlain openly describes his personal life as well as his career in sports, addressing such topics as the personal dislike other players had for him and his impact on the game of basketball, as well as offering his opinion of many of the players who joined him on the court.

Subject(s): Autobiography, Basketball, Sports

997 **Mark L. Chapman**

Christianity on Trial: African-American Religious Thought before and after Black Power
(Maryknoll, NY; Orbis Books, 1996)

Summary: Part of the "Bishop Henry McNeal Turner/Sojourner Truth" series of volumes on black religion, Mark Chapman's *Christianity on Trial: African-American Religious Thought before and after Black Power* examines the question of whether Christianity leads to freedom or oppression. Examining the work of twentieth century theologians that include Benjamin Mays, Delores S. Williams, Albert Cleage, Elijah Muhammad, and James H. Cone, Chapman explores the way Christianity has impacted the Black Power movement, Black Muslims, and womanist theology.

Subject(s): Religion, Christianity, Oppression

998   Chinweizu

The West and the Rest of Us: White Predators, Black Slavers, and the African Elite
(New York, NY; Random House, 1975)

Summary: This book examines the effect that Western expansion has had on the rest of the world, using the "Euro-African Connection," comprising a five-hundred-year period, as its focus. The author considers the role of African complicity in the West's subjugation of the continent. Showing how black slavers prepared Africa for conquest, the work compares them to today's African elite, who, for their own benefit, have failed to promote a decolonization of Third World nations, leaving these countries in a state of underdevelopment. By exploring myths of racism, the author demonstrates how the oppression of Africa has continued.

Subject(s): Africa, Slavery, Colonialism

999   Kenneth B. Clark

Dark Ghetto: Dilemmas of Social Power
(New York, NY; Harper & Row, 1965)

Summary: In *Dark Ghetto: Dilemmas of Social Power* psychologist and educator Kenneth B. Clark recounts his experiences as co-founder and consultant to Harlem Youth Opportunities Unlimited, an organization designed to help inner-city youth succeed within a decaying urban environment. Clark examines the causes for such decay--poverty, crime, the break down of the family, drug abuse, and lack of hope--and argues that those living in America's ghettos are not responsible for the political, economic, and other conditions they are forced to endure. He states that misguided efforts at social engineering have also contributed to the problem.

Subject(s): City and Town Life, Poverty, Urban Affairs

1000   Septima Poinsette Clark

Echo in My Soul
(New York, NY; Dutton, 1962)

Summary: *Echo in My Soul* is the account of Septima Poinsette Clark's experiences of racism in the South of the 1960s. The daughter of a former slave, Clark worked as a schoolteacher from the early twenties until 1956, when, at the age of fifty-eight, she was fired from her teaching position in Charleston, South Carolina, for joining the National Association for the Advancement of Colored People (NAACP). Clark describes the experiences of losing a job--to which she had devoted most of her adult life--as a result of her support of racial equality. A resilient woman, she spent the remainder of her professional life promoting literacy among Tennessee's African American population before joining Dr. Martin Luther King, Jr. in training teachers through King's Southern Christian Leadership Conference.

Subject(s): Autobiography, Civil Rights Movement, Racism

1001   John Henrik Clarke, Editor

Harlem: A Community in Transition
(New York, NY; Citadel Press, 1964)

Summary: This book presents a collection of essays on Harlem. The volume's introduction looks at the history and development of the community. Subsequent essays consider Harlem's literature, music, and theater in addition to its economy and politics. Other essays consider the legacy of Alain Locke, the Harlem Renaissance, and nationalist movements. The collection includes an interview with James Baldwin and two essays by Langston Hughes.

Subject(s): Harlem Renaissance, Music, Black Nationalism

1002   John Henrik Clarke, Editor

Malcolm X: The Man and His Times
(New York, NY; Macmillan, 1969)

Summary: Author and educator John Henrik Clarke created a chronology of the life of Malcolm X by collecting essays about and writings by the African American civil rights leader. The collection, edited by Clarke, shows Malcolm X as seen by others during various stages of his career. A radical separatist before converting to the Muslim faith, who eventually recanted that faith to found the Organization of Afro-American Unity, Malcolm X remains a figure fascinating to many historians of the civil rights movement. Friends and followers provide the preponderance of material in Clarke's book, which results in what some critics have maintained is a sympathetic slant. However, others have praised *Malcolm X: The Man and His Times* as a valuable resource for the study of the many-faceted career of a man who became a folk hero among African Americans.

Subject(s): Civil Rights Movement, Politics, Racial Conflict

1003   John Henrik Clarke, Editor

Marcus Garvey and the Vision of Africa
(New York, NY; Random House, 1974)

Summary: Compiled with the assistance of Amy S. Garvey, *Marcus Garvey and the Vision of Africa* collects writings by and about the black activist, most widely known for spearheading the "Back to Africa" movement of the turn of the twentieth century. Editor John Hendrik Clarke groups the selected essays into five chronological groups, then completes the work with two additional sections: essays about Garvey's relationship with his critics, and essays reflecting recent reappraisals of his contributions to the movement for racial equality in the United States. Overall in agreement with Garvey's philosophy, essayists discuss not only his contributions during the 1920s but also the influence he had on the black nationalism movement of later decades.

Subject(s): Black Nationalism, Africa, Racism

1004 John Henrik Clarke, Editor

William Styron's "Nat Turner": Ten Black Writers Respond

(Boston, MA; Beacon Press, 1968)

Summary: In 1967 novelist William Styron published *The Confessions of Nat Turner*, a novel that would become controversial in its depiction of the nineteenth century black activist. In *William Styron's "Nat Turner": Ten Black Writers Respond*, historian John Henrik Clarke presents critical reaction to Styron's portrayal of Turner as indecisive and with an obsessive erotic preoccupation about white women providing the motivation for his acts of rebellion. Among the essayists are Alvin F. Poussaint, Charles V. Hamilton, and Vincent Harding.

Subject(s): Biography, Literature, American History

1005 Albert B. Cleage, Jr.

The Black Messiah

(New York, NY; Sheed and Ward, 1968)

Summary: *The Black Messiah* is a collection of sermons written by Albert B. Cleage, an ordained minister of the United Church of Christ. Educated at Oberlin College's School of Theology, Cleage worked as a social worker in Detroit during the 1930s before beginning his ministry. The sermons contained in this volume were developed during his ministrations to congregations in Lexington, Kentucky, San Francisco, California, Springfield, Massachusetts, and, finally, Detroit, Michigan where Rev. Cleage led the congregation of the Shrine of the Black Madonna, beginning in 1952.

Subject(s): Religion, Christianity, Community Relations

1006 Eldridge Cleaver

Soul on Ice

(New York, NY; McGraw-Hill, 1968)

Summary: The essay collection *Soul on Ice* was radical civil rights activist Eldridge Cleaver's first published work. Written while its author was imprisoned for a drug and rape conviction and credited with motivating the letter-writing campaign that resulted in his early release, the book was inspired by Cleaver's admiration for Malcolm X, leader of the Black Muslim group of which Cleaver was a member. With a foundation built on Cleaver's study of the political philosophy of figures as diverse as Thomas Paine, Nikolai Lenin, and James Baldwin, *Soul on Ice* finds Cleaver reflecting on both his own descent into violence and the related dilemma faced by African Americans frustrated in their attempts to succeed within U.S. society. The book was praised by reviewers who respected Cleaver's well-reasoned criticisms of a system that alienated people of color and his re-visioning of U.S. society. Cleaver would later be an active member of the Black Panther party.

Subject(s): Resistance Movements, Racism, Violence

1007 Leonard A. Cole

Blacks in Power: A Comparative Study of Black and White Elected Officials

(Princeton, NY; Princeton University Press, 1976)

Summary: In *Blacks in Power: A Comparative Study of Black and White Elected Officials*, author Leonard A. Cole analyzes interviews with 130 elected officials from sixteen New Jersey cities, all with significant black populations. Questions revolved around the qualities of leadership of black versus white officials and the influence of black elected officials on policymaking by a predominately white governing body. Cole also includes, in addition to data tables and other appendices, case studies of busing and zoning issues showing that the African American presence is indeed a factor in city policies.

Subject(s): Government, Urban Affairs, Politics

1008 Patricia Hill Collins

Black Feminist Thought: Knowledge, Consciousness, and the Politics of Empowerment

(Boston, MA; Unwin Hyman, 1990)

Summary: In *Black Feminist Thought: Knowledge, Consciousness, and the Politics of Empowerment* feminist theorist and educator Patricia Hill Collins outlines the ideas of modern black "womanists"--African American feminists--from both academic and nonacademic backgrounds. The first book-length history and analysis of "Black women's ideas," Collins's volume allows readers to view the trappings of modern black culture from a new perspective, particularly as they relate to a woman's vision of self. Essays, which encourage the empowerment of women in modern black society, introduce works by such authors as political activist Angela Davis, novelist Alice Walker, and poet Audre Lorde. *Black Feminist Thought* was published in a revised edition in 1999, updating its focus to include a discussion of black popular culture, the affirmative action debates, and the Anita Hill hearings.

Subject(s): Women's Rights, Popular Culture, Sexism

1009 James P. Comer

Beyond Black and White

(New York, NY; Quadrangle Books, 1972)

Summary: Psychiatrist and author James P. Comer has written several books during his career that promote his theory that the way to improve the academic performance of inner-city young people is to foster a family-like atmosphere within the city's schools. In his *Beyond Black and White*, he meditates on the problems of race relations and discusses his experiences as an African American member of the academic elite. Coming from a working class Chicago family, Comer earned degrees from Indiana University, Howard University, the University of Michigan, and Yale University during the civil rights movement, eventually advancing himself within academia and establishing a long and successful career at Yale's Department of Psychiatry beginning in 1970.

Subject(s): Education, Racism, Academia

1010 Henry Steele Commager, Editor

The Struggle for Racial Equality: A Documentary Record

(New York, NY; Harper & Row, 1967)

Summary: In *The Struggle for Racial Equality: A Documentary Record* noted U.S. historian Henry Steele Commager selects and assembles important primary source materials referencing efforts by both blacks and whites to create a society wherein race ceases to be a dividing line. With the intent of providing the general public with the words and ideas that actually shaped American society and the laws that govern it, Commager's editorial efforts set the race-based strife of the nation's first two centuries--from the arrival of the first slave ships onto North American shores through the volatile years of the civil rights movement--into a context that encourages readers to reassess both the country's history and its future.

Subject(s): Racism, American History, Resistance Movements

1011 James H. Cone

Black Theology and Black Power

(New York, NY; Seabury Press, 1969)

Summary: Considered among the classic documents emanating from the civil rights and Black Power movements of the 1960s, *Black Theology & Black Power* was author James H. Cone's attempt to align Christian salvation with the militant quest for liberation from oppression. Believing the gospels of Jesus Christ to have been distorted in favor of white congregations, Cone provided a unique African American theology that reflected the social conflicts of the civil rights era.

Subject(s): Religion, Racism, Religious Conflict

1012 James H. Cone

For My People: Black Theology and the Black Church

(Maryknoll, NY; Orbis Books, 1984)

Summary: *For My People: Black Theology and the Black Church* is James H. Cone's study of the history of African American religious thought from the civil rights movement of the 1960s to the 1980s. Placing black theology within the context of the black power movement and other breaks with mainstream U.S. culture, the volume also outlines the ideas of leading black religious leaders and includes a discussion of the future direction of Christianity as practiced by African Americans. Finally, the book explores how religion can help deal with the social crises caused by racial conflict.

Subject(s): Religion, Spiritualism, Resistance Movements

1013 James H. Cone

Martin & Malcolm & America: A Dream or a Nightmare

(Maryknoll, NY; Orbis Books, 1991)

Summary: In his *Martin & Malcolm & America: A Dream or a Nightmare* James H. Cone examines the lives of Martin Luther King, Jr., and Malcolm X, the two most influential black leaders of the twentieth century. Contrasting King's vision of U.S. society as "a dream . . . as yet unfulfilled" with the more radical Malcolm X who viewed America as a nightmare, Cone looks beyond the beliefs of the moment to contend that the philosophies of the two leaders—pacifist and radical—would have eventually come into alignment with regard to ways to address issues of class and race.

Subject(s): Civil Rights Movement, Racism, Resistance Movements

1014 James H. Cone

My Soul Looks Back

(Nashville, TN; Abingdon, 1982)

Summary: In this work, the author recounts the development of a black theology of liberation. Beginning with his childhood in Arkansas, Cone describes his father's resistance to racism, his own experience with racial discrimination in graduate school, and his controversial articulation of liberation theology. The author also considers Third World theologies, feminism, and Marxism.

Subject(s): Religion, Racism, Colleges and Universities

1015 James H. Cone

The Spirituals and the Blues: An Interpretation

(New York, NY; Seabury Press, 1972)

Summary: James H. Cone's *The Spirituals and the Blues: An Interpretation* explores two of the most influential aspects of African American culture—Negro spirituals and their offshoot, the blues. Beginning his history with the importance of spirituals among slaves and the children of slaves as a way to affirm their essential humanity and spiritual worthiness against an oppressive white culture, Cone goes on to depict the blues as a "this-worldly" statement of political and cultural rebellion and discusses its influence on modern American music.

Subject(s): Religion, Racism, Music

1016 Harold X. Connolly

A Ghetto Grows in Brooklyn

(New York, NY; New York University Press, 1977)

Summary: *A Ghetto Grows in Booklyn* documents the development of Brooklyn, New York's predominantly African American community. Based on historic records and author Harold X. Connolly's interviews with influential members of the Bedford-Stuyvesant neighborhood, the study is divided into four parts, among them a historic overview, a discussion of community organization, and an analysis of the problems faced by Bedford-Stuyvesant in the areas of education, housing, and crime by the mid-1900s. Praised for its scholarship, Connolly's work also points out the pervasive racism and anti-urban bias undergirding much large-scale public policy measures in New York City.

Subject(s): Urban Affairs, Racism, Politics

1017 Mercer Cook, Editor

The Haitian-American Anthology: Haitian Readings from American Authors

(Port-au-Prince, Haiti; Imprimerie de l'etat, 1944)

Summary: Before he became American ambassador to the African nations Niger and Senegal in the mid-1960s, Mercer Cook was professor of English at the University of Haiti, Port-au-Prince, between 1943 and 1945. As a way of providing his French-speaking students with literature that was relevant to their life experience, he collected and published *Haitian American Anthology: Haitian Readings from American Authors*, which includes short stories and excerpts accompanied by comprehension guides. Cook would publish a number of guides for both teachers and students in Haiti during his three years in that country.

Subject(s): Literature, Education

1018 Mercer Cook
Stephen E. Henderson, Co-author

The Militant Black Writer in Africa and the United States

(Madison, WI; University of Wisconsin Press, 1969)

Summary: Prior to retiring from his position as professor of Romance languages at Howard University, Mercer Cook co-wrote *The Militant Black Writer in Africa and the United States*. Cook and fellow professor Stephen E. Henderson each contributed an essay based on their joint address to the Conference on Afro-American Culture held in 1968 at the University of Wisconsin. For his part, Cook drew on his academic experiences, as well as his experiences as ambassador to Niger and Senegal in the mid-1960s, in discussing the currents of radical political thought underlying literature emanating from Africa. Cook was also aided by his experience as director of Africa's Congress for Cultural Freedom in the early 1960s and as alternate delegate to the U.N. General Assembly in 1963.

Subject(s): Literature, Cultural Conflict, Apartheid

1019 Wayne Cooper

Claude McKay: Rebel Sojourner in the Harlem Renaissance: A Biography

(Baton Rouge, LA; Louisiana State University Press, 1987)

Summary: Wayne Cooper's biography depicts the life of the Jamaican-born McKay (1890-1948), who was considered an iconoclast within the New York intellectual circles that comprised the Harlem Renaissance. Moving to New York City in 1915, McKay involved himself with a succession of political ideologies, including black radicalism, socialism, and communism, before adopting Catholicism in the 1930s. While his 1928 novel *Home to Harlem* was the first novel by a black to achieve bestseller status, his other work failed to follow suit. Making a meager living as an editor, he relied for his support upon the help of his friends and on the generosity of the groups he joined.

Subject(s): Biography, Harlem Renaissance, Poetry

1020 Janet Duitsman Cornelius

"When I Can Read My Title Clear": Literacy, Slavery, and Religion in the Antebellum South

(Columbia, SC; University of South Carolina Press, 1991)

Summary: *"When I Can Read My Title Clear:" Literacy, Slavery, and Religion in the Antebellum South* chronicles the role of religion and education in the struggle for freedom prior to the Civil War. Showing the methods used by blacks to acquire the ability to read despite its prohibition among slaves, Janet Duitsman Cornelius argues that ten percent of the slave population was made literate through the efforts of white missionaries and others. This literacy fueled their desire for freedom; biblical stories shared clandestinely among enslaved Africans then inspired the acts of courage and insurrection of countless slaves. Cornelius bases her study on numerous primary sources, among them slave narratives, church records, and the diaries of slave-owning whites.

Subject(s): Slavery, American South, Resistance Movements

1021 Harold Courlander

Negro Folk Music USA

(New York, NY; Columbia University Press, 1963)

Summary: A student of philosophy, oral history, and folklore, Harold Courlander was fortunate to be able to amass enough grant money to make a thorough study of the music and folk legacy of black Americans of African and West Indian descent. His *Negro Folk Music USA* is one of many results of his efforts. A collection of the songs, spirituals, and other forms of music traditionally created by African Americans, the volume includes both music and background information for each of the songs included.

Subject(s): Music, Folklore, Popular Culture

1022 Stanley Crouch

The All-American Skin Game, or, The Decoy of Race: The Long and Short of It, 1990-1994
(New York, NY; Pantheon Books, 1995)

Summary: *The All-American Skin Game; Or, the Decoy of Race: The Long and Short of It* is the second collection of essays by jazz critic and journalist Stanley Crouch. As he had in 1990's *Notes of a Hanging Judge*, Crouch voices his strong condemnation of African American leaders who advocate black superiority and blame racial oppression for the source of all their ills. A former black nationalist himself, Crouch blames such separatist movements for the breakdown of the process toward civil rights begun by Martin Luther King, Jr. and others during the mid-1900s, and advocates self-reliance among African Americans as a way to put an end to many of America's societal ills.

Subject(s): Civil Rights Movement, Racism, Black Nationalism

1023 Stanley Crouch

Notes of a Hanging Judge: Essays and Reviews, 1979-1989
(New York, NY; Oxford University Press, 1990)

Summary: In *Notes of a Hanging Judge: Essays and Reviews, 1979-1989* jazz critic and political commentator Stanley Crouch delves into subjects ranging from feminism and the Third World to boxing and the films of black director Spike Lee. His common thread is music; his strong political beliefs filter his commentary. Condemning African Americans such as Malcolm X, Stokely Carmichael, Toni Morrison, and Lee for pandering to the self-pitying attitudes of some in the black community, he rejects separatism and other divisive "black power" philosophies in favor of accepting personal responsibility, attaining education, and entering into an educated debate as a means of improving the situation of blacks in U.S. society.

Subject(s): Literacy, Racism, Resistance Movements

1024 James L. Curtis

Blacks, Medical Schools, and Society
(Ann Arbor, MI; University of Michigan Press, 1971)

Summary: In *Blacks, Medical Schools, and Society* African American psychiatrist James L. Curtis examines the problems confronting young blacks desirous of a career in medicine. After providing a history of blacks in medicine, Curtis goes on to examine the dramatic increase in black enrollments to medical schools in the wake of the civil rights movement, and he suggests ways to encourage qualified young people to pursue careers in the medical arts. Also under discussion are the pros and cons of lowering admission criteria for minority students, encouraging blacks to practice medicine in low-income areas where care is most needed, and the effects of attending so-

called "segregated" medical schools such as those at all-black colleges and universities.

Subject(s): Education, Medicine, Segregation

1025 Harlon L. Dalton

Racial Healing: Confronting the Fear between Blacks and Whites
(New York, NY; Doubleday, 1995)

Summary: In Harlon L. Dalton's *Racial Healing: Confronting the Fear between Blacks and Whites* the author suggests that whites and blacks have the potential to share the same communities without regard for the color of one another's skin. Dalton, a professor at Yale Law School, maintains that on an individual level, men and women should openly express their hidden stereotypes, fears, prejudices, and questions, blacks to whites and whites to blacks, thereby gaining a true understanding of racial difference and eradicating the fears and tensions that keep society segregated.

Subject(s): Race Relations, Psychology

1026 Douglas Henry Daniels

Pioneer Urbanites: A Social and Cultural History of Black San Francisco
(Philadelphia, PA; Temple University Press, 1980)

Summary: In *Pioneer Urbanites: A Social and Cultural History of Black San Francisco*, Douglas Henry Daniels provides a compelling portrait of the black men and women who migrated to the West Coast between 1850 and the 1940s. Leaving behind all ties, these courageous individuals used their energy, optimism, and strong work ethic to forge thriving African American communities enhanced by a sophisticated culture and a vibrant social life. In the wake of much scholarship portraying blacks as unwilling or unable to put forth effort on their own behalf, Daniels's portrait refutes such stereotyping. Based on public records as well as interviews with the descendants of San Francisco's black community founders, the work was noted for its ability to show urban development from a personal level.

Subject(s): Urban Affairs, American West

1027 Leon Dash

Rosa Lee: A Mother and Her Family in Urban America
(New York, NY; Basic Books, 1996)

Summary: Based on his Pulitzer Prize-winning profile in the *Washington Post*, journalist Leon Dash brings to life the realities of inner-city life in *Rosa Lee: A Mother and Her Family in Urban America*. Infected with AIDS as a result of drug use, and surviving on welfare in Washington, D.C., Rosa Lee Cunningham personifies the problems facing children raised by single mothers who spend time in jail, fight drug addiction, and link offspring of multiple fathers in one family. While Dash paints a dark picture, he also elicits sympathy for Rosa Lee and hope for her children, some of whom escape the circumstances of their childhoods.

Subject(s): Biography, Poverty, Single Parent Families

1028 Basil Davidson

Black Mother: The Years of the African Slave Trade

(Boston, MA; Little, Brown, 1961)

Summary: Basil Davidson's *Black Mother* describes the commerce in black Africans that was begun during the sixteenth century as a way to find manpower to build an agricultural economy in the New World. Published in several revisions as *The African Slave Trade* beginning in 1965, Davidson's book is part of a series detailing the history of the United States from the time of its discovery through the mid-1800s. Davidson, a well-known popularizer of African history, depicts African culture as far more sophisticated that formerly believed, and relies upon archeological evidence to show the treatment of Africans by European slave traders was based on a lack of respect and understanding for that sophistication.

Subject(s): Slavery, Tribal Life--Africa, American South

1029 Chandler Davidson, Editor

Minority Vote Dilution

(Washington, DC; Howard University Press, 1984)

Summary: Published under the auspices of the Joint Center for Political Studies, *Minority Vote Dilution* contains essays by black attorneys, sociologists, and political scientists that discuss the practice of minority vote dilution: the passage of election laws designed to limit the voting power of blacks and other minorities. Written in the wake of the Voting Rights Act of 1965 and its amendments, essays include a discussion of such practices as at-large elections, gerrymandering, and the hosting of runoff primaries, practices that remain in place in several areas of the South. Taking a scholarly approach, contributors are united in their belief that the Voting Rights Act should be further strengthened and enforcement made mandatory.

Subject(s): Politics, Law, Government

1030 Allison Davis
Burleigh B. Gardner, Co-author
Mary R. Gardner, Co-author

Deep South: A Social Anthropological Study of Caste and Class

(Chicago, IL; University of Chicago Press, 1941)

Summary: Together with Burleigh and Mary Gardner, noted education specialist Allison Davis published *Deep South: A Social Anthropological Study of Caste and Class*. Professor emeritus at the University of Chicago prior to his death in 1983, Davis wrote widely on the influence of social and financial variables to learning and the formation of personality in young

people. *Deep South*, which was republished in 1986 by the University of California, Los Angeles, observes the lives of blacks and whites within a single town in the South and was considered groundbreaking in its approach to understanding the social dynamic of race. Anthropologist Margaret Mead noted of the work that it would "prove an effective background for the kind of thinking which leads to social change."

Subject(s): Education, American South, Segregation

1031 Angela Davis

Angela Davis: An Autobiography

(New York, NY; Random House, 1974)

Summary: The career of one of the most radical black activists of the 1960s is recounted in *Angela Davis: An Autobiography*. Growing up amid the racial tension of Birmingham, Alabama, Davis recalls her middle-class parents' encouragement of her intellectual and political growth. Steeped in African American history through the teachings of her grandmother and a youthful participant in the Civil Rights movement, where she stood as a protester alongside her activist mother, Davis attended a private New York City high school before making her way to Brandeis University and Paris's Sorbonne. The 1963 church bombing in Birmingham, which took the life of several young girls she knew, forged her commitment to actively fight racism, and she joined the legendary Black Panther movement, becoming one of its most vocal spokespeople. Dismissed from a faculty position at the University of California by then-governor Ronald Reagan, Davis eventually found herself on the FBI's most-wanted list when several guns registered in her name were used in a prison break. Captured but ultimately acquitted by 1972, her autobiography closes as she resumes her career as an academic and lecturer on behalf of the rights of black people.

Subject(s): Women's Rights, Racism, Civil Rights Movement

1032 Angela Davis

If They Come in the Morning: Voices of Resistance

(New York, NY; Third Press, 1971)

Summary: In *If They Come in the Morning: Voices of Resistance* civil rights activist Angela Davis and others argue, with Marxist-based logic, that most of the individuals incarcerated in the nation's prisons, jails, reformatories, detention houses, and other lock-ups are political prisoners rather than criminals. Rather than breaking the law, these individuals are the victims of oppression due to race, religion, political beliefs, or other factors. Containing letters, court pleadings, and other writings, the book includes essays by James Baldwin and John Cluchette.

Subject(s): Prisoners and Prisons, Communism, Political Prisoners

1033   Angela Davis

Women, Culture, & Politics
(New York, NY; Random House, 1989)

Summary: Similar to 1981's *Women, Race, & Class*, in *Women, Culture, and Politics* teacher and political activist Angela Davis collects speeches, essays, lectures, and other documents from the period 1983 through 1987. Her overall contentions: "The roots of sexism and homophobia are found in the same economic and political institutions that serve as the foundation of racism in this country." Divided into sections such as "On Women and the Pursuit of Equality and Peace" and "On Education and Culture," Davis marshals facts from historical records that chronicle the efforts of African American women to improve substandard housing and unsafe working conditions for all women of working classes.

Subject(s): Working-Class Life, Women's Rights, Racism

1034   Angela Davis

Women, Race, & Class
(New York, NY; Random House, 1981)

Summary: In *Women, Race, & Class*, radical black activist and former Black Panther Angela Davis presents a study of the U.S. women's movement as it has taken shape within the country from its roots in abolitionist activity prior to the Civil War, through the Civil Rights era, to the early 1980s. In her study, Davis claims that the movement has consistently been restricted due to the racism and class prejudice of its college-educated, white leadership. If the movement for women's equality is to be successful, Davis claims, racial and class prejudices must be ignored and all women must join together in a united front.

Subject(s): Abolition, Women's Rights, Racism

1035   **Arthur Paul Davis,** Editor
Saunders Redding, Co-editor

Cavalcade: Negro American Writing from 1760 to the Present
(Boston, MA; Houghton Mifflin, 1971)

Summary: *Cavalcade: Negro American Writing from 1760 to the Present* was highly influential in its presentation of a discussion of American writers of color who had previously been neglected in literary overviews. A professor of English at Howard University, co-author Arthur Davis was a pioneer in teaching African American literature at the college level. Davis and Saunders Redding's contributions to *Cavalcade* are enhanced by his personal friendships with many writers, particularly Harlem Renaissance poets Langston Hughes and Countee Cullen, and NAACP founder W.E.B. Du Bois.

Subject(s): Literature, Writing, Education

1036   **Arthur Paul Davis,** Editor

From the Dark Tower: Afro-American Writers (1900-1960)
(Washington, DC; Howard University Press, 1974)

Summary: This book collects the prose and poetry of African American writers working in the first half of the twentieth century. Writers included in this anthology by noted educator and literary scholar Arthur P. Davis are Langston Hughes, Richard Wright, and Ralph Ellison. One of several anthologies Davis published in his crusade to introduce the work of black writers into college literature classes, *From the Dark Tower* was used as a textbook in growing numbers of Afro-American literature courses. Highly praised by critics and educators alike, the work was reissued in 1981.

Subject(s): Literature, Harlem Renaissance, Poetry

1037   **Arthur Paul Davis,** Editor
Sterling A. Brown, Co-editor
Ulysses Lee, Co-editor

The Negro Caravan: Writings
(New York, NY; Dryden Press, 1941)

Summary: The first of many anthologies of black writers edited or co-edited by Arthur P. Davis, *The Negro Caravan* stands as a groundbreaking work. Still considered a classic, the anthology was praised as laying the foundation for the study of writings by African Americans that would follow. Presenting the works of many writers of color, including the members of the Harlem Renaissance of the early part of the century, *The Negro Caravan* was one of the first books available for use as a textbook in classes exploring the work of black authors.

Subject(s): Literature, Harlem Renaissance, Writing

1038   **Arthur Paul Davis,** Editor
Michael W. Peplow, Co-editor

The New Negro Renaissance: An Anthology
(New York, NY; Holt, Rinehart and Winston, 1975)

Summary: *The New Negro Renaissance*, compiled by Arthur P. Davis, collects the works of a number of African American writers of the twentieth century, many of whom were now beginning to be included in scholarly discussions of literature due to Davis's work. A professor of English at Howard University, Davis was a pioneer in the introduction of prose and poetry by blacks at the college level, and *The New Negro Renaissance* was used as a textbook around the country as colleges began offering classes in Afro-American literature.

Subject(s): Literature, Poetry, Writing

1039 David Brion Davis

From Homicide to Slavery: Studies in American Culture

(New York, NY; Oxford University Press, 1986)

Summary: In the essay collection *From Homicide to Slavery: Studies in American Culture*, David Brion Davis examines violence, ideology, and national heroes during the battle against slavery that raged in the nineteenth century. His essays focus, in particular, on the ways Americans define themselves through both acts of rebellion and reform movements. Among the essays included are "Slavery and the Post-World War II Historians" and "American Slavery and the American Revolution," as well as a study of James Cropper, head of England's abolition movement. Brion, one of the most noted scholars in the area of New World slavery, has won numerous awards, including a Pulitzer Prize and a National Book Award; his work has been praised for its scholarship, clarity, and fresh insights into the history of "the peculiar institution."

Subject(s): Slavery, History, American South

1040 David Brion Davis

The Problem of Slavery in the Age of Revolution, 1770-1823

(Ithaca, NY; Cornell University Press, 1975)

Summary: *The Problem of Slavery in the Age if Revolution, 1770-1823* continues David Brion Davis's multi-volume study of the institution of slavery as it relates to society at large. Davis focuses his analysis of slavery on the United States, and questions how the shift from acceptance of the institution of slavery to its abhorrence could come about within the space of a generation. Davis compares the U.S. antislavery movement with those in England and Europe, and concludes that the relative success of the British movement lay with that nation's more enlightened--and more flexible--philosophical and religious ideologies.

Subject(s): Slavery, American History, American South

Award(s): National Book Award: History, 1976

1041 David Brion Davis

The Problem of Slavery in Western Culture

(Ithaca, NY; Cornell University Press, 1966)

Summary: *The Problem of Slavery in Western Culture*, part of historian David Brion Davis's series of books on the topic, was honored with the Pulitzer Prize, as well as kudos by critics. Praised for the wealth of information within its pages, the work includes a discussion of the complexities involved in the debate over slavery that would ultimately fractionalize the United States in the mid-1800s. Extending his examination beyond the shores of the United States, Davis details the changes in European philosophy and religion that allowed the anti-slavery movement to take shape, and discusses the Christian concept of "original sin" that was used to justify the servitude of people of color prior to the Age of Enlightenment.

Subject(s): Slavery, History, Philosophy

Award(s): Pulitzer Prize: Nonfiction, 1967

1042 Lenwood G. Davis

The Black Woman in American Society: A Selected Annotated Bibliography

(Boston, MA; G.K. Hall, 1975)

Summary: *The Black Woman in American Society* was compiled by black history scholar and educator Lenwood Davis as a tool for students researching original source material regarding the lives of women of color in the United States. A professor of black history, Davis lists and describes documents from published works to journals and collections of correspondence that are available to fellow scholars through libraries and academic collections. His bibliography encompasses the development of U.S. culture over several centuries, and shows African American women to have been impassioned chroniclers of their families as well as their difficult position in U.S. society.

Subject(s): American History, Women, Family Life

1043 Lenwood G. Davis

Sickle Cell Anemia: A Selected Annotated Bibliography

(Newark, DE; National Black Bibliographic and Research Center, 1978)

Summary: *Sickle Cell Anemia: A Selected Annotated Bibliography* is the work of Lenwood G. Davis, a professor of black history who has been active in collecting information on many aspects of the African American experience. The volume provides information on the wealth of data published on the sometimes fatal disease--an inherited blood condition characterized by a distortion of red blood cells into a hook shape--which is prevalent among African Americans, as well as individuals of both Mediterranean and southwest Asian ancestry. With its entries organized for ease of research and with comments by Davis, the volume was praised for providing both scholars and laypeople with access to materials otherwise difficult to locate and access.

Subject(s): African Americans, Medicine, Genetic Disease

1044 Ruby Dee

My One Good Nerve: Rhythms, Rhymes, Reasons

(Chicago, IL; Third World Press, 1987)

Summary: *My One Good Nerve: Rhythms, Rhymes, Reasons* contains stories, poems, and essays written by actress Ruby Dee. The wife of actor Ossie Davis, Dee has combined a highly praised acting career with work as a playwright, journalist, and editor. *My One Good Nerve* reflects Dee's energetic, positive spirit, strong social consciousness, and mature insight, as well as her excellent ear for dialogue and language, developed over half a century of acting on stage and screen.

Subject(s): Poetry, Writing, Acting

1045 Mamadou Dia
Mercer Cook, Translator

The African Nations and World Solidarity
(New York, NY; Praeger, 1961)

Summary: In a text translated from the French by Mercer Cook, Senegalese prime minister Mamadou Dia discusses the problems facing an economically challenged Africa in *The African Nations and World Solidarity*. Maintaining that morality cannot exist without economic security, Dia adopts a socialist stance, proposing "Mutual Development"--less economically developed nations assisted by more developed nations--as a way to aid emerging African nations and yet avoid the pitfalls of political domination. Dia, who authored several other works on the subject of post-colonial African economics, was praised for his scholarship and his ability to present clearly the dilemma facing African nations to a Western readership.

Subject(s): Africa, Politics, Economics

1046 Ellen Irene Diggs

Black Chronology: From 4000 B.C. to the Abolition of the Slave Trade
(Boston, MA; G.K. Hall, 1983)

Summary: *Black Chronology: From 4000 B.C. to the Abolition of the Slave Trade* provides a chronological overview of the personalities and events that make up black history from the rise of Egyptian civilization onward. Ellen Irene Diggs, a researcher and colleague of W.E.B. Du Bois during the early years of the civil rights movement, ends her study in 1888, the year signaling the end of the Brazilian slave trade, and focuses primarily on nineteenth century history. Included are an extensive bibliography of books written by blacks beginning in the seventeenth century as well as a list of patents issued to black inventors, making the volume a useful research tool for those interested in African American intellectual history. The book is a revision of 1970's *Chronology of Notable Events and Dates in the History of the African and His Descendants during the Period of Slavery and the Slave Trade*.

Subject(s): Slavery, Africa, History

1047 Hasia R. Diner

In the Almost Promised Land: American Jews and Blacks, 1915-1935
(Westport, CT; Greenwood Press, 1977)

Summary: *In the Almost Promised Land: American Jews and Blacks, 1915-1935* presents Hasia R. Diner's contention that Jewish immigrants' active support of the advancement of African American equality provided them with a vehicle whereby they could become an accepted part of American society. Primarily a work of Jewish-American history, Diner chronicles the Jewish involvement in such pro-black organizations as the NAACP, labor unions, and philanthropic organizations that supported the cause of equal rights. Diner's work, which breaks with much scholarship on the subject by not concentrating on black anti-Semitism, was published in a revised edition in 1995.

Subject(s): Civil Rights Movement, Jews

1048 Cheikh Anta Diop

The African Origin of Civilization: Myth or Reality
(New York, NY; L. Hill, 1974)

Summary: Based on earlier works published during the 1950s and 1970s, Senegalese historian and academician Cheikh Anta Diop's *The African Origin of Civilization: Myth or Reality* encompasses much of the author's body of work. Diop presents the theory that Africans played a far more significant role in the origins of civilization than had been previously credited them, and argues that the ancient Egyptians, whose culture reflects an advanced knowledge of science and art, were in fact black. Cheikh Anta Diop began the first carbon-14 dating laboratory in Africa and founded two political parties in his native Senegal that were later banned, but he is best remembered for his historical works about Africa.

Subject(s): Ancient History, Africa, Tribal Life--Africa

1049 Cheikh Anta Diop

Precolonial Black Africa: A Comparative Study of the Political and Social Systems of Europe and Black Africa, from Antiquity to the Formation of Modern States
(Westport, CT; L. Hill, 1987)

Summary: Known for his theories regarding the sophistication of early black African culture and its contribution to the flowering of what students are taught as "Ancient History," Cheikh Anta Diop addresses similar theories in *Precolonial Black Africa*. Stemming from his theory that the origins of civilization lay south of the Sahara desert, Diop argues that prior to the time Europeans invaded Africa and began robbing the continent of its wealth of natural resources, the plateau continent contained a wealth of tribal cultures that were far more sophisticated than white invaders realized. *Precolonial Black Africa* was one of several books to be published shortly after Diop's death in 1986.

Subject(s): Ancient History, Africa, Tribal Life--Africa

1050 Christa Klingbeil Dixon

Negro Spirituals: From Bible to Folk Song

(Philadelphia, PA; Fortress Press, 1976)

Summary: In *Negro Spirituals: From Bible to Folk Song* Christa Dixon presents the results of her interest in the folk music of African Americans. Born in Germany and later becoming a professor at Illinois State University, Dixon obtained a grant to advance her study of spirituals, songs that provided blacks--particularly slaves--with a means to express both their deep emotions and their strong religious beliefs. Such songs often focus on deliverance from life's troubles through Biblical means, such as an exodus, and are noted for their less structured rhythms and rich harmonies. Many examples of spirituals are included in Dixon's work.

Subject(s): Music, Slavery, Religion

1051 Edward F. Dolan, Jr.

Matthew Henson, Black Explorer

(New York, NY; Dodd, Mead, 1979)

Summary: Written for a young audience, Edward F. Dolan's biography *Matthew Henson, Black Explorer* details the life of Henson, the African American explorer who accompanied U.S. Naval Admiral Robert E. Peary to the North Pole. Against daunting temperatures, supply problems, and tremendous odds, Peary and Henson reached the pole on April 6, 1909. Henson would later pen his own recollections of the trip as *A Black Explorer at the North Pole: An Autobiographical Report by the Negro Who Conquered the Top of the World with Admiral Robert E. Peary.*

Subject(s): Biography, Adventure and Adventurers

1052 Molly Crocker Dougherty

Becoming a Woman in Rural Black Culture

(New York, NY; Holt, Rinehart and Winston, 1978)

Summary: This book examines a southern black community and its life cycle passages from the viewpoint of its women. The authors refers to the north central Florida community under study as Edge Crossing. The first part of the work considers the community's use of space as well as its economy, education, and rituals. The following section explores the community's kinship system and childhood socialization. The final section looks at female adolescence within the community; it includes courtship, pregnancy, childbirth, and motherhood.

Subject(s): Rural Life, American South, Women

1053 St. Clair Drake

Black Folk Here and There: An Essay in History and Anthropology. Volume 1

(Los Angeles, CA; Center for Afro-American Studies, University of California, 1987)

Summary: This scholarly work by St. Clair Drake explores contributions by blacks throughout world history. After two introductory chapters in which he discusses "White Racism and the Black Experience" and "Theories of Color Prejudice," Drake focuses his attention on the presence of--and contributions by--blacks in ancient Egypt. Among the topics in this latter section are "Egypt before the Pharaohs" and "The Rise and Fall of the Ethiopian Dynasty."

Subject(s): Africa, History

1054 Phillip T. Drotning

A Guide to Negro History in America

(Garden City, NY; Doubleday, 1968)

Summary: Beginning with the first appearance of African natives on the shores of North America, Philip Drotning's *Guide to Negro History in America* presents, in state-by-state and alphabetical sequence, the many contributions of African Americans to the growth of the United States, connecting most incidents with the many monuments scattered around the nation marking such contributions. The volume was later reprinted as *An American Traveler's Guide to Black History.*

Subject(s): History, Monuments, Travel

1055 Dinesh D'Souza

The End of Racism: Principles for a Multiracial Society

(New York, NY; Free Press, 1995)

Summary: Stirring a great deal of controversy upon its publication, *The End of Racism: Principles for a Multiracial Society* is conservative thinker Dinesh D'Souza's examination of the history and nature of modern-day racism. Taking aim against the mainstay assumption that racism is the primary barrier to African Americans' attainment of a truly equitable position in U.S. society, D'Souza maintains that racism is, instead, a uniquely Western phenomenon--a "neurotic obsession" of the twentieth century promoted by the "civil rights industry"--with a finite influence upon world history. Liberal solutions to the "problem of racism," therefore, are ill-conceived: cultural differences, rather than racism, are responsible for the degree of success people have in finding success within American society.

Subject(s): Racism, Race Relations, Civil Rights Movement

1056 Shirley Graham Du Bois
(Also known as Shirley Graham)

Du Bois: A Pictorial Biography
(Chicago, IL; Johnson Pub. Co., 1978)

Summary: Author Shirley Graham Du Bois was the second wife of famed civil rights leader W.E.B. Du Bois. This book captures the life of this noted leader and founder of the National Association for the Advancement of Colored People, from his childhood and formative years as a Harvard student to his years of social and political activism, ending with his ultimate relocation to Ghana in the early 1960s after openly declaring his Communist sympathies.

Subject(s): Photography, Racism, Civil Rights Movement

1057 Shirley Graham Du Bois
(Also known as Shirley Graham)

Gamal Abdel Nasser, Son of the Nile: A Biography
(New York, NY; Third Press, 1972)

Summary: The second wife of famed civil rights leader W.E.B. Du Bois, Shirley Graham Du Bois authored a series of biographies that included 1972's *Gamal Abdel Nasser*. Prior to his death in 1970, Nasser became president of Egypt in 1954, and his action in assuming control of the Suez Canal a few years later sparked the Israeli-Palestinian conflict. Promoting unity against Israeli, European, and American interests in the Middle East, he formed the United Arab Republic, but his continued efforts were stalled by the fractional politics of the region.

Subject(s): Biography, Middle East, Politics

1058 Shirley Graham Du Bois
(Also known as Shirley Graham)

His Day Is Marching On: A Memoir of W.E.B. Du Bois
(Philadelphia, PA; Lippincott, 1971)

Summary: Author Shirley Graham Du Bois was the second wife of famed civil rights leader W.E.B. Du Bois. Her laudatory biography, *His Day Is Marching On*, recounts the successes of the man who founded the National Association for the Advancement of Colored People and fought the assimilation of blacks into white culture. Educated at Harvard University, Du Bois had a successful career in academia, in addition to founding the NAACP in 1909. The author of numerous books on slavery and the "color problem," the radical Du Bois joined the Communist Party in 1961 and spent his last years in Ghana.

Subject(s): Racism, Civil Rights Movement

1059 Shirley Graham Du Bois
(Also known as Shirley Graham)

Jean Baptiste Pointe de Sable: Founder of Chicago
(New York, NY; J. Messner, 1953)

Summary: The second wife of famed civil rights leader W.E.B. Du Bois, Shirley Graham Du Bois authored a series of laudatory biographies profiling the lives of notable blacks from history with the intention of providing suitable role models to African American young people. Published in 1953, her *Jean Baptiste Pointe de Sable: Founder of Chicago* recounts the exploits of de Sable, an African born in Haiti who, through his explorations south of the Great Lakes in the 1600s, founded what would later be named Chicago as a strategic port for accessing the wealth of the North American interior. Chicago would grow to become the second largest city in the United States by the mid-1900s.

Subject(s): Biography, History

1060 W.E.B. Du Bois
Herbert Aptheker, Editor

The Autobiography of W.E.B. Du Bois: A Soliloquy on Viewing My Life from the Last Decade of Its First Century
(New York, NY; International Publishers, 1968)

Summary: A prolific writer, sociologist W.E.B. Du Bois was at the vanguard of the U.S. civil rights movement. Of French/African descent, he was raised in Massachusetts; due to a childhood free from racial strife, he did not experience racial prejudice until he attended Fisk University in Tennessee. Later, as a student at Harvard, Du Bois began to seriously study the oppression of blacks, voluntarily segregating himself from white students. Published five years after Du Bois's death and edited by historian Herbert Aptheker, *The Autobiography of W.E.B. Du Bois: A Soliloquy on Viewing My Life from the Last Decade of Its First Century*, is one of several memoirs penned by the co-founder of the NAACP in a look back on a long and eventful life.

Subject(s): Civil Rights Movement, Autobiography, Communism

1061 W.E.B. Du Bois

The World and Africa: An Inquiry into the Part Which Africa Has Played in World History
(New York, NY; Viking Press, 1947)

Summary: Of French and African descent, W.E.B. Du Bois graduated from Fisk and Harvard universities and went on to a career as a civil rights activist and educator. In *The World and Africa: An Inquiry into the Part Which Africa Has Played in World History*, which was first published in 1947 and revised in 1964, he presents a sweeping history that paints Africa as having a prominent role in world civilization. The book is a reflection of the Pan-African ideology Du Bois had begun promoting in the early 1920s, an ideology that, while winning him respect internationally, drew increasing criticism in the United States.

Subject(s): History, Africa, Pan-Africanism

1062 **Alan Dundes,** Editor

Mother Wit from the Laughing Barrel: Readings in the Interpretation of Afro-American Folklore
(New York, NY; Garland, 1973)

Summary: Edited by folklorist Alan Dundes, *Mother Wit from the Laughing Barrel: Readings in the Interpretation of Afro-American Folklore* collects a number of essays that explore the roots of traditional African American folk stories and legends. From the widely known "Brer Rabbit" stories to less well-known tales and spirituals, contributors analyze these works with relation to spirituality, the family, and the role of women; draw comparisons with the folklore of other cultures; and comment on the ways folk tales reflect the transition of black culture during its move from an agrarian to an industrial setting over two centuries of U.S. history.

Subject(s): American South, Folklore, Spiritualism

1063 **Katherine Dunham**
Patricia Cummings, Photographer

Dances of Haiti
(Los Angeles, CA; UCLA Center for Afro-American Studies, 1983)

Summary: Noted African American choreographer and dance teacher Katherine Dunham devoted her career to the study and performance of dance from a variety of black cultures. A resident of the West Indian nation of Haiti, she established a dance school in the capital city of Port-au-Prince in 1961. Her *Dances of Haiti* collects the native dances of Haiti, both in an effort to share them with American students and to record native dances before the effects of modernization and immigration take their toll on tradition. For her efforts at promoting Haitian culture, Dunham received several awards, including being named an honorary citizen of Port-au-Prince in 1957.

Subject(s): Culture, Dancing, West Indies

1064 **Katherine Dunham**

Island Possessed: Haiti
(Garden City, NY; Doubleday, 1969)

Summary: Katherine Dunham, a noted African American dancer and choreographer, spent much of her adult life in the West Indian nation of Haiti. In *Island Possessed: Haiti*, the second part of Dunham's autobiography, which began with 1959's *A Touch of Innocence*, she discusses her impression of matters as diverse as Haitian politics and history and traditional voodoo rituals. Dunham also touches on subjects of a more personal nature, such as her search for her cultural roots and a sense of her own identity as a woman of color. Dunham established a dance school in the capital city of Port-au-Prince in 1961, and was named an honorary citizen of that city in 1957.

Subject(s): Autobiography, Travel, West Indies

1065 **Katherine Dunham**

Katherine Dunham's Journey to Accompong
(New York, NY; H. Holt and Company, 1946)

Summary: *Katherine Dunham's Journey to Accompong* recounts the thirty days the author spent in a Maroon village in the mountain region of Jamaica. Maroons, who are descendants of African slaves who rebelled against their Spanish masters centuries before, dislike whites, but they accepted the African American dancer and anthropologist into their community willingly. More journalistic than scholarly, the well-illustrated volume presents detailed portraits of the people, their customs, and their history.

Subject(s): Autobiography, Travel, Anthropology

1066 **Katherine Dunham**

A Touch of Innocence
(New York, NY; Harcourt, Brace, 1959)

Summary: In *A Touch of Innocence* noted African American dancer/choreographer Katherine Dunham chronicles her early life, particularly her teen years. Born into a working-class family in Joliet, Illinois, and encouraged to pursue the arts by her father, a musician, Dunham's childhood was still a difficult one, made more challenging due to the racial prejudice she encountered as a young student of the ballet in Chicago. Dunham would continue her autobiography with 1969's *Island Possessed: Haiti*.

Subject(s): Autobiography, Travel, Adolescence

1067 **Alice Allison Dunningan**

A Black Woman's Experience: From Schoolhouse to White House
(Philadelphia, PA; Dorrance, 1974)

Summary: *A Black Woman's Experience: From Schoolhouse to White House* is the autobiography of Alice Allison Dunnigan, the first African American woman to gain admittance to the White House as a reporter. Recalling her experiences serving as the chief of the Associated Negro Press's Washington bureau from 1947 to 1961, Dunnigan also discusses her childhood in rural Kentucky and her ringside view of many of the newsworthy events of the first half of the twentieth century. In addition to her work as a journalist, she also recounts her experiences working in the political arena, first on the vice-presidential campaign of Lyndon Johnson and later as education consultant to John F. Kennedy's Committee on Equal Employment Opportunity.

Subject(s): Politics, Journalism, Autobiography

1068 Jo Durden-Smith

Who Killed George Jackson?
(New York, NY; Knopf, 1976)

Summary: African American convict George Jackson was the author of *Soledad Brother*, a collection of letters written during his incarceration at California's San Quentin Prison. In *Who Killed George Jackson?* journalist Jo Durden-Smith recounts his investigation into the events surrounding Jackson's death on August 2, 1971. Killed while running across the prison yard, carrying a gun, Jackson had been hailed by Leftist liberals as a true revolutionary. In his analysis, Durden-Smith concludes that such an appraisal was biased by radical ideology and propaganda. In addition to expressing his own growing disenchantment with the black radical movement, the author presents factual evidence consisting of interviews with prison guards and other witnesses and background information regarding Jackson's associates and prime defenders.

Subject(s): Crime and Criminals, Prisoners and Prisons, Violence

1069 Michael Eric Dyson

Reflecting Black: African-American Cultural Criticism
(Minneapolis, MN; University of Minnesota Press, 1993)

Summary: Baptist minister and academic Michael Eric Dyson published the first of several collections of his journalistic essays as *Reflecting Black: African American Cultural Criticism*. Focusing on African American culture between the years 1989 and 1993, Dyson discusses the appeal of popular entertainment figures such as Michael Jackson, Michael Jordan, and Spike Lee, and analyzes the manner in which racism, sexism, politics, and religion influence--and are influenced by--black America's visual arts and music.

Subject(s): Popular Culture, Cultural Conflict, Racism

1070 Christopher F. Edley, Jr.

Not All Black and White: Affirmative Action, Race, and American Values
(New York, NY; Hill & Wang, 1996)

Summary: An advisor to President Bill Clinton, Christopher F. Edley, Jr. addresses one of the most important aspects of U.S. society in *Not All Black and White: Affirmative Action, Race, and American Values*. The book, which is directed toward the general reader through its animated and readable text, analyzes the wealth of relevant legal information, statistical evidence collected by social scientists, legislative activities, and business trends in making a case for the continuation of affirmative action. In framing his argument, Edley is careful to evaluate the evidence within the objective context of U.S. law rather than through the guise of personal, moral, or religious values.

Subject(s): Affirmative Action, Economics, Politics

1071 Thomas Byrne Edsall

Chain Reaction: The Impact of Race, Rights, and Taxes on American Politics
(New York, NY; Norton, 1991)

Summary: In *Chain Reaction: The Impact of Race, Rights, and Taxes on American Politics*, *Washington Post* journalist Thomas B. Edsall discusses the Republican Party's control of the White House in five of six presidential terms of office following 1964. He contends that conservatives have used the issues of race and taxes to fracture the Democratic hold on the office by feeding the frustrations of whites resentful of outlaying tax dollars for public assistance programs that benefit blacks and other minorities. Marshalling a vast quantity of voter and demographic data as well as interviews, Edsall follows the policies of politicians like Barry Goldwater, George Wallace, and former president Richard Nixon that encouraged such divisions between blacks and whites.

Subject(s): Politics, Racism, Economics

1072 Elijah Muhammad

Message to the Blackman in America
(Chicago, IL; Muhammad Mosque of Islam No. 2, 1965)

Summary: In *Message to the Blackman in America*, Nation of Islam leader Elijah Muhammad (1897-1975) addresses such topics as God, the Devil, the Bible and the Holy Qur'an. He also speaks out on race relations, religion, and issues specific to the Nation of Islam. A religious leader, teacher, and self-proclaimed Messenger of Allah, Muhammad was born in Georgia in 1897 and received formal education only until grade three. A charismatic leader, he provided his many followers, who organized into a separatist movement known as the Black Muslims, with a sense of belonging that translated into racial pride.

Subject(s): Religion, Black Nationalism, Muslims

1073 Stanley M. Elkins

Slavery: A Problem in American Institutional and Intellectual Life
(Chicago, IL; University of Chicago Press, 1959)

Summary: Stanley M. Elkins's *Slavery: A Problem in American Institutional and Intellectual Life* was considered highly controversial due to its author's contention that the docility of enslaved blacks was a factor in their continued servitude. Many critics called Elkins's suggestion that certain character traits make blacks unable to strive for freedom misguided. Republished in several editions, the work expands from an examination of the black character to examine the broader question: what made the impact of American slavery on the spirit and resilience of the enslaved far more severe and lasting than in other slave systems?

Subject(s): Slavery, American South, History

Beyond Liberation: The Gospel in the Black American Experience
(Downer's Grove, IL; InterVarsity Press, 1983)

Summary: *Beyond Liberation: The Gospel in the Black American Experience*, authored by theologian Carl F. Ellis, Jr., is the author's effort to develop a theological framework through which African Americans can translate the work of God into a guide for coping with everyday life. In his book he discusses modern culture as it has been transformed by the civil rights movement, and expresses concern over the decreasing influence of religious values in black urban America.

Subject(s): Religion, Community Relations, Urban Affairs

1075 Ralph Ellison

Going to the Territory
(New York, NY; Random House, 1986)

Summary: In his second collection of essays and interviews, African American man of letters Ralph Ellison continues his critique (begun in 1964's *Shadows and Act*) of the relationship between black culture and the predominately white culture of the United States. In *Going to the Territory* Ellison discusses literature, art, and music, includes personal anecdotes, and reviews, and interviews contained in the volume date to 1957, and contain the same sense of humor and irony that Ellison invested in his 1952 novel, *Invisible Man,* which won the National Book Award.

Subject(s): Autobiography, Literature, Cultural Conflict

1076 Ralph Ellison

Shadow and Act
(New York, NY; Random House, 1964)

Summary: In *Shadow and Act* noted African American author Ralph Ellison compiles a collection of essays, reviews, and interviews reflecting his first two decades of social commentary. Stating his purpose "to explore the full range of American Negro humanity and to affirm those qualities which are of value beyond any question of segregation, economics or previous condition of servitude," Ellison examines such topics as art, music, literature, and the influence of the black experience on white U.S. culture. The book also provides insight into Ellison's National Book Award-winning 1952 novel, *Invisible Man,* which recounted the author's early experiences of racial prejudice.

Subject(s): Autobiography, Literature, Cultural Conflict

1077 Eleanor Engram

Science, Myth, Reality: The Black Family in One-Half Century of Research
(Westport, CT; Greenwood Press, 1982)

Summary: The monograph *Science, Myth, Reality: The Black Family in One-Half Century of Research* is author Eleanor Engram's appraisal of the research that has been done on the African American family unit between 1900 and 1950. In reviewing the conclusions of sociologists, as well as the recommendations for public policy that emanated from those recommendations, Engram is highly critical of the fact that research data was judged against the social "norms" of white society and therefore irrelevant within African American culture.

Subject(s): Family Life, City and Town Life, Sociology

1078 Edgar G. Epps, Compiler

Race Relations: Current, Perspectives
(Cambridge, MA; Winthrop Publishers, 1973)

Summary: *Race Relations: Current, Perspectives* presents essays centering on the uneasy peace struck in many urban areas in the wake of the waves of rioting sparked by racial intolerance in the 1960s. Edgar Epps moderates and contributes to the debate on race through this work, which, while dated, reflects the dismal condition of the public schools used by urban blacks and the inflammation of racial tensions through the court-mandated busing that began in 1971 as a means of addressing *de facto* segregation.

Subject(s): Education, Race Relations, Segregation

1079 Dena J. Epstein

Sinful Tunes and Spirituals: Black Folk Music to the Civil War
(Urbana, IL; University of Illinois Press, 1977)

Summary: *Sinful Tunes and Spirituals: Black Folk Music to the Civil War* is the result of a great deal of research on the part of University of Chicago music librarian Dena Epstein. Following her interest in music beginning in 1953, Epstein used her research skills to document the transplantation of African music into the New World, where vestiges of the original tribal music remained in more remote locations for almost a century and a half. She also describes the transformation of African music into hymns, spirituals, and other African American folk songs sung by slaves and other blacks up to the Civil War.

Subject(s): Music, American South, Slavery

Award(s): Chicago Folklore Prize, 1978

1080 **Robert T. Ernst,** Editor
Lawrence Hugg, Co-editor

Black America: Geographic Perspectives
(Garden City, NY; Anchor Press, 1976)

Summary: The approximately twenty-five essays in this 1976 work offer a geographical history of African Americans. The various authors discuss both national trends of the placement and movement of blacks throughout American history and local statistics related to such areas as Mississippi, Miami, Cleveland, and Detroit. Among the issues the book examines are the riots that erupted in several urban black ghettos during the latter 1960s and the Great Migration of rural southern blacks to northern industrial cities during the early and mid-twentieth century.

Subject(s): History, Geography

1081 **E.U. Essien-Udom**

Black Nationalism: A Search for an Identity in America
(Chicago, IL; University of Chicago Press, 1962)

Summary: In *Black Nationalism: A Search for an Identity in America* Nigerian-born E.U. Essien-Udom examines the growth of the black nationalist movement in the United States. Providing a historic background to the movement of the mid-1900s, Essien-Udom outlines the organizations and leadership involved, concentrating particularly on the Nation of Islam and its leader, Elijah Muhammad. He also puts the movement into the larger context of African American history, explaining the significance of black nationalism to the many blacks in search of moral and cultural definition.

Subject(s): Black Nationalism, History, Resistance Movements

1082 **Gwendolyn Etter-Lewis,** Editor

Unrelated Kin: Race and Gender in Women's Personal Narratives
(New York, NY; Routledge, 1996)

Summary: This collection of essays considers race and gender in women's life narratives. The volume positions the stories of non-Western and non-white women at the center of scholarly discourse. Among the voices included in the collection are those belonging to Native American, African American, Asian American, and Latina women.

Subject(s): Women, Race Relations

1083 **James H. Evans, Jr.**

We Have Been Believers: An African-American Systematic Theology
(Minneapolis, MN; Fortress Press, 1992)

Summary: *We Have Been Believers: An African-American Systematic Theology* is the work of James H. Evans, Jr. a Baptist minister and president of Colgate Rochester Divinity School/Bexley Hall/Crozer Theological Seminary. Focusing on issues such as faith and freedom, Evans discusses the growth of a uniquely black theology, stressing the commonality between branches of the Christian faith as various churches have taken root in the commitment to uniting in religious brotherhood African and Caribbean blacks.

Subject(s): Religion, History, American South

1084 **Myrlie Evers**
William Peters, Co-author

For Us, the Living
(Garden City, NY; Doubleday, 1967)

Summary: *For Us, the Living* is the biography of slain civil rights activist Medgar Evers, as written by his wife, Myrlie Evers. Born and raised in Mississippi, Evers worked as a field secretary for the NAACP during the 1950s and 1960s, and his high public profile within the state of Mississippi made him a target of those resistant to the integration of blacks into white society. Undeterred by threats against his personal safety, Evers continued to help blacks register to vote, petition their local governments to integrate public facilities, and join the growing ranks of the NAACP. He was murdered in 1963.

Subject(s): Civil Rights Movement, Biography, American South

1085 **William H. Exum**

Paradoxes of Protest: Black Student Activism in a White University
(Philadelphia, PA; Temple University Press, 1985)

Summary: The late 1960s and early 1970s marked a period of cultural upheaval and changing attitudes in the African American community, as blacks became increasingly frustrated at the enduring racism and oppression in white-dominated America. William H. Exum in this work offers a detailed examination of this changing cultural landscape by focusing on black student activism at University College, on the Bronx campus of New York University. A graduate student and instructor at the college during the period discussed in his book, Exum provides a background discussion of the civil rights movement of the 1950s and 1960s in addition to exploring the details of black student activism at the college between 1966 and 1972.

Subject(s): Colleges and Universities, Civil Rights Movement, Race Relations

1086 **Charles E. Fager**

White Reflections on Black Power
(Grand Rapids, MI; W.B. Eerdmans Pub. Co., 1967)

Summary: Written by a self-described northern white liberal, this brief book examines the rise of the black power movement of the 1960s. During this period, many African American leaders adopted a much more aggressive, hostile tone toward the longstanding racism of American society, some advocating violence or black separatism as appropriate responses. In the book, Fager offers his own analysis of the elements of black power as well as a description of the relationship between white liberals and the black power movement. He concludes that movement is not only legitimate but destined to alter forever race relations in the United States.

Subject(s): Black Nationalism, Race Relations

1087 **Frantz Fanon**
Constance Farrington, Translator

The Wretched of the Earth
(New York, NY; Grove Press, 1963)

Summary: Martinique-born black psychoanalyst and political philosopher Frantz Fanon (1925-1961) was open in his expression of concern for the oppressed peoples of Africa who had suffered much at the hands of colonial rulers, and his books were widely discussed in leftist circles. Considered pioneering in its analysis of the impact of racism on Africa, *The Wretched of the Earth* recounts its author's experiences working in Algeria during that nation's battle for independence from French rule, and he excoriates the region's upper classes for their lack of commitment to their nation's decolonization. He argues that their inaction caused unnecessary bloodshed and violence toward the more populous lower classes. "[T]he unpreparedness of the educated classes, the lack of practical links between them and the mass of the people, their laziness, and, let it be said, their cowardice at the decisive moment of the struggle will give rise to tragic mishaps," Fanon prophetically noted.

Subject(s): Artists and Art, Africa, Colonialism

1088 **Reynolds Farley**
Walter R. Allen, Co-author

The Color Line and the Quality of Life in America
(New York, NY; Russell Sage Foundation, 1987)

Summary: *The Color Line and the Quality of Life in America* is a study of the comparative well-being of blacks and whites in modern U.S. society. Drawing statistical evidence from studies of education, health, employment, earning capacity, morality, family situation, and other demographics, authors Reynolds Farley and Walter R. Allen conclude that economic status is a larger factor than race in the well-being of African Americans. Containing a wealth of statistics and other data gathered between 1900 and the mid-1980s, the volume supports the contention by many blacks that integration within America's cities has not progressed substantially, leaving blacks disadvantaged in terms of education, housing, and employment.

Subject(s): City and Town Life, Economics, Sociology

1089 **James Farmer**

Lay Bare the Heart: An Autobiography of the Civil Rights Movement
(New York, NY; Arbor House, 1985)

Summary: *Lay Bare the Heart: An Autobiography of the Civil Rights Movement* is the autobiography of Texan James Farmer, a civil rights leader who worked alongside Dr. Martin Luther King, Jr., and others to promote the cause of African American equality during the 1950s and 1960s. The son of a preacher, Farmer grew up in Texas, encountering segregated businesses and public places. In reaction he later founded the Congress of Racial Equality (CORE), and in 1942 orchestrated the first sit-in opposing segregation of a public restaurant in Chicago. An adherent to the teachings of Gandhi, Farmer would organize numerous other peaceful protests in the years ahead. While his efforts were overshadowed by the legendary Dr. King, Farmer received the Medal of Freedom from President Bill Clinton in 1998.

Subject(s): Civil Rights Movement, Resistance Movements, Racism

---

1090 **Robert M. Farnsworth**

Melvin B. Tolson, 1898-1966: Plain Talk and Poetic Prophecy
(Columbia, MO; University of Missouri Press, 1984)

Summary: In *Melvin B. Tolson, 1898-1966: Plain Talk and Poetic Prophecy,* author Robert M. Farnsworth chronicles the life of poet, educator, and journalist Tolson, whose studies at Columbia University in the 1930s linked him to other poets of the Harlem Renaissance. A minor figure of that literary movement, Tolson eventually became a columnist for the *Washington Tribune* and an educator. His appointment as poet laureate of the Republic of Liberia came in 1953, thirteen years before his death.

Subject(s): Biography, Harlem Renaissance, Poetry

1091 **Louis Farrakhan**

A Torchlight for America
(Chicago, IL; FCN Pub. Co., 1993)

Summary: In *A Torchlight for America,* Nation of Islam spokesman Louis Farrakhan addresses a readership encompassing many races and religions regarding the present condition of the United States and the possibilities for the future. Answering the national concern over safe neighborhoods, a quality education for the younger generations, and the ability to enjoy basic freedoms within society, Minister Farrakhan urges a course of nonviolence and encourages self-respect and respect for others. Farrakhan, a black nationalist with a reputation for being both anti-Semitic and homophobic, would address many of the same points included here during his speech at the 1995 Million Man March.

Subject(s): Resistance Movements, Muslims, Black Nationalism

1092 Arthur Huff Fauset

Black Gods of the Metropolis: Negro Religious Cults of the Urban North
(Philadelphia, PA; University of Pennsylvania Press, 1944)

Summary: Written by Philadelphia educator Arthur Huff Fauset, *Black Gods of the Metropolis: Negro Religious Cults of the Urban North* presents an analysis of five religious cults in greater Philadelphia, showing both their similarities and differences. Each of the cults, notes Fauset, differs in ritual and commandment, while all break significantly with the traditional Christianity practiced for centuries by blacks in imitation of whites. Written originally as Fauset's thesis at the University of Pennsylvania, the book received criticism for the narrowness of its scope. It was nonetheless praised as the first scholarly work to concentrate on African American cults and was reprinted in 1971.

Subject(s): Religion, Christianity, Sociology

1093 Joe R. Feagin

Racial and Ethnic Relations
(Englewood Cliffs, NJ; Prentice-Hall, 1978)

Summary: Authored by prominent urban sociologist Joe R. Feagin, *Racial and Ethnic Relations* is a sociology text designed for use in courses dealing with cultural diversity issues. Containing a theoretical overview within each of its subject areas--political power; economics; the role of women; methods of adaptation and resistance--the volume is organized around 14 racial and ethnic groups. The volume has gone through several editions, including the fourth edition, with wife, Clairece Booher Feagin, published in 1993, and the fifth edition, published in 1995.

Subject(s): Racism, Cultural Conflict, Resistance Movements

1094 Cain Hope Felder

Troubling Biblical Waters: Race, Class, and Family
(Maryknoll, NY; Orbis Books, 1989)

Summary: In Cain Hope Felder's *Troubling Biblical Waters: Race, Class, and Family*, the author examines the importance of acknowledging a black presence within the Bible as a means of strengthening the presence of the African American church during the struggle for black liberation. Reviewing the sometimes problematic history of the black church in America, Felder maintains that the Bible, while held in the control of white culture for hundreds of years, speaks to black men and women and can provide a source of hope and joy as well as the basis for a dynamic Christian-based spirituality.

Subject(s): Christianity, Family Life, Racism

1095 William Ferris

Blues from the Delta
(London, England; Studio Vista, 1970)

Summary: An expansion of the author's Ph.D. dissertation in folklore, *Blues from the Delta* is a detailed examination of the history and traditions of the blues music of Mississippi's Delta region. Focusing on local musicians living between Vicksburg and Memphis, William Ferris, an expert on folklore and the blues, maintains that, more than being "back-porch" music or a recreational outlet, blues music is a significant part of the lives of those who perform it. Written for the scholar more than the general reader, Ferris's work contains photographs, bibliographies, and the transcript of a blues session performed by local artist Wallace "Pinetop" Johnson in the late 1960s.

Subject(s): Music, Musicians, American South

1096 Fred Fetrow

Robert Hayden
(Boston, MA; Twayne Publishers, 1984)

Summary: In the biography *Robert Hayden*, author Fred Fetrow tells the story of one of the most significant poets of the twentieth century. In his work, which includes such poems as "Aunt Jemima of the Ocean Waves," "The Ballad of Nat Turner," and "Night, Death, Mississippi," Hayden (1913-1980) explores African American history and focuses on themes that include dreams, mortality, the world of nature, travel, and the process of memory. He also composed several poems recounting the lives of such prominent African Americans as Frederick Douglass and Phillis Wheatley, an African-born poet who published her work to the critical approval of a white Boston readership in 1783.

Subject(s): Poetry, Biography, American History

1097 John Hall Fish

Black Power/White Control: The Struggle of the Woodlawn Organization in Chicago
(Princeton, NJ; Princeton University Press, 1973)

Summary: Founded in 1961 by community activists and local clergymen, the Woodlawn Organization in Chicago became a source of political autonomy and commercial development for the black neighborhood bordering the campus of the University of Chicago. In *Black Power/White Control: The Struggle of the Woodlawn Organization in Chicago* author John Hall Fish recounts the history of the organization and describes in detail three programs that it put in place to combat the disintegrating urban environment: the Black Rangers project for young people, the Woodlawn Experimental School project to improve educational opportunities, and the Model Cities project to enhance local neighborhoods. Despite a lack of support from Chicago's governmental agencies, the Woodlawn Organization would serve as a model of how a community could, through its own resources, renew its vitality.

Subject(s): Urban Affairs, City and Town Life, Politics

1098 Miles Mark Fisher

Negro Slave Songs in the United States

(Ithaca, NY; Cornell University Press, 1953)

Summary: In his *Negro Slave Songs in the United States* Miles Mark Fisher views the traditional songs and spirituals of African Americans living in the south before the Civil War as akin to an historical document. Decoding each of these "oral" documents, Fisher contends, unveils clues as to the song's original composer, the time and place of its composition, its composer's plans for escape from slavery, and a passive but articulate protestation against oppression and bondage.

Subject(s): Music, Slavery, Resistance Movements

1099 Robert W. Fogel
Stanley L. Engerman, Co-author

Time on the Cross: The Economics of American Negro Slavery

(Boston, MA; Little, Brown, 1974)

Summary: One of the most controversial books of the 1970s, *Time on the Cross: The Economics of American Negro Slavery* is a critical examination of the traditional assumptions regarding slavery in the United States. Authors Robert W. Fogel and Stanley L. Engerman argue that slavery, which they cite as a highly unprofitable enterprise despite the minor cash outlay required to sustain an enslaved work force, was an inefficient component of agricultural production, and the use of slave labor contributed to the demise of the southern economy prior to the outbreak of the Civil War. Marshalling numerous statistics in support of their argument, the authors received their most heated criticism for their assertion that the living conditions endured by most slaves were not as inhumane as some historians had suggested.

Subject(s): Slavery, Economics, American South

1100 Marshall Frady

Jesse: The Life and Pilgrimage of Jesse Jackson

(New York, NY; Random House, 1996)

Summary: In *Jesse: The Life and Pilgrimage of Jesse Jackson* biographer Marshall Frady profiles one of the most controversial African American politicians of the twentieth century. Beginning with Jackson's illegitimate birth in Greenville, South Carolina, Frady follows Jackson from his role as assistant to Martin Luther King, Jr. through his rise through the political ranks that resulted in two strong bids for the office of president during the 1980s. Dealing with the two sides of Jackson—his tendency toward egomania on the one hand and his continued contributions to social issues by taking the moral high road on the other—Frady paints a compelling picture of a fascinating individual whom he characterizes as "about the

only figure remaining from the classic civil rights days—the last survivor—who is still actively at it."

Subject(s): Politics, Biography, Civil Rights Movement

1101 John Hope Franklin, Compiler

Color and Race

(Boston, MA; Houghton Mifflin, 1968)

Summary: John Hope Franklin's *Color and Race* collects articles originally published in *Daedalus* that focus on the issue of race throughout the world. An esteemed historian, Franklin provides an introduction outlining his thesis: racism and prejudice have not been limited to blacks against whites but have been universal characteristics of human societies coming into contact with other, racially different, societies. Included among the countries examined are Japan, Great Britain, India, Brazil, and the West Indies. Among the contributors are sociologists, historians, and psychologists.

Subject(s): Slavery, Colonialism, Racism

1102 John Hope Franklin
Alfred A. Moss, Jr., Co-author

From Slavery to Freedom: A History of American Negroes

(New York, NY; A.A. Knopf, 1947)

Summary: A noted scholar and professor emeritus at Duke University, John Hope Franklin published *From Slavery to Freedom: A History of American Negroes* in 1947; it appeared in its sixth edition in 1987. The work, co-authored by Alfred A. Moss Jr., is considered by many to be the standard text on African American history. The work attempts to correct the historic record as it pertains to both the contributions of black Americans as a whole and the accomplishments of noted African American individuals, such as nineteenth century historian George Washington Williams who was the first to publish a history of the African American people. The work was revised as *From Slavery to Freedom: A History of African Americans* in 1994.

Subject(s): African Americans, American History, Biography

1103 John Hope Franklin
Loren Schweninger, Co-author

Runaway Slaves: Rebels on the Plantation

(New York, NY; Oxford University Press, 1999)

Summary: In *Runaway Slaves: Rebels on the Plantation* scholars John Hope Franklin and Loren Schweninger argue that many enslaved blacks frequently rebelled against their white masters and attempted to gain their freedom. Drawing on primary sources that include plantation-owner's records, court petitions, and contemporary newspaper accounts, the authors document the repeated efforts of slaves to escape their masters.

The volume also shows the harsh consequences of such actions, as slaveholders banded together to preserve their property.

Subject(s): Slavery, American South, Resistance Movements

1104 **John Hope Franklin**

A Southern Odyssey: Travelers in the Antebellum North

(Baton Rouge, LA; Louisiana State University Press, 1976)

Summary: In *A Southern Odyssey: Travelers in the Antebellum North*, John Hope Franklin examines the motivations of the many southerners who toured the northern states prior to the Civil War. Before 1850, numerous southern whites traveled to the northern states, some to make a new home, others to lobby for the preservation of the plantation way of life amid the growing tide of abolitionist sentiment. In this work Franklin, a noted African American historian, points out the questions remaining for historians regarding this phenomenon, particularly with regard to the preservation of southern business interests and the impressions of the industrial North on these southern travelers.

Subject(s): Slavery, History, American South

Award(s): Jules F. Landry Award, 1975

1105 **V.P. Franklin**

Black Self-Determination: A Cultural History of the Faith of the Fathers

(Westport, CT; L. Hill, 1984)

Summary: In *Black Self-Determination: A Cultural History of the Faith of the Fathers*, V.P. Franklin collects slave narratives, poems, spirituals, sermons, and other works in an effort to show how American blacks have increasingly valued freedom, education, and self-determination as part of the legacy of slavery and Reconstruction. Representing black religious traditions as an expression of both a desire for freedom and a resistance to oppression, Franklin also maintains that self-determination and self-reliance have been the ultimate goals of blacks, evidenced by such things as the move westward in the years following the Civil War. A black nationalist historian, Franklin received some criticism for subverting the historical record in an effort to prove his argument, although critics agreed that his study was a pioneering work in expanding the interpretation of events in African American history.

Subject(s): Black Nationalism, History, Self-Reliance

1106 **V.P. Franklin**

Living Our Stories, Telling Our Truths: Autobiography and the Making of the African-American Intellectual Tradition

(New York, NY; Scribner, 1995)

Summary: Tracing the leadership role of 12 major intellectual leaders in *Living Our Stories, Telling Our Truths: Autobiography and the Making of the African-American Intellectual*

Tradition, author V.P. Franklin reworks black intellectual history as autobiography. Included are the thoughts, impressions, and recollections of Ida Wells Barnett, James Baldwin, James Weldon Johnson, and Richard Wright that, together with others, encompass much of African American literature and thought over two centuries.

Subject(s): History, Autobiography, Philosophy

1107 **V.P. Franklin,** Editor

New Perspectives on Black Educational History

(Boston, MA; G.K. Hall, 1978)

Summary: Conscious of a lack of recently published works in the area of black educational history, a group of young historians decided to publish a book of essays on the topic. The book provides a survey of contemporary research interests in the field. The essays in the collection examine such issues as normal school industrial education, the training of black leadership, and school desegregation. The essays focus on educational institutions such as Fisk University, Howard University School of Law, and Meharry Medical College.

Subject(s): History, Education, Colleges and Universities

1108 **George C. Fraser**

Success Runs in Our Race: The Complete Guide to Effective Networking in the African-American Community

(New York, NY; W. Morrow, 1994)

Summary: Written with the input of motivational speaker Les Brown, business guru George Fraser's *Success Runs in Our Race* provides African American entrepreneurs, professionals, and small business owners with an upbeat take on success. Based on the seven principles of Nguzo Saba, among which are unity, self-determination, collective responsibility, a sense of purpose, faith, and creativity, Fraser guides readers in the use of networking to gather information, gain influence and resources, get a new job, and further the general welfare. He provides tips and anecdotes featuring positive examples from a variety of ethnic groups and lists the twenty-five best places to network.

Subject(s): Business Building, Employment, Community Relations

1109 **E. Franklin Frazier**

The Negro Church in America

(New York, NY; Schocken Books, 1963)

Summary: In his *The Negro Church in America* author E.F. Frazier presents a groundbreaking analysis of the history of the African American church. Beginning with the origins of the church in the Antebellum South, Frazier follows the development of different branches of the church during the massive exodus by blacks from the farm economy of the South to the industrial north. In a republication of Frazier's work in 1989, C. Eric Lincoln supplements this scholarly work with an essay, "The Black Church Since Frazier," in which Lincoln argues that the civil rights movement of the 1950s and 1960s fractured the traditional church that was the subject of Frazier's study. New roles must be found for religion that reflect the new social context of resistance to oppression, according to Lincoln.

Subject(s): Religion, Christianity, History

1110 E. Franklin Frazier

Negro Youth at the Crossways: Their Personality Development in the Middle States

(Washington, DC; American Council on Education, 1940)

Summary: Prepared for the American Youth Commission, E. Franklin Frazier's *Negro Youth at the Crossways: Their Personality Development in the Middle States* describes the day-to-day life experiences of young people of color living in Washington, D.C., and Louisville, Kentucky. Using these as examples of a "middle area," Frazier discusses the problems caused by the shift in family patterns after the abolition of slavery, the transition from the rural life in the South to the industrialized North, and the economic freedom recently acquired by black youth. The work was praised by critics for its scholarship, readability, and objectivity.

Subject(s): City and Town Life, Coming-of-Age, Children

1111 Thomas R. Frazier, Editor

Afro-American History: Primary Sources

(New York, NY; Harcourt Brace Jovanovich, 1971)

Summary: *Afro-American History: Primary Sources* was compiled by Thomas R. Frazier to answer a need by colleges around the nation searching for texts for black history classes. Containing portions of such written documents as slave narratives, published sermons, newspaper editorials, and petitions, the book provides access to many documents not available to the general public. Frazier balances his work with selections of poetry and song and includes the works of such authors as Nat Turner, Frederick Douglass, David Walker, Langston Hughes, Marcus Garvey, W.E.B. Du Bois, and Malcolm X.

Subject(s): History, Colleges and Universities

1112 William W. Freehling

The Reintegration of American History: Slavery and the Civil War

(New York, NY; Oxford University Press, 1994)

Summary: In *The Reintegration of American History*, history professor William H. Freehling presents a revealing look at both owning and being a slave in nineteenth century America and discusses the roots of the Civil War. He objectively demon-

strates the importance of research into local communities and state governments in accessing the many points of view influencing this period of history—from that of white women and poorer European immigrants to Native Americans and blacks themselves—and shows that notions of black inferiority were prevalent in northern abolitionists despite the rhetoric of the period. The difficult and time-consuming process of historical research is also illuminated.

Subject(s): History, Slavery, Research

1113 Sylvia R. Frey

Water from the Rock: Black Resistance in a Revolutionary Age

(Princeton, NJ; Princeton University Press, 1991)

Summary: The formation of the United States of America required radical social, economic, and political change. In *Water from the Rock: Black Resistance in a Revolutionary Age*, historian Sylvia Frey sees the most change occurring in the South, where a black liberation movement had already begun before the American Revolution. She argues that the struggle for independence involved three adversaries: white revolutionaries, whites loyal to Britain, and most of the hundreds of thousands of slaves that occupied the thirteen colonies at the time of the Revolution. Although the slaves' struggle failed during the Revolution, it continued on into the early years of the U.S. in the guise of evangelical religion.

Subject(s): American South, American Revolution, Slavery

1114 Hoyt W. Fuller

Journey to Africa

(Chicago, IL; Third World Press, 1971)

Summary: Hoyt W. Fuller's 1971 memoir begins with his description of the racism and economic disparity that drove him into voluntary exile from America in 1958. After spending a year in France, he decided to travel to Africa. His memoir describes the ten years he spent traveling through the continent, witnessing the living conditions and political situations of countries from Algeria to Senegal to Guinea. He offers a scathing indictment of white Euro-American domination of Africa but yet expresses hope that African nations are beginning to control their own destinies.

Subject(s): Africa, Autobiography, Racism

1115 Kenneth L. Gagala

The Economics of Minorities: A Guide to Information Sources

(Detroit, MI; Gale Research Co., 1976)

Summary: Using sources covering the period 1965 to 1974, Kenneth L. Gagala has organized the existing documentation referencing the economic conditions of blacks and other minorities. In his *The Economics of Minorities* Gagala divides the available information--gleaned from journals, books, and documents from the U.S. Bureau of Labor Statistics and other government institutions--into twelve groups, among them education, consumerism, and the psychology of race, each as they relate to African Americans. Native Americans and Hispanics are also represented in separate sections. Bibliographic information is listed alphabetically under each section, and annotations aid readers in pinpointing specific sources according to the type of information provided.

Subject(s): Economics, Minorities

1116 **David Barry Gaspar,** Editor
Darlene Hine, Co-editor

More than Chattel: Black Women and Slavery in the Americas
(Bloomington, IN; Indiana University Press, 1996)

Summary: In *More than Chattel: Black Women and Slavery in the Americas*, editors Gaspar and Hine collect essays by noted academics that address the issue of gender within the context of slave communities. As the collection illustrates, the experiences of enslaved males were distinguished from those of females due to physiological as well as emotional differences. With greater physical strength, men were able to take a more active role in confronting their captors, while women relied on more subtle means of protest. Because of gender, women's experiences included exploitation as both sexual objects and as surrogate parents to very young white children. The volume highlights the ways in which women as a "weaker sex" managed to resist such abuse and transcend their captivity.

Subject(s): Slavery, American South, Sex Roles

1117 **Henry Louis Gates, Jr.**

Colored People: A Memoir
(New York, NY; Knopf, 1994)

Summary: In *Colored People: A Memoir* Harvard professor Henry Louis Gates, Jr. describes the years he spent growing up in Piedmont, West Virginia. Taking place in the 1950s and 1960s against the backdrop of the civil rights movement (which he viewed mainly on television), Gates writes of his growing awareness of the color line in his small mill town, and of the rich world he was part of despite the racial divide. Unlike Gates' many scholarly works, this volume is written with a sense of nostalgia for perhaps happier times.

Subject(s): Autobiography, American South, Small Town Life

1118 **Henry Louis Gates, Jr.**
Cornel West, Co-author

The Future of the Race
(New York, NY; A.A. Knopf, 1996)

Summary: *The Future of the Race* is a collection of important essays--two by modern black theorists Henry Louis Gates and Cornel West, and the third by NAACP co-founder W.E.B. Du Bois--that focus on the responsibility of what Du Bois had once referred to as that "talented tenth" of the black population.

Gates and West present differing perspectives on the duty of those African Americans who, through a combination of adequate education and other beneficial circumstances, were able to rise above the mainstream, to "uplift the race," as Du Bois had suggested.

Subject(s): Education, Class Conflict, Responsibility

1119 **Henry Louis Gates, Jr.,** Editor
William L. Andrews, Co-editor

Pioneers of the Black Atlantic: Five Slave Narratives from the Enlightenment, 1772-1815
(Washington, DC; Civitas, 1998)

Summary: *Black Pioneers of the Enlightenment: Five Slave Narratives from the Enlightenment, 1772-1815* collects the stories of James Albert Ukawsaw Gronniosaw, John Marrant, Ottobah Cugoano, Olaudah Equiano, and John Jea, five slaves who determined to learn the skills necessary to create a written record of their lives worthy of being made part of the historical record. Known today as the Black Atlantic writers, these men published autobiographical narratives during the late 1800s and into the next century, creating the foundations of the black literary tradition.

Subject(s): Slavery, Literature, Autobiography

1120 **Willard B. Gatewood, Jr.**

Black Americans and the White Man's Burden, 1898-1903
(Urbana, IL; University of Illinois Press, 1975)

Summary: In *Black Americans and the White Man's Burden, 1898-1903*, historian Willard B. Gatewood, Jr. examines the reaction of African Americans to the SpanishAmerican War in 1898. While many blacks, eager to assimilate into mainstream society, joined with U.S. government forces to defend the nation's interest in Cuba against Spain, others felt the daily sting of racism in American's towns and cities. Of particular interest to Gatewood is the inconsistent support of the black press to the U.S. war effort, their argument often being that by focusing attention on the war, less emphasis would fall on the battle against social and economic advancement of blacks in the wake of the Civil War.

Subject(s): Racism, Spanish-American War, Reconstruction

1121 **Addison Gayle, Jr.,** Compiler

Black Expression: Essays by and about Black Americans in the Creative Arts
(New York, NY; Weybright and Talley, 1969)

Summary: *Black Expression: Essays by and about Black Americans in the Creative Arts* was the first published work of educator and author Addison Gayle, Jr. Compiled after Gayle, a lecturer in English at the City College of the City University of New York at the time, found that there were few books focusing on African American contributions to the arts, the book contains both biographies of black artists and writings by men and women of color working in a variety of creative mediums, including the written word. Gayle's motivation for compiling the volume prefigures his future work in promoting a separate black aesthetic as a means of placing a relative value on works of art and literature by blacks.

Subject(s): Literature, Artists and Art, Biography

1122 **Addison Gayle, Jr.**

The Black Situation
(New York, NY; Horizon Press, 1970)

Summary: *The Black Situation* is a collection of nineteen essays by influential literary critic and educator Addison Gayle, Jr. Many of the ruminations Gayle includes in this book describe his youth and the development of his own ideas regarding literature and the arts as they relate to black culture. Other essays reflect the frustration felt by many blacks with regard to the racism that permeated U.S. society during the first half of the twentieth century. At one point Gayle writes: "What Black man, if he is honest with himself, has not dreamed of mass murder, of burning his way across America...?"

Subject(s): Literature, Autobiography, Racism

1123 **Addison Gayle, Jr.**

Claude McKay: The Black Poet at War
(Detroit, MI; Broadside Press, 1972)

Summary: In *Claude McKay: The Black Poet at War* educator and author Addison Gayle, Jr., describes the life of Jamaican-born poet McKay (1890-1948), a temperamental man considered an outsider within the New York intellectual circles that comprised the Harlem Renaissance. Moving to New York City in 1915, McKay became involved with a succession of radical political ideologies, including black radicalism, socialism, and communism, before adopting Catholicism in his forties. While his 1928 work of fiction *Home to Harlem* was the first novel by a black to achieve bestseller status, McKay's poetry failed to achieve critical notice. Forced into a meager living as an editor, McKay relied increasingly on his few friends for his support, as well as on the generosity of his political associates. In his approach, Gayle attempts to judge McKay and his work through a black rather than white aesthetic.

Subject(s): Literature, Biography, Harlem Renaissance

1124 **Addison Gayle, Jr.**

Oak and Ivy: A Biography of Paul Laurence Dunbar
(Garden City, NY; Doubleday, 1971)

Summary: *Oak and Ivy: A Biography of Paul Laurence Dunbar*, recounts the life of one of the preeminent black poets of the twentieth century. The son of former slaves, Dunbar was born in Ohio in 1872. Fascinated by dialect, he published his first collection of verse, *Lyrics of Lowly Life* at the age of

twenty-four, and followed it by more poems and a novel. Within his biography, Gayle is careful to judge the works of Dunbar against what Gayle terms a black aesthetic, one that discounts white cultural or literary standards in favor of those based on an African sensibility.

Subject(s): Literature, Biography, Poetry

1125 **Addison Gayle, Jr.**

Richard Wright: Ordeal of a Native Son
(Garden City, NY; Anchor/Doubleday, 1980)

Summary: *Richard Wright: Ordeal of a Native Son* is the biography of the novelist and critic whose novel, *Native Son*, focuses on a disadvantaged African American youth who, descending into a life of violence, murders a white woman and ultimately dies in the electric chair. Wright was born in 1908 on a Mississippi plantation and was raised in an impoverished and abusive family situation, his adolescence punctuated by racist incidents. Eventually seeking education and philosophical guidance, Wright moved to Paris and adopted the existentialist teachings of Jean Paul Sartre. In line with biographer Addison Gayle, Jr.'s own philosophy, Wright's life is filtered through an African, rather than white European lens, and his work in Gayle's book is judged against a small but growing body of black literature rather than against a "white" literary aesthetic.

Subject(s): Literature, Biography, Racism

1126 **Addison Gayle, Jr.**

Wayward Child: A Personal Odyssey
(Garden City, NY; Anchor Press, 1977)

Summary: *Wayward Child: A Personal Odyssey* recounts educator and author Addison Gayle, Jr.'s eventual rejection of mainstream America's cultural standards in favor of new standards that reflected his own African heritage. Gayle's autobiography follows his transition from "Negro" to "Black" in the wake of the black power movement, and his rise to a position of prominence in academic and literary circles. A tireless and sometimes militant supporter of a black, rather than white, aesthetic as a means to judge the creative works of African Americans, Gayle served in the U.S. Air Force and taught English at the college level for over two decades. Describing his approach to both writing and teaching, Gayle maintained that his work should be approached from a black point of view.

Subject(s): Literature, Autobiography, Cultural Conflict

1127 **Eugene D. Genovese**

Roll, Jordan, Roll: The World the Slaves Made
(New York, NY; Pantheon Books, 1974)

Summary: Marxist historian Eugene Genovese's *Roll, Jordan, Roll: The World the Slaves Made* is an 800-page history of slavery in the United States that is considered among the best books on the subject. Within its four sections, the volume describes the pattern of life created by and for the slaves, and also discusses the masters who oversaw enslaved blacks as they gave structure to their confined world. Common foodstuffs and garments, religious practices, sexual conventions, codes of behavior, and forms of entertainment are all discussed, showing that, while the institution of slavery was an abomination, there existed a more humane level to it than has been studied by scholars. While Genovese agrees that slaves failed to establish a revolutionary tradition, he marks numerous incidents whereby their refusal to act served as a rebellion against their servitude.

Subject(s): Slavery, American South, American History

Award(s): Bancroft Prize, 1975

1128 Walter Gibson

Black Americans: Biological Facts and Fancies
(New York, NY; Vantage Press, 1983)

Summary: Falsehoods about African Americans have underlain white racial attitudes since the arrival of enslaved Africans in North America. In his 1983 work, scholar Walter Gibson offers an engaging look at racism in American society. He deflates numerous myths about blacks' intelligence, behavior patterns, and athletic and sexual skills. Among the book's chapters are "Alleged Differences in 'White' versus 'Black' Brain Structure" and "Sex Organs--Are They Really Larger in Blacks?"

Subject(s): Biology, Racism, Prejudice

1129 Paula Giddings

When and Where I Enter: The Impact of Black Women on Race and Sex in America
(New York, NY; W. Morrow, 1984)

Summary: In *When and Where I Enter: The Impact of Black Women on Race and Sex in America* journalist Paula Giddings presents a history of the contributions made by African American women to the cause of racial and sexual equality. The book includes a history of the development of black women's clubs, suffrage associations, and civil rights groups that proliferated beginning in the early 1890s. She shows how this activism began even before the Civil War, sparked by black women's use of contraceptives and abortion as a means of preventing their offspring from sharing the women's fates as slaves. Giddings maintains that the Victorian ideal of womanhood, which required the "fairer sex" to be submissive and confined to domestic life, had no place in the lives of black women trying to support their families while the men were unable to find work.

Subject(s): Racism, Women's Rights, Sexism

1130 Nikki Giovanni

Gemini: An Extended Autobiographical Statement on My First Twenty-five Years of Being a Black Poet
(Indianapolis, IN; Bobbs-Merrill, 1971)

Summary: In *Gemini: An Extended Autobiographical Statement on My First Twenty-Five Years of Being a Black Poet* noted author Nikki Giovanni includes essays that cover not only her life but her views on literature and politics as well. Describing her childhood in Knoxville, Tennessee, and her experiences as a militant student at Fisk University, Giovanni also discusses the work of black writers such as James Baldwin and Charles W. Chesnutt and expresses her concerns about the relationship between African American men and women in U.S. society. While adopting a revolutionary posture, Giovanni's essays also reflect her relative youth, and the contradictions in her overall message revealed a philosophy that had yet to fully form.

Subject(s): Poetry, Civil Rights Movement, Autobiography

1131 Nikki Giovanni
Margaret Walker, Co-author

A Poetic Equation: Conversations between Nikki Giovanni and Margaret Walker
(Washington, DC; Howard University Press, 1974)

Summary: In *A Poetic Equation*, noted African American writers poets Nikki Giovanni and Margaret Walker talk about their experiences chronicling the shifting landscape of the twentieth century from their perspective as women of color. Walker, who died in 1998, was the author of the novel *Jubilee*, a popular novel portraying the history of an African American family from its roots in slavery. Giovanni is well known as a poet, essayist, and outspoken critic of U.S. culture.

Subject(s): Poetry, Civil Rights Movement, Women's Rights

1132 Nikki Giovanni

Racism 101
(New York, NY; Quill, 1994)

Summary: In *Racism 101* poet and essayist Nikki Giovanni presents readers with a range of political and social perspectives. Examining U.S. life and culture from the point of view of an introspective, educated, independent-minded African American woman, Giovanni ranges from reminiscences on her own upbringing to the role of education and her dismay over the attitudes of affluent blacks such as Supreme Court Justice Clarence Thomas and their rejection of the affirmative action policies that enabled their own successes and those of other blacks during the second half of the twentieth century. *Racism 101* is classic Giovanni in its provocative, sometimes intimate, but often totally unapologetic political slant.

Subject(s): Current Affairs, Civil Rights Movement, Autobiography

1133 Douglas G. Glasgow

The Black Underclass: Poverty, Unemployment, and Entrapment of Ghetto Youth

(San Francisco, CA; Jossey-Bass Publishers, 1980)

Summary: Howard University professor Douglas G. Glasgow's *The Black Underclass: Poverty, Unemployment, and Entrapment of Ghetto Youth* takes as its focus the Watts riots of August, 1965. Based on a four-year study of young men and women between the ages of 18 and 34 who inhabited the impoverished Los Angeles neighborhood after the riots, Glasgow's work analyzes the reasons why social programs have done nothing to diminish the number of African American youths without job skills, education, or a future.

Subject(s): Poverty, Urban Affairs, Racism

1134 Ralph J. Gleason

Celebrating the Duke and Louis, Bessie, Billie, Bird, Carmen, Miles, Dizzy, and Other Heroes

(Boston, MA; Little, Brown, 1975)

Summary: *Celebrating the Duke: And Louis, Bessie, Billie, Bird, Carmen, Miles, Dizzy, and Other Heroes* collects essays by *Rolling Stone* magazine co-founder and journalist Ralph J. Gleason. A jazz aficionado, Gleason entertains readers with stories about musical legends Duke Ellington, Billie Holiday, Miles Davis, Dizzy Gilespie, and other notable musicians, including Louis Armstrong, who Gleason hails as one of the most influential musicians in the history of jazz.

Subject(s): Music, Popular Culture, Jazz

1135 David Emmanuel Goatley

Were You There?: Godforsakenness in Slave Religion

(Maryknoll, NY; Orbis Books, 1996)

Summary: Volume 11 in the "Bishop Henry McNeal Turner/ Sojourner Truth" series, David Emmanuel Goatley's *Were You There?: Godforsakenness in Slave Religion* explores the experience of many enslaved black Africans who felt abandoned by God in the New World. The author contends that this sense of absolute abandonment to a life of indignity was central to the slave experience and served as a foundation of the spirituality and theology that developed among African Americans.

Subject(s): Slavery, Religion, Christianity

1136 Carole Goodwin

The Oak Park Strategy: Community Control of Racial Change

(Chicago, IL; University of Chicago Press, 1979)

Summary: In her 1979 work, Carole Goodwin considers the racial changes of neighborhoods. She examines two neighborhoods: Austin, a community within the Chicago city limits, and Oak Park, a suburb adjacent to Austin. Austin, which was once made up of white residents, become biracial for a brief period before it became resegregated as a black neighborhood. Oak Park, in contrast, experienced a growth in its black population but went through no resegregation. This work considers the strategies developed in Oak Park for dealing with racial change.

Subject(s): Neighbors and Neighborhoods, Segregation

1137 Ruby Berkley Goodwin

Its Good to Be Black

(Garden City, NY; Doubleday, 1953)

Summary: *Its Good to Be Black* is poet and journalist Ruby Berkley Goodwin's memoir of her childhood spent as the daughter of a coal miner. Born and raised in Illinois, she followed her dream of being a writer, eventually working as a Hollywood columnist and as publicist and secretary to African American actress Hattie McDaniel. Affirming both her religious faith and her belief in the abilities of blacks, Goodwin paints a compelling portrait of a closely knit African American family.

Subject(s): Autobiography, Family Life, Writing

Award(s): Commonwealth Award, 1953

1138 Milton M. Gordon

Assimilation in American Life: The Role of Race, Religion, and National Origins

(New York, NY; Oxford University Press, 1964)

Summary: In *Assimilation in American Life: The Role of Race, Religion, and National Origins* educator Milton M. Gordon views the United States as a nation composed of "subsocieties" organized along ethnic lines, with a core society of middle-class white Anglo-Saxons. Rather than a melting pot, he contends that other ethnic groups have assimilated into this core culture, with varying levels of success. Reviewing a number of theories about the process of such assimilation, Gordon concludes that efforts to desegregate housing, rather than the U.S. educational system, should have been employed by liberals intent on eliminating racism.

Subject(s): Education, Race Relations, Housing

1139 Vivian V. Gordon

Black Women, Feminism, and Black Liberation: Which Way?

(Chicago, IL; Third World Press, 1985)

Summary: In *Black Women, Feminism, and Black Liberation: Which Way?* Vivian V. Gordon researched the most significant issues between black men and women to surface in the wake of the women's liberation movement of the 1960s and 1970s.

Gordon includes among these issues the formation of coalition politics between white women and women of color, and the relationship between the civil rights movement and the proliferation of Women's Studies programs on college campuses across the nation. A poll of black women taken by Gordon showed them still unified with regard to the improvement of the entire African American community, rather than just black women, causing Gordon to conclude that unification along lines of race has taken precedence over political alignment by gender.

Subject(s): Women's Rights, Racism, Revolution

1140 Brenda D. Gottschild

Digging the Africanist Presence in American Performance: Dance and Other Contexts
(Westport, CT; Greenwood Press, 1996)

Summary: In *Digging the Africanist Presence in American Performance* Temple University professor Brenda D. Gottschild examines how black culture has influenced the arts in the United States. Dance and the modern ballet of George Balanchine, as well as minstrel shows, jazz, vaudeville, rap and hip hop, and Native American powwows are all the result of such influence, according to Gottschild, who also discusses racism and its impact on the performing arts in general by noting that such black influences have been "invisibilized" in consequence.

Subject(s): Performing Arts, Popular Culture, Racism

1141 Lino A. Graglia

Disaster by Decree: The Supreme Court Decisions on Race and the Schools
(Ithaca, NY; Cornell University Press, 1976)

Summary: In *Disaster by Decree: The Supreme Court Decisions on Race and the Schools* Lino A. Graglia focuses on the landmark 1954 Supreme Court decision handed down in *Brown v. Board of Education,* which disallowed separate-but-equal policies in public schools. While acknowledging the positive impact of the decision, which stemmed from a case brought against the Topeka, Kansas, school system, Graglia argues that the Court's decision also actively enforced racial discrimination and resulted in public furor over forced busing and redistricting of urban schools across the nation.

Subject(s): Judicial System, Education, Racism

1142 Shirley Graham
(Also known as Shirley Graham Du Bois)

Booker T. Washington: Educator of Hand, Head, and Heart
(New York, NY; Messner, 1955)

Summary: The second wife of NAACP founder W.E.B. Du Bois, Shirley Graham Du Bois authored a series of biographies

profiling the lives of notable black Americans that were designed to inspire African American children. Published in 1955, *Booker T. Washington: Educator of Hand, Head, and Heart* tells the story of the man who rose from slavery to become a teacher, author, and lecturer. The biography recounts Washington's 1881 appointment as principal of the Tuskegee Institute, a school founded to provide former slaves with the job skills necessary to enter the trades. The author of *Up from Slavery,* Washington died in 1915.

Subject(s): Biography, Slavery, Education

1143 Shirley Graham
(Also known as Shirley Graham Du Bois)
George D. Lipscomb, Co-author
Elton C. Fax, Illustrator

Dr. George Washington Carver, Scientist
(New York, NY; J. Messner, 1944)

Summary: Even before her marriage in 1951 to famed civil rights leader W.E.B. Du Bois, Shirley Graham Du Bois authored a series of biographies profiling the lives of notable blacks from around the world. Published a year after Carver's death in 1943, *Dr. George Washington Carver, Scientist* recounts the life of the first African American scientist, from his birth to Missouri slaves in 1860 through his many agricultural innovations. Of particular benefit to southern farmers was Carver's development of commercial uses for southern sweet potato and peanut crops like peanut butter which helped stabilize the southern economy.

Subject(s): Biography, Scientific Experiments, Botany

1144 Shirley Graham
(Also known as Shirley Graham Du Bois)

Julius K. Nyerere: Teacher of Africa
(New York, NY; Julian Messner, 1975)

Summary: One of a series of biographies profiling the lives of notable blacks from around the world, Du Bois's *Julius K. Nyerere: Teacher of Africa* gives an account of the socialist politician who earned a degree in economics at the University of Edinburgh before returning to his native Tanganyika. Trained as a teacher, Nyerere organized the nationalist movement that would eventually win his country independence from its colonial rulers. He also negotiated the union with Zanzibar that resulted in the formation of the African state of Tanzania in 1964.

Subject(s): Biography, Africa, Education

1145 Shirley Graham
(Also known as Shirley Graham Du Bois)

Paul Robeson: Citizen of the World
(New York, NY; J. Messner, 1946)

Summary: In a series of biographies, Shirley Graham Du Bois profiled the lives of notable blacks from around the world. Published in 1946, *Paul Robeson: Citizen of the World* tells the story of the African American who abandoned a career as an attorney in favor of life as a performing artist. A noted actor and singer whose stage credits included the role of Othello, Robeson stirred the ire of Cold War watchdogs by stating publicly that the treatment of blacks under communism was fairer than it was under capitalism. The U.S. government responded by invalidating Robeson's passport until 1963.

Subject(s): Biography, Communism, Actors and Actresses

1146 **Shirley Graham**
(Also known as Shirley Graham Du Bois)
Robert Burns, Illustrator

The Story of Phillis Wheatley
(New York, NY; J. Messner, 1949)

Summary: A noted journalist and playwright, Shirley Graham Du Bois authored a series of biographies profiling the lives of notable individuals. *The Story of Phillis Wheatley* recounts the life of the African-born poet who was educated in Latin and other subjects by her Boston owner along with his own children. Beginning writing seriously at the age of thirteen, she published several volumes of verse and spoke on her craft in both England and the United States. Wheatley died in 1785.

Subject(s): Biography, Poetry, American History

1147 **Shirley Graham**
(Also known as Shirley Graham Du Bois)
Mario Cooper, Illustrator

The Story of Pocahontas
(New York, NY; Grosset & Dunlap, 1953)

Summary: As part of her continuing effort to present the lives of notable men and women of color, author Shirley Graham Du Bois profiled the life of the noted Native American princess in *The Story of Pocahontas*. Beginning with her childhood as the daughter of Chief Powhatan, Graham follows Pocahontas as she befriends English captain John Smith upon his arrival in the Chesapeake Bay in 1607, saves him from death at the hands of her father, converts to Christianity, and marries an Englishman who returns with her to Great Britain, although, like many Native Americans, she does not long survive exposure to European diseases.

Subject(s): Biography, Native Americans, American Colonies

1148 **Shirley Graham**
(Also known as Shirley Graham Du Bois)

Your Most Humble Servant
(New York, NY; Messner, 1949)

Summary: Shirley Graham, the wife of civil rights leader W.E.B. Du Bois, wrote several biographies profiling the lives of notable blacks in an effort to provide young African Americans with role models. Published in 1949, her *Your Most

Humble Servant is the inspirational story of the builder of the first clock made in America. Born in 1731, Banneker developed his prototype clock from a cast-off watch; his interest soon expanded to astronomy, where his later studies in the subject led him to correct several longstanding errors in calculations by other astronomers. Graham's biography emphasizes the determination and creativity of this noted American inventor.

Subject(s): Biography, Astronomy, Inventions
Award(s): Anisfield-Wolf Award, 1949

1149 **Joanne Grant,** Editor

Black Protest: 350 Years of History, Documents, and Analyses
(New York, NY; Ballantine, 1968)

Summary: Containing essays about such diverse rebels as John Brown, Stokely Carmichael, Ossie Davis, Frederick Douglass, Lorraine Hansberry, and Rosa Parks, *Black Protest: 350 Years of History, Documents, and Analyses* was compiled by Joanne Grant. Chronicling over three centuries of African American acts of rebellion, Grant concludes that repeated efforts to gain equality between the races through the vote, the judicial system, nonviolent demonstrations, and black nationalism have failed.

Subject(s): Resistance Movements, Politics, Race Relations

1150 **Mildred Denby Green**

Black Women Composers: A Genesis
(Boston, MA; Twayne Publishers, 1983)

Summary: This book looks at twentieth century black American women composers, who have combined the elements of jazz, blues, and spirituals with the traditions of Western European music. The volume considers the work of the following composers: Florence Price, Margaret Bonds, Julia Perry, Evelyn Pittman, and Lena McLin.

Subject(s): Music, Jazz

1151 **Eloise Greenfield**
Alesia Revis, Co-author
George Ford, Illustrator

Alesia
(New York, NY; Philomel Books, 1981)

Summary: *Alesia,* illustrated by George Ford, with photographs by Sandra Turner Bond, is the chronicle of a black teen's acceptance of her altered lifestyle. Injured during her junior year at high school, Alesia spent months in a coma before regaining consciousness and discovering that she had lost use of her legs. Showcasing the young woman's resilient spirit and her ability to transcend the restrictions placed on her by her disability, co-author Eloise Greenfield shows eighteen-year-old Alesia's determination in learning to walk with a brace and cane, ending her emotional story with the walk up to the podium to receive her high school diploma.

Subject(s): Biography, Adolescence

1152 Eloise Greenfield
Jerry Pinkney, Illustrator

Mary McLeod Bethune
(New York, NY; Crowell, 1977)

Summary: *Mary McLeod Bethune*, illustrated by Jerry Pinkney, is the life story of an African American woman who dedicated her life to the education of her people. Born in 1875 and raised in South Carolina, Bethune was able to receive an education that allowed her to teach the children in her community. In Eloise Greenfield's easy-to-read biography, Bethune is presented as a role model for young people in her unflagging and lifelong dedication to promoting education for all children, whatever their race. Bethune died in 1955.

Subject(s): Biography, Education, Children

1153 Eloise Greenfield
Eric Marlow, Illustrator

Rosa Parks
(New York, NY; Crowell, 1973)

Summary: *Rosa Parks* tells the life story of the Montgomery, Alabama seamstress who in 1955 refused to relinquish her seat on a city bus to a white person, in violation of state law. The poor treatment Parks received at the hands of city officials led to a boycott of the bus system, sparking the many marches, boycotts, and other confrontations that would characterize the civil rights movement. In this easy-to-read biography, author Eloise Greenfield shows Parks's continued dedication to the movement her actions helped to inspire. *Rosa Parks* was reissued with new illustrations in 1995.

Subject(s): Biography, Civil Rights Movement, American South

Award(s): National Council for the Social Studies: Carter G. Woodson Book Award, 1974

1154 Dick Gregory
Robert Lipsyte, Co-author

Nigger: An Autobiography
(New York, NY; Dutton, 1964)

Summary: *Nigger* is the autobiography of Dick Gregory, the first African American comic to perform professionally in front of a white audience. Using his impoverished childhood in St. Louis, Missouri as source material, he managed to raise the social consciousness of his audience through nonconfrontative humor, writing in *Nigger:* "I've got to go up there as an individual first, a Negro second. I've got to be a colored funny man, not a funny colored man." Active in civil rights campaigns and politics, Gregory tapped his skill as a performer only after attending college on a track scholarship and doing a stint in the army. A fill-in job at Chicago's Playboy Club in 1961 would make Gregory a household name and increase awareness of the

poverty, segregation, and racial injustice on which he focused his satirical routines.

Subject(s): Autobiography, Performing Arts, Humor

1155 William Grier
Price M. Cobbs, Co-author

Black Rage
(New York, NY; Basic Books, 1968)

Summary: In *Black Rage*, African American psychiatrists William Grier and Price Cobbs discuss the building frustration among people of color in modern society. Seeing similar personality disorders among the patients they counselled in their respective practices, Grier and Cobbs began to study the situation. They correlate increasing amounts of frustration, anger, and even violent outbreaks with the social and cultural demands placed on patients, particularly patients who are black males. The book was released in a second edition in 1992.

Subject(s): Anger, Psychiatry, Family Life

1156 Cyril E. Griffith

The African Dream: Martin R. Delany and the Emergence of Pan-African Thought
(University Park, PA; Pennsylvania State University Press, 1975)

Summary: Martin R. Delany (1812-1885) is often remembered, if at all, as Frederick Douglass's opposite on issues related to the future of blacks in the United States. With Douglass's prominence, Delany's writing fell from favor and was largely ignored for almost a century. With *The African Dream: Martin R. Delany and the Emergence of Pan-African Thought* Cyril E. Griffith attempts to reintroduce Delany's voice into the arguments surrounding abolition and the "Negro Problem." Delany believed in the importance of a united Africa as a possible homeland for those released from the bonds of slavery.

Subject(s): Pan-Africanism, Slavery, Abolition

1157 Alan P. Grimes

Equality in America: Religion, Race, and the Urban Majority
(New York, NY; Oxford University Press, 1964)

Summary: In *Equality in America: Religion, Race, and the Urban Majority* political science professor Alan P. Grimes outlines the political questions surrounding issues of race and religion as they relate to the development of law. The book developed out of Grimes's own effort to understand why the decisions handed down by the U.S. Supreme Court under Justice Earl Warren favored the principle of equality embodied in decisions like *Brown vs. Board of Education*. The book shows the process by which Grimes traced this trend toward equality through the years preceding Warren's appointment to chief justice in 1953.

Subject(s): Racism, Urban Affairs, Religion

1158 William J. Grimshaw

Black Politics in Chicago: The Quest for Leadership, 1939-1979

(Chicago, IL; Loyola University of Chicago, 1980)

Summary: *Black Politics in Chicago: The Quest for Leadership, 1939-1979* is a study by Illinois Institute of Technology professor William J. Grimshaw, who served as political and policy adviser to a former mayor of Chicago. Involved firsthand with numerous political campaigns, Grimshaw presents an account of the relationship between the African American community and Chicago's Democratic machine that has existed since the Great Depression and the implementation of social programs under the New Deal. Griffith's book was updated as *Bitter Fruit: Black Politics and the Chicago Machine, 1931-1991* in 1992.

Subject(s): Poverty, Politics, Urban Affairs

1159 Bernard Grofman, Editor
Chandler Davidson, Co-editor

Quiet Revolution in the South: The Impact of the Voting Rights Act, 1965-1990

(Princeton, NJ; Princeton University Press, 1994)

Summary: The first volume to attempt to quantify the results of civil rights legislation over several decades, *Quiet Revolution in the South: The Impact of the Voting Rights Act, 1965-1990* studies the aftermath of the Voting Rights Act of 1965. Editors Chandler Davidson and Bernard Grofman collect essays that present a historic overview demonstrating that African Americans and other minorities have found the U.S. Constitution to be an excellent tool for access to equal political participation in eight core southern states since the close of the Civil War. Placing particular focus on the second half of the twentieth century, contributors use quantitative methodology in marshalling evidence to show the success of the act in increasing black registration and political participation. A detailed discussion of related legal actions is included.

Subject(s): Civil Rights Movement, Politics, Law

1160 Susan Gubar

Racechanges: White Skin, Black Face in American Culture

(New York, NY; Oxford University Press, 1997)

Summary: Susan Gubar's *Racechanges: White Skin, Black Face in American Culture* explores the history of cross-racial impersonations: whites donning blackface in minstrel shows and blacks "passing" for whites due to their light complexion. Reviewing a host of films, books, music, paintings, and other manifestations of this phenomenon within popular culture, Gubar documents the profound influence black culture has had within the United States as a whole. She contends that white people's adoption of black artistic mannerisms has been both an acknowledgment of the validity of the black aesthetic and a consequence of white guilt over racism.

Subject(s): Racism, Popular Culture, Guilt

1161 Patricia Gurin

Black Consciousness, Identity, and Achievement: A Study of Students in Historically Black Colleges

(New York, NY; Wiley, 1975)

Summary: This work is based on studies made of historically black colleges between 1964 and 1970, a period when the civil rights movement was at its height and black nationalism was in vogue. In analyzing the data, authors Gurin and Epps reveal tensions felt by students between their individual identities and their allegiance to a collective black identity. The authors conclude that solutions must be devised that allow students to integrate their personal identities with their commitment to black community issues.

Subject(s): Colleges and Universities, Black Nationalism, Identity

1162 Patricia Guthrie

Catching Sense: African American Communities on a South Carolina Sea Island

(Westport, CT; Bergin & Garvey, 1996)

Summary: *Catching Sense: African American Communities on a South Carolina Sea Island* is an anthropological study done on St. Helena Island between 1972 and 1992. Describing the history of the island and its inhabitants, Guthrie also discusses the spiritual and emotional aspects of island life. Plantation membership, which is conferred after one has been a resident through twelve years of age, brings with it social and ethical instruction as well as rights and attendant duties. An African American anthropologist, Guthrie maintains that the plantation structure was an offshoot of slavery days, when one's identity was derived from one's plantation rather than one's actual parents.

Subject(s): American South, Slavery, Anthropology

1163 Herbert G. Gutman

The Black Family in Slavery and Freedom, 1750-1925

(New York, NY; Pantheon Books, 1976)

Summary: Best known for his pioneering work in revisionist labor history, particularly with regard to the working classes and racial and ethnic minorities, Herbert G. Gutman authored *The Black Family in Slavery and Freedom, 1750-1925*. Published in 1976, the work challenges the traditional theories and practices employed by the social scientists on whose work governmental social policy decisions are made. In particular, Gutman summons evidence to refute the traditional view that slavery severed the ties binding African family members upon their introduction into slave culture in the United States.

Subject(s): Slavery, Economics, Family Life

1164 Herbert G. Gutman

Slavery and the Numbers Game: A Critique of "Time on the Cross"
(Urbana, IL; University of Illinois Press, 1975)

Summary: Herbert G. Gutman is considered a pioneer in U.S. labor history. In *Slavery and the Numbers Game: A Critique of "Time on the Cross"* he critiques the study Time on the Cross: The Economics of Negro Slavery, published in 1974 by economists Robert W. Fogel and Stanley Engerman. Gutman argues that the previous work—ostensibly an objective study using computer models and statistical evidence--is flawed because it contains errors of fact, incorrect research methods, and a misapplication of data. He disagrees with its overall conclusion that, based on studies of slave work habits, slave markets, social and sexual mores, and other aspects of slavery, the institution of slavery was not as horrific as history has portrayed it. Gutman believes the study is flawed and the work unrevealing of the lives of enslaved African Americans.

Subject(s): Slavery, American South, Economics

1165 John Langston Gwaltney, Editor

Drylongso: A Self-Portrait of Black America
(New York, NY; Random House, 1980)

Summary: "Drylongso" means ordinary, and in *Drylongso: A Portrait of Black America* author/interviewer John Langston Gwaltney sets down the thoughts and feelings of ordinary black men and women collected during his travels around the United States during the 1970s. Anthropologist Gwaltney, who is blind, was able to put his subjects at ease, making this collection compelling for its honesty and candidness as a portrait of those blacks working regular jobs, living in stable families, and relying on traditional values to navigate their lives.

Subject(s): Family Life, Autobiography, Working-Class Life

1166 Andrew Hacker

Two Nations: Black and White, Separate, Hostile, Unequal
(New York, NY; Ballantine Books, 1992)

Summary: In *Two Nations: Black and White, Separate, Hostile, Unequal* political scientist Andrew Hacker uses statistical analysis to help define modern race relations. While some of the examples presented in the book provide only a simplistic portrait of the imbalance between the races in terms of wealth, health, and other measurable criteria, his approach transcends subjective but oft-cited rhetoric to show that the current inabil-

ity of many African Americans to escape poverty is unique and not to be solved by the "hard work and perseverance" that whites maintain blacks are lacking.

Subject(s): Poverty, Race Relations, Urban Affairs

1167 David Halberstam

The Children
(New York, NY; Random House, 1998)

Summary: *The Children* chronicles Pulitzer Prize-winning author David Halberstam's return to Nashville, Tennessee, where he began his career as a twenty-five-year-old journalist covering the civil rights movement for a local newspaper. He documents the years 1960-65--the pivotal years of that movement—through the lives of the young people who rallied to the cause of racial equality, among them Democratic congressman John Lewis, mayor Marion Barry of Washington, D.C., and activist Diane Nash, all of whom were infused with the pacifist teachings of Gandhi by the Reverend James Lawson. Including accounts of lunch counter sit-ins and the freedom rides, Halberstam presents a compelling portrait of young people risking their lives for freedom.

Subject(s): Civil Rights Movement, Biography, Race Relations

1168 Lorraine Hale

Hale House: The House That Love Built
(New York, NY; Hale House, 1991)

Summary: The title of this work refers to a shelter for boys and girls born addicted to drugs in New York City's Harlem neighborhood. Established by Clara Hale around 1970, the shelter cared for hundreds of children during the next few decades. Narrated by Clara Hale's daughter, Lorraine Hale, who was also associated with the operation of Hale House, the book tells the stories of memorable children who passed through Hale House during the 1970s and 1980s.

Subject(s): Drug Abuse, Children, Mothers

1169 John Samuel Haller, Jr.

Outcasts from Evolution: Scientific Attitudes of Racial Inferiority, 1859-1900
(Urbana, IL; University of Illinois Press, 1971)

Summary: In *Outcasts from Evolution: Scientific Attitudes of Racial Inferiority, 1859-1900* scholar John S. Haller studies the scientific "proof" of racial inferiority that circulated in U.S. intellectual circles between the publication of Charles Darwin's *Origin of Species* in 1859 and Gregor Mendel's experiments with genetics forty years later. Illustrating how scientists attempted to adapt the principles of Darwin's theory to morality and the physical attributes of non-white races, Haller draws parallels between such scientific "advances" and contemporary public policy decisions.

Subject(s): Racism, Evolution, Sociology

1170 Warren J. Halliburton

The Picture Life of Jesse Jackson
(New York, NY; F. Watts, 1972)

Summary: Created for young readers, Warren J. Halliburton's *The Picture Life of Jesse Jackson* provides photographs and text of the famed civil rights leader. It begins with his Greenville, North Carolina boyhood and continues from his early years as a Baptist clergyman to his world-famous efforts as a politician and a civil rights activist advancing the cause of racial equality in America. The book was compiled with the assistance of Jackson, who dedicated much of his career to building self-confidence and racial pride in African American youth.

Subject(s): Biography, Photography, Civil Rights Movement

1171 Virginia Hamilton

Paul Robeson: The Life and Times of a Free Black Man
(New York, NY; Harper & Row, 1974)

Summary: In this biography, Virginia Hamilton, the popular author of many books for young readers, details the life of the multi-talented African American Paul Robeson. Robeson (1898-1976) was a noted actor and vocalist who sacrificed a successful career in the United States to advocate on behalf of people of color around the world. Robeson grew up in Princeton, New Jersey, where his father, a pastor, exhorted him to achieve his vast human potential. Robeson did, becoming a scholar of law, excelling at sports, and building a career as a talented singer and thespian on the New York stage as well as in films. His interest in politics grew also, and his favorable impression of Communism as practiced in the U.S.S.R. led to his belief that it could be used as a means of benefiting Africa's many struggling post-colonial black governments. This political stance resulted in the actor's blacklisting during the Communist "Red Scare" of the 1950s. Eventually, Robeson was forced to live abroad; his U.S. passport was declared invalid.

Subject(s): Biography, Communism, Civil Rights Movement

1172 Virginia Hamilton

W.E.B. Du Bois: A Biography
(New York, NY; T.Y. Crowell, 1972)

Summary: Written by noted author Virginia Hamilton, *W.E.B. Du Bois: A Biography* tells the story of the life of the famed civil rights leader in a manner that will make Du Bois an exciting character to younger readers. One of the primary founders of the National Association for the Advancement of Colored People (NAACP) in 1909, Du Bois is introduced to readers as a child growing up in Massachusetts. From his early studies in sociology at Harvard University, to his work documenting the oppression of blacks and attempting to aid in their efforts to attain equality, Hamilton's book shows a Du Bois who was

sometimes egotistical, sometimes weak, yet ultimately a leader; she also paints a vivid portrait of the spirit of his times.

Subject(s): Civil Rights Movement, History, Biography

1173 D. Antoinette Handy

Black Women in American Bands and Orchestras
(Metuchen, NJ; Scarecrow Press, 1980)

Summary: A collection of 112 short biographies of African American woman instrumentalists, *Black Women in American Bands and Orchestras* serves as a valuable addition to the historical record. Dividing her profiles into such areas as orchestra leaders, string players, keyboard players, and administrators, D. Antoinette Handy includes women from vaudeville and minstrel shows, marching bands, jazz ensembles and swing bands, and orchestras, and covers several generations of musicians. Most of the women are working musicians rather than celebrities. In addition to photographs, Handy also includes essays on the development of black ensemble music. The work was updated in 1981.

Subject(s): Music, Musicians, Biography

1174 D. Antoinette Handy

The International Sweethearts of Rhythm
(Metuchen, NJ; Scarecrow Press, 1983)

Summary: In *The International Sweethearts of Rhythm* musicologist D. Antoinette Handy profiles a popular women's jazz band of the 1940s. The International Sweethearts, which was formed at South Carolina's Piney Woods Country Life School, eventually received acclaim as one of the best all-women's swing bands in the nation. Handy's book, which was later revised, includes interviews with members of the band, and the author is careful to document all points of view surrounding controversial aspects of the band's history.

Subject(s): Music, Small Town Life, Popular Culture

1175 Lorraine Hansberry

The Movement: Documentary of a Struggle for Equality
(New York, NY; Simon & Schuster, 1964)

Summary: After twenty-year-old University of Wisconsin student Lorraine Hansberry was told by her theater arts instructor that black women had no future in theater, she decided to begin a career as a journalist and moved to New York City. Gravitating to the theater community, she became acquainted with actor and activist Paul Robeson, and Robeson quickly hired Hansberry to contribute to his journal *Freedom*, which drew on the talents of many other black writers of the 1950s. Hansberry, whose *A Raisin in the Sun* has become a classic of American theater, remained an activist on behalf of racial equality throughout her life. Her recollections of the early years of the civil rights movement, along with several *Freedom* articles, are collected in *The Movement: Documentary of a Struggle for Equality*, which was published a year before Hansberry's death in 1965.

Subject(s): Journalism, Theater, Civil Rights Movement

1176 Vincent Harding

The Other American Revolution

(Los Angeles, CA; UCLA Center for Afro-American Studies, 1980)

Summary: In this book, historian and journalist Vincent Harding offers thirty essays that comment upon the history of African Americans in the United States. Begun as a script for a proposed television series and later recorded on audiotape, Harding's essays reflect his own perspective as a radical activist in the civil rights movement, culminating with the murder of Dr. Martin Luther King, Jr. in 1968. Characterized by an engaging writing style, the work is a document of one man's changing perceptions about politics, people, and race during one of the most tumultuous movements of the twentieth century.

Subject(s): Civil Rights Movement, Autobiography, Race Relations

1177 Vincent Harding

There Is a River: The Black Struggle for Freedom in America

(New York, NY; Harcourt Brace Jovanovich, 1981)

Summary: Likening the fight against racism and oppression to a mighty black river fighting against the prevailing currents of white supremacy, Vincent Harding creates a vivid rendition of African American history. In his work, *There Is a River: The Black Struggle for Freedom in America*, Harding focuses on the black river's main strength: outspoken men and women such as former slaves Sojourner Truth, Nat Turner, Harriet Tubman, and Frederick Douglass, as well as the unsung heroes of the abolitionist cause, whose efforts also powered the struggle for freedom.

Subject(s): Racism, Slavery, Resistance Movements

1178 Sharon Harley, Editor
Rosalyn Terborg-Penn, Co-editor

The Afro-American Woman: Struggles and Images

(Port Washington, NY; Kennikat Press, 1978)

Summary: In their *The Afro-American Woman: Struggles and Images*, editors Sharon Harley and Rosalyn Terborg-Penn collect essays espousing a variety of historical and political perspectives that highlight the racist and sexist experiences of African American women during the last two hundred years. From civil rights activists and educators to artists and blue-collar workers, the women profiled reflect in their changing attitudes the development of both black and white culture in

America. The subjects of the book are studied from both an historical and modern black nationalist viewpoint.

Subject(s): Women's Rights, Sexism, American History

1179 Phillip Brian Harper

Are We Not Men?: Masculine Anxiety and the Problem of African-American Identity

(New York, NY; Oxford University Press, 1996)

Summary: In *Are We Not Men?: Masculine Anxiety and the Problem of AfricanAmerican Identity* author Phillip Brian Harper addresses issues of race and representation and shows that stereotypes and preconceived ideas about African American masculinity have always played a troubled role both in the formation of the black male's sense of self and the manner in which black men are represented in movies, music, and other media.

Subject(s): Movies, Music, Racism

1180 Fred R. Harris, Editor
Roger W. Wilkins, Co-editor

Quiet Riots: Race and Poverty in the United States

(New York, NY; Pantheon Books, 1988)

Summary: In *Quiet Riots: Race and Poverty in the United States*, the editors collect essays examining the outgrowth of the Kerner Report of 1967. Convened by President Lyndon B. Johnson in 1967, the Kerner Commission investigated the increasing numbers of riots breaking out in cities like Tampa, Atlanta, and Detroit in the wake of the civil rights movement. The commission's conclusion--that riots were sparked by white racism--prompted numerous policies designed to counteract this problem. Essayists in *Quiet Riots* view the results of such policies two decades later and deal with the question of whether the Kerner Report, and the actions it prompted, truly addressed the cause of black unrest.

Subject(s): Civil Rights Movement, Race Relations, Urban Affairs

1181 James Haskins

Adam Clayton Powell: Portrait of a Marching Black

(New York, NY; Dial Press, 1974)

Summary: In *Adam Clayton Powell: Portrait of a Marching Black*, author James Haskins tells the story of controversial Harlem congressman Powell (1908-1972) for younger readers. Born and raised in Harlem, the son of the pastor of the nation's largest Baptist church, Powell went from attempting to pass as white while a student at Colgate University to becoming a vocal supporter of African Americans. Coming to the public's notice during his efforts to reform Harlem Hospital, and remaining visible throughout his career for his tumultuous personal and financial dealings, Powell was appointed as an advisor in President Lyndon Johnson's War on Poverty programs during the 1960s.

Subject(s): Biography, Politics, Harlem Renaissance

1182 **James Haskins**
Don Miller, Illustrator

The Creoles of Color of New Orleans
(New York, NY; Crowell, 1975)

Summary: Creole families of color are considered among southern Louisiana's first residents, and, living in close-knit communities and encouraging a strong work ethic, hold an influential role in the economy and culture of New Orleans. James Haskins's *The Creoles of Color of New Orleans* focuses on these descendants of French immigrants and Africans, exploring their history and the unique culture--Mardi Gras, zydeco music, and a colorful "pidgin" language are among its characteristics—that they have preserved due to their relative isolation from the mainstream population.

Subject(s): American South, Popular Culture, Colonialism

1183 **James Haskins**

James Van DerZee: The Picture-Takin' Man
(New York, NY; Dodd, Mead, 1979)

Summary: *James Van DerZee: The Picture-Takin' Man* is a book for young readers that recounts the life of a black photographer whose body of work chronicles the life and culture of black Americans during the twentieth century. Born in Massachusetts in 1886, Van DerZee began taking pictures in 1900. Living in New York City by 1915, he started working as a photographer full-time and worked out of his Harlem studio throughout much of the 1920s and 1930s. Achieving national renown late in life, he was sought out by celebrities such as Bill Cosby, Muhammad Ali, and Miles Davis, each of whom considered a Van DerZee portrait to be an honor. At Van DerZee's death in 1983, he was credited with taking over 125,000 photographs of black America.

Subject(s): Biography, Politics, Photography

1184 **R. Allen Hays**

The Federal Government and Urban Housing: Ideology and Change in Public Policy
(Albany, NY; State University of New York Press, 1985)

Summary: Scholar R. Allen Hays specializes in housing, urban, and social policy issues. This study, one of several works he has authored on home ownership within industrialized countries, was among the first to focus the key issues of home ownership as it has been affected by federal legislation and social policies. Covering the rise and subsequent fall of cities as residential centers, Hays examines the growth of resi-

dential "projects" and other failed efforts to encourage home ownership among the nation's poor and predominately African American population.

Subject(s): Urban Affairs, Poverty, Housing

1185 **Anna Arnold Hedgeman**

The Trumpet Sounds: A Memoir of Negro Leadership
(New York, NY; Holt, Rinehart and Winston, 1964)

Summary: In *The Trumpet Sounds: A Memoir of Negro Leadership* author Anna Arnold Hedgeman recounts her experiences as an activist in the civil rights movement during the early twentieth century. Born in the North, Hedgeman would encounter overt racism only after moving south to Mississippi to teach at an all-black college there; her experiences would cause her to dedicate herself to the fight for racial equality. Her detailed description of the movement between the years 1922 and 1963 provides a wealth of information for students of modern black history.

Subject(s): Civil Rights Movement, Racism, American South

1186 **Tony Heilbut**

The Gospel Sound: Good News and Bad Times
(New York, NY; Simon and Schuster, 1971)

Summary: This book offers a portrait of the nation's gospel singers. Having experienced the poverty, discrimination, and violence of the Depression-era South, these singers are presented as expressing their religious faith in music. The author includes portraits of the major figures in gospel music, including Mahalia Jackson, Sallie Martin, Thomas A. Dorsey, and the Dixie Hummingbirds.

Subject(s): Music, American South, Racism

1187 **Willa Mae Hemmons**

Black Women in the New World Order: Social Justice and the African American Female
(Westport, CT; Praeger, 1996)

Summary: In *Black Women in the New World Order: Social Justice and the African American Female* lawyer and sociologist Willa Mae Hemmons analyzes the relationship between social institutions and black women. Studying changes in the political process, education, government funded social services, the family, health care, and the criminal justice system following the Cold War, Hemmons sees black women as increasingly disadvantaged due to both the sexism and racism that will intensify as ethnic competition increases and world resources diminish.

Subject(s): Economics, Women's Rights, Racism

1188 **David Henderson**

Jimi Hendrix: Voodoo Child of the Aquarian Age
(Garden City, NY; Doubleday, 1978)

Summary: *Jimi Hendrix: Voodoo Child of the Aquarian Age* is the story of psychedelic guitarist Hendrix, who taught himself to play guitar as a way of escaping the poverty of his childhood. Born in Seattle, Hendrix mixed blues, jazz, and his own uninhibited guitarwork to become what many still consider the best guitarist in rock history. Spending his peak years in England with his group, The Jimi Hendrix Experience, Hendrix died as the result of a drug and alcohol overdose in 1970.

Subject(s): Biography, Popular Culture, Musicians

1189 **David Henderson**

'Scuse Me While I Kiss the Sky: The Life of Jimi Hendrix
(New York, NY; Bantam Books, 1981)

Summary: *'Scuse Me While I Kiss the Sky: The Life of Jimi Hendrix* recounts the life of one of the most famous rock guitarists of the twentieth century. A legendary performer even while he was alive, Hendrix's death of a drug overdose raised him to cult-figure status. In this, his second Hendrix biography, author David Henderson takes readers from Hendrix's childhood in Seattle, Washington, to his stint in the army, to his life as a rock superstar and his death at age twenty-seven. Henderson augments his story with numerous photographs.

Subject(s): Biography, Popular Culture, Musicians

1190 **Frank Hercules**

American Society and Black Revolution
(New York, NY; Harcourt Brace Jovanovich, 1972)

Summary: In his *American Society and Black Revolution*, West Indian-born educator and author Frank Hercules provides an international perspective on the racism existing in U.S. society. His conclusion is that as an inherently racist society, America has sabotaged its own economic growth by systematically excluding blacks from the industrial process. He also critiques African American leaders, such as Booker T. Washington and W.E.B. Du Bois, concluding that change has been slow in coming due to the bourgeois habit employed by black leaders attempting to work within the status quo. Improvement in the African American lot, holds Hercules, will come from the ability to "rise above the past and transcend the present so as to command the future."

Subject(s): Minorities, Economics, Race Relations

1191 **Calvin C. Hernton**

Sex and Racism in America
(New York, NY; Grove Press, 1965)

Summary: *Sex and Racism in America* is a serious study of a somewhat closeted topic: the racist myths that have taken shape in the minds of both whites and blacks of both genders regarding the sexual mores, characteristics, or deviancies of members of other races. Written by Calvin C. Hernton, the volume was hailed for both its research and its restraint, and it is still considered a classic study in its field. The work was reissued in 1988.

Subject(s): Racism, Sexism, Prejudice

1192 **Richard J. Herrnstein**
Charles Murray, Co-author

The Bell Curve: Intelligence and Class Structure in American Life
(New York, NY; Free Press, 1994)

Summary: One of the most controversial books of its decade, *The Bell Curve: Intelligence and Class Structure in American Life* equates intelligence with race. Mustering data showing a positive correlation between the variation in scores between African Americans, Caucasians, and Asian Americans on standardized intelligence tests and the test-taker's race, authors Murray and Herrnstein contend that while "nurture" in the form of a rich social, economic, and intellectual environment can positively influence scores, "intelligence still seems to be strongly influenced by the genes of one's forebears." A continuation of the status quo, the authors fear, will result in a stratified society topped by a technological elite.

Subject(s): Economics, Sociology, Education

1193 **Neil Hickey**
Ed Edwin, Co-author

Adam Clayton Powell and the Politics of Race
(New York, NY; Fleet Pub. Corp., 1965)

Summary: In *Adam Clayton Powell and the Politics of Race*, authors Hickey and Edwin profile the politics of Powell (1908-1972), the headline-making African American congressman who represented Harlem during the civil rights era. A charismatic preacher in the Baptist faith, Powell rose to national prominence as a civil rights figurehead by orchestrating civil agitation and electoral politics. Among his moves as a Democratic legislator was the so-called "Powell Amendment" denying federal funds to projects or organizations that practiced discrimination. Appointed chairman of the House Committee on Education and Labor in 1960, Powell became an embarrassment to both parties, in part a result of his unwillingness to commit to his own party's platform.

Subject(s): Politics, Race Relations, Civil Rights Movement

1194 A. Leon Higginbotham, Jr.

Shades of Freedom: Racial Politics and Presumptions of the American Legal Process
(New York, NY; Oxford University Press, 1996)

Summary: In *Shades of Freedom: Racial Politics and Presumptions of the American Legal Process* noted African-American jurist and legal scholar A. Leon Higginbotham, Jr. examines the history of the interaction between the law and the oppression of blacks and other minorities in the United States. He contends that the judiciary, which was entrusted with dispensing justice, often dispensed the means through which blacks were relegated to inferior positions within society. Citing the *Dred Scott* case as well as *Plessy v. Ferguson,*, Higginbotham shows how the highest court in the land legitimized racial bias in America.

Subject(s): Racism, Segregation, Judicial System

1195 Anita Hill

Speaking Truth to Power
(New York, NY; Doubleday, 1997)

Summary: *Speaking Truth to Power* is law professor Anita Hill's account of the background to her 1991 revelations before the Senate hearings confirming the nomination of Clarence Thomas to the U.S. Supreme Court. She explains, in depth, her charges of sexual harassment toward Thomas and frames them within the larger issues of racial and sexual discrimination. Born in rural Oklahoma, Hill describes the work it took to gain the education needed to work in the legal field and the obstacles that were put in her path due to both her race and gender. One such obstacle was Thomas, Hill contends, and she devotes a substantial portion of her book to chronicling the discussions of sexual prowess, presentations of pornography, and repeated requests for dates that characterized her working relationship with Thomas at the Equal Employment Opportunity Commission.

Subject(s): Sexual Harassment, Sexism, Autobiography

1196 George H. Hill

Black Media in America: A Resource Guide
(Boston, MA; G.K. Hall, 1984)

Summary: George H. Hill's *Black Media in America: A Resource Guide* performs a service crucial to the African American legacy: recording publications by blacks. From *Freedom's Journal*--with its initial publication date of 1827, believed to be the first such publication--to newspapers and magazines printed in the late twentieth century, more than 3,500 African American publications have circulated within the United States. Some were motivated by an individual's need to protest, others as a business. Hill's book lists all documents preserved on microfilm or other format, allowing researchers and the general public to tap into one of the black community's most eloquent voices.

Subject(s): Journalism, Reference, African Americans

1197 Robert A. Hill, Editor

The Marcus Garvey and Universal Negro Improvement Association Papers. Volumes 1-2
(Berkeley, CA; University of California Press, 1983)

Summary: Edited by Robert A. Hill, *The Marcus Garvey and Universal Negro Improvement Association Papers* began an extended work in collecting and making available to scholars the letters, speeches, articles, and other documents relating to nineteenth century black nationalist activist Marcus Garvey (1887-1940) and his Universal Negro Improvement Association. Founded in the early 1900s, the UNIA was a foundation in the largest Pan-African mass movement of all time, encompassing both the United States and the Caribbean in its dedication to secure a homeland for all men and women of African descent. With the two initial volumes covering the years 1824-1919 and 1919-1920 respectively, the entire work was projected to encompass ten volumes and 30,000 documents.

Subject(s): Education, Black Nationalism, Migration

1198 Chester Himes

The Autobiography of Chester Himes: My Life of Absurdity
(Garden City, NY; Doubleday, 1976)

Summary: Concluding the autobiography that had been published four years earlier with the subtitle *The Quality of Hurt*, African American novelist Chester Himes (1909-1984) chronicled his later years in this work. Living in Paris as an expatriate, Himes finally found the personal and artistic freedom required to continue his writing. He would pen his most popular works while living abroad, including the popular *Cotton Comes to Harlem* and other detective novels that have Harlem, New York City, as their setting.

Subject(s): Autobiography, Writing, Europe

1199 Chester Himes

The Autobiography of Chester Himes: The Quality of Hurt
(Garden City, NY; Doubleday, 1972)

Summary: The first of two volumes of autobiography by African American expatriate novelist Chester Himes, this book recounts his early years. Raised in a respectable, middle-class southern family, Himes rebelled against the strictures of his parents and teachers, eventually retreating into lawlessness and finally, an eight-year prison sentence as a result of an armed robbery attempt. Himes would eventually move to France to escape the restrictive mores of U.S. readers. Among his more notable works is the detective novel *Cotton Comes to Harlem*, which is part of a series of books taking place in Harlem.

Subject(s): Autobiography, Writing, Rebellion

1200 Arnold R. Hirsch

Making the Second Ghetto: Race and Housing in Chicago, 1940-1960
(New York, NY; Cambridge University Press, 1983)

Summary: In *Making the Second Ghetto: Race and Housing in Chicago, 1940-1960* historian Arnold Hirsch argues that efforts to renew Chicago's urban landscape mid-century were channeled by racial strife into efforts at segregation. This racial strife was a result of the influx of southern blacks looking for factory work during the 1940s, creating a growing population sector that threatened to displace white residents whose population was also booming after World War II. Segregated housing was the result, aided and abetted by both the public and private sectors, with the city initiating action on many segregation concepts during the urban renewal of the 1950s.

Subject(s): Racism, Poverty, Working-Class Life

1201 Graham Russell Hodges, Editor

Black Itinerants of the Gospel: The Narratives of John Jea and George White
(Madison, WI; Madison House, 1993)

Summary: Reprinted in this work are the autobiographies of two nineteenth century African American preachers. White's narrative, titled "A Brief Account of the Life, Experience, Travels and Gospel Labours of George White," describes the resistance he encountered from white Methodist congregations and his eventual founding of a separate black congregation termed "African Methodist Episcopal Zion." Jea's autobiography ("The Life, History, and Unparalleled Sufferings of John Jea, the African Preacher") is a more picaresque narrative in which he relates his travels in the United States; like White, he also formed his own African American congregation.

Subject(s): Religion, Racism, Autobiography

1202 Joseph Winthrop Holley

You Can't Build a Chimney from the Top: The South through the Life of a Negro Educator
(New York, NY; William-Frederick Press, 1948)

Summary: In this autobiography, the author sees his life as the story of the education of blacks in the South from a time of no formal instruction to the period when the state recognized its responsibility to educate blacks at the university level. The author also presents his insights on suffrage, fair employment practice, sharecropping, lynching, and segregation.

Subject(s): American South, Education, Segregation

1203 bell hooks

Ain't I a Woman: Black Women and Feminism
(Boston, MA; South End Press, 1981)

Summary: Considered bell hooks' most controversial work, *Ain't I a Woman* reflects the author's continuing efforts to define the place of women of color within U.S. history and culture. Focusing on the historic experiences of black women, hooks--who writes under the name of her own great grandmother--places the struggles of African American women from the nineteenth century onward within the wider struggle of women to attain equality. While criticized for containing a number of historical inaccuracies in its portrayal of the lot of black woman during the last two hundred years, *Ain't I a Woman* is revered in feminist circles as perhaps the first book to place African American woman into a feminist movement that had its origins in the agenda of upper-class, educated, white women.

Subject(s): American History, Women's Rights, Poverty

1204 bell hooks
Cornel West, Co-author

Breaking Bread: Insurgent Black Intellectual Life
(Boston, MA; South End Press, 1991)

Summary: In *Breaking Bread: Insurgent Black Intellectual Life,* prominent intellectual theorists and educators bell hooks and Cornel West set forth their thoughts on racism, gender discrimination, and the cult of the individual so prevalent within contemporary culture. Included among their focus are such aspects of modern black culture as fashion, Rap music, and other art forms. The essays are informed by hooks strong political views and West's Marxist approach to history as well as the authors' optimistic view of the future of the African American people.

Subject(s): Popular Culture, Sexism, Cultural Conflict

1205 bell hooks

Feminist Theory: From Margin to Center
(Boston, MA; South End Press, 1984)

Summary: The twentieth-century feminist movement comes under assault in this work from bell hooks, who continues the critique begun in her controversial *Ain't I a Woman* in *Feminist Theory: From Margin to Center*. While hooks lauds the movement's white, college-educated, relatively affluent founders-- such women as Gloria Steinem and Betty Friedan--she also argues that true feminism should encompass women from all social, cultural, racial, and economic backgrounds. African American women should become aware of the unique perspective afforded by their "marginality" and use that perspective to call attention to U.S. society's racist and class-based culture, a hegemony that is also prevalent within the feminist movement.

hooks also encourages women of color to "envision and create a counter-hegemony."

Subject(s): Women's Rights, Class Conflict, Cultural Conflict

---

1206   bell hooks

Killing Rage: Ending Racism
(New York, NY; H. Holt and Co., 1995)

Summary: A collection of essays in which bell hooks vents her anger at white cultural arrogance, *Killing Rage: Ending Racisim* expresses the discontent felt, in particular, by some members of the African American middle class toward what they see as U.S. society's continued domination by an economic elite that is predominately white. But hooks also aims her anger toward that same black middle class, which she faults for their continued insistance upon laying the blame for their disadvantaged status at the feet of racism rather than class domination. In addition, while many affluent blacks have assimilated into the predominately white culture—embracing the American dream and chasing the "white" goals of wealth, status, and a nice big house in the suburbs--their increased leverage within society has been put to little use in ending racism. On the contrary, the American Dream has been pursued at the expense of the black community at large: the intellectual and financial resources possessed by blacks who have "made it" in a white world have been removed from inner city communities and those African Americans who still remain trapped in them.

Subject(s): Class Conflict, Racism, Women's Rights

1207   Gerald Horne

Black and Red: W.E.B. Du Bois and the Afro-American Response to the Cold War, 1944-1963
(Albany, NY; State University of New York Press, 1986)

Summary: In *Black and Red: W.E.B. Du Bois and the Afro-American Response to the Cold War, 1944-1963*, author Gerald Horne examines the role of blacks in the political climate of Cold War America following World War II. Focusing on civil rights leader W.E.B. Du Bois and Du Bois's adoption of Communism, Horne presents an in depth and intriguing analysis of the role played by African Americans such as Du Bois, and the reason why Du Bois and other black leaders, such as Benjamin Davis, gravitated toward a socialist political agenda. Information is also included about the U.S. Communist Party's active support of blacks' struggle for equality.

Subject(s): Communism, Civil Rights Movement

1208   Joseph C. Hough

Black Power and White Protestants: A Christian Response to the New Negro Pluralism
(New York, NY; Oxford University Press, 1968)

Summary: *Black Power and White Protestants: A Christian Response to the New Negro Pluralism* is a study of U.S. race relations since 1900. Increasingly militant demands for racial justice were made by blacks during the Black Power movement of the 1960s, and these demands were perceived as threatening by whites. Joseph C. Hough directs his remarks toward white Protestant churchgoers, counseling these men and women to recognize their responsibility as Christians, continue to "love" blacks, and turn the other cheek despite the rhetoric of rebellion that vilified all whites and dismissed them as bigots.

Subject(s): Racism, Christianity, Race Relations

1209   Gene L. Howard

Death at Cross Plains: An Alabama Reconstruction Tragedy
(University, AL; University of Alabama Press, 1984)

Summary: *Death at Cross Plains: An Alabama Reconstruction Tragedy* chronicles an event from the Reconstruction era that took place in Cross Plains, a town in the hills of the northeastern portion of Alabama, in July of 1870. In recounting the history of Canadian educator William Luke and his efforts to educate young freed African Americans before he was captured and lynched by a local outpost of the Ku Klux Klan, author Gene L. Howard brings to life the fear and courage that overshadowed many small black communities following the Civil War. In addition to showing the injustice of the Klan's actions, Howard also illustrates the insensitivity of many northern reformers in descending on a spiritually broken region without considering the resentment that their efforts would engender.

Subject(s): Reconstruction, Lynching, American South

1210   Victor B. Howard

Black Liberation in Kentucky: Emancipation and Freedom, 1862-1884
(Lexington, KY; University Press of Kentucky, 1983)

Summary: In *Black Liberation in Kentucky: Emancipation and Freedom, 1862-1884*, historian Victor B. Howard marshals a quantity of evidence to show that slaves living in Kentucky during the Civil War made repeated and consistent attempts to seek freedom by escaping to the Union outposts that dotted the borderlands near the Ohio River. While federal policy did not encourage troops to assist these runaways, many Union soldiers did, and male slaves often joined the Union army as a way of gaining their freedom. By the end of the war, maintains Howard, a shortage of slave labor existed in the state due to the mass exodus of slave families, paving the way for a system of paid labor by war's end.

Subject(s): American South, Civil War, Slavery

1211 Nathan Irvin Huggins

Black Odyssey: The Afro-American Ordeal in Slavery
(New York, NY; Pantheon, 1977)

Summary: A study of the actual experiences of men, women, and children brought forcibly to the new world to serve as slaves, *Black Odyssey: The Afro-American Ordeal in Slavery* by Nathan Irvin Huggins has been highly praised for its graceful portrayal of a sometimes horrific subject. In addition to recounting the physical treatment of slaves both in the terrifying "Middle Passage"--the slave route between Africa and the West Indies--and at their final home in the United States, Huggins also examines the psychological effects of enslavement and the breaking down of traditional family units.

Subject(s): Slavery, History, American South

1212 Langston Hughes
Roy DeCarava, Photographer

The Sweet Flypaper of Life
(New York, NY; Simon and Schuster, 1955)

Summary: Set against a text written by poet Langston Hughes, photographer Roy DeCarava documents life in Harlem through the eyes of Sister Mary Bradley, an elderly black woman. Praised for its accuracy in reflecting the day-to-day life in the northern section of Manhattan, the volume contains both humor and insight into African American life as observed through Bradley's eyes. Optimistic in her outlook, she sees her community with both a sense of its past and a sense of hope at its future, a future it will share with her many grandchildren.

Subject(s): City and Town Life, Family Life, Photography

1213 Gloria T. Hull, Editor
Barbara Smith, Co-editor
Patricia Bell Scott, Co-editor

All the Women Are White, All the Blacks Are Men, but Some of Us Are Brave: Black Women's Studies
(Old Westbury, NY; Feminist Press, 1982)

Summary: Feminists Barbara Smith, Patricia Bell Scott, and Gloria T. Hull's *All the Women Are White, All the Blacks Are Men, but Some of Us Are Brave* is a volume designed to establish the "frameworks in which Black Women's Studies can be most successfully taught" on the college level. Collecting essays and articles encompassing music, health care, literature, and social issues as they each relate to African American women, *All the Women Are White* demonstrated a convincing need for a Black Women's curriculum at a time when such a curriculum was still considered a novelty on college campuses. One of the first anthologies of its kind, this work would be used as a text in many of the same courses it helped to create.

Subject(s): Women's Rights, Education

1214 Florence Jackson

The Black Man in America
(New York, NY; F. Watts, 1970)

Summary: In her series of reference books collectively titled *The Black Man in America*, author Florence Jackson profiles the life and times of African Americans throughout various periods of their nation's history. Dividing her collection into segments containing various numbers of years--1619-1790; 1791-1861; 1861-1877; 1877-1905; 1905-1932; 1932-1954; and 1954-1979--Jackson focuses on both the social and political events that affected the lives of African Americans as well as people of note who lived during each time segment covered. The series was published from 1970-1979 and was formatted to serve as an attractive reference for younger readers.

Subject(s): History, Slavery, Biography

1215 George Jackson

Soledad Brother: The Prison Letters of George Jackson
(New York, NY; Coward-McCann, 1970)

Summary: Convicted of armed robbery and incarcerated at California's Soledad Prison, George Jackson became a national celebrity and a figurehead of the black struggle after his involvement in a raid on the Marin County Courthouse in 1970. In *Soledad Brother: The Prison Letters of George Jackson,* his correspondence with family members, activist Angela Davis, and others reflects the rage of centuries of blacks forced to live as slaves to white men and embodies much of the rhetoric of the black revolutionary of the 1970s. Self-educated, Jackson was admired for his ability to channel his extreme bitterness into a compelling statement reflecting the feelings of many blacks. Jackson was killed during an attempted prison break in August of 1971.

Subject(s): Prisoners and Prisons, Resistance Movements, Race Relations

1216 C.L.R. James
Scott McLemee, Editor

C.L.R. James on the "Negro Question"
(Jackson, MS; University Press of Mississippi, 1996)

Summary: *C.L.R. James on the "Negro Question"* collects selected essays, articles, and other writings of Trinidad-born writer, historian, journalist, Marxist, and intellectual C.L.R. James. Spanning a wide range of topics, including colonialism, race, international political issues, and Marxism, the book presents the writings of James in a context that allows readers to follow his developing philosophy regarding the plight of blacks living in a primarily white culture. Sources for each selection are also provided.

Subject(s): Race Relations, Colonialism, Politics

1217 **Charles Richard Johnson**
Patricia Smith, Co-author

Africans in America: America's Journey through Slavery
(New York, NY; Harcourt Brace, 1998)

Summary: An accompanying text to a Public Television broadcast of the same name, *Africans in America: America's Journey through Slavery* by novelist Charles Johnson and poet and former *Boston Globe* columnist Patricia Smith has been highly praised for both its prose and insight. The well-researched text, which is interspersed with a dozen short stories by Johnson, finds within the history of slavery in the United States a common humanity among Americans. The book includes illustrations composed of rare documents, letters, advertisements from slaveholders, slave-ship cargo diagrams, drawings, and paintings.

Subject(s): Slavery, History, Civil War

1218 **Michael P. Johnson**
James L. Roark, Co-author

Black Masters: A Free Family of Color in the Old South
(New York, NY; Norton, 1984)

Summary: A biography of nineteenth century black planter William Ellison, *Black Masters: A Free Family of Color in the Old South* details the life of a man who, after gaining his freedom in 1816, used his talent for building cotton gins to become the richest black man in South Carolina. A companion work to the authors' *No Chariot Let Down, Black Masters* details Ellison's economic success as owner of a plantation worked by thirty slaves, his purchase of family members from bondage, and his family's gradual decline at the turn of the century. Michael P. Johnson and James L. Roark were commended by many critics for their compelling portrayal of Ellison and for their painstaking efforts at researching the Ellison family through public and private documents to accurately reflect an era where the concept of race was vastly different from that of a century later.

Subject(s): Slavery, American South, Civil War

1219 **Michael P. Johnson,** Editor
James L. Roark, Co-editor

No Chariot Let Down: Charleston's Free People of Color on the Eve of the Civil War
(Chapel Hill, NC; University of North Carolina Press, 1984)

Summary: *No Chariot Let Down: Charleston's Free People of Color on the Eve of the Civil War* includes thirty-four letters written by members of the family of William Ellison between 1848 and 1864. Ellison, a planter living in Stateburg, was the richest free black in South Carolina; his relatives' correspondence reflects the same concerns as those of affluent white families up until the time when the Civil War caused freed blacks to fear the threats of Charleston officials to enslave all people of color not in possession of certain "proofs" of their freedom.

Subject(s): American South, Letters, Civil War

1220 **Samuel M. Johnson**

Often Back: The Tales of Harlem
(New York, NY; Vantage Press, 1971)

Summary: Samuel M. Johnson's 1971 work is an intellectual and cultural history of Harlem, the New York City neighborhood that became home to large numbers of African Americans in the twentieth century. In chapters such as "Religion," "Politics," "Police and Crime," and "Night and the Area," Johnson explores the ingredients that have made Harlem a center of African American achievement in this century.

Subject(s): Cultural Identity, Urban Affairs, City and Town Life

1221 **Jacqueline Jones**

Labor of Love, Labor of Sorrow: Black Women, Work, and the Family from Slavery to the Present
(New York, NY; Vintage Books, 1986)

Summary: In *Labor of Love, Labor of Sorrow: Black Women, Work, and the Family from Slavery to the Present* Jacqueline Jones examines the complex relationships between work, sex, race, and class in the lives of several centuries of African American women. While addressing several racial and sexist stereotypes in American life, the book also examines the changing role of African American women and the black family. Both roles have altered in the twentieth century due to rapidly changing social norms, as well as such factors as the decline of the U.S. city and the women's liberation movement of the 1970s.

Subject(s): Women's Rights, Slavery, Working-Class Life

Award(s): Brown Publication Prize, 1987

1222 **LeRoi Jones**
(Also known as Amiri Baraka)

Blues People: Negro Music in White America
(New York, NY; Morrow, 1963)

Summary: In *Blues People: Negro Music in White America* noted African American writer LeRoi Jones (later known as Amiri Baraka) examines the sociological aspects of the blues. He traces the African American experience through this uniquely American musical form, beginning with the music of African-born slaves who gave the blues its melancholy roots.

Subject(s): Music, Sociology, Racism

1223 Reginald L. Jones, Editor

Black Psychology

(New York, NY; Harper & Row, 1972)

Summary: Groundbreaking in its effort to unite in a single volume writings by new black psychologists of the time and other black social and behavioral scientists, this book begins by considering black psychology as a discipline. Subsequent chapters examine the psychological assessment of blacks, problems of personality and motivation in blacks, psychological perspectives on racism, and psychology in the community.

Subject(s): Psychology, Racism

1224 June Jordan

Affirmative Acts: Political Essays

(New York, NY; Doubleday, 1998)

Summary: Activist, poet, and educator June Jordan collects her most noted essays from the 1990s in *Affirmative Acts,* which like her earlier volume, *Civil Wars,* covers subjects like politics, race relations, women's health care, and the debate over affirmative action. Written without academic jargon, essays such as "We Are All Refugees," "My Mess and Ours," and "Notes on a Model of Resistance" showcase Jordan's eloquence, her skill as a writer, and her commitment to fight racial injustice.

Subject(s): Affirmative Action, Racism, Politics

1225 June Jordan

Civil Wars: Selected Essays, 1963-1980

(Boston, MA; Beacon Press, 1981)

Summary: The early works of poet, feminist, and civil rights activist June Jordan are collected in *Civil Wars: Selected Essays, 1963-1980.* Ranging in subject from U.S. politics, urban blight, and the growing feminist movement to the unequal treatment of blacks in American society and the rise of the Black Power movement, Jordan shows her humanistic approach to the civil unrest of the period and her skills as a writer. The work was reissued in 1996.

Subject(s): Women's Rights, Racism, Politics

1226 Winthrop D. Jordan

White over Black: American Attitudes toward the Negro, 1550-1812

(Chapel Hill, NC; University of North Carolina Press, 1968)

Summary: In *White over Black: American Attitudes toward the Negro, 1550-1812* author Winthrop D. Jordan examines the "origins, meaning and explanation of Negro debasement in America." In 612 pages, he details the mythos developed by whites in reaction to their fear of blacks, correlating such myths with still-existing stereotypes and with the unwillingness of many whites to welcome blacks as equals in American society.

While daunting because of its length, the work was highly praised for its objective, scholarly analysis of a vast body of historical detail.

Subject(s): Racism, Fear, History

1227 Gloria I. Joseph

Common Differences: Conflicts in Black and White Feminist Perspectives

(New York, NY; Anchor Press/Doubleday, 1981)

Summary: This work examines the differences that exist between black and white women in the women's movement in the United States. The authors consider sexism, racism, and classism as the major influences affecting women's attitudes. In addition, the book explores women's status through history and discusses the issues where differences occur: sexuality, men and marriage, mothers and daughters, media images, as well as the direction of the women's movement itself. The volume includes interviews with women from a variety of backgrounds.

Subject(s): Women's Rights, Racism, Sexism

1228 Charles W. Joyner

Down by the Riverside: A South Carolina Slave Community

(Urbana, IL; University of Illinois Press, 1984)

Summary: In his *Down by the Riverside: A South Carolina Slave Community,* historian Charles W. Joyner reconstructs life in the All Saints Parish of Georgia's low country. Noted for some of the richest land in the United States, the region boasted a ratio of nine blacks for every white due to the vast work force necessary to harvest rice from this fertile soil. Focusing on transplanted African slaves' efforts to develop a new life for themselves, Joyner examines local folklore and religious expression, language, and other cultural elements, as well as the treatment blacks received at the hands of masters and slave traders.

Subject(s): Slavery, Popular Culture, Family Relations

1229 Ernest Kaiser, Editor

A Freedomways Reader: Afro-America in the Seventies

(New York, NY; International Publishers, 1976)

Summary: *A Freedomways Reader: Afro-America in the Seventies* collects articles and essays published in the noted African American journal *Freedomways,* which was founded in 1961. Edited by *Freedomways* co-founder and associate editor Ernest Kaiser, the volume collects the thoughts and viewpoints of black writers and educators analyzing African American society, culture and politics within the context of the 1970s.

Subject(s): History, Journalism, Race Relations

1230 **Maulana Karenga**

Introduction to Black Studies

(Inglewood, CA; Kawaida Publications, 1982)

Summary: This work has received significant praise for filling the need for an interdisciplinary textbook for Black Studies. The author presents an Afrocentric analysis of authors and literature in several subject areas, which include black history, religion, social organization, politics, economics, creative production, and psychology.

Subject(s): Education, History, Religion

1231 **Maulana Karenga**

Kwanzaa: Origin, Concepts, Practice

(Inglewood, CA; Kawaida Publications, 1977)

Summary: In *Kwanzaa: Origin, Concepts, Practice* author Maulana Karenga explains the history of the African American holiday of Kwanzaa, which is celebrated by almost 20 million people each December. The rituals of the holiday are clearly presented including the lighting of seven candles--one each night--that represent each of the seven Kwanzaa principles. Kwanzaa symbols are reviewed, and the origin, application, and celebration of the Seven Principles of the holiday are discussed in their historic context.

Subject(s): Holidays, Africa, Family Life

1232 **Michael B. Katz**

The Undeserving Poor: From the War on Poverty to the War on Welfare

(New York, NY; Pantheon, 1989)

Summary: In *The Undeserving Poor: From the War on Poverty to the War on Welfare* historian Michael B. Katz examines the preconceptions, beliefs, and ideals that have molded the welfare system since the "War on Poverty" began during the 1960s. This "War on Poverty" has become a "War on Welfare," according to Katz, who argues that the poverty debate has become increasingly self-defeating with the rise of conservatism. He suggests a constructive solution to the problems facing America's poor.

Subject(s): Poverty, Urban Affairs, Racism

1233 **Shlomo Katz,** Editor

Negro and Jew: An Encounter in America

(New York, NY; Macmillan, 1967)

Summary: Based on a symposium sponsored by the Jewish journal *Midstream*, *Negro and Jew: An Encounter in America* collects articles that attempt to determine the source of black anti-Semitism. Presenting a predominately Jewish perspective on the debate, the work presents a wide variety of opinions, among which are the belief that blacks equate Jewish men and women with landlords and businessmen who attempt to take advantage of them, or that African American religion is drawn from an earlier, less tolerant Christian base than white Christianity.

Subject(s): Religion, Anti-Semitism, Race Relations

1234 **William Loren Katz**

Teachers' Guide to American Negro History

(Chicago, IL; Quadrangle Books, 1968)

Summary: One of the first manuals designed to aid teachers in broadening their standard curriculum to include African Americans, William Loren Katz's *Teachers' Guide to American Negro History* provides factual information on crucial time periods in U.S. history. From the African slaves, whose activities sparked the most notice during the colonial years to black cowboys aiding the move westward, to heroism shown by African Americans such as the members of the Massachusetts 52nd Regiment, who defended the nation during the Civil War, Katz organizes his material topically, and suggests ways of integrating it into the standard history curriculum.

Subject(s): History, American Revolution, Civil War

1235 **David M. Katzman**

Before the Ghetto: Black Detroit in the Nineteenth Century

(Urbana, IL; University of Illinois Press, 1973)

Summary: *Before the Ghetto: Black Detroit in the Nineteenth Century* was sociologist David M. Katzman's dissertation at the University of Michigan in 1969. In it he argues that despite the abolition of slavery in the state of Michigan by 1837, existing and new laws would continue to place blacks in an inferior social and economic position relative to whites. Portraying race relations within nineteenth century Detroit as resembling a caste system, Katzman presents factual evidence showing blacks' occupations, lifestyle habits, and religious and political preferences, which he contends reflect divisions among the city's African American population that were more oppressive than those between black and white.

Subject(s): Race Relations, Urban Affairs, City and Town Life

1236 **Ira Katznelson**

Black Men, White Cities: Race, Politics, and Migration in the United States, 1900-30, and Britain, 1948-68

(London, England; Oxford University Press, 1973)

Summary: This book considers the incorporation of black migrants into the political life of the northern United States and Britain during formative periods of interracial contact in these nations. Focusing on the "immigrant-colonial amalgam," the author explores similar race relation patterns between the nations. The volume examines the cities of New York, Chicago, and Nottingham.

Subject(s): Migrant Labor, Colonialism, Race Relations

1237 Charles Keil

Urban Blues
(Chicago, IL; University of Chicago Press, 1966)

Summary: *Urban Blues* had its source in an M.A. thesis by Charles Keil, whose interest in the unique sounds of jazz music led him to a study of black culture in the 1960s. Profiling African American trends in music, art, literature, and politics, the volume shows blacks expressing their creativity in ways distinct from those of Western-influenced "white" Americans. *Urban Blues* includes information on noted black men and women, from musician John Coltrane to civil rights leader Malcolm X, and illustrates their unique approach to art and life. The book, which has been translated into Japanese, was revised in 1992.

Subject(s): Popular Culture, Artists and Art, Cultural Conflict

1238 Charles Flint Kellogg

NAACP: A History of the National Association for the Advancement of Colored People. Volume 1
(Baltimore, MD; Johns Hopkins Press, 1967)

Summary: In this book, author Charles Flint Kellogg provides a history of an organization that, through negotiation, litigation, and legislation, has become one of the strongest defenders of civil rights and equality between the races. Founded by W.E.B. Du Bois and several other influential blacks and whites between 1909 and 1911, the organization has, among other things, focused its attention on attaining voting rights for blacks in 1915; lobbying for an anti-lynching bill in 1922; addressing continual housing and transportation concerns; and challenging the segregation of public schools.

Subject(s): Justice System, Civil Rights Movement

1239 George D. Kelsey

Racism and the Christian Understanding of Man
(New York, NY; Scribner, 1965)

Summary: In *Racism and the Christian Understanding of Man* theologian George D. Kelsey develops the unique argument that racism is a form of idolatry in which men deify their own racial group. Addressing his book to clergyman attempting to cope with churchgoing whites who openly express their racist sentiments, Kelsey provides suggested ways in which those calling themselves Christians can be made to see the contradiction between their attitude and the teachings of Jesus. His arguments are girded by the writings of such notable scholars and theologians as Karl Barth, Martin Buber, Ruth Benedict, and Gunnar Myrdal.

Subject(s): Racism, Religion, Intolerance

1240 John Oliver Killens

Black Man's Burden
(New York, NY; Trident Press, 1965)

Summary: A collection of political essays by civil rights activist and writer John Oliver Killens, *Black Man's Burden* covers subjects that include white paternalism, labor unions, passive resistance, religion, black nationalism, Africa, and the right of self-defense. Killens argues that passive acceptance of racial oppression will only encourage the proliferation of race-based violence, and he concludes that the only way for African Americans to end the cycle of racial violence will be to answer violence with violence.

Subject(s): Race Relations, Resistance Movements, Violence

1241 Martin Luther King, Jr.

Strength to Love
(New York, NY; Harper & Row, 1963)

Summary: *Strength to Love* is one of several collections of sermons published by noted civil rights leader Martin Luther King, Jr. Known for his Christian beliefs and his pacifism, King was an ordained Baptist minister who served as pastor of Montgomery, Alabama's Dexter Avenue Baptist Church, from 1954 until 1960, when he joined his father at Atlanta's Ebenezer Baptist Church. His sermons, which have been collected in many anthologies, reflect King's adherence to the nonviolent philosophy of Mahatma Gandhi, who helped bring an end British rule in India. Imbued with social, as well as religious concerns, King's texts show him as a talented and compelling orator.

Subject(s): Religion, Civil Rights Movement, Racism

1242 Martin Luther King, Jr.

Stride toward Freedom: The Montgomery Story
(New York, NY; Harper, 1958)

Summary: *Stride toward Freedom: The Montgomery Story* recounts civil rights leader Martin Luther King, Jr.'s first public attempt to change society through nonviolent means. Leading a local protest against the arrest of African American Rosa Parks after her refusal to relinquish her seat on a Montgomery, Alabama, bus to a white man, King organized a bus boycott that lasted more than a year. Despite threatening phone calls, arrest, and the bombing of his home, King won; the U.S. Supreme Court declared Montgomery's bus segregation laws illegal in late 1956. *Stride toward Freedom* was hailed as an important documentary of the civil rights movement, and also reflects the personal beliefs of one of the greatest individuals of the twentieth century.

Subject(s): Religion, Civil Rights Movement, Racism

Award(s): Anisfield-Wolf Award, 1958

1243 Martin Luther King, Jr.

Where Do We Go from Here: Chaos or Community?
(New York, NY; Harper & Row, 1967)

Summary: In this book, pacifist civil rights leader Martin Luther King, Jr. sought to address the growing "black power" movement that he believed would destroy his dream of nonviolent desegregation. Although King approved of black power leaders' efforts to foster pride and community relations among African Americans, he was concerned that the slogan, coined by Stokely Carmichael, caused white Americans to fear black efforts at integration. He also railed against the movement's support of violence as a means to that integration, as well as its nihilism and pessimism and support of racial separatism.

Subject(s): Violence, Civil Rights Movement, Racism

1244 Martin Luther King, Jr.

Why We Can't Wait
(New York, NY; Harper & Row, 1964)

Summary: This work documents civil rights leader Martin Luther King, Jr.'s desegregation of Birmingham, Alabama, which he termed "the most segregated city in America." Training followers in the techniques of nonviolent protest, King prepared demonstrators to react to the "harsh language and physical abuse of the police and self-appointed guardians of the law" by teaching them "to resist without bitterness; to be cursed and not reply; to be beaten and not hit back." The protest peaked on May 3, 1963, as protestors--many of them children and teens--were repelled by fire hoses and police dogs. Horrified, President John F. Kennedy took action that resulted in the desegregation of lunch counters, restrooms, and drinking fountains throughout the city. *Why We Can't Wait* includes the "Letter from Birmingham Jail," which King wrote in the cell he occupied during the protest.

Subject(s): American South, Civil Rights Movement, Racism

1245 Mel King

Chain of Change: Struggles for Black Community Development
(Boston, MA; South End Press, 1981)

Summary: In *Chain of Change,* Mel King considers changes and developments in the black community of Boston from the 1950s through the 1970s. He explores issues of economic development, housing, politics, and community-controlled education. Other topics addressed include desegregation, racism in the unions, and urban gentrification. The volume concludes with a community development strategy for the 1980s.

Subject(s): City and Town Life, Housing, Education

1246 Daisuke Kitagawa

The Pastor and the Race Issue
(New York, NY; Seabury Press, 1965)

Summary: Christian ministry within a social and cultural context of racial tensions is the central issue of Kitagawa's 1965 book. Addressed to pastors, the book examines the historical background of the race issue. In addition to an exploration of preaching on the race issue, the author looks at the theology of race. The book also includes sections on pastoral counseling and Christian action on the race issue.

Subject(s): Racism, Religion, Christianity

1247 Richard Kluger

Simple Justice: The History of Brown v. Board of Education and Black America's Struggle for Equality
(New York, NY; Knopf, 1976)

Summary: Richard Kluger's well-researched study of African Americans and the American educational system focuses on the historic High Court decision that ended separate but equal education in the United States. Kluger provides readers with an historic backdrop of U.S. race relations before explaining the complex process by which five separate court cases were joined and accepted for judgement by the Supreme Court. Finally, Kluger describes the way the Court, under a great deal of political pressure, reached the decision that would change education in the United States.

Subject(s): Judicial System, Racism, Education

1248 Thomas Kochman

Black and White Styles in Conflict
(Chicago, IL; University of Chicago Press, 1981)

Summary: In Thomas Kochman's *Black and White Styles in Conflict,* communication styles between blacks and whites are analyzed with regard to their potential in creating misunderstanding. Among the areas discussed in Kochman's book are the development of African American culture, colloquialisms, the way individuals of different genders relate to each other through speech, and the use of spoken language in educational situations. Among the differences cited within the work is the white male's emotional reserve in social settings, as opposed to African American men who evidence a more boastful, animated, often sexually explicit persona.

Subject(s): Sociology, Communication, Popular Culture

1249 Thomas Kochman, Editor

Rappin' and Stylin' Out: Communication in Urban Black America
(Urbana, IL; University of Illinois Press, 1972)

Summary: In *Rappin' and Stylin' Out: Communication in Urban Black America*, Thomas Kochman collects essays focusing on African American communications. Through his selections, Kochman attempts to illustrate the cultural and social factors that affect communications between blacks, and also the communication across races. The speech patterns of urban blacks, including slang and jargon, and other elements of communication are discussed in a volume that is both anthropological and activist in its approach.

Subject(s): Popular Culture, Language, Media

1250 Rajni Kothari

Footsteps into the Future: Diagnosis of the Present World and a Design for an Alternative

(New Delhi, India; Orient Longman, 1974)

Summary: In his 1974 study, Rajni Kothari analyzes the contemporary international geo-political scene and devises a plan to change it for the better. Specifically, Kothari argues that a strategy must be developed to assist Third World nations in their attempts to overcome poverty and to reduce violence throughout the world. A prominent Indian political scientist, Kothari provides both an intellectual framework for a potential new international design and specific steps that members of the world community must take to achieve that new design.

Subject(s): Poverty, Violence, Government

1251 Jonathan Kozol

Amazing Grace: The Lives of Children and the Conscience of a Nation

(New York, NY; Crown, 1995)

Summary: As he has in such previous books as *Death at an Early Age*, Jonathan Kozol published *Amazing Grace: The Lives of Children and the Conscience of a Nation* to alert the nation to the problems facing Americans living below the poverty line. The book follows a group of children from the South Bronx, New York, one of America's biggest racially segregated communities of poor people. Kozol spent a year in the South Bronx, learning about the children, their friends and families, their day-to-day activities, their dreams, and their beliefs. He also searches for the means by which they retain their childlike innocence in the face of such violence and adversity.

Subject(s): Urban Affairs, Poverty, Education

1252 Jonathan Kozol

Death at an Early Age: The Destruction of the Hearts and Minds of Negro Children in the Boston Public Schools

(Boston, MA; Houghton Mifflin, 1967)

Summary: *Death at an Early Age: The Destruction of the Hearts and Minds of Negro Children in the Boston Public Schools* is an account of the months Jonathan Kozol spent teaching in Boston's ghetto schools. Kozol wrote the book after he was fired from his teaching position, ostensibly for reading his fourth-grade class a poem by black poet Langston Hughes that was not on the approved curriculum material list. Written before Boston began integrating its schools, the book addresses the concerns raised in contemporary debates on desegregation. Kozol focuses in particular on teaching methods he was instructed to use that reinforced a separate and unequal education. Kozol has gone on to write several more books focusing on the conditions of the poor in America.

Subject(s): Urban Affairs, Poverty, Education

Award(s): National Book Award: Nonfiction, 1967

1253 Barry Krisberg

Crime and Privilege: Toward a New Criminology

(Englewood Cliffs, NJ; Prentice-Hall, 1975)

Summary: In this work, the author argues that traditional methods of punishment and correction in the United States actually promote the suppression of individuals who threaten the status quo. These individuals are mainly minorities. In effect, the justice system has created a social climate that favors the privileged. The author presents a case for reform based on a new criminology that responds to the expectations of the privileged as well as the needs of the oppressed.

Subject(s): Crime and Criminals, Minorities

1254 Jawanza Kunjufu

Countering the Conspiracy to Destroy Black Boys

(Chicago, IL; Afro-Am Pub. Co., 1983)

Summary: In his multi-volume *Countering the Conspiracy to Destroy Black Boys* Jawanza Kunjufu addresses the growing dilemma facing young boys growing up in single-parent families headed by either a mother or grandmother. They are usually raised in impoverished circumstances without a positive male role model to guide them. Citing the institutional systems and social constraints that perpetuate the cycle of poverty and lead to dropping out of school and opting for a life on the streets, Kunjufu calls for a renewed effort by black fathers to care for their children. He appeals to parents and teachers to instill the self-discipline that leads to heightened self-esteem. Each volume of the work includes a reference and index.

Subject(s): Education, Fathers and Sons, Self-Reliance

1255 Jawanza Kunjufu

Developing Positive Self-Images and Discipline in Black Children

(Chicago, IL; African World Press, 1984)

Summary: Jawanza Kunjufu's *Developing Positive Self-Images and Discipline in Black Children* is intended as a guide for parents, teachers, and others working with African American youth. In his discussion of the relationship between self-esteem and success in academics, personal relationships, and public ventures such as jobs and community involvement, Kunjufu emphasizes the need for early and continued structure in both school and home life as the key to a child's success.

Subject(s): Education, Self-Discipline, Self-Reliance

1256 Jawanza Kunjufu

Motivating and Preparing Black Youth for Success

(Chicago, IL; African Images, 1986)

Summary: Jawanza Kunjufu considers issues such as the high school dropout rate in *Motivating and Preparing Black Youth for Success*. Kunjufu is the author of a number of books designed to guide teachers, parents, and other adults who work with black youth in raising self-disciplined, educated, and well-adjusted young men despite the poverty and other problems that plague many African American families. The author examines the reasons for the steady decrease in a black child's motivation for learning as his or her age increases, and he questions whether schools are committed to educating young people or are merely engaged in vocational training.

Subject(s): Education, Self-Discipline, Single Parent Families

1257 Kenneth L. Kusmer

A Ghetto Takes Shape: Black Cleveland, 1870-1930

(Urbana, IL; University of Illinois Press, 1976)

Summary: *A Ghetto Takes Shape: Black Cleveland, 1870-1930* chronicles the history of Cleveland, Ohio, within the context of the migration of southern blacks to northern cities at the turn of the twentieth century. Including biographies of several of the city's notable African American residents, author Kenneth L. Kusmer also offers a brief history of the city and a discussion of Garveyism and other social movements affecting blacks. With its wealth of maps, census data, and other information, Kusmer's work presents a compelling portrait of the genesis and growth of a black urban ghetto.

Subject(s): Urban Affairs, Migration, Race Relations

1258 Elizabeth Kytle

Willie Mae

(New York, NY; Knopf, 1958)

Summary: The author's first book tells the story of a black woman's struggle in Georgia during the early part of the twentieth century. The book was primarily based on interviews with a woman whom Kytle knew. The author added some invention to this woman's experiences for literary reasons. *Willie Mae* explores the significance of being black and female in the American South.

Subject(s): American South, Women, Racism

Award(s): Martha King Cooper Ohioana Library Association: Ohioana Award, 1958

1259 William Labov

Language in the Inner City: Studies in the Black English Vernacular

(Philadelphia, PA; University of Pennsylvania Press, 1972)

Summary: *Language in the Inner City: Studies in the Black English Vernacular* is based on linguistic and sociological fieldwork undertaken beginning in 1965 in New York's Harlem area. William Labov includes nine topics for analysis, among them the structure of black vernacular compared to other types of black English; language as it is tolerated and taught in urban schools; and a sociological portrait of the modern U.S. city. Highly technical, the work nonetheless is useful for educators willing to perceive black English as a dialect rather than a biological defect.

Subject(s): Language, Children, Education

1260 Joyce A. Ladner, Editor

The Death of White Sociology

(New York, NY; Random House, 1973)

Summary: A collection of essays, *The Death of White Sociology* is a condemnation of the manner in which sociologists have approached and represented the African American community. Criticized by some observers for being pro-black rather than balanced in their approach, contributing essayists agree overwhelmingly that objective studies free of embedded prejudice are not possible. Instead, in order to be valid, blacks must oversee such sociological studies themselves, thereby eliminating the basic assumption underlying "white" studies: that blacks are somehow defective socially because of their race.

Subject(s): Sociology, Race Relations, City and Town Life

1261 Hope Landrine
Elizabeth A. Klonoff, Co-author

African American Acculturation: Deconstructing Race and Reviving Culture

(Thousand Oaks, CA; Sage Publications, 1996)

Summary: In *African American Acculturation: Deconstructing Race and Reviving Culture* clinical psychologists and co-authors Hope Landrine and Elizabeth A. Klonoff argue that African Americans and European Americans are actually ethnic groups, not races, making the differences between white and black Americans conflicts of culture. In an effort to deconstruct the concept of "race" as a point of social conflict, they theorize a process of African American acculturation as a way of understanding the differences between blacks and the country's dominant "white" culture. Appendices are included that address the specific needs of psychologists by providing survey data and other clinical information.

Subject(s): Cultural Conflict, Racism, Psychology

1262 Arnold Laubich, Compiler
Ray Spencer, Compiler

Art Tatum: A Guide to His Recorded Music

(Metuchen, NJ; Scarecrow Press, 1982)

Summary: *Art Tatum: A Guide to His Recorded Music* provides a discography and other valuable information regarding Art Tatum (1909-1956), one of the most prominent pianists of the swing era. In their volume, authors Laubich and Spencer include not only Tatum's major label recordings with producer Norman Granz and the Columbia label, among others, but also his live performances and after-hours tapes. Blind in one eye, Tatum was a musical prodigy whose complex, almost florid style would greatly influence the bop generation that followed him.

Subject(s): Reference, Music, Jazz

1263 Martha F. Lee

The Nation of Islam: An American Millenarian Movement

(Lewiston, NY; E. Mellen Press, 1988)

Summary: *The Nation of Islam: An American Millenarian Movement* chronicles the history of the Nation of Islam, from its roots as a separatist organization to its present-day incarnation as the Black Muslims. Founded in 1930 by W.D. Fard and Elijah Muhammad, the organization based its ideology on the supposition that African Americans are the descendants of an ancient Muslim tribe. In its first decades, its leaders advocated the adoption of a Muslim name and pressed for a separate black nation as reparation for the enslavement of past generations. Later organization leaders, including Malcolm X, have gradually moderated the group's position and now embrace a quasi-traditional Muslim ideology.

Subject(s): Muslims, Religion, Black Nationalism

1264 Julius Lester

All Is Well

(New York, NY; Morrow, 1976)

Summary: Noted children's author Julius Lester tells his story in *All Is Well.* Born in 1939 and raised in Missouri as the son of a Methodist minister, Lester turned his back on his father's faith as a young man and embraced the civil rights movement. He based many of his works for children on African American folk tales and other original documents, creating stories that educated young black readers about their heritage and provided young people with a grounding in what Lester referred to as the "usable past" to serve as both a moral and political compass. Searching for spiritual guidance in his later years, Lester himself would embrace Judaism in 1983.

Subject(s): Autobiography, Folklore, Literature

1265 Ellen Levine

Freedom's Children: Young Civil Rights Activists Tell Their Own Stories

(New York, NY; Putnam, 1993)

Summary: *Freedom's Children: Young Civil Rights Activists Tell Their Own Stories* collects the memoirs of thirty black men and women who were growing up amid the racial unrest of the mid-twentieth century. Contributors describe the consequences involved in their choice to fight against segregationist Jim Crow laws in the South, consequences that included the threat of bodily harm, harassment, arrest, and even death. The entries are based on interviews and are accompanied by black-and-white photographs that allow young readers to identify with the men and women depicted.

Subject(s): Civil Rights Movement, Autobiography, Adolescence

1266 Lawrence W. Levine

Black Culture and Black Consciousness: Afro-American Folk Thought from Slavery to Freedom

(New York, NY; Oxford University Press, 1977)

Summary: In *Black Culture and Black Consciousness: Afro-American Folk Thought from Slavery to Freedom* author Lawrence W. Levine focuses on the long tradition of the spoken word within African American culture. In a well-researched, scholarly presentation, Levine examines both sacred and secular music performed by blacks, as well as folktales, forms of humor, and legends. He argues that this analysis of culture demonstrates the development of value systems for eighteenth and nineteenth century African Americans.

Subject(s): Slavery, Music, American History

1267 Florence Hamlish Levinsohn, Editor
Benjamin Drake Wright, Co-editor

School Desegregation: Shadow and Substance

(Chicago, IL; University of Chicago Press, 1976)

Summary: A collection of papers originally published in an issue of *School Review, School Desegregation: Shadow and Substance* provides an overview of the state of school desegregation since it was first implemented by law in 1954. Including perspectives by educators, policy makers, and social scientists, the diverse essays reevaluate the benefits of desegregation and review the different policies put into place around the nation as a way to address the imbalance in America's public schools. Among the contributors are Alvin Poussaint, Lillian Rubin, Charles Bullock, and Harry Gottlieb.

Subject(s): Education, Race Relations, Sociology

1268 Eugene Donald Levy

James Weldon Johnson: Black Leader, Black Voice

(Chicago, IL; University of Chicago Press, 1973)

Summary: In *James Weldon Johnson: Black Leader, Black Voice* Eugene Levy presents the life story of the famous civil rights leader. A co-founder--with W.E.B. Du Bois, Mary White Ovington, and over forty others--of the National Association for the Advancement of Colored People (NAACP), Johnson helped advance the cause of racial equality and human rights through not only his activism but also in his songs, poems, speeches, and books such as *Black Manhattan*. Johnson published his autobiography, *Along This Way*, in 1933.

Subject(s): Biography, Civil Rights Movement, Writing

1269 David L. Lewis

King: A Critical Biography

(New York, NY; Praeger, 1970)

Summary: In his biography of Martin Luther King, Jr., David L. Lewis focuses on the civil rights leader's intellectual and public life. Careful not to ignore King's failings, Lewis maintains that while his personal courage was immense, King's success was in part a result of the unique combination of circumstances in which he found himself. For example, King's pacifism was an outgrowth of the constant exhortations of friend Bayard Rustin rather than a product of King's own deep-seated beliefs. Lewis's work was the first major biography to be written about King, and the author reveals an objective stance and a familiarity with the community in which King lived during his formative years.

Subject(s): Biography, Civil Rights Movement, Race Relations

1270 David L Lewis

When Harlem Was in Vogue

(New York, NY; Knopf, 1981)

Summary: In *When Harlem Was in Vogue*, Daniel Levering Lewis draws readers back to the time of the Harlem Renaissance, a flowering of African American artistic expression, experimentation, and collaboration that began at the close of World War I and lasted until the onset of the Depression. Focusing on the contributions of such artists as Langston Hughes, Zora Neale Hurston, and Paul Robeson to the development of not only black culture but U.S. culture as a whole, Lewis brings extensive research to his study of this fleeting moment in which black artistic expression was validated by white culture.

Subject(s): City and Town Life, Popular Culture, Harlem Renaissance

1271 John Lewis
Michael D'Orso, Co-author

Walking with the Wind: A Memoir of the Movement

(New York, NY; Simon & Schuster, 1998)

Summary: John Lewis, now a Georgia congressman, left the cotton farm on which he was raised to join the fight for black civil rights. In *Walking with the Wind* he recounts his story, imbued with the passionate advocacy of nonviolence that made him one of the movement's guiding figures. After leading the sit-ins in Nashville, he participated in 1961's Freedom Rides, was arrested, and after his release joined Martin Luther King, Jr.'s March on Washington in 1963. His speech there led to his election as national chairman of the Student Nonviolent Coordinating Committee (SNCC), although after 1965's "Bloody Sunday"--where state troopers attacked and beat Lewis and other protesters in Selma, Alabama--he turned over power of the SNCC to more militant activists. In 1986 he ran a successful campaign against former SNCC colleague Julian Bond, which earned him a congressional post.

Subject(s): Civil Rights Movement, Race Relations, American South

1272 C. Eric Lincoln

The Black Muslims in America

(Boston, MA; Beacon Press, 1961)

Summary: C. Eric Lincoln's *The Black Muslims in America* details the formation and development of the Black Muslim movement in the United States through its wide-ranging expressions in America during the second half of the twentieth century. Focusing especially on Louis Farrakhan's movement as the true successor to the original Nation of Islam founded by Elijah Muhammad, the book is considered a classic of sociological inquiry. *The Black Muslims in America* was based on Lincoln's Ph.D. thesis at Boston University; it was revised in 1982.

Subject(s): Sociology, Islam, Religion

1273 C. Eric Lincoln, Editor

Is Anybody Listening to Black America?

(New York, NY; Seabury Press, 1968)

Summary: This book looks at the perceptions that Americans have of themselves and their place in society in regards to race. The volume collects excerpts from a variety of sources to explore the racial crisis. The first part of the work considers the views of black leaders. Subsequent sections present the opinions of ordinary black Americans and responses by white Americans.

Subject(s): Race Relations, Identity

1274 George Lipsitz

Rainbow at Midnight: Labor and Culture in the 1940s

(Urbana, IL; University of Illinois Press, 1994)

Summary: In *Rainbow at Midnight: Labor and Culture in the 1940s,* author George Lipsitz explores the strike wave that rocked U.S. industry in the years following World War II. Detailing the labor unrest and its fallout from the perspective of assembly line workers and their communities, the book takes its title from a country and western song from the period that echoes workers' beliefs in a better life in an egalitarian society. Lipsitz has noted that his work "concerns the way in which ordinary people make history and are made by it. The history of public institutions--governments, economic systems, and armies--makes most sense when viewed in the light of the ways in which it intersects the hopes and aspirations of ordinary people." The book is a revision of Lipsitz' 1981 volume, *Class and Culture in Cold War America: A Rainbow at Midnight.*

Subject(s): Working-Class Life, Popular Culture, World War II

1275 Leon F. Litwack

Been in the Storm So Long: The Aftermath of Slavery

(New York, NY; Knopf, 1979)

Summary: Leon F. Litwack's *Been in the Storm So Long* examines the aftereffects of the abolition of slavery in the American South. Focusing on the experiences of black men and women in their transition from slavery to freedom, Litwack highlights their many efforts to build churches, schools, and communities in an attempt to gain a legitimate seat at the table in U.S. society and politics. Source material includes newspapers, letters, and other public archives, as well as the numerous slave narratives collected via the Federal Writers' Project during the 1930s. In these narratives, former slaves express their feelings upon gaining their freedom, and they tell of the hardships encountered during the Reconstruction period that followed the end of the Civil War.

Subject(s): Slavery, History, Reconstruction

Award(s): Pulitzer Prize: History, 1980

1276 Leon F. Litwack

North of Slavery: The Negro in the Free States, 1790-1860

(Chicago, IL; University of Chicago Press, 1961)

Summary: *North of Slavery: The Negro in the Free States, 1790-1860* is considered to be a groundbreaking work of scholarship in author Leon F. Litwack's attempt to uncover the true meaning of race in the northern U.S. prior to the Civil War. Bucking the prevailing belief in a liberal north, Litwack reveals segregation, legal obstacles to equality, and accepted cultural practices that kept free blacks an underclass. Litwack includes numerous contemporary accounts to bolster his argument, and his analysis has held up well under academic scrutiny.

Subject(s): Slavery, History, Civil War

1277 Rayford W. Logan, Editor

W.E.B. Du Bois: A Profile

(New York, NY; Hill and Wang, 1971)

Summary: In *W.E.B. Du Bois: A Profile,* Rayford W. Logan recounts the life of the civil rights pioneer who was one of the primary founders of the National Association for the Advancement of Colored People in 1909. Raised in Massachusetts and educated at Harvard University, Du Bois was a sociologist who dedicated his life to documenting the oppression of blacks and attempting to aid in their efforts to attain equality. Well-illustrated, Logan's biography was useful in introducing Du Bois's contributions to social justice to a new generation of Americans.

Subject(s): Biography, Civil Rights Movement, Affirmative Action

1278 Louis E. Lomax

The Negro Revolt

(New York, NY; Harper, 1962)

Summary: Beginning with a brief history of race relations, Louis E. Lomax's *The Negro Revolt* presents in a clear, easy-to-follow format the transformation of black attitudes from the days before slavery to the increasing militancy expressed in the wake of the Montgomery, Alabama, bus boycotts of the mid-1950s. Including discussions of the formation of the NAACP, the implementation of sit-ins and the Freedom Rides, and the evolution of such groups as the Black Muslims, the volume also includes a great deal of behind-the-scenes information gleaned from Lomax's work as a journalist.

Subject(s): Civil Rights Movement, History, Race Relations

1279 Charles H. Long

Significations: Signs, Symbols, and Images in the Interpretation of Religion

(Philadelphia, PA; Fortress Press, 1986)

Summary: In the essay collection *Significations: Signs, Symbols, and Images in the Interpretation of Religion* Charles H. Long draws on the connection between the "other" as a sacred being in theological discussions and the "other" referenced by intellectuals in discussing oppressed people, particularly women and non-whites. Beginning with a history of academic religious studies, Long examines several black and other ethnic religions before outlining his central thesis. According to Long, the metaphysical representation of the "other" in religious studies allows for the best understanding of the worldly, oppressed "other." Written from a theoretical viewpoint and full of complex arguments, Long's essays are not designed for the general reader.

Subject(s): Religion, Academia

1280 Audre Lorde

Sister Outsider: Essays and Speeches
(Trumansburg, NY; Crossing Press, 1984)

Summary: Activist and poet Audre Lorde assembled the first of two collections of her essays and speeches on topics that included lesbianism, the trials and tribulations of motherhood, and the power of anger to transform. Speaking before student groups and promoting her agenda for social change in various journals, Lorde considers the differences between people as a cause for celebration and a hope for the future. Race, sexual orientation, political agendas, and socio-economic distinctions: these and other differences should be recognized rather than ignored, and alternative points of view accepted and tolerated for society to flourish.

Subject(s): Women's Rights, Homosexuality/Lesbianism, Race Relations

1281 Audre Lorde

Zami: A New Spelling of My Name
(Trumansburg, NY; Crossing Press, 1982)

Summary: Black feminist-activist Audre Lorde tells her life story in *Zami: A New Spelling of My Name*. Terming her work a "biomythography" rather than an autobiography, Lorde places the events of her own life and the relationships she has had within a larger context: the community of all women. Beginning with her birth in New York City, Lorde allows readers to follow her academic career and her continued excitement at viewing the world through a poet's eyes. A marriage, two children, and several volumes of poetry would follow before Lorde's voice became more stridently political; in her later work her perspective became increasingly feminist. Diagnosed with cancer in the late 1970s, Lorde transformed her battle with breast cancer into a life-transforming experience, drawing on a renewed energy to survive and to continue the creative process that sparked the "unfolding of [her] life and loves" in *Zami*.

Subject(s): Women's Rights, Homosexuality/Lesbianism, Autobiography

1282 Glenn C. Loury

One by One from the Inside Out: Essays and Reviews on Race and Responsibility in America
(New York, NY; Free Press, 1995)

Summary: In *One by One from the Inside Out: Essays and Reviews on Race and Responsibility in America*, black intellectual Glenn C. Loury examines a number of social issues as they relate to race and poverty, among them the cult of victimization, black-Jewish relations, the shrinking middle class, liberalism, and affirmative action. He calls for Americans to discard philosophical labels and address issues on the basis of logic and

fairness. Showing blacks in conflict between the self-actualization philosophy of Booker T. Washington on the one hand and the separatist ideology of W.E.B. Du Bois that has guided most civil rights agendas, Loury urges African Americans to lobby for economic, social, and legal rights. He believes that once a flat playing field has been achieved, blacks will be able to compete on their individual merits as a means of retaining a true democratic system.

Subject(s): Civil Rights Movement, Self-Reliance, Economics

1283 John Lovell, Jr.

Black Song: The Forge and the Flame; The Story of How the Afro-American Spiritual Was Hammered Out
(New York, NY; Macmillan, 1972)

Summary: The songs and spirituals of African Americans are recognized as unique and valuable contributions to U.S. culture. However, spirituals and songs of the antebellum South were more than simply musical expression. They were "documents" of oral historical value reflecting the traditions of many diverse people of color. Embedded within spirituals and related folk songs of the seventeenth and eighteenth century is information respecting songs' authors, dates, places of origin, plans regarding flights to freedom, and subtle protests against slavery. In *Black Song* John Lovell, Jr. tells the story of the spiritual from its earliest incarnation in the songs of Africans disembarking from slave ships upon the New World.

Subject(s): Music, Folklore, Spiritualism

1284 Samuel Lubell

White and Black: Test of a Nation
(New York, NY; Harper & Row, 1964)

Summary: *White and Black: Test of a Nation* was the work of reporter and political analyst Samuel Lubell. Viewing the methods undertaken to resolve racial tensions in the years since the Civil War, Lubell argues that the racial problem was defined by two crucial junctures wherein no meeting of the minds was reached. He contends that the problem should be dealt with in different ways in the North and South: in the North through more equitable housing and in the South through integrated schools and a ban on public displays of racism.

Subject(s): Race Relations, Education

1285 J. Anthony Lukas

Common Ground: A Turbulent Decade in the Lives of Three American Families
(New York, NY; Knopf, 1985)

Summary: Taking as its subject the court-ordered implementation of school busing in the city of Boston, J. Anthony Lukas' award-winning *Common Ground: A Turbulent Decade in the Lives of Three American Families* frames the social and political upheaval of that time within class rather than race. Beginning with the assassination of Martin Luther King, Jr., journalist Lukas profiles the events in Boston that culminated in the 1974 riots following the forced busing of students to integrate the city's public schools. Two working-class families--one headed by an Irish-American widow, the other by an African American mother--and a middle-class family serve to reflect the diverse feelings and motivations of Bostonians during that period.

Subject(s): Race Relations, Integration, Judicial System

Award(s): Pulitzer Prize: Nonfiction, 1986

1286 Duncan J. MacLeod

Slavery, Race, and the American Revolution

(London, England; Cambridge University Press, 1974)

Summary: In his 1974 study, Duncan J. MacLeod examines the impact of the ideology of the American Revolution upon conceptions of the place of slavery in the nation's society. While the northern states abolished slavery, southern states followed a different course. The author shows how southern slaveholders promoted the view of blacks as morally and intellectually inferior to white people. In creating the perception that blacks were a threat to free white society, slavery advocates advanced the "peculiar institution" as the means to contain that threat.

Subject(s): American Revolution, American South, Slavery

1287 Haki R. Madhubuti

Enemies: The Clash of Races

(Chicago, IL; Third World Press, 1978)

Summary: Noted writer Haki R. Madhubuti in this collection of essays presents an analysis of the African American condition and the struggle of blacks in the United States as well as "Afrika." The essays consider such issues as black nationalism, the Pan-Afrikan Congress, food as a white weapon of control, and black art and white critics. Other writings examine contemporary economic problems, why blacks should limit contact with whites, and the necessity of force.

Subject(s): Africa, Black Nationalism, Art

1288 Malcolm X

The Autobiography of Malcolm X

(New York, NY; Grove Press, 1965)

Summary: In *The Autobiography of Malcolm X*, noted popular novelist Alex Haley teams with the famous civil rights leader to produce a work that profiles Malcolm's path from minister's son to armed felon to a key member of the Nation of Islam under Elijah Muhammad. His twelve-year service as an influential Muslim confident to Muhammad ended when Malcolm rejected the black separatist leader and his philosophy. Condemning his own misspent youth, Malcolm X concludes his autobiography by discussing the changes in outlook and personal spirituality following his break with Elijah Muhammad and the Black Muslims.

Subject(s): Autobiography, Black Nationalism, Islam

1289 Malcolm X

Malcolm X on Afro-American History

(New York, NY; Merit Publishers, 1967)

Summary: *Malcolm X on Afro-American History* collects speeches by controversial civil rights activist Malcolm X (1925-1965). An influential leader and compelling orator, Malcolm X rose to prominence in the mid-1950s as the outspoken representative of the Nation of Islam, a religious sect led by Elijah Muhammad. Malcolm came out in opposition to the efforts of Martin Luther King, Jr., instead advocating black separatism and promoting acts of violence as necessary to effectively combat racism. His later speeches, made in the last five years of his life, would find him repudiating his former stance and embracing the more peaceable tenets of conventional Islam.

Subject(s): Violence, Race Relations, Islam

1290 Jay R. Mandle

The Roots of Black Poverty: The Southern Plantation Economy after the Civil War

(Durham, NC; Duke University Press, 1978)

Summary: In *The Roots of Black Poverty: The Southern Plantation Economy after the Civil War*, Marxist economist Jay R. Mandle argues that the plantation economy supported by slave labor prior to the Civil War continued in a modified form after emancipation because lack of employment opportunities forced freed blacks to remain tied to the land as tenant farmers. While critics found much to dispute in Mandle's assumptions--the presence of white tenant farmers in numbers equal to blacks, to cite one example--his line of argument was considered noteworthy in presenting factual evidence of African American economic disadvantage within a new framework.

Subject(s): Reconstruction, Economics, Poverty

1291 Manning Marable

From the Grassroots: Essays toward Afro-American Liberation

(Boston, MA; South End Press, 1980)

Summary: This book originated as a series of political essays written by the author for black community and student newspapers. The volume seeks to interpret the diverse parts of the contemporary black social movement. The book begins with a theoretical look at grassroots liberation in the United States. Subsequent sections examine black politics within the nation's capitalist economy, culture and consciousness, the "Southern Question," and state, race, and society.

Subject(s): Civil Rights, Politics, American South

1292 **Manning Marable**

How Capitalism Underdeveloped Black America: Problems in Race, Political Economy, and Society
(Boston, MA; South End Press, 1963)

Summary: In *How Capitalism Underdeveloped Black America: Problems in Race, Political Economy, and Society*, historian and educator Manning Marable presents an analysis of African American history under capitalism. Marable is know for his insightful analysis of the manner in which race, class, and gender disempower many Americans, as well as for the economic and social truths behind the rhetoric defending the status quo in the United States. In this comprehensive Marxist analysis of the economics of black America, Marble shows the many ways blacks have been oppressed by a racist state.

Subject(s): Economics, Sociology, Race Relations

1293 **Manning Marable**

Race, Reform and Rebellion: The Second Reconstruction in Black America, 1945-1982
(Jackson, MS; University Press of Mississippi, 1984)

Summary: This book considers the role of African Americans in political struggles in the United States since 1945. The work opens with a look at the legacy of the post-Civil War Reconstruction period. The chapters that follow examine the effect of the Cold War on desegregation campaigns, subsequent demands for reform, the civil rights movement and growth of black nationalism in the 1960s, the election of thousands of black officials in the 1970s, and the white political backlash, which was marked by the election of Ronald Reagan. The book also recognizes the contributions of major figures including Martin Luther King, Jr., Malcolm X, Stokely Carmichael, and Jesse Jackson.

Subject(s): Reconstruction, Civil Rights Movement, Segregation

1294 **Manning Marable**

Speaking Truth to Power: Essays on Race, Resistance, and Radicalism
(Boulder, CO; Westview Press, 1996)

Summary: In this book, Manning Marable collects his views on the causes of the discrimination, chronic unemployment, and poverty endured by most African Americans. Drawn from speeches and interviews as well as from his many writings, author Marable traces the impact of race upon domestic social policy issues since the 1950s. His essays reflect his developing ideas, which have expanded to consider the possibility of a truly multicultural democratic government dispensing social justice.

Subject(s): Politics, Civil Rights Movement, Race Relations

1295 **Waldo E. Martin, Jr.**

The Mind of Frederick Douglass
(Chapel Hill, NC; University of North Carolina Press, 1984)

Summary: In his work *The Mind of Frederick Douglass*, Waldo E. Martin, Jr. examines the influences and experiences that shaped the thoughts and beliefs of one of the most noted abolitionists of the nineteenth century. Born into slavery in 1818, Douglass was taught to read at a young age. His observation of urban life and the educated classes—gained while working at a Baltimore shipyard—furthered his personal aspirations as well as his interest in politics and intellectual debate. Fleeing slavery in 1838, Douglas took up the cause of abolition and, later, women's suffrage. Also, as Martin notes, his oratory broadened in philosophic scope, to eventually encompass the hypocrisy of some religions and an analysis of the liberties guaranteed by the U.S. Constitution.

Subject(s): Abolition, Politics, Psychology

1296 **Gary T. Marx**

Protest and Prejudice: A Study of Belief in the Black Community
(New York, NY; Harper & Row, 1967)

Summary: Based on a survey of African Americans taken in the early 1960s, *Protest and Prejudice: A Study of Belief in the Black Community* presents an overview and analysis of the attitude of African Americans with regard to other segments of U.S. society. Addressing issues of racial and ethnic prejudice, class differences, and other cultural stereotypes, Gary T. Marx's interpretation of the data is clearly set forth, his conclusions defended with intelligent analysis. Reflecting a panorama of impressions, beliefs, stereotypes, and misunderstandings regarding whites, Jews, and other segments of U.S. society, *Protest and Prejudice* helped to dispel a wide range of unfounded generalizations about the attitude of the nation's blacks.

Subject(s): Prejudice, Rebellion, African Americans

1297 **Katja May**

African Americans and Native Americans in the Creek and Cherokee Nations, 1830s to 1920s: Collision and Collusion
(New York, NY; Garland, 1996)

Summary: Part of a series of books focusing on African American history, Katja May's *African Americans and Native Americans in the Creek and Cherokee Nations, 1830s to 1920s: Collision and Collusion* is a study of the relationship between freed African slaves and the Creek and Cherokee Native Americans. May bolsters her study with oral accounts of the effect of Indian removal and the common ground defended by the two groups during the Green Peach War and the Crazy Snake Uprising, and includes census data from the early 1900s, as well as federal documents detailing the demographics of both tribal Indians and black communities.

Subject(s): American History, Native Americans, Miscegenation

1298 Benjamin E. Mays

Born to Rebel: An Autobiography of Benjamin E. Mays
(Athens, GA; University of Georgia Press, 1986)

Summary: *Born to Rebel* is the life story of prominent African American Benjamin E. Mays, a clergyman, educator, civil rights activist, and writer. Born in South Carolina in 1894 to a sharecropper and his wife, Mays rose to become the president of Atlanta's Morehouse College, one of the nation's leading black colleges. Among the college's alumni were Andrew Young, Julian Bond, and Martin Luther King, Jr. Known for his tireless support of civil rights issues, Mays sought the path of compromise and searched for a common ground. While president of Morehouse, Mays introduced King to Gandhi's philosophy of nonviolence; he would also deliver the eulogy at King's funeral following the civil rights leader's 1968 assassination.

Subject(s): Religion, Civil Rights Movement, Autobiography

1299 Benjamin E. Mays

Quotable Quotes of Benjamin E. Mays
(New York, NY; Vantage Press, 1963)

Summary: *Quotable Quotes of Benjamin E. Mays* collects the words and writings of prominent African American civil rights activist and teacher Benjamin E. Mays. Mays's academic writings of the 1930s were among the first to record important aspects of black American religious life. His philosophy of conciliation and search for a peaceful solution would influence his protege, Martin Luther King, Jr., while King was under Mays's tutelage at Atlanta's Morehouse College in the late 1940s. A widely praised orator, Mays would deliver the eulogy at King's funeral in 1968. As Mays once noted: "I cannot and would not apologize for being a Negro. We have a great history; we have a greater future...we have a rendezvous with America."

Subject(s): Religion, Civil Rights Movement, Autobiography

1300 Ali A. Mazrui
Alamin M. Mazrui, Co-author

The Power of Babel: Language and Governance in the African Experience
(Chicago, IL; University of Chicago Press, 1998)

Summary: In *The Power of Babel: Language and Governance in the African Experience,* noted Kenyan scholar, author, and educator Ali A. Mazrui examines the complex interplay between language and cultural identity in Africa. Together with his son, Alamin M. Mazrui, he explores the threat to native

African languages in countries where most discourse is conducted in the Eurocentric languages of international commerce: English, French, and Spanish. The Mazruis' book recounts the history of Africa's oral traditions as well as the influence of English, Arabic, and other languages in promoting literacy and fostering a political ideology based on the European nation-state. They note that African American English speakers could help forestall the destruction of African cultures through "African counter-penetration": using their mastery of English to educate the West about Africa.

Subject(s): Africa, Language, Politics

1301 Ali A. Mazrui

Towards a Pax Africana: A Study of Ideology and Ambition
(Chicago, IL; University of Chicago Press, 1967)

Summary: In *Towards a Pax Africana: A Study of Ideology and Ambition* political scientist Ali A. Mazrui examines the possibilities of lasting peace in Africa since colonial powers relinquished their hold on the continent. Praised as one of the first successful theoretical analyses of the subject, the book approaches the problem from an African perspective, outlining the issues of race, region, and political sovereignty that make Africa's situation so compelling. Mazrui, a member of a wealthy Kenyan family, at one time held the political science chair at Makerere University, Uganda.

Subject(s): Africa, Politics, Peace

1302 Ali A. Mazrui

World Culture and the Black Experience
(Seattle, WA; University of Washington Press, 1974)

Summary: Part of the World Order Models Project, whose goal was to examine global trends and make proposals for world reform, this book considers the effect of a widespread European culture on the black peoples of Africa and its diaspora. Specifically, the author looks at the impact of the following: world religions, particularly Judaism, Christianity, and Islam; the technological superiority of European civilization; and the rise of English and French as world languages.

Subject(s): Culture, Africa, Religion

1303 Harriette Pipes McAdoo, Editor

Black Families
(Beverly Hills, CA; Sage Publications, 1981)

Summary: In *Black Families,* editor Harriette Pipes McAdoo has compiled a selection of essays reviewing the current literature and analyzing issues of importance to African American families during the early 1980s. Essays are arranged in sections that include the historical and theoretical basis of the black family: economics; social customs among families; gender relations; and state and other intervention policies. Among the many issues touched upon in this early work are religion and ethics, the role of the African American male, single parenting, and the effects of the women's movement. The work was updated and revised in 1996.

Subject(s): Family Life, Family Relations, Family Problems

1304 William S. McFeely

Frederick Douglass
(New York, NY; Norton, 1991)

Summary: Based on copious research through historic archives, William S. McFeely's in-depth biography *Frederick Douglass* profiles the life and legacy of arguably the most noted abolitionist of the nineteenth century. Born into slavery in 1818, Douglass received enough education at an early age to fuel his intellectual curiosity and feed his desire to better both his own circumstances and those of all African Americans. Escaping to freedom at the age of twenty, Douglass used his skill as a compelling orator to advance both the abolitionist cause in the United States and in England, as well as on behalf of women's suffrage following the Civil War.

Subject(s): Abolition, Biography, History

1305 Linda McMurry

Recorder of the Black Experience: A Biography of Monroe Nathan Work
(Baton Rouge, LA; Louisiana State University Press, 1985)

Summary: *Recorder of the Black Experience* is the biography of Monroe Nathan Work (1866-1945), an African American sociologist and bibliographer who received his primary education at the University of Chicago. As director of the Department of Records and Research at Tuskegee Institute, Work amassed a wealth of articles and other primary source material, making him an international expert on the African American experience. In Linda McMurry's biography, his accomplishments as an aide to Institute founder Booker T. Washington are also chronicled.

Subject(s): Biography, Sociology, Education

1306 Lawrence M. Mead

Beyond Entitlement: The Social Obligations of Citizenship
(New York, NY; Free Press, 1986)

Summary: Authored by scholar Lawrence M. Mead, *Beyond Entitlement: The Social Obligations of Citizenship* sparked a shift in the debate over welfare reform. Rather than looking at welfare as a drain on the U.S. economy--providing funds to individuals unable to meet basic needs with no expectation of a return--Mead asks more fundamental questions about public assistance: what is its ultimate goal? And what is the corresponding duty of welfare recipients? Mead contends that the return on investment to the government should be returning recipients to productivity; the corresponding duty should be to strive for self-reliance and accept the responsibilities of citizenship.

Subject(s): Poverty, Politics

1307 August Meier
Elliott M. Rudwick, Co-author

From Plantation to Ghetto: An Interpretive History of American Negroes
(New York, NY; Hill and Wang, 1966)

Summary: In *From Plantation to Ghetto: An Interpretive History of American Negroes* authors Meier and Rudwick explore black political and social ideologies from the colonial era to the mid-1900s. Focusing in particular on the rise of such movements as the Black Muslims and the Back to Africa Movement promoted by Marcus Garvey, the book also highlights the inner workings of the slave system in place prior to the Civil War. Although several critics have found their work in this area to be imbued with factual inaccuracies and a radical Left bias, the volume was recommended highly as a text on black history for undergraduate students.

Subject(s): History, Race Relations, Resistance Movements

1308 August Meier, Editor
Elliott M. Redwick, Co-editor

The Making of Black America: Essays in Negro Life & History
(New York, NY; Atheneum, 1969)

Summary: *The Making of Black America: Essays in Negro Life & History* begins with the history of African Americans from their removal from Africa through Reconstruction. Editors Meier and Rudwick then turn their attention to black political thought, specifically as it has developed into militant and radical ideologies such as those promoted by the Black Muslims. Including essays by such noted scholars as John Hope Franklin and Benjamin Quarles, the work provides a chronological perspective on the development of black political and social consciousness.

Subject(s): History, Resistance Movements, Race Relations

1309 Richard M. Merelman

Representing Black Culture: Racial Conflict and Cultural Politics in the United States
(New York, NY; Routledge, 1996)

Summary: In *Representing Black Culture: Racial Conflict and Cultural Politics in the United States* University of Wisconsin professor Richard M. Merelman looks at the way in which both blacks and whites represent and project images of African American culture within the U.S. cultural mainstream. Citing examples from movies, popular music, literature, education, television, and the government—sources guilty of the "tweaking" of society—Merelman argues that a more responsible and more positive image campaign has the potential to substantially reduce racial conflict.

Subject(s): Politics, Cultural Conflict, Race Relations

1310 Kweisi Mfume

No Free Ride: From the Mean Streets to the Mainstream

(New York, NY; Ballantine Books, 1996)

Summary: *No Free Ride: From the Mean Streets to the Mainstream* is the inspiring autobiography of Kweisi Mfume, who rose from a life of poverty and crime to political leadership and the presidency of the NAACP. Raised by a single mother in a poor section of Baltimore, Maryland, Mfume was forced to quit school and take to the streets after his mother died of cancer. In Mfume's mind, the turmoil of the world of street gangs was augmented by the ongoing violence of the Vietnam War in which several of his friends were killed. For several years he descended into a life of crime and violence. But in his mid-twenties he had a life-altering revelation; he changed his name and his perspective. Earning his GED, he enrolled in college and entered a life of activism, using his role as a popular radio talkshow personality to help him win a seat on Baltimore's City Council. This facility for leadership extended into Congress, where Mfume chaired the Congressional Black Caucus, and thence to the NAACP.

Subject(s): Poverty, Civil Rights, Autobiography

1311 Floyd J. Miller

The Search for a Black Nationality: Black Emigration and Colonization, 1787-1863

(Urbana, IL; University of Illinois Press, 1975)

Summary: Floyd J. Miller's *The Search for a Black Nationality: Black Emigration and Colonization, 1787-1863* studies the activities of groups such as the American Colonization Society, active during the nineteenth century, the primary focus of which was to find a solution to the "Negro Problem." The most successful effort was the ACS's establishment of the nation of Liberia as early as 1817, with that country's first settlement of free or emancipated blacks located at Monrovia by 1822. Miller also examines similar efforts to return blacks to Africa, a solution defended by noted abolitionist Martin Delany.

Subject(s): Abolition, Africa, Emigration and Immigration

1312 Loren Miller

The Petitioners: The Story of the Supreme Court of the United States and the Negro

(New York, NY; Pantheon, 1966)

Summary: In *The Petitioners: The Story of the Supreme Court of the United States and the Negro* California judge Loren Miller presents what many critics hailed as the definitive work on blacks and the law. The son of a slave, Miller remains objective in his analysis of the high court's treatment of cases involving African Americans between 1789 and the 1960s, highlighting the shift in court opinion from a pro-slavery stance in the early nineteenth century to a pro-civil rights approach by the mid-twentieth century. Including the constitution-based tactics of NAACP attorney Thurgood Marshall's defense of black equality and the momentum toward equality created by the Labor movement in the wake of the Great Depression, Miller's book is solidly grounded in legal citations.

Subject(s): Racism, History, Judicial System

1313 Henry H. Mitchell

Black Belief: Folk Beliefs of Blacks in America and West Africa

(New York, NY; Harper & Row, 1975)

Summary: *Black Belief: Folk Beliefs of Blacks in America and West Africa* presents the argument of author Henry H. Mitchell that the Christian traditions of the descendants of enslaved Africans are not solely a distillation of the results of their ancestor's proselytization by whites. Rather, Mitchell argues, distinct influences can been seen in the religion of West Africa. Considered a pioneering work in black theology due to its review of black religion "from the inside," *Black Belief* is a unique document in an area that has since been the subject of much scrutiny.

Subject(s): Religion, Africa, Spiritualism

**1314 Henry H. Mitchell
Nicholas C. Cooper-Lewter,** Co-author

Soul Theology: The Heart of American Black Culture

(San Francisco, CA; Harper & Row, 1986)

Summary: In *Soul Theology: The Heart of American Black Culture,* Nicholas C. Cooper-Lewter and Henry H. Mitchell examine the underlying spiritual and philosophic beliefs that have enabled African Americans to endure the hardships of life in North America through several generations. Focusing on the importance of a core belief system, the authors provide suggestions for using such core beliefs as reference points to develop a positive relationship to everyday events, as well as to strengthen one's personal relationship with God.

Subject(s): Religion, Christianity

1315 Clarence L. Mohr

On the Threshold of Freedom: Masters and Slaves in Civil War Georgia

(Athens, GA; University of Georgia Press, 1986)

Summary: The product of ten years' research, *On the Threshold of Freedom: Masters and Slaves in Civil War Georgia* focuses on the "peculiar institution" of slavery in the years following the Secession of the Southern States that precipitated the Civil War. The Old South, author Clarence L. Mohr argues, concealed basic aggressions beneath its lazy facade, and those aggressive tendencies were driven to the surface in wartime, resulting in a changing relationship between blacks and whites throughout the Confederate states. He profiles that new relationship in microcosm, studying events in the state of Georgia throughout the war and into Reconstruction.

Subject(s): Slavery, Reconstruction, American South

1316 Ashley Montagu

Race, Science and Humanity

(Princeton, NJ; Van Nostrand, 1963)

Summary: An esteemed anthropologist known for his work in relating cultural factors to the patterns of human evolution, Ashley Montagu addressed the issue of racism in numerous books written over his lengthy career. In *Race, Science and Humanity* he reiterates an argument made in his groundbreaking 1942 work, *Man's Most Dangerous Myth*. The myth is that race is an absolute designation that embodies qualities beyond skin tone and physiognomy, among them character and intelligence. In this book, Montagu reviews the large body of work accumulated by scientists in this area and shows the inadequacies of much scientific methodology in dealing with this controversial topic.

Subject(s): Science, Racism, Anthropology

1317 Esteban Montejo
Miguel Barnet, Editor

The Autobiography of a Runaway Slave

(London, England; Bodley Head, 1966)

Summary: Based on interviews Cuban author Miguel Barnet had with former slave Esteban Montejo in the 1960s, *The Autobiography of a Runaway Slave* was widely translated, appearing in the United States and England as one of the first narratives to present the history of Latin American slavery from a non-white viewpoint. Born in 1858, Montejo escaped slavery to fight in Cuba's War of Independence in the late 1890s. Barnet's book, written to illuminate the history of black Cubans, contains information on African-Cuban folklore and traditions, religious practices, and social life.

Subject(s): Slavery, Colonialism, Biography

1318 Daniel J. Monti

A Semblance of Justice: St. Louis School Desegregation and Order in Urban America

(Columbia, MO; University of Missouri Press, 1985)

Summary: Written thirty years after the *Brown vs. the Board of Education* decision, this book considers the social implications of desegregation. Specifically, the work examines the efforts to desegregate the public school system in St. Louis, a process involving both voluntary and mandatory plans. The

author views desegregation as part of a tradition of reform movements in American urban areas to assimilate diverse elements of the population.

Subject(s): Segregation, Education, Race Relations

1319 Cherrie Moraga, Editor
Gloria Anzaldua, Co-editor

This Bridge Called My Back: Writings by Radical Women of Color

(Watertown, MA; Persephone Press, 1981)

Summary: Chicana writers Gloria Anzaldua and Cherrie Moraga edited *This Bridge Called My Back: Writings by Radical Women of Color.* Considered a groundbreaking work, *This Bridge* grew out of Moraga's master's degree thesis at San Francisco State University. Beginning by stating the feminist philosophy of its editors--that the women's movement needs to expand beyond its initial agenda, which supports only educated white women, to encompass the specific oppression endured by both straight and lesbian women of a variety of races and economic groups--the book gives a voice to minority women of color by addressing Third World feminism. Translated into Spanish, the anthology received the 1986 Before Columbus Foundation's American Book Award.

Subject(s): Racism, Hispanic Americans, Women's Rights

Award(s): Before Columbus Foundation: American Book Award, 1986

1320 Edmund S. Morgan

American Slavery, American Freedom: The Ordeal of Colonial Virginia

(New York, NY; Norton, 1975)

Summary: In the highly controversial *American Slavery, American Freedom: The Ordeal of Colonial Virginia,* historian Edmund S. Morgan argues that it was the practice of owning slaves that spurred Virginians to pull free of British rule, thus precipitating revolution. Within the studied rhetoric of Virginians regarding the threat of "slavery" and the danger to their "liberties" from British policies of the 1760s and 1770s, Morgan sees in such lines a connection to the very real freedom they enjoyed, the bondage they imposed on others, and the enlightened republicanism drifting in from France.

Subject(s): American Revolution, Slavery, American Colonies

1321 Philip D. Morgan

Slave Counterpoint: Black Culture in the Eighteenth-Century Chesapeake and Lowcountry

(Chapel Hill, NC; University of North Carolina Press, 1998)

Summary: *Slave Counterpoint: Black Culture in the Eighteenth-Century Chesapeake and Lowcountry* is Philip D. Morgan's reconstruction of life in the pre-Civil War South. The work focuses on differences between slavery in Virginia and

Maryland, on the one hand, and in South Carolina and Georgia, on the other. In the Lowcountry South slaves were more isolated from their owners than in the Chesapeake and consequently were able to retain their African customs longer, "enjoy" a greater measure of economic independence, and have discretionary time. Including examinations of living conditions, family structure, population shifts, and race relations, Morgan's work underscores his contention that slavery was "a fundamental, acceptable, thoroughly American institution."

Subject(s): Slavery, History, American South

1322 Toni Morrison, Editor

Race-ing Justice, En-Gendering Power: Essays on Anita Hill, Clarence Thomas, and the Construction of Social Reality
(New York, NY; Pantheon Books, 1992)

Summary: In *Race-ing Justice, En-Gendering Power: Essays on Anita Hill, Clarence Thomas, and the Construction of Social Reality,* editor Toni Morrison collects eighteen essays that focus on the Thomas-Hill conflict that saturated the U.S. media in 1991. The essayists include men and women--both whites and people of color, drawn from the academic community. They reflect on the personal, public, sexual, and legal issues raised by the accusations of sexual harassment leveled by Hill at Supreme Court nominee Thomas during his confirmation hearings before the U.S. Senate, and put the events in historical perspective.

Subject(s): Sexual Harassment, Law, Sociology

1323 Wilson Jeremiah Moses

Afrotopia: The Roots of African American Popular History
(New York, NY; Cambridge University Press, 1998)

Summary: Afrocentrism has often been controversial because of what some people consider its glorification of achievements by members of African civilizations, most notably those of ancient Egyptian origin. The controversy stems from non-Afrocentric scholars' contention that Afrocentric scholars make extravagent claims for which they have no credible sources, and use fabricated historical details to attribute achievements to blacks that were actually made by other races. Others argue that Afrocentrism is merely rectifying the Eurocentric view of history that has deleted blacks from the record. In *Afrotopia,* Wilson Moses offers an objective view of both sides of the controversy and seeks to examine the myths and realities. He begins with the origins of the Afrocentric view in black intellectual thought during the eighteenth century and continues to the present day.

Subject(s): History, Popular Culture, Education

1324 Charles C. Moskos
John Sibley Butler, Co-author

All That We Can Be: Black Leadership and Racial Integration the Army Way
(New York, NY; Basic Books, 1996)

Summary: In *All That We Can Be: Black Leadership and Racial Integration the Army Way* sociologists Charles C. Moskos and John Sibley Butler highlight the successes experienced by many African Americans who chose a career within the U.S. Army. Citing the success story of Joint Chief of Staff chairman Colin Powell, as well as statistics that show the ranks of noncommissioned Army officers to be forty percent black, the authors describe the successful effort at racial integration undertaken by the Army since the 1970s. They state that this has been achieved by including a "supply-side" affirmative action policy dedicated to the belief that training can open more doors than quotas or lowered standards and argue that the same strategy might be applied in the private sector with equal results.

Subject(s): Affirmative Action, Armed Forces, Employment

1325 Robert W. Mullen

Blacks in America's Wars: The Shift in Attitudes from the Revolutionary War to Vietnam
(New York, NY; Monad Press, 1973)

Summary: In *Blacks in America's Wars: The Shift in Attitudes from the Revolutionary War to Vietnam,* author Robert W. Mullen traces the history of African Americans in the U.S. military throughout the nation's history. Blacks risked their lives, hoping that their participation during wartime and their heroism in battle would win them complete emancipation and social standing equal to the whites that shared their battle lines. However, after emancipation and well into the twentieth century, many blacks have resisted risking their lives for a nation that they contend does not extend them total equality.

Subject(s): Vietnam War, History, Military Life

1326 Gilbert H. Muller

John A. Williams
(Boston, MA; Twayne Publishers, 1984)

Summary: In *John A. Williams,* Muller outlines the life and work of the African American novelist and journalist who has been called one of the most original as well as controversial black writers of the twentieth century. Beginning Williams's biography with his childhood in Syracuse, New York, Muller follows the writer through his college career, his service with the U.S. Navy, and the publication of his first novel, *The Angry Ones,* in 1960. Later works of fiction would express Williams's increasing frustration over the treatment of blacks in white society.

Subject(s): Biography, Race Relations, Writing

1327 Michael Mullin

Africa in America: Slave Acculturation and Resistance in the American South and the British Caribbean, 1736-1831
(Urbana, IL; University of Illinois Press, 1992)

Summary: Part of the "Blacks in the New World" series, Michael Mullin's *Africa in America: Slave Acculturation and Resistance in the American South and the British Caribbean, 1736-1831* exposes the roots of African American societies in both the American South and the British West Indies. Illuminating the realities of slave family life, finances, and religious beliefs, Mullin also describes various patterns of resistance: sudden violent uprisings reflective of African warfare followed by a period of withdrawal and subtle noncompliance, and then open rebellions led by assimilated blacks knowledgeable of the ways of white society and politics.

Subject(s): American Colonies, Slavery, Resistance Movements

1328 Charles Murray

Losing Ground: American Social Policy, 1950-1980
(New York, NY; Basic Books, 1984)

Summary: Basing his conclusions on a thirty-year study, Charles Murray contends that slashing public assistance spending would be of greater benefit than the current welfare system. Including extensive data to support his contentions, Murray claims that African Americans in particular have suffered under the current system, and he cites several trends during the 1970s and 1980s--the increasing numbers of unemployed young black males, the increase in the illegitimate birth rate among blacks, and the increase in violent crimes involving African Americans--as support for his position. As a solution, Murray proposes the complete abolition of almost all social programs, leaving the majority of the poor to find work and the rest to depend on private charity.

Subject(s): Economics, Labor and Labor Classes, Social Services

1329 Gunnar Myrdal

An American Dilemma: The Negro Problem and Modern Democracy
(New York, NY; Harper & Brothers, 1944)

Summary: A classic work of scholarship and a defining book in the history of U.S. race relations, *An American Dilemma: The Negro Problem and Modern Democracy* by Gunnar Myrdal is an essential work on U.S. culture and society. Swedish-born scholar Myrdal profiles the status of American blacks at midcentury, including segregation practices and lynch laws still in force, but also expressing optimism at the shift in attitudes that would lead to the civil rights movement of the 1950s and 1960s. A new printing of the book in 1996 provided stu-

dents with an opportunity to see how far U.S. society had come in changing the status quo regarding race.

Subject(s): Race Relations, Segregation, History

1330 Gary B. Nash

Red, White, and Black: The Peoples of Early America
(Englewood Cliffs, NJ; Prentice-Hall, 1974)

Summary: In this 1974 work, acclaimed historian Gary B. Nash offers a cultural perspective of the early centuries of American history. Specifically, he examines how North America was peopled prior to the arrival of Christopher Columbus in 1492 and after, when Spanish and English settlers began to arrive and then eventually brought enslaved Africans to the continent. Nash stresses how the intermixing of American Indians, whites, and Africans helped forge a unique American culture by the middle of the eighteenth century, as American independence from England was achieved.

Subject(s): History, Culture, Race Relations

1331 Truman Nelson, Editor

Documents of Upheaval: Selections from William Lloyd Garrison's "The Liberator", 1831-1865
(New York, NY; Hill and Wang, 1966)

Summary: *Documents of Upheaval: Selections from William Lloyd Garrison's "The Liberator," 1831-1865* was penned by Truman Nelson, an actor and novelist. Turning to nonfiction in mid-career, Nelson specialized in writing books focusing on little studied areas of black history. In his profile of the abolitionist publisher of *The Liberator*, Nelson follows the newspaper's colorful career as a vehicle for Garrison's anti-slavery message. Despite never becoming profitable, through Garrison's efforts--twelve-hour days were common--the paper produced stories that were picked up and spread by other newspapers both in the United States and England. Selections from the newspaper, published between 1831 and 1865, are included.

Subject(s): Journalism, Abolition, Rebellion

1332 Dorothy K. Newman, Editor

Protest, Politics, and Prosperity: Black Americans and White Institutions, 1940-75
(New York, NY; Pantheon Books, 1978)

Summary: The product of five researchers working under a grant from the Carnegie Foundation, *Protest, Politics, and Prosperity: Black Americans and White Institutions, 1940-75* examines such factors as employment, housing, medical care, and income within the context of racial discrimination. While many policymakers considered anti-black discrimination to have been resolved as a result of legislation passed during the 1950s and 1960s, a review of the available data shows that advances in the relative position of African Americans were small by the mid-1970s, and that those advances were achieved due to the efforts of blacks themselves rather than through any significant increase in opportunities provided by an ostensibly more equitable social system.

Subject(s): Sociology, Race Relations, Economics

1333 Huey P. Newton

Revolutionary Suicide
(New York, NY; Harcourt Brace Jovanovich, 1973)

Summary: *Revolutionary Suicide* is Black Panther leader Huey Newton's explanation of the life events that prompted him to support the militant separatist rhetoric of the Black Power movement after the assassination of Dr. Martin Luther King, Jr. After an underprivileged childhood, Newton attended college, where the ideology advanced by fellow Panther Bobby Seale prompted the movement that would be targeted by both police and national law enforcement agencies until its break-up. The dissolution of the group came several years after the publication of this volume due to the ideological differences of its leadership. Newton ends this volume on an optimistic note, writing: "We will touch God's heart; we will touch the people's heart, and together we will move the mountain."

Subject(s): Resistance Movements, Violence, Biography

1334 Robert J. Norrell

Reaping the Whirlwind: The Civil Rights Movement in Tuskegee
(New York, NY; Knopf, 1985)

Summary: In *Reaping the Whirlwind: The Civil Rights Movement in Tuskegee,* author Robert J. Norrell focuses on Macon County, Alabama, during the Civil Rights era, and shows the region's successful efforts at integration. Tuskegee was the home of Booker T. Washington; his Tuskegee Institute was an all-black school organized under Washington's guiding philosophy of concentrating on economic, rather than social, gains in the fight for equality. Norrell shows Macon County's progress away from Washington's beliefs, and how the community eventually adapted to the concept of integration.

Subject(s): Education, Work, Civil Rights Movement

1335 Aletta J. Norval

Deconstructing Apartheid Discourse
(New York, NY; Verso, 1996)

Summary: Written in the wake of South Africa's apartheid society, Aletta Norval's *Deconstructing Apartheid Discourse* examines the nature of the racist measure and the personal and social identities it created in generations of black South Africans. Norval presents a history of this racially based means of dividing society from its early stages in the 1970s through its demise in the mid-1980s under F.W. DeKlerk's government. Employing both post-Marxist and post-structuralist approaches, Norval analyzes the positions of the white govern-

ment as well as the African National Congress, and she posits the potential for a colorblind political future.

Subject(s): Apartheid, Politics

1336 Russel Blaine Nye

Fettered Freedom: Civil Liberties and the Slavery Controversy, 1830-1860
(East Lansing, MI; Michigan State College Press, 1949)

Summary: In his *Fettered Freedom: Civil Liberties and the Slavery Controversy, 1830-1860,* Pulitzer Prize-winning historian Russel Blaine Nye examines freedom of thought and intellectual growth, freedom of the press, and freedom from oppression within the context of the move to abolish slavery in the early to mid-1800s. After a close examination of the historical record, Nye shows that the growing abolitionist movement created fear in advocates of the status quo which resulted in an effort to stifle the media as well as educational institutions with regard to the slave issue. In addition to demonstrating that there were efforts to halt the spread of abolitionist sentiment by placing restrictions on the use of the U.S. mail, Nye shows that vigilantism and mob rule also gained a foothold in American society during the pre-Civil War era.

Subject(s): Slavery, History, Violence

1337 Constance E. Obudho

Black-White Racial Attitudes: An Annotated Bibliography
(Westport, CT; Greenwood Press, 1976)

Summary: This book presents annotations of articles and books concerned with various aspects of the racial attitudes held by blacks and whites in the United States. The works presented offer information on the attitudes of blacks and whites toward their own groups as well. The works covered, which were published between 1950 and 1974, also consider factors associated with racial attitudes and examine attitude formation and change in children and adults.

Subject(s): Racism, Race Relations, Identity

1338 John U. Ogbu

Minority Education and Caste: The American System in Cross-Cultural Perspective
(New York, NY; Academic Press, 1978)

Summary: In his *Minority Education and Caste: The American System in Cross-Cultural Perspective,* Nigerian-born anthropologist and educator John U. Ogbu studies U.S. society from a Third World perspective. In his work he examines the ethnic stratification that makes up caste within American politics and society, focusing on the nature of caste and the problems it presents for minorities in a white-dominated culture. Particularly, Ogbu sees the U.S. education system as perpetuating the existing, albeit covert, caste system.

Subject(s): Anthropology, Class Conflict, History

1339 **Femi Ojo-Ade,** Editor

Of Dreams Deferred, Dead or Alive: African Perspectives on African-American Writers
(Westport, CT; Greenwood Press, 1996)

Summary: Edited by University of Maryland professor Femi Ojo-Ade, *Of Dreams Deferred, Dead or Alive* is a collection of thirteen essays by prominent critics from several African nations that provides a unique viewpoint on the work of African American writers. Showcasing the complex relationship between African Americans and their ethnic origins in Africa, the essays touch on such subjects as similarities and differences, major influences, the role of women in society, slavery and colonialism, and writing as an act of exploring one's past. The critical anthology was praised for providing insight into the African perspective on African American philosophy and culture.

Subject(s): Africa, Criticism, Literature

1340 **Gilbert Osofsky**

Harlem; The Making of a Ghetto: Negro New York, 1890-1930
(New York, NY; Harper & Row, 1966)

Summary: This work is a social history by Gilbert Osofsky that recounts how a former upper-middle-class Manhattan suburb was transformed into the largest segregated community in the nation, and thence into a slum, all within the space of only four decades. Osofsky uses as backdrop to Harlem's history the role of African Americans within New York culture prior to their move to Harlem. He cites the influences of shifts in race relations near the turn of the twentieth century as causes for the changes in demographics.

Subject(s): City and Town Life, Segregation

1341 **William A. Owens**

Slave Mutiny: The Revolt on the Schooner Amistad
(New York, NY; J. Day Co., 1953)

Summary: *Slave Mutiny: The Revolt on the Schooner Amistad* recounts the story of Cinque, an African slave who, during his passage to America, gained control of the ship transporting himself and other blacks. Ultimately captured by U.S. authorities off the coast of Connecticut, the charismatic Cinque and his fellow rebels were tried in a case that illustrates the conflicting beliefs and prejudices of northern citizens, both pro-slavery and abolitionists. Written by William A. Owens, *Black Mutiny* draws readers in like an adventure novel and was praised as one of the most compelling records of these historic events.

Subject(s): Slavery, Judicial System, Africa

1342 **Nell Irvin Painter**

Exodusters: Black Migration to Kansas after Reconstruction
(New York, NY; Knopf, 1976)

Summary: A history of the relocation efforts by African Americans westward following the Civil War, *Exodusters: Black Migration to Kansas after Reconstruction* draws heavily on written sources of the period. Author Nell Irvin Painter cites as motivation the economic oppression of southern blacks--enforced by usurious landlord-tenant farming contracts--in motivating many newly freed slaves and their families to undertake the arduous journey to Kansas in a mass exodus in 1879. Painter views this migration as a grass-roots protest movement sparked by dashed hopes of receiving equality in society, rather than an unstudied reaction to the machinations of unethical land speculators.

Subject(s): Reconstruction, American South, Emigration and Immigration

1343 **David Parks**

GI Diary
(New York, NY; Harper & Row, 1968)

Summary: The son of noted African American photographer and film director Gordon Parks, David Parks captured his experiences on the battlefields of Southeast Asia in *GI Diary*. Published in 1968, the book chronicles the human aspects of warfare as seen through the eyes of Parks, a young black man whose talents as a photographer bring the horrors of war to life. Awarded the Purple Heart during his tour of duty, Parks returned to the United States after the Vietnam War and began a career as a photographer.

Subject(s): Photography, Violence, Vietnam War

1344 **Gordon Parks**

A Choice of Weapons
(New York, NY; Harper & Row, 1966)

Summary: In his *A Choice of Weapons*, photographer Gordon Parks recounts his life, from his poverty-stricken early years, to his journey from rural Kansas to Minnesota in 1928 when he was sixteen, to his eventual move to Harlem to involve himself in the flowering of African American culture known as the Harlem Renaissance. Talented, ambitious, and believing in the American ideal—that hard work fosters success—Parks fought numerous odds, including racism, to achieve acclaim as an award-winning photographer.

Subject(s): Photography, Autobiography, Harlem Renaissance

1345 **Lydia Parrish,** Compiler

Slave Songs of the Georgia Sea Islands
(New York, NY; Creative Age Press, 1942)

Summary: In *Slave Songs of the Georgia Sea Islands*, compiler and folklorist Lydia Parrish includes the result of a quarter century of research into the music of African Americans living on the islands off the Georgia coast. Including 59 songs, the collection is divided into several sections: shout songs; ring-play, dance, and fiddle songs; religious songs; and work songs. Including a bibliography and numerous photographs, Parrish's volume represents a valuable contribution to the folklore of the region and a compelling argument for further efforts at its preservation.

Subject(s): Music, Folklore, Slavery

1346 Theresa Perry, Editor

Teaching Malcolm X
(New York, NY; Routledge, 1996)

Summary: Theresa Perry's anthology *Teaching Malcolm X* is a guide to educators seeking a multicultural approach to the works of radical civil rights activist Malcolm X. Covering the introduction of Malcolm's speeches and writings to both public school and college students, Perry assembles the insight of a variety of educators regarding Malcolm X's works, his historical importance, and ways his work can contribute in other academic areas.

Subject(s): Criticism, Education, Civil Rights Movement

1347 Caryl Phillips

The European Tribe
(New York, NY; Farrar, Straus, Giroux, 1987)

Summary: This collection of essays is the result of the international journeys that the author made to learn more about racism as well as his own African-European heritage. In the book, Phillips assesses the relationships that European nations have with their minorities, especially those who have immigrated from former European colonies. He also links Europe's anti-Semitism with the racism focused on immigrant communities. By making judgments on the various European nations that he visits, the author subverts the traditional European travelogue. The collection also features some postcolonial interpretations of major European works, such as William Shakespeare's plays *The Merchant of Venice* and *Othello*. Phillips concludes the book by affirming his cultural relation to the West.

Subject(s): Racism, Colonialism, Anti-Semitism

Award(s): Martin Luther King Memorial Prize, 1987

1348 Alphonso Pinkney

The Myth of Black Progress
(New York, NY; Cambridge University Press, 1984)

Summary: In *The Myth of Black Progress*, liberal educator and sociologist Alphonso Pinkney presents an analysis of the change in the overall condition of African Americans within U.S. society during the twentieth century. Focusing his attention on the role of race versus class as a determining factor in the general welfare of black families, Pinkney addresses many criticisms of the relatively new phenomenon of the upwardly mobile black. Sparking criticism due to his controversial position and his unwillingness to take into account contradictory research, Pinkney argues that blacks have not made the advances that they should have by this point in time, and he concludes with a discussion of the changes that must be made to allow them to do so.

Subject(s): Sociology, Race Relations, Economics

1349 Alphonso Pinkney

Red, Black, and Green: Black Nationalism in the United States
(New York, NY; Cambridge University Press, 1976)

Summary: Educator and sociologist Alphonso Pinkney examines a number of organized movements toward African American unity in his *Red, Black, and Green: Black Nationalism in the United States*. Viewing nationalism as a desire for unity and autonomy that is combined with racial pride, Pinkney looks at the history of such nationalist manifestations as the "Back to Africa" movement inspired by activist Marcus Garvey and then draws comparisons to more recent manifestations of black nationalism occurring in the 1960s and 1970s. While the black nationalist movement had lost its momentum by the 1950s, the ethnic pride and desire for self-direction that it inspired has aided the cause of equality by promoting racial solidarity within a growing segment of the U.S. population.

Subject(s): Politics, Black Nationalism, Africa

1350 Anthony M. Platt

E. Franklin Frazier Reconsidered
(New Brunswick, NJ; Rutgers University Press, 1991)

Summary: *E. Franklin Frazier Reconsidered* is a biography of the African American left-wing sociologist and author whose active role in the civil rights movement brought him into contact with such figures as Paul Robeson and W.E.B. Du Bois. Concentrating primarily upon Frazier's early life, author Anthony M. Platt based his volume on an in-depth reading of his subject's written work, as well as interviews with Frazier's friends, colleagues, and students, and Frazier's personal papers. Platt's book was praised for placing Frazier squarely in the company of the twentieth century's most significant intellectuals.

Subject(s): Biography, Sociology

1351 Alvin F. Poussaint

Why Blacks Kill Blacks
(New York, NY; Emerson Hall Publishers, 1972)

Summary: The essays in this 1972 work address the problems faced by blacks. The first part of the work considers the rise of black power. This section includes essays on psychiatry and the black patient and obstacles to black solidarity. The second part of the book looks at problems related to whites and includes the essay "Why Blacks Kill Blacks." This section also presents chapters on suicide, sexuality, and advice for both black and white parents. The book features an introduction by the Reverend Jesse Jackson and dialogues between the author and Jackson on self-hatred and separatism.

Subject(s): Racism, Psychiatry, Suicide

1352 Colin Powell

My American Journey
(New York, NY; Random House, 1995)

Summary: One of the most widely respected African Americans of the late twentieth century, General Colin L. Powell authored *My American Journey* as a means of sharing his road to success with others. Raised in the Bronx, Powell entered into a military career during the Vietnam Era and rose through the ranks to his appointment as Chairman of the Joint Chiefs of Staff under President Ronald Reagan. Pressed to run for the presidency himself, Powell declined due to family considerations; the same sense of responsibility is revealed in his engaging and personable autobiography.

Subject(s): Autobiography, Military Life, Politics

1353 Richard J. Powell

Black Art and Culture in the 20th Century
(New York, NY; Thames & Hudson, 1997)

Summary: Art historian Richard Powell's, *Black Art and Culture in the 20th Century* covers painting, computer-aided art, and other visual arts, as well as music and performance art, that has been created by or about black Americans. The volume includes nearly 180 illustrations, artist profiles, and interpretive essays focusing on the social and cultural contexts for each art form, making it a valuable resource for art historians. Beginning his discussion of black art by noting its basis in the "African diasporal experiences" that resulted from the slave trade and European colonial expansion, Powell traces the philosophical and social forces that have shaped a black diasporal presence.

Subject(s): Popular Culture, Performance Art, Art

1354 Samuel D. Proctor

The Young Negro in America, 1960-1980
(New York, NY; Association Press, 1966)

Summary: Basing his analysis on personal observations, Samuel D. Proctor views the position of blacks a century after the Civil War in *The Young Negro in America, 1960-1980*. Showing the divergence by younger generations of African Americans with the separatist sentiments of the NAACP and the militancy of the black power movement of the 1960s, Proctor sets forth the way in which young blacks can gain admittance to mainstream U.S. society, citing education as the most effective means. A former college president and Peace Corps

volunteer, Proctor remains optimistic about the course of race relations through the end of the century.

Subject(s): Race Relations, Education, Civil Rights Movement

1355 Roderick W. Pugh

Psychology and the Black Experience
(Monterey, CA; Brooks/Cole Pub. Co., 1972)

Summary: Inspired by developments in the 1960s, this book considers the relationship of professional psychology to the black experience. The first part of the work examines the "Black Revolution" of the 1960s, in particular black student activism. The book then looks at the concerns of two black clinical psychologists, one who treats individual patients and another who works with an urban black community. Two subsequent chapters present autobiographical recollections from two black psychologists. The volume concludes with a treatment of the issue of a "black psychology."

Subject(s): Psychology, Civil Rights Movement

1356 Benjamin Quarles

Frederick Douglass
(Washington, DC; Associated Publishers, 1948)

Summary: One of the first modern biographies of the famed nineteenth-century abolitionist, *Frederick Douglass* augment's the former slave's own autobiographical accounts. Authored by Benjamin Quarles, the volume briefly covers Douglass's childhood in slavery and his escape from his Baltimore slave-owners. Quarles concentrates more attention on Douglass's speaking tour in Britain, where he removed himself for several years when the notoriety caused by publication of his *Narrative of the Life of Frederick Douglass* sparked efforts at his capture.

Subject(s): Biography, Abolition, History

1357 Lee Rainwater

Behind Ghetto Walls: Black Families in a Federal Slum
(Chicago, IL; Aldine Pub. Co., 1970)

Summary: *Behind Ghetto Walls: Black Life in a Federal Slum* examines the quality of life experienced by African American families living in government-subsidized housing projects. Based on a study of the Pruitt-Igoe housing project in St. Louis, Missouri, Lee Rainwater's book presents ghetto life in anthropological terms. Its brutality is a response to the white power structure that created the project and its social confines. Interviews with project residents make plain the poverty, antagonism, and helplessness endured by many ghetto-dwellers and shows how such feelings translate into actions and attitudes that further their downward spiral.

Subject(s): Poverty, Anthropology, Urban Affairs

1358 Lee Rainwater
William L. Yancey, Co-author

The Moynihan Report and the Politics of Controversy: A Trans-action Social Science and Public Policy Report
(Cambridge, MA; M.I.T. Press, 1967)

Summary: Authored by sociology professors William L. Yancey and Lee Rainwater, *The Moynihan Report and the Politics of Controversy* includes both the controversial report, which outlined the status of the black family during the administration of President Lyndon B. Johnson, and commentary. Including a number of newspaper articles written in response to the report as well as papers given at a conference following distribution of the document, the volume gains value due to its inclusion of the text of a speech given by Johnson at Howard University and an essay describing the fallout from Daniel Patrick Moynihan's conclusions. The work also includes a discussion of the conflicting interests of civil rights leaders, social scientists, and government policymakers.

Subject(s): Politics, Sociology, Race Relations

1359 Paul Ramsey

Christian Ethics and the Sit-In
(New York, NY; Association Press, 1961)

Summary: In his book, Princeton University educator Paul Ramsey examines the ethical aspects of the pacifist resistance technique known as the sit-in. Ramsey notes that the sit-in was intended for use by clergy in referencing such actions within a Christian context, and he draws on the concept of the Creation-Covenant as well as the necessity of Christians to obey the existing system of laws. He also contrasts such active protests as sit-ins with such things as economic embargoes supported on behalf of the cause of ending racial oppression.

Subject(s): Religion, Ethics, Resistance Movements

1360 Alan Read, Editor

The Fact of Blackness: Frantz Fanon and Visual Representation
(Seattle, WA; Bay Press, 1996)

Summary: Growing out of a conference at the Institute of Contemporary Arts in London, *The Fact of Blackness: Frantz Fanon and Visual Representation* explores the legacy of Martinique-born psychoanalyst/political philosopher Frantz Fanon that surfaces in the works of multicultural arts practitioners and critics. Born in 1925, Fanon was among the more noted black intellectuals of his day to voice his concern over the oppressed. His books, which included *The Wretched of the Earth* and *Black Skin, White Masks,* were widely discussed in leftist circles. In Alan Read's anthology, essays, discussions, and photographs are combined to show how Fanon's works have been reinterpreted since his death in 1961.

Subject(s): Artists and Art, Multicultural, Intolerance

1361 L.D. Reddick

Crusader Without Violence: A Biography of Martin Luther King, Jr.
(New York, NY; Harper, 1959)

Summary: *Crusader without Violence: A Biography of Martin Luther King, Jr.* is a profile of the life of the Civil Rights leader written by L.D. Reddick, a former curator of the Schomburg Collection of Negro Literature at the New York Public Library as well as a highly respected educator. Published when King was only thirty years old, Reddick's volume focuses on King's interpretation of the passive resistance advocated by Indian leader Mahatmas Gandhi and King's efforts to promote integration through boycotts of city buses and sit-ins at lunch counters that would not service African Americans. Four years after this volume was published, King organized the March on Washington, an event that brought him to national attention.

Subject(s): Segregation, American South, Biography

1362 Edwin S. Redkey

Black Exodus: Black Nationalist and Back-to-Africa Movements, 1890-1910
(New Haven, CT; Yale University Press, 1969)

Summary: In *Black Exodus: Black Nationalist and Back-to-Africa Movements, 1890-1910,* historian and educator Edwin S. Redkey examines the movement spearheaded by Bishop Henry M. Turner in the late 1800s. Redkey credits organizations like the American Colonization Society and the International Migration Society with increasing solidarity among African Americans. He also draws comparisons with the back-to-Africa movements, supported by poorer blacks who had lost hope in the possibility of social and political equality, and both the migration of Europeans to the United States during the same period and the movements initiated by Marcus Garvey that followed.

Subject(s): Migration, History, Africa

1363 Adolph L. Reed, Jr.

The Jesse Jackson Phenomenon: The Crisis of Purpose in Afro-American Politics
(New Haven, CT; Yale University Press, 1986)

Summary: In *The Jesse Jackson Phenomenon: The Crisis of Purpose in Afro-American Politics,* author Adolph L. Reed, Jr. discusses the failed 1984 presidential campaign of Jesse Jackson and its effect on the growing African American presence within U.S. politics. Likening Jackson's campaign style to the charismatic leadership that served blacks during the civil rights era, Reed contends that the use of such protest rhetoric now impacts the black community negatively. He believes the community has become too large and too diverse to be represented in that manner. The book is noteworthy for successfully refuting the commonly held belief that the black community is socially, politically, and economically homogenous.

Subject(s): Politics, Community Relations

1364 Joe M. Richardson

A History of Fisk University, 1865-1946

(University, AL; University of Alabama Press, 1980)

Summary: *A History of Fisk University, 1865-1946* recounts the interesting story of one of the most noted black colleges in the United States. Founded by missionaries in Nashville, Tennessee, in 1866, the school had its roots in the parallel school system where schools were segregated between blacks and whites. In 1930 it became the first black institution to gain accreditation, and it remains firmly entrenched in the liberal arts tradition, its competitive admissions process reflected in the many notable African Americans who have graduated from its halls. Among the college's many alumni are W.E.B. Du Bois, who received his bachelor's degree from Fisk in 1890. The school is also noted for the Jubilee Singers, formed in 1871 to raise money for the college, who toured the world and introduced Europe to the sounds of spirituals.

Subject(s): Colleges and Universities, Education, Schools

1365 Marilyn Richardson

Black Women and Religion: A Bibliography

(Boston, MA; G.K. Hall, 1980)

Summary: This bibliography represents the first effort to catalogue books, articles, music, art, videos, and other items related to black women and religion. Author Marilyn Richardson includes an appendix of autobiographies and biographies of important black women.

Subject(s): Religion, Bibliography, Women

1366 Jonathan Rieder

Canarsie: The Jews and Italians of Brooklyn against Liberalism

(Cambridge, MA; Harvard University Press, 1985)

Summary: *Canarsie: The Jews and Italians of Brooklyn against Liberalism* focuses on the animosity between the Democratic, working-class population of Brooklyn and both the African Americans and other racial minorities that benefit from public assistance programs voted into law by liberal-minded, intellectual elites from other parts of the city. Basing his book on a study made during the 1970s of Canarsie, in the southern section of Brooklyn's Jamaica Bay, Rieder demonstrates that racism is sometimes grounded in everyday interaction between the races rather than abstract hatemongering. He profiles the feelings and realities of men and women forced to deal with the consequences of high-minded liberal legislation such as the school busing legislation supported by whites in more affluent suburbs.

Subject(s): Prejudice, Race Relations, Politics

1367 Gregory U. Rigsby

Alexander Crummell: Pioneer in Nineteenth-Century Pan-African Thought

(New York, NY; Greenwood Press, 1987)

Summary: In *Alexander Crummell: Pioneer in Nineteenth-Century Pan-African Thought*, biographer Gregory U. Rigsby profiles Crummell's Pan-African theories as well as his spirituality. Providing comprehensive documentation, Rigsby divides Crummell's life into four periods, following the activist through his childhood in New York City, his studies at Oneida Institute and then Cambridge University, his ordination as an Episcopalian priest in 1840, and his extensive missionary work, which included raising funds for black settlement in Liberia. Crummell returned to the United States at the age of fifty, serving as pastor of St. Luke's Episcopal Church in Washington, D.C., until his death in 1898.

Subject(s): Biography, Emigration and Immigration

1368 Paul Robeson

Here I Stand

(New York, NY; Othello Associates, 1958)

Summary: Paul Robeson (1898-1976) was a noted actor and vocalist who became one of the most accomplished African Americans of the twentieth century. *Here I Stand* is Robeson's explanation to his many fans worldwide, who could not comprehend why the actor's efforts to gain racial equality around the world should result in his banishment from his own country. Beginning with his childhood in Princeton, New Jersey, Robeson describes the expectations of his demanding father, a pastor, and his later achievements as a scholar, a talented thespian on the New York stage, a renowned singer, and an influential political activist. His support of the Soviet Union eventually resulted in his forced exit from the United States during the Communist "Red Scare" of the 1950s.

Subject(s): Communism, Cold War, Actors and Actresses

1369 Paul Robeson

Paul Robeson, The Great Forerunner

(New York, NY; Dodd Mead, 1978)

Summary: *The Great Forerunner* collects essays by and about actor, singer, and activist Paul Robeson (1898-1976), an African American icon who was blacklisted for much of his career because of his outspoken support of Communism. In addition to Robeson's own writings on racism and other topics relating to U.S. society, commentaries on his work, politics, and life are provided. The book, created by the editors of *Freedomways* magazine as a posthumous tribute to a great African American, would be updated in 1998 to honor Robeson's birth.

Subject(s): Communism, Race Relations, Politics

1370 J.A. Rogers

World's Great Men of Color. Volumes 1-2

(New York, NY; J.A. Rogers, 1946)

Summary: In this two volume work, J.A. Rogers provides a comprehensive guide to black history and hundreds of biographies from 3000 B.C. to 1946 A.D. The first volume details the lives of blacks from Africa and Asia; the second volume covers Europe, the Americas, and the West Indies. Eminent figures, from Hannibal to Marcus Garvey, are contained in this work.

Subject(s): History, Biography, Education

1371 Judith Rollins

Between Women: Domestics and Their Employers

(Philadelphia, PA; Temple University Press, 1985)

Summary: Judith Rollins's *Between Women: Domestics and Their Employers* examines the multi-faceted relationship between black female domestics and their white female employers. While domestic work was once an occupation rife with exploitation of the employee, it has evolved to one in which the norm is for both employer and domestic to treat each other with respect. Rollins did most of the research for her book in and around Boston; from her study she concludes that the domestic-homeowner relationship no longer supports the gender, racial, and class strata that it once did.

Subject(s): Working-Class Life, Working Mothers, Women

1372 Willie Lee Rose

Rehearsal for Reconstruction: The Port Royal Experiment

(Indianapolis, IN; Bobbs-Merrill, 1964)

Summary: *Rehearsal for Reconstruction: The Port Royal Experiment* recounts the situation confronting the slave population of the Sea Islands off the South Carolina coast after Union troops captured the region and vacillated between giving the rich cotton-growing lands to the freed slaves or selling them to private concerns. Noting the wide-scale betrayal of southern blacks that would characterize the subsequent Reconstruction Era, Rose's work draws on primary source material to show the conflicted interests of the Sea Island residents, philanthropists, politicians, missionaries, and business interests.

Subject(s): Slavery, Reconstruction, Civil War

Award(s): Society of American Historians: Allan Nevins History Prize, 1964

1373 Theodore Rosengarten, Compiler

All God's Dangers: The Life of Nate Shaw

(New York, NY; Knopf, 1974)

Summary: Theodore Rosengarten's *All God's Dangers: The Life of Nate Shaw* profiles a man born into freedom in Alabama shortly after the close of the Civil War. As a boy he worked the cotton fields for thirty-five cents an hour. At the age of forty-seven Shaw would courageously rise above the oppression of a quality of life only a few notches above the slavery his parents had known. Confronting a group of white deputies intent on confiscating a friend's cotton crop, he was arrested, brutalized, and spent the next twelve years in a southern prison. Rosengarten recounts Shaw's life through recording long talks with Shaw, who was by then in his mid-eighties.

Subject(s): Biography, Courage, American South

1374 Carl T. Rowan

The Coming Race War in America: A Wake-Up Call

(Boston, MA; Little, Brown, 1996)

Summary: Journalist and civil rights advocate Carl T. Rowan sounds the alarm about the growing tension between blacks and whites in *The Coming Race War in America*. Citing increasing incidents of hate crimes across the Unites States, Rowan accuses academics, members of the media, and government officials of encouraging racial antagonisms, sometimes inadvertently, by interjecting race into unrelated issues or giving unwarranted attention to racial aspects of larger issues. Reviewing the influence of such figures as Louis Farrakhan and Rush Limbaugh within the context of a volatile social fabric, Rowan also contrasts the public perception of O.J. Simpson and General Colin Powell: two African Americans who have inspired extreme reactions within the American populace.

Subject(s): Race Relations, Violence, Journalism

1375 Bayard Rustin

Strategies for Freedom: The Changing Patterns of Black Protest

(New York, NY; Columbia University Press, 1976)

Summary: *Strategies for Freedom: The Changing Patterns of Black Protest* outlines the beliefs of civil rights activist Bayard Rustin. Active from the 1930s, first in the American Communist Party's youth group, then as head of the pacifist War Resisters' League, and during the late 1950s and early 1960s as special assistant to Dr. Martin Luther King, Jr., Rustin was influenced by his Quaker upbringing as well as his pragmatism in advocating a peaceful, nonviolent alteration of society. Rustin discusses his resistance to the radical aspects of the civil rights movement, including black political violence, in favor of the passive resistance he practiced throughout his career.

Subject(s): Civil Rights Movement, Black Nationalism

1376 William Ryan

Blaming the Victim

(New York, NY; Pantheon, 1971)

Summary: In his work *Blaming the Victim,* sociologist William Ryan outlines the prejudices and misunderstandings embedded within the attitudes of the U.S. middle class with regard to minorities, the poor, and other members of society who in the view of some are unable to succeed in modern society due to a lack of their own efforts. Focusing particularly on the 1960s, Ryan views the attitudes of suburbanites with regard to the less affluent, densely populated urban areas they surround, and he examines the lack of communication and information flow that fosters the anger on both sides of the barriers constructed by race, poverty, and ethnicity.

Subject(s): Urban Affairs, Prejudice, Cultural Conflict

1377 Arnold Schuchter

Reparations: The Black Manifesto and Its Challenge to White America
(Philadelphia, PA; Lippincott, 1970)

Summary: In the late 1960s James Forman and the leadership of the Black Economic Development Conference issued a request for some sort of economic redress for the exploitation of black Americans by whites. In *Reparations: The Black Manifesto and Its Challenge to White America* author Arnold Schuchter suggests that, in response to feelings of guilt felt by many white Christians, affluent white churches should take the initiative in creating a program of reparations. Such a program for national reform should, with government sponsorship, replace the military-industrial complex as a national priority, in Schuchter's view.

Subject(s): Slavery, Economics, Race Relations

1378 Flip Schulke, Editor

Martin Luther King, Jr.: A Documentary, Montgomery to Memphis
(New York, NY; Norton, 1976)

Summary: Containing an introductory essay by Coretta Scott King, *Martin Luther King, Jr.: A Documentary, Montgomery to Memphis* is a photographic essay of the late civil rights leader, from his boyhood in Alabama to his work throughout the South and the nation on behalf of African Americans. Concentrating on King's developing philosophy of nonviolence and his many noteworthy achievements, the volume also contains the text of several of his most famous speeches. Rather than a scholarly work, the book provides general readers with a glowing tribute to King and his legacy.

Subject(s): Biography, Photography, Civil Rights Movement

1379 Howard Schuman
Charlotte Steeh, Co-author
Lawrence Bobo, Co-author

Racial Attitudes in America: Trends and Interpretations
(Cambridge, MA; Harvard University Press, 1985)

Summary: *Racial Attitudes in America: Trends and Interpretations* received critical praise for its balanced, well-documented presentation of the shift in racial attitudes in the United States during the second half of the twentieth century. Basing their work on demographic and regional studies, the editors divide their analysis of racial attitudes into principles of equality, government implementation of those principles, and social distance. The volume was revised and updated in 1998, adding a discussion of both affirmative action and the basis of inequality.

Subject(s): Race Relations, History

1380 John Anthony Scott

Woman against Slavery: The Life of Harriet Beecher Stowe
(New York, NY; Crowell, 1978)

Summary: Written for younger readers, John Anthony Scott's *Woman against Slavery: The Life of Harriet Beecher Stowe* profiles the author whose *Uncle Tom's Cabin* rocked the United States upon its publication in 1852 and inflamed the growing northern abolitionist movement. Stowe was born in Connecticut in 1811, became the wife of a minister, and was a journalist prior to the publication of her classic work. Stowe penned *Uncle Tom's Cabin* in response to the passage of the Fugitive Slave Law of 1850, which allowed runaway slaves to be returned to their southern masters.

Subject(s): Biography, Slavery, Abolition

1381 Max Seham

Blacks and American Medical Care
(Minneapolis, MN; University of Minnesota Press, 1973)

Summary: Written by a white physician, this book examines the problems involving blacks and medical care in the United States. The work considers the difficulties that black Americans face in getting medical care, in receiving medical training, and in practicing as physicians. A pediatrician himself, the author pays particular attention to the problems related to the medical care of black children. The author argues that an effort to eradicate racism and poverty is necessary to confront the black health crisis.

Subject(s): Medicine, Poverty, Racism

1382 **Leopold Sedar Senghor**

African Socialism
(New York, NY; American Society of African Culture, 1959)

Summary: Leopold Senghor's *African Socialism* reflects his political beliefs and his desire to promote a united view of African culture and history. Born in 1906, Senghor was one of the first great leaders of twentieth century Africa. Known as both a poet and philosopher, he became Senegal's first president in 1960 and was repeatedly reelected until his retirement in 1980.

Subject(s): Pan-Africanism, Africa, Socialism

1383 **David K. Shipler**

A Country of Strangers: Blacks and Whites in America
(New York, NY; Knopf, 1997)

Summary: In *A Country of Strangers: Blacks and Whites in America*, Pulitzer Prize-winning author and journalist David K. Shipler explores the psychological aspects of racial interaction within the United States. Among the issues covered in Shipler's work are the manner in which members of other races are viewed and judged, and how their language and means of social interaction are interpreted across racial and cultural lines. Covert prejudice, stereotyping, physical differences, the efforts by some blacks to move between two cultures, the attempts by members of different races to enter into relationships and create families and other outgrowths of our multiracial society are discussed by Shipler. The book forces readers to re-examine the foundation of their own attitudes regarding race in America.

Subject(s): Race Relations, Minorities, Miscegenation

1384 **Ann Allen Shockley**
Sue P. Chandler, Co-author

Living Black American Authors: A Biographical Directory
(New York, NY; R.R. Bowker Co., 1973)

Summary: Teacher and archivist Ann Allen Shockley teams with co-author Sue P. Chandler to publish *Living Black American Authors,* one of the first books of its kind in the United States. Modeled on traditional literary reference books focusing on well-established authors of the Western literary cannon, this work covers writers ranging from colonial America to the late twentieth century. Responding to the absence of such a book in academic as well as public libraries, the authors succeed in formalizing the panorama of black literary history by suggesting trends and schools of literary activity among black women authors, while also helping to define the literary traditions of succeeding generations of women writers.

Subject(s): Literature, Harlem Renaissance, Biography

1385 **Alan Shucard**

Countee Cullen
(Boston, MA; Twayne, 1984)

Summary: In his study, author Alan Shucard discusses the life and work of one of the most prolific poets to be associated with the Harlem Renaissance movement of the 1920s. Reflecting the rhetoric of black leaders such as W.E.B. Du Bois in his espousal of a unique African American aesthetic, Cullen (1903-1946) wrote not only poems but novels, plays, and essays as well. Though a student of Romantic poets such as John Keats, he broke away from stylistic conventions in much of his verse. In his biography, Shucard notes of Cullen that he was "led...to fabricate various pasts" due to his desire for acceptance within various social circles, making his brief life, as well as his writing, a unique creation.

Subject(s): Poetry, Literary Criticism, Harlem Renaissance

1386 **Charles E. Silberman**

Crisis in Black and White
(New York, NY; Random House, 1964)

Summary: *Crisis in Black and White* sets forth author Charles E. Silberman's contention that if all discrimination against blacks were to end immediately, the position of African Americans relative to whites in American society would be seen to have been unchanged since the early 1800s. The reason, maintains Silberman, is that blacks have been robbed of the initiative and ambition that would enable them to compete with whites on an equal playing field. In order for any social welfare programs to be effective, blacks need to be reinspired with such drives; being given control over such programs would be one way to aid in that effort. In reinforcing his argument for such claims, Silberman cites the efforts of neighborhood activist Saul Alinsky in revitalizing Chicago's Woodlawn area.

Subject(s): Slavery, Self-Actualization, Economics

1387 **Rawle Simpson**

Adventure into the Unknown
(New York, NY; Carlton Press, 1969)

Summary: This work recounts the author's journey throughout the Western Hemisphere. From the West Indian nations of Barbados and Trinidad, Simpson travels to the South American nations of Colombia and Venezuela and the countries of Central America. His trip across North America, encompassing Mexico, Canada, and the United States, culminates in New York City. Along the way, the author offers analyses of national characters, provides portraits of individuals he meets, and describes the discriminatory practices he observes and experiences along the way.

Subject(s): Travel, Prejudice

1388 **Janet L. Sims,** Compiler

The Progress of Afro-American Women: A Selected Bibliography and Resource Guide
(Westport, CT; Greenwood Press, 1980)

Summary: In *The Progress of Afro-American Women: A Selected Bibliography and Resource Guide,* author Janet L. Sims includes four thousand references to the lives and contributions of African American women living in the nineteenth and twentieth centuries. The contents of the volume are arranged according to subject areas, each divided by subtopics. An index allows researchers to find authors and subjects with ease.

Subject(s): Reference, Women's Rights, Race Relations

1389 **Naomi Sims**
Harvey Boyd, Illustrator

All about Health and Beauty for the Black Woman
(Garden City, NY; Doubleday, 1976)

Summary: *All about Health and Beauty for the Black Woman* is written by Naomi Sims, the first high-profile African American model in the United States and the first black woman to appear in *Vogue* magazine. Written several years after Sims left modeling to start her own business, this book was one of the first to approach the world of beauty from the black perspective, focusing on the unique health concerns and beauty problems of African American women.

Subject(s): Health Care, Beauty, African Americans

1390 **Naomi Sims**

All about Success for the Black Woman
(Garden City, NY; Doubleday, 1982)

Summary: In 1967, Naomi Sims became the first black woman to enter the world of high fashion. A model for *Vogue* as well as other fashion magazines, at age twenty-four Sims opted to leave modeling and start her own business. Her *All about Success for the Black Woman* is a book of tips for working women, written in response to meeting many African Americans during her travels who felt frustrated with their lives and careers.

Subject(s): Women, Employment, African Americans

1391 **Wesley G. Skogan**

Disorder and Decline: Crime and the Spiral of Decay in American Neighborhoods
(New York, NY; Free Press, 1990)

Summary: In *Disorder and Decline: Crime and the Spiral of Decay in American Neighborhoods,* author Wesley G. Skogan examines inner-city crime and its relation to community activism in improving neighborhood well-being. Based on a study of six cities and forty urban neighborhoods, the volume presents a wealth of statistical data for use by sociologists and those engaged in the field of urban studies. An analysis of the methods currently enacted to forestall urban decay causes Skogan to conclude that the most effective means of stopping the downward spiral is through community policing: the creation of neighborhood-based police squads that sustain a high public profile through their involvement in community activities but that also perform their anti-crime duties.

Subject(s): Urban Affairs, Poverty, Crime and Criminals

1392 **JoAnn Skowronski**

Black Music in America: A Bibliography
(Metuchen, NJ; Scarecrow, 1981)

Summary: Compiled by JoAnn Skowronski, *Black Music in America: A Bibliography* provides detailed information on books and articles on the music of African Americans in the United States from colonial times through the 1970s. Including both famous and less well-known musicians, the book provides readers with a look at the important role blacks have played in the evolution of "American" music.

Subject(s): Music, Musicians, African Americans

1393 **C. Freeman Sleeper**

Black Power and Christian Responsibility: Some Biblical Foundations for Social Ethics
(Nashville, TN; Abingdon Press, 1969)

Summary: *Black Power and Christian Responsibility* presents an analysis of the Biblical traditions out of which a response to the militant Black Power movement might appropriately be drawn. Beginning by stating the Christian imperative to serve as agents of God's will in establishing a just peace between the races, author C. Freeman Sleeper goes on to explain how such agentry might be implemented by concerned whites in the face of sometimes frightening militancy by African American radicals. Written for a white Christian audience, the volume contains numerous interpretations of Biblical passages as well as a scholarly discussion of what it means to be a Christian.

Subject(s): Religion, Resistance Movements, Christian Life

1394 **Barbara Smith,** Editor

Home Girls: A Black Feminist Anthology
(New York, NY; Kitchen Table: Women of Color Press, 1983)

Summary: Published by activist publisher Kitchen Table: Women of Color Press and edited by Kitchen Table founder Barbara Smith, *Home Girls: A Feminist Anthology* includes writings by such African American feminists as Audre Lorde, Gloria T. Hull, and Angela Davis.

Subject(s): Women's Rights, Politics, Homosexuality/Lesbianism

1395 **Barbara Smith**

Toward a Black Feminist Criticism
(Brooklyn, NY; Out & Out Books, 1980)

Summary: First published in *Conditions 2* magazine in 1977, Barbara Smith's *Toward a Black Feminist Criticism* asserts the validity of a black female-penned literature within the traditional literary canon dominated by dead white males. Including Third World women writers as well as other marginalized groups--such as lesbians of color--in the expanding literary establishment, Smith envisions a new literary criticism inspired by African American women's unique perspective. Based in the culture of black America, such a criticism would then allow themes, references, archetypes, and other insights relevant to the black experience to be identified for study within a literary context.

Subject(s): Women's Rights, Criticism, Homosexuality/Lesbianism

1396 **Edward D. Smith**

Climbing Jacob's Ladder: The Rise of Black Churches in Eastern American Cities, 1740-1877
(Washington, DC; Smithsonian Institution Press, 1988)

Summary: Focusing on the rise of some of the nation's oldest black congregations, this book presents an illustrated history of the development of the institutional black church in America. The work begins with a consideration of the roots of Afro-American Christianity. Subsequent chapters examine the emergence of black congregations before the nineteenth century and look at antebellum congregations in both the North and slave-holding South. The final section of the volume depicts the growth of black congregations in the South during the Civil War and Reconstruction.

Subject(s): Christianity, Slavery, American South

1397 **Warren Thomas Smith**

John Wesley and Slavery
(Nashville, TN; Abingdon Press, 1986)

Summary: In *John Wesley and Slavery* historian Warren Thomas Smith discusses the role played by British theologian John Wesley in promoting the abolitionist movement. Wesley, the founder of Methodism, harshly criticized the practice of keeping slaves in his *Thoughts upon Slavery,* distributed in the United States in 1775. Wesley's attitudes found their reflection in those of other notable intellectuals of the day, including economist Adam Smith, Thomas Clarkson, and others.

Subject(s): Slavery, Philosophy, Religion

1398 **Mechal Sobel**

Trabelin' On: The Slave Journey to an Afro-Baptist Faith
(Westport, CT; Greenwood Press, 1979)

Summary: In Mechal Sobel's *Trabelin' On: The Slave Journey to an Afro-Baptist Faith,* the author provides a history of the religious practices of both slaves and free blacks prior to the Civil War. Sobel argues that under the hardships of slavery, the beliefs of African slaves were preserved as an underpinning to Christianity. Beliefs incorporating spirits and soul-travels are among these beliefs, states Sobel, who supports her case within a convincing and well-documented anthropological, sociological, and historical framework.

Subject(s): Slavery, Religion, Christianity

1399 **Mechal Sobel**

The World They Made Together: Black and White Values in Eighteenth-Century Virginia
(Princeton, NJ; Princeton University Press, 1987)

Summary: In *The World They Made Together: Black and White Values in Eighteenth-Century Virginia,* historian Mechal Sobel argues that both black and white southerners shared a common culture. Going against prevailing scholarship, Sobel culls documentary and other evidence from colonial Virginia in the 1700s to demonstrate that the social mores and values as well as the organization and activities of both communities and individual family units of the area's white inhabitants were mirrored by the region's slave population.

Subject(s): Slavery, History, American South

1400 **Allan H. Spear**

Black Chicago: The Making of a Negro Ghetto, 1890-1920
(University of Chicago Press; 1967)

Summary: Considered one of the groundbreaking works in twentieth century urban studies, *Black Chicago: The Making of a Negro Ghetto, 1890-1920* examines the forces that led to the creation of an isolated black community within the city of Chicago. History professor Allan Spear draws much of his background data from primary statistical sources as well as from the Chicago Commission on Race Relations report on the status of Chicago blacks, first published in 1922. Within the thirty-year period under investigation, Spear demonstrates that interaction between the races degenerated in the face of increasing segregationist and discriminatory policies. This, coupled with a rise in nationalistic sentiment among black leaders, resulted in an acceptance of all-black urban communities, according to Spear.

Subject(s): Racism, Urban Affairs, Black Nationalism

1401 Carol B. Stack

All Our Kin: Strategies for Survival in a Black Community
(New York, NY; Harper & Row, 1974)

Summary: Author Carol B. Stack presents the difficulties faced by inner-city black communities and the resourcefulness of people working together to overcome those difficulties. Taking as her central focus the African American family, Stack profiles the strong "kinship" network that cements not only extended families but neighborhoods as well.

Subject(s): City and Town Life, Family Relations

1402 Kenneth M. Stampp

The Peculiar Institution: Slavery in the Ante-Bellum South
(New York, NY; Knopf, 1956)

Summary: Considered groundbreaking in its approach, *The Peculiar Institution: Slavery in the Ante-Bellum South* profiles the institution of slavery as it related to the economic decline of the southern economy. Praised for his research, his logic, and his courage in examining slavery from an objective viewpoint, historian Kenneth Stampp summoned a wealth of statistical evidence to show the enslavement of black African Americans as not only a detriment to the economic well-being of the region but one of the greatest injustices of the nation. Stampp's book was one of the first liberal revisionist studies of slavery to be published.

Subject(s): Slavery, American South, Economics

1403 Robert Staples

Black Masculinity: The Black Man's Role in American Society
(San Francisco, CA; Black Scholar Press, 1982)

Summary: In *Black Masculinity: The Black Man's Role in American Society* Robert Staples discusses the sexual and social lives of black men as they conflict with the pressures wrought by feminism and other shifts in the late twentieth century social landscape. Deflating a number of myths about black men--including their threatening sexuality and their propensity toward violence--Staples goes on to deal with the problems of urban violence and single-parent families, arguing that these are the result of institutional racism.

Subject(s): Sex Roles, Racism, Violence

1404 Shelby Steele

The Content of Our Character: A New Vision of Race in America
(New York, NY; St. Martin's Press, 1990)

Summary: In his award-winning *The Content of Our Character: A New Vision of Race in America,* conservative black scholar Shelby Steele sparked heated debate over his indict-ment of the liberal policies and social attitudes towards race that have proliferated in the United States in the wake of the civil rights movement. Within the book's nine essays, Steele argues against victimization and for personal responsibility, and against social policies that exacerbate rather than diminish racial conflict and inequalities.

Subject(s): Race Relations, Politics

Award(s): National Book Critics Circle Award: Nonfiction, 1991

1405 Shelby Steele

A Dream Deferred: The Second Betrayal of Black Freedom in America
(New York, NY; HarperCollins Publishers, 1998)

Summary: In *A Dream Deferred: The Second Betrayal of Black Freedom in America* Shelby Steele argues that the civil rights agenda of the late twentieth century was not motivated by a desire to promote equality between the races; rather, it was an effort by stigmatized white liberals to expiate their moral guilt through support of policies like affirmative action. Steele, a black conservative, expresses his frustration at the growth of the "victim-focused" racial identity that has resulted from set-aside programs and entitlements, arguing that it conflicts with the successes blacks could achieve through self-reliance and being allowed a level playing field.

Subject(s): Race Relations, Self-Perception, Politics

1406 Dorothy Sterling, Editor

The Trouble They Seen: Black People Tell the Story of Reconstruction
(Garden City, NY; Doubleday, 1976)

Summary: In her *The Trouble They Seen: Black People Tell the Story of Reconstruction,* editor Dorothy Sterling introduces young readers to the aftermath of the Civil War from a slightly different historical perspective. Viewing the years of rebuilding both the physical landscape and the economy from the perspective of African Americans newly released from slavery, Sterling shows that many blacks were worse off than before the war due to the activities of carpetbaggers--individuals from the northern U.S. who moved south, bought up land, and grew rich off the misfortune of others. By the late 1870s, many blacks had left the area, preferring to make a start in western states such as Kansas.

Subject(s): Reconstruction, Emigration and Immigration, Economics

1407 Paul Stoller, Editor

Black American English: Its Background and Its Usage in the Schools and in Literature
(New York, NY; Dell Pub. Co., 1975)

Summary: This comprehensive study of black American English explores black vernacular from a linguistic, historical, and literary perspective. In the book's three chapters--"History and Structure of Black Speech"; "Black Speech and Education"; and "Black Speech and Literature"-various essays discuss such matters as "Some Linguistic Features of Negro Dialect" and "Talking Black in the Classroom." The final chapter includes selections from novels by Al Young, Martie Charles, and June Jordan. The issue of black speech being used to educate African American students in American public schools--in a system known as "Ebonics"--would spark controversy more than two decades after the publication of this book.

Subject(s): Education, Literature, Language

1408 Margie Sturgis

Let the Record Show: Memoirs of a Parole Board Member

(Hicksville, NY; Exposition Press, 1978)

Summary: Margie Sturgis, in her 1978 memoir, tells of her stint as a member of the Illinois Parole and Pardon Board. During her term on the Board, Sturgis witnessed how political infighting, bigotry, and personal agendas compromised the Board's effectiveness and its fairness. Sturgis's term occurred during the mid-1970s, when crime rates reached historic levels in many American states and cities.

Subject(s): Racism, Prisoners and Prisons

1409 Henry Louis Suggs, Editor

The Black Press in the Middle West, 1865-1985

(Westport, CT; Greenwood Press, 1996)

Summary: Edited by Clemson University professor Henry Louis Suggs, *The Black Press in the Middle West, 1865-1985* is considered the first detailed study of the efforts of newspapermen and women of color in the Midwest. Beginning with the publication of America's first black newspaper, *Freedom's Journal*, the book's ten contributors contend, African Americans had a large voice in molding the character and politics of the region. Playing an active role in young communities where larger presses had yet to become institutionalized, black newspapers were free to push openly for educational reforms and advance other policies and philosophies of their editorial staffs.

Subject(s): City and Town Life, Journalism, Newspapers

1410 James Summerville

Educating Black Doctors: A History of Meharry Medical College

(University, AL; University of Alabama Press, 1983)

Summary: In *Educating Black Doctors: A History of Meharry Medical College* author James Summerville describes the roots of the largest predominately African American medical school in the United States. Founded in 1876 by Samuel Meharry, a Nashville, Tennessee, businessman, the school was graduating more than half the nation's black physicians by the mid-1950s. Summerville noted that by the 1980s, black acceptance in medical schools across the nation was up, and while Meharry no longer produced the bulk of the nation's black doctors, its facilities, adjacent to Fisk University, had begun attracting white students.

Subject(s): Education, Segregation, Doctors

1411 Ibrahim K. Sundiata

From Slaving to Neoslavery: The Bight of Biafra and Fernando Po in the Era of Abolition, 1827-1930

(Madison, WI; University of Wisconsin Press, 1996)

Summary: In *From Slaving to Neoslavery: The Bight of Biafra and Fernando Po in the Era of Abolition, 1827-1930* Brandeis University professor Ibrahim K. Sundiata relates the history of the West African island of Fernando Po, the homeland of the Bantu-speaking Bubi tribe. Colonized by westernized blacks in the late 1800s, the island developed a plantation economy similar to that of the pre-Civil War South. Culminating his analysis of labor relations with the virtual extinction of the native Bubi culture, Sundiata argues against the traditional economic model in which free labor ultimately displaces slavery, instead positing influences such as environment, disease, and political alliances in determining slavery's survival.

Subject(s): Slavery, Economics, Africa

1412 Leonard I. Sweet

Black Images of America, 1784-1870

(New York, NY; Norton, 1976)

Summary: *Black Images of America, 1784-1870* presents author Leonard I. Sweet's contention that African Americans in leadership positions prior to the Civil War did not view their interests as apart from those of white Americans. Through copious research, Sweet shows that a belief in the American Dream--accepting both progress and a sense of divine mission as their inevitable destiny--bound black leaders closely with whites and overshadowed any consideration of racial differences.

Subject(s): Race Relations, History, Self-Perception

1413 Karl E. Taeuber
Alma F. Taeuber, Co-author

Negroes in Cities: Residential Segregation and Neighborhood Change

(Chicago, IL; Aldine Pub. Co., 1965)

Summary: In *Negroes in Cities: Residential Segregation and Neighborhood Change* Karl and Alma Taeuber merge their doctoral research undertaken in the area of segregation and desegregation in U.S. cities. Basing their study on census data and a vast body of other statistical evidence, the Taeubers present what was acclaimed as an objective historical overview of the trends in population as it relates to race within urban residential areas during the civil rights era. Notable in the Taeubers' work is their emphasis on the process by which urban neighborhoods were transformed into enclaves of blacks, whites, and other racial minorities.

Subject(s): Urban Affairs, Segregation, Sociology

1414 Ellen Tarry

The Third Door: The Autobiography of an American Negro Woman
(New York, NY; D. McKay Co., 1955)

Summary: This volume recounts the life of Ellen Tarry, a journalist and writer. Beginning her career at the Birmingham, Alabama, *Truth,* Tarry moved north to New York City, where she was introduced to major literary figures of the Harlem Renaissance, including Claude McKay, Countee Cullen, and Langston Hughes. She also worked at Friendship House, an interracial justice center in Harlem. Tarry also had a successful career as a children's book writer.

Subject(s): Autobiography, Harlem Renaissance

1415 Brook Thomas, Editor

"Plessy v. Ferguson," with Documents
(New York, NY; St. Martin's Press, 1996)

Summary: *"Plessy v. Ferguson," with Documents* provides students of the civil rights movement with primary documents related to one of the most notable legal precedents to be battled during the twentieth century: the concept of "separate but equal" as a viable alternative to integration in society. Based on an 1896 U.S. Supreme Court decision negating Homer Plessy's argument that his prohibition from riding in the "white" train car violated his rights under the 14th Amendment, *Plessy v. Ferguson* would ultimately be overturned in the early 1950s by *Brown v. Board of Education.*

Subject(s): Judicial System, Segregation, Law

1416 Becky Thompson, Editor
Sangeeta Tyagi, Co-editor

Names We Call Home: Autobiography on Racial Identity
(New York, NY; Routledge, 1996)

Summary: *Names We Call Home: Autobiography on Racial Identity* collects a number of essays that supplement and expand the academic discussion begun with 1995's *A Theory of Textuality: The Logic and Epistemology.* A reflection of more moderate views, the essays explore such issues as the identity and function of writers and readers, geography and culture as a foundation of racial identity, and identity as it is created by whites, Native Americans, blacks, and other minorities within a textual sphere.

Subject(s): Literature, Academia, Identity

1417 Emory J. Tolbert

The UNIA and Black Los Angeles: Ideology and Community in the American Garvey Movement
(Los Angeles, CA; Center for Afro-American Studies, University of California, 1980)

Summary: *The UNIA and Black Los Angeles: Ideology and Community in the American Garvey Movement* discusses Marcus Garvey's Universal Negro Improvement Association (UNIA) as the group affected the African American community of Los Angeles in the early part of the twentieth century. In the early 1920s Garvey captured the attention of many blacks by proclaiming his dream of going "back to Africa," a dream that would end in ruin with the financial collapse of his Black Star Line but that would spark other "back to Africa" ideologies in later generations.

Subject(s): Africa, Emigration and Immigration

1418 David Toop

The Rap Attack: African Jive to New York Hip Hop
(Boston, MA; South End Press, 1984)

Summary: In David Toop's well-illustrated *The Rap Attack: African Jive to New York Hip Hop* the rap phenomenon is traced from its African roots through the street culture of the early twentieth century to its modern incarnation as a commercialization of the sounds of the original politically conscious street DJs of the 1970s and early 1980s. Originating in New York City, hip hop is a culture that embodies rap music, break dancing, and a streetwise attitude as a way of life. While hip hop has been seen by some as derivative, Toop views hip hop as promoting creativity through the reconfiguring and re-use of existing songs and instrumental recordings. Providing a revealing and accessible treatment of his subject, Toop's book was highly praised; it would be revised in the late 1990s as *Rap Attack 2.*

Subject(s): Music

1419 Dempsey J. Travis

An Autobiography of Black Jazz
(Chicago, IL; Urban Research Institute, 1983)

Summary: Written by Chicago businessman and journalist Dempsey J. Travis, *An Autobiography of Black Jazz* is about Chicago jazz as well as the city that created it, including the night life, politics, and racial mix that has influenced numerous jazz musicians. Travis includes numerous anecdotes, local history, legends and city lore in an effort to enrich jazz fans' appreciation and enjoyment of music produced in the Windy City.

Subject(s): Music, Jazz, Popular Culture

1420 U.S. National Advisory Commission on Civil Disorders

The Kerner Report

(New York, NY; Bantam Books, 1968)

Summary: One of the most influential documents to come out of the civil rights movement, *The Kerner Report* was the result of the Commission on Civil Disorders appointed by President Lyndon B. Johnson in 1967 to investigate the cause of the riots that had broken out in U.S. cities during the 1960s. Among its conclusions, the Commission cited white racism as the cause of most urban unrest and warned that the nation was becoming segregated along racial and economic lines. Among the Commission's recommendations were the creation of new jobs, job-training programs, enhanced neighborhood schools, low-income and subsidized housing, welfare reform, and a national income supplementation, as well as laws against discrimination in employment and access to housing.

Subject(s): Segregation, Race Relations, Civil Rights Movement

1421 William L. Van Deburg

New Day in Babylon: The Black Power Movement and American Culture, 1965-1975

(Chicago, IL; University of Chicago Press, 1992)

Summary: In his *New Day in Babylon: The Black Power Movement and American Culture, 1965-1975*, professor William L. Van Deburg of the University of Wisconsin in Madison undertakes the mammoth task of locating, documenting, and interpreting documents reflecting an era during which the United States underwent significant social and political change. Praised for its scholarship, *New Day* also was cited as a road map for the future of race relations.

Subject(s): Race Relations, Cultural Conflict, History

1422 Richard C. Wade

Slavery in the Cities: The South, 1820-1860

(New York, NY; Oxford University Press, 1964)

Summary: In his *Slavery in the Cities: The South, 1820-1860*, historian Richard C. Wade attempts to "find out what happened to slavery in an urban environment and to reconstruct the texture of life of the Negroes who lived in bondage in the cities." Examining records in the urban areas of the South, as well as in newer settlements along the Mississippi Valley, Wade highlights the differences in character between urban slavery and that characteristic of southern plantations. The book sparked some controversy among critics due to its attempt to draw parallels between life in the early 1800s and life in urban America in the mid-1900s.

Subject(s): Slavery, Urban Affairs, History

1423 Anne Kendrick Walker

Tuskegee and the Black Belt: A Portrait of a Race

(Richmond, VA; Dietz Press, 1944)

Summary: *Tuskegee and the Black Belt: A Portrait of a Race* profiles the legacy of Booker T. Washington. Beginning with a description of Washington's early years, author Ann Kendrick Walker describes the founding of Tuskegee University and then moves forward in time to discuss the "Negro's Bill of Grievances," the debate over the poll tax, the role of blacks in both world wars, and the debate over the government's efforts to create more jobs for African Americans, an intervention considered unwelcome by many southern whites. Walker, a southern white herself, was praised for her open-minded approach to black history.

Subject(s): Race Relations, American South, History

1424 Margaret Walker
Maryemma Graham, Editor

On Being Female, Black, and Free: Essays by Margaret Walker, 1932-1992

(Knoxville, TN; University of Tennessee Press, 1997)

Summary: *On Being Female, Black, and Free: Essays by Margaret Walker, 1932-1992* collects speeches, essays, and other writings by noted poet and novelist Walker. A major figure in twentieth century African American letters, Walker reflects on her personal creative process as well as that of other women writers, and she discusses issues of education, politics, race, and culture.

Subject(s): Politics, Social Conditions, Women's Rights

1425 Peter F. Walker

Moral Choices: Memory, Desire, and Imagination in Nineteenth-Century American Abolition

(Baton Rouge, LA; Louisiana State University Press, 1978)

Summary: In *Moral Choices: Memory, Desire, and Imagination in Nineteenth-Century American Abolition* historian Peter F. Walker takes a psycho-biographical approach in his six essays on abolitionists who worked on the sidelines of the nineteenth-century movement to abolish slavery. In well-wrought prose, Walker takes the controversial stance that female abolitionists joined the movement in response to their repressed sexual urges, and he makes the equally controversial judgment that Frederick Douglass was fueled in his career by a secret desire to be a white man.

Subject(s): Slavery, Abolition, Biography

1426 **Vanessa Siddle Walker**

Their Highest Potential: An African American School Community in the Segregated South

(Chapel Hill, NC; University of North Carolina Press, 1996)

Summary: In *Their Highest Potential: An African American School Community in the Segregated South* Vanessa Siddle Walker focuses on the Caswell County, North Carolina community school prior to its last year of segregation in 1969. While showing through a series of interviews the school's under-funding relative to white schools in the region and its inadequate facilities, staffing, and supplies, Walker argues that segregation was a benefit to the black children of Caswell County in that they were not required to confront racism or internalize their minority status. Instead, she maintains, the school provided an excellent learning environment as a result of the combined efforts of school officials, teachers, parents, and students.

Subject(s): Education, American South, Segregation

1427 **Michele Wallace**

Black Macho and the Myth of the Superwoman

(New York, NY; Dial Press, 1979)

Summary: Published in 1976, when its author, Michele Wallace, was only twenty-six years old, *Black Macho and the Myth of the Superwoman* was hailed by feminist critics as groundbreaking. The volume is divided into two parts: the first deals with the Black Power movement of the late 1960s, while the second examines the changing role of African American women during that movement. According to Wallace, in response to feelings of powerlessness within society at large, black men adopted primitive attitudes toward their female companions: "women as possessions, women as the spoils of war." Challenging this stereotype of the valueless black woman, Wallace counters with the superwoman, who holds the family together both emotionally and financially while her man, suffering poor self-esteem, hunts around for a paying job. While praised in some circles for challenging the black status-quo, *Black Macho* also received its share of criticism for its attack on an African American community already divided by racial strife.

Subject(s): Women's Rights, Civil Rights Movement, Racial Conflict

1428 **Ronald G. Walters**

The Antislavery Appeal: American Abolitionism after 1830

(Baltimore, MD; Johns Hopkins University Press, 1976)

Summary: In *The Antislavery Appeal: American Abolitionism after 1830* historian Ronald G. Walters argues that abolitionists were united in their vision of a future United States as a moral, God-fearing nation, its progress fueled by capitalism and egalitarianism. Despite the surface differences among abolitionists and their organizations, Walters shows that most of the men and women who worked to end slavery were drawn to the movement as a replacement for evangelical religion. More than just battling against slavery, abolitionists were attempting to direct a culture in transition, according to Walters.

Subject(s): Abolition, History, Resistance Movements

1429 **Joseph R. Washington, Jr.**

The Politics of God

(Boston, MA; Beacon Press, 1967)

Summary: In Joseph R. Washington's *The Politics of God* the author continues the exploration of the development of American religion he began in 1964's *Black Religion*. Beginning by arguing that racism serves as the core of the nation's white Christian doctrine, Washington goes on to contend that blacks, as God's chosen servants, have been entrusted with the task of "freeing" themselves as well as their captors. Indeed, claims Washington, African American churches will prove to be the salvation of the United States.

Subject(s): Religion, Christianity, Race Relations

1430 **A.I. Waskow**

From Race Riot to Sit-In, 1919 and the 1960s: A Study in the Connections between Conflict and Violence

(Garden City, NY; Doubleday, 1966)

Summary: In his 1966 study, liberal socialist theorist A.I. Waskow contrasts the different methods protestors have used to challenge discrimination through the first part of the twentieth century. Combining historical and sociological analysis, Waskow summarizes in detail the non-violent methods employed by civil rights activists in the 1960s in an effort to initiate interracial reform by challenging discrimination.

Subject(s): Race Relations, Civil Rights Movement, Rebellion

1431 **Enoch P. Waters**

American Diary: A Personal History of the Black Press

(Chicago, IL; Path Press, 1987)

Summary: Written by journalist Enoch P. Waters, *American Diary: A Personal History of the Black Press* is a history of African American newspapers and periodicals in the United States. Executive editor for the Chicago *Defender*, one of the largest black-owned dailies in the United States, Waters worked for many other papers as well as the Associated Press during his long career. His first-hand experience as a journalist, as well as his familiarity with the business side of journalism through his ownership of a newspaper, gives *American Diary* its insightful view of the business of the press as a crucial part of American history.

Subject(s): Journalism, History, Newspapers

1432 Thomas L. Webber

Deep like the Rivers: Education in the Slave Quarter Community, 1831-1865

(New York, NY; Norton, 1978)

Summary: Based on the author's masters' thesis, *Deep like the Rivers: Education in the Slave Quarter Community, 1831-1865* presents U.S. society and culture as it was understood and navigated by the men and women brought over as slaves from Africa and other places. Adopting the "voice" of both slaves and former slaves, author Thomas L. Webber attempts to reflect the unique worldview of blacks learning from a variety of sources in an effort to align their religion and traditions with those in place in America.

Subject(s): Education, Slavery, American South

1433 Robert E. Weems, Jr.

Black Business in the Black Metropolis: The Chicago Metropolitan Assurance Company, 1925-1985

(Bloomington, IN; Indiana University Press, 1996)

Summary: In *Black Business in the Black Metropolis: The Chicago Metropolitan Assurance Company, 1925-1985*, part of the series "Blacks in the Diaspora," Robert E. Weems, Jr. examines one of the many black-owned and -operated insurance companies to spring up in response to African Americans' desire for insurance that was not made available to them by white-owned companies in the early years of the twentieth century. While many black-owned insurance providers had their roots in mutual aid societies, Chicago's Metropolitan Assurance Company was originally funded by gambling income. Considered well researched, Weems's work presents an in-depth look at both black entrepreneurship and a growing black community.

Subject(s): Economics, Urban Affairs

1434 Robert E. Weems, Jr.

Desegregating the Dollar: African American Consumerism in the Twentieth Century

(New York, NY; New York University Press, 1998)

Summary: In *Desegregating the Dollar: African American Consumerism in the Twentieth Century*, Robert E. Weems, Jr. profiles the economic stability of the African American family in an age of consumerism. Including interviews with African American public relations and marketing specialists, Weems outlines the history of the targeting of black consumers, which began after rural southern blacks migrated north to industrial cities and better paying jobs. He shows that while consumer options have increased, a more "integrated" market has often destroyed successful ethnic-oriented black businesses. Weems maintains that new strategies must be employed by African American businesses to ensure that at least part of the $500 mil-

lion spent by blacks each year remains in their own communities.

Subject(s): Economics, Urban Affairs

1435 Robert G. Weisbord

Genocide?: Birth Control and the Black American

(Westport, CT; Greenwood Press, 1975)

Summary: In *Genocide? Birth Control and the Black American* author Robert G. Weisbord examines the argument, made by some, that birth control is actually a covert effort to diminish the African American population. From a history of similar efforts that dot the American past and an overview of the position of black leaders spanning radical groups like the Black Panthers to more conservative groups like C.O.R.E., Weisbord concludes that while such a concern may be well-founded, the availability of modern birth control has been a voluntary system, and that it has been black women themselves who have steadily demanded its availability.

Subject(s): Women's Rights, Genocide

1436 Cornel West

Race Matters

(Boston, MA; Beacon Press, 1993)

Summary: In the essay collection *Race Matters* noted scholar and educator Cornel West cements his reputation as one of the foremost writers on racial issues in the late twentieth century. His writings focus on such issues as how groups of a variety of political and racial identities have perpetuated the racial strife within the United States. Following his critique of the race problem with solutions, West recommends opening lines of communication, redistributing wealth, and pushing for implementation of government-sponsored help in implementing such programs.

Subject(s): Race Relations, Government

1437 Deborah Gray White

Ar'n't I a Woman?: Female Slaves in the Plantation South

(New York, NY; Norton, 1985)

Summary: In *Ar'n't I a Woman? Female Slaves in the Plantation South*, scholar Deborah Gray White presents a groundbreaking study of the lives of slave women in the Old South. Burdened with responsibilities extending far beyond those traditionally expected to be borne by women in the eighteenth and nineteenth century, African American women labored under both racism and sexism, their sex often subsumed by their role as chattel. White extends her study to the years following the Civil War, as black women gained new freedoms but also labored to hold their families together amid a chaotic culture debased and devastated by war. A new edition was published in 1999.

Subject(s): Slavery, American South, Women's Rights

1438 Evelyn D. White, Compiler

Selected Bibliography of Published Choral Music by Black Composers
(Washington, DC; White, 1975)

Summary: *Choral Music by Black Composers: A Selected, Annotated Bibliography* contains information on published and unpublished choral works by some one hundred African American composers and arrangers. Compiled by Evelyn D. White, the volume includes works representative of a variety of musical styles, from classical to contemporary. Included are an annotated list of compositions organized alphabetically by composer's name, a listing of collections, biographical sketches, a discography, and addresses of relevant publishers and composers.

Subject(s): Music, Reference

1439 Walter White

A Man Called White: The Autobiography of Walter White
(New York, NY; Viking Press, 1948)

Summary: *A Man Called White: The Autobiography of Walter White* is the life story of Walter White (1893-1955), an author, activist, and co-founder of the National Association for the Advancement of Colored People. White was a significant figure in the Harlem Renaissance and was the author of several highly regarded novels. From the time he began working alongside W.E.B. Du Bois at the NAACP in 1918 until he was elected executive secretary of that organization thirteen years later, White remained a tireless advocate for equal treatment among the races. He also served as a consultant to Presidents Harry S. Truman and Franklin D. Roosevelt.

Subject(s): Harlem Renaissance, Civil Rights Movement, Autobiography

1440 Cynthia Willett

Maternal Ethics and Other Slave Moralities
(New York, NY; Routledge, 1995)

Summary: *Maternal Ethics and Other Slave Moralities* is a postmodernist examination of the narratives of slaves set down in the eighteenth and nineteenth centuries by blacks who, often without the help of whites, learned to read and write as a means of immortalizing their experiences. Author Cynthia Willett examines how such narratives reflect a development of a variety of moral codes, and she studies those moralities through the lens of such intellectuals as Julia Kristeva, Daniel Stern, Luce Irigaray, and others.

Subject(s): Academia, Biography, Slavery

1441 Chancellor Williams

The Destruction of Black Civilization: Great Issues of a Race from 4500 B.C. to 2000 A.D.
(Dubuque, IA; Kendall/Hunt Pub. Co., 1971)

Summary: In the controversial *The Destruction of Black Civilization: Great Issues of a Race from 4500 B.C. to 2000 A.D.* historian Chancellor Williams surveys the traditional culture of over one hundred language groups. Basing his conclusions on the results of a two year study undertaken in the early 1960s, Williams contends that among the reasons why Africans are considered less politically and culturally sophisticated than other ethnic groups is the African people's lack of guile. African's openness to strangers led to the countless invasions by marauding Europeans and others that robbed the continent of the natural resources that would have made it among the wealthiest of nations. Williams ends with an overview of black history, which he hopes will allow blacks to learn from their past, organize, and reclaim their destiny as a great people.

Subject(s): Africa, History

Award(s): Black Academy of Arts and Letters: Book Award, 1971

1442 Delores S. Williams

Sisters in the Wilderness: The Challenge of Womanist God-Talk
(Maryknoll, NY; Orbis Books, 1993)

Summary: Considering religion from a black feminist or "womanist" perspective, Delores S. Williams's *Sisters in the Wilderness: The Challenge of Womanist God-Talk* challenges the male bias inherent in traditional Christian theologies as well as the patriarchal aspects of several African American denominations. In her argument for the increased participation of women within black churches, Williams uses the symbol of Hagar, the mother of Ishmael, who, sent out into the wilderness by Abraham and Sarah, found God's protection. Like Hagar, Williams sees modern black women as self-reliant, independent, and surviving against overwhelming odds.

Subject(s): Women's Rights, Religion, Christianity

1443 Juan Williams

Thurgood Marshall: American Revolutionary
(New York, NY; Times Books, 1998)

Summary: *Thurgood Marshall: American Revolutionary* is a biography of the first African American ever appointed to the U.S. Supreme Court. Written by news correspondent Juan Williams, the book focuses on Marshall's early years as an attorney for the NAACP, including his tumultuous relationship with organization founder W.E.B. Du Bois. Successful in his defense of desegregation of U.S. public schools in *Brown v. Board of Education*, Marshall rose through the legal ranks to solicitor general, and from there to his historic appointment by President Lyndon Johnson to a 24-year term on the high court.

Subject(s): Biography, Law, Judicial System

1444 Patricia J. Williams

The Alchemy of Race and Rights: Diary of a Law Professor

(Cambridge, MA; Harvard University Press, 1991)

Summary: In *Alchemy of Race and Rights: Diary of a Law Professor,* Patricia J. Williams characterizes her years as a student at Harvard University's prestigious school of law as a period during which she felt "invisible." As both a black and a female, Williams, who went on to teach law at New York City's Columbia University, was keenly aware of the marked absence of both groups among Harvard's faculty. The book details its author's growing perception of how issues of race, gender, and class have combined to influence U.S. law, and how those laws, by their implementation, have defined and continue to mold society. Illustrating her argument with specific instances of what she terms the "disenfranchisement" of African Americans, Williams argues that even Constitutional law has been interpreted by a white male elite, with the resulting rights under that law clearly benefiting its interpreters--at the expense of blacks, the poor, and women.

Subject(s): Racism, Criminal Justice, Civil Rights

1445 Joel Williamson

New People: Miscegenation and Mulattoes in the United States

(New York, NY; Free Press, 1980)

Summary: *New People: Miscegenation and Mulattoes in the United States* is Joel Williamson's analysis of the interracial relationships between whites and blacks that have produced "new people." Beginning his examination of miscegenation in the pre-Revolutionary War era, Williamson shows how this intermingling of the races has affected U.S. society and culture, distinguishing between the social significance of being a mulatto in earlier centuries and the relative insignificance of being mixed-race in the twentieth century.

Subject(s): Miscegenation, Race Relations, Interracial Marriage

1446 Deborah Willis, Editor

Picturing Us: African American Identity in Photography

(New York, NY; New Press, 1994)

Summary: In *Picturing Us: African American Identity in Photography,* editor and photography historian Deborah Willis assembles photographs selected by black writers, critics, and filmmakers. She also includes an essay describing the personal significance of the photographic image, with an eye to creating an overview of the black experience in twentieth century Amer-

ica. Among those included in this volume linking art and society are Edward P. Jones, Lise Hamilton, and Angela Davis.

Subject(s): Photography, Social Conditions, Artists and Art

1447 Emily Herring Wilson

Hope and Dignity: Older Black Women of the South

(Philadelphia, PA; Temple University Press, 1983)

Summary: For *Hope and Dignity: Older Black Women of the South* cultural historian Emily Herring Wilson interviewed more than twenty older African American women living in the southern United States. Drawing on memories of the past, these oral histories provide readers with information about the day-to-day lives of past generations and the beliefs and attitudes that allowed these strong women to survive the inevitable tragedies that touch each of us. Through these women's own words, readers are introduced to women's capacity to perform a variety of roles in life. Wilson's text is accompanied by photographs by Susan Mullally and a foreword by Maya Angelou.

Subject(s): Women, Working-Class Life, Old Age

1448 William J. Wilson

The Declining Significance of Race: Blacks and Changing American Institutions

(Chicago, IL; University of Chicago Press, 1978)

Summary: In *The Declining Significance of Race: Blacks and Changing American Institutions* sociologist William J. Wilson follows the thread of black history from slavery to the mid-1900s to demonstrate the success of efforts to exclude African Americans from the social and political mainstream. While the civil rights movement would eliminate many of the mechanisms that created such exclusion, Wilson argues that the disparity between income levels within the black community has now resulted in a new hierarchy that continues to disadvantage many blacks, this one based on class rather than race.

Subject(s): Sociology, Economics, History

1449 William J. Wilson

The Truly Disadvantaged: The Inner City, the Underclass, and Public Policy

(Chicago, IL; University of Chicago Press, 1987)

Summary: Selected by the *New York Times* as one of the best books of 1987, William J. Williams's *The Truly Disadvantaged: The Inner City, the Underclass, and Public Policy* contends that the rise in the poverty level in U.S. cities during the late 1900s was not the result of racist attitudes or policies. Instead, shifts in the U.S. economy as a result of the nation's movement from a manufacturing to a service economy have created a labor force not tied to urban centers, while entitlement programs and other race-based policies have stabilized the suburban middle classes.

Subject(s): Economics, Race Relations, Labor Conditions

Award(s): C. Wright Mills Award, 1998

1450 **Peter H. Wood**

Black Majority: Negroes in Colonial South Carolina from 1670 through the Stono Rebellion

(New York, NY; Knopf, 1974)

Summary: *Black Majority: Negroes in Colonial Carolina from 1670 through the Stono Rebellion* presents an overview of South Carolina's African American culture from the onset of slavery through the slave rebellion that took place in 1740. Including information on both free and enslaved blacks, Wood includes a discussion of the "Gullah" dialect characteristic of the region, a discussion of the dominant influences of blacks upon South Carolina's white society, and the growing fear of whites as blacks attained strength in numbers compared to whites. The work is notable for Wood's emphasis on work as a determining factor in an individual's self-image and reaction to slavery.

Subject(s): Slavery, Rebellion, American South

1451 **C. Vann Woodward**

The Strange Career of Jim Crow

(New York, NY; Oxford University Press, 1955)

Summary: Based on a series of lectures given at the University of Virginia in 1954, *The Strange Career of Jim Crow* traces the history of segregation in the American South. Professor C. Vann Woodward argues that Jim Crow laws did not go into effect immediately after the withdrawal of Union troops, but rather evolved over the next few decades, with poll taxes, literacy and property requirements going into effect only in 1895. Unlike many historians on the subject, Woodward portrays southern whites as less insidious in their efforts to keep blacks down than others.

Subject(s): History, Reconstruction, American South

1452 **John Wesley Work**

American Negro Songs

(New York, NY; Howell, Soskin & Company, 1940)

Summary: John Wesley Work's *American Negro Songs* serves as a comprehensive collection of 230 folk songs, religious songs, blues melodies, and spirituals. Including easy-to-play arrangements in addition to lyrics, Work, a professor of music at Fisk University, augmented his collection with chapters outlining the origins and nature of different types of song and commenting on the music's African origins. A continuation of several other volumes of African American music, *American Negro Songs* served as a major contribution to black folklore.

Subject(s): Music, Slavery, Folklore

1453 **George C. Wright**

Life behind a Veil: Blacks in Louisville, Kentucky, 1865-1930

(Baton Rouge, LA; Louisiana State University Press, 1985)

Summary: A study of black life between the Civil War and the Depression years, *Life behind a Veil: Blacks in Louisville, Kentucky, 1865-1930* tracks the influences of black emancipation. George C. Wright discusses reconstruction, segregationist policies, and the rise of Marcus Garvey and his "back to Africa" movement. While examining several facets of black city life, author Wright limits his focus to the regional political sphere, drawing conclusions based on the activities of the NAACP and the National Urban League, the changing platforms and leadership of the two political parties, and items of interest to the African American press.

Subject(s): History, American South, Reconstruction

1454 **Nathan Wright**

Black Power and Urban Unrest: Creative Possibilities

(New York, NY; Hawthorn Books, 1967)

Summary: In his *Black Power and Urban Unrest: Creative Possibilities* author Nathan Wright, Jr. depicts the Black Power movement of the 1960s as a crucial stage in the movement toward racial harmony in the United States. Stressing the importance of allowing blacks to assume leadership of the fight for equality, Wright encourages white-run churches and businesses to aid blacks in their struggle, claiming that churches, in particular, have the most to gain from a self-sufficient black constituency. The book includes a statement on black power issued by the National Committee of Negro Churchmen in 1966.

Subject(s): Religion, Self-Reliance, Race Relations

1455 **Tinsley E. Yarbrough**

Judge Frank Johnson and Human Rights in Alabama

(University, AL; University of Alabama Press, 1981)

Summary: Written by historian Tinsley E. Yarbrough, *Judge Frank Johnson and Human Rights in Alabama* describes a state court judge and his steadfast support of civil rights in tumultuous Alabama from 1955 to 1979. While Yarbrough portrays Justice Johnson as a staunch Republican, he broke from party lines to follow his conscience. Conservative on fiscal, criminal, and personal matters, he remained unflinching in his determination to follow the letter of the Constitution and uphold the Bill of Rights by supporting racial integration.

Subject(s): American South, Segregation, Judicial System

1456 Al Young

Bodies & Soul: Musical Memoirs
(Berkeley, CA; Creative Arts Book Co., 1981)

Summary: *Bodies and Soul: Musical Memoirs* is one of a series of essay collections by Al Young, a poet, novelist, and author of short fiction who focuses on African Americans trying to find their way in twentieth century black society. In each selection, Young is inspired by a favorite piece of music--jazz, blues, pop, and classical--and writes about the memories or emotions that are unlocked by that particular melody or score.

Subject(s): Music, Autobiography

1457 Al Young

Kinds of Blue: Musical Memoirs
(San Francisco, CA; D.S. Ellis, 1984)

Summary: A gradually unfolding autobiography linked to sound, *Kinds of Blue: Musical Memoirs* is one of several essay collections written by poet, novelist, and author of short fiction Al Young, who focuses on African Americans trying to find their way in twentieth century black society. Inspired by individual fragments of music, be they jazz, blues, pop, or classical, Young explores his personal views and creative vision.

Subject(s): Music, Autobiography

1458 Andrew Young
Lee Clement, Editor

Andrew Young at the United Nations
(Salisbury, NC; Documentary Publications, 1978)

Summary: Clergyman, congressman, and civil rights activist Andrew Young rose to international prominence in 1977 when he became President Jimmy Carter's choice for ambassador to the United Nations. In *Andrew Young at the United Nations* editor Lee Clement uses Young's addresses, essays and other materials to chronicle Young's efforts to advance the cause of human rights through attacks on South Africa's apartheid policies and other human rights violations around the world. Considered a radical by many in the United States, Young upheld his convictions, with Carter's support, until he was forced to resign in 1979 as the result of a meeting with a representative of the Palestine Liberation Organization, a meeting that was prohibited by the U.S. State Department.

Subject(s): Politics, Peace

1459 Andrew Young

An Easy Burden: The Civil Rights Movement and the Transformation of America
(New York, NY; HarperCollins Publishers, 1996)

Summary: In *An Easy Burden: The Civil Rights Movement and the Transformation of America* former U.N. ambassador Andrew Young recalls his personal experiences during the 1950s and 1960s. A former member of the staff of Martin Luther King, Jr., Young provides insight into the relationship between King and presidents Kennedy and Johnson and explains the evolution of his own beliefs about the movement after Dr. King's assassination. Beginning the book with his college experiences at Howard University and his work as a minister with the United Church of Christ, Young ends with a vision of the nation's future as a country free of racial tension.

Subject(s): Race Relations, Autobiography, Civil Rights Movement

1460 Margaret Young

The Picture Life of Martin Luther King, Jr.
(New York, NY; F. Watts, 1967)

Summary: *The Picture Life of Martin Luther King, Jr.* is intended to serve as an introduction for young people to the life of the noted civil rights leader. Author Margaret Young focuses all her works on inspiring readers' interest in African American men and women; in her biography of King, she accomplishes this through the use of many pictures. She depicts King as an eloquent man passionate about his mission to gain racial equality and staunch in his belief that such a goal could be accomplished through non-violent means, an important lesson for young students.

Subject(s): Civil Rights Movement, Violence, Rebellion

1461 Whitney M. Young, Jr.

Beyond Racism: Building an Open Society
(New York, NY; McGraw-Hill, 1969)

Summary: Written while its author was executive director of the National Urban League, *Beyond Racism: Building an Open Society* reflects Whitney M. Young's efforts to increase civil rights for blacks through traditional establishment channels. Calling white racism "a disease that is tearing America apart," Young sets forth his ideas for solving the problems of racism by working within the system. Outlining concrete actions that could be taken on local, state, and national levels of government, Young emphasizes the need for a dialogue on individual responsibility as well as the necessity of respecting group identity.

Subject(s): Civil Rights Movement, Race Relations, Racism

Award(s): Christopher Book Award, 1970

Renate Zahar
Willfried F. Feuser, Translator

Frantz Fanon: Colonialism and Alienation: Concerning Frantz Fanon's Political Theory
(New York, NY; Monthly Review Press, 1974)

Summary: Renate Zahar's *Frantz Fanon: Colonialism and Alienation* examines the life and ideas of social philosopher Frantz Fanon (1925-1961). Born in Guadeloupe and trained in France, Fanon rejected French colonialism and joined the Algerian liberation movement in the 1950s. Fanon's ideas, which encompass such areas as politics, philosophy, feminism, psychology, and revolution, have impacted the study of African culture, feminism, and postcolonialism, and were particularly influential during the philosopher's own lifetime. In this work, Zahar also examines the diverse ways in which Fanon's works have been re-interpreted by scholars in the years since his death.

Subject(s): Philosophy, Sociology, Colonialism

Howard Zinn

SNCC: The New Abolitionists
(Boston; Beacon Press, 1964)

Summary: Political scientist Howard Zinn draws on his experiences in the trenches of the civil rights movement in *SNCC: The New Abolitionists*. Focusing on the activities of the Student Nonviolent Coordinating Committee, a protest organization with which he was affiliated during the 1950s, Zinn examines the resistance movements of the 1960s and the role of nonviolent protest.

Subject(s): Civil Rights Movement, Rebellion, Race Relations

Poetry

The period from 1940 to the present saw a number of phases of African American poetry. The era from the 1940s to the 1950s included the emergence of major poetic voices such as Robert Hayden and Gwendolyn Brooks. Hayden and Brooks were both influenced by a number of sources such as the politics of the thirties, Vachel Lindsay, Robert Frost, and modernist poets such as T.S. Eliot and Ezra Pound. Brooks' skills as a poet were recognized by blacks and whites; she won several awards, two Guggenheim Fellowships, and in 1950 became the first African American to win a Pulitzer Prize for poetry with her book *Annie Allen*. During the late fifties and early sixties, the poetry of the beat movement appeared and both Amiri Baraka (also known as LeRoi Jones at this period) and Bob Kaufman were associated with this movement. Though Baraka became increasingly alienated from this movement and later became involved with the Black Arts movement, Kaufman was a beat poet who continued friendships with, and was influenced by, Jack Kerouac and others known as the beats.

The politics of the sixties and the seventies spawned the radical Black Arts movement that attracted poets such as Amiri Baraka, Nikki Giovanni, and Sonia Sanchez. Despite their Black Nationalist roots, these poets were also influenced by the beat movement, e.e. cummings, and modernist poets such as Ezra Pound. Though all three of these poets have moved away from the Black Nationalist stance, they continue to write and publish important poetical work dealing with racial issues. Giovanni and Sanchez now utilize themes of women's rights as well as race in creating their poetry.

Since the seventies, poets with a wide range of styles and subject matter have had both popular and critical success. They include eclectic poets of history such as Michael Harper and Jay Wright, as well as female poets such as Maya Angelou, formalist-symbolist Rita Dove, and feminist poets like Audre Lorde. In this period black poets have become an important literary presence in American culture. Dove not only was the second African American woman to win the Pulitzer Prize for poetry in 1987, but was also poet laureate of the United States from 1993 until 1995. A number of poets, such as Angelou, Hayden, Harper, and Dove have taught or now teach at major American universities. Their poems are published not only in black literary journals such as *Callaloo* but also in mainstream literary journals such as *Poetry, Antaeus* and others. Moreover, African American poets such as Brooks, Hayden, and Dove have held important honorific positions.

Ai

"Blue Suede Shoes: A Fiction"
Sin: Poems
(Boston, MA; Houghton Mifflin, 1986)

Summary: In this poem, Ai inhabits the mind and dreams of Senator Joseph McCarthy, who presided over anti-Communist trials during the 1950s. The majority of the poem concerns McCarthy's relations with his family, but toward the end of the piece McCarthy's thoughts grow more obsessed with America, with the "Reds" (as he calls Communists), and with his own power—he revels in his ability to "stomp" his enemies' souls out of them.

Subject(s): Communism

Ai

"Conversation: For Robert Lowell"
Sin: Poems
(Boston, MA; Houghton Mifflin, 1986)

Summary: As its subtitle suggests, this poem concerns American poet Robert Lowell (1917-77). The narrator quizzes Lowell about how death feels; the poet answers with a metaphor suggesting that death is like looking down on life from high on a perch, trapped in "horrible" solitude. The conversation implies tension and unease between the narrator and Lowell.

Subject(s): Death, Poetry

1466 Ai

"Endangered Species"

Greed
(New York, NY; Norton, 1993)

Summary: In an angry critique of the American criminal justice system and of the racism that is still so entrenched in American society, Ai here inhabits a college professor who is stopped by the police in his car not because he committed any infraction but because he is black. The monologue casts a cynical eye on the ability of the white-dominated establishment to change its ways and move beyond its racist attitudes.

Subject(s): Racism, Race Relations, Judicial System

1467 Ai

"Evidence: From a Reporter's Notebook"

Fate: New Poems
(Boston, MA; Houghton Mifflin, 1991)

Summary: One of the longest pieces in *Fate,* this poem explores the power of the media while confronting themes of racism, sexism, and abuse of power. The monologue is a television reporter's rumination on a story that he was first to report and that made headlines: a black woman contended that she was raped by a white man in a racially motivated crime. However, the reporter presents evidence that calls the woman's story into question. In a wide-ranging poem that mentions figures from Franz Kafka to Oprah Winfrey, Ai offers a chilling portrait of life in modern urban America.

Subject(s): Media, Race Relations, Rape

1468 Ai

"Family Portrait, 1960"

Greed
(New York, NY; Norton, 1993)

Summary: This "portrait" is a monologue that depicts the entrenched poverty experienced by a single family living in Los Angeles. In the poem, a man relates everyday events from his life with his wife and two daughters. In an interesting contrast with the majority of the other monologues in the collection, this piece features a man who cooks, cleans, and cares for his family in small but important ways; while he may not evince deep love for his family, he does help fend off "chaos."

Subject(s): Family Life, Poverty

1469 Ai

"General George Armstrong Custer: My Life in the Theater"

Fate: New Poems
(Boston, MA; Houghton Mifflin, 1991)

Summary: In its use of the metaphor of theater while treating the life of a historic American figure, this poem epitomizes the works in *Fate.* In this poem, famed Indian fighter George

Custer ruminates on his defeat and death at the Battle of the Little Big Horn in 1876, when warriors under the command of Sioux chief Sitting Bull vanquished Armstrong's Seventh Cavalry. Ai uses the imagery of blood and warfare to evoke Custer's reaction to his defeat.

Subject(s): War, Indians of North America

1470 Ai

"Go: For Mary Jo Kopechne and Edward Kennedy"

Fate: New Poems
(Boston, MA; Houghton Mifflin, 1991)

Summary: The opening piece of Ai's fourth collection of poetry, "Go" reflects the poet's continuing use of the dramatic monologue to explore the nature of America and its people. As its subtitle suggests, the poem deals with the relationship between Edward Kennedy and Mary Jo Kopechne, who drowned after the automobile she and Kennedy were traveling in crashed into the water off Chappaquiddick, Massachusetts in 1967; Kennedy swam to safety but gained the reputation of a coward or murderer for not saving Kopechne. Inhabiting Kopechne's post-death voice, the narrator expresses both anger at and sympathy toward Kennedy: anger at his cowardly act and his inability to deal honestly with it, and sympathy toward him for the permanent damage the accident did to his life.

Subject(s): Death, Automobile Accidents, Anger

1471 Ai

"The Good Shepherd: Atlanta, 1981"

Sin: Poems
(Boston, MA; Houghton Mifflin, 1986)

Summary: Like most of Ai's poems, this one is a dramatic monologue. It is told from a child murderer's point of view (numerous children were murdered by a serial killer in Atlanta in the late 1970s and early 1980s) in even, deadpan language; the poet chronicles the man's thoughts and actions following one murder. Using the dramatic monologue to devastating purpose, Ai conveys the murderer's feelings with such imagination that he becomes sympathetic to the reader.

Subject(s): Murder, Children

1472 Ai

"Hoover, J. Edgar"

Greed
(New York, NY; Norton, 1993)

Summary: This monologue is told from the viewpoint of J. Edgar Hoover, the legendary lawman who was one of the most powerful men in America during his fifty-year stint as head of the Federal Bureau of Investigation. In the poem, Hoover revels in his power, accumulated through secret investigations of his enemies, including President John F. Kennedy, Martin Luther King, Jr., and later President Lyndon Johnson. As Ai did repeatedly in her earlier collections, she here casts an unsparing spotlight on the abuse of power.

Subject(s): Crime and Criminals, Judicial System

1473 Ai

"Jack Ruby on Ice"
Greed
(New York, NY; Norton, 1993)

Summary: The title of this poem refers to the gunman who killed Lee Harvey Oswald two days after Oswald was arrested for the murder of President John F. Kennedy in 1963. The poem's epigraph is a quote from organized crime figures Sam and Chuck Giancana, long rumored to have ties to the Kennedy assassination, implying that Ruby and Oswald were lovers. Ai explores that implication in the poem, imagining Ruby as having some affection for Oswald but more allegiance to the people who orchestrated Kennedy's murder. Thus, Ruby is willing to kill Oswald when ordered to do so, so that the official version of Kennedy's assassination—that Oswald acted alone—can be preserved. Ruby's last assertion in the poem is that it is America itself that has been killed, not any particular person.

Subject(s): Assassination, Homosexuality/Lesbianism, Crime and Criminals

---

1474 Ai

"Jimmy Hoffa's Odyssey"
Fate: New Poems
(Boston, MA; Houghton Mifflin, 1991)

Summary: Ai continues her examination of America by imagining the journey of Jimmy Hoffa, former head of the Teamsters' Union, whose mysterious disappearance and probable death was likely engendered by organized crime figures. Ai presents a scenario in which Hoffa joins space aliens after his death; at the end of the poem, Hoffa displays his trademark swagger and vows to return to the picket line. As in other interior monologues in *Fate*, Ai presents Hoffa as a flawed man obsessed with power even after his death; nonetheless, her use of the first person monologue elicits sympathy for the subject of the poem.

Subject(s): Crime and Criminals, Death

1475 Ai

"Knockout: For Desiree Washington and Mike Tyson"
Greed
(New York, NY; Norton, 1993)

Summary: This poem takes it title from the incident in which famed boxer Mike Tyson was convicted of raping a Miss America pageant contestant, Desiree Washington. Narrated by a poor, African American prostitute, however, the poem is essentially an impassioned attack on the second-class status of all women in a male-dominated society. The speaker warns the

beautiful, well-educated and "special" Washington that her attributes will not be enough to prevent her domination by men.

Subject(s): Prostitution, Rape

1476 Ai

"Lyndon Libre"
Fate: New Poems
(Boston, MA; Houghton Mifflin, 1991)

Summary: In this poem the narrator is former President Lyndon Johnson, speaking in 1989—sixteen years after his death. He laments his failure to win the war in Vietnam; his inability to overcome Robert F. Kennedy—even after Kennedy's assassination—to give himself a chance to win the 1968 election; and the aborted "Great Society" program with which he hoped to combat poverty. Ai presents Johnson as a vain, deluded man who was utterly unable to control the forces shaping America in the late 1960s and who was destroyed by those forces.

Subject(s): Poverty, Vietnam War, Politics

1477 Ai

"The Man with the Saxophone"
Sin: Poems
(Boston, MA; Houghton Mifflin, 1986)

Summary: Set on a cold winter morning in New York City, this poem is a rumination on poverty and solitude. It takes as its central figure a homeless man—who may or may not be the narrator—standing on a street corner playing a saxophone. Like most of the poems in *Sin*, "The Man with the Saxophone" deals in personal, specific tones with the promise and problems of America.

Subject(s): Homelessness, Poverty

1478 Ai

"More: For James Wright"
Sin: Poems
(Boston, MA; Houghton Mifflin, 1986)

Summary: The narrator of this short poem relates a dream about America in which he affirms the value of the country (worth "more" than love), despite its flaws. Toward the end of the piece, he longs to overcome his illness/death and know life again, rising like Lazarus from the dead. As with many of the poems in *Sin*, in "More" Ai examines death and imagines what it is like to be beyond death, looking back at life and the living.

Subject(s): Death

1479 Ai

"Respect, 1967"
Greed
(New York, NY; Norton, 1993)

Summary: The title of this poem is a reference to the well-known song of the same name made popular by Aretha Franklin. In the song, Franklin sings in forceful and defiant terms about the respect she and all women demand of men. In contrast, the male speaker of this monologue throws that demand back at women, lashing out at all things female. He brags about bullying his wife and other women, spewing rage at women for robbing men of their manhood. The poem is clearly an indictment of male rage and of the mistaken notion of manhood that engenders it.

Subject(s): Anger, Women's Rights

1480   Ai

"Riot Act, April 29, 1992"

Greed
(New York, NY; Norton, 1993)

Summary: Ai begins her fifth collection of poetry with a dramatic monologue about the riots in south central Los Angeles in 1992, which erupted after several policemen were acquitted in the beating of a black motorist, Rodney King, even though the beating was caught on videotape. The poem's voice belongs to a poor, African American male who intends to join in the looting and rioting. Highlighting the intense poverty that engendered the riots and the media that fueled them, Ai critiques an America in which poor urban blacks are shut out of the American dream; when they finally decide to seize that dream anyway, they are thwarted by the justice system.

Subject(s): Media, Race Relations, Poverty

1481   Ai

"Self Defense: For Marion Barry"

Greed
(New York, NY; Norton, 1993)

Summary: In this poem, Ai imagines the voice of Marion Barry, longtime mayor of Washington, D.C. One of the most visible big-city African American mayors, Barry was convicted in 1990 of drug possession—he was caught in a sting operation in a motel room, using crack cocaine in the company of a prostitute—and eventually served four years in prison. The monologue is infused with the racial hostility and fighting spirit that characterized Barry's 20-year reign, and it epitomizes a collection that is angrier and more disturbing than Ai's previous works.

Subject(s): Drug Abuse, Race Relations, Politics

1482   Ai

"Two Brothers: A Fiction"

Sin: Poems
(Boston, MA; Houghton Mifflin, 1986)

Summary: This dramatic monologue, separated into 3 parts, is a conversation between John F. Kennedy and his brother, Robert F. Kennedy ("Bobby" in the poem). Parts 1 and 3 are told in John's voice; Part 2 consists of John relating a story by Bobby. In the poem, John muses about his death and life; about his pride and the envy it evoked; and about his ability as a showman and his aspiration to sainthood. The poem opens Ai's 1986 collection, *Sin*, a wide-ranging examination into the nature of male power.

Subject(s): Assassination, Presidents

1483   Maya Angelou

"Africa"

Oh Pray My Wings Are Gonna Fit Me Well
(New York, NY; Random House, 1975)

Summary: This poem is an ode to Africa—its beauty and riches, the theft of its resources and people by foreign powers, and its slow awakening. In three stanzas of eight, nine, and eight lines, respectively, Angelou pays homage to the African continent, comparing it to a sleeping beauty that is now moving forward after having lain dormant for years. Among the themes that Angelou addresses are Africa's legacy of colonization and the institution of slavery.

Subject(s): Africa, Colonialism, Slavery

1484   Maya Angelou

"America"

Oh Pray My Wings Are Gonna Fit Me Well
(New York, NY; Random House, 1975)

Summary: In ten couplets followed by two single-line stanzas, Angelou builds on the imagery of "Request" by exploring the unfulfilled promise of America and its penchant for hiding failure in legends of heroic achievement. Angelou highlights racism, poverty, and injustice, imploring readers to look past the easy triumphs of America's mythology and instead discover a deeper and more genuine story about the country.

Subject(s): Poverty, Racism

1485   Maya Angelou

"Awaking in New York"

Shaker, Why Don't You Sing?
(New York, NY; Random House, 1983)

Summary: This one-stanza poem, which opens Angelou's fifth collection of poetry, is a deceptively simple piece about dawn in New York City. Its direct language and uncomplicated imagery are hallmarks of all of Angelou's poetry, as is its focus on everyday issues.

Subject(s): Nature, City Life

1486   Maya Angelou

"Caged Bird"

Shaker, Why Don't You Sing?
(New York, NY; Random House, 1983)

Summary: This poem, in both title and subject, recalls Angelou's hugely popular 1970 autobiography, *I Know Why* *the Caged Bird Sings.* In that volume, Angelou recalls her unhappy childhood in Arkansas, during which she endured numerous travails and even lost the ability to speak. In this poem, Angelou addresses the anger and longing that cause the caged bird to sing, contrasting its anguished song with the exhilaration known by the free bird.

Subject(s): Childhood

1487   **Maya Angelou**

"Changes"

Shaker, Why Don't You Sing?
(New York, NY; Random House, 1983)

Summary: In this poem, Angelou addresses the tenuous nature of comfort, peace, and confidence. She compares the elusive states to birds that hop from one branch to another, not knowing the damage they do as they frolic about. The poem consists of thee stanzas of seven, seven, and six lines, respectively, filled with Angelou's trademark use of everyday images to fashion direct and intimate poetry.

Subject(s): Poetry

1488   **Maya Angelou**

"Faces"

Just Give Me a Cool Drink of Water 'fore I Diiie: The Poetry of Maya Angelou
(New York, NY; Random House, 1971)

Summary: This brief poem from Angelou's first collection of poetry recalls the forgotten delights of childhood. In Angelou's direct verse, the poem becomes a plea to the reader to replace the hate of adulthood with love remembered from one's youth.

Subject(s): Love, Childhood

1489   **Maya Angelou**

"The Gamut"

Just Give Me a Cool Drink of Water 'fore I Diiie: The Poetry of Maya Angelou
(New York, NY; Random House, 1971)

Summary: This poem consists of three quatrains. In her trademark simple language, Angelou describes the range of emotions that accompany the arrival, speech, and departure of her "true love."

Subject(s): Love

1490   **Maya Angelou**

"In a Time"

Just Give Me a Cool Drink of Water 'fore I Diiie: The Poetry of Maya Angelou
(New York, NY; Random House, 1971)

Summary: Though using the direct language that is the hallmark of this collection, this poem's subject is more oblique than most of the pieces in the book. In three quatrains, Angelou chronicles emotions ranging from pain to loss to betrayal.

Subject(s): Poetry

1491   **Maya Angelou**

"Insignificant"

I Shall Not Be Moved
(New York, NY; Random House, 1990)

Summary: A brief poem of two stanzas, "Insignificant" perhaps speaks to a woman learning of her pregnancy, a development that she does not welcome. In typical fashion, Angelou uses images from nature such as salt and bees to evoke irony and disappointment.

Subject(s): Pregnancy, Nature

1492   **Maya Angelou**

"Known to Eve and Me"

I Shall Not Be Moved
(New York, NY; Random House, 1990)

Summary: In this poem from her 1990 collection of poetry, Angelou uses Biblical imagery from the story of Adam and Eve to construct a piece about spiritual love and strength. The poem consists of two stanzas, one of thirteen lines and the other of eighteen lines. Unlike her earlier poetry, Angelou here makes less use of rhyme, instead veering toward a freer verse.

Subject(s): Bible

1493   **Maya Angelou**

"Late October"

Just Give Me a Cool Drink of Water 'fore I Diiie: The Poetry of Maya Angelou
(New York, NY; Random House, 1971)

Summary: An ode to the colors and sounds of autumn, this two-stanza poem showcases Angelou's ability to use simple, direct language to evoke emotion and memory in her reader. The poem appears in the first section of the collection, titled "Where Love Is a Scream of Anguish."

Subject(s): Seasons

1494   **Maya Angelou**

"Love Letter"

I Shall Not Be Moved
(New York, NY; Random House, 1990)

Summary: This short free verse poem, as the title suggests, consists of a woman addressing her lover. As is the case with the majority of her poetry, Angelou here eschews political or social commentary in favor of an intimate, emotionally charged poem about love.

Subject(s): Love, Letters

1495 Maya Angelou

"Martial Choreograph"

Shaker, Why Don't You Sing?
(New York, NY; Random House, 1983)

Summary: In this four-stanza poem, Angelou addresses a young sailor in an airport whose dancing and mirth reveal his ignorance of warfare and its ravages. The poet uses images of dancing and choreography to depict a young man who is obviously unaware of the horrors that may yet await him in battle.

Subject(s): War, Dancing

1496 Maya Angelou

"Nothing Much"

I Shall Not Be Moved
(New York, NY; Random House, 1990)

Summary: A free verse poem consisting of sixteen lines, this poem may be a reference to Angelou's rape as a child, an incident depicted in her 1970 autobiography, *I Know Why the Caged Bird Sings*. Although in this 1990 collection Angelou uses less formal rhyme and more free verse than in her earlier work, she continues to rely on sparse language and simple imagery to construct her poetry.

Subject(s): Rape

1497 Maya Angelou

"Passing Time"

Oh Pray My Wings Are Gonna Fit Me Well
(New York, NY; Random House, 1975)

Summary: This poem, which opens the second section of Angelou's 1975 collection, is a brief poem consisting of three stanzas with two lines each. The speaker of the poem addresses a lover on the impermanence of love itself: like the poem, love is brief and "passing."

Subject(s): Love

1498 Maya Angelou

"Picken Em Up and Layin Em Down"

Oh Pray My Wings Are Gonna Fit Me Well
(New York, NY; Random House, 1975)

Summary: The opening piece in Angelou's second collection of poems is about the fear of commitment. The speaker, a man, muses about meeting and loving women from San Francisco to Detroit. At every juncture, however, he cuts short his affairs—regardless of the love he may feel—to go in search of other women in other places. The poem, with its repeating lines at the close of every stanza, has the feel of a song. It showcases Angelou's focus on themes of love and relationships and her continuing use of direct language and simple imagery in her poetry.

Subject(s): Love

1499 Maya Angelou

"Preacher, Don't Send Me"

I Shall Not Be Moved
(New York, NY; Random House, 1990)

Summary: Consisting of four stanzas of eight lines each, this poem is a wry appeal for a heaven of one's own choosing. The speaker highlights items that she does not want to see in her paradise: rats, grits, milk, gold. Instead, she asks for jazz music and autumnal weather along with "loyal" families and "nice" strangers. The poem is a trademark Angelou creation: simple rhymes and spare language seeking a direct emotional impact.

Subject(s): Seasons, Family

1500 Maya Angelou

"Request"

Oh Pray My Wings Are Gonna Fit Me Well
(New York, NY; Random House, 1975)

Summary: This poem begins the third section of the collection, and signals a departure from the previous two sections. After a series of poems about relationships, Angelou begins to focus on more worldly concerns. In this poem, which consists of one eleven-line stanza, Angelou compares America to an illegitimate child, implying that it is somehow incomplete in its development. The piece sets the stage for a more direct poem about America later in the section.

1501 Maya Angelou

"Riot: 60's"

Just Give Me a Cool Drink of Water 'fore I Diiie: The Poetry of Maya Angelou
(New York, NY; Random House, 1971)

Summary: This poem references the riots that broke out in the late 1960s in inner-city African American neighborhoods in Detroit, Newark, Los Angeles, and elsewhere. In six stanzas, Angelou depicts the fire and looting that marked the riots; the anger and hopelessness that fueled them; and the racist reactions of the police and National Guard in response to the riots. Each stanza begins with pleasant, ironic imagery before giving way to language that reflects the hostility and conflict that infused the riots.

Subject(s): Law Enforcement, Racial Conflict, Racism

1502 Maya Angelou

"Senses of Insecurity"

Oh Pray My Wings Are Gonna Fit Me Well
(New York, NY; Random House, 1975)

Summary: Once again eschewing issues of race or injustice in favor of a focus on love and relationships, Angelou here examines the shocking effect of love. In a single eight-line stanza, the poem's speaker relates how love has heightened her sense of insecurity.

Subject(s): Love

1503 **Maya Angelou**

"Shaker, Why Don't You Sing?"

Shaker, Why Don't You Sing?
(New York, NY; Random House, 1983)

Summary: In the title poem to her 1983 collection, Angelou offers a bittersweet examination of waning love. The speaker of the poem, which consists of two fairly long stanzas and two one-line stanzas, addresses her sleeping lover by recalling their past love and hoping for that love's return. However, the speaker's lover remains silent and still, while love itself remains a memory.

Subject(s): Love, Memory

1504 **Maya Angelou**

"To a Freedom Fighter"

Just Give Me a Cool Drink of Water 'fore I Diiie: The Poetry of Maya Angelou
(New York, NY; Random House, 1971)

Summary: This poem is directed at a "freedom fighter." Though the nature of the fight is unclear, this collection was written and published at the height of the Black Nationalist movement in the late 1960s and early 1970s, when the older, noncombative style of black activism had been replaced by a more militant and hostile version. Thus, the poem can be read as a testament to the new generation of fighters who remember, even in their sleep, the ravages of slavery.

Subject(s): Black Nationalism, Slavery

1505 **Maya Angelou**

"Worker's Song"

I Shall Not Be Moved
(New York, NY; Random House, 1990)

Summary: This "song," the opening piece in Angelou's 1990 collection, is a testament to the laborers who built America's railways, planes, automobiles, and ships. The poem consists of three stanzas, each with a similar closing refrain meant perhaps to signify the sound of a train bringing the workers justice and recognition for their efforts.

Subject(s): Labor and Labor Classes

1506 **Amiri Baraka**

(Also known as LeRoi Jones)

"Das Kapital"

Hard Facts: Excerpts
(Newark, NJ; People's War, 1975)

Summary: This poem reflects Baraka's shift in the mid-1970s from espousing Black Nationalism to advocating for third world socialism. By this time, Baraka had repudiated Black Nationalism as racist and destructive and had begun focusing his energies on poverty, economic disparity, and the rights of third-world populations. Despite the shift in his thematic concern, Baraka's poetry at this time still shows his skill in creating evocative free verse filled with dense imagery.

Subject(s): Racism, Black Nationalism, Poverty

1507 **Amiri Baraka**

(Also known as LeRoi Jones)

"A Poem for Deep Thinkers"

Hard Facts: Excerpts
(Newark, NJ; People's War, 1975)

Summary: This poem reflects Baraka's newfound advocacy of class struggle and his movement away from strictly racial matters in his poetry. In addition to Baraka's focus on economic concerns and his call for socialist upheaval, "A Poem for Deep Thinkers" also displays the poet's increasing use of urban black dialect in his poetry.

Subject(s): Poverty, Class Conflict, Race Relations

1508 **Gwendolyn Brooks**

"After Mecca"

In the Mecca: Poems
(New York, NY; Harper & Row, 1968)

Summary: The second and final section of Brooks's 1968 collection, which follows the lengthy title piece, contains ten shorter poems. The poems in this section reveal Brooks's commitment in the late 1960s to the ideas espoused by Black Nationalism. In poems depicting influential figures such as Malcolm X and Medgar Evers, in addition to anonymous characters from her home in Chicago, Brooks calls for unity and courage in the face of the struggle for social, racial, and economic justice.

Subject(s): Black Nationalism

1509 **Gwendolyn Brooks**

"The Anniad"

Annie Allen
(New York, NY; Harper, 1949)

Summary: The centerpiece to Brooks's Pulitzer-Prize winning collection is a mock epic poem whose title recalls Virgil's famous epic, "The Aeneid," which has long been considered a central part of the Western literary canon. In her poem, Brooks follows her heroine from childhood to marriage to motherhood, a journey that crushes dreams and provides harsh lessons in the reality of life for a poor black woman. The poem's 43 stanzas— each with 7 rhyming lines—display Brooks's erudition and stylistic brilliance, even as she highlights contemporary themes of racial and sexual injustice.

Subject(s): Women's Rights, Poverty, Racism

1510 Gwendolyn Brooks

"The Ballad of Rudolph Reed"

The Bean Eaters
(New York, NY; Harper, 1960)

Summary: This poem, which consists of 16 quatrains, tells the story of a black man who moves his family out of a roach-infested inner-city ghetto to a white suburb in the hopes of a better life. There, the whites react with hostility to their new black neighbors. After a rock is thrown through the Reeds' window, wounding Rudolph's daughter Mabel, he goes outside to confront the white vandals. A fight erupts, and Rudolph wounds four white men before they kill him.

Subject(s): Racial Conflict, Urban Affairs

1511 Gwendolyn Brooks

"The Bean Eaters"

The Bean Eaters
(New York, NY; Harper, 1960)

Summary: This short poem, the title poem in Brooks's 1960 collection, epitomizes the volume in its depiction of lives stunted by poverty. The elderly couple in the poem have little in their lives except memories.

Subject(s): Poverty, Aging

1512 Gwendolyn Brooks

"A Bronzeville Mother Loiters in Mississippi. Meanwhile, a Mississippi Mother Burns Bacon"

The Bean Eaters
(New York, NY; Harper, 1960)

Summary: This poem was inspired by the 1955 murder of Emmett Till, an African American teenager who was murdered by a white man for allegedly whistling at white girl; the man was acquitted. In the poem, the man's wife realizes with horror that her husband considers himself a hero for murdering the boy. In addition to highlighting the physical differences of the grown man and his babyfaced victim, Brooks depicts the racist views of a southern white man who snubs his nose at the idea of black civil rights. This poem works as a companion piece to "The Last Quatrain of the Ballad of Emmett Till," which appears in this same collection.

Subject(s): Murder, Racism, Racial Conflict

1513 Gwendolyn Brooks

"The Chicago Defender Sends a Man to Little Rock, Fall, 1957"

The Bean Eaters
(New York, NY; Harper, 1960)

Summary: This poem refers to a Chicago reporter being sent to Little Rock, Arkansas, in 1957 to examine the integration of the local school district, an event in which federal troops were dispatched to the city to enforce a court ruling in the face of intense local hostility to integration. The heart of the poem is the reporter's realization that the people in Little Rock, with their daily routines and standard convictions, loves, and prejudices, are the same as people everywhere.

Subject(s): Schools, Racial Conflict

1514 Gwendolyn Brooks

"The Explorer"

The Bean Eaters
(New York, NY; Harper, 1960)

Summary: The opening poem in Brooks's 1960 collection reflects the search for meaning in a hostile and cruel world, a search that animates many of the characters in this collection. The title character in this poem searches for meaning with decreasing likelihood of success. Unlike her earlier collections, which contained deeply personal poems along with pieces that commented on worldly affairs, *The Bean Eaters* is far more concerned with social issues such as poverty, racial injustice, and hatred.

Subject(s): Poverty

1515 Gwendolyn Brooks

"Gay Chaps at the Bar"

A Street in Bronzeville
(New York, NY; Harper & Brothers, 1945)

Summary: This twelve-stanza poem features a World War II serviceman speaking of the horrors of war. As in the first poem in this 1945 collection, "A Street in Bronzeville", Brooks here gives each stanza its own title. Although this poem highlights the racism that African American soldiers experienced during the war, Brooks moves beyond a critique of racism to a condemnation of war and its devastating consequences.

Subject(s): World War II, Racism

1516 Gwendolyn Brooks

"In the Mecca"

In the Mecca: Poems
(New York, NY; Harper & Row, 1968)

Summary: This long poem is the centerpiece to the 1968 collection of the same name. It refers to the dilapidated Chicago apartment building in which Brooks worked for a brief period in the 1930s; the building housed the spiritual advice empire of Dr. E.N. French, and Brooks worked as his secretary. Brooks hated the job, and she later tried unsuccessfully to incorporate her experiences there into her poetry. Brooks began working on this long poem in the early 1960s but didn't complete it until late 1967 or early 1968, when she had been energized by her introduction to Black Nationalism and her association with many of the artists who espoused its defiant philosophy, such as LeRoi Jones (Amiri Baraka) and Margaret Danner. In startling free-form verse, Brooks examines the hope, despair, and cruelty that suffuses the lives of the poverty-stricken inhabitants of the Mecca.

Subject(s): Poverty, Black Nationalism, Urban Affairs

1517 Gwendolyn Brooks

"The Last Quatrain of the Ballad of Emmett Till"
The Bean Eaters
(New York, NY; Harper, 1960)

Summary: A companion piece to "A Bronzeville Mother Loiters in Mississippi. Meanwhile, a Mississippi Mother Burns Bacon," this poem continues Brooks's examination into the brutal, senseless murder of a black teenager by a white man. In the poem, Brooks imagines the acts of the boy's mother after his death and burial. The two companion poems were inspired by the real-life murder of Emmett Till, a Chicago teenager, in 1955 by a white man who was later acquitted of the murder.

Subject(s): Murder, Racism, Racial Conflict

1518 Gwendolyn Brooks

"The Lovers of the Poor"
The Bean Eaters
(New York, NY; Harper, 1960)

Summary: A scathing depiction of naive and shallow intentions, this poem examines a group of wealthy white women in suburban Chicago who decide to help the poor and venture to an inner-city slum. Shocked by the decay, dirt, and smells of the location as well as by the haggard appearances of the people who live there, the ladies lose their resolve and quickly leave; perhaps, they decide, they can find a cleaner and neater slum to help, or maybe they can simply give money to the poor by mail. With its focus on social ills rather than personal issues, this poem is representative of the work in *The Bean Eaters* and highlights Brooks's determination to comment upon the injustices in the world around her.

Subject(s): Poverty, Urban Affairs

1519 Gwendolyn Brooks

"My Little 'Bout-Town Gal"
The Bean Eaters
(New York, NY; Harper, 1960)

Summary: Among the themes that Brooks mines in her 1960 collection is the spirit-crushing nature of the ghetto, and "My Little 'Bout-Town Gal" is representative of that theme. In the poem, a man describes the flashy dress of his wandering girlfriend while also revealing his own infidelity. The poem portrays the woman's appearance and the man's behavior as ineffectual, even doomed, attempts at happiness.

Subject(s): Poverty, Clothes, Sexual Behavior

1520 Gwendolyn Brooks

"Negro Hero"
A Street in Bronzeville
(New York, NY; Harper & Brothers, 1945)

Summary: Here, for the first time in her opening collection, Brooks directly addresses the injustice of racism and the rage that it engenders in its victims. The speaker of the poem is an African American veteran of World War II. In ironic and bitter tones, he remembers the grudging acceptance of his help—the help of all black soldiers—by the white establishment during the war. He wonders aloud at the wisdom of fighting on behalf of a political system that oppresses him but ultimately decides that the fight was a worthwhile one. The portrait that emerges of him is not one of victimhood but rather of a proud, defiant man who sees himself as morally superior to fellow Americans who would discriminate against him because of his skin color.

Subject(s): World War II, Racism

1521 Gwendolyn Brooks

"Notes from the Childhood and the Girlhood"
Annie Allen
(New York, NY; Harper, 1949)

Summary: The opening poem in Brooks's 1949 collection introduces readers to the book's title character, Annie Allen, in vignettes that describe her parents, the death of an elderly relative, and some early life lessons. The book marked an advancement and maturity in Brooks's craft and earned the author the Pulitzer Prize for poetry in 1950, the first time the award had been given to an African American.

Subject(s): Childhood

1522 Gwendolyn Brooks

"Old Mary"
The Bean Eaters
(New York, NY; Harper, 1960)

Summary: Another brief but powerful piece depicting the effects of poverty, this poem is narrated by an old woman. In six lines, Brooks evokes the woman's unrealized dreams and her resignation at having nothing left with which to battle life but her words.

Subject(s): Poverty, Aging

1523 Gwendolyn Brooks

"A Street in Bronzeville"
A Street in Bronzeville
(New York, NY; Harper & Brothers, 1945)

Summary: The opening section of Brooks's first collection of poetry is actually a multi-part poem that contains eleven distinct pieces within it. With titles such as "The Mother," "Hunchback Girl: She Thinks of Heaven," and "The Independent Man," these pieces introduce readers to the poor urban landscape of Chicago's south side. Brooks depicts the characters in this landscape with precision and sympathy, revealing the dreams and hopes that inspire them but that rarely become reality. The themes that Brooks examines in this section—poverty, racial injustice, sexual prejudice—reoccur throughout most of her later work.

Subject(s): Poverty, Racism, Women's Rights

1524 **Gwendolyn Brooks**

"Strong Men Riding Horses: Lester after the Western"

The Bean Eaters
(New York, NY; Harper, 1960)

Summary: This poem contrasts the vision of masculine strength depicted in Western movie characters with the less noble traits of the poem's speaker, a poor black man. With a mixture of irony and resignation, Lester readily admits that he possesses none of the bravery of the hero he has just witnessed on screen. Rather, he has to display servitude and subterfuge just to stay alive.

Subject(s): Poverty, Film, Sex Roles

1525 **Gwendolyn Brooks**

"The Sundays of Satin-Legs Smith"

A Street in Bronzeville
(New York, NY; Harper & Brothers, 1945)

Summary: This poem begins a series of five poem-portraits that make up the second section of Brooks's 1945 collection. "The Sundays of Satin-Legs Smith" depicts a beautifully dressed dandy who glories in his clothes (especially on Sunday), flowers, scents, furniture, and women—a wealth of possessions that contrast with the poverty of his surroundings on Chicago's south side. At 159 lines, this poem is the longest in the book.

Subject(s): Poverty, Clothes

1526 **Gwendolyn Brooks**

"We Real Cool: The Pool Players. Seven at the Golden Shovel"

The Bean Eaters
(New York, NY; Harper, 1960)

Summary: A devastating portrait of black men living in a ghetto, "We Real Cool" is probably the most-famous poem in *The Bean Eaters*. The poem is short: eight lines, with the first seven lines containing 3 words each and the final line containing only 2 words, all displaying Brooks's mastery in evoking the mixture of bravado and hopelessness that characterizes her subjects.

Subject(s): Poverty, Sex Roles, Adolescence

1527 **Gwendolyn Brooks**

"The Womanhood"

Annie Allen
(New York, NY; Harper, 1949)

Summary: This lengthy section in Brooks's Pulitzer Prize-winning collection contains several sections, each with distinct poems. In its focus on poverty and racism on Chicago's south side, the section recalls the author's earlier volume, *A Street in Bronzeville*. Here, Brooks presents a searing portrait of the lives of poor black women.

Subject(s): Women's Rights, Poverty, Racism

1528 **Owen Dodson**

The Confession Stone: Song Cycles
(London, England; P. Breman, 1970)

Summary: *The Confession Stone: Song Cycles* is considered to be Owen Vincent Dodson's finest work of poetry. A drama coach and educator, Dodson wrote the work in retirement, while he was living in New York City. Composed as a series of monologues spoken by the Holy Family in a simple language that appeals to young listeners, *The Confession Stone* follows the early life of Jesus. Traditionally performed during Easter services by Baptist congregations around the country, Dodson's verses show the young savior as a boy like any other boy; at one point his mother, Mary, tells him not to stop and play with Judas and his friends while on an errand for the family.

Subject(s): Music, Biblical Story, Family Life

1529 **Owen Dodson**
James Van DerZee, Photographer
Camille Billops, Illustrator

The Harlem Book of the Dead
(Dobbs Ferry, NY; Morgan & Morgan, 1978)

Summary: In *The Harlem Book of the Dead* drama coach, author, and educator Owen Dodson contributed poems to a collection of funeral photographs by Harlem photographer James Van Der Zee enhanced by visual graphics by artist Camille Billops. The work contains Dodson's highly acclaimed poem "Allegory of Seafaring Black Mothers," a work that shows the poet's gift for interweaving abstract thoughts with startling visual imagery: "How many mothers with their grit / with their bony and long dreams / have dared to splash with us out to sea?"

Subject(s): Death, Photography

1530 **Rita Dove**

"A L'Opera"

Grace Notes
(New York, NY; Norton, 1989)

Summary: This poem from the final section of Dove's 1989 collection reflects the suggestion of the book's title, which refers to the embellishment of a musical melody. Inspired by the poet's travels—this time in France—the poem describes a simple scene of heartbreak witnessed by the poet on a street corner.

Subject(s): Music, Travel

1531 **Rita Dove**

"And Counting: Bellagio: Italy"

Grace Notes
(New York, NY; Norton, 1989)

Summary: An autobiographical travel poem, in this case inspired by a trip to Italy, "And Counting" ranges widely in its musings—from fountains to poetry to tennis to the Virgin Mary. Cryptic in the manner of much confessional poetry, this piece nevertheless showcases Dove's lyric skills and fresh and surprising imagery.

Subject(s): Tennis

1532 **Rita Dove**

"Banneker"

Museum: Poems
(Pittsburgh, PA; Carnegie-Mellon University Press, 1983)

Summary: The subject of this poem is Benjamin Banneker (1731-1806), the famed African American mathematician and astronomer who was part of a group that surveyed and planned the building of Washington, DC. In the poem, Dove describes Banneker's quirky habits and quiet personal life and imagines a night in which he envisioned the layout of the nation's capital. Dove does not often address racial issues in this collection, and here she makes no mention of race other than to explore the life of an African American man.

1533 **Rita Dove**

"Courtship"

Thomas and Beulah: Poems
(Pittsburgh, PA; Carnegie-Mellon University Press, 1986)

Summary: This poem from Dove's 1986 collection describes the central relationship in the volume: the marriage between Dove's grandparents, Thomas and Beulah. In this poem, the pair is seen courting in a poem told from Thomas's point of view. The wise and warm depiction of her grandparents, which earned Dove tremendous critical praise, is on full display in this poem.

Subject(s): Love, Romance

1534 **Rita Dove**

"David Walker (1785-1830)"

The Yellow House on the Corner
(Pittsburgh, PA; Carnegie-Mellon University Press, 1980)

Summary: In this poem from her 1980 collection, Dove utilizes the dramatic monologue to tell the story of noted American abolitionist David Walker, whose 1829 pamphlet "Walker's Appeal" called on slaves to fight for their freedom. The four-stanza poem includes several phrases and sentences from Walker's writings and ends with his death in 1830.

Subject(s): Abolition, Slavery

1535 **Rita Dove**

"Dog Days, Jerusalem"

Grace Notes
(New York, NY; Norton, 1989)

Summary: A brief account of a summer evening in Israel, this poem grew out of Dove's travels in the Middle East. The poem's two stanzas of quiet, carefully rendered free verse are quintessential Dove work, which make no mention of racial matters but instead drive at the truth in small, everyday details.

Subject(s): Travel, Middle East

1536 **Rita Dove**

"Dusting"

Thomas and Beulah: Poems
(Pittsburgh, PA; Carnegie-Mellon University Press, 1986)

Summary: This poem, from Dove's celebrated 1986 collection about her grandparents, describes Beulah's remembrance of a boyfriend she had when she was young. While remembering, Beulah is cleaning a piece of wooden furniture, thus the "dusting" of the poem's title. This volume of lyrical narrative verse won Dove the Pulitzer Prize for Poetry in 1987, making her only the second African American to win the prize (following Gwendolyn Brooks).

Subject(s): Love, Memory

1537 **Rita Dove**

"The Event"

Thomas and Beulah: Poems
(Pittsburgh, PA; Carnegie-Mellon University Press, 1986)

Summary: The first poem of Dove's Pulitzer Prize-winning 1986 collection describes her grandfather's migration from Tennessee on a riverboat. Dove portrays Thomas's carefree nature as he began his two-year stint on a riverboat before he finally landed in 1921 in Akron, Ohio. There, he met his future wife and Dove's grandmother, Beulah. The collection is divided into two sections, the first told from Thomas's point of view and the second told from Beulah's point of view. After Dove became only second African American since Gwendolyn Brooks to win the Pulitzer Prize for Poetry, she was catapulted to the front ranks of American poets. She later became the nation's first African American Poet Laureate.

Subject(s): Family, Travel

1538   Rita Dove

"Fantasy and Science Fiction"

Grace Notes
(New York, NY; Norton, 1989)

Summary: This poem contains three stanzas which on the surface deal with three entirely separate subjects, but which on further inspection relate intimately to the poem's title—and to one another. The first stanza features a young girl imagining entering a neighborhood house about which she knows nothing. The second is a cryptic parable-like section about a skyscraper in a forest, surrounded by Native Americans, which comes tumbling down when Ben Franklin discovers the lightning rod. The third addresses the imagination of children.

Subject(s): Childhood, Indians of North America

1539   Rita Dove

"Genetic Expedition"

Grace Notes
(New York, NY; Norton, 1989)

Summary: In "Genetic Expedition," Dove explores the geography of her body, naming its qualities and identifying the ways in which her child shares—or doesn't share—those qualities. The poem consists of four six-line stanzas followed by a single line at the poem's end.

Subject(s): Parent and Child, Anatomy

1540   Rita Dove

"Grape Sherbet"

Museum: Poems
(Pittsburgh, PA; Carnegie-Mellon University Press, 1983)

Summary: This poem is from the section of *Museum* titled "My Father's Telescope." Appropriately, the poem recalls a holiday from Dove's childhood during which her father made grape sherbet for the family. Subtle and lyrical, the poem reflects Dove's precise use of language. As is frequently the case in her poetry, Dove here eschews overtly racial themes, instead offering a snapshot of her life that becomes a universal meditation on family and childhood.

Subject(s): Family Life, Childhood

1541   Rita Dove

"Nexus"

The Yellow House on the Corner
(Pittsburgh, PA; Carnegie-Mellon University Press, 1980)

Summary: This brief autobiographical poem, the title of which means "link" or "connection," provides a glimpse into the creation of Dove's poetry. She describes writing on a warm evening, beset by the noise from insects and even the grass. Dove's sparkling language and subtle imagery are fully evident in this poem.

Subject(s): Poetry, Nature

1542   Rita Dove

"Nigger Song: An Odyssey"

The Yellow House on the Corner
(Pittsburgh, PA; Carnegie-Mellon University Press, 1980)

Summary: This poem's use of the word "nigger" in its title and throughout its three stanzas signals a rare instance in which Dove addresses race head-on in her poetry. The poem describes a group of six friends riding through the night in their car, with laughter and safety in abundance.

Subject(s): Friendship

1543   Rita Dove

"Night Watch"

The Yellow House on the Corner
(Pittsburgh, PA; Carnegie-Mellon University Press, 1980)

Summary: Another poem drawn from Dove's travels, "Night Watch" describes a night at a house in Mexico. Dove notes the stucco house, the noise of castanets, the presence of lizards, and the shanties of the poor on a nearby mountainside.

Subject(s): Mexicans, Travel

1544   Rita Dove

"Notes from a Tunisian Journal"

The Yellow House on the Corner
(Pittsburgh, PA; Carnegie-Mellon University Press, 1980)

Summary: A poem drawn from Dove's travels in northern Africa, "Notes from a Tunisian Journal" exhibits the poet's ability to craft a compelling portrait of a place with a few brief images. Dove's interest in travel is seen in much of her subsequent poetry.

Subject(s): Travel, Africa

1545   Rita Dove

"O"

The Yellow House on the Corner
(Pittsburgh, PA; Carnegie-Mellon University Press, 1980)

Summary: The final poem in Dove's 1980 collection is a cryptic reflection on change. The poem's title refers to a character in the Swedish alphabet. Spoken in a typical American neighborhood, Dove notes that a simple Swedish word changes everything in unexpected ways. Also included in the poem is a mention of "the yellow house on the corner" of the volume's title.

Subject(s): Change

1546   Rita Dove

"Obbligato"

Grace Notes
(New York, NY; Norton, 1989)

Summary: This poem is prefaced by a quote from the French composer Hector Berlioz (1803-1869) in which he declares his undying love for a woman. The poem itself is cryptic; the title, "Obbligato," refers in music to an element of a composition that is indispensable and must be retained.

Subject(s): Music, Love

1547 Rita Dove

"Parsley"

Museum: Poems
(Pittsburgh, PA; Carnegie-Mellon University Press, 1983)

Summary: The seemingly innocuous title of this poem belies its violent subject, the brutal murder of 20,000 Haitian field workers in October 1957. The mass murder was ordered by Rafael Trujillo (1891-1961), the dictator of the Dominican Republic, when he became enraged that the Haitians could not pronounce the letter "r" in *parejil,* the Spanish word for parsley. The poem is divided into two sections, "The Cane Fields" (which tells the story of the field workers) and "The Palace" (which explores the mindset of Trujillo).

Subject(s): Murder, Racial Conflict

1548 Rita Dove

"Robert Schumann: Or: Musical Genius Begins with Affliction"

The Yellow House on the Corner
(Pittsburgh, PA; Carnegie-Mellon University Press, 1980)

Summary: This poem from Dove's first major collection of poetry focuses on Robert Schumann (1810-1856), the noted German composer whose career was cut short by mental illness. Key in the poem is Dove's use of the letter "A" as a foundation for the images she presents. In this early poem, Dove does not address racial issues but instead focuses on language, imagery, and universal human themes—a quality found in much of her subsequent poetry.

Subject(s): Music, Mental Illness

1549 Rita Dove

"Stitches"

Grace Notes
(New York, NY; Norton, 1989)

Summary: This autobiographical poem from Dove's 1989 collection describes an incident in which the poet accidentally cut herself and had the wound stitched up by a doctor. In its free-verse lines, the poem reflects Dove's ability to convey complex and unexpected emotion through simple imagery.

Subject(s): Illness

1550 Rita Dove

"Summit Beach, 1921"

Grace Notes
(New York, NY; Norton, 1989)

Summary: This poem, which appears almost as a preface to Dove's 1989 collection, relates the experience of a young black woman sitting by a fire on a beach. While brushing aside the attention of the young men around her, the woman recalls breaking her leg as a child and having to fortify herself with an equal stubbornness to deal with the discomfort.

Subject(s): Childhood

1551 Rita Dove

"Sunday Night at Grandfather's"

Museum: Poems
(Pittsburgh, PA; Carnegie-Mellon University Press, 1983)

Summary: Nostalgia and subtle views of parent-child relationships are themes reflected in this poem from Dove's 1983 collection. While the poem's first stanza explores the narrator's remembrance of her childhood, the second stanza shifts unexpectedly to an implication of the grandfather's pained relationship to his own son. Dove's quiet lyricism, so evident in this poem, has been instrumental in her emergence as one of America's best-known poets.

Subject(s): Family Life, Childhood

1552 Rita Dove

"Taking in Wash"

Thomas and Beulah: Poems
(Pittsburgh, PA; Carnegie-Mellon University Press, 1986)

Summary: The second section of the Pulitzer Prize-winning *Thomas and Beulah,* which focuses on the life of Dove's grandmother, introduces Beulah as a little girl. The poem strikes a note of discord, as Dove reveals the drunken threat posed by Beulah's father and the stern protective stance taken by Beulah's mother.

Subject(s): Family Relations

1553 Nikki Giovanni

"Beautiful Black Men: With Compliments and Apologies to All Not Mentioned by Name"

Black Feeling, Black Talk, Black Judgement
(New York, NY; W. Morrow, 1970)

Summary: This poem from Giovanni's 1970 collection celebrates the beauty of African American men, who in the late 1960s began to cultivate a look and dress that clashed with and defied the styles popular among the dominant white culture. Featuring colorful clothing and a hairstyle known as an "Afro," some of the men Giovanni mentions by name include singer Wilson Pickett and the musical group Temptations.

Subject(s): Music, Clothes, Popular Culture

1554 Nikki Giovanni

"Black Power: For All the Beautiful Black Panthers East"

Black Feeling, Black Talk, Black Judgement
(New York, NY; W. Morrow, 1970)

Summary: In this poem from her 1970 collection, Giovanni recollects an incident in which she and a group of friends were harassed by a white law enforcement officer. Unexpectedly, one of her friends then assaulted the officer. Giovanni celebrates the assault, in keeping with her advocacy of violence as a means to achieving social justice and freedom for African Americans. The poet's militancy put her at the forefront of the "Black Arts" movement and brought her widespread recognition.

Subject(s): Black Nationalism, Civil Rights Movement, Racial Conflict

1555 Nikki Giovanni

"Ego Tripping: There May Be a Reason Why"

Re:Creation
(Detroit, MI; Broadside Press, 1970)

Summary: This poem from Giovanni's third collection is an ironic rumination on being divine. In the poem, Giovanni muses about building pyramids in Egypt, creating an ice age in Europe, granting oil to the Arab world, and making the Earth round.

Subject(s): Earth

1556 Nikki Giovanni

"The Funeral of Martin Luther King, Jr."

Black Feeling, Black Talk, Black Judgement
(New York, NY; W. Morrow, 1970)

Summary: In this poem about Martin Luther King, Jr., Giovanni dismisses the work of one of the chief figures of the black civil rights movement of the 1960s. Like others in the "Black Arts" movement and the political advocates of Black Nationalism, Giovanni rejected King's nonviolent approach to civil rights as ineffectual and insufficient. In this poem, she avers that only black militancy can create a world in which blacks can be free in life, not just death.

Subject(s): Black Nationalism, Civil Rights Movement, Racial Conflict

1557 Nikki Giovanni

"Poem: No Name No. 3"

Black Feeling, Black Talk, Black Judgement
(New York, NY; W. Morrow, 1970)

Summary: This poem from Giovanni's 1970 collection, which includes her first two volumes of poetry, illustrates the defiant voice that brought Giovanni immediate fame. A leader of the "Black Arts" movement, whose members advocated a militant approach to civil rights in the manner of the Black Nationalist preachings of Malcolm X, Giovanni warns African Americans that they had better join the "Black Revolution." If the revolution fails, notes the poet, the white reaction to it will almost certainly vanquish blacks. Giovanni references the Holocaust, the Vietnam War, and the Arab-Israeli conflict in addition to mentioning black cultural figures such as Stokely Carmichael and LeRoi Jones (later known as Amiri Baraka).

Subject(s): Black Nationalism, Civil Rights Movement

1558 Nikki Giovanni

"Poem for Aretha"

Re:Creation
(Detroit, MI; Broadside Press, 1970)

Summary: In this poem from her third original volume of poetry, Giovanni pays tribute to singer Aretha Franklin. Giovanni portrays Franklin as a musical genius who is being devoured by a greedy public. She also praises Franklin for not capitulating to the white mainstream but instead following her own musical instincts and leading the way for other black artists from Nancy Wilson to Ray Charles.

Subject(s): Music, Jazz

1559 Nikki Giovanni

"Revolutionary Dreams"

Re:Creation
(Detroit, MI; Broadside Press, 1970)

Summary: In her trademark free verse style, Giovanni in this poem dreams about how to achieve black liberation and end white racism. She remarks that she has given up her "militant" and "radical" dreams of revolutionary methods for a simpler method: being and acting as a "natural woman." This poem signals a moderation from Giovanni's earliest poetry, when she was at the forefront of the "Black Arts" movement and advocated violent revolution.

Subject(s): Racism, Civil Rights Movement

1560 Michael S. Harper

"Buck"

Nightmare Begins Responsibility
(Urbana, IL; University of Illinois Press, 1975)

Summary: This poem from Harper's 1975 collection is an ode to a family friend whose past ties to the boxing world still inspire his present. The poem includes other autobiographical elements as well, particularly Harper's reference to the deaths of two of his own sons. Among the boxing heroes named in the poem is Joe Louis.

Subject(s): Family Relations, Death, Boxing

1561 Michael S. Harper

"Cannon Arrested"

Images of Kin: New and Selected Poems
(Urbana, IL; University of Illinois Press, 1977)

Summary: This poem from Harper's 1977 collection showcases his continued interest in jazz music as inspiration, myth, and as a reconciling force between people of differing sensibilities. Though not named in the poem, famed jazz trumpeter Miles Davis figures prominently in it; the titles of two of his recordings (*Somethin' Else* and Kind of Blue) begin the poem.

Subject(s): Jazz

1562 Michael S. Harper

"Crossing Lake Michigan"

Images of Kin: New and Selected Poems
(Urbana, IL; University of Illinois Press, 1977)

Summary: Harper's "Crossing Lake Michigan" uses an innocuous ferry-crossing to examine racial tensions. Describing a trip on the Lake Michigan ferry to buy auto parts for his broken-down car, Harper relates comments made by other ferry passengers about the assassination of Martin Luther King, Jr., in 1968. Sometimes criticized for writing poems from the dual vantage points of an American and a black man, Harper here creates a questioning, yet illuminating, poem about race relations in America.

Subject(s): Race Relations, Poetry

1563 Michael S. Harper

"Grandfather"

Nightmare Begins Responsibility
(Urbana, IL; University of Illinois Press, 1975)

Summary: "Grandfather" is a masterful poem that fuses the twin themes of family life and societal racism. In the poem, Harper describes his grandfather's life, including an incident in 1915 when he stared down a white mob intent on setting fire to his house and running him out of the neighborhood. Though he triumphed over that mob and lived the rest of his life in dignity and strength, the white nation surrounding him—symbolized in the noted film *Birth of a Nation*—ignored him and refused to budge from its comfortable racism.

Subject(s): Family Relations, Racism

1564 Michael S. Harper

"Healing Song"

Images of Kin: New and Selected Poems
(Urbana, IL; University of Illinois Press, 1977)

Summary: This poem from Harper's acclaimed 1977 collection epitomizes his interest in analyzing and establishing ties to other writers and artists. In this poem, he includes a stanza devoted to poet Robert Hayden. As is typical for him, Harper does not shower Hayden with unfiltered praise but ultimately affirms his own connection and admiration for Hayden. Among other references in this wideranging, free-verse poem is one to Abraham Lincoln.

Subject(s): Poetry, Friendship

1565 Michael S. Harper

"Heartblow: Messages"

Debridement
(Garden City, NY; Doubleday, 1973)

Summary: This poem from the second section of Harper's 1973 collection focuses on writer Richard Wright, author of such seminal works as *Native Son* and *Black Boy*. While Wright is often celebrated as the finest African American writer of the twentieth century, Harper's opinion of him is complicated: Harper criticizes Wright's reliance on stereotypes relating to black sexuality and aggression. Nonetheless, Harper presents Wright as a hero. At the end of the poem, Harper wonders about Wright's sad and lonely death.

Subject(s): Sexuality, Literature, Death

1566 Michael S. Harper

"Kin"

Nightmare Begins Responsibility
(Urbana, IL; University of Illinois Press, 1975)

Summary: In this poem from his 1975 collection, Harper examines the tensions of parent-child relationships. He describes the emotions drawn forth when his wife gets news that her mother has broken her hip and been hospitalized. Among those emotions are painful memories of her father and of her son, both of whom are now dead. The poem consists of three free-verse stanzas.

Subject(s): Family Relations, Death

1567 Michael S. Harper

"The Meaning of Protest"

Debridement
(Garden City, NY; Doubleday, 1973)

Summary: Harper's 1973 collection focuses on myth, racism, and stereotypes through three primary subjects: abolitionist John Brown, writer Richard Wright, and boxer Joe Louis. In "The Meaning of Protest," Harper makes references to both Brown and Wright in a poem that explores the nature of protest and the history of racism in America. The poem's imagery ranges from Harriet Beecher Stowe's famous nineteenth century anti-slavery novel, *Uncle Tom's Cabin,* to Richard Wright's *Pagan Spain* to the Black Power movement of the 1960s.

Subject(s): Racism, Slavery

1568 Michael S. Harper

"We Assume: On the Death of Our Son, Reuben Masai Harper"

Dear John, Dear Coltrane
(Pittsburgh, PA; University of Pittsburgh Press, 1970)

Summary: This poem from Harper's first collection of poetry is an ode to his deceased son Reuben, who died shortly after being born. In the poem, Harper describes Reuben's life, which consisted of 28 hours spent in an oxygen tent. The poem is one of several autobiographical poems in Harper's oeuvre that deal with the deaths of Reuben and another son, Michael.

Subject(s): Death, Children

1569 Robert Hayden

"Aunt Jemima of the Ocean Waves"

Words in the Mourning Time
(New York, NY; October House, 1970)

Summary: In this poem, Hayden engages an African American folk symbol—Aunt Jemima—in his own unique way. Never comfortable inhabiting a folk world, as many other black poets have done, Hayden often addressed folk issues with some distance. In this case, Hayden removes the folk symbol from its traditional habitat and infuses it with history and complexity.

Subject(s): Folk Tales

1570 Robert Hayden

"The Ballad of Remembrance"

A Ballad of Remembrance
(London, England; P. Breman, 1962)

Summary: Set in New Orleans, Louisiana, during the Mardi Gras celebration, the title poem to Hayden's 1962 collection offers a dense stylistic mix of colorful imagery and ornate verbiage. In the poem, the poet recoils at the surreal costumes and dizzying atmosphere of Mardi Gras, before he is finally rescued by a friend: Mark Van Doren (1894-1972), a respected critic and editor.

Subject(s): Friendship, Celebrations

1571 Robert Hayden

"The Ballad of Sue Ellen Westerfield"

A Ballad of Remembrance
(London, England; P. Breman, 1962)

Summary: A ballad about love doomed by racism, this poem grew out of the stories of Hayden's adoptive mother (whose maiden name was Sue Ellen Westerfield). In the poem, Sue Ellen recalls her experiences working as a riverboat chambermaid on the Ohio River after the Civil War. She relates an incident in which a riverboat on which she was riding caught fire. A white man rescued her, and the two began an affair. Their relationship did not last, though, as the racial divide in Reconstruction-era America proved too burdensome. Though criticized by other black writers for not using his poetry to argue for black civil rights, Hayden often explored themes related to African American history and culture in his work.

Subject(s): Civil Rights Movement, Reconstruction, Civil War

1572 Robert Hayden

"Belsen, Day of Liberation"

A Ballad of Remembrance
(London, England; P. Breman, 1962)

Summary: The horrors of the Holocaust are suggested in this poem from Hayden's 1962 collection. Belsen is a village in Germany that was the sight of a concentration camp during the Nazi regime. In the poem, a young girl who is a prisoner at the camp in 1945 watches as foreign soldiers liberate the camp's survivors.

Subject(s): World War II, Nazis, Childhood

1573 Robert Hayden

"Crispus Attucks"

Angle of Ascent: New and Selected Poems
(New York, NY; Liveright, 1975)

Summary: This brief poem (four lines in length) is about Crispus Attucks (1723?-1770), an African American patriot who was one of several people killed during the Boston Massacre on March 5, 1770. The incident, in which British troops fired into a crowd of demonstrators, was a key event on the road to the eventual declaration of independence by the American colonies. Though Attucks was perhaps the leader of the group of demonstrators, very little is known about his life. In Hayden's poem, Attucks is a silent historical figure whose vague life is used by later generations for their own purposes.

Subject(s): American Revolution, British Colonies

1574 Robert Hayden

"The Diver"

A Ballad of Remembrance
(London, England; P. Breman, 1962)

Summary: A description of exploring a shipwreck while scuba diving, "The Diver" epitomizes Hayden's spare verbiage and restrained imagery. The 1962 collection in which this poem appears was the first for which Hayden received widespread recognition from the literary establishment. However, this new-found acclaim was tempered by fierce criticism during the 1960s from members of the "Black Arts" movement, who felt that Hayden's refusal to devote his poetry to racial and social-cultural concerns was shortsighted. For his part, Hayden refused to cast aside his traditional aesthetic concerns in favor of a politically oriented poetry.

Subject(s): Shipwrecks, Scuba Diving

1575 Robert Hayden

"Electrical Storm"

A Ballad of Remembrance
(London, England; P. Breman, 1962)

Summary: This description of a severe thunderstorm and its effects is also a rumination on spiritual belief. In the poem, Hayden juxtaposes his educated understanding of the causes of thunderstorms with the folk belief that such storms are a divine event. Saved from danger by a seemingly random occurrence, Hayden wonders which explanation—scientific or religious—is correct.

Subject(s): Weather, Religion, Folk Tales

1576 Robert Hayden

"For a Young Artist"

Angle of Ascent: New and Selected Poems
(New York, NY; Liveright, 1975)

Summary: A somewhat fantastical poem about an angel fallen to Earth, "For a Young Artist" presents an unflattering portrait of the heavenly creature. Old, dirty, and sweat-stained, the angel is used as a sideshow attraction before he is finally able to find the proper "angle of ascent" and return to the air. Like much of his later poetry, Hayden here eschews rhyme and avoids strict meter, although the poem is not fully free verse in technique.

Subject(s): Poetry, Angels

1577 Robert Hayden

"Frederick Douglass"

A Ballad of Remembrance
(London, England; P. Breman, 1962)

Summary: This poem is an ode to Frederick Douglass (1817-1895), the escaped slave who became a prominent journalist and abolitionist. Consisting of a single stanza with fourteen lines, the poem pays homage to Douglass by arguing that when true freedom for African Americans finally arrives, he will be remembered for his courage and foresight.

Subject(s): Slavery, Abolition

1578 Robert Hayden

"Free Fantasia: Tiger Flowers: For Michael"

Angle of Ascent: New and Selected Poems
(New York, NY; Liveright, 1975)

Summary: This poem from Hayden's 1975 collection is an elegy to a deceased man whom Hayden admired as a boy. The poem displays Hayden's trademark poetic traits: his short lines, combination of free verse and formal verse techniques, and his verbal restraint. Always concerned with the technical craft of his poetry and reluctant to use that craft for what he viewed as propagandist purposes—such as overt references to social or political issues—Hayden here presents a precise and unsentimental portrait of inner-city black life.

Subject(s): Poetry

1579 Robert Hayden

"From A Snow Lamp"

American Journal
(Taunton, MA; Effendi Press, 1978)

Summary: The subject of this poem is the 1909 expedition to the North Pole by Robert Peary and Matthew A. Henson. During the expedition, Henson became legendary among the Inuit people of Greenland. The Inuit came to consider Henson one of their own and named him "Miypaluk." The poem is told in three parts; the first part suggests an Inuit song-poem.

Subject(s): Eskimos, Exploration

1580 Robert Hayden

"Full Moon"

A Ballad of Remembrance
(London, England; P. Breman, 1962)

Summary: In this poem from his 1962 collection, Hayden examines the moon, from its long history as an object of folk tales to its future potential as a military outpost. The poem consists of seven three-line stanzas, a formal structure that was a hallmark of Hayden's poetry. The linking of the moon with militarism in the poem's last stanza reflects a concern with war—especially nuclear war—that is seen in much of Hayden's later poetry.

Subject(s): Astronomy, Military Bases, Folk Tales

1581 Robert Hayden

"Homage to the Empress of the Blues"

A Ballad of Remembrance
(London, England; P. Breman, 1962)

Summary: The "Empress" of this poem's title is Bessie Smith (1894?-1937), the legendary blues singer. The poem's imagery is itself blues-tinged, although it does not aspire to the literary blues style of Langston Hughes, in which Hughes crafted poems that approximated blues lyrics. This poem consists of four stanzas, alternating between four-line stanzas and briefer two-line refrains.

Subject(s): Music, Poetry

1582 Robert Hayden

"Kodachromes of the Island"

Words in the Mourning Time
(New York, NY; October House, 1970)

Summary: As its title suggest, "Kodachromes of the Island" contains verbal snapshots of a foreign land. Divided into three sections, each containing four three-line stanzas, the poem's imagery ranges from beggar children to local fisherman. At the end of the poem, Hayden invokes one of his literary heroes, William Butler Yeats (1865-1939). The poem illustrates Hayden's enduring interest in aesthetic concerns and his refusal to be categorized as a "black poet," instead claiming all English poetry as his domain.

Subject(s): Poetry, Fishing, Travel

1583 Robert Hayden

"A Letter from Phillis Wheatley: London, 1773"

American Journal
(Taunton, MA; Effendi Press, 1978)

Summary: A dramatic monologue featuring Phillis Wheatley (1753?-1784), an African-born slave who became a renowned poet, this poem is told in the form of a letter. In the letter, Wheatley describes a journey to London, England, where her first book of poetry was in the process of being published—a landmark event because it was the first book ever published by an African American. After her return from England, Wheatley was emancipated by her owner, John Wheatley.

Subject(s): Slavery, Poetry

1584 Robert Hayden

"Locus"

Words in the Mourning Time
(New York, NY; October House, 1970)

Summary: Hayden infuses this poem with strong Native American thematic concerns. The poem is mostly a description of a spot in a wilderness, one overflowing with trees and flowers and history. This "locus" is filled with life but is also a transformational place in which death comes frequently.

Subject(s): Indians of North America, Nature

1585 Robert Hayden

"Middle Passage"

A Ballad of Remembrance
(London, England; P. Breman, 1962)

Summary: One of Hayden's most-celebrated poems, the title of this piece refers to the route traveled by slave ships between Africa and the West Indies. In the poem, a variety of voices depict the horrifying conditions on the ships, where African slaves suffered fever, blindness, and death while packed onto the ships like "cattle." The poem closes with a narrative account of the slave mutiny on the ship *Amistad*. The mutiny was led by a slave known as Cinque. Tricked into landing on the coast of America, the slaves were defended in their actions by former U.S. President John Quincy Adams.

Subject(s): Slavery

1586 Robert Hayden

"Monet's 'Waterlilies'"

Words in the Mourning Time
(New York, NY; October House, 1970)

Summary: The title of this poem refers to one of a series of nature paintings by French Impressionist Claude Monet (1840-1926). In the poem, the speaker journeys to a museum to gaze upon this painting and to escape the cascade of crises in the contemporary world, from the Vietnam War to the city of Selma, Alabama, long a flashpoint in the African American civil rights movement.

Subject(s): Vietnam War, Painting, Civil Rights Movement

1587 Robert Hayden

"Names"

American Journal
(Taunton, MA; Effendi Press, 1978)

Summary: This autobiographical poem from Hayden's last original volume of poetry highlights two painful aspects of his life. First, he recalls being taunted as a child by peers because of his poor eyesight and his need to wear glasses. Second, he relates his confusion upon learning, while in his forties, that his adopted parents had never legally adopted him or changed his name. The poem consists of three stanzas of six, five, and six lines, respectively.

Subject(s): Childhood, Adoption

1588 Robert Hayden

"On Lookout Mountain"

Words in the Mourning Time
(New York, NY; October House, 1970)

Summary: In this poem Hayden visits the site of a battle during the American Civil War. Fought in November 1863 near Chattanooga, Tennessee, the battle was a turning point for Union forces, whose soldiers performed feats of bravery in driving Confederate forces from the area. Hayden combines his reflections on the battle with an observation of the modern-day character of the mountain, which has become a place where tourists buy cheap and trivial trinkets.

Subject(s): Civil War, Commerce

1589 Robert Hayden

"The Peacock Room: In Memory of Betsy Graves Reyneau"

The Night-Blooming Cereus
(London, England; Paul Breman, 1972)

Summary: Ranging widely from introspection to elegy to historical reference, "The Peacock Room" is fundamentally an ode to a deceased friend. A key reference is to the artist James Abbott McNeill Whistler (1834-1903), who designed the restaurant of the poem's title.

Subject(s): Death, Artists and Art

1590 Robert Hayden

"A Plague of Starlings: Fisk Campus"

Words in the Mourning Time
(New York, NY; October House, 1970)

Summary: In this poem, Hayden ruminates on the deaths of small birds on the campus of Fisk University in Nashville, Tennessee (where Hayden taught for many years). The deaths were caused by construction workers, and Hayden juxtaposes the starlings' deaths with his class lectures on the Greek philosopher Socrates (470?-399 B.C.).

Subject(s): Birds, Philosophy

1591 Robert Hayden

"Richard Hunt's 'Arachne'"

The Night-Blooming Cereus
(London, England; Paul Breman Ltd., 1972)

Summary: This poem from Hayden's 1972 collection focuses on a theatrical production about Arachne, a figure from Greek mythology who was turned into a spider for challenging Athena to a weaving match. The poem consists of impressionistic phrases, and its thematic focus is on the transformational power of death.

Subject(s): Death, Mythology

1592 Robert Hayden

"Runagate Runagate"

A Ballad of Remembrance
(London, England; P. Breman, 1962)

Summary: One of a series of historical-themed poems from Hayden's 1962 collection, "Runagate Runagate" focuses on runaway slaves. Striving desperately to reach free territory, the slaves are pursued by men and bloodhounds and gripped by fear. Hayden tells a story with the poem, using varying points of view and structures it intricately, with a mixture of dense stanzas followed by indented single lines and couplets set apart. Toward the end of the poem, Hayden makes references to numerous historical figures, including Harriet Tubman, John Brown, and William Lloyd Garrison.

Subject(s): Slavery

1593 Robert Hayden

"Smelt Fishing"

The Night-Blooming Cereus
(London, England; Paul Breman, 1972)

Summary: This three-part poem from Hayden's 1972 collection, like most of the other poems in the volume, focuses on death and transformation. The first two stanzas are both in the form of a haiku, a Japanese lyric form that consists of three lines of five, seven, and five syllables, respectively. The third stanza is not quite a haiku, as the first and third lines contain only four syllables each. Hayden experimented with various traditional poetic forms throughout his career.

Subject(s): Death, Fishing

1594 Robert Hayden

"Snow"

A Ballad of Remembrance
(London, England; P. Breman, 1962)

Summary: This brief poem about snow, consisting of three two-line stanzas, reflects Hayden's preoccupation with aesthetic matters. His focus on the craft of poetry—on word use, meter, and structure—and his wide-ranging thematic concerns earned him significant acclaim from the literary establishment. During the tumultuous 1960s, though, when the black civil rights movement was at its peak and when the "Black Arts" movement emerged, many African American artists criticized Hayden for not directly addressing socio-political issues in his poetry.

Subject(s): Civil Rights Movement, Poetry, Nature

1595 Robert Hayden

"Sphinx"

Words in the Mourning Time
(New York, NY; October House, 1970)

Summary: This poem from Hayden's 1970 collection is on the surface cryptic and even impenetrable. The poem's speaker ruminates on a riddle that he cannot solve, one that causes him pain and that places him in a spot from which he cannot escape. Some critics believe that this poem is one of several in which the poet confronts his lifelong fears about his own homosexual feelings.

Subject(s): Homosexuality/Lesbianism

1596 Robert Hayden

"Those Winter Sundays"

A Ballad of Remembrance
(London, England; P. Breman, 1962)

Summary: In this poem from his 1962 collection, Hayden relates bittersweet memories of his childhood. He would greet his father in the morning with indifference, despite the fact that his father had risen early to build fires to warm the house before polishing his son's shoes. The father Hayden depicts in this poem is actually his adoptive father, William Hayden, who took the poet into his home when Robert Hayden was two years old.

Subject(s): Childhood, Parent and Child

1597 Robert Hayden

"Witch Doctor"

A Ballad of Remembrance
(London, England; P. Breman, 1962)

Summary: A four-part narrative poem, "Witch Doctor" follows a dubious evangelist through his pre-sermon preparations to his false and cynical triumph on the altar. Depicting the preacher as a calculating, greedy fake, Hayden casts a scornful eye on a man who professes to cure his followers' pain and sorrows, as if he himself were divine. Though Hayden criticized certain self-styled preachers, he himself was an ardent follower of the Baha'i faith, which preaches a unity of all religions and service to one's fellow humans.

Subject(s): Religion, Greed

1598 Langston Hughes

Ask Your Mama: 12 Moods for Jazz

(New York, NY; Knopf, 1961)

Summary: One of Hughes's last original volumes of poetry is also one of his most important. Combining poetry and jazz and exploring the major themes of his long career—humanity, racism, nationalism, poverty—Hughes presents verse alongside musical direction. In the volume's pieces, Hughes focuses heavily on musicians, writers, and other artists, alluding to Louis Armstrong, Ralph Ellison, Marian Anderson, Lena Horne, and Sidney Poitier, among others.

Subject(s): Jazz, Poverty, Racism

1599 Langston Hughes

"Harlem Sweeties"

Shakespeare in Harlem
(New York, NY; A.A. Knopf, 1942)

Summary: In his 1942 collection, Hughes left behind the political radicalism that had marked his work in the 1930s to return to many of the themes that he had explored in the 1920s, such as literary blues. "Harlem Sweeties" is a sensual ode to beautiful women in Harlem, told in musical verse with sparkling imagery that focuses on taste through Hughes's use of words such as "honey-gold," "sugar," "caramel," "chocolate," and "cinnamon."

Subject(s): Love, Food

1600 Langston Hughes

"I Dream a World"

Teamwork magazine
(February 1945)

Summary: This poem appeared in the libretto for *Troubled Island,* the opera on which Hughes collaborated with William Grant Still. Set during the Haitian Revolution of the late 1700s and early 1800s, the opera premiered in New York City in 1949, although Hughes and Still had worked on the piece since the 1930s. "I Dream a World" is a brief ode to freedom and tolerance.

Subject(s): Haitians, Opera

1601 Langston Hughes

"Madam and the Number Writer"

Contemporary Poetry magazine
(Autumn 1943)

Summary: This poem, originally published with the title "Madam and the Number Runner," is a humorous depiction of life in a poverty-stricken inner city in the 1940s. The narrator, "Madam," appears in numerous Hughes poems of the 1940s. Here, determined to foreswear gambling, she succumbs to the number runner's clever plea and bets once more. As usual, she loses. The poem ends with Madam again swearing that she will gamble no more until she reaches heaven. The number runner's response: "suppose / You goes to hell?"

Subject(s): Gambling, Poverty

1602 Langston Hughes

Montage of a Dream Deferred

(New York, NY; Holt, 1951)

Summary: In a brief preface to this 1951 book-length poem, Hughes explains that the work is marked by qualities found in African American musical forms such as jazz, blues, ragtime, and be-bop. All of the pieces in the poem, regardless of their musical inspiration, feature characters in contemporary Harlem in New York City. Hughes emphasizes the folk elements of his chosen subject, from poverty to childhood to racism.

Subject(s): Jazz, Poverty, Racism

1603 LeRoi Jones
(Also known as Amiri Baraka)

"Black Art"

Black Art
(Newark, NJ; Jihad Productions, 1966)

Summary: This title poem to a 1966 collection by Jones displays the inflammatory language for which he became famous during the 1960s. In the poem, Jones makes a plea for an explicitly black art that does not cater to white or bourgeois tastes. Among those whom Jones disparages in the poem are Jews, "negroleader[s]" who serve whites, prostitutes, the police, and gays. The poem reflects Jones' increasing radicalism following the murder of Black Nationalist leader Malcolm X in 1965.

Subject(s): Black Nationalism, Anti-Semitism, Prostitution

1604 **LeRoi Jones**

(Also known as Amiri Baraka)

"Black People!"

Black Magic
(New York, NY; Morrow, 1967)

Summary: The inflammatory language of this poem epitomizes Jones' "Black Arts" phase during the late 1960s and early 1970s. In the poem, Jones urges blacks to vandalize, steal, and even kill—all in an overtly anti-white rhetoric containing epithets such as "whitey." The "Black Arts" movement coincided with the rise of Black Nationalism, which likewise advocated violence as an acceptable method of achieving social justice. In the mid-1970s, Baraka would repudiate his Black Nationalist beliefs as racist and destructive.

Subject(s): Racial Conflict, Black Nationalism, Violence

1605 **LeRoi Jones**

(Also known as Amiri Baraka)

"Hymn for Lanie Poo"

Preface to a Twenty Volume Suicide Note
(New York, NY; Totem Press/Corinth Books, 1961)

Summary: This early Jones poem clearly reflects the influence of the "Beat" poets, who often used surreal imagery in their work. The poem includes a strange mix of images, and while the language itself is clear, the meaning of the images is not; in its totality, however, the poem appears to bemoan the monotony of everyday life. In keeping with the other poems in this collection, Jones' technical skill is evident, but there are no hints of the later fiery rhetoric of the Black Nationalist radical.

Subject(s): Black Nationalism

1606 **LeRoi Jones**

(Also known as Amiri Baraka)

"Leroy"

Black Magic
(New York, NY; Morrow, 1967)

Summary: This poem's title alludes to Jones' given name, LeRoi, as well as to his father's middle name—spelled "Leroy" as in the poem's title. In the poem, Jones recalls a yearbook photograph of his mother in her college days. He also displays his "Black Arts" aesthetic vision, referring to his mother's black knowledge and consciousness inherited from her ancestors and passed on to him, and which he in turn hopes to pass on to future generations of blacks.

Subject(s): Race Relations, Family, Knowledge

1607 **LeRoi Jones**

(Also known as Amiri Baraka)

"Letter to E. Franklin Frazier"

Black Magic
(New York, NY; Morrow, 1967)

Summary: Displaying the bitterness and alienation that are hallmarks of Jones' poetry in the late 1960s, this poem also shows the poet's skill with imagery and language. Nonetheless, many white critics dismissed Jones' poetry of this period as being too preoccupied with racial and political matters.

Subject(s): Poetry, Race Relations

1608 **LeRoi Jones**

(Also known as Amiri Baraka)

"Notes for a Speech"

Preface to a Twenty Volume Suicide Note
(New York, NY; Totem Press/Corinth Books, 1961)

Summary: In this poem from his 1961 collection, Jones examines the meaning of Africa and his relationship to it. He calls Africans his "people" but admits that in the end Africa is a "foreign" land and that he is wholly American. The admission is bittersweet, since his true homeland—America—remains thoroughly racist. By the end of the 1960s, Jones would become far more strident and bitter when describing America.

Subject(s): Africa

1609 **LeRoi Jones**

(Also known as Amiri Baraka)

"Poem for Halfwhite College Students"

Black Magic
(New York, NY; Morrow, 1967)

Summary: In this poem, Baraka clearly articulates his vision of the "Black Arts" movement, a new black cultural aesthetic based on black rather than white standards of art and beauty. Referring to college students listening to him speak, Baraka chastises the black students for remaining beholden to white standards as epitomized by actors such as Elizabeth Taylor, Richard Burton, and Steve McQueen.

Subject(s): Race Relations, Art, Beauty

1610 **LeRoi Jones**

(Also known as Amiri Baraka)

"A Poem for Willie Best"

The Dead Lecturer: Poems
(New York, NY; Grove Press, 1964)

Summary: The man named in the title of this poem, Willie Best, was an African American character actor whose Hollywood name was Sleep'n'eat. The poem itself is divided into eight sections, with Jones' free verse ranging widely among images and language suggesting sex and violence. With this 1964 collection, Jones' poetry became noticeably more bitter toward white America, while the author displayed an increasing affinity for political action and social change.

Subject(s): Sexuality, Violence, Race Relations

1611 LeRoi Jones

(Also known as Amiri Baraka)

"A Poem Some People Will Have to Understand"

Black Magic
(New York, NY; Morrow, 1967)

Summary: This poem from his 1967 collection shows Jones in his "Black Arts" phase, embracing violence as an acceptable method of social change. Admitting with irony that "I am no longer a credit to my race," Jones dismisses traditional methods for achieving racial harmony and justice. The "Black Arts" cultural movement dovetailed with the rise of Black Nationalism, a defiant political ideology espoused by leaders such as Malcolm X.

Subject(s): Black Nationalism, Anger, Violence

1612 LeRoi Jones

(Also known as Amiri Baraka)

"Preface to a Twenty Volume Suicide Note"

Preface to a Twenty Volume Suicide Note
(New York, NY; Totem Press/Corinth Books, 1961)

Summary: This poem, the title poem of Jones' first published collection of poetry, is dedicated to his daughter, Kellie Jones. In the poem, the speaker ruminates on feelings of emptiness and depression, mentioning everyday events such as running to catch a bus, walking the dog, and counting stars. The poem closes with an unexpected view of the speaker's daughter, in her room praying to an unseen God. The poem reveals the technical and stylistic strength that marked Jones' poetry from the beginning, but the increasingly radical and political tones that would predominate his work as the 1960s progressed are nowhere to be found. Instead, Jones' bohemian outlook and the influence of the "Beat" poets take center stage.

Subject(s): Children, Depression

1613 LeRoi Jones

(Also known as Amiri Baraka)

"Rhythm & Blues (1: For Robert Williams, in Exile"

The Dead Lecturer: Poems
(New York, NY; Grove Press, 1964)

Summary: In this free-verse poem, divided into three sections, Baraka displays his increasing distance from the Beat poets, who heavily influenced his early poetry. Cryptic and dense in its imagery, the poem nevertheless suggests the poet's anger and bitterness toward America and his growing radicalism.

Subject(s): Poetry, Anger

1614 LeRoi Jones

(Also known as Amiri Baraka)

"Western Front"

Black Magic
(New York, NY; Morrow, 1967)

Summary: Nowhere is Jones' repudiation of his early Beat-influenced style more apparent than in this poem, in which he refers to "fools like Allen Ginsberg." Ginsberg was one of the leaders of the Beat poets, who had a profound influence on the literary establishment in the late 1950s and early 1960s, but here Jones dismisses the Beats as irrelevant and naive. By the time of this collection, Jones had begun to theorize a new black literary aesthetic—the "Black Arts" movement—that called for black artists to reject white cultural standards in favor of their own and that advocated the violent destruction of America's white-dominated society.

Subject(s): Violence, Race Relations

1615 June Jordan

Who Look at Me

(New York, NY; Crowell, 1969)

Summary: In this book-length poem, June Jordan considers the interaction between whites and blacks by using the moment of eye contact as a central image. The title refers to the white persons "who look at me." The poem first considers how blacks are defined through the eyes of whites then changes its approach to define blacks using their own historical and artistic traditions. Slavery is treated as a source of strength gained through survival. In its original volume, the poem is accompanied by a series of paintings, which by calling attention to the act of looking, enhance the work's message.

Subject(s): Racism, Slavery

1616 Bob Kaufman
Gerald Nicosia, Editor

Cranial Guitar: Selected Poems

(Minneapolis, MN; Coffee House Press, 1996)

Summary: This collection of poems by Bob Kaufman contains his most famous works from the 1950s to the 1980s. Kaufman came to be considered the "be-bop man" of the Beat poets. Kaufman's poetry is based on jazz rhythms and is usually written in either a symbolist or surrealist style. Much of it is intended to be sung or read to music. A Buddhist who demonstrated his opposition to the war in Vietnam by taking a vow of silence until it was over, Kaufman neither spoke nor wrote poetry for ten years. Many of his poems before and after are politically charged. Subjects covered in his work include love, jazz, revolution, and odes to famous personalities from Hart Crane to Ray Charles.

Subject(s): Revolution, Jazz

1617 Haki R. Madhubuti

Killing Memory, Seeking Ancestors
(Detroit, MI; Lotus Press, 1987)

Summary: A collection of poems, *Killing Memory, Seeking Ancestors* reflects poet Haki R. Madhubuti's continuing explorations of black consciousness. Formerly writing under his birth name of Don L. Lee, Madhubuti examines black awareness through such works as "Always Remember Where You Are" and "Negro: An Updated Definition Part 368." An educator and editor of Third World Press, Madhubuti is a student of African culture and poetry.

Subject(s): Identity, Self-Perception

1618 Leonard A. Slade, Jr.

I Fly Like a Bird: The Poetry of Leonard A. Slade, Jr.
(Nashville, TN; Winston-Derek Publishers, 1992)

Summary: The author's third book of poetry is divided into four parts, dealing with themes of flight, strength, dreams, and journeys. Among the collection's pieces are poems celebrating the black woman, Nelson Mandela, and Martin Luther King, Jr.

Subject(s): Apartheid, Civil Rights Movement

1619 Arthur Lee Smith

The Break of Dawn
(Philadelphia, PA; Dorrance, 1964)

Summary: This collection of poetry considers the African American experience and includes a diverse selection of works. "Sisyphus" uses the Greek myth to explore the concept of liberty. "On Fred Douglas" addresses the black abolitionist. Other significant figures are also dealt with: Martin Luther King, Jr. ("Advice from King"), Medgar Evers ("Death of Medgar Evers"), James Baldwin ("On James Baldwin"), and John F. Kennedy ("In Memory of John Kennedy"). Other poems address black music ("The Beat"), civil rights ("Birmingham"), and Islam ["Of Another (Muslims)"].

Subject(s): Abolition, Civil Rights Movement, Muslims

1620 Quincy Troupe

Avalanche: Poems
(Minneapolis, MN; Coffee House Press, 1996)

Summary: In *Avalanche*, a poetry collection imbued with both jazz and political overtones, award-winning poet Quincy Troupe blends metaphor and a unique rhythm with images of African American culture. Among the works included are "Conjuring against Alien Spirits," "For Malcolm Who Walks in the Eyes of Our Children," and "A Response to All You Angry White Males." Troupe, co-author of an autobiography of Miles Davis, commemorates the world-famous jazz musician in the work "Back to the Dream Time: Miles Speaks from the Dead." The collection is illustrated by Jose Bedia.

Subject(s): Poetry, Music, Politics

1621 Jay Wright

"The Albuquerque Graveyard"
Soothsayers and Omens
(New York, NY; Seven Woods Press, 1976)

Summary: Wright, who was born and raised in Albuquerque, New Mexico, here recounts a visit to a local cemetery. He encounters the graves of men and women whom he encountered while growing up. Like many of the poems in Wright's 1976 collection, "The Albuquerque Graveyard" connects the poet's own history with a larger African American culture, so that the poem functions as a quest for identity in both personal and cultural terms.

Subject(s): Death, Identity

1622 Jay Wright

"Baptism in the Lead Avenue Ditch"
Soothsayers and Omens
(New York, NY; Seven Woods Press, 1976)

Summary: This poem from Wright's 1976 collection depicts the poet's search for religious meaning. "Baptism" is one of several poems in *Soothsayers and Omens* in which Wright is seen to be on a spiritual quest, a quest that takes him from his childhood in the American Southwest to his traveling days in Mexico and later to a maturity in which he combines African spiritual images with his own history.

Subject(s): Religion, Africa

1623 Jay Wright

"The Birthday"
Soothsayers and Omens
(New York, NY; Seven Woods Press, 1976)

Summary: In this poem, Wright recounts a childhood birthday, describing it as an event that marks the period "between one age and another." The poem contains the restrained language and quiet, astute imagery that are the hallmarks of Wright's work. Like much of the rest of the collection, "The Birthday" reveals the poet on a spiritual quest for meaning as a man and as an African American.

Subject(s): Religion, Childhood

1624 Jay Wright

"Crispus Attucks"
The Homecoming Singer
(New York, NY; Corinth Books, 1971)

Summary: In this poem from his first collection, Wright examines the life of Crispus Attucks, an African American who was one of the people killed in the Boston Massacre of 1770. In that incident, British troops opened fire on a crowd of people protesting the American colonies' treatment by the British. The incident inflamed the colonies' sentiment against the British and helped propel the colonies toward declaring their independence from Great Britain, which they did in 1776.

Subject(s): Rebellion, History, American Colonies

1625 **Jay Wright**

"Homecoming: Guadalajara-New York, 1965"

Soothsayers and Omens
(New York, NY; Seven Woods Press, 1976)

Summary: As its subtitle suggests, this poem relates Wright's arrival back in New York City after living in Mexico. In the poem, Wright mixes English, Spanish, and Italian in addition to combining images of life in Mexico and America. At the end of the poem, Wright implies that the spiritual transformation that he has been moving toward throughout the collection is complete.

Subject(s): Religion, Travel

1626 **Jay Wright**

"The Homecoming Singer"

The Homecoming Singer
(New York, NY; Corinth Books, 1971)

Summary: The title poem from Wright's first major collection imagines a homecoming celebration at a traditionally black college in Nashville, Tennessee. The poem combines naturalistic themes with fanciful images and is considered by critics to be one of Wright's best works.

Subject(s): College Life

1627 **Jay Wright**

"An Invitation to Madison County"

The Homecoming Singer
(New York, NY; Corinth Books, 1971)

Summary: The Madison County of this poem's title is in Mississippi, and the poem is a chronicle of the alienation Wright felt when visiting the poor, rural community there. Describing himself as urbane and educated yet ignorant of the ways of the South, a "poet with matching socks and tie," Wright discovers a gentle hospitality in the poor blacks he meets there.

Subject(s): American South, Poverty, Rural Life

1628 **Jay Wright**

"Logbook of Judgments"

Dimensions of History
(Santa Cruz, CA; Kayak, 1976)

Summary: Using African religious mythology in combination with imagery from the Americas, Wright in *Dimensions of History* creates a complex, demanding poetry. The four-part "Logbook of Judgments" is divided into sections titled "What Is Good," "What Is True," "What Is Beautiful," and "Meta-A

and the A of Absolutes." Relying heavily on images from nature, these sections treat the figures of mother and lover as mythological ideals, both erotically and spiritually.

Subject(s): Religion, Africa

1629 **Jay Wright**

"Sketch for an Aesthetic Project"

The Homecoming Singer
(New York, NY; Corinth Books, 1971)

Summary: This poem, which begins with a quote from writer Thomas Kinsella, relates Wright's sense of alienation while living in Mexico. The poem is one of several in *The Homecoming Singer* that depict life in Mexico, a geographical terrain that Wright would return to in later poems.

1630 **Jay Wright**

"Wednesday Night Prayer Meeting"

The Homecoming Singer
(New York, NY; Corinth Books, 1971)

Summary: This poem from Wright's 1971 collection reflects the poet's recollection of Wednesday evenings spent at church while growing up in the Southwest. In the poem, Wright discusses the weekly rituals followed by young and old at the church, rituals whose validity Wright regards with deep skepticism. Written in a single, lengthy stanza of free verse, the poem represents one of Wright's early explorations of the meaning of religious life—a theme he would return to in his later work.

Subject(s): Religion, Christianity

Drama

Black theatre began to gain impetus in the 1940s and 1950s. Langston Hughes produced important plays, and Richard Wright's seminal novel *Native Son* was transformed into a play. The forties also saw the emergence of the Howard University playwright Owen Dodson. In the fifties Lorraine Hansberry wrote the acclaimed *Raisin in the Sun,* which opened on Broadway in 1959 and won the New York Drama Critics Circle Award. This play and others, like Ossie Davis' 1961 work *Purlie Victorious,* have been popularized through transformations into musicals. The "Black Arts" movement gave impetus to theatre in the sixties and seventies, with playwrights like Ed Bullins writing important works during this period and developing outlets for black theatre. During the 1960s and 1970s, Bullins was the director of the New Lafayette Theatre group and later founded a theatre in memory of his son and a theatre workshop. Several other theatrical groups were founded during the "Black Arts" movement of the 1960s and 1970s. In 1965, Amiri Baraka, with the help of other black activists, created the Black Arts Repertory Theatre/School (BARTS). Playwright and actor Douglas Turner Ward, along with Robert Hooks and Gerald Krone, founded The Negro Ensemble Company in

1967, at the pinnacle of the "Black Arts" movement. Some of their most well-known productions include *The River Niger* by Joseph Walker and *A Soldier's Play* by Charles Fuller. This theatre group continues to produce a wide variety of black plays and musicals, both with American and international themes, for a black audience. Feminism brought the work of women such as Ntozake Shange to the forefront of the 1970s theatrical scene. Her play *for colored girls who have considered suicide/ when the rainbow is enuf* was a Broadway hit and won several awards. More recently, during the 1980s and 1990s, August Wilson and Adrienne Kennedy have achieved status as major playwrights. Wilson started the Black Horizon Theatre Company and has won Pulitzer Prizes for drama with his plays *Fences* and *The Piano Lesson*. Adrienne Kennedy has been a pioneer of avant-garde and experimental theatre.

1631 Ed Bullins

The Duplex: A Black Love Fable in Four Movements

(New York, NY; Morrow, 1971)

Summary: This play is notable not only for its literary merits but for the controversy that attended its 1972 production at Lincoln Center in New York City. Bullins, who was at the forefront of the black arts movement of the 1960s and 1970s, directed his provocative and highly political plays at an African American audience. As in his other plays of this period, Bullins presents a searing portrait of the violence that plagued inner-city black lives. The three central characters are Steve Benson, the chief male character, who also appears in other Bullins plays; Velma, a battered wife with whom Benson develops a tender love affair; and Velma's sadistic husband. The play premiered in 1970 at the New Lafayette Theatre in Harlem, the landmark institution that Bullins helped create and at which he produced several of his plays. When a new production opened in 1972 at the mainstream Lincoln Center, however, Bullins disavowed any connection with the production, charging the producer (Jules Irving) and director (black director Gilbert Moses) with turning the play into a "coon show." Bullins's angry public rhetoric exemplified the split between separatist black artists and mainstream artists and institutions.

Subject(s): Black Nationalism, Working-Class Life, Spouse Abuse

1632 Ed Bullins

How Do You Do: A Nonsense Drama

(Mill Valley, CA; Illuminations Press, 1967)

Summary: This play, Bullins's first, reflects the influence of absurdist writers such as Franz Kafka and Eugene Ionesco on Bullins. The play revolves around a pretentious couple, Doris and Roger, whose social and economic aspirations elicit ridicule by Paul, a down-and-out man. From his park bench, Paul comments on Doris and Roger's behavior throughout the short play. While Bullins eventually left behind absurdist techniques for the most part, he did use absurdist elements in some of his later plays. Thematically, however, *How Do You Do* represents the start of a primary feature of many works by Bullins: the cri-

tique of bourgeois, assimilationist elements in the African American community. The play was produced at San Francisco's Firehouse Repertory Theatre in 1965.

Subject(s): Class Conflict

1633 Alice Childress

Wine in the Wilderness

Black Theater U.S.A.: Forty-Five Plays by Black Americans, 1847-1974
(New York, NY; Free Press, 1974)

Summary: Set during the civil rights movement of the 1960s, *Wine in the Wilderness* focuses on the issues of class and race consciousness. In the play, Childress sets three middle-class characters--an artist, a writer, and a social worker--in contrast to an elderly "roustabout" and a young factory worker. The factory worker, a woman named "Tommy," is the play's moral center: honest, compassionate and proud, she is a heroine unlike earlier dramatic depictions of African American females that were typically older "mother" figures. In the play, the three middle-class characters are exposed for their arrogance and for their artificial natures, as Childress comments on bourgeois African Americans whose values undermine the fight for black civil rights. The drama was first produced by Boston's WGBH-TV in 1969.

Subject(s): Civil Rights Movement, Class Conflict

1634 Countee Cullen
Arna Bontemps, Co-author

St. Louis Woman

(New York, NY; Dodd, 1971)

Summary: This musical premiered in New York City in 1946 amid controversy. Adapted by Countee Cullen and Arna Bontemps from Bontemps's novel *God Sends Sunday*, *St. Louis Woman* depicts the pursuit of a caustic beauty, Della Greene, by two men: gambler Bigelow Brown and jockey Lil Augie. Originally slated to premiere in 1945, the musical was delayed after NAACP head Walter White attacked it for showing seamy aspects of lower-class black life such as gambling and drinking. It finally premiered in March of 1946, making a star of Pearl Bailey. Unfortunately, Cullen died three months before the work's premiere.

Subject(s): Gambling, Working-Class Life

1635 Ossie Davis

Escape to Freedom: A Play about the Young Frederick Douglass

(New York, NY; Viking, 1978)

Summary: This award-winning play written for children tells the story of Frederick Douglass, from his childhood in the 1820s as a slave in Maryland, to his escape to New York and to freedom in 1838. Davis depicts Douglass's early determination to learn to read (despite laws against allowing slaves to read), his realization that his education was the key to his freedom, and his eventual escape, achieved by using a free man's pass to gain a seat on a train bound for New York. The play was produced at New York City's Town Hall in 1976.

Subject(s): Slavery, Education, Biography

Award(s): American Library Association: Coretta Scott King Book Award, 1979; Jane Addams Peace Association: Jane Addams Children's Book Award, 1979

1636 Ossie Davis

Purlie Victorious

(New York, NY; Samuel French, 1961)

Summary: This highly successful play features an indictment of southern racism couched within a comic, sometimes farcical framework. The play's central character, Purlie Victorious Judson, returns home to Waycross, Georgia, and attempts to buy and restore an abandoned barn. Standing in his way is Ol' Cap'n Cotchipee, a stereotypical bigot. Purlie hatches an outlandish scheme to get the money needed to buy the barn, using a local woman who personifies sweetness and beauty, Lutiebelle Gussiemae Jenkins. Purlie eventually gets the barn with the help of Ol' Cap'n's liberal son, and at the end of the play Ol' Cap'n dies and is buried, signifying the death of southern racism. Produced on Broadway in 1961, a few years before the rise of black nationalism, the play is important because of its attack, however cautious, on white bigotry and the non-violent way in which the good-humored Purlie succeeds. The play was turned into a movie, *Gone Are the Days*, in 1963 and a Broadway musical, *Purlie*, in 1970.

Subject(s): Black Nationalism, Comedy, Racism

1637 Owen Dodson

Bayou Legend

Black Drama in America: An Anthology
(Greenwich, CT; Fawcett, 1971)

Summary: This free verse drama is an adaptation of Henrik Ibsen's classic play, *Peer Gynt*. Dodson's version is set in a Louisiana bayou amid a poor, rural African American population and displays Dodson's interest in exploring the African American tradition of oral storytelling. Folk legend and spiritual belief also play a major role in the play, which was first produced in 1948 at Howard University's noted theater.

Subject(s): Spiritualism, Storytelling, Folk Tales

1638 Owen Dodson

Divine Comedy

Black Theater, U.S.A.: Forty-Five Plays by Black Americans,
1847-1974
(New York, NY; Free Press, 1974)

Summary: This 1938 play is an attack on self-styled religious prophets and on the naive people who give both belief and wealth to such false prophets. Written and produced while Dodson was in graduate school at Yale University's Drama School, the play features a central character, Father Divine, who claims to be God. The play is based on an incident in Dodson's childhood. The play won the prestigious Maxwell Anderson Award for Verse Drama.

Subject(s): Religion

Award(s): Maxwell Anderson Award: Verse Drama, 1940

1639 Owen Dodson

Everybody Join Hands

Theatre Arts
(September 1943)

Summary: This play grew out of Dodson's experience as a seaman serving in the racially segregated Great Lakes Naval Training Station during World War II. Dodson's commander at the station, Daniel Armstrong, asked Dodson to produce a series of plays about naval history to raise the morale of black seamen at the station. *Everybody Join Hands* was one of two plays, out of a total of eight written for this purpose and staged at the Naval Training Station, to be published in the prestigious theatrical monthly, *Theatre Arts*. The play tells the story of the heroic struggle by the Chinese against their Japanese oppressors during the late 1930s and early 1940s.

Subject(s): World War II, Oppression, War

1640 Randolph Edmonds

Earth and Stars

Black Drama in America: An Anthology
(Greenwich, CT; Fawcett, 1971)

Summary: One of a group of Edmonds plays classified as "social problem" dramas, this 1946 play follows a minister, Rev. Joshua H. Judson, as he leaves his home in Ohio to journey to a southern city. There, he sets up a "social action" church that is devoted not just to the afterlife but also to justice and health here on Earth. As in his other "social problem" plays, Edmonds here uses drama to espouse progressive ideas for African Americans.

Subject(s): Religion, Social Conditions

1641 Lonne Elder, III

Ceremonies in Dark Old Men

(New York, NY; Farrar, Straus, 1969)

Summary: This tragi-comic exploration of black family life won numerous awards and catapulted Elder into the front ranks of American dramatists. The play features a poor family in Harlem trying to escape the poverty and hopelessness of their situation by making and selling illegal corn liquor. The father and two sons who hatch the scheme are balanced by the daughter, who despairs of having to work hard to support the men in her family, just as her mother had to do before her. Originally produced in 1965, a revised version was produced at New York City's St. Mark's Playhouse in 1969. The drama was later turned into a teleplay and broadcast on ABC in 1975.

Subject(s): Poverty, Working-Class Life, Family Life

Award(s): Stanley Drama Award: Playwriting, 1965; Vernon Rice Drama Desk Award, 1970; Outer Circle Critics Award: Drama, 1970

1642 Lonne Elder, III

Charades on East Fourth Street

Black Drama Anthology
(New York, NY; New American Library, 1971)

Summary: More challenging and disturbing than Elder's *Ceremonies in Dark Old Men*, this play features a gang of black and Hispanic youth kidnapping a white policeman whom they accuse of brutalizing their friends. The youths hold the policeman in a movie-house basement, where they interrogate and torture him. The policeman eventually confesses to crimes that he is innocent of, adding an element of irony to the play. Elder infuses this drama with more anger and racial tension than are evident in *Ceremonies*. The play was produced in 1967.

Subject(s): Violence, Gangs, Black Nationalism

1643 Charles Fuller

A Soldier's Play

(New York, NY; Samuel French, 1982)

Summary: Set at a Louisiana army base during World War II, this acclaimed drama centers around the mysterious death of an African American sergeant and the subsequent investigation into the murder. While notorious elements in the local white community—including the KKK—may have committed the murder, Fuller also examines the possibility that other blacks on the army base may have killed the unpopular sergeant. A complex exploration of race relations between blacks and whites, this play was awarded the Pulitzer Prize for drama—only the second time the award had gone to an African American playwright.

Subject(s): World War II, Race Relations

Award(s): Pulitzer Prize: Drama, 1982; New York Drama Critics Award: Best American Play, 1982; Audelco Award: Best Play, 1982

1644 Charles Fuller

Zooman and the Sign

(New York, NY; Samuel French, 1981)

Summary: Set in inner-city Philadelphia, the play—produced in 1979—presents the aftermath of the murder of a little girl who was playing on her porch. From the girl's grieving family to the arrogant teenage killer, the play examines issues of urban poverty, community relations, and human nature. Winner of an Obie Award for best play, *Zooman* signaled Fuller's arrival as a talented voice in American drama and set the stage for his Pulitzer Prize-winning triumph with his next play, *A Soldier's Play*.

Subject(s): Urban Affairs, Murder, Community Relations

Award(s): Obie Award: Best Play, 1981; Audelco Award: Best Writing, 1981

1645 Lorraine Hansberry
Robert Nemiroff, Co-author

Les Blancs

(New York, NY; Samuel French, 1972)

Summary: Produced five years after Hansberry's 1965 death, this unfinished play was essentially completed by Hansberry's ex-husband, Robert Nemiroff. Set in a mythical African country, the play explores themes of colonialism, violent revolution, and oppression. The major characters are Tshembe Matoseh, a black intellectual who leaves behind his white wife and child in London to take part in liberating the country from its white-dominated, colonial government, and Charlie Morris, a white reporter who decides that the only possible course of liberation for the people is through armed struggle. Though most of the plotting and dialogue were written by Hansberry, the finishing elements were completed by Nemiroff based on conversations with Hansberry before she died.

Subject(s): Revolution, Oppression

1646 Lorraine Hansberry

The Drinking Gourd

Les Blancs: The Collected Last Plays of Lorraine Hansberry
(New York, NY; Random House, 1972)

Summary: Written as part of an NBC teleplay project that never materialized, this play examines the dehumanizing effects of slavery. The play revolves around a struggling Kentucky plantation owned by Hiram Sweet, and three slaves on the plantation: Hannibal; his mother, Rissa; and his girlfriend, Sarah. Faced with overwork and brutality, the three slaves find they have no choice but to escape. Meanwhile, the whites on the plantation—including Hiram as well as a poor white overseer, Zeb—are horrified by what they have to do to maintain their livelihoods. With the play, which was inspired by tales of Hansberry's own grandparents, Hansberry makes a passionate statement against the devastating effects of the institution of slavery.

Subject(s): Slavery, Oppression, Freedom

1647 Lorraine Hansberry

A Raisin in the Sun

(New York, NY; Random House, 1959)

Summary: The first play by an African American playwright to be produced on Broadway, *A Raisin in the Sun* recalls Hansberry's own childhood, when her family fought a lengthy battle for the right to live in a white Chicago neighborhood. In the play, following the death of their father, a black family decides to use the father's life insurance proceeds to move out of the Chicago housing projects and into a white, middle-class neighborhood in the suburbs. Doing so, however, prompts resistance from the white neighbors and comes at a personal cost: one son,

Walter Lee, has to give up his dream to open his own business, which he had planned to do with the insurance money. The play was the first by an African American writer to win New York Drama Critics Circle Award for best play.

Subject(s): Race Relations, Community Relations

Award(s): New York Drama Critics Award: Best Play, 1959

1648 Lorraine Hansberry

The Sign in Sidney Brustein's Window
(New York, NY; Random House, 1965)

Summary: Set in New York City's Greenwich Village, this play is notable in that it does not focus explicitly on African American issues or characters. Instead, Hansberry examines a group of white intellectuals and artists. The title character is a Jewish intellectual caught between social protest and utter despair at the social problems he encounters. With the play Hansberry declared her independence as an artist to focus on themes that were important to her, regardless of whether the arts establishment—both black and white—thought that she should restrict her attention to explicitly African American matters. Neither a popular nor critical success, the play nevertheless ran on Broadway for more than 100 performances, closing January 12, 1965, the day Hansberry died from cancer at the age of thirty five.

Subject(s): Social Conditions

1649 Lorraine Hansberry

What Use Are Flowers?
Les Blancs: The Collected Last Plays of Lorraine Hansberry
(New York, NY; Random House, 1972)

Summary: This drama is a powerful anti-nuclear play that explores the effects of a nuclear war. In the play, some of the few children that survive the war encounter a dying man who teaches them about beauty and inspires them to hope and plan for a better future. The play was written in 1962, following a period of intense social action by Hansberry. In addition to protesting Senator Joseph McCarthy's anti-Communist proceedings, she spoke out against the Cuban missile crisis of that year, when the United States and the Soviet Union nearly engaged in a nuclear conflict.

Subject(s): Nuclear Warfare, Children and War

1650 Abram Hill

Walk Hard
Black Theater U.S.A.: Forty-Five Plays by Black Americans, 1847-1974
(New York, NY; Free Press, 1974)

Summary: Abram Hill, one of the founders of New York City's legendary American Negro Theater, set this play in 1939 amid the boxing world of New York. *Walk Hard*, produced in 1944, is an exploration of the stereotype of black men as physically strong but mentally inferior to whites. In the play, Hill depicts the exploitation of a young African American boxer by

a gangster. The play captures the street lingo of 1940s America while exploring the lingering racial stereotypes that have impacted race relations in the United States.

Subject(s): Boxing, Race Relations

1651 Langston Hughes

Booker T. Washington in Atlanta
Radio Drama in Action: Twenty-Five Plays of a Changing World
(New York, NY; Farrar & Rinehart, 1945)

Summary: Written on the occasion of the United States Post Office issuing a stamp honoring Booker T. Washington, this radio play describes Washington's preparations for and delivery of a speech at the opening of a cotton exposition in Atlanta, Georgia. While preparing the speech, Washington reminisces about his childhood days in slavery; his later work as a coal miner, during which he taught himself to read; attending college; and founding the Tuskegee Institute. In his speech, he emphasizes the beliefs for which he is best known: advancement through work and education for blacks, and prosperity for whites who assist blacks in their efforts.

Subject(s): Education, Slavery

1652 Langston Hughes

Simply Heavenly
(New York, NY; Dramatists Play Service, 1959)

Summary: This 1957 play was adapted from Hughes's book *Simple Takes a Wife*, which was part of a series of works featuring Hughes's everyman folk hero, Jesse B. Semple, known as "Simple." A rural southern man who has landed in the big city, Simple spends his time ruminating in comic terms about serious subjects. Although the character of Simple was hugely popular in Hughes's prose books, he translated poorly to the stage, where much of Simple's musings were replaced by action. Nonetheless, in the play as in his books, Hughes paints a warm portrait of a funny man who succeeds in life through his humanity and common sense.

Subject(s): Comedy, Working-Class Life

1653 Elizabeth Maddox Huntley

Legion, the Demoniac
American Literature by Negro Authors
(New York, NY; Macmillan, 1950)

Summary: This brief, simple one-act play addresses belief in Christianity. The title character is a man possessed by devils. During a trip through the forest, his grief-stricken mother and brother meet two field workers and tell them about Legion. The workers suggest that only Jesus can chase away the devils. Shortly thereafter, Jesus does indeed heal Legion, and the play closes with the characters singing a hymn.

Subject(s): Christianity, Devil

1654 Adrienne Kennedy

A Beast Story

Cities in Bezique
(New York, NY; Samuel French, 1969)

Summary: Produced in 1966 and later in tandem with *An Owl Answers*, *A Beast Story* is a hallucinatory, dreamlike play that focuses on sexual repression. In the play, a young woman awakens to reality on the morning after her wedding. She then murders someone, but whether that someone is her child, her husband, who raped her the night before, her lover, or her father is not clear. Though considered by many critics to be a lesser drama than its companion piece, *A Beast Story* clearly demonstrates Kennedy's avant-garde style of interior drama and experimental form.

Subject(s): Marriage, Rape, Sexuality

1655 Adrienne Kennedy

Funnyhouse of a Negro

(New York, NY; Samuel French, 1969)

Summary: Kennedy's first produced work and one of her most important dramas, *Funnyhouse of a Negro* derives its title from an amusement park in Cleveland, Ohio, where two large white statues stood outside the door of a funhouse, mocking those who entered. The play's protagonist is Sarah, a confused and despairing young black woman. In a style that would become her trademark, Kennedy portrays Sarah and the play's other figures as multi-faceted, even multi-person: Sarah is haunted by memories of her lives as Queen Victoria and the Duchess of Hapsburg. She is particularly disturbed by the figure of Patrice Lumumba, also called the "father/husband," a flawed character who ignores his calling to save his people and instead focuses his attention on his white friends. At the end of the play, Sarah commits suicide and is the subject of a ridiculing eulogy by her landlady and her Jewish boyfriend. With the influence and support of Edward Albee, the play was produced off-Broadway in 1964 and won an Obie Award for distinguished play.

Subject(s): Race Relations, Suicide

Award(s): Obie Award: Distinguished Play, 1964

1656 Adrienne Kennedy

An Owl Answers

Cities in Bezique
(New York, NY; Samuel French, 1969)

Summary: Originally produced in 1963 and later paired with *A Beast Story* in a landmark 1969 production at the New York Shakespeare Festival (under the title *Cities in Bezique*), *An Owl Answers* is one of Kennedy's most influential plays. An exploration of identity, the drama features a central character, Clara Passmore, who struggles to understand her background as the illegitimate daughter of a black cook and a wealthy white Englishman. Adopted by a black minister and his wife, Clara searches for her roots and herself, in so doing coming into contact with several famous English forebears, including William

Shakespeare and Anne Boleyn. Kennedy's trademark experimental style presents characters that shift in and out of selves and identities.

Subject(s): Adoption, Identity

1657 Adrienne Kennedy

A Rat's Mass

New Black Playwrights
(Baton Rouge, LA; Louisiana State University Press, 1968)

Summary: This complicated, surreal drama grew out of a dream the author had in which she was pursued by bloodied rats. Kennedy traced the dream to the death of her brother in a car accident. In the play, two rats—brother and sister—profess their adoration for one another and for their former friend, a woman named Rosemary who is a "descendant of the Pope and Julius Caesar and the Virgin Mary." The play (produced in 1966) is heavily infused with Catholic symbolism and has the aura of a parodied mass.

Subject(s): Catholicism, Religion, Death

1658 Adrienne Kennedy

Sun: A Poem for Malcolm X Inspired by His Murder

Spontaneous Combustion: Eight New American Plays
(New York, NY; Winter House, 1972)

Summary: This brief, esoteric work pays tribute to political leader Malcolm X, who was assassinated in 1965. *Sun* is essentially a prose-poem, filled with passages of poetry in combination with more conventional dramatic passages. Thematically, the work is highly symbolic, containing images of magic and mythology that focus on a world of pain and terror.

Subject(s): Race Relations, Assassination

1659 Ron Milner

The Warning: A Theme for Linda

A Black Quartet: Four New Black Plays
(New York, NY; New American Library, 1970)

Summary: This 1969 play is an exploration of manhood told through the eyes of female characters. The protagonist, Linda, is a seventeen-year-old growing up in a family of women in inner-city Detroit. Continually warned about the treachery of men by her grandmother and mother, Linda gradually makes her own peace with the men in her life, determined to give them a chance to match her own strength and integrity.

Subject(s): Family Relations

1660 Ron Milner

What the Wine Sellers Buy

(New York, NY; Samuel French, 1974)

Summary: A searing 1973 drama about life in inner-city black ghettoes during the 1970s, this play revolves around seventeen-year-old Steve Carlton. Steve finds himself under pressure from a pimp in his Detroit neighborhood to become a hustler himself and turn his own girlfriend into a prostitute. The pimp argues that the financial gains cannot be matched, but Steve eventually resists the pressure and temptations. Widely produced around the country, the play was a tremendous commercial and critical success for Milner.

Subject(s): Family Relations, Urban Affairs, Prostitution

1661 Ron Milner

Who's Got His Own

Black Drama Anthology
(New York, NY; Columbia University Press, 1972)

Summary: Milner's first play to be produced in New York City, *Who's Got His Own* is a family drama that focuses on Tim Bronson, Jr. and the effect his deceased father had on his life and on the lives of his sister and mother. Both hated and feared, Tim's father leaves a legacy of mystery and dysfunction. The combative Tim, Jr. struggles to come to grips with his father's life, a job that is complicated by the revelations that his mother makes about his father after his father's death. While infused with the rage that characterized black theater in the 1960s, this 1966 drama also foreshadows Milner's later creation of works that are less overtly political and more focused on issues of human nature and black community.

Subject(s): Family Relations, Fathers and Sons

1662 Roi Ottley

The Negro Domestic

Radio Drama in Action: Twenty-Five Plays of a Changing World
(New York, NY; Farrar & Rinehart, 1945)

Summary: Ottley's sentimental World War II drama exposes the hypocrisy and racism prevalent among whites during the era. The drama centers on Martha, who works as a maid and nanny for a white family. Although the family appreciates Martha's hard work, they nonetheless cling to old stereotypes about her racial inferiority. When Martha realizes how deeply rooted these stereotypes are, she abruptly quits and finds other work. Ottley also highlights the anger felt by black servicemen who fought for world democracy during World War II, but yet remained second-class citizens in their own country.

Subject(s): World War II, Servants, Racism

1663 Thomas Desire Pawley, III

Jedgement Day

Humanities through the Black Experience
(New York, NY; Dryden, 1941)

Summary: First published in 1941, this humorous play by Pawley pokes fun at both religion and human nature. In the play, Minerva tries unsuccessfully to get her lazy husband, Zeke, out of bed to go to church. Even after the local reverend comes by and makes an appeal as well, Zeke refuses to leave his bed. Minerva and the reverend warn Zeke about the wrath

of God and then leave for church. Shortly thereafter, Zeke has a dream in which Judgement Day indeed begins and he is slated to be torn apart because of his pitiful soul. He wakes, inspired to get up and go to church, but at the play's close decides to take one last nap before getting up.

Subject(s): Religion, Humor

1664 Thomas Desire Pawley, III

The Tumult and the Shouting

Black Theater U.S.A.: Forty-Five Plays by Black Americans, 1847-1974
(New York, NY; Free Press, 1974)

Summary: For this 1969 play, Thomas Pawley examined a milieu not usually treated in African American literature: the world of educated southern blacks in the period between the first and second world wars. The play's protagonist, David Sheldon, Sr., is a college teacher who believes in education as the way to ensure that young blacks can provide for themselves in a hostile America. Despite his beliefs, Sheldon finds himself devastated by racism and by economic forces beyond his control.

Subject(s): American South, Racism, Education

1665 Willis Richardson

The House of Sham

American Literature by Negro Authors
(New York, NY; Macmillan, 1950)

Summary: In *The House of Sham*, a seemingly well-to-do businessman shocks his family when he is forced to admit that he has incurred deep debts so that the family can enjoy a comfortable lifestyle. Richardson heaps scorn upon those who lie, cheat, and steal in order to appear to be wealthier than they are.

Subject(s): Money, Wealth, Dishonesty

1666 Ntozake Shange

For Colored Girls Who Have Considered Suicide, When the Rainbow Is Enuf: A Choreopoem

(San Lorenzo, CA; Shameless Hussy, 1975)

Summary: This groundbreaking work, only the second by an African American woman to be produced on Broadway, was a huge success upon its initial production in New York City in 1975 and subsequent production on Broadway. A mixture of poetry, music, and dance, the piece consists of seven women who perform twenty poems examining gender, psychological pain, love, and self-esteem. The work won numerous awards and was nominated for Tony, Emmy, and Grammy awards.

Subject(s): Women, Love, Poetry

Award(s): Obie Award, 1977; Outer Critics Circle Award, 1977; Audelco Award, 1977

1667 Anna Deavere Smith

Fires in the Mirror: Crown Heights, Brooklyn, and Other Identities

(New York, NY; Anchor Books/Doubleday, 1993)

Summary: Anna Deavere Smith pioneered a distinctive dramatic form in the 1980s and 1990s, winning numerous accolades and extending the cultural debate about race relations in America. In creating her pieces, Smith interviews dozens of people about a particular topic or event, then acts out the exact words and mannerisms of her subjects to create a unique dramatic pastiche. *Fires in the Mirror*—produced in 1992—takes as its subject the 1991 riots between Orthodox Jews and African Americans in the Brooklyn, New York neighborhood of Crown Heights. The riots erupted after a car driven by a Jewish man hit and killed a black child in the neighborhood; during the riots, a Jewish rabbinical student was stabbed to death. Smith used her technique to expose the racial tensions at the heart of the riots.

Subject(s): Racial Conflict

Award(s): *Village Voice*: Obie Award, 1993; Drama Desk Award, 1993; Lucille Lortel Award, 1993

1668 Anna Deavere Smith

Twilight--Los Angeles, 1992 on the Road: A Search for American Character

(New York, NY; Anchor Books, 1994)

Summary: Using the words and mannerisms of dozens of interview subjects, Anna Deavere Smith creates unique documentary-dramas that explore race relations in America. In *Twilight*, Smith examines the riots that erupted in Los Angeles in 1992 following the acquittal of white policemen on trial for beating a black motorist, Rodney King. The personas that Smith inhabits in her show range from black gang members to Korean storeowners to white politicians. Smith's work was originally produced in 1993.

Subject(s): Racial Conflict, Violence

Award(s): *Village Voice*: Obie Award, 1994; Drama Desk Award, 1994; New York Drama Critics Circle Award: Best Play, 1994

1669 Joseph A. Walker

The River Niger

(New York, NY; Hill and Wang, 1973)

Summary: This award-winning play focuses on the travails of contemporary black males, a thematic concern present in most of Walker's plays. The drama's protagonist, Johnny Williams, is a middle-aged painter and poet who despairs at his many unfulfilled dreams. He places his hopes in his son Jeff, but is soon disappointed again when Jeff abandons his military career and returns home to resume his former gang life. Later in the play, Johnny dies in a shootout with one of Jeff's enemies, but not before he takes the responsibility for the gang's actions, in essence giving the gang members—and his son—a

new lease on life. Walker presents a hopeful vision of the future of black males, as embodied in the idea that all African Americans share an unbroken bond with their African ancestors.

Subject(s): Gangs

Award(s): Obie Award, 1971; Tony Award, 1973

1670 Douglas Turner Ward

Brotherhood

(New York, NY; Dramatists Play Service, 1970)

Summary: This piercingly satiric play exposes the phony nature of certain black-white relationships. In the play, a white couple invites a black couple to their home for dinner. The white couple, though polite throughout dinner, has covered up furniture and artwork in an attempt to mask feelings of superiority toward blacks. For their part, the black couple behaves equally politely, but they also mask their true feelings of hate toward whites behind misleading smiles. The play, produced in 1970, displays Ward's biting wit and interest in exposing racism and phoniness regardless of where they lie.

Subject(s): Comedy, Race Relations

1671 Douglas Turner Ward

Happy Ending

(New York, NY; Dramatists Play Service, 1966)

Summary: This play, along with *Day of Absence*, was produced in 1965 as a double-bill and was one of the first productions of the influential Negro Ensemble Company, a theater company co-founded by Ward and for which Ward servd as artistic director and occasional actor. The plays feature Ward's trademark combination of satiric humor and social commentary. *Happy Ending* features a pair of sisters, both of them domestic servants for a wealthy white couple, who despair at the breakup of their employers' marriage. When the sisters' proud nephew berates them for their servile attitude, they respond by making him understand that his own comfortable lifestyle is made possible only by their jobs. In *Day of Absence*, Ward depicts the panic that besets the white residents of a southern town when none of the town's black citizens show up for work one day. The play displays the dependence of middle- and upper-class whites on the black men and women whose hard work make their lives function smoothly.

Subject(s): Working-Class Life, Comedy, Race Relations

Award(s): Vernon Rice Drama Desk Award, 1966; Obie Award, 1966; Tony Award, 1969

1672 Douglas Turner Ward

The Reckoning: A Surreal Southern Fable

(New York, NY; Dramatists Play Service, 1970)

Summary: Somewhat grimmer than his other plays, this work nonetheless displays Ward's ability to critique social conditions through comedy. In the play, a black pimp blackmails the governor of a southern state over the governor's liaison with a prostitute. The pimp, Scar, and his girlfriend force the governor to allow and publicly welcome a black march on the state capitol. Ward complicates the play's message about moral integrity and social justice by making the pimp a hero. Ward both wrote and acted in the play's 1969 off-Broadway premier and won an Obie Award for his performance.

Subject(s): Comedy, Race Relations, Prostitution

1673 Richard Wesley

The Mighty Gents
(New York, NY; Dramatists Play Service, 1979)

Summary: Known for mixing elements of the 1960s militant black nationalist drama movement and the 1970s "theatre of experience," in *The Mighty Gents* Wesley depicts the members of a former gang in Newark, New Jersey. Out of work, poorly educated, and with limited options for improving their lives, the men relive the "victories" of their teenage gang years. The play was produced in 1974.

Subject(s): Urban Affairs, Poverty, Gangs

Award(s): National Association for the Advancement of Colored People: Image Award, 1977

1674 Richard Wesley

The Sirens
(New York, NY; Dramatists Play Service, 1975)

Summary: The title of this 1974 play recalls the "Sirens" of Greek legend, beguiling figures whose songs lured sailors into shipwrecks. In this drama, however, Wesley focuses on three women who attract men like the Greek figures, but it's the women themselves who are likely to experience a shipwreck. Mavis and Pepper are both prostitutes who cling tenuously to men from their past and present in the hopes of better lives. Mavis's niece, Betty, lives a precarious existence based on vague promises from her boyfriend. The play is a representative example of Wesley's exploration of the poverty and hopelessness that pervaded the lives of those trapped in inner-city black ghettoes during the 1970s.

Subject(s): Urban Affairs, Poverty, Prostitution

Award(s): National Association for the Advancement of Colored People: Image Award, 1974

1675 August Wilson

Fences: A Play
(New York, NY; New American Library, 1986)

Summary: August Wilson, considered one of the most important American dramatists of the 1980s and 1990s, set this Pulitzer Prize-winning play in an anonymous big city during the 1950s. The play focuses on the troubled relationship between Troy Maxson, a hard-working former athlete, and his son Cory, who seeks to go to college on an athletic scholarship. Comic, sad, and gripping, the play combines sparkling dialogue and

naturalistic intensity with a skilled use of allegory and myth. The Yale Repertory Theatre hosted a production in 1985. In addition to winning the Pulitzer Prize and several other major awards, *Fences* also had a successful run on Broadway.

Subject(s): Family Problems

Award(s): Pulitzer Prize: Drama, 1987; Tony Award: Best Play, 1987; New York Drama Critics Circle Award: Best Play, 1986

1676 August Wilson

The Piano Lesson
(New York, NY; New American Library, 1990)

Summary: When this play won the Pulitzer Prize in 1990, August Wilson became only the seventh American dramatist to win the award twice. Set during the Great Depression of the 1930s, *The Piano Lesson* tells the story of a familial conflict between a brother and sister, Boy Willie and Berniece. At issue is the family piano, which Willie wants to sell to buy land and which Berniece thinks is too valuable as a family heirloom to part with. In the end, the piano serves as a symbol of the friction between honoring the past and living in the present. Along with Wilson's other plays, *The Piano Lesson* is part of a projected ten-play cycle about twentieth century African American life, with each play focusing on a different decade.

Subject(s): Family Problems, Depression (Economic)

Award(s): Pulitzer Prize: Drama, 1990; Tony Award: Best Play, 1990; New York Drama Critics Circle Award: Best Play, 1990

1677 George C. Wolfe

The Colored Museum
(New York, NY; Grove Press, 1988)

Summary: Acclaimed as a playwright as well as a theatrical director and producer, George C. Wolfe drew numerous accolades--and significant criticism--for this play. In eleven vignettes, Wolfe satirizes and exposes various elements of African American culture, from the "mammy" stereotype to homophobia to black men who chronically see themselves as "victims" of white society. Though some critics accosted Wolfe for what they viewed as a self-hating play, others lauded the author for creating a witty yet serious play that is ruthless in its search for truth. The work was produced in 1985.

Subject(s): African Americans, Racism, Comedy

Award(s): Dramatists Guild: Elizabeth Hull-Kate Warriner Award, 1986

1678 Richard Wright
Charles K. O'Neill, Adapter

Fire and Cloud
American Scenes
(New York, NY; John Day Company, 1941)

Summary: O'Neill adapted this radio play from a short story by Wright. The play is set in a small southern town during the Great Depression of the 1930s. The central character is Reverend Taylor, who is beseeched by members of his congregation to support their planned march down the town's main street; hungry and angry, their goal is to protest their living conditions. Taylor eschews their requests, feeling that he cannot give his support to a march that may end in the lynching of the marchers by angry white townspeople. However, after the Reverend himself is abducted and savagely beaten by local whites, he decides to lead the march himself. As the marchers descend on city hall, asking for nothing but bread, they are joined by sympathetic whites.

Subject(s): American South, Depression (Economic), Lynching

1679 **Richard Wright**
Paul Green, Co-author

Native Son (the Biography of a Young American): A Play in Ten Scenes
(New York, NY; Harper, 1941)

Summary: Richard Wright and Paul Green adapted this play from Wright's much celebrated novel of the same name. Like the novel, the play tells the story of Bigger Thomas, a black man who murders a white woman in Chicago. The play was first produced on Broadway in 1941 in a production directed by Orson Welles and starring Canada Lee as Bigger Thomas.

Subject(s): Murder, Racism, Judicial System

Literary Criticism

African American literary criticism gained institutional stature with the 1941 publication of Sterling A. Brown, Arthur P. Davis, and Ulysses Lee's *The Negro Caravan,* a comprehensive anthology of African American literature. The major mode of literary criticism that emerged in the forties and fifties was the explication of individual texts. This technique was pioneered in the essays of Arthur P. Davis, who also continued to edit anthologies that highlighted major African American writers. In the fifties and sixties, African American literature received an important boost with the publication of literary histories such as Robert Bone's *Negro Novel in America* (1958). Essays from figures such as Blyden Jackson, Darwin Turner, Charles T. Davis, and a host of others propelled blacks into recognition as writers of literary criticism.

The nationalist period of the late sixties and the early seventies was exemplified by the Black Arts or Black Aesthetic movement, which produced a more political and race-oriented group of critics. These included Amiri Baraka and Larry Neal, who co-edited the 1968 work *Black Fire,* and Addison Gayle, who edited the defining book of criticism by authors of the movement, *The Black Aesthetic.* In this collection of essays by

black artists, the predominant theme is that white aesthetics should not be used as a basis for judging black art.

Finally, the integration of the elite universities in the late sixties and early seventies, plus the onset of the feminist movement, led to the growth of a new generation of critics. These included Houston A. Baker, Jr., Henry Louis Gates, Jr., Robert Stepto, Deborah McDowell, and bell hooks. Gates' book of literary criticism *The Signifying Monkey* won the 1988 American Book Award.

African American literary criticism has at present reached the status of a standard aspect of literary studies in the academic establishment of America. Black literary critics participate in major literary conferences, academic organizations, and in groups such as the Modern Language Association and the National Council of Teachers in English. Articles on black literature are regularly published in the leading literary and literary criticism journals, signaling that this type of work is now part of mainstream American literature.

1680 **Sandra Adell**

Double Consciousness/Double Bind: Theoretical Issues in Twentieth-Century Black Literature
(Urbana, IL; University of Illinois Press, 1994)

Summary: In her 1994 work, Adell examines problematic issues in literary criticism about modern African American literature, from the issue of feminist criticism to a discussion of black vernacular in modern criticism. One of the major issues that Adell explores is the distinctness of African American literary criticism, which is called into question when such criticism relies heavily on white European modes of thought. Among the specific works that Adell treats is the classic *The Souls of Black Folk* by W.E.B. Du Bois.

Subject(s): Literature

1681 **William L. Andrews,** Editor

Sisters of the Spirit: Three Black Women's Autobiographies of the Nineteenth Century
(Bloomington, IN; Indiana University Press, 1986)

Summary: This 1986 book contains three autobiographical works by black women: Jarena Lee, Zilpha Elaw, and Julia A.J. Foote. Though not as well known as other nineteenth century black women such as Sojourner Truth or Harriet Tubman, these women nevertheless forged reputations as influential social and religious activists. Andrews includes a lengthy introduction to the three texts.

Subject(s): Autobiography, Religion

1682   William L. Andrews　,

To Tell a Free Story: The First Century of Afro-American Autobiography, 1760-1865

(Urbana, IL; University of Illinois Press, 1986)

Summary: Early literature by African Americans was dominated by autobiography, and Andrews offers a comprehensive study of the first hundred years of African American autobiography. Most of the works discussed by Andrews are slave narratives by such writers as Harriet Jacobs, Nat Turner, and Frederick Douglass. At the end of the book, Andrews offers an annotated bibliography of African American autobiography and biography.

Subject(s): Autobiography, Slavery

1683   Houston A. Baker, Jr., Editor
Patricia Redmond, Co-editor

Afro-American Literary Study in the 1990s

(Chicago, IL; University of Chicago Press, 1989)

Summary: Co-edited by noted literary critic Houston A. Baker, Jr. and Patricia Redmond, this volume of essays grew out of a 1987 conference at the University of Pennsylvania titled "The Study of Afro-American Literature: An Agenda for the 1990s." Included in the book are seven contributions to that conference along with discussions of the issues raised.

Subject(s): Literature

1684   Houston A. Baker, Jr.

Black Studies, Rap, and the Academy: Issues in Black Literature and Criticism

(Chicago, IL; University of Chicago Press, 1993)

Summary: Baker weaves together black studies with rap music in this provocative 1993 work. He discusses the emergence of black studies on university campuses during the tumultuous 1960s, then offers a critical analysis of the 1990 obscenity trial of the rap group "2 Live Crew." Ultimately, while suggesting that the group's album *As Nasty as They Wanna Be* was rightfully banned, Baker celebrates the creative explosion of rap music and argues that African American academics should witness, study, and respect rap music as a compelling force in American culture.

Subject(s): Music, Judicial System, Cultural Identity

1685   Houston A. Baker, Jr.

Blues, Ideology, and Afro-American Literature: A Vernacular Theory

(Chicago, IL; University of Chicago Press, 1984)

Summary: In this 1984 work, Baker uses the blues--the musical form that was originated by blacks in the rural South--as a paradigm with which to study African American literary expression. According to Baker, this particular musical form, because it serves as a crossroads for themes of folklore, sexuality, and economic matters, offers critics a useful structure from which to study black literature.

Subject(s): Music, Literature, American South

1686   Houston A. Baker, Jr.

The Journey Back: Issues in Black Literature and Criticism

(Chicago, IL; University of Chicago Press, 1980)

Summary: Extending his examination of black autobiography begun in *Long Black Song*, Houston A. Baker here shows how African American verbal expression is used by black writers to establish order and thus postulate the existence of a unique African American culture. He also explores the manner in which African American writers alter--and in turn are altered by--the dominant white literary tradition in America.

Subject(s): Literature, Autobiography

1687   Houston A. Baker, Jr.

Long Black Song: Essays in Black American Literature and Culture

(Charlottesville, VA; University Press of Virginia, 1972)

Summary: This work, which is Baker's first published work of literary criticism, establishes the framework on which much of his later work is based. As the subtitle suggests, Baker argues here that black literature cannot be discussed separately from black culture. Among the texts that Baker examines are works by Frederick Douglass, W.E.B. Du Bois, Richard Wright, and Ralph Ellison.

Subject(s): Literature

1688   Houston A. Baker, Jr.

Modernism and the Harlem Renaissance

(Chicago, IL; University of Chicago Press, 1987)

Summary: In his 1987 work, Baker argues that writers of the Harlem Renaissance did indeed experiment with elements of literary modernism—the early twentieth century movement usually associated with Anglo-American authors such as T.S. Eliot and James Joyce. Previous critics have categorized the Harlem Renaissance as "provincial" in style and outlook, but Baker shows that writers such as Jean Toomer, Countee Cullen, and W.E.B. Du Bois were influenced by modernist principles.

Subject(s): Literature, Harlem Renaissance

1689 Toni Cade Bambara

Deep Sightings and Rescue Missions: Fiction, Essays, and Conversations

(New York, NY; Pantheon Books, 1996)

Summary: Along with several works of Bambara's short fiction and interviews with and by Bambara, this work includes a number of essays of criticism by the author. Among the subjects she examines in the book's critical essays are the "blaxploitation" film era of the 1970s as well as filmmakers Julie Dash and Spike Lee. This work includes a preface by Bambara's friend, Nobel laureate Toni Morrison.

Subject(s): Film, Literature

1690 Richard K. Barksdale

Praisesong of Survival: Lectures and Essays, 1957-89

(Urbana, IL; University of Illinois Press, 1992)

Summary: A compendium of lectures and essays covering three decades, *Praisesong of Survival* offers a significant overview of Barksdale's career as a prominent literary critic and intellectual. The collection is divided into six thematic sections, among them "Literary Canons and Blackness," "The Humanities beyond Literary Canons," and "Literary Forms of Historic Survival." The last two sections include several essays about notable writers, including Toni Morrison, Margaret Walker, and Langston Hughes.

Subject(s): Literature

1691 Rebecca Chalmers Barton

Black Voices in American Fiction, 1900-1930

(Oakdale, NY; Dowling College Press, 1976)

Summary: In her 1976 work, Rebecca Chalmers Barton begins by offering a detailed analysis of race consciousness. She then turns her attention to how race consciousness has manifested itself in fictional works by African American authors between 1900 and 1930. As part of her study, Barton considers the urban-rural dynamic at work in African American life during the period, and she also focuses on individual identity in the works of authors such as Rudolph Fisher, Claude McKay, Jessie Fauset, and Jean Toomer.

Subject(s): City and Town Life, Rural Life, Identity

1692 Bernard W. Bell

The Afro-American Novel and Its Tradition

(Amherst, MA; University of Massachusetts Press, 1987)

Summary: This critical work became the definitive study of the African American novel upon its publication in 1987. Beginning with William Wells Brown's 1853 novel, *Clotel*, and ending with Ishmael Reed's 1972 novel, *Mumbo Jumbo*, Bell examines more than 150 works and 40 writers.

Subject(s): Literature

1693 Judith R. Berzon

Neither White Nor Black: The Mulatto Character in American Fiction

(New York, NY; New York University Press, 1978)

Summary: Promoted as "the first comprehensive study of the mulatto character in American fiction," Berzon's work, originally written as a thesis in 1974, offers a detailed description of the social, political, and cultural forces that have contributed to the American fascination with mixed-race identity. Berzon also provides a thorough analysis of key nineteenth and twentieth century authors including Mark Twain, Langston Hughes, William Faulkner, and John A. Williams. Among the archetypal themes that Berzon identifies in the works of these authors are the "tragic mulatto," the "mulatto as black bourgeois," the "mulatto as race leader," and the "mulatto as existential man."

Subject(s): Class Conflict, Race Relations, Identity

1694 Robert Bone

The Negro Novel in America

(New Haven, CT; Yale University Press, 1958)

Summary: This 1958 book by Robert Bone is considered a classic text of African American literary criticism. In the book, Bone surveys black literature in chronological fashion, beginning with the period of 1890 to 1920, during which such authors as Sutton Griggs, Charles W. Chesnutt, and Paul Laurence Dunbar were active. Bone then examines the decade of the 1920s, which featured the rise of the "New Negro" literature (also known as the Harlem Renaissance) and such authors as Langston Hughes and Nella Larsen; the 1930s, when William Attaway and Richard Wright began working; and the 1940s and early 1950s, when James Baldwin secured his literary reputation.

Subject(s): Literature, Harlem Renaissance

1695 Melba Joyce Boyd

Discarded Legacy: Politics and Poetics in the Life of Frances E.W. Harper, 1825-1911

(Detroit, MI; Wayne State University Press, 1994)

Summary: Boyd's critical study of the life and work of Frances E.W. Harper focuses on reclaiming Harper's modern legacy as a writer and as an activist. Boyd examines Harper's pioneering work as an abolitionist and feminist from the mid-1800s to the end of her life; she also argues for a retrieval of Harper's legacy, which languished in obscurity during much of the twentieth century. In addition to discussing Harper's life, Boyd offers detailed analyses of Harper's major works, including *Iola Leroy* and *Sketches of Southern Life.*

Subject(s): Literature, Women's Rights, Abolition

1696 Jerry H. Bryant

Victims and Heroes: Racial Violence in the African American Novel
(Amherst, MA; University of Massachusetts Press, 1997)

Summary: The issue of violence, specifically the manner in which African American writers have treated the issue in their fiction, is the focus of Bryant's 1997 study. Bryant discusses the work of nineteenth century writers such as Martin Delany and Sutton Griggs as well as twentieth century authors including Chester Himes, Ishmael Reed, and Toni Morrison. In the end, Bryant argues that the overwhelming presence of violence by whites toward blacks in American history has produced an ambiguous response in African American fiction.

Subject(s): Literature, Violence

1697 Keith E. Byerman

Fingering the Jagged Grain: Tradition and Form in Recent Black Fiction
(Athens, GA; University of Georgia Press, 1985)

Summary: In his 1985 critical work, Byerman focuses on the fiction of African American writers of the 1970s and 1980s. Unlike the writers of the "black arts" movement of the 1960s, who focused primarily on the social and political issues surrounding African Americans, these later writers valued aesthetic concerns such as form and craftsmanship. In addition, they sought to reclaim elements of folk culture in their work. Among the writers whom Byerman features are Ernest J. Gaines, Alice Walker, Toni Morrison, and Clarence Major.

Subject(s): Literature, Folklore

1698 John F. Callahan

In the African-American Grain: The Pursuit of Voice in Twentieth-Century Black Fiction
(Urbana, IL; University of Illinois Press, 1988)

Summary: A well-regarded work about twentieth century black fiction, this critical study focuses on the relationship between the black oral storytelling tradition and modern African American fiction. Callahan adds a distinctive political note to his argument, discussing such issues as "democratic identity" and "politics and the restoration of voice in *Meridian*." Among the writers he discusses are Jean Toomer and Ralph Ellison.

Subject(s): Literature, Politics, Storytelling

1699 Jane Campbell

Mythic Black Fiction: The Transformation of History
(Knoxville, TN; University of Tennessee Press, 1986)

Summary: Each chapter of Campbell's 1986 critical study examines two classic novels written by African Americans. In addition, each chapter is focused on a different theme, allowing Campbell to explore the creation of a distinct mythology by African American writers. Among the themes and works featured are "Celebrations of Escape and Revolt," in which Campbell addresses William Wells Brown's *Clotel* and Arna Bontemps's *Black Thunder*; "Female Paradigms" in Frances E.W. Harper's *Iola Leroy* and Pauline Hopkins's *Contending Forces*; and "Ancestral Quests" in Toni Morrison's *Song of Solomon* and David Bradley's *The Chaneysville Incident.*

Subject(s): Literature, Mythology

1700 Katie Cannon

Katie's Canon: Womanism and the Soul of the Black Community
(New York, NY; Continuum, 1995)

Summary: Cannon here examines the role and place of women in African American history, including literary history. Consisting of essays written during a ten-year period, the book includes several pieces devoted to author Zora Neale Hurston.

Subject(s): Literature, Women's Rights

1701 Hazel V. Carby

Reconstructing Womanhood: The Emergence of the Afro-American Woman Novelist
(New York, NY; Oxford University Press, 1987)

Summary: In the eight essays contained in this 1987 work, Hazel V. Carby examines the development of African American women writers. She begins with women who wrote narratives about their existence as slaves, then examines subsequent major writers such as Frances E.W. Harper and Pauline Hopkins. She also includes a bibliography of works by black women authors in addition to a general bibliography about black literature.

Subject(s): Slavery, Literature, Women

1702 Rebecca Carroll

I Know What the Red Clay Looks Like: The Voice and Vision of Black Women Writers
(New York, NY; Crown Trade Paperbacks, 1994)

Summary: A collection of interviews with and excerpts by several contemporary African American women writers, this work is a companion volume to Carroll's *Swing Low: Black*

Men Writing. Here, writers such as Nikki Giovanni, Rita Dove, Gloria Naylor, and J. California Cooper discuss their lives, their work, and their literary influences.

Subject(s): Literature

1703 **Rebecca Carroll,** Compiler

Swing Low: Black Men Writing
(New York, NY; Carol Southern Books, 1995)

Summary: This companion volume to Carroll's *I Know What the Red Clay Looks Like,* contains interviews with and excerpts by sixteen African American male writers. Among the authors included in the collection are Leon Forrest, Henry Louis Gates, Jr., Ishmael Reed, and August Wilson.

Subject(s): Literature

1704 **Barbara Christian**

Black Women Novelists: The Development of a Tradition, 1892-1976
(Westport, CT; Greenwood Press, 1980)

Summary: Barbara Christian begins her 1976 study with three chapters that trace the historical development of African American women writers. In particular, Christian shows how stereotypical images imposed on black women by the dominant white male society impacted black women writers. In the book's second half, Christian shows how three twentieth century writers--Paule Marshall, Toni Morrison, and Alice Walker--dealt with and eventually transcended these images in their work.

Subject(s): Literature, Women

1705 **James W. Coleman**

Blackness and Modernism: The Literary Career of John Edgar Wideman
(Jackson, MS; University Press of Mississippi, 1989)

Summary: Acclaimed author John Edgar Wideman is the focus of this 1989 critical work by Coleman. In examining Wideman's life, Coleman argues that Wideman overcame feelings of alienation from the black community and eventually became fully engaged in African American culture. So too with his fiction, notes Coleman, who divides Wideman's career into three stages: his early books (including *Hurry Home* and *The Lynchers*); his "Homewood" trilogy; and his more recent novels (*Brothers and Keepers* and *Reuben*). The book also includes an interview that Coleman conducted with Wideman.

Subject(s): Literature

1706 **Michael G. Cooke**

Afro-American Literature in the Twentieth Century: The Achievement of Intimacy
(New Haven, CT; Yale University Press, 1984)

Summary: In this work, Cooke examines how modern African American writers have rejected the detached and isolated voice of much contemporary fiction, instead grappling with the issue of intimacy in their work. Focusing on writers such as Nella Larsen, Eldridge Cleaver, Alice Walker, and James Baldwin, Cooke analyzes their treatment of issues such as suicide, magic, and materialism.

Subject(s): Literature, Suicide, Magic

1707 **John R. Cooley**

Savages and Naturals: Black Portraits by White Writers in Modern American Literature
(Newark, DL; University of Delaware Press, 1982)

Summary: Cooley offers a detailed analysis of the works of eight white American writers, and he categorizes the writers by the metaphors of the "savage" and the "natural" as seen in their works. Thus, in the works of Stephen Crane, Vachel Lindsay, Eugene O'Neill, and Waldo Frank, Cooley discusses how their works portray black characters as savages. On the other hand, in examining the works of William Faulkner, Eudora Welty, Norman Mailer, and Kurt Vonnegut, Jr., Cooley shows how these authors have utilized the motif of the black "natural" in their writings. In both instances, notes Cooley, white authors have insisted on representing blacks as primitives—either to denigrate them as savages or to elevate them as somehow untouched by modern troubles.

Subject(s): Racism, Literature

1708 **Stelamaris Coser**

Bridging the Americas: The Literature of Paule Marshall, Toni Morrison, and Gayl Jones
(Philadelphia, PA; Temple University Press, 1995)

Summary: In analyzing the works of Paule Marshall, Toni Morrison, and Gayl Jones, Brazilian-born critic Stelamaris Coser makes comparisons between these authors and prominent modern Latin American writers such as Gabriel Garcia Marquez and Carlos Fuentes. Coser concludes that the literature of Marshall, Morrison, and Jones restructures the boundaries of American writing by going beyond conventional notions of gender, race, and nationality.

Subject(s): Literature

1709 **Angelo Costanzo**

Surprizing Narrative: Olaudah Equiano and the Beginnings of Black Autobiography
(New York, NY; Greenwood Press, 1987)

Summary: Focusing on the slave narrative of Olaudah Equiano, Costanzo here emphasizes the slave narrative as a distinct literary genre and as the beginning of African American literature. Costanzo points out that the slave narrative introduced into black literature such elements as the religious sermon form and the picaresque character. While Equiano is the book's central figure, Costanzo also discusses slave narratives by Ottobah Cugoano and John Marrant, among others.

Subject(s): Slavery, Autobiography, Literature

1710 **David Dabydeen,** Editor

The Black Presence in English Literature
(Dover, NH; Manchester University Press, 1985)

Summary: The ten essays in Dabydeen's 1985 work focus on black issues in British literature, from black characters in William Shakespeare's dramas to black writers during the eighteenth and nineteenth centuries. Other essays discuss the "problematic presence" of "the colonial other" in works by Rudyard Kipling and Joseph Conrad and the existence of blacks in works about the former British empire.

Subject(s): Africa, Literature, Colonialism

1711 **Walter C. Daniel**

"De Lawd: ichard B. Harrison and "The Green Pastures"
(New York, NY; Greenwood Press, 1986)

Summary: Daniel's 1986 work examines the dramatic phenomenon of *The Green Pastures,* a religious play by Marc Connelly that toured the United States during the Great Depression of the 1930s with an all-black cast of nearly 100 people. During the play's run, the character of God was played by Richard B. Harrison, who emerges as the central figure of this critical study. Daniel also discusses earlier contributions by black artists to the American theater.

Subject(s): Depression (Economic), Drama, Religion

1712 **Carole Boyce Davies**

Black Women, Writing, and Identity: Migrations of the Subject
(New York, NY; Routledge, 1994)

Summary: The "migrations of the subject" that Davies explores in this work refer to the manner in which black women occupy several spheres of identity by migrating from one to another. These spheres include not only race but also gender and nationality. In making her argument, Davies examines black writers in America, Africa, and the Caribbean. Among the writers she includes in her study is Ama Ata Aidoo.

Subject(s): Literature, Africa

1713 **Charles T. Davis**
Henry Louis Gates, Jr., Editor

Black Is the Color of the Cosmos: Essays on Afro-American Literature and Culture, 1942-1981
(New York, NY; Garland Pub., 1982)

Summary: This collection of Davis's essays from a forty-year period is divided into three sections: "Theories of Black Literature and Culture"; "The Structure of the Afro-American Literary Tradition"; and "On Wright, Ellison, and Baldwin." In section one, Davis treats such topics as the Harlem Renaissance and the "black arts" movement of the 1960s. In section two, he discusses Paul Laurence Dunbar, Jean Toomer, and slave narratives. Finally, in section three, he examines three titanic twentieth century writers.

Subject(s): Literature, Harlem Renaissance

1714 **Thadious M. Davis**

Faulkner's "Negro": Art and the Southern Context
(Baton Rouge, LA; Louisiana State University Press, 1983)

Summary: Novelist William Faulkner (1897-1962) is considered one of the most important writers in twentieth century American literature. In this 1983 work, critic Thadious M. Davis examines the presence of African Americans in Faulkner's writings, arguing that the "Negro" character derived from Southern stereotypes "is a central imaginative force in Faulkner's fiction." Among the works that Davis addresses are *The Sound and the Fury, Light in August,* and *Absalom, Absalom!*

Subject(s): American South, Literature, Racism

1715 **Thadious M. Davis**

Nella Larsen, Novelist of the Harlem Renaissance: A Woman's Life Unveiled
(Baton Rouge, LA; Louisiana State University Press, 1994)

Summary: Nella Larsen (1891-1964), the focus of Davis's 1994 biography, was a key figure in the Harlem Renaissance cultural flowering of the 1920s. Her first two novels, *Quicksand* (1928) and *Passing* (1929), brought her instant recognition. In 1930, however, she was accused of plagiarism, and thereafter she withdrew from the literary world and worked mainly as a nurse. Davis examines how Larsen's mixed-race heritage influenced her life and her art.

Subject(s): Biography, Harlem Renaissance

1716 Jacqueline De Weever

Mythmaking and Metaphor in Black Women's Fiction

(New York, NY; St. Martin's Press, 1991)

Summary: In this work, De Weever studies seventeen novels by African American women writers such as Toni Morrison, Alice Walker, and Gayl Jones. Exploring the manner in which these authors use myth and metaphor, De Weever highlights their use of European, African, African American, and Native American myths in their works.

Subject(s): Literature, Mythology

1717 Dorothy Hamer Denniston

The Fiction of Paule Marshall: Reconstructions of History, Culture, and Gender

(Knoxville, TN; University of Tennessee Press, 1995)

Summary: In her 1995 work, Denniston focuses on the Afrocentric elements in the work of noted African American writer Paule Marshall. Examining Marshall's career chronologically in seven chapters, Denniston covers the author's early writings in the 1950s, her work during the Black Nationalist movement of the 1960s, and her later work in the 1970s, 1980s, and 1990s. Denniston offers innovative readings of Marshall's work that explore the way in which the issue of class intersects the issues of race and gender in Marshall's fiction.

Subject(s): Literature, Black Nationalism

1718 Melvin Dixon

Ride Out the Wilderness: Geography and Identity in Afro-American Literature

(Urbana, IL; University of Illinois Press, 1987)

Summary: As this work's subtitle suggests, Dixon explores the relationship between geography and identity in the formation of African American literature. Dixon argues that black writers, who have been alienated from mainstream literary culture, have created alternative literary landscapes in which they fully explore their racial and cultural identities. After examining the significance of real-life geographical places in slave songs and narratives, Dixon goes on to study the role of symbolic landscapes such as the mountaintop, the wilderness, and the underground in twentieth-century works by authors including Toni Morrison, Jean Toomer, and James Baldwin.

Subject(s): Literature, Geography, African Americans

1719 Laura Anne Doyle

Bordering on the Body: The Racial Matrix of Modern Fiction and Culture

(New York, NY; Oxford University Press, 1994)

Summary: Doyle examines the issues of race and gender in the works of several twentieth century experimental writers, including Virginia Woolf, Jean Toomer, James Joyce, Ralph Ellison, and Toni Morrison. Drawing on fields as diverse as biology, anthropology, and psychology, Doyle argues that even works by white male authors such as Joyce cannot be properly understood without an analysis of race and gender.

Subject(s): Literature

1720 Madhu Dubey

Black Women Novelists and the Nationalist Aesthetic

(Bloomington, IN; Indiana University Press, 1994)

Summary: In her 1994 work, feminist literary critic Madhu Dubey examines the works of three seminal contemporary black female writers: Toni Morrison, Alice Walker, and Gayl Jones. Dubey's purpose is to restructure the black nationalist criticism that arose in the 1960s--in which race was viewed as the primary element in critiquing literature--so that gender receives due consideration as a fundamental factor in literary criticism.

Subject(s): Women's Rights, Black Nationalism

1721 Ann duCille

The Coupling Convention: Sex, Text, and Tradition in Black Women's Fiction

(New York, NY; Oxford University Press, 1993)

Summary: duCille's aim in her 1993 work is to reclaim fictional works by black women writers that treat the issue of "coupling," or marriage. duCille argues that such works have been systematically excluded from critical discourse in two ways. First, white critics have ignored such works because the authors were black; second, black feminist critics have ignored the works because of their thematic terrain. Among the authors that duCille examines are Harriet Jacobs, Frances E.W. Harper, Zora Neale Hurston, and Dorothy West.

Subject(s): Literature, Marriage

1722 Arlene A. Elder

The "Hindered Hand": Cultural Implications of Early African-American Fiction

(Westport, CT; Greenwood Press, 1978)

Summary: In examining three notable early African American authors—Sutton E. Griggs, Paul Laurence Dunbar, and Charles W. Chesnutt—Arlene A. Elder shows how their works exemplified the literature written by blacks during the period. In discussing the work of Griggs, Elder focuses on his treatment of class issues. Elder offers an analysis of Dunbar's "triumph of the tradition" that is typified by his work. When focusing on

Chesnutt, Elder explores the issue of whether his literary output amounted to "art or assimilation."

Subject(s): Class Conflict, Literature

1723 John Ernest

Resistance and Reformation in Nineteenth-Century African-American Literature: Brown, Wilson, Jacobs, Delany, Douglass, and Harper
(Jackson, MS; University Press of Mississippi, 1995)

Summary: In this 1995 work, Ernest offers a broad survey of African American literature in the nineteenth century. Ernest discusses the way in which the history of African Americans influenced the work of authors such as Martin Delany, William Wells Brown, and Frances E.W. Harper, who turned that history into fiction and myth. Nonetheless, notes Ernest, such literature remained preoccupied with the injustice of slavery and oppression and focused on avenues of social change.

Subject(s): Literature, Slavery, History

1724 James H. Evans, Jr.

Spiritual Empowerment in Afro-American Literature: Frederick Douglass, Rebecca Jackson, Booker T. Washington, Richard Wright, Toni Morrison
(Lewiston, NY; E. Mellen Press, 1987)

Summary: Volume 6 in the "Studies in Art and Religious Interpretation" series, this 1987 work explores the interaction between African American literature and religion "as types of cultural expression." In addressing this issue, Evans examines Frederick Douglass's famous autobiography; the fictional work of Rebecca Jackson and Booker T. Washington; Richard Wright's classic twentieth century novel, *Native Son;* and Toni Morrison's acclaimed novel *Song of Solomon.*

Subject(s): Religion, Literature

1725 Frances Smith Foster

Written by Herself: Literary Production by African American Women, 1746-1892
(Bloomington, IN; Indiana University Press, 1993)

Summary: Foster's 1993 work treats nearly 150 years of writings by African American female writers, including such authors as Phillis Wheatley, Frances E.W. Harper, Harriet Jacobs, and Harriet Wilson. Foster addresses the issues of race, gender, and class in examining various works and their authors.

Subject(s): Literature

1726 H. Bruce Franklin

The Victim as Criminal and Artist: Literature from the American Prison
(New York, NY; Oxford University Press, 1978)

Summary: The subject of this 1978 critical work is the literature of minority artists—primarily African Americans—whose work grew out of their experience of being defined by society as criminals and who were physically incarcerated at some point in their lives. Franklin discusses slave narratives, writers such as Chester Himes, whose work focuses on the prison experience, and Malcolm X.

Subject(s): Slavery, Crime and Criminals

1727 Joanne V. Gabbin

Sterling A. Brown: Building the Black Aesthetic Tradition
(Westport, CT; Greenwood Press, 1985)

Summary: Poet and critic Sterling A. Brown is the focus of Gabbin's 1985 critical study. In the work, Gabbin argues that Brown has been the principal architect of the black aesthetic tradition through both his acclaimed poetry and his influential criticism. Brown, notes Gabbin, "has made the necessary connections between oral folk culture and self-conscious literature, identifying in his own poetry and the writings of others their debt to the folk."

Subject(s): Folklore, Literature, Poetry

1728 Henry Louis Gates, Jr.

Figures in Black: Words, Signs, and the "Racial" Self
(New York, NY; Oxford University Press, 1987)

Summary: Arguing that too much of black literature has been focused on advocating ideas at the expense of aesthetic form, Gates examines classic black narratives from a new perspective. Gates utilizes a myriad of critical perspectives as he draws new parallels between African American texts from the nineteenth and twentieth centuries.

Subject(s): Literature

1729 Henry Louis Gates, Jr.

Loose Canons: Notes on the Culture Wars
(New York, NY; Oxford University Press, 1992)

Summary: In the various essays in this book, Henry Louis Gates, Jr., argues for greater diversity in American arts. Criticizing both the conservative right for trying to protect an outmoded canon modeled on Western cultural works, and the liberal left for advocating a canon based heavily on gender and racial matters, Gates concludes that only cultural tolerance and understanding can result in a workable modern literary canon.

Subject(s): Literature

1730 Henry Louis Gates, Jr., Editor

Reading Black, Reading Feminist: A Critical Anthology

(New York, NY; Meridian Books, 1990)

Summary: This 1990 anthology consists of twenty-six essays focusing on black and feminist issues in literature. The essays are divided into two sections: "Constructing a Tradition" and "Reading Black, Reading Feminist." Among the contributors are Barbara E. Johnson, Jewelle Gomez, bell hooks, and Deborah E. McDowell. The book also includes an introduction by Henry Louis Gates, who edited the collection, as well as two interviews—one with Rita Dove and another with Jamaica Kincaid.

Subject(s): Literature, Women, Women's Rights

1731 Henry Louis Gates, Jr.

The Signifying Monkey: Towards a Theory of Afro-American Literary Criticism

(New York, NY; Oxford University Press, 1988)

Summary: The term "Afro-American" is at the heart of this 1988 work; Gates attempts to show continuities of form and content from African Yoruba folk tales to contemporary African American literature. The book contains an extended examination of the "talking book," a form seen in the earliest slave narratives as well as in twentieth century writings by authors such as Zora Neale Hurston and Ralph Ellison.

Subject(s): Literature, Africa, Folk Tales

Award(s): American Book Award, 1989; Anisfield-Wolf Award for Race Relations, 1989

1732 Addison Gayle, Jr., Editor

The Black Aesthetic

(Garden City, NY; Doubleday, 1971)

Summary: Addison Gayle's 1971 work examines the way in which twentieth century black artists moved toward an aesthetic philosophy that reflected a unique African American culture, as opposed to merging their work with a larger American culture. Divided into sections such as "Theory," "Music," "Poetry," "Drama," and "Fiction," the book includes pieces by a wide range of thinkers, from Alain Locke and W.E.B. Du Bois to Larry Neal and Dudley Randall.

Subject(s): Literature, African Americans, Culture

1733 Addison Gayle, Jr., Editor

Bondage, Freedom, and Beyond: The Prose of Black Americans

(Garden City, NY; Zenith Books, 1971)

Summary: Educator and critic Addison Gayle, Jr. authored several groundbreaking books profiling the life and work of African American writers as a means of introducing students to what he termed the "black aesthetic"--a perspective on black culture that was unique from the Western approach used to judge white cultural achievements. In his *Bondage, Freedom, and Beyond: The Prose of Black Americans* Gayle compiled selected criticisms and excerpts focusing on the works of notable African American writers, among them Paul Laurence Dunbar and Richard Wright.

Subject(s): Literature, Biography, Cultural Conflict

1734 Addison Gayle, Jr.

The Way of the New World: The Black Novel in America

(Garden City, NY; Anchor Press, 1975)

Summary: In *The Way of the New World*, prominent literary critic Addison Gayle, Jr., offers a panoramic view of fiction by and about blacks from the 1850s to the 1970s. Gayle incorporates a combined literary-sociological viewpoint into his readings of various texts, arguing against either a purely literary or historical approach to analyzing literature. Among the writers whom Gayle discusses are James Baldwin, John A. Williams, Norman Mailer, and Chester E. Himes.

Subject(s): Literature, History

1735 Donald B. Gibson, Editor

Five Black Writers: Essays on Wright, Ellison, Baldwin, Hughes, and LeRoi Jones

(New York, NY; New York University Press, 1970)

Summary: The essays in this 1970 critical work discuss five landmark black authors of the twentieth century: Richard Wright, Ralph Ellison, James Baldwin, Langston Hughes, and LeRoi Jones (later known as Amiri Baraka). The various contributors to the book explore the thematic, stylistic, and political nature of the five authors' writings, from Ellison's *Invisible Man* to Wright's *Native Son* to LeRoi Jones's work in the "Black Arts" movement of the 1960s.

Subject(s): Literature, Politics

1736 Donald B. Gibson

The Politics of Literary Expression: A Study of Major Black Writers

(Westport, CT; Greenwood Press, 1981)

Summary: In his 1981 work, Donald B. Gibson explores the works of five important African American authors: Richard Wright, Ralph Ellison, James Baldwin, Charles W. Chesnutt, and Jean Toomer. The writings of these authors span much of the twentieth century, beginning with Chesnutt's popular works of the early 1900s. Toomer is considered a major figure of the Harlem Renaissance cultural flowering of the 1920s, while Wright, Ellison, and Baldwin produced groundbreaking fiction during the middle part of the century.

Subject(s): Literature, Harlem Renaissance

1737 J. Lee Greene

Blacks in Eden: The African American Novel's First Century
(Charlottesville, VA; University Press of Virginia, 1996)

Summary: Rather than a standard history of the African American novel in its first century (1850 to 1960), this work of literary criticism focuses on the "Eden myth" in African American novels of the period. Greene examines characters, chapters, and key passages from various novels in essays covering such topics as "Black Female Subjectivity and the Social Skin," "Black Man, New Man: Chesnutt's John (Walden) Warwick," and "Configurations of a Southern Fictive World."

Subject(s): Literature, Mythology

1738 Farah Jasmine Griffin

"Who Set You Flowin'?": The African-American Migration Narrative
(New York, NY; Oxford University Press, 1995)

Summary: The title quotation from this 1995 work by Griffin comes from the Jean Toomer novel *Cane*. It refers to the great migration of blacks from the rural South to the urban North during the early decades of the twentieth century. Griffin takes an interdisciplinary approach to her subject, examining not only literature but also music and visual arts such as photography and painting. Aside from Toomer, Griffin discusses artists such as Richard Wright, Billie Holiday, and Dorothy West.

Subject(s): Literature, American South, City and Town Life

1739 Seymour L. Gross, Editor
John Edward Hardy, Co-editor

Images of the Negro in American Literature
(Chicago, IL; University of Chicago Press, 1966)

Summary: This critical work contains sixteen essays by various scholars about how blacks have been portrayed by American authors, both black and white. Critics and writers such as Milton Cantor, Ralph Ellison, Irving Howe, and Robert A. Bone examine a wide variety literary authors, works, and eras, from "The Image of the Negro in Colonial Literature" to "The Early Harlem Novel" to authors including Herman Melville, Mark Twain, Langston Hughes, Eudora Welty, and Richard Wright.

Subject(s): Literature

1740 Donna Akiba Sullivan Harper

Not So Simple: The "Simple" Stories by Langston Hughes
(Columbia, MO; University of Missouri Press, 1995)

Summary: The focus of Harper's 1995 study is the fictional character invented by Langston Hughes: Jesse B. Semple, or "Simple." In numerous works, Hughes used Simple to depict the lives of common African Americans. By using a middle-class narrator to record the musings of the poor but wise Simple, Hughes was able to express class tensions that intersected other issues such as race.

Subject(s): Literature, Working-Class Life, Class Conflict

1741 Michael S. Harper, Editor
Robert B. Stepto, Co-editor

Chant of Saints: A Gathering of Afro-American Literature, Art, and Scholarship
(Urbana, IL; University of Illinois Press, 1979)

Summary: This collection of material by thirty prominent twentieth century African American writers first appeared as a special issue of the *Massachusetts Review*. The work includes essays, poems, and fictional selections by (and often interviews with) such writers as Toni Morrison, Ralph Ellison, Sherley A. Williams, and Derek Walcott. Included in the book is a foreword written by acclaimed historian John Hope Franklin, who compares the volume to Alain Locke's pioneering 1925 anthology, *The New Negro*, which heralded the beginnings of the Harlem Renaissance.

Subject(s): Literature, Poetry

1742 Norman Harris

Connecting Times: The Sixties in Afro-American Fiction
(Jackson, MS; University Press of Mississippi, 1988)

Summary: The Vietnam War, the civil rights movement, and the black power movement are three key events whose impact during the 1960s was deeply felt among black writers. In his 1988 work, Norman Harris examines that impact by analyzing a host of novels. Part I focuses on "Novels of the Vietnam War," including such works as *Captain Blackman* by John A. Williams and *Tragic Magic* by Wesley Brown. In Part II, Harris turns his attention to "Novels of the Civil Rights and Black Power Movements," discussing novels including Alice Walker's *Meridian* and Ishmael Reed's *The Last Days of Louisiana Red*.

Subject(s): Black Nationalism, Civil Rights Movement, Vietnam War

1743 Trudier Harris

Black Women in the Fiction of James Baldwin

(Knoxville, TN; University of Tennessee Press, 1985)

Summary: In her 1985 critical study of the writings of James Baldwin, Trudier Harris shows how Baldwin's depiction of black women changed during his thirty year career. In his early writings, Harris argues, Baldwin's black female characters were one-dimensional characters who were bound by the church's conception of proper female roles—wives, mothers, sisters, and lovers. As Baldwin matured, however, he began to depict black women characters with more fully realized lives, eventually creating sympathetic black women characters.

Subject(s): Literature, Women, Religion

1744 Trudier Harris

Exorcising Blackness: Historical and Literary Lynching and Burning Rituals

(Bloomington, IN; Indiana University Press, 1984)

Summary: The long history of violence perpetrated by whites against African Americans—a subject treated in numerous fictional works by black authors from the 1850s to the present—is the focus of this critical work. In Harris's view, the presentation of violent incidents such as lynching, burning, raping, and castrating in black authors' works signals the perpetuation of a black oral history designed to ensure the survival of the race. While discussing early African American authors such as Charles W. Chesnutt and Paul Laurence Dunbar, Harris also shows how modern authors from Toni Morrison to John Edgar Wideman have attempted to move beyond the emphasis on violence prevalent in their works.

Subject(s): Literature, Violence, Racism

1745 Trudier Harris

Fiction and Folklore: The Novels of Toni Morrison

(Knoxville, TN; University of Tennessee Press, 1991)

Summary: Nobel laureate Toni Morrison is known for her ability to fuse folkloric elements with naturalistic ones in her work. In her 1991 study of Morrison's novels, Trudier Harris argues that Morrison uses folklore to achieve a "reversal" in her work: the incredible becomes commonplace. Through this technique, argues Harris, Morrison is able to blend fiction and folklore, history and legend in a powerful manner. Among the novels that Harris considers are *The Bluest Eye, Tar Baby, Sula, Song of Solomon,* and *Beloved.*

Subject(s): Literature, Folklore

1746 Trudier Harris

From Mammies to Militants: Domestics in Black American Literature

(Philadelphia, PA; Temple University Press, 1982)

Summary: In her first published book of literary criticism, acclaimed scholar Trudier Harris explores the subject of "domestics"--maids, housekeepers, gardeners, and so on--in African American literature. Harris examines twenty-four works, among them Toni Morrison's first novel, *The Bluest Eye,* as well as Richard Wright's story "Man of All Work."

Subject(s): Literature, Labor Conditions, Servants

1747 Trudier Harris

The Power of the Porch: The Storyteller's Craft in Zora Neale Hurston, Gloria Naylor, and Randall Kenan

(Athens, GA; University of Georgia Press, 1996)

Summary: Oral storytelling is the prime focus of this 1996 work by Harris. Using works by Zora Neale Hurston, Gloria Naylor, and Randall Kenan, Harris examines the art of storytelling as seen in porch conversations in fictional works set in the South. Harris shows how oral tradition and folklore--particularly the tradition of the magical "trickster" in literature--combine to create a potent storytelling culture.

Subject(s): Literature, American South, Storytelling

1748 Paul Carter Harrison

The Drama of Nommo

(New York, NY; Grove Press, 1972)

Summary: In his introductory essay to this 1972 study, an essay he titles "Praeforce," Paul Carter Harrison explains that the most important aspect for blacks in the theater is their understanding of and ability to marshal "Nommo," or the spiritual life force. In the main text, Harrison devotes chapters to "Nommo on the Block," "Nommo and the Black Messiah," "Look Out, Niggahs! Freud Will Get Yo' Momma," "The Single Face of the Invisible Man," and "The Drama of Nommo."

Subject(s): Drama, Spiritualism

1749 Robert Hayden, Editor
Frederick Glaysher, Co-editor

Collected Prose

(Ann Arbor, MI; University of Michigan Press, 1984)

Summary: Robert E. Hayden is considered one of the foremost African American poets of the twentieth century. In this work, editor Frederick Glaysher compiles a selection of Hayden's prose works. The book's three parts are titled "Addresses and a Play"; "Essays and Introductions"; and "Interviews and Conversations."

Subject(s): Poetry

1750 Robert Hayden
Frederick Glaysher

Conscientious Sorcerers: The Black Postmodernist Fiction of LeRoi Jones/ Amiri Baraka, Ishmael Reed, and Samuel R. Delany

(New York, NY; Greenwood Press, 1987)

Summary: The subjects of this study are three influential African American writers who emerged from the 1960s: Amiri Baraka (formerly known as LeRoi Jones), Ishmael Reed, and Samuel R. Delany. While Fox discusses the issue of race as it is treated in the fictional works of the three authors, he moves beyond race to consider how "American" the work of these authors ultimately is.

Subject(s): Literature

1751 Robert E. Hemenway

Zora Neale Hurston: A Literary Biography

(Urbana, IL; University of Illinois Press, 1977)

Summary: In this 1977 work, Robert E. Hemenway blends straightforward biography with literary criticism to illuminate the life of Zora Neale Hurston (1903-1960), one of the most prominent African American writers of the twentieth century. Hemenway follows Hurston's emergence as a leading figure of the Harlem Renaissance cultural movement of the 1920s through her literary career and to her death in dire poverty in 1960, at which point she was buried in an unmarked grave in a Florida cemetery. The book includes a foreword by acclaimed writer Alice Walker.

Subject(s): Harlem Renaissance, Literature, Women

1752 Herbert Hill, Editor

Anger, and Beyond: The Negro Writer in the United States

(New York, NY; Harper & Row, 1966)

Summary: This 1966 anthology includes ten essays by writers such as Saunders Redding, LeRoi Jones (later Amiri Baraka), Arna Bontemps, and Albert Murray. It also includes an interview with poet Melvin B. Tolson and a chapter devoted to Richard Wright, who elevated American literature to new heights during his career. The anthology serves as a companion to Hill's 1968 work *Soon, One Morning*.

Subject(s): Literature, Poetry

1753 Herbert Hill, Editor

Soon, One Morning: New Writing by American Negroes, 1940-1962

(New York, NY; Knopf, 1963)

Summary: Herbert Hill selected the pieces that appear in this anthology and wrote an introductory essay as well. He divides the anthology into sections of essays, fictional works, and poetry. Among those whose work appears here are John Hope Franklin, Langston Hughes, Gwendolyn Brooks, Ralph Ellison, Robert Hayden, and Paul Vesey.

Subject(s): Literature, Poetry

1754 Lynda Marion Hill

Social Rituals and the Verbal Art of Zora Neale Hurston

(Washington, DC; Howard University Press, 1996)

Summary: One of a flood of recent critical works about the life and art of Zora Neale Hurston, this 1996 study focuses on the folkloric source of Hurston's writings. Hurston, who was a leading figure of the Harlem Renaissance of the 1920s, drew upon both African as well as African American folk culture in her work.

Subject(s): Harlem Renaissance, Folklore

1755 W. Lawrence Hogue

Discourse and the Other: The Production of the Afro-American Text

(Durham, NC; Duke University Press, 1986)

Summary: In his preface to this 1986 study, W. Lawrence Hogue describes his aim as an attempt to understand how Afro-American literary texts come to be "produced"—written, published, reviewed, and labeled. The book's eight chapters explore such topics as the relationship between African American texts and the American literary establishment; 1960s' social movements and their impact on African American texts; and developments after 1970. In addition, he devotes several chapters to studying particular works by African American writers, including Ernest J. Gaines's *The Autobiography of Miss Jane Pittman*, Alice Walker's *The Third Life of Grange Copeland*, and Toni Morrison's *Sula*.

Subject(s): Literature, Books and Reading

1756 Karla F.C. Holloway

The Character of the Word: The Texts of Zora Neale Hurston

(New York, NY; Greenwood Press, 1987)

Summary: In this critical study of Zora Neale Hurston's four major novels, Holloway focuses on two elements: Hurston's use of the black oral storytelling tradition in her work, and her use of standard American English. In discussing these elements, Holloway describes Hurston's university education, including her work with anthropologist Franz Boaz at Columbia University. The result is the first major critical work to focus on the language of Hurston's art.

Subject(s): Storytelling, Literature, Language

1757 **Karla F.C. Holloway**

Moorings & Metaphors: Figures of Culture and Gender in Black Women's Literature

(New Brunswick, NJ; Rutgers University Press, 1992)

Summary: Holloway studies the connections between West African and African American women's literature in her 1992 work. According to the author, a common thread between the two literatures is the utilization of a goddess/ancestor metaphor, a linguistic device whereby African American authors recall the spirituality of their African ancestors. Among the authors whose work Holloway features are Paule Marshall, Gayl Jones, Gloria Naylor, and Toni Cade Bambara.

Subject(s): Literature, Spiritualism

1758 **Sylvia Wallace Holton**

Down Home and Uptown: The Representation of Black Speech in American Fiction

(Rutherford, NJ; Fairleigh Dickinson University Press, 1984)

Summary: In her 1984 work, Sylvia Wallace Holton examines the use of Black English in American literary history. Holton first traces the origins of Black English; some experts view Africa as the origin while others consider Black English a regional dialect that grew out of Anglo-African interaction. In the book's central section, Holton makes a detailed study of how Black English has appeared in American fiction during the past two hundred years. Holton considers texts by authors such as Harriet Beecher Stowe, William Faulkner, Ralph Ellison, and Toni Morrison.

Subject(s): Language, Literature

1759 **Maureen Honey,** Editor

Shadowed Dreams: Women's Poetry of the Harlem Renaissance

(New Brunswick, NJ; Rutgers University Press, 1989)

Summary: The Harlem Renaissance of the 1920s represented a turning point for African American writers, who from that time forward moved increasingly into the mainstream of American literature. Notable during the Renaissance was the emergence of women writers, including many of the writers featured in this collection. Among those whose poems are reprinted are Angelina Weld Grimke, Jessie Redmon Fauset, Georgia Douglas Johnson, and Anne Spencer.

Subject(s): Harlem Renaissance, Poetry, Women

1760 **Fred Lee Hord**

Reconstructing Memory: Black Literary Criticism

(Chicago, IL; Third World Press, 1991)

Summary: Fred Lee Hord in his 1991 work argues that contemporary African Americans have lost their memory of the black experience, and he uses African American literature to illustrate his thesis. The task of reconstructing this memory is made more difficult, notes Hord, by a white establishment that acts essentially as a colonial force in relation to African Americans--repressing blacks' cultural past and assaulting their collective identity. Among the authors whose work Hord examines are Paul Laurence Dunbar and Ralph Ellison.

Subject(s): Identity, Colonialism, Literature

1761 **Dolan Hubbard**

The Sermon and the African American Literary Imagination

(Columbia, MO; University of Missouri Press, 1994)

Summary: Arguing that the black church has been a fundamental force in African American culture, Hubbard examines how the black sermon has influenced both the themes and the styles of works by African American writers. In defining the black sermon, Hubbard focuses on the elements of oral delivery and ritual performance that have long characterized sermons by African American preachers. He then explores texts by writers such as Richard Wright, Frances E.W. Harper, James Baldwin, and Toni Morrison.

Subject(s): Literature, Religion

1762 **Theodore R. Hudson**

From LeRoi Jones to Amiri Baraka: The Literary Works

(Durham, NC; Duke University Press, 1973)

Summary: This 1973 study of Amiri Baraka (formerly known as LeRoi Jones) begins with an in-depth examination of his aesthetic framework, including chapters devoted to "perceptions, conceptions, stances" and "form, technique, style." In part two of his work, Hudson analyzes Baraka's nonfiction prose, his fiction, his poetry, and his drama. Overall, Hudson provides the earliest critical study of one of the most important figures in African American letters from the latter half of the twentieth century.

Subject(s): Literature

1763 Carl Milton Hughes

(Pseudonym of John Milton Charles Hughes)

The Negro Novelist: A Discussion of the Writings of American Negro Novelists, 1940-1950

(New York, NY; Citadel Press, 1953)

Summary: As its title suggests, this work of literary criticism focuses on the decade between 1940 and 1950. In discussing various novels of the period, Hughes draws heavily on biographical information about the authors of the novels. Richard Wright, Chester Himes, Curtis Lucas, Ann Petry, Alden Bland, Zora Neale Hurston, and Carl Offord are but a few of the writers Hughes treats as he explores his topic.

Subject(s): Literature

1764 Gloria T. Hull

Color, Sex, and Poetry: Three Women Writers of the Harlem Renaissance

(Bloomington, IN; Indiana University Press, 1987)

Summary: The three Harlem Renaissance writers featured by Hull in this volume are Alice Dunbar-Nelson, Angelina Weld Grimke, and Georgia Douglas Johnson. These three writers distinguished themselves during the 1920s in a variety of genres, from poetry to drama to fiction. They also made their mark on the vibrant social scene of 1920s Harlem, with Johnson hosting a "Saturday Nighters" salon at her home every Saturday evening, an event that numerous artistic and intellectual luminaries of the period attended. Hull closes her study with a brief essay about black women writers who followed Johnson, Dunbar-Nelson, and Grimke and who made use of their rich legacy.

Subject(s): Women, Harlem Renaissance, Literature

1765 George Hutchinson

The Harlem Renaissance in Black and White

(Cambridge, MA; Belknap Press of Harvard University Press, 1995)

Summary: In his critical work about the Harlem Renaissance cultural movement of the 1920s, Hutchinson argues that the interactions between white and black intellectuals during the period had a profound and positive effect on American culture in the twentieth century. According to Hutchinson, the dialogue between black and white intellectuals during the Harlem Renaissance established a diverse, inclusive cultural debate as the primary American form of discourse during the remainder of the century.

Subject(s): Literature, Harlem Renaissance, Race Relations

1766 Chidi Ikonne

From Du Bois to Van Vechten: The Early New Negro Literature, 1903-1926

(Westport, CT; Greenwood Press, 1981)

Summary: Although the literature of the "New Negro"—also known as Literature of the Harlem Renaissance—is chiefly identified with the 1920s, Ikonne traces its roots to the early 1900s. In the book's early sections, Ikonne examines long-standing racial prejudices as seen in works by playwright Eugene O'Neill and writer and critic Gertrude Stein and discusses turn-of-the-century black writers such as Paul Laurence Dunbar and W.E.B. Du Bois. Ikonne then focuses on the prime figures of the Harlem Renaissance, including Jean Toomer, Countee Cullen, and Zora Neale Hurston. The author also includes a chapter about the central periodicals associated with the Harlem Renaissance: *Opportunity, The Crisis, The Messenger* and *Fire*.

Subject(s): Literature, Harlem Renaissance

1767 Madelyn Jablon

Black Metafiction: Self-Consciousness in African American Literature

(Iowa City, IA; University of Iowa Press, 1997)

Summary: In this work, Jablon examines the tradition of "self-consciousness" in ten contemporary novels by African Americans, including works by Leon Forrest, Charles Johnson, Rita Dove, and Octavia Butler. Jablon's aim is to reformulate established theories about metafiction by previous scholars working in the fields of Anglo-American and African American literature.

Subject(s): Literature

1768 Blyden Jackson

A History of Afro-American Literature. Volume 1

(Baton Rouge, LA; Louisiana State University Press, 1989)

Summary: This volume, which is the first of four projected volumes, covers the early period of literature by African Americans. Jackson divides his study into two sections, the "Age of Apprenticeship," during which African slaves had to learn to express themselves in the foreign language of English; and the "Age of Abolitionists," during which blacks began to protest their treatment by white America. Jackson discusses slave narratives, poetry, novels, and folk literature before concluding with a lengthy bibliographic essay.

Subject(s): Slavery, Africa, Abolition

1769 Blyden Jackson

The Waiting Years: Essays on American Negro Literature

(Baton Rouge, LA; Louisiana State University Press, 1976)

Summary: Critic and novelist Blyden Jackson in this 1976 work examines several landmark black authors of the twentieth century, including Langston Hughes, Richard Wright, and Jean Toomer. The work also includes essays about the Harlem Renaissance of the 1920s and a book review of J.L. Dillard's *Black English*, a study about African American speech patterns.

Subject(s): Literature, Harlem Renaissance, Language

1770 Abby Arthur Johnson
Ronald M. Johnson, Co-author

Propaganda and Aesthetics: The Literary Politics of Afro-American Magazines in the Twentieth Century

(Amherst, MA; University of Massachusetts Press, 1979)

Summary: The rich history and literary culture of twentieth century African American magazines is the focus of this 1979 work by Johnson and Johnson. Among the periodicals discussed by the authors are *Voice of the Negro*, *The Crisis*, *Opportunity*, *Phylon* and *Harlem Quarterly*. The book is arranged chronologically, beginning with the period from 1900 to 1910 and ending with an examination of "Black Aesthetic Revolutionary Little Magazines" from 1960 to 1976.

Subject(s): Periodicals

1771 Charles Richard Johnson

Being & Race: Black Writing since 1970

(Bloomington, IN; Indiana University Press, 1988)

Summary: Though best known for his fiction, novelist Charles Johnson here offers a critical study of recent literature by African Americans. Johnson begins his work with a philosophical discussion of the issues of race, fiction, and form, before going on to examine major male and female authors after 1970. Among those whose work Johnson discusses are Octavia E. Butler, Jamaica Kincaid, Gloria Naylor, Alice Walker, John A. Williams, David Bradley, James Alan McPherson, and Leon Forrest.

Subject(s): Literature

1772 Gayl Jones

Liberating Voices: Oral Tradition in African American Literature

(Cambridge, MA; Harvard University Press, 1991)

Summary: Prominent novelist Jones here examines the way in which modern African American writers have made use of folk forms for aesthetic purposes. Focusing on twentieth cen-

tury authors such as Toni Morrison, Ernest J. Gaines, and Alice Walker, Jones blends critical insights with folk tradition to create an ambitious literary history of African American writers. Jones offers analysis of novels, short stories, and poetry in the work.

Subject(s): Literature, Folk Tales, Storytelling

1773 LeRoi Jones, Editor
(Also known as Amiri Baraka)
Larry Neal, Co-editor

Black Fire: An Anthology of Afro-American Writing

(New York, NY; Morrow, 1968)

Summary: This 1968 anthology appeared at the height of the "Black Arts" movement, in which many black writers and artists advocated an art that relied on race as a central theme and that had as its purpose the immediate end of racism and the dawn of social justice for African Americans. The movement occurred simultaneously with the rise of the Black Nationalist philosophy of political leader Malcolm X. LeRoi Jones, who co-edited this volume with Larry Neal, was at the forefront of the "Black Arts" movement. Among those whose work appears in the volume are Stokely Carmichael, Sonia Sanchez, David Henderson, Jay Wright, and Carol Freeman.

Subject(s): Literature, Racism, Black Nationalism

1774 Robert B. Jones

Jean Toomer and the Prison-House of Thought: A Phenomenology of the Spirit

(Amherst, MA; University of Massachusetts Press, 1993)

Summary: In this critical study of Jean Toomer, author of the landmark 1923 novel *Cane*, Robert B. Jones explores the various aesthetic, psychological, and religious influences in Toomer's life. Jones divides his book into three sections, ultimately showing that the single greatest factor in Toomer's art was his feeling of alienation--from society, from other African Americans, and from himself--despite his continual efforts to portray himself as having transcended conventional boundaries of race and ethnicity.

Subject(s): Literature

1775 Donald Franklin Joyce, Compiler

Blacks in the Humanities, 1750-1984: A Selected Annotated Bibliography

(New York, NY; Greenwood Press, 1986)

Summary: Joyce's aim in this bibliography is to provide a ready reference source for researchers seeking information about contributions by African Americans in eleven different disciplines: philosophy; religion; journalism; libraries and librarianship; folklore; linguistics; art; music; performing arts; literary criticism; and cultural and intellectual history. Following an opening chapter devoted to general works in the humanities by African Americans, the book offers eleven chapters, each devoted to one of the aforementioned disciplines.

Subject(s): African Americans, Bibliography

1776 Joyce Ann Joyce

Ijala: Sonia Sanchez and the African Poetic Tradition
(Chicago, IL; Third World Press, 1996)

Summary: In four lengthy essays, Joyce Ann Joyce offers a critical appraisal of the poetry of Sonia Sanchez, one of the leading poets of the "Black Arts" movement of the late 1960s and early 1970s as well as an influential poet of the 1980s and 1990s. Sanchez is known for her poetry readings, and Joyce honors this tradition with the book's title; *Ijala* is the Yoruba word for a highpitched voice. Joyce discusses the West African roots of much of Sanchez's poetry; relatives her verse to the African American poetic legacy in general; and follows her artisic developmnt through the 1980s.

Subject(s): Africa

1777 Joyce Ann Joyce

Richard Wright's Art of Tragedy
(Iowa City, IA; University of Iowa Press, 1986)

Summary: Joyce Ann Joyce's 1986 work is an analysis of Richard Wright's pioneering novel, *Native Son,* in which Wright offered scathing indictments of American racism and its dehumanizing effects. Joyce examines the stylistic and thematic elements of the novel to show how Wright used his craft and imagination to forge a work that stands as one of the most important American novels of the twentieth century. In addition to her own theoretical arguments, Joyce also discusses previous critical studies of the novel.

Subject(s): Literature, Racism

1778 Ronald A.T. Judy

(Dis)Forming the American Canon: African-Arabic Slave Narratives and the Vernacular
(Minneapolis, MN; University of Minnesota Press, 1993)

Summary: The central text of Judy's 1993 study is a nineteenth slave narrative by Ben Ali, an African Muslim who was a slave on Sapelo Island in Georgia. In examining this text and other such African-Arabic texts, Judy argues that they "disform" the perceived mainstream American literary canon, as do more conventional (and well-known) slave narratives such as that by Frederick Douglass.

Subject(s): Slavery, Literature

1779 Phillipa Kafka

The Great White Way: African American Women Writers and American Success Mythologies
(New York, NY; Garland Pub., 1993)

Summary: Kafka traces the "American success mythologies" referred to in the subtitle of her 1993 study to the white, male, European presence in America. Examining this mythology as it influenced early African American women writers such as Phillis Wheatley, Kafka notes that many subsequent women writers have also had to deal with this success mythology in their work. Kafka also addresses a related mythology—that of the Cinderella myth. Among those whose work Kafka examines are Harriet A. Jacobs, Zora Neale Hurston, and Alice Walker.

Subject(s): Literature, Mythology, Women

1780 Carolyn L. Karcher

Shadow over the Promised Land: Slavery, Race, and Violence in Melville's America
(Baton Rouge, LA; Louisiana State University Press, 1980)

Summary: In her 1980 work, Carolyn L. Karcher attempts to re-fashion decades of literary criticism about the works of famed American author Herman Melville (1819-1891). While previous critics ignored the themes of slavery and race as they applied to Melville's works, Karcher shows that they were of central importance to such Melville novels as *Redburn, White-Jacket, The Confidence-Man,* and *Moby-Dick.* Karcher's work to re-examine standard texts by white American authors in terms of race was part of a larger effort among critics and intellectuals during the 1980s and 1990s; Toni Morrison made similar re-evaluations in *Playing in the Dark: Whiteness and the Literary Imagination.*

Subject(s): Race Relations, Slavery, Violence

1781 Samira Kawash

Dislocating the Color Line: Identity, Hybridity, and Singularity in African American Narrative
(Stanford, CA; Stanford University Press, 1997)

Summary: *Dislocating the Color Line* is an analysis of racial boundaries in African American literature. In the work, Kawash examines works by Harriet Jacobs, Zora Neale Hurston, and several members of the Harlem Renaissance to show how the concept of a color line has pervaded black American literature from the slavery period to the present.

Subject(s): Literature, Harlem Renaissance

1782 Gunilla Theander Kester

Writing the Subject: Bildung and the African American Text

(New York, NY; P. Lang, 1995)

Summary: Kester in this work explores the differences between the European and African American *bildungsroman* (the term for a coming-of-age novel whose principal theme is the emotional and intellectual development of a young protagonist). Discussing works by authors such as Ralph Ellison, Toni Morrison, Gayl Jones, and Sherley Anne Williams, Kester focuses on issues of subjectivity, gender, and history.

Subject(s): Coming-of-Age, Literature

1783 Martin Klammer

Whitman, Slavery and the Emergence of "Leaves of Grass"

(University Park, PA; Pennsylvania State University Press, 1995)

Summary: First published in 1855, *Leaves of Grass* is the most important work of poetry by American author Walt Whitman. In this 1995 study, Klammer argues that the book was pioneering in its author's attitude toward and handling of racial issues. Klammer follows Whitman from his early pro-slavery stance to his eventual sympathy with slaves, depicting the influence that race relations had on Whitman's development as a poet.

Subject(s): Slavery, Poetry, Race Relations

1784 Phyllis Rauch Klotman

Another Man Gone: The Black Runner in Contemporary Afro-American Literature

(Port Washington, NY; Kennikat Press, 1977)

Summary: In this 1977 work, Klotman sets her study of flight in black literature firmly within a Western and American context, discussing such white writers as Herman Melville and John Updike. Klotman argues that the figure of the running man in black literature first represented the literal need to flee from slavery; in the twentieth century, however, that figure shifted to one seeking—often without success—to find equality, manhood, and identity. James Baldwin, Ralph Ellison, William M. Kelley, and Ronald Fair are a few of the writers whom Klotman examines in the work.

Subject(s): Literature, Slavery, Identity

1785 Missy Dehn Kubitschek

Claiming the Heritage: African-American Women Novelists and History

(Jackson, MS; University Press of Mississippi, 1991)

Summary: Kubitschek examines the way in which female protagonists in works by black American women writers use the past in order to construct their identities. One key ancestral image, notes Kubitschek, is the image of the "mother." Among the writers whose works Kubitschek examines are Nella Larsen, Octavia Butler, Toni Morrison, and Gayl Jones.

Subject(s): Literature, Identity

1786 Vera M. Kutzinski

Against the American Grain: Myth and History in William Carlos Williams, Jay Wright, and Nicol£s Guill£n

(Baltimore, MD; Johns Hopkins University Press, 1987)

Summary: Although the three authors at the heart of this 1987 work are typically viewed as being from separate literary cultures—Anglo-American in the case of Williams; African American in the case of Wright; Latin American in the case of Guill£n—Kutzinski argues that they actually share a common cultural thread. Kutzinski terms this thread "New World writing" and places its origin in the approach to New World themes that each poet has taken. According to the author, New World writing rejects a Euro-centric view of literary ancestry, instead choosing to locate literary ancestry in places that are separate from typical national or ethnic boundaries. Kutzinski titles her essay about Wright "The Black Limbo: Jay Wright's Mythology of Writing."

Subject(s): Poetry

1787 Dominick LaCapra, Editor

The Bounds of Race: Perspectives on Hegemony and Resistance

(Ithaca, NY; Cornell University Press, 1991)

Summary: This work brings together a collection of essays that originated at a conference hosted by LaCapra at Cornell University. Each of the essays deals in some way with the issue of race in black literature, whether in Africa, Europe, or the Americas. Among the scholars who contributed to this book are Henry Louis Gates, Jr., Hortense J. Spillers, Kwame Anthony Appiah, and Anne McClintock.

Subject(s): Literature, Africa

1788 Charles R. Larson

Invisible Darkness: Jean Toomer & Nella Larsen

(Iowa City, IA; University of Iowa Press, 1993)

Summary: This double biography focuses on two major figures of the Harlem Renaissance literary movement of the 1920s. Larson describes only one meeting between Jean Toomer and Nella Larsen in their lifetimes, but he relates how their literary careers flourished simultaneously in the 1920s. In so doing, he sheds light on two neglected figures in twentieth century American letters as well as on the African origins in their work.

Subject(s): Literature, Harlem Renaissance

1789 **A. Robert Lee,** Editor

Black Fiction: New Studies in the Afro-American Novel since 1945
(London, England; Vision Press, 1980)

Summary: This collection of eleven critical essays focuses on African American novels between 1945 and 1980. Written by both American and British critics, the various essays cover such authors as Richard Wright, Langston Hughes, Amiri Baraka, Toni Morrison, Alice Walker, Ishmael Reed, and John O. Killens.

Subject(s): Literature

1790 **Geta LeSeur**

Ten Is the Age of Darkness: The Black Bildungsroman
(Columbia, MO; University of Missouri Press, 1995)

Summary: LeSeur's stated aims in this critical study are to illustrate the similarities in experience among black writers in American and the Caribbean; to emphasize the importance of childhood experiences in the lives of young blacks; and to show how black writers have adapted the literary form of the European "bildungsroman" in their own work. (A bildungsroman is a novel that focuses on the intellectual and emotional development of a central character who is usually young in age.) Among the writers whose work LeSeur examines are George Lamming, James Baldwin, Gwendolyn Brooks, and Ntozake Shange.

Subject(s): Literature, Coming-of-Age, Childhood

1791 **Robert S. Levine**

Martin Delany, Frederick Douglass, and the Politics of Representative Identity
(Chapel Hill, NC; University of North Carolina Press, 1977)

Summary: Levine in this work examines the ideals and ideas of two seminal nineteenth century African Americans: Martin Delany (1812-1885) and Frederick Douglass (1818-1895). Throughout their lives, the two men debated and argued passionately, often espousing differing notions about how to achieve emancipation for black slaves and about the best path for social justice after emancipation. Delany worked for the return of freed slaves to Africa, where they might create their own nations, while Douglass believed in America as a legitimate home for blacks. In his work, Levine explores the ways in which the two men--and the society around them--saw themselves as representative of all blacks.

Subject(s): Slavery, Abolition, Africa

1792 **David Littlejohn**

Black on White: A Critical Survey of Writing by American Negroes
(New York, NY; Grossman, 1966)

Summary: David Littlejohn's 1966 critical study offers a chronologically ordered analysis of black literature. He divides his work into two distinct stages: the period before Richard Wright's *Native Son* (published in 1940) and the period after it. Ultimately, Littlejohn examines how black writers have forged self-respect and a sense of identity from an oppressed, violent past.

Subject(s): Racism, Literature, Identity

1793 **Helen Lock**

A Case of Mis-Taken Identity: Detective Undercurrents in Recent African American Fiction
(New York, NY; P. Lang, 1994)

Summary: In this 1994 work, Lock focuses on black detective fiction. However, she does not concentrate on mystery writers such as Chester E. Himes and Walter Mosely. Rather, she analyzes the way in which black detective fiction has been treated in the work of more mainstream African American writers such as Ralph Ellison and Toni Morrison. In presenting her arguments, Lock demonstrates the connection between black detective fiction and African American folklore.

Subject(s): Literature, Mystery, Folklore

1794 **Alain Locke**

The New Negro: An Interpretation
(New York, NY; A. and C. Boni, 1925)

Summary: Few anthologies in American literature have had as much impact as *The New Negro*, which is considered the work that placed the Harlem Renaissance movement of the 1920s onto the nation's cultural map. Containing a wide variety of poems, short stories, and articles by such writers as Countee Cullen, Langston Hughes, Angelina Weld Grimke, and Claude McKay, the anthology illustrated the enormous creative output produced by writers associated with New York City's Harlem neighborhood.

Subject(s): Literature, Poetry, Harlem Renaissance

1795 **Audre Lorde**

A Burst of Light: Essays
(Ithaca, NY; Firebrand Books, 1988)

Summary: In this volume of five essays, noted writer and critic Audre Lorde addresses subjects ranging from black lesbian and gay writers; the relationship between apartheid-era South Africans and African Americans; and her years-long battle with cancer, to which she eventually succumbed. The essay about black lesbian and gay literature, titled "I Am Your

Sister: Black Women Organizing across Sexualities," seeks to establish links among writers such as Langston Hughes, Alice Dunbar Nelson, and Angelina Weld Grimke.

Subject(s): Literature, Homosexuality/Lesbianism, Cancer

1796 John Lowe

Jump at the Sun: Zora Neale Hurston's Cosmic Comedy
(Urbana, IL; University of Illinois Press, 1994)

Summary: Zora Neale Hurston was one of the leading figures of the Harlem Renaissance cultural movement of the 1920s, and her work pulsates with comic elements. In this 1994 work, John Lowe explores the roots and nature of those comic elements. Lowe argues that Hurston drew heavily upon African American religious imagery and folklore for her comic inspiration and that she used her comedy for a serious purpose: to highlight the strength of an oppressed people.

Subject(s): Comedy, Harlem Renaissance, Folklore

1797 Clarence Major

The Dark and Feeling: Black American Writers and Their Work
(New York, NY; Third Press, 1974)

Summary: This 1974 critical work by Clarence Major, an acclaimed writer in his own right, offers numerous essays about modern black poets and novelists, from Richard Wright and James Baldwin to June Jordan and John A. Williams. The work also includes two interviews with Major (one of which is a "self interview").

Subject(s): Literature, Poetry

1798 Reginald Martin

Ishmael Reed and the New Black Aesthetic Critics
(New York, NY; St. Martin's Press, 1988)

Summary: Reginald Martin in this work attempts to define the idea of a "black aesthetic"--a literary form unique to black literature--for modern readers. He does so by examining the works of Ishmael Reed, considered one of the most important black writers of the latter half of the twentieth century. Despite his widespread acclaim, Reed has also come under attack by some black critics, including Amiri Baraka, for his views of black art.

Subject(s): Literature

1799 Deborah E. McDowell

"The Changing Same": Black Women's Literature, Criticism, and Theory
(Bloomington, IN; Indiana University Press, 1995)

Summary: McDowell maps the black female literary tradition from the "Women's Era" of the 1890s through the Harlem Renaissance of the 1920s and to the "New Black Renaissance" of the 1970s and 1980s. Discussing works by such authors as Toni Morrison, Alice Walker, Jessie Redmon Fauset, and Nella Larsen, McDowell examines representations of slavery, sexuality, and homoeroticism as well as modern African American feminist writing. The title of McDowell's work comes from an essay by Amiri Baraka.

Subject(s): Literature, Women's Rights, Harlem Renaissance

1800 D.H. Melhem

Heroism in the New Black Poetry: Introductions & Interviews
(Lexington, KY; University Press of Kentucky, 1990)

Summary: In her 1990 work, Melhem introduces and interviews six leading African American poets: Gwendolyn Brooks, Dudley Randall, Haki R. Madhubuti, Sonia Sanchez, Jayne Cortez, and Amiri Baraka. Melhem's overriding theme is that of the poet hero or leader. Among the issues she raises in her interviews with the six poets are nationalism, sexual identity, separatism, and religion.

Subject(s): Poetry, Religion, Sexuality

1801 R. Baxter Miller

The Art and Imagination of Langston Hughes
(Lexington, KY; University Press of Kentucky, 1989)

Summary: Langston Hughes, one of the dominant figures in twentieth century American letters, is the subject of Miller's 1989 critical study. In his analysis, Miller examines Hughes's fiction, poetry, drama, and autobiographical writings in an attempt to understand the sources of the author's portrayals of black women, his political opinions, and his stylistic achievements in tragicomedy.

Subject(s): Literature, Biography

1802 R. Baxter Miller, Editor

Black American Poets between Worlds, 1940-1960
(Knoxville, TN; University of Tennessee Press, 1986)

Summary: Among the poets who are featured in this 1986 critical work are Melvin Tolson, Robert Hayden, Dudley Randall, Margaret Walker, and Gwendolyn Brooks. In virtually all cases, these poets were children during the Harlem Renaissance cultural movement of the 1920s; middle-aged writers during the Korean conflict of the early 1950s; and mature artists by the time of the civil rights movement of the 1960s. The various critical voices in the book examine the poets' works, their themes, and their stylistic evolutions.

Subject(s): Poetry, Harlem Renaissance, Civil Rights Movement

1803 Angelyn Mitchell, Editor

Within the Circle: An Anthology of African American Literary Criticism from the Harlem Renaissance to the Present
(Durham, NC; Duke University Press, 1994)

Summary: Mitchell's anthology of African American literary criticism begins with essays by Harlem Renaissance figures such as Alain Locke, Langston Hughes, and Zora Neale Hurston. It then moves to the "Humanistic/Ethical Criticism and Protest Tradition" as seen in essays by such writers as Margaret Walker and James Baldwin; "The Black Arts Movement" of the 1960s; "Structuralism, Post-Structuralism, and the African-American Critic"; and finally to a discussion of "Gender, Theory, and African-American Feminist Criticism," including contributions by Alice Walker and Barbara Smith.

Subject(s): Literature, Harlem Renaissance

1804 Maxine Lavon Montgomery

The Apocalypse in African-American Fiction
(Gainesville, FL; University Press of Florida, 1996)

Summary: Analyzing seven classic novels by African American writers, Montgomery shows how the notion of apocalypse has been treated in the works. Among the novels Montgomery examines are Richard Wright's *Native Son*, James Baldwin's *Go Tell It on the Mountain*, Toni Morrison's *Sula*, and Gloria Naylor's The Women of Brewster Place. Montgomery argues that apocalypse in these works is often viewed as a desired way to end present suffering.

Subject(s): Literature, Religion

1805 Toni Morrison

Playing in the Dark: Whiteness and the Literary Imagination
(Cambridge, MA; Harvard University Press, 1992)

Summary: Though best known for her award-winning fiction, Toni Morrison in this work produced an influential and widely read work of literary criticism. Her aim is the re-examination of standard works by white American authors such as Ernest Hemingway, Mark Twain, and Willa Cather. Whereas the literary establishment historically treated such works as completely devoid of any influence by or concern with African American issues, Morrison argues that the works were profoundly influenced by a concern with blacks and black issues. *Playing in the Dark,* which grew out of lectures that Morrison gave at Harvard University, reflected a trend among literary critics to reconsider white canonical texts in light of black issues and history.

Subject(s): Literature

1806 Albert L. Murray

The Omni-Americans: New Perspectives on Black Experience & American Culture
(New York, NY; Outerbridge & Dienstfrey, 1970)

Summary: Later editions of *The Omni-Americans* have a different subtitle which further illuminates the focus of Murray's 1970 work: "Some Alternatives to the Folklore of White Supremacy." In the work's essays about literature, music, and culture, Murray offers provocative opinions on the ethnic differences between American whites and blacks, including the opinion that mainstream society often mistakenly emphasizes those differences in certain cultural areas. Among other issues, Murray discusses black cultural studies, the black middle class, and literary works by such authors as Claude Brown, Gordon Parks, and James Baldwin.

Subject(s): Literature, Culture, Music

1807 Larry Neal
Michael Schwartz, Editor

Visions of a Liberated Future: Black Arts Movement Writings
(New York, NY; Thunder's Mouth Press, 1989)

Summary: This posthumously published collection of Larry Neal's essays and poetry deal with the "Black Arts" movement of the late 1960s and early 1970s. During the movement, writers and intellectuals argued for art that was based on the black experience and that engaged issues of political and social justice. Neal was an influential figure in the "Black Arts" movement, which paralleled the rise of Black Nationalism and Malcolm X. In addition to essays and poems, the book includes a section of Neal's play *The Glorious Monster in the Bell of the Horn.* Amiri Baraka, one of the leading writers of the "Black Arts" movement, contributed a foreword to the book.

Subject(s): Racism, Literature, Black Nationalism

1808 Aldon Lynn Nielsen

Black Chant: Languages of African-American Postmodernism
(New York, NY; Cambridge University Press, 1997)

Summary: Nielsen's 1997 work focuses on recovering neglected major works produced by black poets during the previous three decades. Among the poets whose work Nielsen discusses are William Melvin Kelley, Norman Pritchard, Lloyd Addison, and Jayne Cortez. Virtually all of the writers examined by Nielsen are not treated in major anthologies of black verse published during the 1990s.

Subject(s): Poetry

1809 Aldon Lynn Nielsen

Reading Race: White American Poets and the Racial Discourse in the Twentieth Century

(Athens, GA; University of Georgia Press, 1988)

Summary: An analysis of poetry written by white American poets about Africa, Africans, and African Americans, *Reading Race* argues that white poets have relied on cultural stereotypes to reinforce the myth of white superiority. Nielsen shows how white poets have alternated between overtly racist images of blacks and subtler--but still racist--expressions that treat blacks and black art as exotic and primitive. In addition, Nielsen examines non-racist literary efforts by white writers such as Herman Melville and Gertrude Stein.

Subject(s): Poetry, Racism, Africa

1810 Aldon Lynn Nielsen

Writing between the Lines: Race and Intertextuality

(Athens, GA; University of Georgia Press, 1994)

Summary: Nielsen's 1994 work explores the relationships between works by black and white writers. Rather than viewing black literature as a distinct canon or in relationship to the white American literary canon, Nielsen focuses on the fluidity between racial boundaries for both white and black writers. His focus is primarily on twentieth century writers such as Amiri Baraka and James Weldon Johnson.

Subject(s): Literature, Race Relations

1811 Michael North

The Dialect of Modernism: Race, Language, and Twentieth-Century Literature

(New York, NY; Oxford University Press, 1994)

Summary: North focuses on two literary movements in his 1994 work: the modernist movement founded by such white writers as Joseph Conrad and Gertrude Stein, and the Harlem Renaissance movement, as exemplified by Claude McKay, Jean Toomer, and Zora Neale Hurston. Both movements appeared in the early 1920s, and according to North, the interconnectedness between the two makes it impossible to consider either in isolation from the other.

Subject(s): Literature

1812 John O'Brien, Editor

Interviews with Black Writers

(New York, NY; Liveright, 1973)

Summary: This 1973 volume contains interviews with seventeen prominent African American novelists and poets. In the interviews, the writers discuss the themes found in their works, catalog their major literary influences, and offer opinions about their respective styles and aims. Among those interviewed are Ishmael Reed and Arna Bontemps.

Subject(s): Literature, Poetry

1813 Sondra A. O'Neale

Jupiter Hammon and the Biblical Beginnings of African-American Literature

(Metuchen, NJ; Scarecrow Press, 1993)

Summary: In this book of criticism, O'Neale features and analyzes the works of the man who is considered by many to be the first African American writer, Jupiter Hammon (1711-179?). A slave, Hammon wrote a sermon, two essays, and four poems during his lifetime. O'Neale reprints these works and offers critical opinions of them.

Subject(s): Slavery, Literature, Poetry

1814 Philip Page

Dangerous Freedom: Fusion and Fragmentation in Toni Morrison's Novels

(Jackson, MS; University Press of Mississippi, 1995)

Summary: In this study of Nobel laureate Toni Morrison's novels, Philip Page identifies three contexts in which to discuss Morrison's work: American culture, African American culture, and the critical theory of deconstruction. Page analyzes previous critical studies of Morrison in addition to drawing upon elements of psychoanalysis to offer his own distinct critical vision of the author. The six Morrison novels that Page discusses are *The Bluest Eye, Sula, Song of Solomon, Tar Baby, Beloved,* and *Jazz.*

Subject(s): Literature

1815 Ladell Payne

Black Novelists and the Southern Literary Tradition

(Athens, GA; University of Georgia Press, 1981)

Summary: The interconnection of black and white southern writers is Payne's focus in this critical work. Payne examines five key black writers from the South: Charles W. Chesnutt, James Weldon Johnson, Jean Toomer, Richard Wright, and Ralph Ellison. In the process, he asserts the kinship between these writers and their white southern counterparts, including William Faulkner.

Subject(s): Literature, American South

1816 Kim Pereira

August Wilson and the African American Odyssey
(Urbana, IL; University of Illinois Press, 1995)

Summary: Playwright August Wilson is one of the most acclaimed theatrical writers of the 1980s and 1990s, having won Pulitzer Prizes for both *Fences* and *The Piano Lesson*. In this critical study, Pereira offers a detailed analysis of those two works plus two others by Wilson, *Ma Rainey's Black Bottom* and *Joe Turner's Come and Gone*. Pereira focuses on the themes of family, migration, and reconciliation in Wilson's works.

Subject(s): Drama, Family

1817 Margaret Perry

Silence to the Drums: A Survey of the Literature of the Harlem Renaissance
(Westport, CT; Greenwood Press, 1976)

Summary: Perry's 1976 critical study begins with a chapter devoted to the background of the cultural movement of the Harlem Renaissance, in which African American writers and artists working in the 1920s burst into the American cultural mainstream. Perry then discusses those who helped shape the movement, including literary critic Alain Locke. She goes on to examine the poets, novelists, and short story writers who defined the age. These latter writers include Claude McKay, Langston Hughes, Jessie Fauset, and Zora Neale Hurston.

Subject(s): Harlem Renaissance, Culture

1818 Bernard L. Peterson, Jr.

Contemporary Black American Playwrights and Their Plays: A Biographical Directory and Dramatic Index
(New York, NY; Greenwood Press, 1988)

Summary: In this 1988 study, Bernard L. Peterson, Jr. offers a comprehensive study of African American playwrights active during the 1960s, 1970s, and 1980s. The work is arranged alphabetically by the last name of each playwright. As the sub-title suggests, however, the work is more than a biographical study; Peterson also offers summaries and critical analyses of the major works by each of the playwrights discussed.

Subject(s): Drama

1819 Carla L. Peterson

"Doers of the Word": African-American Women Speakers and Writers in the North (1830-1880)
(New York, NY; Oxford University Press, 1995)

Summary: Peterson's 1995 work focuses not only on slavery-related issues of the period between 1830 and 1880, such as the slave narrative of Harriet Jacobs, but also other literary efforts by a variety of African American women. For instance, the author examines the post-Civil War speeches about women's rights by noted abolitionist Sojourner Truth, showing that issues of gender and class also engaged intellectuals during the period. Other writers and speakers discussed by Peterson include Frances E.W. Harper, Charlotte Forten, and Maria Stewart.

Subject(s): Literature, Slavery, Women's Rights

1820 Donald A. Petesch

A Spy in the Enemy's Country: The Emergence of Modern Black Literature
(Iowa City, IA; University of Iowa Press, 1989)

Summary: In the first part of his 1989 study, Petesch examines the nineteenth century literary, historical, and social conditions from which modern African American literature grew. Petesch argues that these conditions compelled writers before the twentieth century to focus on literature of moral persuasion, in which the theme of "masking" was omnipresent. In the book's second part, the author examines the work of five modern black writers: Charles W. Chesnutt, James Weldon Johnson, Wallace Thurman, Nella Larsen, and Jean Toomer, whose literature continued the art of masking and became preoccupied with issues of self and identity.

Subject(s): Literature, Identity

1821 Deborah G. Plant

Every Tub Must Sit on Its Own Bottom: The Philosophy and Politics of Zora Neale Hurston
(Urbana, IL; University of Illinois Press, 1995)

Summary: In this study's six chapters, Deborah G. Plant examines Zora Neale Hurston's sense of self, her intellectual grounding, her use of folk culture, and her political philosophy. Hurston was a treasured figure of the Harlem Renaissance cultural movement of the 1920s and later an icon for feminist and lesbian scholars, and Plant discusses Hurston's antipathy toward labels, particularly as they applied to notions of womanhood.

Subject(s): Literature, Harlem Renaissance, Sex Roles

1822 Dorothy Porter, Compiler

Early Negro Writing, 1760-1837
(Boston, MA; Beacon Press, 1971)

Summary: In addition to discussing fiction and poetry, Porter's 1971 anthology features a wide array of essays, sermons, addresses, and other nonfiction writings. One chapter includes the constitutions and bylaws of mutual aid and fraternal organizations between 1792 and 1833, while another features articles taken from "Societies for Educational Improvement" between 1808 and 1836. Among the writers whose works are included are Phillis Wheatley, Jupiter Hammon, and Benjamin Banneker.

Subject(s): Education, Literature

1823 William H. Robinson

Black New England Letters: The Uses of Writing in Black New England

(Boston, MA; Trustees of the Public Library of the City of Boston, 1977)

Summary: This work consists of lectures given by literary scholar William H. Robinson at the Boston Public Library. In the work, Robinson explores such black New England writers as Phillis Wheatley and W.E.B. Du Bois in addition to examining the papers of the "Free African Union Society" in Newport, Rhode Island, between 1780 and 1824.

Subject(s): Literature

1824 Lawrence R. Rodgers

Canaan Bound: The African-American Great Migration Novel

(Urbana, IL; University of Illinois Press, 1997)

Summary: During the early decades of the twentieth century, a huge number of African Americans migrated from the rural South to urban centers in the North, fleeing generations of southern racism and seeking better economic opportunities. In *Canaan Bound*, Lawrence R. Rodgers shows how this migration was utterly connected to a search for identity. Among the authors whose work Rodgers examines are Paul Laurence Dunbar, Waters Turpin, William Attaway, and George W. Henderson.

Subject(s): Identity, American South, City and Town Life

1825 Alan Henry Rose

Demonic Vision: Racial Fantasy and Southern Fiction

(Hamden, CT; Archon Books, 1976)

Summary: Alan Henry Rose's subject in his 1976 book is the literary figure of the black man as devil. Studying white literature about the American South between 1830 and 1930, Rose finds this figure represented again and again. In Rose's view, this literary "demonic vision" grew out of whites' fear of disorder and eventually became mingled with whites' fear of Native Americans, before Native Americans were wiped out in the social and cultural landscape. The author finds images of black devils in the works of Mark Twain, William Faulkner, and Thomas Wolfe, before a new generation of white southern writers after World War II broke free of this mythic stereotype and offered a new vision of African Americans.

Subject(s): American South, Literature, Racism

1826 Roger Rosenblatt

Black Fiction

(Cambridge, MA; Harvard University Press, 1974)

Summary: In this 1974 work, Roger Rosenblatt examines the way in which black protagonists in American fiction have fought against the historical forces pressing upon them from a hostile world. Rosenblatt argues that while the black hero may try to escape these forces, he ultimately fails, only to realize that such escape was not only impossible but also undesirable. In his analysis, Rosenblatt reassesses previous literary criticism by such authors as Addison Gayle, Jr. and J. Saunders Redding.

Subject(s): Racism, Literature

1827 Lorraine Elena Roses
Ruth Elizabeth Randolph, Co-author

Harlem Renaissance and Beyond: Literary Biographies of 100 Black Women Writers, 1900-1945

(Cambridge, MA; Harvard University Press, 1990)

Summary: Among the 100 women writers included in this work are well-known figures of the Harlem Renaissance such as Zora Neale Hurston and Nella Larsen, along with lesser-known writers such as May Miller and Hazel Vivian Campbell. Presented in alphabetical order, the various biographies each include a select bibliography as well as a list of secondary sources about the author.

Subject(s): Harlem Renaissance, Literature, Women

1828 Sandi Russell

Render Me My Song: African-American Women Writers from Slavery to the Present

(New York, NY; St. Martin's Press, 1990)

Summary: This comprehensive critical work about black women writers covers virtually all major African American writers from the eighteenth century to the present. Russell structures her work chronologically, beginning with early works by writers such as Phillis Wheatley, Sojourner Truth, and Frances E.W. Harper. She then moves through early twentieth century authors including Angelina Weld Grimke and Zora Neale Hurston and ultimately discusses modern writers such as Toni Morrison, Maya Angelou, Rita Dove, and June Jordan.

Subject(s): Literature

1829 Wilfred D. Samuels
Clenora Hudson-Weems, Co-author

Toni Morrison

(Boston, MA; Twayne Publishers, 1990)

Summary: Toni Morrison, the subject of this literary biography, is one of the most celebrated American authors of the twentieth century and the first African American to win the Nobel Prize for literature. In seven chapters, co-authors Samuels and Hudson-Weems examine the five Morrison novels that were written prior to 1990: *The Bluest Eye, Sula, Song of Solomon, Tar Baby,* and the Pulitzer Prize-winning *Beloved.* In their preface to the work, Samuels and Hudson-Weems note, "Morrison's spellbinding prose/poetry..., coupled with the mysticism, black folklore, and mythology woven into her fictional worlds have led many critics to append the label 'Black Magic' to her craftsmanship."

Subject(s): Literature, Folklore, Biography

1830 Leslie Catherine Sanders

The Development of Black Theater in America: From Shadows to Selves
(Baton Rouge, LA; Louisiana State University Press, 1988)

Summary: The five prominent playwrights at the center of this 1988 work are Willis Richardson, Randolph Edmonds, Langston Hughes, LeRoi Jones (later Amiri Baraka), and Ed Bullins. Sanders argues that the history of black theater in America required that black artists utilize and transform dramatic conventions from white European culture; once that was accomplished, a realistic African American stage presence emerged.

Subject(s): Drama, African Americans, Culture

1831 Keith A. Sandiford

Measuring the Moment: Strategies of Protest in Eighteenth-Century Afro-English Writing
(Selinsgrove, PA; Susquehanna University, 1988)

Summary: Keith Sandiford in this work focuses on the impact of three African-English writers of the 1700s: Ignatius Sancho (1729-1780); Ottobah Cugoano (1757-?); and Olaudah Equiano (1745-1797). Sandiford argues that the work of these three writers contributed greatly to the successful movement to emancipate slaves in the British West Indian colonies. Sancho's letters, Cugoano's antislavery treatise, and Equiano's autobiographical narrative, notes the author, reached a wider audience than had long been believed and established the three writers as leading abolitionist figures.

Subject(s): Slavery, Abolition, Colonialism

1832 Noel Schraufnagel

From Apology to Protest: The Black American Novel
(Deland, FL; Everett/Edwards, 1973)

Summary: Schraufnagel's influential 1973 work is a panoramic study of black novels from the publication of Richard Wright's *Native Son* in 1940 through the protest novels of the late 1960s, when the "Black Arts" movement flourished. In a chronological discussion of black novels in the 1940s, 1950s,

and 1960s, Schraufnagel examines the development of the black novel within its historical American context.

Subject(s): Literature, History

1833 Charles Scruggs

The Sage in Harlem: H.L. Mencken and the Black Writers of the 1920s
(Baltimore, MD; Johns Hopkins University Press, 1984)

Summary: During his lifetime, critic and editor H.L. Mencken (1880-1956) exerted an enormous influence over American letters. Later in the twentieth century, however, critics dismissed him as a bigoted, poorly educated figure whose work was superficial and whose impact was overstated. Scruggs offers a new critical perspective of Mencken, arguing in particular that despite the offensive racist rhetoric he often employed, he was instrumental in helping many black writers during the 1920s. During this era, which is known as the Harlem Renaissance, black writers entered the American literary mainstream as never before.

Subject(s): Harlem Renaissance, Literature, Racism

1834 Charles Scruggs

Sweet Home: Invisible Cities in the Afro-American Novel
(Baltimore, MD; Johns Hopkins University Press, 1993)

Summary: Scruggs's 1993 work is a sociological study of the rise of urban black America as seen through twentieth century African American literature. Scruggs discusses W.E.B. Du Bois's *The Philadelphia Negro* as well as Alain Locke's influential 1925 collection, *The New Negro,* in which Locke described the "New Negro" cultural movement sweeping through New York City's Harlem neighborhood, a movement that would come to be known as the Harlem Renaissance. He also examines several seminal novels, including James Baldwin's *Go Tell It on the Mountain,* Ralph Ellison's *Invisible Man,* and Toni Morrison's *Beloved.*

Subject(s): Urban Affairs, Harlem Renaissance, City and Town Life

1835 Sandra G. Shannon

The Dramatic Vision of August Wilson
(Washington, DC; Howard University Press, 1995)

Summary: Pulitzer Prize-winning playwright August Wilson is the focus of Shannon's 1995 critical study. Analyzing Wilson's plays, Shannon shows how he has tapped into elements of black history, including the great migration of rural southern blacks to northern cities during the first decades of the twentieth century. The book includes an interview that Shannon conducted with Wilson.

Subject(s): Drama

1836 Ann Allen Shockley

Afro-American Women Writers, 1746-1933: An Anthology and Critical Guide

(Boston, MA; G.K. Hall, 1988)

Summary: In her 1988 work, Ann Allen Shockley offers an extensive cross-section of literary works by African American women writers from Lucy Terry—considered the first black woman poet in America—to the end of the Harlem Renaissance. Shockley divides the book into four sections: 1746-1862; 1868-1899; 1900-1923; and 1924-1933. Within each section, the author provides critical essays that place the writers within their political, social, and cultural context.

Subject(s): Literature, Women

1837 David R. Shumway

Creating American Civilization: A Genealogy of American Literature as an Academic Discipline

(Minneapolis, MN; University of Minnesota Press, 1994)

Summary: This 1994 work focuses on how the study of American literature began and developed. Shumway places the discipline's origins in the 1880s with writers such as William Dean Howells and Barrett Wendell. In discussing the twentieth century, Shumway follows the beginnings of the study of literature at American universities; the establishment of programs in American and cultural studies; and the rise of schools of literary critics grounded in the "New Criticism" and Marxism, among other dogmas.

Subject(s): Literature, Colleges and Universities

1838 **Amritjit Singh,** Editor
William S. Shiver, Co-editor
Stanley Brodwin, Co-editor

The Harlem Renaissance: Revaluations

(New York, NY; Garland, 1989)

Summary: This 1989 critical work offers a re-examination of the Harlem Renaissance cultural movement of the 1920s, when African American writers and artists burst into the American cultural mainstream as never before. In addition to examining standard major figures of the period such as Langston Hughes, Alain Locke, and Nella Larsen, the work also offers views of less well-known aspects of the period such as "White Writers and the Harlem Renaissance" and "Philadelphia's Literary Circle and the Harlem Renaissance."

Subject(s): Harlem Renaissance, Literature, Music

1839 Amritjit Singh

The Novels of the Harlem Renaissance: Twelve Black Writers, 1923-1933

(University Park, PA; Pennsylvania State University Press, 1976)

Summary: The Harlem Renaissance cultural movement of the 1920s and early 1930s catapulted numerous African American writers into the American literary mainstream. In his 1976 critical study, Amritjit Singh examines the most important novels of twelve of these writers, including Countee Cullen, Jessie Fauset, Langston Hughes, Nella Larsen, and Jean Toomer. Singh focuses on common themes among the works discussed: class, race, and self-definition.

Subject(s): Literature, Harlem Renaissance, Race Relations

1840 Valerie Smith

Self-Discovery and Authority in Afro-American Narrative

(Cambridge, MA; Harvard University Press, 1987)

Summary: Smith's 1987 work focuses on how early African American slave narratives influenced later black writing and, in particular, how the issue of literacy is treated by black authors. She argues that by telling the stories of their lives, the writers of slave narratives as well as later authors establish an authority that is missing in their real lives. After an opening chapter in which she examines three classic slave narratives, Smith devotes chapters to James Weldon Johnson, Richard Wright, Ralph Ellison, and Toni Morrison.

Subject(s): Slavery, Identity

1841 Werner Sollors
Maria Diedrich, Editor

The Black Columbiad: Defining Moments in African American Literature and Culture

(Cambridge, MA; Harvard University Press, 1994)

Summary: This collection of essays by thirty-five American, European, and African critics focuses on the issue of African culture as it is represented in the culture of the African diaspora, specifically of Africans in America. The work is divided into three sections: nineteenth century, twentieth century, and the contemporary period. Among the authors whose works are discussed are Melvin Dixon, Zora Neale Hurston, Ishmael Reed, and Charles Johnson.

Subject(s): Africa, Literature

1842 Catherine Juanita Starke

Black Portraiture in American Fiction: Stock Characters, Archetypes, and Individuals
(New York, NY; Basic Books, 1971)

Summary: Following an opening chapter in which she outlines the context for her study of black figures in American fiction, Juanita Starke identifies and examines numerous character types. As "stock characters," she identifies such figures as "accommodative slaves," "brutes," and "buffoons." In the chapter devoted to "archetypal patterns," she comments on such figures as "mulattoes," "mammies," and "primitives." Finally, she discusses "black individuals" in fictional figures including "youthful males in search of self" and "black avengers."

Subject(s): Literature

1843 Eric J. Sundquist

The Hammers of Creation: Folk Culture in Modern African-American Fiction
(Athens, GA; University of Georgia Press, 1992)

Summary: Sundquist in this work analyzes the role of folk culture in three novels by African Americans from the early twentieth century: James Weldon Johnson's *The Autobiography of an Ex-Coloured Man,* Zora Neale Hurston's *Jonah's Gourd Vine,* and *Arna Bontemps's Black Thunder.* Discussing such cultural happenings as slavery, black spirituals and jazz, and religious expression, Sundquist shows how each of the three writers was able to highlight and preserve fundamental elements of African American history.

Subject(s): Literature, Folklore, History

1844 Eric J. Sundquist

To Wake the Nations: Race in the Making of American Literature
(Cambridge, MA; Harvard University Press, 1993)

Summary: Sundquist takes the title of this large-scale work about African American literature from a well-known black spiritual song. In the work, Sundquist focuses on nineteenth and early twentieth century works to examine how race emerged as a factor in writings by both white and black Americans of the period. Among the authors whom Sundquist discusses are Frederick Douglass, Mark Twain, Charles W. Chesnutt, and Joel Chandler Harris.

Subject(s): Literature, History

1845 Wylie Sypher

Guinea's Captive Kings: British Anti-Slavery Literature of the XVIIth Century
(Chapel Hill, NC; University of North Carolina Press, 1942)

Summary: While the eighteenth century saw massive importation of enslaved Africans to the United States, it also witnessed a similar importation of slaves to the British colonies in the West Indies. As the century progressed, numerous writers and intellectuals in Britain began agitating for and end to this importation and for the abolition of all slavery in British colonies. In his 1942 work, Wylie Sypher analyzes works by such writers as Daniel Defoe, Thomas Bellamy, and Alexander Pope.

Subject(s): Slavery, Abolition

1846 Ronald T. Takaki

Violence in the Black Imagination: Essays and Documents
(New York, NY; Putnam, 1972)

Summary: Through an analysis of three important black writers of the pre-Civil War era, Martin Delany, William Wells Brown, and Frederick Douglass, Ronald T. Takaki provides a critical opinion of the nature of pre-war America. Takaki focuses on the themes of slave rebellion and violence against whites in the writings of the three authors. In doing so, he explores the relationship between these authors and the racist American establishment.

Subject(s): Violence, Civil War, Slavery

1847 Claudia C. Tate

Psychoanalysis and Black Novels: Desire and the Protocols of Race
(New York, NY; Oxford University Press, 1998)

Summary: Arguing that traditional theories of race and gender are insufficient frameworks with which to analyze many black novels, Tate in this work uses psychoanalytic techniques to examine five novels. Among those works are Emma Dunham Kelley's *Meqda,* W.E.B. Du Bois' *Dark Princess,* Richard Wright's *Savage Holiday,* Nella Larsen's *Quicksand,* and Zora Neale Hurston's *Seraph on the Suwanee.* Ultimately, Tate offers an untapped avenue for the critical analysis of African American literature.

Subject(s): Psychology, Literature

1848 H. Nigel Thomas

From Folklore to Fiction: A Study of Folk Heroes and Rituals in the Black American Novel
(New York, NY; Greenwood Press, 1988)

Summary: Folklore has played a crucial role in the development of African American literature, and numerous critics have examined the issue. In this 1988 work, H. Nigel Thomas focuses on writers from the turn of the twentieth century to the 1980s, showing how folk elements have made their way into works by such writers as Paul Laurence Dunbar, Leon Forrest, and Toni Morrison. Among the folk-inspired characters identified by Thomas are the preacher and the trickster.

Subject(s): Literature, Folklore

1849 Tyrone Tillery

Claude McKay: A Black Poet's Struggle for Identity
(Amherst, MA; University of Massachusetts Press, 1992)

Summary: The subject of this literary biography is Claude McKay, who wrote numerous poems in addition to such novels as *Banjo* and *Home to Harlem*. Tillery examines McKay's childhood in Jamaica, his later immigration to the United States, his long sojourn in Europe and Africa during the 1920s and 1930s, and his eventual homecoming to New York City. In presenting the details of McKay's life, Tillery shows how the author's experiences and his cultural milieu influenced his art.

Subject(s): Literature, Biography

1850 Nancy M. Tischler

Black Masks: Negro Characters in Modern Southern Fiction
(University Park, PA; Pennsylvania State University Press, 1969)

Summary: Analyzing southern fiction written after 1900, Nancy M. Tischler in her 1969 work finds that previous stereotypical black characters have been altered (the tragic mulatto) or eliminated (the comic Negro). In addition, Tischler recognizes new character types, such as the black Christ, which became popular in the 1920s, and the black proletarian, which arose during the Great Depression of the 1930s.

Subject(s): Literature, Depression (Economic), American South

1851 Steven C. Tracy

Langston Hughes & the Blues
(Urbana, IL; University of Illinois Press, 1988)

Summary: One of the most important American authors of the twentieth century, and a key figure in the Harlem Renaissance, Langston Hughes was greatly influenced by blues music. In his poetry, the structures, sounds, imagery, and rhythms of the blues idiom are clearly visible. Steven C. Tracy's 1988 work explores this connection, offering an in-depth examination of Hughes's poetry and its blues in-spired nature.

Subject(s): Music, Poetry, Harlem Renaissance

1852 Darwin T. Turner

In a Minor Chord: Three Afro-American Writers and Their Search for Identity
(Carbondale, IL; Southern Illinois University Press, 1971)

Summary: In his 1973 study, Darwin T. Turner offers critical essays about three major figures of the Harlem Renaissance cultural movement of the 1920s: Jean Toomer, author of the landmark work *Cane*; the renowned poet Countee Cullen; and Zora Neale Hurston, now considered an icon in both feminist and African American literary circles.

Subject(s): Literature, Poetry, Harlem Renaissance

1853 William L. Van Deburg

Slavery & Race in American Popular Culture
(Madison, WI; University of Wisconsin Press, 1984)

Summary: In this 1984 work, William Van Deburg focuses on how slavery and race have been perceived and presented in novels, historical works, poems, films, and songs. The author begins with an examination of the period 1619-1830, in which white writers relied on stereotypes such as the "Noble Captive." He then covers the growing debate about abolition that occurred from 1830 until the beginning of the Civil War in 1861, including the appearance of numerous black writers whose work served as a corrective to white observations. He concludes with chapters devoted to the periods 1861-1965 ("From Slave to Citizen") and 1965-1980 ("The Debate Continues").

Subject(s): Slavery, Popular Culture

1854 Gloria Wade-Gayles

No Crystal Stair: Visions of Race and Sex in Black Women's Fiction
(New York, NY; Pilgrim Press, 1984)

Summary: Struggling under the burden of their dual minority status, black women authors have created compelling characters that highlight their unique place in American society. In this 1984 edition (revised in 1997), Wade-Gayles offers insights into the work of such authors as Gwendolyn Brooks, Toni Morrison, Dorothy West, and Gayl Jones. In the book's essays, Wade-Gayles focuses on black women's lives as seen in their literary incarnations as mother, wife, hopeless refugee, and radical challenger.

Subject(s): Women, African Americans, Literature

1855 Jean Wagner
Kenneth Douglas, Translator

Black Poets of the United States: From Paul Laurence Dunbar to Langston Hughes
(Urbana, IL; University of Illinois Press, 1973)

Summary: Jean Wagner's 1973 work offers a detailed analysis of African American poets from the late 1800s to the middle of the 1900s. Seven major authors are discussed: Paul Laurence Dunbar, Claude McKay, Jean Toomer, Countee Cullen, James Weldon Johnson, Langston Hughes, and Sterling Brown. In addition to examining the work and impact of these writers, Wagner also offers contextual analysis that places the writers within their respective cultural eras.

Subject(s): Poetry

1856 **Melissa Walker**

Down from the Mountaintop: Black Women's Novels in the Wake of the Civil Rights Movement, 1966-1989
(New Haven, CT; Yale University Press, 1991)

Summary: The diverse and substantial outpouring of novels by African American women since the 1960s is the focus of Walker's 1991 critical work. Dividing her study into thematic discussions of the literature of slavery and Reconstruction; the period between World War I and World War II; Harlem; and the civil rights movement of the 1950s and 1960s, Walker examines works by such authors as Toni Morrison, Alice Walker, Toni Cade Bambara, Ntozake Shange, Alice Childress, and Rosa Guy.

Subject(s): Literature, Civil Rights Movement, Women

1857 **Cheryl A. Wall**

Women of the Harlem Renaissance
(Bloomington, IN; Indiana University Press, 1995)

Summary: As its title suggests, this work focuses on the women writers who were part of the Harlem Renaissance movement of the 1920s and into the 1930s—Wall uses an expansive definition of the movement's period. Three writers occupy center stage in Wall's study: Jessie Redmon Fauset, Nella Larsen, and Zora Neale Hurston. Other authors whose work is discussed by Wall include Marita Bonner and Georgia Douglas Johnson.

Subject(s): Literature, Harlem Renaissance, Women

1858 **Kenneth W. Warren**

Black and White Strangers: Race and American Literary Realism
(Chicago, IL; University of Chicago Press, 1993)

Summary: The late 1800s and early 1900s, the years during which the literary genre of realism flourished in America, are the focus of this critical study by Warren. In his work, Warren examines texts by black writers of the period such as Frances E.W. Harper and W.E.B. Du Bois and also re-reads texts by white writers such as Henry James to examine how the issue of race factored into their work. Warren's re-examination of seminal texts by white authors in order to focus on the subject of race is but one of many such works written in the 1990s by literary critics.

Subject(s): Literature

1859 **Carole McAlpine Watson**

Prologue: The Novels of Black American Women, 1891-1965
(Westport, CT; Greenwood Press, 1985)

Summary: Watson's 1985 work is a critical survey of writing by African American women from 1891 to 1965. Watson presents her analysis in chronological fashion, covering the periods from 1891 to 1920, 1921 to 1945, and 1946 to 1965. Among the writers whose work Watson examines are Frances E.W. Harper, Pauline Hopkins, Paule Marshall, and Jessie Fauset. In the book's preface, Watson admits that her motivation for writing the book grew out of the "Black Arts" movement of the 1960s, when black artists forged a new aesthetic concept that was based on race-centered art.

Subject(s): Women, Literature

1860 **Jerry Gafio Watts**

Heroism and the Black Intellectual: Ralph Ellison, Politics and Afro-American Intellectual Life
(Chapel Hill, NC; University of North Carolina Press, 1994)

Summary: Throughout his career, Ralph Ellison struggled with the issue of whether to place his primary focus on developing his craft as a writer or on working to alleviate racial oppression. Early on in his career, he moved among Socialist intellectual circles, but later he renounced such ties to emphasize his obligations to his own artistic development. Dealing mainly with the author's nonfiction essays rather than his fiction, Watts examines the criticism heaped on Ellison by many in the African American literary establishment for his adherence to aesthetic concerns. Ellison's struggle was shared by numerous African American writers of the twentieth century and was at the center of the rise of the "Black Arts" movement of the 1960s, when a new generation of writers such as Amiri Baraka argued that no black writer could ignore injustice and racism in his or her work. Later writers such as Toni Morrison and Ishmael Reed, however, sought to move beyond such limiting confines, again placing aesthetic concerns at the center of their art.

Subject(s): Literature, Racism

1861 **Gay Wilentz**

Binding Cultures: Black Women Writers in Africa and the Diaspora
(Bloomington, IN; Indiana University Press, 1992)

Summary: In this work, Wilentz argues that black women's literature in Africa and America looks back to the oral storytelling of previous generations of black mothers in Africa and beyond. Wilentz examines the work of six writers: Flora Nwapa, Efua Sutherland, and Ama Ata Aidoo from West Africa and Toni Morrison, Alice Walker, and Paule Marshall from America.

Subject(s): Literature, Africa, Storytelling

1862 **Pontheolla T. Williams**

Robert Hayden: A Critical Analysis of His Poetry

(Urbana, IL; University of Illinois Press, 1987)

Summary: Considered the most comprehensive study of twentieth century black writer Robert Hayden, this work contains a brief introduction to Hayden's life and his literary, cultural, and political influences. The remainder of the book offers a detailed analysis of Hayden's major poetical works.

Subject(s): Literature, Biography

1863 **Cary D. Wintz**

Black Culture and the Harlem Renaissance

(Houston, TX; Rice University Press, 1988)

Summary: This study of the Harlem Renaissance cultural movement of the 1920s seeks to place the movement within its historical context. In the work, Wintz examines the demographic and social history of African Americans during the period; the intellectual and artistic achievements of black writers and thinkers; and the critics and promoters whose work brought the Harlem Renaissance to the attention of mainstream American culture.

Subject(s): Literature, Harlem Renaissance, History

1864 **Henry B. Wonham,** Editor

Criticism and the Color Line: Desegregating American Literary Studies

(New Brunswick, NJ; Rutgers University Press, 1996)

Summary: Beginning with a 1989 essay by Toni Morrison exhorting literary critics to re-examine standard works by white American authors to see how race influenced the texts, this collection of articles reveals a widespread effort by critics to do so in the 1990s. Among the white writers discussed are Edgar Allan Poe, Mark Twain, and Gertrude Stein; among the African American writers featured are Richard Wright and Booker T. Washington.

Subject(s): Literature, Race Relations

1865 **Lee Alfred Wright**

Identity, Family, and Folklore in African American Literature

(New York, NY; Garland Pub., 1995)

Summary: Wright's 1995 critical study examines representations of the disintegration of the black family in America from the slavery period to the present. Drawing upon other analysis by such critics as Houston A. Baker, Jr. and Henry Louis Gates, Jr., Wright focuses on works from the nineteenth century through the present. Among the writers whose work Wright discusses are Alice Walker and Toni Morrison.

Subject(s): Literature, Family, Folklore

1866 **James O. Young**

Black Writers of the Thirties

(Baton Rouge, LA; Louisiana State University Press, 1973)

Summary: This well-regarded critical study of African American writers during the 1930s covers such writers as Langston Hughes and Richard Wright as well as critics such as E. Franklin Frazier. Young places these writers in the intellectual and cultural context of the period, when the United States experienced the Great Depression and Adolf Hitler rose to power in Germany.

Subject(s): Literature, Depression (Economic)

1867 **Mary E. Young**

Mules and Dragons: Popular Culture Images in the Selected Writings of African-American and Chinese-American Women Writers

(Westport, CT; Greenwood Press, 1993)

Summary: Young's 1993 work compares and contrasts pop culture stereotypes of Chinese American and African American women. In constructing her argument, Young offers historical and literary accounts of the development of such stereotypes. Among the writers featured in the study are Harriet Wilson, Amy Tan, Frances E.W. Harper, and Alice Walker.

Subject(s): Literature, Popular Culture, Asian Americans

Index

E

O

U

V

W